HARRODS

A selection from Harrods General Catalogue
1929

David & Charles

British Library Cataloguing in Publication Data

Harrods
   Harrods : a selection from the General Catalogue of 1929.
   1. Harrods—History   2. Harrods—Catalogs
   I. Title
   381.1′09421′34   HF5465.G74H3

   ISBN 0-7153-8784-7

Printed in Great Britain
by Redwood Burn Limited, Trowbridge, Wiltshire
for David & Charles (Publishers) Limited
Brunel House   Newton Abbot   Devon

Published in the United States of America
by David & Charles Inc
North Pomfret   Vermont 05053   USA

Publisher's Note

This volume will surely stop countless conversations in many homes, provide endless diversion and amusement, and add a touch of knowledge to those interested in social and economic history. We have had great pleasure producing it, but have to admit that it has wasted much time, remarks like 'Fancy that,' 'Were they really doing that then,' and 'That would have been expensive in those days' always punctuating the turning of pages in the editorial and production processes.

We are publishing it partly to celebrate our own twenty-fifth birthday, having successfully published reprints of a number of store catalogues earlier in our short history. One was in fact of the oldest known Harrods' catalogue to have survived, that for 1895, but our reprint has become so scarce that I have been unable to replace the copy that mysteriously disappeared from my own shelves. Each reprint was greeted with the same amazement: 'Who would possibly want to buy a reprint of an old catalogue,' immediately followed by 'Oh, I know who would like this' and a string of comments on the contents of successive pages. Normally it is hard enough to persuade booksellers to sample the books they are being offered to buy; with these catalogues the problem is preventing them endlessly gazing at the pages.

Why the fascination? Well, most of us (whatever our religion, politics, jobs or place in society) spend much of our lives collecting artefacts and using them – for better or worse. So when you go into someone else's home, you cannot help noticing items that are the same as yours and those that are quite different. Who does not comment on a neighbour or relative who has stylish furniture or way-out taste – or allows his or her home to deteriorate into a museum of bits and pieces that most people would have long discarded?

Here you can decide what your parents and grandparents would probably have chosen, even if you do not recognise the very items that they did – and maybe are gaining value up in the attic at this very moment. You can peep endlessly into the domestic life of the more fortunate fifth of society who might have been tempted to patronise Harrods. Familiar values and sentiments, as well as familiar physical shapes, leap out at you from almost every page. You can almost hear and smell some of the goods, and remember the joys and sorrows that were attached to them.

Essentially we offer the reprint for fun, but there will also be a more serious usage for collectors of yesterday's everyday items and for those who have to comment on the age or portray it on stage or screen.

Harrods, occasionally described by overseas children as the capital of Britain, was by 1929 firmly in a class of its own, larger than Selfridges and more determined to make its services as well as its goods unbeatable. Like so many businesses, it had started almost by accident. Henry Charles Harrod began earning his living as a miller in Clacton. Later becoming a tea merchant, he extended long credit to a Brompton grocer who ultimately failed so that he took his business over. That was in 1849. In 1861, Harrod's son, Charles Digby, took control, and broke from the tradition of allowing credit to the cream of society and concentrated on cash business. Things went well until a disastrous fire in 1883; all the Christmas stock was lost, but even then customers were kept waiting only a few days for replacement goods. Progress was quickly resumed, partly driven on by competition with other stores setting out to provide a high level of service.

Harrods cast their net ever wider, the telegraphic address becoming *Everything London*, and department upon department opening as the premises were extended, now occupying a site where dozens of separate establishments once stood. And in Edwardian days the store also increasingly led the way in fashion. Harrods had become 'a recognised social rendezvous; in fact, one of the few smart rendezvous acknowledged and patronised by Society.' People visited it for the experience as well as to choose the best and the latest; they ordered goods from it by telephone; and from all over the Empire the orders came pouring in by mail. By the mid-1920s, the arrival of the Harrods' catalogues was one of the year's highspots in the lives of thousands of families at home and abroad. They eagerly studied the latest fashions and models – and also Harrods' methods of doing business.

Many pages reproduced here tell us about the latter, and well might you envy those who were fortunate enough to be able to patronise Harrods when deliveries were so frequent, interest rates so low, and prices (especially of hand-made items) beyond belief for today's younger shoppers. You will quickly find the areas where prices have changed fastest and slowest, some goods that still seem familiar (even though their prices are not) and many that have long ceased to be sold. And you are bound to wonder what people in fifty-five years might be thinking of the goods we buy today and the prices we pay for them. Enjoy it – and share it among young and old! There is much here for everyone.

DAVID ST JOHN THOMAS

BY APPOINTMENT TO
HER MAJESTY
THE QUEEN OF ITALY

BY APPOINTMENT TO
HER MAJESTY
THE QUEEN

BY APPOINTMENT TO
HIS MAJESTY
THE KING

BY APPOINTMENT TO
HER MAJESTY
THE QUEEN OF NORWAY

BY APPOINTMENT TO
THEIR MAJESTIES THE
KING & QUEEN OF THE BELGIANS

HARRODS

LIMITED

LONDON

PARIS   MANCHESTER

ISSUED SHARE CAPITAL £6,213,820

Divided into 4,000,000 $7\frac{1}{2}$ % Cumulative Preference Shares of £1 each and

2,213,820 Ordinary Shares of £1 each

Reserve £1,000,000

Directors

SIR WOODMAN BURBIDGE, Bart., C.B.E.
Chairman and Managing Director

EDGAR COHEN

SIR HARRY K. NEWTON, Bart.

FRANK R. CHITHAM

ALLAN HEPWORTH

CHARLES E. WILES

THOMAS ANTHONY

JOHN TAYLOR

RICHARD BURBIDGE
General Manager

Chief Accountant

ROBERT ASHWORTH, F.C.A., F.S.A.A.

Secretary

R. H. GRIFFITH

FOREWORD

TO THE 1929 EDITION

THE hundreds of letters received from recipients of our last volume were encouraging testimonies that Harrods General Catalogue has achieved its object, and has been a well thumbed book upon the book shelves of many a home, enabling thousands of country customers to enjoy the convenience of shopping at Harrods without even setting foot in Brompton Road.

¶ With more than ordinary pleasure, therefore, we present this the 1929 edition of our work and hope that it will prove of ever increasing value.

¶ The task of revision has been careful and complete; all prices have been checked; all illustrations brought up to date and much new merchandise has been added to its pages.

¶ The constant and rapid 'turnover' of Harrods immense stocks is of itself an assurance of the freshness and newness of all merchandise offered, an advantage to the customer not possible under ordinary trading conditions.

¶ Particularly would we draw attention to the benefits offered by our 'Deposit Order Account' Scheme, which not only eliminates the risk, trouble and expense of sending cheques, postal orders or money orders through the post, but means a $2\frac{1}{2}$ per cent. (6d. in the £) saving on all purchases.

¶ A specially trained staff deals with all orders sent by post, and helpful, experienced and impartial advice is freely available concerning any detail upon which fuller information than that offered in this book may be desired.

¶ Apart from this volume and the many seasonable catalogues, booklets and brochures published during the year, 'Harrods News' is sent to some forty thousand homes every week, and places before its readers much that is new in things to wear and use, as well as a supplement of current food prices. We shall be pleased to send a specimen copy of 'Harrods News' on request and place your name upon the regular list, if desired.

BUSINESS ARRANGEMENTS

OBJECT

The object of the Company is to supply its Customers with the best goods at the lowest possible prices

HOURS OF BUSINESS

From 9 a.m. to 6 p.m. and 1 p.m. on Saturdays ; Closed on all Bank Holidays

CREDIT ACCOUNTS

On receipt of a satisfactory Trade reference or Bankers reference a Credit Account can be opened at Harrods. Accounts are rendered and are payable monthly. Weekly Accounts can also be arranged, if desired. Separate Accounts payable monthly for both Town and Country are arranged for Drapery and Personal items. Monthly accounts are payable on or before the 10th of the month following that in which goods are supplied

TERMS OF PAYMENT

Except where accounts have been opened are Cash with Order. Goods cannot be sent by our own vans for payment on delivery

CHEQUES

Cheques and Post Office or Postal Orders should be made Payable to Harrods Ltd. and crossed Barclays Bank Limited, not negotiable

BANKING

Deposit Accounts and Current Accounts opened and Interest allowed. Full particulars on application

CORRESPONDENCE

(a) All letters should be addressed to the Company
(b) The Name and Title should be distinctly written
(c) The mention of the Account Register Number ensures greater promptitude in replying
(d) Order forms are only supplied for writing out orders, and consequently if used for any other purpose a delay arises in dealing with them

ORDERS FOR GOODS

A Special Staff is in attendance day and night to deal with Post and Telephone Orders, so that Meat, Poultry, Fish, etc., may be sent out by the early vans

VERBAL ORDERS

For Customers having large orders to place for Groceries, etc., an Order Office is provided, thus saving them the trouble of visiting the various counters. The Order Office is situated in the Royal Exchange in the centre of the building

COLLECTION OF CUSTOMERS' ORDERS

Standing orders can be placed for regular delivery of Groceries, Fish, Meat, etc., and for the convenience of customers Carmen when delivering may bring back written orders

ORDER BOOKS

For writing orders in duplicate, Order Books are supplied free. When writing orders, none but words descriptive of the Goods required should be used. The embodiment of such quotations as ' Please send,' ' Kindly deliver,' etc., constitutes a letter which is surcharged accordingly by the Post Office officials—a procedure which entails delay in the delivery of the letter, and in the execution of the order. In order to facilitate delivery Customers are requested to give their nearest Railway Station on all orders

TIME OF POSTING

Order Forms intended to reach Harrods by the early morning post must be posted in London and Suburbs before 3.30 p.m. the previous day

PERISHABLE PROVISIONS

Customers will find it to their advantage to order Fish, Meat, Poultry, Fruit and Dressed Provisions separately from the General Orders ; this will ensure more prompt despatch. When orders cannot be despatched by Goods Train in time to meet Customers' special requirements they will at the discretion of the company be despatched by Passenger Train, Carriage Paid, and the difference between Goods and Passenger rates debited to customer's accounts

TELEPHONE ORDERS

An efficient staff of Order Clerks is kept in constant attendance for the purpose of receiving orders. Since they are provided with the morning quotations for Fish and other articles of daily consumption they can give any information as to the most seasonable goods, prices, etc., etc.

COUNTRY ORDERS 24 HOUR SERVICE

Every endeavour is made in order to ensure Country Customers receiving their Goods within 24 hours of posting the order

TELEPHONE SLOANE 1234 (Day and Night)

AN ALL NIGHT TELEPHONE SERVICE

is in force at Harrods, and a Special Staff in attendance ensures the reception of Orders from Customers at any hour Night or Day

TELEPHONE ORDERS

received after business hours will be executed and delivered by the first delivery after the receipt of the Order

TELEGRAPHIC ORDERS

Customers are advised to make use of the Departmental Initials and numbers which are quoted throughout the catalogue

PUBLIC TELEPHONES

are provided on the 3rd floor for the use of Customers at the usual public charge

TELEGRAMS

Customers sending telegraphic enquiries respecting purchases would save delay by naming the goods that have been ordered ; the words ' Parcels,' ' Goods,' etc., being altogether inadequate to afford any assistance in tracing or identifying them
It would greatly assist us if Customers would add address when signing a Telegram of Enquiry

TELEGRAPHIC ADDRESS ' Everything Harrods London '

EXPORT ORDERS

Special attention is given to the execution and shipment of export orders to customers abroad. Shipping instructions will be received and enquiries answered at the Export Office. See Export Price List and Rules

ENQUIRY OFFICE

This office is intended not only to answer enquiries but also to make a note of complaints and bring them under

the notice of the Managing Director or General Manager. It is particularly requested that any incivility or want of attention on the part of employees be at once reported

SALES

Harrods hold two Annual Clearance Sales with the object of disposing of the season's surplus stock. These each last for one week only, the Summer Sale in July and the Winter Sale in January

---

HARRODS LTD   LONDON S W 1

CARRIAGE ARRANGEMENTS

DELIVERIES—LONDON AND SUBURBS

Goods are delivered free of charge in London and the Suburbs to any address within the wide radius of Harrods Motor Service. A full list of these Free Deliveries will be sent on request. Suburban orders received not later than 4 p.m. are delivered the following day. Orders received by 12 o'clock on Saturday are delivered on Monday or by the earliest delivery in the following week. A special staff is always in attendance (day and night) for telephone orders

DRAPERY AND WEARING APPAREL, TEA, COFFEE, CONFECTIONERY, AND PERFUMERY

Purchases of 10/- value or over are sent Carriage Paid. If sent by Parcels Post they are delivered free to any address in Great Britain. If sent by rail, Carriage is Paid to nearest Goods Station in Great Britain, or to any Port in the Channel Islands having direct steamer communication with London

GENERAL GOODS

Subject to a few exceptions, purchases of 20/- value or over are sent Carriage Paid to any Goods Station in England or Wales, or (if within the limits of 11 lbs. in weight when packed) Post Free to any address in Great Britain. Purchases of £2 value or over are sent Carriage Paid to any Goods Station in Scotland, or to any Port in the Channel Islands having direct steamer communication with London

GROCERIES, PROVISIONS AND WINES

Subject to a few exceptions, purchases of £1 value or over are sent Carriage Paid to any Goods Station in England and Wales. Purchases of £3 value or over are sent Carriage Paid to any Goods Station in Scotland, or to any Port in the Channel Islands having direct steamer communication with London

Note.—Carriage cannot be paid on one order where the goods have to go to two or more addresses

PERISHABLE GOODS

Patrons living beyond the radius of Harrods Motor Deliveries should state whether Perishable Goods are to be forwarded by Parcels Post or Passenger Train. Perishable Goods for which orders are received at Harrods on Saturday for delivery in districts over 50 miles from London, cannot be sent by Post to arrive the same day. Such orders will be sent by Passenger Train

PARCELS POST

Postage will be paid on purchases of the values already mentioned (not exceeding 11 lbs. in weight when packed) to anywhere in Great Britain. When it is desired that goods exceeding the limit of 11 lbs. in weight should be sent in several parcels, postage on one parcel only will be paid. As it often occurs that goods ordered to be sent by Parcels Post are too large or too heavy for this method of transit, it is always advisable to give the Rail Address as well as the Post Town

FURNITURE AND CARPETS

Purchases of £5 value or over are sent Carriage Paid to any Goods Station in England and Wales. Purchases of £10 value or over are sent Carriage Paid to any Goods Station in Scotland, or to any Port in the Channel Islands having direct steamer communication with London. Complete House Furnishings are delivered free by Harrods Vans as follows : to value of £50, 50 miles ; to value of £100, 120 miles ; to value of £200, 150 miles : to value of £300, 200 miles

PASSENGER TRAIN

Carriage on heavy goods ordered by Passenger Train cannot be paid where the amount of carriage exceeds the Goods Train rates, but an allowance will be made equivalent to the cost of transit by Goods Train

CASH ON DELIVERY

Cash should accompany all orders unless you have a Registered Shopping Account. Purchases can be sent ' Cash on Delivery ' if desired. Goods sent C.O.D. are subject to our ordinary carriage arrangements, but where the Goods ordered C.O.D. amount in value to £1 or over, Harrods pay the C.O.D. fees

CARRIAGE TO NORTHERN IRELAND AND THE IRISH FREE STATE

Drapery, Wearing Apparel, Tea, Coffee, Confectionery and Perfumery. Purchases value 10/- and over Post or Rail free

Groceries, Provisions and Wines. Purchases value £5 or over, Carriage Forward and an allowance of 5 per cent. made in lieu of Carriage, or Carriage Paid at our option. Other Goods. Purchases value £2 or over, Carriage Forward and an allowance of 5 per cent. made in lieu of Carriage or Carriage Paid at our option

PACKING CASES

Groceries, Provisions and Wines are packed in non-returnable Cases, free of charge

Cases and Crates for Furniture, Pictures, China, Glass, Toys, etc., are charged at cost but credited in full if returned Carriage Paid and received in good condition

GOODS ON APPROVAL

Drapery Goods, except those of a delicate and fragile nature, are sent on approbation to any part of Great Britain upon payment of the necessary deposit (if no Account has been opened) and upon the understanding that goods not approved are returned immediately and received by Harrods in perfect condition. Goods on approval are insured both ways, subject to a Certificate of Posting or Registration being obtained when the return parcel is handed over to the Post Office. Customers are requested to retain the Certificate in the event of a claim being made on the Insurance Company

ADDITIONAL ORDERS

Additional orders too late for inclusion with original orders will be treated as separate orders, and if under 10/- in value will be sent carriage forward

STATION CLOAK ROOMS

Parcels may be sent to the Cloak Room of any London Station and booked free of charge provided the customer gives a reasonable time to admit our Vans delivering by the time mentioned in the order

GOODS REPORTED MISSING

All orders are most carefully checked before despatch, and where goods have apparently been omitted a careful search in the straw or packing is respectfully recommended as often the goods are discovered to have been received but overlooked

GOODS DAMAGED IN TRANSIT

Should it be discovered that goods have been damaged, or articles stolen from packages during transit, Customers are advised to give information at once to the Station Master or local agent from whom the goods are received, thus affording an opportunity of inspecting the damaged goods. The Company, however, does not hold itself responsible for any damage or loss sustained after goods have been delivered to the Railway Company or carrier

LEFT PARCELS OFFICE

For the convenience of customers a Parcels Office has been opened near the Chief Cashier's Office and customers are invited to leave their coats, umbrellas, parcels or hand baggage there. Should they wish to take their purchases with them, the assistants will send them to the Parcel Office on request

LOST PROPERTY

Lost Property, Money or Jewellery is at once taken to the ' Secretary's Office ' where it is retained by the Lost Property Officer until claimed

HARRODS BANKING DEPARTMENT

COMPLETE BANKING FACILITIES

The convenience of having a banking account in the very place where one's shopping is done, and the genuine interest and courtesy shewn towards each customer, are but a few of the advantages which Harrods offer. You are cordially invited to call and discuss banking arrangements for your personal or business needs

CURRENT ACCOUNTS: Current Accounts are opened for Shareholders and Customers or friends introduced by them. Interest at the rate of 2½ per cent. per annum, credited annually, is allowed upon the minimum monthly balance, provided it is not under £20

No Commission charged for keeping Accounts, but the opening lodgment must not be under £20, nor the minimum balance less than £10

DEPOSIT ACCOUNTS: Money is received on deposit in sums of £1 up to £500 subject to seven days' notice of withdrawal. Higher amounts subject to arrangement. Interest is allowed from date of deposit to date upon which withdrawal notice expires, and is credited or paid, at customers' option, half-yearly, 30th June and 31st December The Directors reserve to themselves the power to return deposits or change the rate of interest Deposit Accounts may not be drawn upon by Cheque

BANKING HOURS: 9 a.m. to 6 p.m. Saturdays: 9 a.m. to 1 p.m.

OPENING AN ACCOUNT: Customers residing at a distance, who wish to open an Account, should write for an application form

FOREIGN EXCHANGE: Circular Notes and Letters of Credit issued for Travellers to all parts of the World. American and Canadian Express Cheques cashed and foreign money exchanged

CHILDREN'S SAVINGS BANK: Accounts may be opened by children, or by parents or guardians acting on their behalf

Accounts to be opened with not less than 5s. upon receipt of which Harrods Supply a Home Safe and a Bank Pass Book

Interest is allowed on each complete £1 up to £50 from date of Deposit, at the rate of 5 per cent., and is added to the account half-yearly on June 30th and December 31st

For any sum in excess of £50 interest will be paid at the ruling rate for Harrods Bank Deposits Sums not exceeding £10 may be withdrawn without notice. Higher amounts subject to arrangement

HARRODS LTD

Telephone SLOANE 1234
Telegrams 'EVERYTHING HARRODS LONDON'

LONDON S W 1

A DEPOSIT ORDER ACCOUNT
SAVES $2\frac{1}{2}\%$

The Ideal Method of Shopping

WHETHER you shop by post or in person you will appreciate the convenience and economy of Harrods Deposit Order Account which may be opened on receipt of £5 and upwards, to be renewed as exhausted

---

A Bonus of $2\frac{1}{2}\%$

is allowed on sums of £5 and upwards deposited in prepayment for goods

If £**5** is received	- **2/6** is added	
,, £**10** ,,	- **5/-**	,,
,, £**20** ,,	- **10/-**	,,

and larger amounts at the same rate

By this method all your shopping can be done under one roof and you save both the time and the inconvenience of paying cash for each purchase

Accounts are rendered regularly, showing the extent to which the Account has been drawn

Why not open an Account To-day?

HARRODS LTD

Telephone SLOANE 1234
Telegrams 'EVERYTHING HARRODS LONDON'

LONDON S W 1

Deferred Payments

HARRODS EASY PAYMENT SCHEME FOR THE PURCHASE OF HOME FURNISHINGS

—✦—

HARRODS Deliver Furniture and Furnishing Purchases value £20 and upwards, provided that the actual Furniture constitutes at least half of the total value of the order, on a first payment of one-tenth of the full price, the balance, plus $2\frac{1}{2}\%$ per annum, being payable over one, two or three years, according to the amount of purchase

---

This Example Explains

	£	s	d
Cash Value of Furniture, say	£100	0	0
You Deposit one-tenth	10	0	0
Balance	90	0	0
Add Interest at $2\frac{1}{2}$ % for 2 years	4	10	0
Leaving 24 monthly payments of	3	18	9
Or add Interest at $2\frac{1}{2}$ % for 3 years... ...	6	15	0
Leaving 36 monthly payments of	2	13	9

EVERY HOME NEED INCLUDED

Under Harrods Easy Payment Scheme your purchases may include Furniture, Carpets, Upholstery, Curtains, Bedsteads, Bedding, China, Glass, Linens, Turnery and Ironmongery.

Examples of some of the Special Purchases included in the Deferred Payment Plan

	TERMS		TERMS
Bicycles ... Typewriters ... Perambulators ... Sewing Machines (to the value of £5 and over)	12 equal monthly instalments and 5% interest is added to Cash Price.	New Motor Cars	A deposit of not less than one-fifth of the cash price and the balance plus 5% interest per annum by twelve or eighteen equal monthly instalments.
Motor Cycles	A deposit of not less than one-fourth of the list price and the balance plus 8% interest by twelve monthly instalments.	Second-Hand Cars	A deposit of not less than one-third of the cash price and the balance plus 5% interest per annum by twelve or eighteen equal monthly instalments.
Pianos ... ... See Page 120. Gramophones ... ,, ,, 136.			

HARRODS MOTOR DELIVERIES

TOWN, SUBURBAN AND COUNTRY DELIVERIES

Our Own Motors Deliver in the Following Districts

Daily Except where Otherwise Stated

TOWN DELIVERIES

4 DELIVERIES DAILY—Knightsbridge, West Brompton, Belgravia, St. James', Chelsea, South Kensington, Pimlico, Mayfair, Earls Court, Hyde Park, Marylebone, Bayswater, Victoria, St. James' Park, Westminster, Brompton, Charing Cross

3 DELIVERIES DAILY—Hampstead, St. John's Wood, Kilburn, Regent's Park, Campden Hill, West Kensington, North Kensington, Notting Hill, Strand, Hammersmith, Holland Park, Paddington, Kilburn Park, Westbourne Park, Haverstock Hill, Primrose Hill, Finchley Road (up to and including Nos. 619 (odd) and 448 (even)) (see Suburban), Queens Park, Royal Oak, Shepherds Bush, Roslyn Park, Swiss Cottage, Hampstead Heath, Ravenscourt Park, Barons Court, Parliament Hill, Parliament Hill Fields

2 DELIVERIES DAILY—Fulham, Euston, Walham Green, Hurlingham, Gower Street, Clerkenwell, Pentonville (South side of Pentonville Road only) (see Suburban), Parsons Green, St. Pancras, Soho, Bloomsbury

1 DELIVERY DAILY—Liverpool Street (City), Farringdon Street (City), Cannon Street (City), St. Pauls (City), Holborn, Broad Street (City), Moorgate Street (City), Mansion House (City), Monument (City), St. Giles

SUBURBAN AND COUNTRY DELIVERIES

DAILY DELIVERY
Including Mondays

Acton (Middx.)
Acton Green
Alexandra Park
Alleyn Park
  (Dulwich)
Amherst Park
Anerley

Balham
Balls Pond
Barnes
Barnsbury
Battersea
Bedford Park
Bermondsey
Beulah Hill
Blackheath
Borough
Bounds Green
Bowes Park
Brixton
Brockley
Brondesbury
Bruce Grove
Burnt Ash (Lee)

Camberwell
Camden Town
Canonbury
Catford
Central Hill
  (Norwood)
Chalk Farm
Champion Hill
Child's Hill
Chiswick
Cintra Park
  (Dulwich)
Clapham
Clapham Com.
Clapham Park
Clapton
Clissold Park
Collier's Wood
Colney Hatch
Cottenham Park
Cricklewood
Crofton Pk., S.E.
Crouch End
Crouch Hill
Crystal Palace

Dalston
Dartmouth Park
Denmark Hill
Deptford
Dollis Hill
Drayton Pk., N.
Dulwich

Ealing
Earlsfield
East Dulwich
East Finchley
East Sheen
Edmonton
Elephant &
  Castle

Finchley
  (Church End)
Finchley Road
  (Above Nos. 619
  and 448)
  (See Town)
Finchley, North
Finsbury Park
Forest Hill
Fortis Green
Friern Barnet

Gipsy Hill
Golder's Green
Gospel Oak

Green Lanes
Greenwich
Grove Park
  (Camberwell)
Grove Park
  (Chiswick)
Grove Park (Lee)
Gunnersbury

Hackney
Hackney Downs
Hackney Wick
Hampstead
  Garden Suburb
Hanger Hill
Hanwell
Harlesden
Harringay
Hatcham
Herne Hill
Highbury
Highgate
Hither Green
Holloway
Honor Oak
Hornsey
Hornsey Rise

Islington

Kennington
Kensal Green
Kentish Town
Ken Wood,
  Highgate
Kew
King's Cross
Kingsland
Knights Hill

Ladywell
Lambeth
Lavender Hill
Laurie Park
Lee (Kent)
Lee Green
Lewisham
Lordship Park
Loughboro' Park
Lower Clapton
Lower Norwood
Lower Sydenham
Lower Tooting

Merton (Surrey)
Merton Abbey
Merton Park
Mildmay Park
Mill Hill Park
Mitcham
Morden (Surrey)
Muswell Hill

Neasden
New Cross
Newington
Newington Butts
New Southgate
Noel Park, N.
Norbury (Surrey)
Northfields
Norwood (Surrey)
Nunhead

Old Kent Road
Old Oak Com.
Old Oak Estate

Palmer's Green
Park Royal
Peckham
Peckham Rye
Penge

DAILY DELIVERY
Including Mondays—continued.

Pentonville
  (North side of
  Pentonville
  Road and
  North thereof.
  See Town)
Perivale
Petersham
Putney (twice
  daily)

Raynes Park
Richmond
Roehampton
  (twice daily)
Roehampton Vale
  (twice daily)
Rotherhithe
Rushey Green

Seven Sisters
Sheen (Surrey)
Shoot-up Hill
Southfields
Southgate (Middx.)
South Hackney
South Norwood
Southwark
Stamford Hill
Stockwell
Stoke Newington
Stonebridge
  Park (Middx.)
Streatham
  Com.
Streatham Hill

Stroud Green
Sydenham
Sylvan Hill

Thornton Heath
Tollington Park
Tooting, Upper
  and Lower
Tottenham
Tufnell Park
Tulse Hill
Turnham Green

Upper Clapton
Upper Norwood
Upper Sydenham
Upper Tolling-
  ton Park

Vauxhall

Walworth
Wandsworth
Wandsworth
  Com.
Waterloo
West Norwood
Willesden
Willesden Green
Wimbledon
Wimbledon
  Com.
Winchmore Hill
Wood Green
Wood Park
  (Dulwich)

EXCEPT MONDAYS

Abbey Wood
Abbots Langley
Addington
Addiscombe
Addlestone
Aldenham
Alperton
Amersham
Apsley End
Arkley
Ascot
Ashford (Middx.)
Ashtead

Banstead
Barnet
Barnet Gate
Batchworth
Batchworth
  Heath
Bayford
Beaconsfield
Bean
Beckenham
Beddington
Bedfont
Bell Bar
Bellingham
Belmont (Surrey)
Belvedere
Bengeo (Herts.)
Bentley Heath
Berkhamsted
Bessell's Green
Betchworth
Bexley
Bexley Heath
Bickley (Kent)
Biggin Hill
Binfield
Bisham
Bisley
Bitchet Green
Black Fen
Blendon

Bletchingley
Blindley Heath
Bookham
Boreham Wood
Bourne End
Boveney
Bovingdon (Herts.)
Bovingdon Green
  (Herts.)
Bovingdon Green
  (Bucks.)
Box Hill
Boxmoor
Bracknell
Brasted
Bray
Bray Wick
Brentford
Brickendon
Bricketwood
Brimsdown
Broadoak End
  (Hertford)
Brockham Green
Bromley (Kent)
Broxbourne
Buckhurst Hill
Buckland
Bulls Cross
Bulstrode Park
Burchett's Green
Burford Bridge
Burgh Heath
Burham Beeches
Burnham (Bucks.)
Bushey
Bushey Heath
Bush Hill Park
Byfleet

Callendars Gate
Cambridge Park
Carshalton
Cassio Bridge
Cassiobury Park

DAILY DELIVERY
Except Mondays—continued

Castle Hill
Caterham
Chaldon
Chalfont St. Giles
Chalfont St. Peter
Chalvey
Chandlers Cross
Charlton (Kent)
Charterhouse
Cheam
Chelsfield
Chelsham
Chenies
Chertsey
Chesham
Chesham Bois
Cheshunt
Chessington
Chevening
Chingford
Chipperfield
Chipping Barnet
Chipstead (Kent)
Chipstead
  (Surrey)
Chislehurst
Chobham
Chorley Woods
Church Cobham
Cippenham
Claybury
Claygate
Ciewer
Cobham
Cockfosters
Cole Green
Coles Hill
Colnbrook
Colney St.
  (St. Albans)
Compton
Cookham
Cookham Dean
Coombe (Surrey)
Coombe Hill
Coombe Warren
Couisdon
Cowley
Cox Green
Cranford (Middx.)
Crastock
Crayford
Crockham Hill
Crockenhill
Crofton
Crowthorne
Croxley Green
Croydon
Cuddington
Cudham

Dartford
Datchet
Dedworth
Denham
Digswell
Dorking
Dormans
Dormans Land
Dormans Park
Dorney
Dorney Reach
Downe
Dropmore
Dunton Green

Earlswood
East Barnet
East Bedfont
Eastbury (Middx.)
East Clandon
Eastcote (Middx.)

Easthampstead
East Horsley
East Molesey
East Wick
Edgware
Effingham
Egham
Elmers End
Elstree
Eltham
Enfield
Enfield Lock
Englefield Green
Epsom
Epsom Downs
Erith
Esher
Essendon (Herts.)
Eton
Eton Wick
Ewell (Surrey)
Eynsford

Farleigh
Farnborough
  (Kent)
Farnham Com.
Farnham Royal
Farningham
Fawkham
Felden
Feltham
Fetcham
Fifield
Flaunden
Fouts Cray
Forty Hill
Four Elms
Fulmer
Fulwell (Middx.)
Furze Platt

Ganwick
Garston
Gatton
Gerrard's Cross
Godalming
Godden Green
Godstone
Goff's Oak
Gordon Boys'
  Home
Great Amwell
Great Bookham
Great Marlow
Greenford
Green St. Green
Guildford

Hackbridge
Hadham Cross
Hadley (Herts.)
Hadley Woods
  (Middlesex)
Haileybury
  College
Halliford
Halsted
Ham (Surrey)
Hampton (Middx.)
Hampton Court
Hampton Hill
Hampton Wick
Hanworth
  (Middlesex)
Harefield
Harlington
  (Middlesex)
Harmer Green
Harmondsworth
Harrow
Harrow Weald
Hatch End

DAILY DELIVERY
Except Mondays—continued

Hatchford
Hatfield (Herts.)
Hatton (Middx.)
Hawley (Kent)
Hawthorne Hill
Hayes (Kent)
Hayes (Middx.)
Headley
Hedgerley
Hedsor
Hemel Hempstead
Hendon
Heronsgate
Hersham
Hertingfordbury
Hertford
Hertford Heath
Heston
Hextable
  (Nr. Swanley)
Highams Park
High Barnet
Highwood Hill
Hildenborough
Hill End
  (St. Albans)
Hillingdon
Hitcham (Bucks.)
Hoddesdon
Holyport
Hook (Surrey)
Hook Heath
Horsell
Horsley
Horsemoor Green
Horton (Bucks.)
Horton (Surrey)
Horton Kirby
Hounslow
How Green
Hunsdon
Hunton Bridge

Ickenham
Ide Hill
Ightham
Inkermann
  Barracks
Isleworth
Iver
Iver Heath
Ivy Hatch

Jordans

Kemsing
Kenley
Kent House
Kenton
Keston
Kidbrook
Kingsbury
King's Langley
Kingston (Surrey)
Kingston Hill
Kingston Vale
Kingswood
Kippington
Knaphill
Knockholt
Knotty Green

Laleham
Lamorbey
  (Kent)
Lampton
Langley (Bucks.)
Langley Marish
Langley Park
Latimer
Leatherhead
Leavesden
Leaves Green

Leigh (Surrey)
Lessness Heath
Letchmore Heath
Limpsfield
Lingfield
Little Amwell
Little
  Berkhamsted
Little Bookham
Little Heath
Little Marlow
Littleton (Middx.)
Littlewick Green
Locks Bottom
London Colney
Long Cross
Long Ditton
Longford (Middx.)
Loughton
Lower Halliford
Lower Kingswood
Lyne (Surrey)

Maidenhead
Maidenhead
  Thicket
Malden
Marlow
Marlow Common
Maybury
Mayford
Merstham
Mickleham
Mill Hill (Middx.)
Mogador
Monken Hadley
Moor Park
Mortlake
Motspur Park
Mottingham
Much Hadham

New Barnet
Newchapel
New Egham

New Eltham
Newhaw
New Malden
New Oxted
Northaw
North Cray
North End (Herts.)
North Mimms
Northolt
Northwood
  (Middlesex)
Norwood Green
Nutfield

Oakleigh Park
Oakley Green
Oatlands Park
  (Surrey)
Ockham
Old Charlton
Old Windsor
Orpington
Osterley Park
Otford
Ottershaw
Ovendon
Oxhey
Oxshott
Oxted

Park Street
  (St. Albans)
Penn (Bucks.)
Penton Hook
Pinkney's Green
Pinner
Plaistow (Kent)
Plumstead

SUBURBAN and COUNTRY DELIVERIES—*continued*

DAILY DELIVERY
Except Mondays—*continued*

DAILY DELIVERY
Except Mondays—*continued*

DAILY DELIVERY
Except Mondays—*continued*

DAILY DELIVERY
Except Mondays—*continued*

Ponders End
Potter's Bar
Preston (Middlesex)
Purley
Puttenham (near Guildford)
Pyrford
Radlett
Ranmore Com.
Redhill
Reigate
Riching Park
Rickmansworth
Riddlesdown
Ridge (Herts.)
Ripley
Riverhead
Roe Green
Ruislip
Rye Park
St. Albans
St. John's
St. Margaret's (Middlesex)
St. Mary Cray
St. Paul's Cray
Salt Hill
Sanderstead

Sarratt
Seal
Seal Chart
Seer Green
Selhurst
Selsdon
Send
Sevenoaks
Sewardstone
Shalford
Shenley (Herts.)
Shepperton (Middlesex)
Shirley
Shooter's Hill
Shoreham (Kent)
Shortlands
Sidcup
Sipson
Slades Green
Slough
Snaresbrook
Southall
South Darenth
South Godstone
South Mimms
South Nutfield
South Penge Park
Spring Grove
Staines

Stanmore
Stanstead (St. Margaret's)
Stanstead Abbott
Stanwell
Stoke, nr. Guildford
Stoke d'Abernon
Stoke Poges
Stone Street
Stoughton
Strawberry Hill
Street Cobham
Sudbury (Middx.)
Sunbury
Sundridge
Sunningdale
Sunninghill
Surbiton
Sutton (Middx.)
Sutton (Surrey)
Sutton-at-Hone
Sutton Green
Swanley
Swanley Junc.
Tadworth
Tandridge
Tangley Park
Taplow

Tatsfield
Teddington
Thames Ditton
Theydon Bois
Thorpe (Surrey)
Titsey
Tolworth
Totteridge (Herts.)
Turnford
Twickenham
Under River
Upper Halliford
Upper Warlingham
Upton (Bucks.)
Uxbridge
Vanburgh Park
Virginia Water
Waddon (Surrey)
Wallington (Surrey)
Waltham Abbey
Waltham Cross
Walton Heath
Walton-on-the-Hill

Walton-on-Thames
Wanstead
Ware
Wareside
Warfield
Warlingham
Watford
Wealdstone
Welham Green
Well End
Well Hall (Kent)
Welling (Kent)
Wellington College
Welwyn
Welwyn Garden City
Wembley
Wentworth
West Byfleet
Westcombe Park
Westcott
West Drayton
Westerham
West Green
West Horsley
West Humble
West Hyde
West Molesey
West Wickham

Wexham
Weybridge (Surrey)
Whetstone (Middx.)
White Webbs Park
Whitton (Middx.)
Whyteleafe
Widford (Herts.)
Widmore (Kent)
Wilmington (Kent)
Windlesham
Windsor
Windsor Forest
Winkfield
Wisley
Woking
Wokingham
Woldingham
Wooburn
Wooburn Green
Woodford
Woodford Green
Woodford Wells
Woodham (Surrey)
Woodmansterne
Woolwich
Worcester Park
Wormley (near Broxbourne)

Wormley Hill (nr. Broxbourne)
Worplesdon
Wraysbury

Wrotham
Yarne
Yeading
Yiewsley

MONDAYS ONLY

Copthorne (near Crawley)
Crawley
Cuckfield
East Grinstead
Felbridge

Forest Row
Haywards Heath
Horley
Ifield
Staplefield
Three Bridges

WEDNESDAYS & FRIDAYS

Arborfield
Barkham

Farley Hill
Finchampstead

WEDS. & SATS.

Cuffley

THURSDAYS

Pirbright

Suburban Orders received not later than 4 p.m. are delivered the following day. Orders received by 12 o'clock on Saturday are delivered on Monday or by the earliest delivery in the following week

---

SPECIAL NOTICES—TOWN ONLY

Customers are respectfully asked to give their orders for *Mineral Waters, Potatoes, Firewood* and *Oil* early in the week, as the pressure on our Delivery Department is extremely heavy on Fridays and Saturdays

EMPTIES are collected daily, Saturdays excepted

DELIVERY of *Ice* and *Paraffin* :—Orders must be given at least one day prior to that upon which delivery is required

For other conditions of Delivery see page 5

ENTRUST YOUR ADVERTISING TO

HARRODS

HARRODS Advertising Agency undertakes every branch of Advertising and accepts advertisements for papers published in any part of the world

Long experience and scientific methods of advertising enable them to provide for advertisers, not only the most practical methods of publicity but also the most advantageous positions for advertisements

It is by such means only that the competitive element so predominant in the modern business world to-day can be met on level terms

Harrods will be glad to submit estimates on any branch of Advertising

HARRODS ADVERTISING AGENCY
32 HANS CRESCENT LONDON SW1

POST AND TELEGRAPH OFFICE

Situated on the third Floor near the Theatre and Railway Ticket Offices

All postal facilities

Savings Bank

Telegrams and Letters may be despatched from this Department

POST OFFICE
THIRD FLOOR
Hours of collection
10 a.m. to 6 p.m.

HARRODS INCOME TAX DEPARTMENT

Expert advice and assistance to all Income Tax Payers

Moderate charges

An assurance of absolute confidence in all transactions

INCOME TAX
DEPARTMENT
Repayment claims prepared and submitted

Do your shopping
by *telephone*

IF for any reason you find it inconvenient to shop in person you may obtain through our thoroughly efficient Telephone Order Office any purchase or information you require

No matter what time of the day or night your 'phone order is received, there are specially trained Order Clerks ready to deal promptly and accurately with orders and enquiries

Urgent orders telephoned during business hours are executed and despatched without delay and orders received after the closing hour are sent off by the early morning delivery vans and mails next day

Phone SLOANE *1234 for anything at any time of the day or night*

Harrods Limited London S W 1

HARRODS

EXPORT AND SHIPPING DEPARTMENT

Telegrams : 'EVERYTHING, HARRODS, LONDON '—Telephone, Sloane 1234 (101 lines). Open Day and Night

CODES : A.B.C. 5th Edition and Western Union

Merchandise and Stores of every description Packed and Shipped Abroad

Expeditions completely equipped for all parts of the world

Goods packed for Mule or Camel Loads. Marine Insurance effected

HARRODS Export Service has developed during the last few years to such an extent that no matter in what remote corner of the globe you live you may rest assured that your most exacting requirements will be fulfilled. Every order has the personal supervision of the Departmental Manager concerned and the packing is carried out by expert packers with the utmost care and despatch

The staff of the Export Section is composed of men whose sole business is to attend to the needs of customers abroad and who make such needs their especial care and interest

Harrods supply complete outfits for ordinary wear and for Expeditions of every kind

Residences furnished and equipped in all parts of the World

Officers' Messes and Clubs and Institutions provisioned with the best English and Foreign foodstuffs

TERMS OF PAYMENT

Full payment by Sight Draft or International Money Order on London, crossed ' Barclays Bank Ltd.' should accompany orders, unless a deposit account has been opened. For orders value £10 or over Harrods will, if desired, on receipt of 25 per cent. of amount, give instructions for bills of lading, etc., to be handed over by their bankers on payment of balance

HARRODS LTD   LONDON S W 1

World Wide Service

HARRODS SHIPPING CORRESPONDENTS
AND CLEARING AGENTS ABROAD

ADELAIDE ..	..	H. GRAVES & CO.
ALEXANDRIA	..	JOHN ROSS & CO.
BEIRA	..	THE MANICA TRADING CO.
BOMBAY	..	COX & KING'S AGENCY.
CALCUTTA ..	..	BALMER, LAWRIE & CO.
CAPETOWN ..	..	DIVINE GATES & CO.
COLOMBO ..	..	E. B. CREASY & CO.
DURBAN ..	..	PARRY LEON & HAYHOE LTD.
KARACHI ..	..	MACKINNON, MCKENZIE & CO.
MADRAS ..	..	BINNY & CO. (MADRAS) LTD.
MELBOURNE	..	MULLALY BYRNE (PTY.) LTD.
MOMBASA ..	..	THE MOMBASA BONDED WAREHOUSE CO.
NEW YORK ..	..	WOOD NIEBUHR & CO.
PORT ELIZABETH..		NEALE, WILKINSON & RENNIE LTD.
PORT SUDAN	..	GELLATLY, HANKEY & CO.
RANGOON ..	..	ADAM SCOTT & CO.
SINGAPORE ..	..	PATERSON, SIMONS & CO.
SYDNEY ..	..	FRANK CRIDLAND (CARRIERS LTD.)
NEW ZEALAND	..	NEW ZEALAND EXPRESS CO.

Customers are advised to have their goods consigned to the Firms mentioned, as a saving in shipping charges can generally be effected and delivery expedited

Harrods do not hold themselves responsible for any difficulties which may arise in connection with the importation of Goods into any country

A DEPOSIT ACCOUNT

Harrods strongly recommend you to open a Deposit Order Account, which saves considerable time, trouble and expense. A Deposit Order Account may be opened upon a receipt of £5 and upwards, to be renewed as exhausted. A Bonus of 2½ per cent. is allowed on sums of £5 and upwards, on a regular running Account, provided a Credit balance is maintained

INSURANCE

Insurance covering ordinary Marine risks, Pilferage, Theft, and Breakage on China and Glass, etc., is effected unless instructions to the contrary are given at the time of purchase. Harrods do not accept responsibility once a consignment has been safely handed over to a Shipping Company, Post Office or Forwarding Agent, and it is therefore essential that all consignments should be fully covered by insurance

Goods under 10s. in value sent by Parcel, Letter or Book Post, will not be insured without your special instructions

If on arrival any package shows signs of having been tampered with, the weight should be compared with that shown on the invoice before a receipt is given. The contents should then be checked up as quickly as possible, and the Shipping Company, Forwarding Agent, or Carrier advised of any loss or damage discovered. In the event of shortage in the number of packages delivered, claim should be sent immediately to the Shipping Company, Agent or Carrier. Notice of claims, supported wherever possible by documentary evidence, should be forwarded to Harrods, who will inform the Underwriters on your behalf and remit the amount received in settlement

PARCELS POST

If you wish to take advantage of the C.O.D. System (where it is in operation), you should remit one-third of the total value of the order

Parcels within the prescribed limits may be sent by Parcels Post wherever the Service extends

FORWARDING CHARGES

If you have no account at Harrods, please add 15 per cent. to Remittance to cover Packing, Freight, Insurance. Any balance will be adjusted

CUSTOMS CHARGES

Harrods cannot undertake to pre-pay Customs charges, but if desired will arrange with Agents at port of arrival to clear and deliver. Customs charges on postal packets are usually collected by Post Office at destination

OUTSIDE PACKAGES

For your convenience small packages will be received for enclosure with goods purchased from Harrods. These must be securely and properly packed when delivered, as no responsibility can be accepted by Harrods. The packages should also be marked clearly with the name and address of sender, and addressed to Export Packing Department, Harrods Ltd. In every instance a form of declaration of contents must be signed. A small commission will be charged for this Service, in proportion to the weight and bulk of the package

HARRODS LTD

LONDON SW1

JEWELLERY DEPARTMENT
Gems of Rare Beauty

J 465/23
Diamond Brooch, Platinum settings
£85 0 0

J 71/70
Pearl and Diamond Earrings
Platinum settings
£235 0 0

J 370/4
Emerald and Diamond Brooch. Finely set in Platinum
£110 0 0

J 73/47
Diamond Earrings. Platinum settings
£75 0 0

J 477/35
Platinum, Sapphire and Diamond Bracelet
£152 10 0

J 360/17
Diamond Bow Brooch, Platinum setting
£97 10 0

J 467/27
Emeralds, Diamond and all Platinum Brooch
£175 0 0

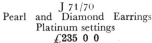

J 465/25
Sapphire and Diamond Brooch. Platinum setting
£60 0 0

J 467/24
Sapphire and Diamond Brooch. Platinum setting
£145 0 0

J 181/8
All Diamond Brooch. Platinum setting
£57 10 0

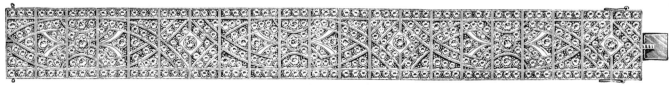

J 477/13
Diamond and Platinum Bracelet
£500 0 0

DIAMOND MOUNTING, JEWELLERY ALTERATIONS AND REPAIRS BY SKILLED WORKMEN

ALL PRICES ARE SUBJECT TO MARKET FLUCTUATIONS

HARRODS LTD

Telephone SLOANE 1234
Telegrams 'EVERYTHING HARRODS LONDON'

LONDON S W 1

JEWELLERY DEPARTMENT
Inexpensive Gem Set Rings
CAREFULLY SELECTED STONES BEAUTIFULLY
MOUNTED AND FINISHED

J 100 1
Diamonds and Rubies
Platinum setting
£11 15 0

J 100 2
Ruby and Diamonds
Platinum setting
£13 10 0

J 100/3
All Diamond cluster, set
in Platinum
£7 15 0

J 100 4
Diamonds set in Platinum
Gold shank
£15 0 0

J 100/5
All Diamonds, Platinum
setting
£7 15 0

J 100/6
Diamonds set in Platinum
18-ct. White Gold shank
£15 15 0

J 100/7
Sapphire and Diamonds
Platinum setting
£15 0 0

J 100/8
Emerald and Diamonds
set in Platinum
£9 10 0

J 100/9
Diamonds set in Platinum
Diamond shoulders
£7 15 0

J 100/10
Emeralds and Diamonds
mounted Platinum and
White Gold
£10 0 0

J 100/11
Diamonds finely matched
set in Platinum
£14 10 0

J 100/12
Sapphire and Diamonds
Platinum set, Gold shank
£8 17 6

J 100/13
Sapphire and Diamonds
finely set in Platinum
£9 10 0

J 100/14
Diamond five stone
Platinum settings
£6 0 0

J 100/15
Diamonds and Sapphires
Platinum setting
Diamond shoulders
£16 17 6

J 100/16
Diamond three stone
Platinum settings
£15 15 0

J 100/17
All Diamonds, set in
Platinum
£7 15 0

J 100/18
Diamond four stone
Platinum settings
£10 10 0

J 100/19
Sapphire and Diamonds
mounted Platinum and
Gold
£10 10 0

J 100/20
Sapphires and Diamonds
mounted Platinum and
White Gold
£17 0 0

J 100/21
Emeralds and Diamonds
Platinum setting
£9 0 0

J 100/22
Diamond two stone, set
in Platinum
£8 10 0

J 325/69
Diamond necklet snap
set Platinum and White
Gold
£2 7 6

J 325/53
Diamond necklet snap
mounted Platinum and
White Gold
£8 0 0

J 326/53
Pearl and Diamond necklet snap, Platinum setting
£10 10 0

22-ct. Solid Gold Wedding Rings

J 301
From **60/-**

J 302
From **50/-**

J 303
From **70/-**

J 304
From **45/-**

J 305
From **35/-**

J 306
From **25/-**

J 307
From **30/-**

J 308
From **17/6**

A large selection of Platinum Wedding Rings from £3 15 0

J 325/67
Diamond necklet snap
Platinum setting
£4 0 0

J 325/64
Diamond and Sapphire
necklet snap, Platinum
setting
£5 0 0

J 325/44
Emerald and Diamond
necklet snap, Platinum
setting
£10 15 0

ALL PRICES ARE SUBJECT TO MARKET FLUCTUATIONS

HARRODS LTD

Telephone SLOANE 1234
Telegrams 'EVERYTHING HARRODS LONDON'

LONDON S W 1

JEWELLERY DEPARTMENT
15-Carat Solid Gold Sporting Brooches

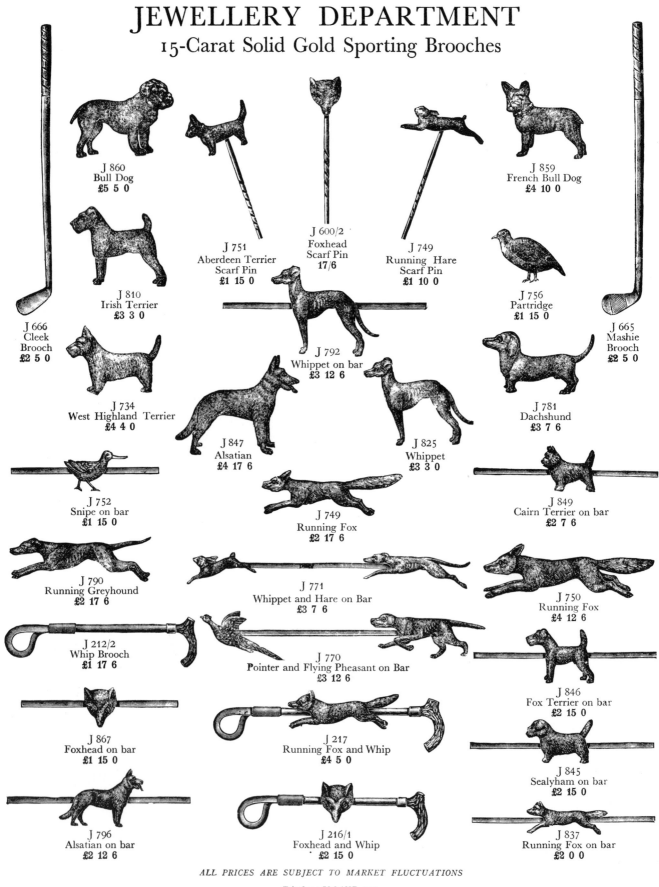

J 860
Bull Dog
£5 5 0

J 751
Aberdeen Terrier
Scarf Pin
£1 15 0

J 600/2
Foxhead
Scarf Pin
17/6

J 749
Running Hare
Scarf Pin
£1 10 0

J 859
French Bull Dog
£4 10 0

J 810
Irish Terrier
£3 3 0

J 756
Partridge
£1 15 0

J 666
Cleek
Brooch
£2 5 0

J 665
Mashie
Brooch
£2 5 0

J 734
West Highland Terrier
£4 4 0

J 792
Whippet on bar
£3 12 6

J 781
Dachshund
£3 7 6

J 752
Snipe on bar
£1 15 0

J 847
Alsatian
£4 17 6

J 825
Whippet
£3 3 0

J 849
Cairn Terrier on bar
£2 7 6

J 790
Running Greyhound
£2 17 6

J 749
Running Fox
£2 17 6

J 771
Whippet and Hare on Bar
£3 7 6

J 750
Running Fox
£4 12 6

J 212/2
Whip Brooch
£1 17 6

J 770
Pointer and Flying Pheasant on Bar
£3 12 6

J 846
Fox Terrier on bar
£2 15 0

J 867
Foxhead on bar
£1 15 0

J 217
Running Fox and Whip
£4 5 0

J 845
Sealyham on bar
£2 15 0

J 796
Alsatian on bar
£2 12 6

J 216/1
Foxhead and Whip
£2 15 0

J 837
Running Fox on bar
£2 0 0

ALL PRICES ARE SUBJECT TO MARKET FLUCTUATIONS

HARRODS LTD

Telephone SLOANE 1234
Telegrams 'EVERYTHING HARRODS LONDON'

LONDON S W 1

JEWELLERY DEPARTMENT

9-ct. Solid Gold Vanity Bags and Cases of Beautiful Workmanship

J 63102
9-ct. Gold with 'grey' Gold stripes, 6¼ ins. wide **£65 0 0**
18-ct. Gold **£110 0 0**

J 62782
9-ct. plain 'green' Gold 5½ ins. wide **£37 10 0**
18-ct. Gold **£82 0 0**

J 62600
9-ct. Gold with 'grey' Gold stripes, 3½ ins. wide **£50 0 0**
18-ct. Gold **£75 0 0** Extra fine expanding mesh

J 131/59
9-ct. Solid Gold Lip Salve Case .. **£4 4 0**

J 514
9-ct. Solid Gold Vanity Box, with glass inside lid Size 1⅞ × 1⅞ ins.
Engine Turned **£6 0 0**
Plain **£5 10 0**

J/R 1
9-ct. Solid Gold Powder Case with glass inside lid
Diam. 1½ ins. **£3 0 0**
,, 1⅞ ins. **£4 0 0**
,, 2⅛ ins. **£5 10 0**

Selections of Jewellery sent on approval on request

J 21
9-ct. Solid Gold combination Cigarette and Vanity Case, size 3 1/16 × 1⅞ ins.
£16 10 0

J/R 2
9-ct. Solid Gold book marker, fitted any initial
Engine Turned **£1 7 6**
Plain .. **£1 5 0**

J 19314
9-ct. Solid woven coloured Gold Fob for Ladies' wear
£2 7 6

J 63276
9-ct. Solid Gold Powder and Lip Salve Stick Box Finely Engine Turned **£10 10 0**

J/R 3
9-ct. Solid Gold box to take 'Poudre Houbigant'
Small size .. **£5 10 0**
Large size .. **£9 9 0**

UNLESS OTHERWISE STATED EACH ARTICLE ILLUSTRATED IS THE EXACT SIZE

J 133
New design. Thin model 9-ct. solid Gold Powder and Puff Box, with glass inside lid **£10 10 0**

ALL PRICES ARE SUBJECT TO MARKET FLUCTUATIONS

HARRODS LTD

Telephone SLOANE 1234
Telegrams 'EVERYTHING HARRODS LONDON'

LONDON S W 1

JEWELLERY DEPARTMENT
Sleeve Links in 9-ct. and 18-ct. Solid Gold
MASONIC LINKS TO ORDER

J 2951
9-ct.	..	30/-
18-ct.	..	75/-

J 2963
9-ct.	..	30/-
18-ct.	..	75/-

J 98/44
9-ct.	..	29/3
18-ct.	..	72/6

J 8816
Mother of Pearl
Platinum border **105/-**

J 2970
9-ct.	..	27/6
18-ct.	..	63/-

J 116F
9-ct.	..	25/-
18-ct.	..	67/6

J 113
9-ct.	..	17/6
18-ct.	..	42/-

J 135F
9-ct.	..	15/-
18-ct.	..	40/-

J 115
9-ct.	..	22/6
18-ct.	..	47/6

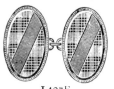

J 127F
9-ct.	..	30/-
18-ct.	..	77/6

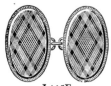

J 115F
9-ct.	..	22/6
18-ct.	..	47/6

J 2947
9-ct.	..	45/-
18-ct.	..	95/-

J 244
9-ct.	..	22/6
18-ct.	..	55/-

J 132F
9-ct.	..	32/6
18-ct.	..	85/-

J 108F
9-ct.	..	17/6
18-ct.	..	40/-

J 8054
18-ct. Gold, Black and
White Enamel .. **105/-**

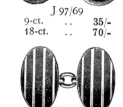

J 119/42
18-ct. Gold
Fine Enamel .. **175/-**

J 116/41
18-ct. Gold, Enamelled
Crystal .. **140/-**

J/A 35
18-ct. Gold
Fine Enamel .. **175/-**

J 115/1
9-ct. Gold, Enamelled
Blue, Red, Green or
Black **37/6**

J 97/70
9-ct.	..	32/6
18-ct.	..	70/-

J 105/41
Platinum and
18-ct. Gold .. **110/-**

J 97/69
9-ct.	..	35/-
18-ct.	..	70/-

J 105/66
Platinum and
18-ct. Gold .. **97/6**

J 115A
9-ct.	..	22/6
18-ct.	..	47/6

J 8932
18-ct. Gold, Black and
White Enamel .. **105/-**

J 117/70
9-ct. Gold and Blue
Enamel **37/6**

J 115/2
9-ct. Gold, Enamelled
Blue, Red, Green, or
Black **37/6**

J 5187
9-ct.	..	27/6
18-ct.	..	63/-

J 117/69
9-ct. Gold, Enamelled
Red or Blue .. **37/6**

J 2961
9-ct.	..	22/6
18-ct.	..	52/6

J 2941
9-ct.	..	30/-
18-ct.	..	75/-

J 8187
18-ct. Gold,
Blue Enamel .. **95/-**

J 85/1
9-ct.	..	27/6
18-ct.	..	75/-

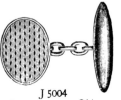

J 5004
9-ct.	..	21/-
18-ct.	..	52/6

ALL PRICES ARE SUBJECT TO MARKET FLUCTUATIONS

HARRODS LTD

Telephone SLOANE 1234
Telegrams 'EVERYTHING HARRODS LONDON'

LONDON SW1

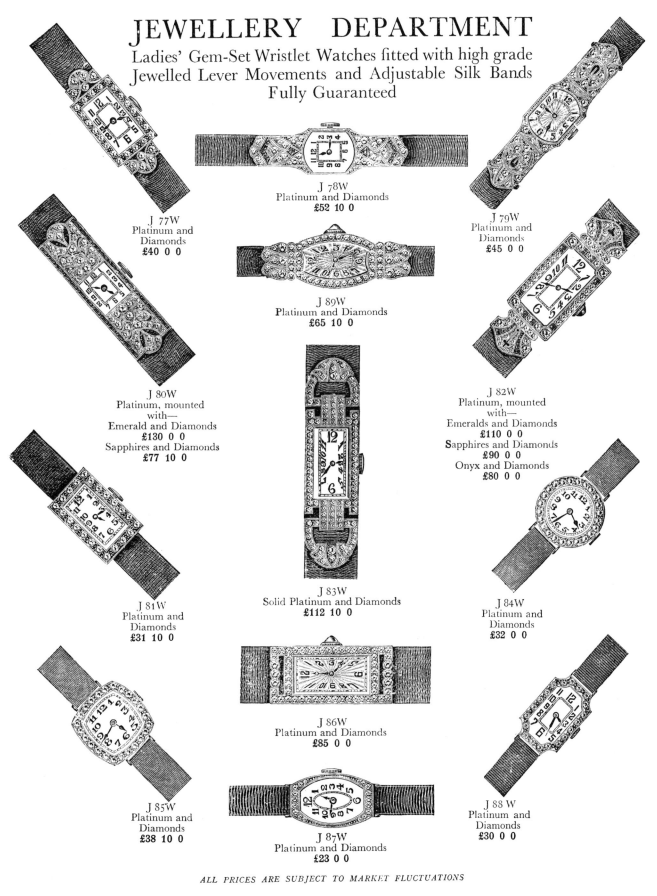

JEWELLERY DEPARTMENT
Ladies' Gem-Set Wristlet Watches fitted with high grade Jewelled Lever Movements and Adjustable Silk Bands
Fully Guaranteed

J 78W
Platinum and Diamonds
£52 10 0

J 77W
Platinum and
Diamonds
£40 0 0

J 79W
Platinum and
Diamonds
£45 0 0

J 89W
Platinum and Diamonds
£65 10 0

J 80W
Platinum, mounted
with—
Emerald and Diamonds
£130 0 0
Sapphires and Diamonds
£77 10 0

J 82W
Platinum, mounted
with—
Emeralds and Diamonds
£110 0 0
Sapphires and Diamonds
£90 0 0
Onyx and Diamonds
£80 0 0

J 83W
Solid Platinum and Diamonds
£112 10 0

J 81W
Platinum and
Diamonds
£31 10 0

J 84W
Platinum and
Diamonds
£32 0 0

J 86W
Platinum and Diamonds
£85 0 0

J 85W
Platinum and
Diamonds
£38 10 0

J 87W
Platinum and Diamonds
£23 0 0

J 88 W
Platinum and
Diamonds
£30 0 0

ALL PRICES ARE SUBJECT TO MARKET FLUCTUATIONS

HARRODS LTD

Telephone SLOANE 1234
Telegrams 'EVERYTHING HARRODS LONDON'

LONDON S W 1

JEWELLERY DEPARTMENT

An interesting page of Watches including the New Rolex 'Oyster' Watches

J 143W 9-CT. GOLD OPEN FACE WATCH

Fine quality, jewelled lever movement ..	**£8 10 0**
Higher grade	**£10 15 0**
18-ct. Gold	**£17 0 0**
Silver .. **£3 0 0** **£4 10 0** and	**£5 15 0**

J 144W 9-CT. GOLD HALF HUNTER WATCH

Jewelled lever movement. Fully Guaranteed	**£11 10 0**
Higher grade	**£15 0 0**
18-ct. Gold .. .. **£21 10 0** and	**£23 10 0**
Silver .. .. **£3 15 0** **£5 15 0** and	**£7 0 0**

J 145W CHRONOGRAPH WATCH

Fine quality jewelled lever movement. Registering minutes, seconds and fifths of seconds up to 30 minutes
Silver **£6 15 0**
9-ct. Gold .. **£16 0 0** 18-ct. Gold **£25 0 0**

J 146W SILVER WRISTLET WATCH

With Leather straps. Fine quality lever movement
£2 0 0

Higher grade { **£2 15 0** **£3 10 0** **£5 10 0**

J 147W LADIES' SILVER WRISTLET WATCH

With either Suede or Silk Wristlet **£1 10 0**
Higher grade **40/-, 57/6, 75/-**

J 148W THE GOLFER'S WATCH
Hunter case of pure White Metal. Can be carried loose in the pocket without danger of breaking the glass. Jewelled lever movement **£2 15 0**
Silver **£3 15 0**

ROLEX 'OYSTER' WATCHES DEFY THE ELEMENTS

J 149W
LADIES' SILVER WATCH
Fine quality jewelled lever movement, with Black Silk Wristlet **£4 4 0**

J 150W 9-CT. GOLD WRISTLET WATCH

Very flat; jewelled lever movement, Suede straps
£5 0 0

Rolex 'Oyster' Watches are definitely dust-proof, water-proof, and immune to changes in temperature. They are hermetically sealed by the specially designed pendant and by the screwed-in back and front cases

All Rolex 'Oyster' Watches are immersed for several hours in water as a final test. The high-grade, jewelled lever movements are fully guaranteed

J 151W 'OYSTER' WATCH

Silver, with Leather strap	.. ..		**£5 15 0**
9-ct. Gold .. **£10 10 0**	18-ct. Gold		**£15 15 0**

Smaller sizes for ladies, at same prices, with Suede or Silk wristlets

J 152W 9-CT. GOLD 'OYSTER' DRESS WATCH
Flat model **£15 15 0**

J 153W 'OYSTER' WATCH

Silver, with Leather strap	.. ..		**£5 15 0**
9-ct. Gold .. **£10 10 0**	18-ct. Gold		**£15 15 0**

Smaller sizes for ladies, at same prices, with Suede or Silk wristlets

ALL PRICES ARE SUBJECT TO MARKET FLUCTUATIONS

CLOCK DEPARTMENT

Inlaid and Carved Grandfather Clocks—London made

The illustrations contained in these pages are representative of a few of the designs offered from Harrods large collection. Every type of Clock can be obtained, whether for Presentation purposes, or personal requirements, and clocks can be specially made in accordance with customers' own designs

REPAIRS—Clocks and Watches of every kind are repaired at Harrods by a staff of competent workmen

Avail yourself of Harrods Clock-Winding Service. Winding and Regulating of any number of clocks undertaken in the London Area, at the rate of **£2** per annum for six clocks, and **4/6** per annum for each additional clock

C 73
Height 7 ft. 4 ins. Three sets of chimes on tubes, three-train movement, chiming Westminster, Whittington and St. Michael. Oak Case
£120 0 0

C 61
Height 6 ft. 5 ins. Nine tube, two train, Westminster, Whittington and St. Michael Chime. Mahogany Case
£80 0 0

C 48
Height 7 ft. Westminster chimes on rods .. **£47 10 0**
Striking hours only **£40 0 0**

C 9
Height 7 ft. 6 ins. Jacobean Oak. Chiming Whittington and Westminster on nine tubes
£85 0 0

ALL PRICES ARE SUBJECT TO MARKET FLUCTUATIONS

Telephone SLOANE 1234

Telegrams 'EVERYTHING HARRODS LONDON'

HARRODS LTD

LONDON SW1

CLOCK DEPARTMENT
Folding Clocks, Alarm Clocks and Novelty Clocks

C 203 RELIABLE CUCKOO CLOCKS

30-hour weight-driven movement .. **£1 15 0**

Others 45/-, 55/-, 75/-

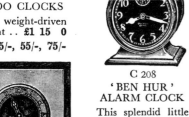

C 198/22 SOLID IVORY 8-DAY CLOCK

Tortoiseshell border. Tortoiseshell dial, also in Green Shagreen. Luminous figures and hands .. **£3 17 6**

C 55/18 FOLDING CLOCK

Reliable 8-day lever movement **£5 15 0**

With Alarm .. **£7 15 0**

BAROMETER AND TIMEPIECE

Combination 8-day Clock and Aneroid Barometer in real leather folding case **£6 10 0, £7 15 0 £8 15 0**

C 208 'BEN HUR' ALARM CLOCK

This splendid little Alarm Clock is fully guaranteed

Luminous dial **19/6**

Plain dial .. **14/-**

C 160/13

The smallest 8-DAY LEVER CLOCK made. Height 1½ ins. Shagreen Tortoiseshell and Enamel. Various colours Complete .. **£6 15 0**

> *Travelling Clocks as on left Various colour cases from* **£2 15 0**

C 214 BOUDOIR OR TABLE CLOCK

(Illustrated left)

Lacquer on Real Tortoiseshell and Ivory—wonderfully effective. 8-Day lever movement. Luminous dial. Fully guaranteed. Height 3¾ ins. **£4 5 0**

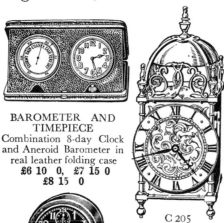

C 205

Reproduction of CROMWELLIAN or 'LANTERN' CLOCK

English made case, finest French lever movements

10 × 3¾ ins. **£4 10 0**
11 × 4½ ins. **£6 0 0**

With striking movements from .. **£7 7 0**

C 163/13 MARINE CLOCKS

Thoroughly reliable 8-day lever movement. 6-in. dial. Brass case. English lever movement **£3 15 0** and **£4 4 0**

French lever movement with centre second hand, suitable for Racing **£6 15 0**

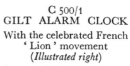

C 90/9 Richly gilt **8-DAY ALARM CLOCK**

Complete in case .. **£3 7 6**

Luminous Dial .. **£3 12 6**

C 162/26 BAROMETER AND TIMEPIECE Solid Brass case. Finely Gilt **£8 10 0**

FRENCH ALARM CLOCK

Fully guaranteed Prettily toned colourings of Mauve, Blue or Burgundy **6/6**

Luminous Dial .. **8/6**

C 500/2 GILT ALARM CLOCK

This Clock has the celebrated French 'Lion' movement

Round Gilt Dial **18/6**

Luminous Dial **21/-**

Cases extra ... **5/-**

> *Clocks Wound and Regulated by Harrods*

C 500/1 GILT ALARM CLOCK

With the celebrated French 'Lion' movement

(Illustrated right)

Square gilt dial .. **21/-**

Luminous dial .. **23/6**

Cases, extra .. **5/-**

C 218

The Wonderful **800-DAY CLOCK**

Guaranteed to keep accurate time for 800 days without attention. A new battery can then be fitted at cost of 3/6, and clock will start off for another 800 days. Height 10 ins. Mahogany base, Brass movement .. **£3 7 6**

C 502

Fine reliable **ALARM CLOCK 11/6**

Other Prices range from **5/6 to 27/6**

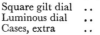

C 209/32A FOLDING CLOCK

30-hour movement, in Leather case. Luminous dial **£1 10 0**

ALL PRICES ARE SUBJECT TO MARKET FLUCTUATIONS

SILVER, ELECTRO-PLATE AND CUTLERY DEPARTMENTS

Wedding and Birthday Gifts, Christening Presents and Silverware for Presentations of every kind

Harrods Silver Salon offers not only a magnificent collection of Antique and Modern Silver, but also a choice of Everyday Plate and Cutlery of the finest quality and workmanship

Harrods specialize in
SPORTS TROPHIES
and
PRIZES

SPECIAL DESIGNS,
INSCRIPTIONS, Etc.,
ON REQUEST

PS 5720 Massive Silver CHALLENGE CUP AND COVER after the style of the famous Silversmith, Paul Lamerie. Beautifully chased and finished, this Cup is altogether a superb example of the Silversmith's craft

Total height of Cup and Cover, exclusive of Pedestal, 9½ inches ..	£30	0	0
,, ,, ,, ,, ,, ,, 14 inches ..	£63	0	0

Prices include Pedestal

ALL PRICES ARE SUBJECT TO MARKET FLUCTUATIONS

HARRODS LTD

Telephone SLOANE 1234
Telegrams 'EVERYTHING HARRODS LONDON'

LONDON S W 1

SILVER AND ELECTRO-PLATE DEPARTMENT
Salvers and Trays, Reproductions from the Antique

SILVER BLOWPIPES FOR EXTINGUISHING LAMPS

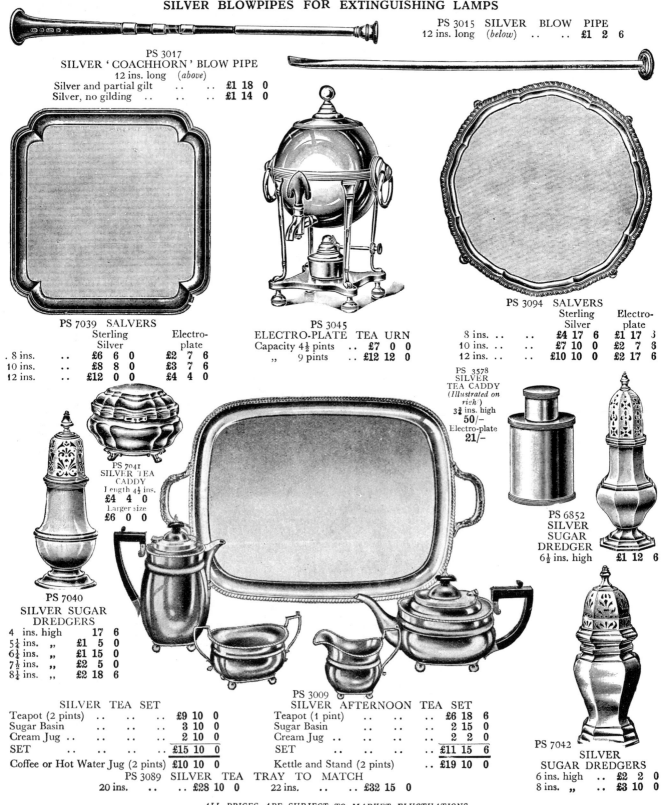

PS 3015 SILVER BLOW PIPE
12 ins. long (below) **£1 2 6**

PS 3017
SILVER 'COACHHORN' BLOW PIPE
12 ins. long (above)

Silver and partial gilt	£1 18	0
Silver, no gilding	£1 14	0

PS 7039 SALVERS

	Sterling Silver	Electro-plate
. 8 ins. ..	£6 6 0	£2 7 6
10 ins. ..	£8 8 0	£3 7 6
12 ins. ..	£12 0 0	£4 4 0

PS 3045
ELECTRO-PLATE TEA URN

Capacity 4½ pints ..	£7 0 0
„ 9 pints ..	£12 12 0

PS 3094 SALVERS

	Sterling Silver	Electro-plate
8 ins.	£4 17 6	£1 17 3
10 ins.	£7 10 0	£2 7 3
12 ins.	£10 10 0	£2 17 6

PS 3578 SILVER TEA CADDY
(Illustrated on right)
3¾ ins. high
50/-
Electro-plate
21/-

PS 7041 SILVER TEA CADDY
Length 4½ ins.
£4 4 0
Larger size
£6 0 0

PS 6852 SILVER SUGAR DREDGER
6½ ins. high **£1 12 6**

PS 7040 SILVER SUGAR DREDGERS

4 ins. high		17	6
5¼ ins. „	£1	5	0
6¼ ins. „	£1	15	0
7¼ ins. „	£2	5	0
8¼ ins. „	£2	18	6

SILVER TEA SET

Teapot (2 pints)	£9 10	0
Sugar Basin	3 10	0
Cream Jug	2 10	0
SET	£15 10	0
Coffee or Hot Water Jug (2 pints)	£10 10	0

PS 3009
SILVER AFTERNOON TEA SET

Teapot (1 pint)	£6 18	6
Sugar Basin	2 15	0
Cream Jug	2 2	0
SET	£11 15	6
Kettle and Stand (2 pints)	£19 10	0

PS 3089 SILVER TEA TRAY TO MATCH

20 ins. ..	.. £28 10 0	22 ins. ..	.. £32 15 0

PS 7042 SILVER SUGAR DREDGERS

6 ins. high	..	£2 2	0
8 ins. „	..	£3 10	0

ALL PRICES ARE SUBJECT TO MARKET FLUCTUATIONS

HARRODS LTD

Telephone SLOANE 1234
Telegrams 'EVERYTHING HARRODS LONDON'

LONDON S W 1

SILVER AND ELECTRO-PLATE DEPARTMENT

Tea and Coffee Services

Sterling Silver and Electro-plate

PS 5090
SUGAR BASIN WITH SIFTER
Dia. 3 ins.
Sterling Silver ..£2 5 0
Electro-plate .. 16 6

PS 6023
STERLING SILVER CREAM JUG
2¾ ins. high .. 17/6

PS 6322
ELECTRO-PLATE SUGAR BASKET
With Blue Glass Lining
1½ ins. dia. .. 17/6

PS 6022
STERLING SILVER SUGAR BASIN
3¼ ins. dia. .. 17/6

PS 3006 OCTAGONAL TEA AND COFFEE SERVICE

	Sterling Silver	Superfine Electro-plate
Coffee or Hot Water Jug, 2 pints	£12 12 0	£6 0 0
Teapot, 2 pints	£13 15 0	£4 15 0
Sugar Basin	£5 5 0	£3 3 0
Cream Jug	£4 7 6	£2 17 6
Kettle with Stand and Lamp (3 pints)	£28 10 0	£10 10 0

PS 6756
STERLING SILVER SUGAR BASIN
With tongs and CREAM JUG in Velvet lined case
complete £4 4 0

Order by post with confidence, Harrods guarantee your satisfaction

PS 4605
KETTLE ON STAND
With powerful regulating lamp

	Electro-plate	Sterling Silver
1½ pints	£3 15 6	£15 7 6
2 pints	£4 0 0	£16 0 0
2½ pints	£4 12 6	£16 15 0
3 pints	£5 5 0	£20 0 0

PS 6925
STERLING SILVER CREAM JUG
Nominal capacity
½ pint .. £1 7 6
¼ pint .. £2 2 0

PS 6743 MASSIVE STERLING SILVER TEA AND COFFEE SERVICE
Adapted from early English Silver as made in the reign of George II

Coffee Pot £19 10 0	Tea Tray, 20 ins. £65 0 0
Teapot £21 0 0	Kettle, to match £42 0 0
Sugar Basin and Cover .. £11 10 0	Hot Water Jug, to match .. £18 0 0
Cream Jug £9 0 0	

PS 6926
STERLING SILVER CREAM JUG
Of heavy make, total
height 4¼ ins. .. £3 3 0

ALL PRICES ARE SUBJECT TO MARKET FLUCTUATIONS

SILVER AND ELECTRO-PLATE DEPARTMENT
Electro-plate Table Heaters, Vegetable Dishes and Dish Covers

PS 6460 ROUND HOT WATER PLATES and Covers

Electro-plate on Britannia Metal, with Porcelain Plate

10-in. Plate	..	..	£1 8 6
Cover	..	..	18/6
8-in. Plate	..	..	£1 1 0
Cover	..	..	12/6

Electro-plate on Nickel Silver

All metal 10-in. Plate	..	..	£2 10 0
Cover	..	..	18/6
8-in. Plate	..	..	£1 15 0
Cover	..	..	12/6

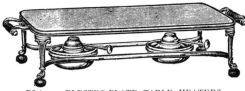

PS 6790 ELECTRO-PLATE TABLE HEATERS

With ornamental legs, and non-conducting fibre feet and handles. Fitted with powerful spirit lamps and patent extinguishers

11 × 8 ins., with 1 lamp	..	..	£4 10 0
18 × 9 ins., with 2 lamps	..	..	£6 16 6
26 × 9 ins., with 3 lamps	..	..	£8 12 6

PS 6319 VEGETABLE DISHES

In Electro-plate, Round shape, with Divider for two vegetables and Side Handle

9 ins. dia...	£3 10 0
Without Side Handle, 9 ins. dia.	£2 15 0
Without Side Handle, 8 ins. dia.	£2 7 6
Without Side Handle, 7 ins. dia.	£1 17 6

PS 6922
ELECTRO-PLATE TABLE HEATERS
With aluminium top

11 × 7½ ins., with 1 lamp	£2 2 0
18 × 9 ins., with 2 lamps	£3 11 0
26 × 9 ins., with 3 lamps	£5 2 6

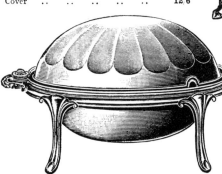

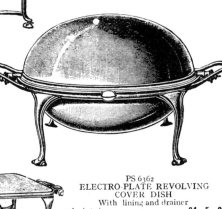

PS 3202
REVOLVING COVER DISH
With lining and drainer

	Electro-plate	Sterling Silver (to order)
1½ pint size	£4 17 6	£35 0 0
2 ,, ,,	£5 10 0	£40 0 0
2½ ,, ,,	£6 6 0	£48 0 0

PS 6362
ELECTRO-PLATE REVOLVING COVER DISH
With lining and drainer

1½ pint size	.. .. ..	£4 5 0
2 ,, ,,	.. .. ..	£4 17 6
2½ ,, ,,	.. .. ..	£5 10 0

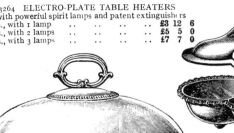

PS 3264 ELECTRO-PLATE TABLE HEATERS
Fitted with powerful spirit lamps and patent extinguishers

11 × 8 ins., with 1 lamp	..	..	£3 12 6
18 × 9 ins., with 2 lamps	..	..	£5 5 0
26 × 9 ins., with 3 lamps	..	..	£7 7 0

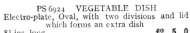

PS 6924 VEGETABLE DISH
Electro-plate, Oval, with two divisions and lid which forms an extra dish

8½ ins. long	..	..	£2 5 0
10 ins. ,,	..	..	£3 3 0
11 ins. ,,	..	..	£3 15 0

PS 3195 MEAT DISH COVERS

	Electro-plate on Nickel Silver		Electro-plate on Britannia Metal
	Gadroon Edges	Plain Edges	Plain
	£ s. d.	£ s. d.	£ s. d.
8 ins. ..	2 0 0	1 15 0	1 2 6
10 ins. ..	2 10 0	2 5 0	1 7 6
12 ins. ..	3 3 0	2 17 6	1 15 0
14 ins. ..	3 15 0	3 10 0	2 5 0
16 ins. ..	4 15 0	4 10 0	2 17 6
18 ins. ..	5 17 6	5 10 0	3 10 0

PS 5690 VEGETABLE DISH
Electro-plate, with removable handle and three divisions £5 12 6
With Hot Water Part £6 15 0

PS 5701 ROUND CHOP DISH
Electro-plate, with reversible cover, 7¼ ins. dia. £2 5 0

PS 6923 ELECTRO-PLATE CHEESE DISH
9½ ins. long £2 2 0

ALL PRICES ARE SUBJECT TO MARKET FLUCTUATIONS

HARRODS LTD

Telephone SLOANE 1234
Telegrams 'EVERYTHING HARRODS LONDON'

LONDON S W 1

SILVER AND ELECTRO-PLATE DEPARTMENT
Flower Centres, Pickle and Sauce Stands, Meat Plates and Dishes

PS 7006 FLOWER CENTRE
Electro-plate and Glass, 18½ ins. high
£2 17 6

PS 5759 PICKLE STAND
Electro-plate and Cut Glass
with Fork **£2 0 0**

**PS 5190
SAUCE FRAME**
Electro-plate, to take
2 bottles .. **£1 6 6**

PS 7007 FLOWER CENTRE
Electro-plate and Glass, 15 ins. high .. **£2 2 0**

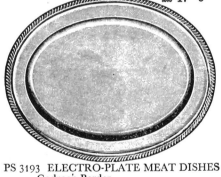

PS 3193 ELECTRO-PLATE MEAT DISHES

	Gadroon Border as illustrated		Plain Border	
	A Quality	A1 Quality	A Quality	A1 Quality
10 ins.	£1 10 0	£1 15 0	£1 5 0	£1 8 6
12 ins.	1 18 6	2 3 6	1 12 6	1 16 6
14 ins.	2 9 6	2 15 0	2 2 0	2 7 6
16 ins.	3 5 0	3 8 6	2 15 0	3 2 6
18 ins.	3 17 6	4 2 6	3 5 0	3 13 6
20 ins.	4 10 0	5 0 0	3 15 0	4 5 0

PS 7008 MEAT PLATES
Electro-plate
10 ins. dia. **£1 10 0**
12 ins. ,, ... **£1 18 6**
With Gadroon Border
10 ins. dia. **£1 18 6**
12 ins. ,, ... **£2 5 0**

**PS 5294
SAUCE BOTTLE
STAND**
Electro-plate **18/6**

**PS 5299
SAUCE BOTTLE
STAND**
Electro-plate **17/6**

PS 7009 FLOWER CENTRE
Sterling Silver, 9¾ ins. high
£8 18 6

**PS 5296
SAUCE BOTTLE
STAND**
Electro-plate **18/6**

**PS 6503
PICKLE STAND**
Electro - plate and
Glass, 7¼ ins. high.
Complete with Fork
£1 1 0

ALL PRICES ARE SUBJECT TO MARKET FLUCTUATIONS

HARRODS LTD

Telephone SLOANE 1234
Telegrams 'EVERYTHING HARRODS LONDON'

LONDON S W 1

SILVER AND ELECTRO-PLATE DEPARTMENT
Breakfast Table Appointments

PS 5229
NUT OR FRUIT DISH
Electro-plate, 9¼ ins. dia.
£1 5 6

PS 5588
EGG CUP WITH SPOON
Electro-plate, with White China Saucer
4/6
With Coloured China Saucer.. .. **5/6**

PS 3301
EGG STAND
Electro-plate, with four cups and spoons **£1 15 0**
With six cups and spoons **£2 10 0**

PS 6006
EGG STEAMER
Electro-plate, for 4 eggs .. **£1 10 0**

PS 5028 EGG STEAMER
Electro-plate, for 4 eggs
£2 12 6
Price in Silver on application

PS 6741
EGG STAND
Superfine Electro-plate, with four cups and spoons **£4 5 0**
Sterling Silver .. **£10 10 0**

PS 6930
EGG COOKER
Electro-plate, will steam or poach eggs
£2 5 0

PS 5756
EGG STAND
Electro-plate, with four cups and spoons **£2 12 6**
With six cups and spoons **£3 15 0**

PS 6863
VACUUM JUG
Electro-plate, will keep liquids hot for nine hours, or cold for 48 hours. Hygienic Patent Stopper (no cork) Nominal capacity one pint .. **£3 3 0**

PS 6933
HOT WATER JUG
Electro-plate
¾ pint .. **£1 12 6**
1 ,, .. **£1 17 6**
1½ ,, .. **£2 4 0**

PS 6009
HOT WATER JUG
Electro-plate on Britannia Metal
1 pint .. **£1 0 0**
1½ ,, .. **£1 5 0**
2 ,, .. **£1 10 0**

PS 6928
HOT WATER JUG
Electro-plate, 1½ pints
£2 18 6
Sterling Silver
£7 15 0

PS 6931
HOT WATER JUG
Electro-plate, capacity, 1½ pints **£2 17 6**

PS 4777
THE 'UNIVERSAL' COFFEE MACHINE, ELECTRO-PLATE
1 pint size **£2 3 0**
1½ ,, ,, ... **£2 8 0**
2½ ,, ,, ... **£2 12 0**
4 ,, ,, ... **£3 3 0**

PS 6564
NUT OR FRUIT DISH
Electro-plate, 8 ins. dia. with two Nut Crackers
£1 15 0

PS 6929 COFFEE MAKER
Electro-plate, with regulating lamp
1½ pint **£3 0 0**
2 ,, ... **£3 10 0**

ALL PRICES ARE SUBJECT TO MARKET FLUCTUATIONS

HARRODS LTD

Telephone SLOANE 1234
Telegrams 'EVERYTHING HARRODS LONDON'

LONDON SW1

SILVER AND ELECTRO-PLATE DEPARTMENT

Tea and Coffee Spoons, Menu Stands and Liqueur Tots

PS 3071 SIX SILVER COFFEE SPOONS
With bean handles, in Velvet-lined
case 10/6
Electro-plate 5/-

PS 6778
SIX SILVER TEA SPOONS
WITH TONGS
In Velvet-lined case .. £1 9 6
Six Spoons only in case .. £1 1 0

PS 6461
SIX SILVER COFFEE
SPOONS WITH TONGS
In Velvet-lined case
£1 7 6
Six Spoons only in
case £1 0 0

PS 6154 SIX ELECTRO-PLATE TEA SPOONS
In strong Velvet-lined box Various patterns .. **9/6**

PS 3069
SIX SILVER TEA SPOONS WITH TONGS
In Velvet-lined case.. .. .. £1 16 0
Twelve Silver Tea Spoons with Tongs, in
case £3 3 0
Six Silver Tea Spoons only, in case £1 9 6

PS 6955
STERLING
SILVER
OWL
MENU HOLDERS
Each **11/6**

PS 6956
STERLING
SILVER
MENU HOLDERS
Each **7/6**

PS 6957
STERLING
SILVER
MENU HOLDERS
Each **8/6**

PS 3068
SIX SILVER TEA SPOONS WITH TONGS
In Velvet-lined case £1 10 0
Twelve Silver Tea Spoons with Tongs, in
case £2 16 6
Six Silver Tea Spoons only, in case £1 4 0

PS 3436 STERLING SILVER MENU HOLDERS

Four in Velvet-lined case	£2 2 6	
Four larger size, in case	£3 5 6	
Singly..	Each	9/-
Singly, larger size	,,	14/6

PS 6968
SIX STERLING SILVER
LIQUEUR TOTS
In Velvet-lined case £5 17 6

PS 6953
SIX SILVER MOUNTED
GLASS LIQUEUR TOTS
In Velvet-lined case £3 3 0

PS 6954
SIX WORCESTER CHINA COFFEE CUPS
WITH SAUCERS
Black and Gold exteriors and Plain Gold interiors
With Silver Gilt Enamelled Spoons to match in
Velvet-lined case £9 12 6

PS 5203
SIX SILVER MOUNTED COFFEE CUPS
WITH SAUCERS
In Velvet-lined case £5 5 0

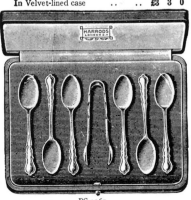

PS 3061
SIX SILVER TEA SPOONS WITH TONGS
In Velvet-lined case £1 16 0
Twelve Silver Tea Spoons with Tongs, in case
£3 3 0
Six Silver Tea Spoons only, in case .. £1 9 6

ALL PRICES ARE SUBJECT TO MARKET FLUCTUATIONS
Telephone SLOANE 1234
Telegrams 'EVERYTHING HARRODS LONDON'

HARRODS LTD   LONDON S W 1

SILVER AND ELECTRO-PLATE DEPARTMENT
Silver and Silver Mounted Toilet Table Appointments

PS 7011
SILVER MOUNTED CUT GLASS PUFF JARS
4 ins. dia. .. £1 2 6
5 ins. ,, £1 11 6
6 ins. ,, £1 18 6

PS 6386
SILVER AND INLAID TORTOISESHELL BRUSH TRAY
Length 12 ins. £9 18 6
For Brushes, etc., to match, see page 77.

PS 7010
SILVER MOUNTED CUT GLASS SCENT BOTTLE
3½ ins. dia .. £1 12 6

PS 5545
SILVER MOUNTED PUFF JAR
3¾ ins. dia. .. £1 5 0

PS 6836
SCENT BOTTLE
Silver and Enamel Top, Cut Glass, 'Princess Mary' Blue
3½ ins. dia. .. £2 10 0

PS 5907
SILVER MOUNTED MANICURE SETS
In Velvet-lined cases
5-piece, Plain .. £1 10 0
Engine Turned .. £2 0 0
7-piece, Plain .. £1 19 6
Engine Turned .. £2 10 0

PS 6301
SILVER LETTER BALANCE
Weighs up to 12 oz.
height 3 ins. £1 5 0

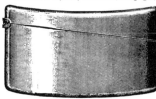

PS 7015   GENTLEMAN'S CARD CASE
Silver £1 2 6
Engine Turned.. .. £1 6 6

PS 7157
Silver and Inlaid Tortoiseshell mounted
SMELLING SALTS BOTTLE
2⅞ ins. high .. 12/6
Ditto without Inlay 11/-

PS 6470
SILVER MOUNTED MANICURE SETS
In Velvet-lined cases
Plain £1 17 6
Engine Turned .. £2 5 0

PS 6767
SILVER MOUNTED MANICURE POLISHERS
In Glass Troughs, 4½ ins. long
Plain 14/6
Engine Turned 17/6

PS 7027
SILVER BUTTON HOOK AND SHOE LIFT
Combined
8 ins. long £1 5 0
10 ins. ,, £1 12 6

PS 3926
SHOE LIFT
Silver handled
Length 6⅜ ins.,
5/6
BUTTON HOOK
to match 5/6

PS 7028   SILVER MOUNTED SALTS BOTTLE
1½ ins. dia. 19/6
1⅝ ins. ,, ... £1 10 0
2½ ins. ,, ... £2 7 6

PS 6001
SHOE LIFT
Silver and Tortoiseshell Mounted. Length 6¾ ins.
10/-

BUTTON HOOK
to match .. 10/-

PS 7013
SILVER AND CUT GLASS HAIR PIN BOX
5¼ ins. long £1 12 6
With plain lid £1 8 6

PS 6455
BUTTON HOOK and SHOE LIFT.
Silver handled
In Velvet-lined case .. 10/-
Engine Turned 12/6

PS 7014   SILVER PIN TRAY
4½ ins. long 13/6
Engine Turned 18/6

PS 7012
LADY'S SILVER CARD CASE
Engine Turned .. £2 15 0
Plain £2 7 6

PS 5544
SILVER MOUNTED CUT GLASS SCENT BOTTLE
4½ ins. high £1 7 6

PS 6838   PIN BOX
Silver and Enamel Top, Cut Glass, 'Princess Mary' Blue,
length 4 ins... .. £2 5 0

PS 6886
PUMP SCENT BOTTLE
Silver Mounted
5½ ins. high .. 18/-

PS 6388
CUT GLASS SCENT BOTTLE
Silver and Inlaid Tortoiseshell Mounted
3¾ ins. dia. .. £2 7 6

PS 6772
SILVER AND ENAMEL MANICURE SETS
Blue, Pink, Mauve and other colours.
In Velvet-lined cases
5-piece £3 7 6
7-piece £4 10 0

ALL PRICES ARE SUBJECT TO MARKET FLUCTUATIONS

HARRODS LTD

Telephone SLOANE 1234
Telegrams 'EVERYTHING HARRODS LONDON'

LONDON S W 1

SILVER AND ELECTRO-PLATE DEPARTMENT
Sterling Silver Smoking Accessories

PS 7029
SILVER CIGARETTE CASES

4⅜ × 3⅞ ins.		£3 10 0
3⅝ × 3⅜ ins.		£3 0 0
2⅞ × 3⅜ ins.		£2 10 0

PS 6294
SILVER CIGARETTE CASES

5 × 3¾ ins.		£3 12 6
4½ × 3⅜ ins.		£2 18 0
3¼ × 3¼ ins.		£2 10 0
2⅞ × 3⅜ ins.		£1 17 6

PS 6766
SILVER CIGARETTE CASES

3⅝ × 3¼ ins.		£2 10 0
3¼ × 3¼ ins.		£2 2 0
2⅞ × 3⅜ ins.		£1 10 0

PS 5553
SILVER MATCH BOXES

Engine Turned 12/6
Plain 10/-

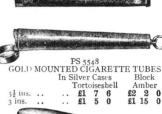

PS 5548
GOLD MOUNTED CIGARETTE TUBES

	In Silver Cases	Block
	Tortoiseshell	Amber
3½ ins. ..	£1 7 6	£2 2 0
3 ins. ..	£1 5 0	£1 15 0

PS 6651
SILVER CIGARETTE CASES

5 × 3½ ins.		£4 0 0
3¾ × 3¼ ins.		£3 3 0
2⅝ × 3¼ ins.		£2 10 0
2½ × 3¼ ins.		£2 0 0

PS 6463
SILVER CIGARETTE CASES

	Engine Turned	Plain
3¼ × 3¼ ins.	£2 17 6	£2 2 0
2⅝ × 3¼ ins.	£2 8 6	£1 17 6
2¼ × 3¼ ins.	£1 19 6	£1 11 6

PS 6060
SILVER CIGARETTE CASES
2⅝ × 3⅜ ins.

Engine Turned ..		£1 5 0
Plain ..		£1 1 0
Single and Double Row same prices

PS 7032
SILVER 'GRENADE' CIGAR LAMPS

2¾ ins. dia.		£2 15 0
2¼ ins. dia.		£2 2 0

PS 4127
SILVER CIGARETTE BOXES

	Cedar lined Plain	Engine Turned
7⅞ × 3½″ to hold 100	£3 12 6	£4 12 6
5⅝ × 3½″ ,, 75	£3 0 0	£3 17 6
4½ × 3½″ ,, 50	£2 10 0	£3 5 0

PS 6052
CIGARETTE BOX
Silver Gilt Mounted Onyx

6 × 4 ins. £7 17 6

PS 6131
SILVER 'BOOK' MATCH CASES

Engine Turned ..		12/6
Plain		10/-

PS 6186
SILVER 'BOOK' MATCH CASES

Engine Turned ..		10/6
Plain		9/-

PS 6779
SILVER 'BOOK' MATCH CASE
14/6

PS 6469
STERLING SILVER MATCH AND ASH STAND

Dia. of ash tray 2½ ins. 12/6
   ,,   ,,   3¼ ins. 25/-

PS 6613
SILVER CIGARETTE BOXES
Cedar lined. Size 5½ × 3⅜ ins.

Engine Turned ..		£2 12 6
Plain ..		£2 2 0

PS 6355
SILVER MOUNTED 'MOORCROFT' CHINA ASH TRAY

Diameter 4¼ ins. .. 15/-

PS 6279
SILVER MOUNTED GLASS MATCH STANDS

4 ins. diam. ..		10/9
2½ ins. ,,		5/6

PS 7031
SILVER MOUNTED DOULTON MATCH STANDS

5 ins. diam.	£1 1 0
4½ ins. ,, ..		17 6
3½ ins. ,, ..		12 6
3 ins. ,, ..		10 0

PS 6356
SILVER ASH TRAY
With three rests

Diameter 4⅜ ins. .. £1 2 6

PS 6288
SILVER CIGARETTE BOX
Cedar lined
3¼ × 3¼ ins., to hold 25 cigarettes £1 5 0

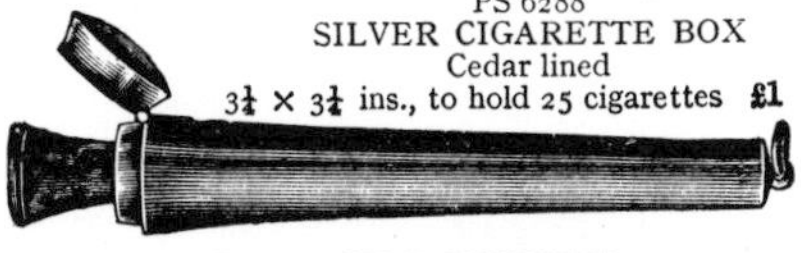

PS 7030
SILVER 'ROMAN LAMP' CIGAR LIGHTERS

Total length 5½ ins.
£4 4 0
Total length 4½ ins.
£2 17 6

PS 6608
HAMMERED SILVER CIGAR LAMP

'There is no herb like it
under the canopy of Heaven'
Total length 5½ ins. £2 7 6

PS 6610
SILVER CIGAR LAMP
Total length 5¾ ins.
£2 5 0

PS 7034 GOLD MOUNTED TORTOISESHELL CIGARETTE TUBES
In Silver Cases

4 ins. .. £1 7 6 3½ ins. .. £1 5 0

PS 7033 SILVER CIGAR LAMP
Approximate length 15 ins.

With Ivory Tusk handle ..	.. ..	£5 15 6
With Ibex Horn handle ..	.. ..	£4 18 6

ALL PRICES ARE SUBJECT TO MARKET FLUCTUATIONS

HARRODS LTD

Telephone SLOANE 1234
Telegrams 'EVERYTHING HARRODS LONDON'

LONDON S W 1

SILVER AND ELECTRO-PLATE DEPARTMENT

Engraving of Silver, Electro-plate and Cutlery a Speciality

SPECIMENS

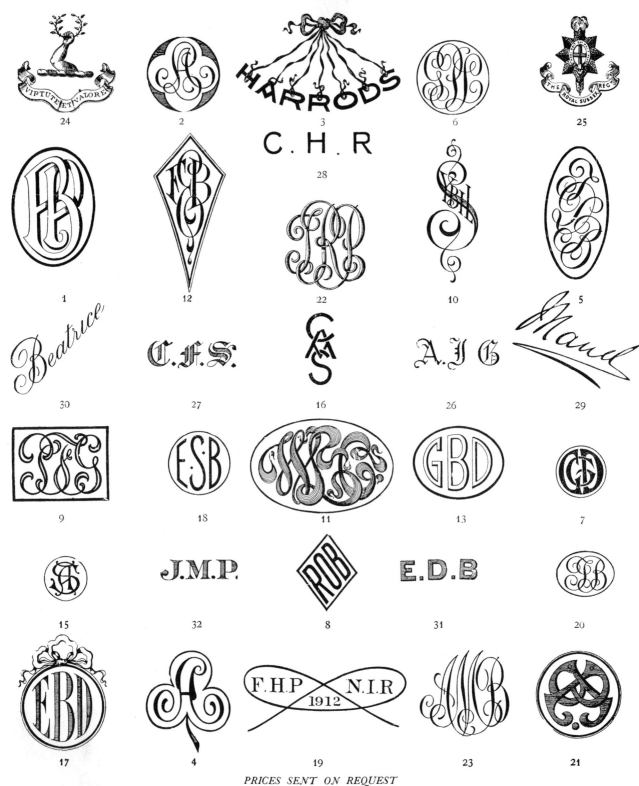

C . H . R
28

Beatrice
30

C.F.S.
27

A.J G
26

Maud
29

J.M.P.
32

E.D.B
31

PRICES SENT ON REQUEST

HARRODS LTD

Telephone SLOANE 1234
Telegrams 'EVERYTHING HARRODS LONDON'

LONDON S W 1

CUTLERY DEPARTMENT
Patterns of Electro-plate Spoons and Forks

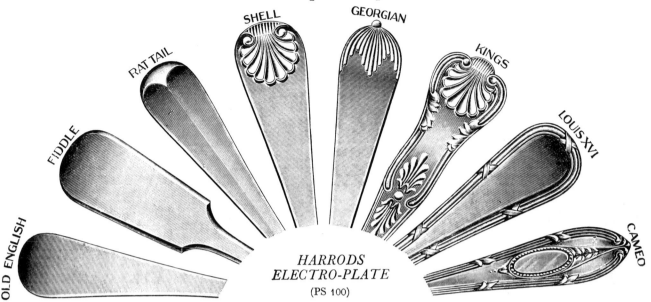

SHELL GEORGIAN KINGS RAT TAIL LOUIS XVI FIDDLE CAMEO OLD ENGLISH

HARRODS ELECTRO-PLATE
(PS 100)

HARRODS ELECTRO-PLATE SPOONS AND FORKS are made to the specification of an expert; they are heavily silver-plated on superior nickel silver and represent the highest standard of excellence

		Old English & Fiddle patterns		Rat tail, Shell & Georgian patterns	Kings, Louis & Cameo patterns
		A. qual.	A. 1 qual.	A. 1 qual.	A. 1 qual.
Table Spoons or Forks ..	per doz.	30/-	37/6	45/-	55/-
Dessert Spoons or Forks ..	,,	22/-	27/6	35/-	42/-
Soup Spoons (round bowls)	,,	31/6	40/-	47/-	57/6
Tea Spoons (breakfast size)	,,	12/-	15/-	20/-	22/6
Tea Spoons (afternoon size)	,,	11/6	14/-	17/6	18/-
After Dinner Coffee Spoons	,,	10/6	11/6	13/-	15/-
Egg Spoons (Gilt bowls) ..	,,	18/-	21/-	24/-	26/-
Salt Spoons (Gilt bowls) ..	,,	16/6	18/6	21/-	22/6
Mustard Spoons (Gilt bowls)	,,	17/6	20/-	23/-	25/-
Gravy Spoons ..	each	6/-	7/6	8/6	10/-
Soup Ladles ..	,,	9/-	11/6	12/6	15/-
Sauce Ladles ..	,,	3/-	4/-	4/6	5/6
Butter Knives (medium size)	,,	1/9	2/6	2/9	3/-
Sugar Tongs (large size) ..	,,	2/6	3/3	3/9	4/-
Sugar Tongs (medium size)	,,	2/-	2/9	3/3	3/6
Sugar Sifters (Gilt bowls)..	,,	—	4/6	5/-	5/6
Sugar Spoons ..	,,	—	2/-	2/3	2/9
Pickle Forks ..	,,	—	2/3	2/6	3/-
Oyster Forks ..	per doz.	—	33/-	35/-	36/-
Jam Spoons ..	each	—	2/6	2/9	3/-
Salad Servers ..	pair	—	12/6	14/-	15/6
Asparagus Servers ..	each	16/6	18/6	20/-	22/6
Asparagus Eating Tongs ..	,,	—	3/6	3/9	4/-
Cheese Scoops ..	,,	—	4/6	4/9	5/-
Marrow Scoops ..	,,	—	5/-	—	—
Caddy Spoons ..	,,	—	1/6	1/9	2/-

No. 3 ELECTRO-PLATE SPOONS AND FORKS Old English Pattern
Harrods have introduced these for secondary use. They are of Nickel Silver with a pure silver surface and will wear white throughout

Table Spoons or Forks Per dozen **22/-**   Dessert Spoons or Forks Per dozen **16/-**   Tea Spoons Per dozen **9/6**

HARRODS PRIMO NICKEL SPOONS AND FORKS Old English Pattern
Extremely hard, very white, and stain-resisting to a remarkable degree

Table Spoons or Forks Per dozen **15/-**   Dessert Spoons or Forks Per dozen **11/6**   Tea Spoons Per dozen **6/-**

HARRODS STAINLESS SILVER STEEL SPOONS AND FORKS Old English Pattern
Made from genuine 'Firth Staybrite' Steel. They constitute the latest advance in the development of rust-resisting steels and are entirely unaffected by food acids

Tea Spoons—

Table Spoons or Forks Per dozen **21/-**   Dessert Spoons or Forks Per dozen **15/-**   Breakfast size Per dozen **8/6**   Small size Per dozen **7/6**

For Tea and Coffee Spoons in Cases, see page 71

ALL PRICES ARE SUBJECT TO MARKET FLUCTUATIONS

HARRODS LTD

Telephone SLOANE 1234
Telegrams 'EVERYTHING HARRODS LONDON'

LONDON SW1

CUTLERY DEPARTMENT
Cutlery Cabinets in Mahogany, Oak and Walnut

PS 6082

PS 6098

POLISHED MAHOGANY CHIPPENDALE
CUTLERY CABINET (*on right*)

Perfectly finished Cabinet with five drawers. Folding Glass-panelled doors with Silk curtains. All drawers contain a separate division for each piece and are lined with Velvet. Total height 48 inches. Contains Electro-plate Spoons and Forks (Chippendale pattern) and Best Sheffield Stainless Cutlery with Hard-soldered Electro-plate Handles

24 Table Knives	4 Salt Spoons
12 Cheese Knives	1 Mustard Spoon
1 Pair Meat Carvers	1 Soup Ladle
1 Pair Game Carvers	2 Sauce Ladles
1 Steel	2 Gravy Spoons
24 Table Forks	1 Sugar Tongs
12 Dessert Forks	1 Sugar Sifter
12 Soup Spoons	1 Butter Knife
6 Table Spoons	1 Pair Knife Rests
12 Dessert Spoons	12 Pairs Fish Knives and Forks
12 Tea Spoons	1 Pair Fish Servers
6 Egg Spoons	12 Pairs Dessert Knives and Forks

Cabinet Complete **£79 15 0**

PS 6082
FUMED OAK 'JACOBEAN' CUTLERY CABINET
(*on left*)

Beautifully made Cabinet with four fitted drawers, covered by folding doors, and one spare drawer. Total height 40 inches. Contains A1 quality Electro-plate Spoons and Forks (Rat-tail pattern) and Best Sheffield Stainless Cutlery with imitation Ivory Handles, as follows :—

24 Table Knives	12 Tea Spoons
12 Cheese Knives	6 Egg Spoons
1 Pair Game Carvers	4 Salt Spoons
1 Pair Meat Carvers	2 Mustard Spoons
1 Steel	1 Pair Fish Carvers
12 Pairs Fish Knives and Forks	2 Sauce Ladles
12 Table Spoons	1 Soup Ladle
24 Table Forks	1 Sugar Tongs
12 Dessert Forks	1 Butter Knife
12 Dessert Spoons	1 Gravy Spoon

Complete **£47 17 6**

Similar CABINET with Real Ivory-Handled Cutlery
£59 7 6

PS 6098

ALL PRICES ARE SUBJECT TO MARKET FLUCTUATIONS

HARRODS LTD

Telephone SLOANE 1234
Telegrams 'EVERYTHING HARRODS LONDON'

LONDON S W 1

CUTLERY DEPARTMENT
Cabinets fitted with Harrods Cutlery and Electro-plate

Any of the Electro-plate Spoons, Forks, etc., in these Canteens, may be obtained separately at the following prices :—

			Old English & Fiddle patterns	
			A qual.	A1 qual.
Table Spoons or Forks	..	per doz.	30/-	37/6
Dessert Spoons or Forks	..	,,	22/-	27/6
Soup Spoons (round bowls)	..	,,	31/6	40/-
Tea Spoons (breakfast size)	..	,,	12/-	15/-
Tea Spoons (afternoon size)	..	,,	11/6	14/-
After Dinner Coffee Spoons	..	,,	10/6	11/6
Egg Spoons (Gilt bowls)	..	,,	18/-	21/-
Salt Spoons ,,	..	,,	16/6	18/6
Mustard Spoons ,,	..	,,	17/6	20/-
Gravy Spoons ..	..	each	6/-	7/6
Soup Ladles ..	..	,,	9/-	11/6
Sauce Ladles ..	..	,,	3/-	4/-
Butter Knives (medium size)	..	,,	1/9	2/6
Sugar Tongs (large size)	..	,,	2/6	3/3

Canteens can be made and fitted to Customers' own requirements to take any quantities

Prices of Sterling Silver Spoons and Forks which vary from day to day are quoted on request

PS 6601 Fumed OAK CABINET with one drawer, fitted with fine quality Stainless Steel Cutlery with imitation Ivory handles, and Harrods celebrated 'A' Quality Electro-plate, 'Old English' Pattern

Contents
6 Table Knives	6 Table Forks	6 Tea Spoons
6 Cheese Knives	6 Dessert Forks	2 Sauce Ladles
1 Pair Joint Carvers	6 Table Spoons	1 Sugar Tongs
1 Steel	6 Dessert Spoons	

COMPLETE **£10 0 0**

Price with Sterling Silver Spoons and Forks and Real Ivory handled Cutlery about **£45 0 0** COMPLETE

PS 6602 Fumed OAK CANTEEN with one lift-out tray, fitted superior quality Stainless Steel Cutlery with imitation Ivory handles, and Harrods 'A' Quality Electro-plate, 'Old English' Pattern

Contents
12 Table Knives	12 Table Forks	12 Tea Spoons
12 Cheese Knives	12 Dessert Forks	1 Soup Ladle
1 Pair Joint Carvers	6 Table Spoons	2 Sauce Ladles
1 Steel	12 Dessert Spoons	

COMPLETE **£15 0 0**

Oak, Mahogany, Walnut and other Woods may be obtained to match existing Furniture

TABLE CUTLERY

PS 6737 Harrods superfine Sheffield made Table Cutlery, with mirror polished Stainless Steel blades and finest quality imitation Ivory handles. In velvet-lined Mahogany case

12 Table Knives
12 Cheese Knives
1 Pair Joint Carvers
1 Pair Poultry Carvers
1 Steel

COMPLETE **£10 10 0**

PS 6599 Fumed OAK CANTEEN with two lift-out trays, fitted superior quality Stainless Steel Cutlery with imitation Ivory handles and Harrods 'A' quality Electro-plate Spoons and Forks, 'Old English' Pattern. For twelve persons

Contents
12 Table Knives	12 Table Forks	12 Tea Spoons
12 Cheese Knives	12 Dessert Forks	6 Egg Spoons
1 Pair Joint Carvers	6 Table Spoons	1 Gravy Spoon
1 Pair Poultry Carvers	12 Soup Spoons	1 Soup Ladle
1 Steel	12 Dessert Spoons	2 Sauce Ladles

COMPLETE **£20 0 0**

PS 6600 Fumed OAK CABINET with two drawers, fitted with superfine quality Stainless Steel Cutlery with mirror-polished blades and finest quality imitation Ivory handles. Harrods famous 'A1' quality Electro-plate Spoons and Forks, 'Old English' Pattern

Contents
12 Table Knives	12 Table Forks	12 Tea Spoons
12 Cheese Knives	12 Dessert Forks	6 Egg Spoons
1 Pair Joint Carvers	6 Table Spoons	1 Gravy Spoon
1 Pair Poultry Carvers	12 Soup Spoons	1 Soup Ladle
1 Steel	12 Dessert Spoons	2 Sauce Ladles

COMPLETE **£25 0 0** With real Ivory handled Cutlery **£33 0 0**

With Sterling Silver Spoons and Forks and real Ivory handled Cutlery about **£72 10 0** COMPLETE

ALL PRICES ARE SUBJECT TO MARKET FLUCTUATIONS

HARRODS LTD

Telephone SLOANE 1234
Telegrams 'EVERYTHING HARRODS LONDON'

LONDON S W 1

SILVER, ELECTRO-PLATE AND CUTLERY

Butter Knives, Cake Knives, Sugar Tongs, Pickle Forks, etc.

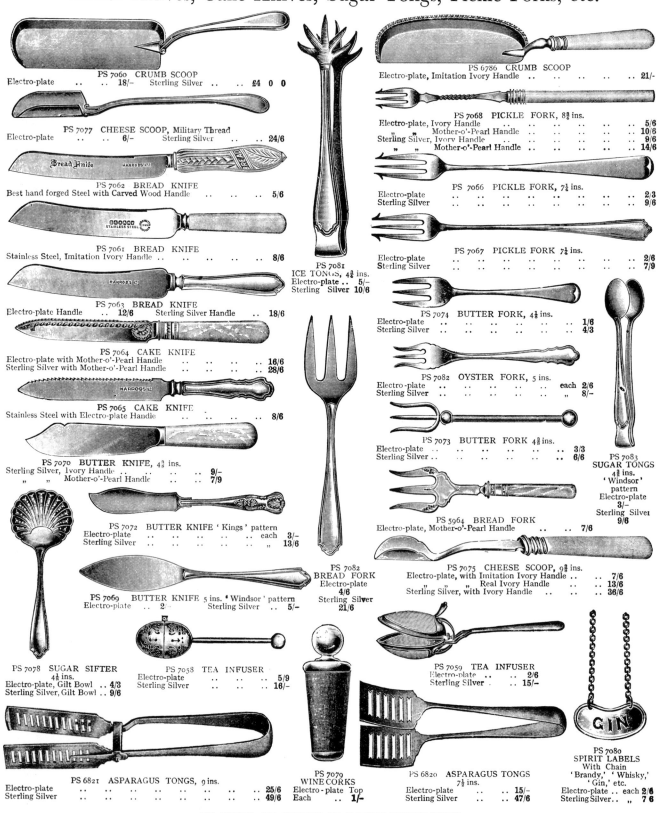

PS 7060 CRUMB SCOOP
Electro-plate .. .. 18/- Sterling Silver £4 0 0

PS 7077 CHEESE SCOOP, Military Thread
Electro-plate .. .. 6/- Sterling Silver 24/6

PS 7062 BREAD KNIFE
Best hand forged Steel with **Carved** Wood Handle 5/6

PS 7061 BREAD KNIFE
Stainless Steel, Imitation Ivory Handle 8/6

PS 7063 BREAD KNIFE
Electro-plate Handle .. 12/6 Sterling Silver Handle .. 18/6

PS 7064 CAKE KNIFE
Electro-plate with Mother-o'-Pearl Handle 16/6
Sterling Silver with Mother-o'-Pearl Handle 28/6

PS 7065 CAKE KNIFE
Stainless Steel with Electro-plate Handle 8/6

PS 7070 BUTTER KNIFE, 4¾ ins.
Sterling Silver, Ivory Handle 9/-
" " Mother-o'-Pearl Handle 7/9

PS 7072 BUTTER KNIFE 'Kings' pattern
Electro-plate .. .. .. each 3/-
Sterling Silver .. .. " 13/6

PS 7069 BUTTER KNIFE 5 ins. 'Windsor' pattern
Electro-plate .. 2/- Sterling Silver .. 5/-

PS 7078 SUGAR SIFTER 4¼ ins.
Electro-plate, Gilt Bowl .. 4/3
Sterling Silver, Gilt Bowl .. 9/6

PS 7058 TEA INFUSER
Electro-plate 5/9
Sterling Silver 16/-

PS 6821 ASPARAGUS TONGS, 9 ins.
Electro-plate 25/6
Sterling Silver 49/6

PS 7081 ICE TONGS, 4¾ ins.
Electro-plate .. 5/-
Sterling Silver 10/6

PS 7082 BREAD FORK
Electro-plate 4/6
Sterling Silver 21/6

PS 7079 WINE CORKS
Electro-plate Top
Each .. 1/-

PS 6786 CRUMB SCOOP
Electro-plate, Imitation Ivory Handle 21/-

PS 7068 PICKLE FORK, 8¾ ins.
Electro-plate, Ivory Handle 5/6
" " Mother-o'-Pearl Handle 10/6
Sterling Silver, Ivory Handle 9/6
" " Mother-o'-Pearl Handle 14/6

PS 7066 PICKLE FORK, 7¼ ins.
Electro-plate 2/3
Sterling Silver 9/6

PS 7067 PICKLE FORK 7¼ ins.
Electro-plate 2/6
Sterling Silver 7/9

PS 7074 BUTTER FORK, 4⅛ ins.
Electro-plate 1/6
Sterling Silver 4/3

PS 7082 OYSTER FORK, 5 ins.
Electro-plate .. .. each 2/6
Sterling Silver .. .. " 8/-

PS 7073 BUTTER FORK 4⅜ ins.
Electro-plate 3/3
Sterling Silver 6/6

PS 5964 BREAD FORK
Electro-plate, Mother-o'-Pearl Handle 7/6

PS 7075 CHEESE SCOOP, 9⅜ ins.
Electro-plate, with Imitation Ivory Handle 7/6
" " Real Ivory Handle 13/6
Sterling Silver, with Ivory Handle 36/6

PS 7059 TEA INFUSER
Electro-plate 2/6
Sterling Silver .. 15/-

PS 6820 ASPARAGUS TONGS 7½ ins.
Electro-plate 15/-
Sterling Silver .. 47/6

PS 7083 SUGAR TONGS 4¾ ins. 'Windsor' pattern
Electro-plate 3/-
Sterling Silver 9/6

PS 7080 SPIRIT LABELS
With Chain
'Brandy,' 'Whisky,' 'Gin,' etc.
Electro-plate .. each 2/6
Sterling Silver.. " 7/6

ALL PRICES ARE SUBJECT TO MARKET FLUCTUATIONS

HARRODS LTD
Telephone SLOANE 1234
Telegrams 'EVERYTHING HARRODS LONDON'
LONDON S W 1

SILVER, ELECTRO-PLATE AND CUTLERY
Important Details for the Perfectly-Appointed Table

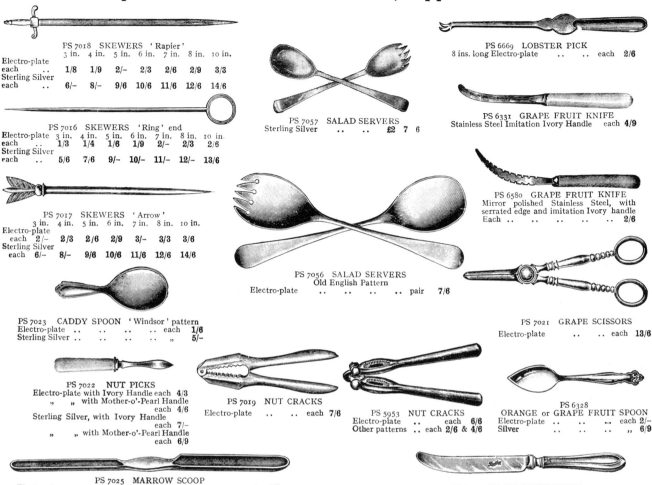

PS 7018 SKEWERS 'Rapier'

	3 in.	4 in.	5 in.	6 in.	7 in.	8 in.	10 in.
Electro-plate each ..	1/8	1/9	2/-	2/3	2/6	2/9	3/3
Sterling Silver each ..	6/-	8/-	9/6	10/6	11/6	12/6	14/6

PS 7016 SKEWERS 'Ring' end

	3 in.	4 in.	5 in.	6 in.	7 in.	8 in.	10 in.
Electro-plate each	1/3	1/4	1/6	1/9	2/-	2/3	2/6
Sterling Silver each ..	5/6	7/6	9/-	10/-	11/-	12/-	13/6

PS 7017 SKEWERS 'Arrow'

	3 in.	4 in.	5 in.	6 in.	7 in.	8 in.	10 in.
Electro-plate each	2/-	2/3	2/6	2/9	3/-	3/3	3/6
Sterling Silver each ..	6/-	8/-	9/6	10/6	11/6	12/6	14/6

PS 7023 CADDY SPOON 'Windsor' pattern
Electro-plate .. .. .. each **1/6**
Sterling Silver .. .. .. ,, **5/-**

PS 7022 NUT PICKS
Electro-plate with Ivory Handle each **4/3**
 ,, ,, with Mother-o'-Pearl Handle each **4/6**
Sterling Silver, with Ivory Handle each **7/-**
 ,, ,, with Mother-o'-Pearl Handle each **6/9**

PS 7025 MARROW SCOOP
Electro-plate .. .. each **3/9**
Sterling Silver .. .. ,, **12/9**

PS 7057 SALAD SERVERS
Sterling Silver **£2 7 6**

PS 7056 SALAD SERVERS
Old English Pattern
Electro-plate .. .. pair **7/6**

PS 7019 NUT CRACKS
Electro-plate .. .. each **7/6**

PS 5953 NUT CRACKS
Electro-plate .. .. each **6/6**
Other patterns .. each **2/6 & 4/6**

PS 6669 LOBSTER PICK
8 ins. long Electro-plate .. .. each **2/6**

PS 6331 GRAPE FRUIT KNIFE
Stainless Steel Imitation Ivory Handle .. each **4/9**

PS 6580 GRAPE FRUIT KNIFE
Mirror polished Stainless Steel, with serrated edge and imitation Ivory handle
Each **2/6**

PS 7021 GRAPE SCISSORS
Electro-plate .. .. each **13/6**

PS 6328 ORANGE or GRAPE FRUIT SPOON
Electro-plate .. .. .. each **2/-**
Silver .. .. .. ,, **6/9**

PS 6597 GRAPE FRUIT KNIFE
Stainless Steel with Electro-plate Handle .. .. .. each **3/6**

SILVER AND PLATE REPAIRS EXECUTED BY SKILLED WORKMEN AT MODERATE CHARGES

REPAIRS TO SILVER HAIR BRUSHES
New Bristles fitted to Customer's own Mounts. All Pure Bleached Bristle
'XA' quality 38/6   'A' 32/6   'B' 25/6   'C' 21/6

TEA AND COFFEE SERVICE REPAIRS
New Handles to Pots, Ebony or Boxwood	from	6/6 each
Herculite Handles. Unbreakable. In Black or Brown ..	,,	8/9 ,,
Rewickering Handles	,,	4/6 ,,
Ivory Non-Conductors	,,	3/- ,,
New Spout to Pots, Hard Metal..	,,	12/6 ,,
Plating and cleaning inside Pots..	,,	6/- ,,

REPAIRS AND NEW PARTS TO CUTLERY
	Best	Second Quality
Table Knives Rebladed, Rustless	4/- each	3/- each
Cheese ,, ,, ...	3/6 ,,	2/6 ,,
Joint Carvers ,, ,, ...	9/6 ,,	8/6 ,,
Game ,, ,, ,, ...	6/9 ,,	6/- ,,

Table and Cheese Knives rebladed. Ordinary Steel about 6d. each less
Carvers about 2/6 each less

Trophies of all kinds mounted under expert supervision
Glass linings of every description fitted to Customer's Silver and Plated articles

SILVERSMITHS' CHESTS IN OAK OR TEAK
Estimates on Request

REPLATING

The following List will serve as an indication of Harrods most moderate Prices
Any article quoted for on request

		A1 Quality Replating	A Quality Replating
Biscuit Boxes	from	17/6 each	15/- each
Cruets	,,	7/6 ,,	6/6 ,,
Coffee Pots	,,	15/6 ,,	12/6 ,,
Dessert Eaters	,,	50/- per doz. prs.	45/- per doz. prs.
Entree Dishes..	,,	37/6 each	32/- each
Hot Water Jugs	,,	15/6 ,,	12/6 ,,
Nut Cracks	,,	3/6 pair	3/- pair
Salt Cellars	,,	8/- ,,	7/- ,,

Spoons and Forks, plain patterns—		A1 Quality Replating	A Quality Replating
Table size	..	25/- doz.	21/- doz.
Dessert ,, ...	..	20/- ,,	17/9 ,,
Tea Spoons	..	11/6 ,,	10/- ,,
Sugar Basins	from	10/6 each	8/6 each
Tankards	,,	10/- ,,	8/- ,,
Tea Trays	,,	47/6 ,,	42/- ,,
Tea Caddies	,,	8/6 ,,	7/- ,,
Tea Kettles on Stands, complete ..	,,	32/6 ,,	28/6 ,,
Tea Urns..	,,	32/- ,,	27/- ,,
Tea Pots..	,,	17/6 ,,	15/- ,,
Toast Racks	,,	4/- ,,	3/6 ,,

ALL PRICES ARE SUBJECT TO MARKET FLUCTUATIONS

HARRODS LTD

Telephone SLOANE 1234
Telegrams 'EVERYTHING HARRODS LONDON'

LONDON S W 1

CUTLERY DEPARTMENT
Safety Razors, Stropping Machines & Assorted Scissors Sets

PS 6668
SHEFFIELD-MADE LIBRARY SCISSORS
With Letter-opener and Sheath. Various colours 15/-

PS 6531
STAINLESS STEEL FRUIT KNIFE
With Mother-o'-Pearl scales
Length 3¼ ins. .. each 8/6

PS 6657
HARRODS EXCLUSIVE COMPACT SCISSORS SET
Containing 3 best Sheffield Scissors with chased Bows, Spring measure, Silver Thimble and Pincushion 32/6

PS 3856
THE SELF-ADJUSTING 'NEW GILLETTE' SAFETY RAZOR
Complete with ten Blades in Leather Case .. 21/-
Wood or Metal Case 21/-
Extra Blades, packet of 10 3/6 ; 5 for 1/9

PS 6411 HARRODS 'PRINCESS' SCISSORS CASE
The case is of Leather in various colourings. When closed it is 7 ins. high. Fittings include three fine quality Sheffield-made Scissors, with Chased Bows, steel-lined Silver Thimble, packets of Needles, reels of coloured Silks and small Pincushion 48/6
A similar case with plain Scissors 39/6
Protected by Royal Letters Patent, and exclusive to Harrods

PS 6338 Fine Embroidery SCISSORS and Silver THIMBLE in case
18/6

PS 6038 POCKET FRUIT KNIFE
With Silver Blades and Mother-o'-Pearl scales .. 12/6

PS 6952 SHEFFIELD SCISSORS
Three complete in case .. 29/6
Four in case 37/6

BLADES FOR ALL SAFETY RAZORS

Auto-Strop Blades,	5 for 2/3, 10 for 4/6
Gillette Blades ..	5 for 1/9, 10 for 3/6
7 o'clock Blades ..	.. 6 for 2/6
'Ever Ready' Blades	5 for 1/8 10 for 3/4
Clemak Blades ..	.. 7 for 2/6
Wilkinson Blades ..	.. each 4/-
'Darwin' for Gillette	.. 5 for 2/3
	10 for 4/6
Also John Watts' Sheffield-made Blades for Gillette ..	6 for 1/9, 12 for 3/6
Blades for Durham Duplex ..	5 for 2/3

PS 3845
LEATHER CASE OF FINEST SHEFFIELD HOLLOW GROUND RAZORS

Seven Razors, Black scales ..	£5 0 0
Seven " Ivory " ..	£6 6 0
Four " Black " ..	£3 3 0
Four " Ivory " ..	£3 18 6
In case complete	

PS 6967 'THE PALL MALL' CUSHION RAZOR STROP
2/6, 3/6, and 6/-

PS 6536 LADIES' 'CARMEN' RAZOR
Silver-plated with seven Blades
Complete in case 10/6
Spare Blades each 5d

PS 6662 'VALET' AUTO STROP SAFETY RAZOR
Nickel Set. Contains heavily Silver-plated razor, 12 blades and horse-hide strop in highly polished Nickel case, lined Velvet and Satin 21/-
Also in Leatherette Case .. 21/-
Travelling Set with Brush and Soap 32/6
Extra Strops .. each 2/6

PS 6664 THE ROLLS RAZOR
This is self-contained and automatically strops and hones the blade, which is guaranteed for five years
'Imperial' Silver plated £1 7 6
Cheaper quality Nickel plated £1 1 0
Extra Blades 6/- each

PS 6966 HANGING RAZOR STROP
Leather and Canvas, 2/6, 4/6 and 6/6

PS 5196 THE 'TWINPLEX' STROPPING MACHINE
For Gillette Blades in Black Enamel 12/6
Super Model, all Nickel Plated .. 21/-
Also made for Durham Duplex Blades at above prices

PS 6313 THE 'ALLEGRO' Automatic Honer and Stropper for Gillette and Auto-Strop Blades. Makes every blade a good blade and keeps it good Price, in neat cardboard box 15/6

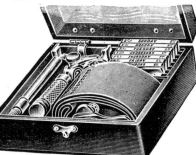

PS 6890 THE 'WILKINSON' Hollow Ground Safety Shaver. Fitted in neat wood case with one Blade .. 8/6 One Blade and Stropper .. 21/-
Three Blades & Stropper 27/6 Seven Blades & Stropper, as illustration 42/-

ALL PRICES ARE SUBJECT TO MARKET FLUCTUATIONS

HARRODS LTD

Telephone SLOANE 1234
Telegrams 'EVERYTHING HARRODS LONDON'

LONDON S W 1

OPTICAL DEPARTMENT

Oculists' Prescriptions carefully and Accurately Dispensed

Harrods Optical Department is under the direct control of an experienced and certified optician assisted by a staff of certified and qualified assistants who are thoroughly trained in every branch of optics, including *Sight Testing*

O 25
Best London Made Tortoiseshell
Spectacle Frame with Patent Gold
joints **67/6**
Imitation Shell with Rolled Gold
joints **23/6**
Lenses extra

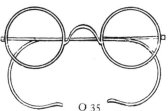

O 35
Rolled Gold Spectacles with Xylo
covered rims **12/6**
Lenses extra

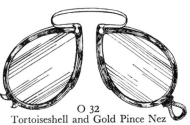

O 32
Tortoiseshell and Gold Pince Nez
Folding pattern **42/-**
Solid Gold **50/-**
Lenses extra

O 31
Rimless Finger Pince Nez with
spherical lenses, best Rolled Gold
mount **13/6**

O 30
Tortoiseshell Lorgnette from **35/-**
Imitation Shell Lorgnette from
13/6
Lenses extra

> Special attention given to *FITTING*
> to ensure the *maximum amount of
> comfort*
> *Charges are strictly moderate*

O 26
Rolled Gold Louis from
18/6
Platinised Silver from
35/-
Platinised Silver and
Marcassite from **55/-**
Solid Gold from **60/-**
Lenses extra

> ### REPAIRS
> Repairs and alterations of
> every description are com-
> pleted promptly and satis-
> factorily. Please do not
> include case when forward-
> ing glasses for repairs

O 33
Tortoiseshell and Gold Pince Nez
40/-
Imitation Shell and Rolled Gold
Pince Nez **17/6**
Lenses extra

O 36
Imitation Tortoiseshell Spectacle
Frame **13/6**
Tortoiseshell Frame .. **20/-**
Tortoiseshell, lighter colours from
30/- to **100/-**
Lenses extra

O 27
Steel Frames with Lenses .. **6/6**
Rolled Gold with Lenses .. **12/6**
Solid Gold with Lenses .. **40/-**

O 29
Gallery Oxford, Gold .. **21/-**
Gallery Oxford, Rolled Gold **5/6**
Lens extra

O 28
Tortoiseshell Pivot
Lorgnette .. **38/6**
Imitation Shell
Lorgnette .. **18/6**
Lenses extra

O 34
Rimless Pince Nez with Spherical
Lenses, Gold mount .. **23/6**

O 37
Tortoiseshell Spectacle with Gold
curl sides **37/6**
Imitation Shell with Rolled Gold
sides **17/6**
Lenses extra

ALL PRICES ARE SUBJECT TO MARKET FLUCTUATIONS

HARRODS LTD
Telephone SLOANE 1234
Telegrams 'EVERYTHING HARRODS LONDON'
LONDON SW1

OPTICAL DEPARTMENT
Magnifying and Protective Eye Glasses and Cases

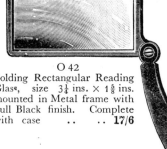

O 40
Silver Mounted Reading Glass
2⅛ ins. **17/6**   2½ ins. **23/6**
3 ins. **33/-**   3½ ins. **38/6**
4¼ ins. **75/-**

O 41 Brocade Spectacle
Case in various colours,
with Rolled Gold serrated
edges.. .. .. **16/6**
Black Moire Silk Case with
Silver serrated edges
13/6

O 42
Folding Rectangular Reading
Glass, size 3¼ ins. × 1⅝ ins.
mounted in Metal frame with
dull Black finish. Complete
with case **17/6**

O 43
Reading Glass with White
Metal rim and Black handle
2⅛-in. dia. **4/6**   2¾-in. dia. **5/3**
2⅞-in. dia. **6/9**   3½-in. dia. **8/-**
4-in. dia. **11/-**   5-in. dia. **18/-**

O 44
Automatic Eye Glass
guards, with Black Enamel
front **3/-**
Oxidized or Moire Silk covered
front **6/-**
Rolled Gold front .. **7/6**
White Rolled Gold front .. **10/6**

O 45
Reading Glass, mounted in adjustable stand, dull Black finished.
Suitable for use on desk, table or
easel. 3¾ in. dia., **45/-**   4¼-in.
dia. **48/9**

Optical purchases of
20/- value or over
are sent Post Free
in England and
Wales. Purchases of
£2 value or over are
sent Post Free in
Scotland

O 48 Lasin : the best preventative against moisture
or steam forming upon lenses, wind screens, mirrors, etc.
Pencil Form **1/-**   Book Form **2/-**   Auto Lasin **2/6**

O 46
Aluminium Circular
Reading Glass
2⅛-in. **8/6** 3-in. **9/6**
3½-in. **12/3** 4-in. **15/-**
4½-in. **17/6**

SPECIAL
QUOTATIONS

Whilst there may be
many optical instru-
ments omitted from
this list Harrods are
always ready to make
special quotations for
any optical instru-
ment

O 47 Silver Pince Nez Case
Plain **23/6**
Engine Turned **30/-**
Silver Spectacle Case for curl sides
Plain **35/-**
Engine Turned **42/-**
Gold Pince Nez Cases from **£7 10 0**

CROOKES'
GLASS
For those who require
spectacles as a pro-
tection from 'glare'
we strongly recom-
mend the use of Sir
William Crookes'
Glass, which is not
only an adequate
protection, but is
also adaptable for
any type of lens

O 49
Milanese Embossed
Leather Spectacle
Case **11/6**

O 51
Aluminium Rectangu-
lar Reading Glass
Spherical Lenses
3 × 2 ins. .. **11/9**
3½ × 2¼ ins. .. **15/-**
4 × 2½ ins. .. **19/6**
Cylindrical Lens giving
a flatter field
3 × 2 ins. .. **16/-**
3½ × 2¼ ins. .. **20/-**
4 × 2½ ins. .. **24/-**

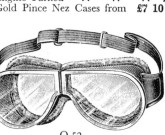

O 52
Triplex Motor Goggle, feather-
weight model
White Glass **25/-**
Tinted **26/-**
White, with Flying Mask .. **42/-**
Triplex Motor Goggles from **12/6**

O 50
Triple Lens Magnifier
in Vulcanite. Powerful
Lenses suitable for
Botany, etc. .. **3/-**

O 53
Folding Pocket Mag-
nifier with excep-
tionally good lens,
in neat Suede case
2-in. diameter **4/6**
3-in. diameter **7/6**

ALL PRICES ARE SUBJECT TO MARKET FLUCTUATIONS

OPTICAL DEPARTMENT
Telescopes, Microscopes, Compasses and Pedometers

STUDENT'S MICROSCOPE
With rack adjustment, triple power objective, condenser, Iris diaphragm and reflecting mirror. Complete in case with forceps and slides   **£4 10 0**

YOUTH'S TELESCOPE
A good practical telescope of useful magnification
$\times$ 11 $\times$ 15 $\times$ 20 $\times$ 25
Diameter of O.G. 1 in. **18/-**, $1\frac{1}{4}$ ins. **22/6**, $1\frac{1}{2}$ ins. **30/-**, $1\frac{3}{4}$ ins. **39/-**

CADET TELESCOPE
'OFFICER OF THE WATCH'
Covered in Brown Leather, with leather cap for object glass **£3 5 0**

ZEISS 'ASSEROS' TELESCOPE
(*Not illustrated*)   This instrument is so constructed that by simply turning a collar a choice of magnifications from 4 to 20 is obtainable. Size of O.G. 2 ins., length $20\frac{1}{2}$ ins. **£21 0 0**

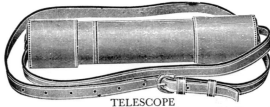

TELESCOPE
Three drawers, $1\frac{3}{8}$-in. diameter, O.G. brass body, covered in Brown Leather With caps, and sling. A well constructed and inexpensive telescope, magnifies 22 times.   Length closed, 10 ins., open, 30 ins.   ..   **£3 15 0**

Microscope **£4 10 0**	Magnifies 40 and 80 and 120	Microscope 23/-	Magnifies $\times$ 30, 50 and 70
,, 15/-	,, $\times$ 30	,, 52/6	,, $\times$ 30, 50 and 70
,, 19/-	,, $\times$ 30, 50 and 70	,, 67/6	,, $\times$ 50, 80 and 110

MAP MEASURE
For measuring any distances, whether straight or curved, such as lengths of roads, rivers, etc. Suitable for any scale map **4/6**

SCHOOL MICROSCOPE
With sliding adjustment and mirror reflector
Single power   ..   **15/-**
Triple power   ..   **19/-**
Triple power and condenser **23/-**

TRANSPARENT COMPASS
With luminous cardinal points Reverse shows divided circle to 5°. The glass, being curved, acts as a magnifier. Mounted in bronzed bezel, $1\frac{1}{2}$-in. diameter **21/-** Prices of Gold and Silver Mounts on application

Repairs and adjustments accurately and skilfully executed

POCKET COMPASS
A useful and thoroughly reliable compass which can be easily carried in the pocket without injury to the instrument 1 in. diameter luminous dial In Hunter Case **6/6**

YOUTH'S MICROSCOPE
With rack adjustment, 3-power objective reflecting mirror. Complete in case with forceps and slides, **52/6**; Larger model **67/6**

POCKET COMPASS
Mounted in gymbal. $1\frac{1}{4}$-in. diam. dial. A useful instrument for motor boats, etc.   ..   **£2 5 0**

PEDOMETER
For measuring the distance walked.   Up to 12 miles **10/6**   100 miles **12/6**
100 miles in yards **15/6**

SERVICE LIQUID PRISMATIC COMPASS
Regulation W.O. pattern, 2-in. diam. Complete in sling and belt case **£6 15 0**

ALL PRICES ARE SUBJECT TO MARKET FLUCTUATIONS

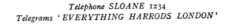

HARRODS LTD   *Telephone SLOANE 1234*
Telegrams 'EVERYTHING HARRODS LONDON'   **LONDON S W 1**

PHOTOGRAPHIC DEPARTMENT

Cameras and Accessories, Optical Lanterns, Cinematograph Apparatus and Everything Appertaining to Photography

DEVELOPING, PRINTING AND ENLARGING A SPECIALITY

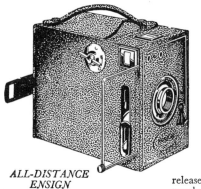

ALL-DISTANCE ENSIGN

ALL-DISTANCE ENSIGN

For Roll Films 2¼B (2¼″ × 3¼″)

EQUALLY SUITABLE FOR 'CLOSE-UPS' AND DISTANT VIEWS

BOX MODEL

BODY—Made entirely of metal, crystalline enamel finish—fittings nickel-plated. Back section hinged for easy loading Leather handle

FILM FLATTENER—A metal pressure plate is fitted to the body, which is operated by an external lever covering the sight hole. When an exposure is being made this plate presses upon the film and keeps it absolutely flat. When the film is wound to the next number the plate is automatically released and the film winds easily and smoothly. As soon as the next number appears the sight hole cover is replaced, applying pressure to the film

LENS—Gives crisp definition at all distances. Hooded

SHUTTER—Time and instantaneous, provided with 3 stops

VIEW FINDERS—Direct vision with sighter plate for eye level pictures. Reflex type for waist line position

SIZE—4¾ × 3 × 4¼ ins. Weight, 22 ozs.

PRICE **£1 5 0**

ALL-DISTANCE POCKET ENSIGN

POCKET MODEL

Has all the advantages of the Box Model, and will fit into a Sports Jacket Pocket **37/6**

ENSIGN CARBINE No. 6

For Roll Films (2¼ × 3¼ ins.)

BODY—All metal, covered in first quality leather; fitted with leather handle and two tripod bushes. Solid leather bellows.

FRONT—Solid aluminium, fitted with thumb grips and rising front.

FOCUSSING MOVEMENT—By radial lever, moved in accordance with a scale for short distances—very fine focussing obtained

SPOOL HOLDERS—Improved; no loose parts

WINDER—Very strong and simple in use

VIEW FINDERS—Large brilliant, reversible, also direct vision with a view plate

SIZE—Closed, 6½ × 3⅜ × 1½ ins. Weight, 22 ozs.

Including wire release and 24-page instruction booklet

Aldis Uno Anastigmat	*f/7·7*	3-speed Shutter	..	**£4 15 0**
Aldis-Butcher ,,	*f/6·3*	6-speed	.. ..	**6 17 6**
Aldis Uno ,,	*f/4·5*	Compur	.. ..	**7 7 0**
Aldis-Butcher ,,	*f/4·5*	Compur	.. ..	**8 17 6**

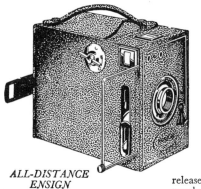

No. 4 ENSIGN CARBINE

TROPICAL MODELS

Supplied in chamois leather bag

For Roll Films 2¼ × 3¼ ins.

Aldis Uno Anastigmat *f/7·7*

3-speed Shutter .. **£4 15 0**

Aldis Uno Anastigmat *f/6·3*

3-speed Shutter .. **£5 5 0**

A REMARKABLE ACHIEVEMENT

ENSIGN SPEED FILM REFLEX WITH FOCAL PLANE SHUTTER

For Roll Films 2¼ × 3¼ inches

Made of mahogany, with Morocco Leather covering. Incorporates the patent film registering device which ensures perfect flatness of film. Surface-silvered mirror and leather handle. Focal-plane shutter with speeds of 1/25th, 1/50th, 1/250th, 1/500th second and Time. Aldis-Butcher guaranteed anastigmats giving perfect covering and pin sharp definition

Fitted with Aldis-Butcher Guaranteed Anastigmats—*f/4·5* **£10 10 0**

,, ,, ,, ,, *f/3·4* **£12 12 0**

ALL PRICES ARE SUBJECT TO MARKET FLUCTUATIONS

PHOTOGRAPHIC DEPARTMENT

Roll-film and Plate Cameras fitted with Goerz-Zeiss and Voigtländer Lenses

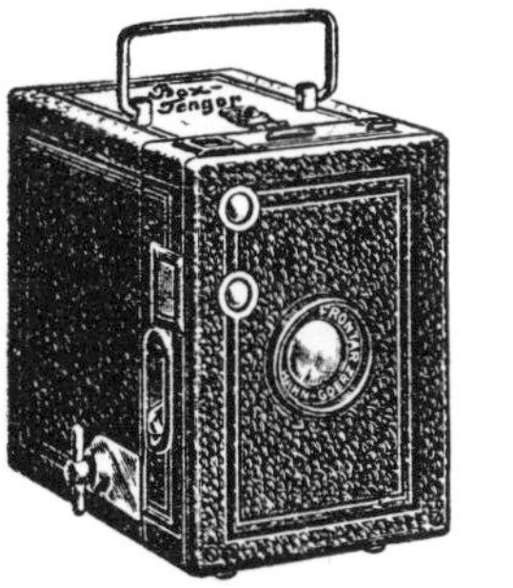

BOX TENGOR

A light ALL METAL box Camera for every make of roll film. Fitted with Goerz Frontar lens F11, and finished in artificial leather. Two good finders. The snapshots taken with the Box Tengor are very sharp and clear and give sparkling lively prints. In three sizes for pictures

3 × 2 ins.	£1	1	0
3¼ × 2¼ ins.	£1	1	0
4¼ × 2½ ins.	£1	10	6

The prices of 3¼ × 2¼ ins. and 4¼ × 2½ ins. sizes include portrait lenses making them 'all focus' cameras. The 3 × 2 ins. does not require any special lens for portraits as everything over 5 ft. is focussed sharply in the picture

ICARETTE

Fitted with the renowned Zeiss Tessar lenses, they will produce negatives full of detail which can be enlarged to almost any size. The Icarettes are fitted with both ordinary and direct vision finders. Covering and bellows of the finest quality leather

Model 488 for pictures 2½ × 1⅝ ins., with Zeiss Tessar & Compur F4.5 .. £11 0 0

Model 500-1 for pictures 3¼ × 2¼ ins., with Zeiss Tessar & Compur F4.5 .. £12 0 0

Model 501, for pictures 4¼ × 2½ ins., with Zeiss Tessar & Compur F4.5 .. £12 7 6

Model 500-2 This is a special model with Double Extension bellows and equipped with a combined back which allows plateholders, focussing screen and film packs to be used if desired. Price with Tessar F4.5 and Compur Shutter (slides and focussing screen extra) £14 12 6

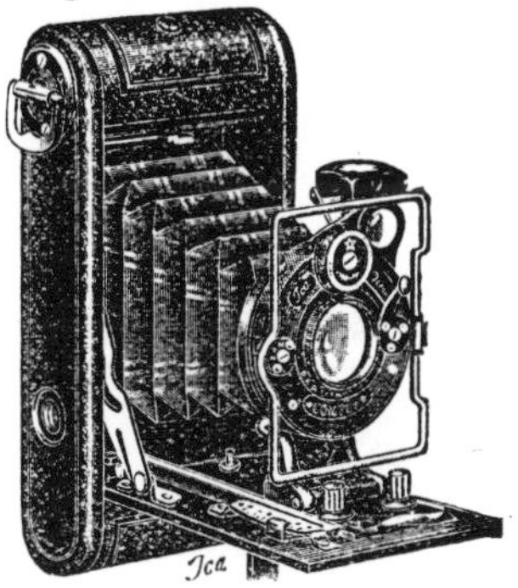

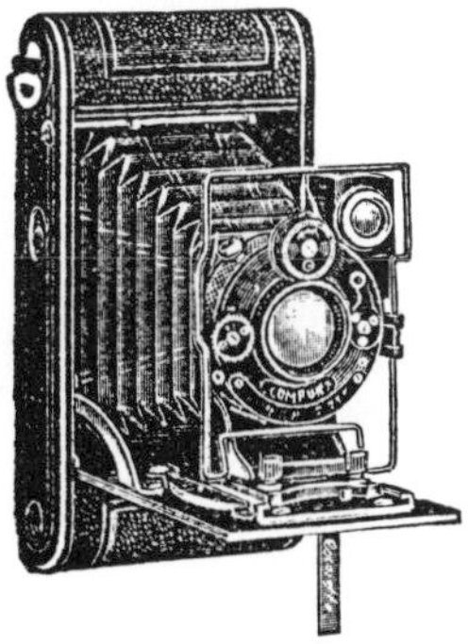

COCARETTE

An excellent Camera at a moderate price made by Messrs. Zeiss Ikon. Folding pattern, leather bellows, beautiful inlaid finish, accurate speeded time, instantaneous shutter, and rapid lenses. Takes all standard films

Model 207, 3 × 2 ins. (*as illustrated*)

With 3-speed shutter and F6.8 Anastigmat £4 12 6

With Compur shutter and F4.9 Zeiss Tessar £10 5 0

Model 206, 3 × 2 ins.

As above, but simple finish and with reflecting finder only. F11 lens £3 2 6

Ditto F6.8 Anastigmat .. £3 12 6

Model 210, 3¼ × 2¼ ins., specification as 206

F11 lens	£3	0	0
F6.8 Anastigmat	£3	10	0
Compur shutter, F4.5 Anastigmat	£7	0	0

Model 220, 4¼ × 2½ ins., specification as 206

F11 lens	£3	7	6
F6.8 Anastigmat	£3	17	6

TRONA
Models 110 & 212

Model 110 for 3¼ × 2¼ ins. for Plates and Film Packs.

Model 212 for 4¼ × 3¼ ins. for Plates and Film Packs.

The Trona is a Zeiss Ikon camera made to minimum dimensions and weight, and is made of metal throughout.

Double extension leather bellows by rack and pinion, rising and cross front, reversible reflecting and direct vision frame finders, hinged 'U' front, leather covering and bellows.

Prices include three single slides and hooded focussing screen.

PRICES	3¼×2¼ ins.	4¼×3¼ ins.
F/4.5 Dominar in Compur shutter	£9 5 0	£11 5 0
F/6.3 Zeiss Tessar in Compur shutter	9 17 6	12 0 0
F/4.5 Ditto. ditto	10 12 6	13 0 0
Extra 3¼ × 2¼ ins. slides		1/9
Extra 4¼ × 3¼ ins. slides		2/-
Extra 3¼ × 2¼ ins. film pack adapter		7/3
Extra 4¼ × 3¼ ins. film pack adapter		8/-

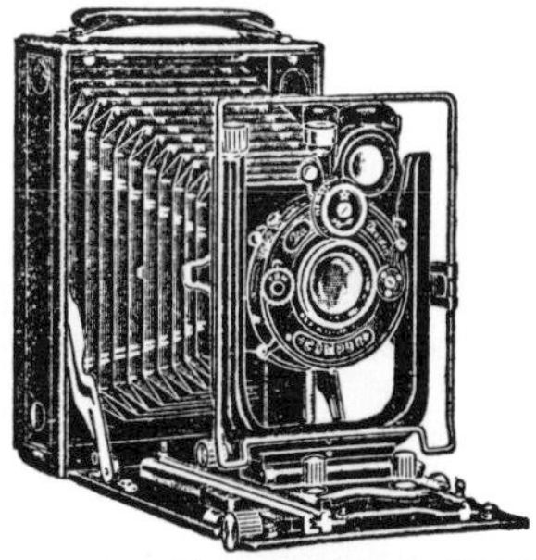

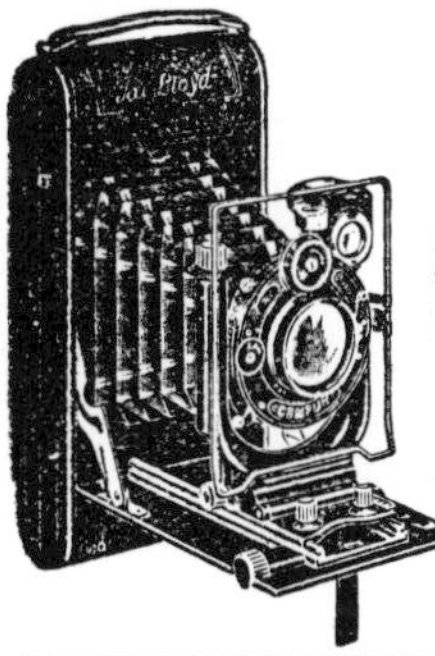

MADE BY ZEISS IKON

THE LLOYD ROLL FILM CAMERAS

Model 510/1 for Roll Films and Plates 4¼″×3¼″

A splendid Camera. Focussing is performed by rack and pinion. The back is adapted to take a focussing screen, and slides for plates, which can be supplied at a slight extra cost. Prices, 4¼ × 3¼ ins.—

With F/4.5 Dominar and Compur shutter	£12	5	0
„ F/6.3 Zeiss Tessar „ „	13	0	0
„ F/4.5 „ „ „	14	0	0

The ZEISS IKON NIXE is a similar precision made Camera to the Lloyd, but equipped with Double Extension Bellows. Prices, with F/4.5 Zeiss Tessar and Compur Shutter

For 4¼ × 3¼ ins. pictures	£16	2	6
„ 5½ × 3¼ ins. „	18	7	6

MIROFLEX FOLDING REFLEX

4¼″ × 3¼″ or 9 × 12 cm. for Plates and Film Packs

The Miroflex is the latest folding reflex brought out by the Zeiss Ikon Company. It is a marvel of mechanical construction, being equally suitable for use as a focal plane camera or folding reflex.

The focal plane shutter is speeded from 1/3rd to 1/2000th of a sec., which speeds are obtained by a special gearing arrangement; one knob entirely controls the working of the shutter.

The reflex hood when folded down enables the camera to be used exactly like the usual focal plane type.

The Miroflex body is made of hard wood covered with morocco leather. Focussing by means of focussing mount.

PRICES—Including six single slides

With F/4.5 Zeiss Tessar	£39	12	6
With F/2.7 Zeiss Tessar	60	7	6

Extra slides 2/- each. Film pack adapter 8/-

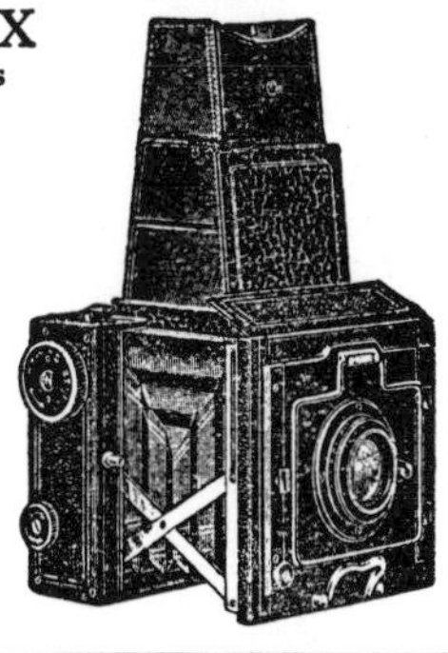

THREE OF THE VOIGTLÄNDER CAMERAS

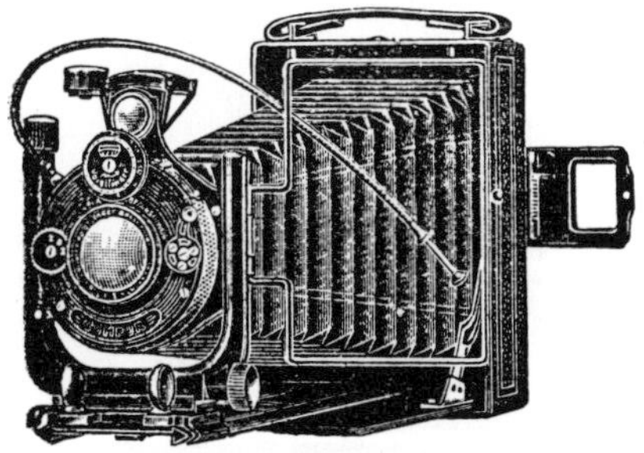

AVUS CAMERA

An extremely well-made camera at a popular price. **Full** double extension, rack rising and cross front, **brilliant** and direct vision view-finders.

With Voigtländer F/4.5 Skopar lens and Compur **Shutter**

3¼ × 2½ ins.	£8	8	0
4¼ × 3¼ ins.	10	0	0

ROLL FILM CAMERA

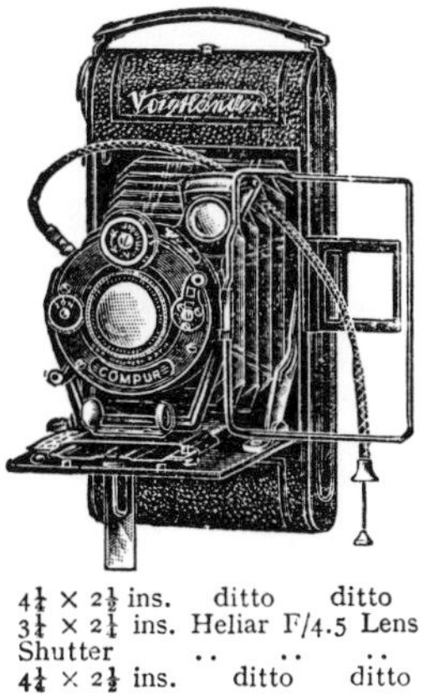

Voigtländer Lenses have excelled for the past 170 years and we offer this new model roll film Camera with the greatest confidence. Perfectly made throughout, it has the highest grade quality lens and shutter

For Standard Roll Films, 3¼ × 2¼ ins., F/4.5 Voigtländer Skopar Lens and Compur Shutter

£6 17 6

3 × 2 ins. do. do.

£6 0 0

4¼ × 2½ ins. ditto ditto	£7	12	6
3¼ × 2¼ ins. Heliar F/4.5 Lens and Compur Shutter	9	12	6
4¼ × 2½ ins. ditto ditto	10	15	0

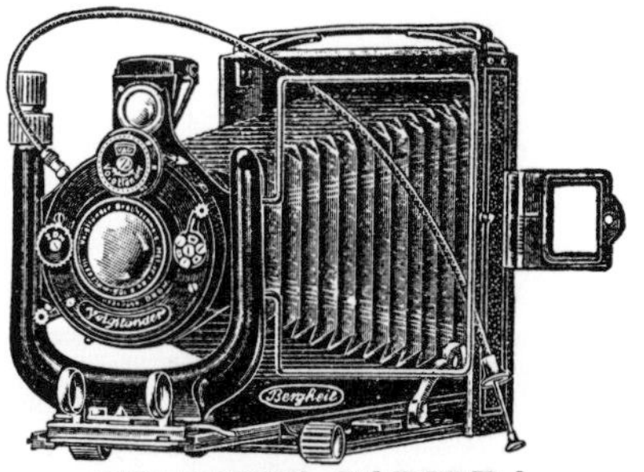

TOURIST CAMERA

Possesses many unique features exclusive to this model. Struts which prevent camera being accidentally closed, double rack and pinion, spirit levels sunk in milled heads, etc. Perfect workmanship throughout.

With Compur Shutter and 3 Slides

Voigtländer Heliar F/4.5, 3¼ × 2¼ ins.	£16	0	0
Ditto 4¼ × 3¼ ins.	16	0	0
Heliar F/3.5, 3¼ × 2¼ ins.	16	0	0
Ditto 4¼ × 3¼ ins. (6 ins. F/4.5)	17	10	0

ALL PRICES ARE SUBJECT TO MARKET FLUCTUATIONS

HARRODS LTD

Telephone SLOANE 1234
Telegrams '*EVERYTHING HARRODS LONDON*'

LONDON S W 1

PHOTOGRAPHIC DEPARTMENT

Harrods Cinemas for the Home are Perfectly Constructed and Easy to Operate

THE CINÉ - 'KODAK' Model B

A hand camera which enables the amateur to make his own motion pictures as easily as he can make snapshots with a 'Kodak.' Pictures are made by holding the camera against the body or at eye level, centring the subject in the finder and pressing the release. A spring motor than makes the exposures

Price :

Ciné - ' Kodak ' Model B, with f6.5 lens	..	..	£18	18	0
,, ,, ,, ,, f3.5 lens	..	..	£25	0	0
,, ,, ,, ,, f1.9 lens	..	..	£31	10	0

THE CINÉ - 'KODAK,' Model A

A compact motion picture camera, equipped in every way to meet the needs of the advanced amateur. It is supplied with ' Kodak ' Anastigmat Lens f1.9, a lens which makes cinematography possible on dull days and enables the making of slow motion pictures

Price :

Ciné - ' Kodak ' Model A, complete with Cine - 'Kodak ' Tripod and with f1.9 lens £60 0 0

CINÉ-'KODAK' FILM 100 feet (including cost of developing) **30/-**

'KODASCOPE' Model B

The 'Kodascope' Model B is almost human. It is self-threading. You merely start the motor, slip the end of the film into a slot, and the self-threading device does the rest. Other outstanding features are : The Framing Device ; the Mechanical Rewind ; Still Picture Device ; and Heat Absorbing Screen and the Reversing Device for running the film backwards without stopping the motor

Price :

' Kodascope ' Model B with Velvet - lined carrying case, two 400 ft. Reels, one Humidor Can, two 200 Watt Lamps, Splicing Outfit and an Oiling Outfit .. .. 100 volt	£89	10	0
200 volt	£92	17	6

'KODASCOPE' Model C

A compact and inexpensive machine for projecting Cine - 'Kodak' pictures. It is extremely simple to use. A small electric motor supplies the power and a special 100-Watt Lamp the illumination. Current for both motor and lamp is obtained from the ordinary House supply (a rheostat is necessary where current is above 120 volts)

Prices :

' Kodascope,' Model C, complete with electric motor and lamp	£18	0	0
Rheostat		27/6	

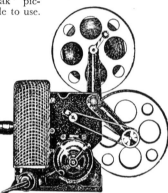

BELL AND HOWELL CINÉ CAMERAS AND PROJECTORS

FILMO No. 75 CAMERA

Takes pictures equal in every respect to those seen at the best picture theatres. Yet so wonderfully is it constructed that it can be operated by a child. Sight the subject and press the button—that's all there is to it. Camera, with lens, and case .. £30 0 0

THE EYEMO CAMERA FOR STANDARD FILMS

A real hand camera. Requires no tripod Weighs only 7 lbs. Daylight loading, entirely automatic. Takes 100 feet film at one load. Complete with lens £82 10 0

FILMO PROJECTOR

The finest piece of mechanism the world has produced. Entirely self-operating. Shows absolutely flickerless pictures on a screen in your own home. Variable speeds, reversing device for rewinding or repeating a section of the film. Filmo projector, like other Filmo apparatus, is fully guaranteed. Complete with carrying case .. £61 10 0

The New Photography—

'Cinematography in the Home'

AN IDEAL COMBINATION

The 16 mm. ' Victor ' Movie camera fitted with 1 in. f/3.5 Dallmeyer lens, incorporating ' slow motion,' and the 16 mm. ' De Vry ' projector with Dallmeyer projection lens, a really portable projector, at an extremely moderate price. Write for details of this apparatus or call for a demonstration

De Vry projector with Dallmeyer projection lens £30
Carrying case .. £2 10 0
Variable voltage resistance £1 12 6

Carriage paid on all purchases 20/- and over to any part of Great Britain

' Victor ' camera with Dallmeyer lens £46 0 0
Leather case £3 10 0
Supplementary lenses—price on application

ALL PRICES ARE SUBJECT TO MARKET FLUCTUATIONS

HARRODS LTD

Telephone SLOANE 1234
Telegrams 'EVERYTHING HARRODS LONDON'

LONDON S W 1

PHOTOGRAPHIC DEPARTMENT

For the Photographer who does His Own Developing

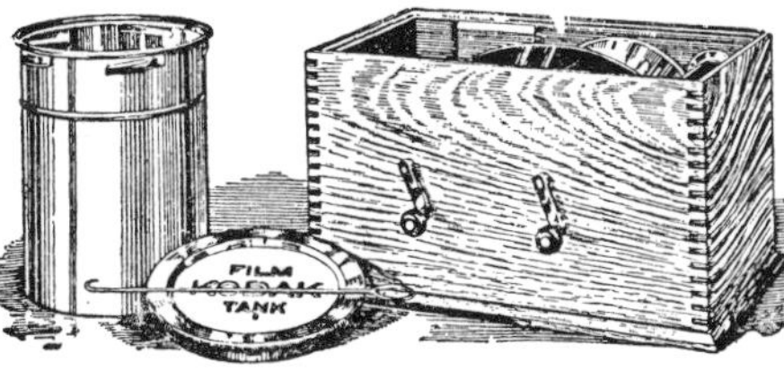

'KODAK' FILM DEVELOPING TANK FOR CORRECTLY DEVELOPED NEGATIVES

The 'Kodak' Film Tank enables the Amateur to develop his films without the inconvenience of a dark room. Ensures perfect results by the Time and Temperature method of development

		Prices
No. 2	For $2\frac{1}{4}$ ins. Films or less	£0 18 6
No. 3	For $2\frac{1}{2}$ ins. Films or less	£1 4 0
No. 4	For $3\frac{1}{2}$ ins. Films or less	£1 8 6

'Kodak' Tank Developing Powders for—

No. 2 Tank In Packets of six	9d
No. 3 Tank In Packets of six	1/3
No. 4 Tank In Packets of six	1/3
'Kodak' Acid Fixing Per $\frac{1}{2}$ lb. Tin	$10\frac{1}{2}$d
'Kodak' Acid Fixing Per 1 lb. Tin	1/6
'Kodak' Thermometer	2/6

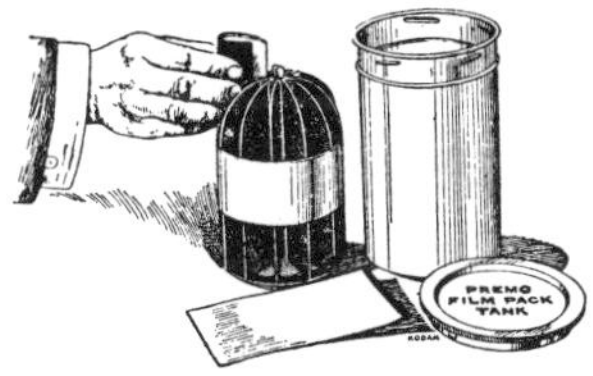

'KODAK' FILM-PACK TANK

Provides a simple and certain method of developing all or part of a 'Kodak' Film Pack at one time and getting negatives of uniform quality

No. 1 For $3\frac{1}{4} \times 2\frac{1}{4}$ ins., $4\frac{1}{2} \times 6$ C/M Films .. 8/6
No. 2 For $3\frac{1}{4} \times 2\frac{1}{4}$ ins., $4\frac{1}{4} \times 2\frac{1}{2}$ ins., $4\frac{1}{4} \times 3\frac{1}{4}$ ins. $5\frac{1}{2} \times 3\frac{1}{4}$ ins. or 5×4 ins. Films 15/-
No. 3 For $6\frac{1}{2} \times 4\frac{3}{4}$ ins., 7×5 ins., Films 17/6

'KODAK' DEVELOPING POWDER

No. 1 Tank In Packets of six	1/-
No. 2 Tank In Packets of six	1/6
No. 3 Tank In Packets of six	1/9

Expert Advice given on all Photographic questions

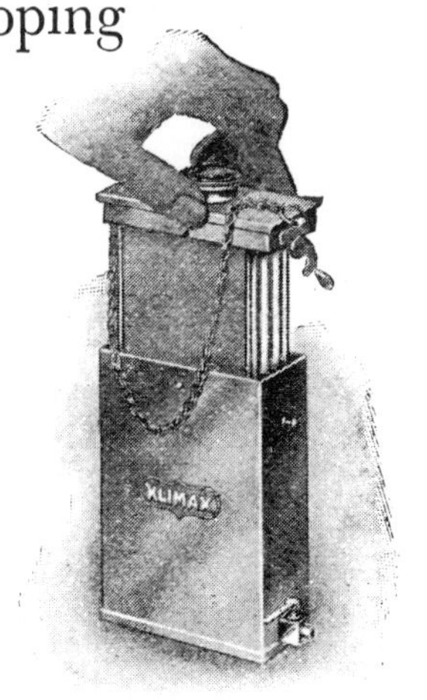

'KLIMAX' FILM-PACK DEVELOPING TANK

For the daylight development of film-packs and plates. Loading only takes a few minutes in the dark room. Other operations can be done in daylight. Fitted with water-tight lid for reversing Tank. The Films are inserted in carriers and left there until dry. Constructed of strong Copper and Brass, heavily nickel-plated, with loose rack

FOR DEVELOPING FILM PACKS
Or Twelve Plates

No. 1	$3\frac{1}{4} \times 2\frac{1}{4}$ ins.	24/-
No. 2	$4\frac{1}{4} \times 3\frac{1}{4}$ ins.	25/-
No. 3	$5\frac{1}{2} \times 3\frac{1}{4}$ ins.	27/-

DEVELOPING POWDERS

For No. 1 Tank In Packets of six	1/6
For No. 2 Tank In Packets of six	2/3
For No. 3 Tank In Packets of six	3/-

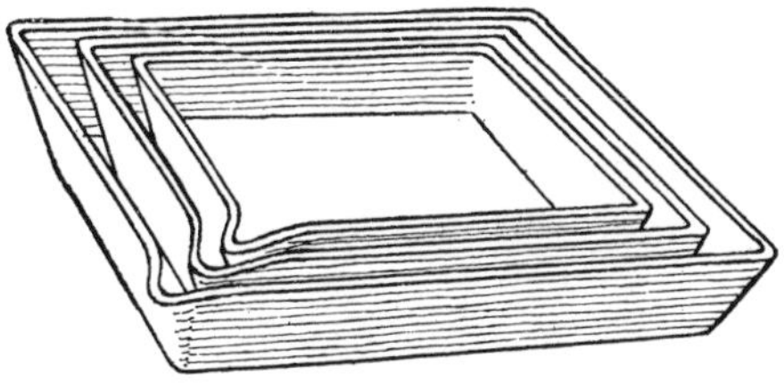

DEVELOPING DISHES

	Porcelain	Enamelled Steel	Xylonite
$3\frac{1}{4} \times 2\frac{1}{4}$ ins.	—	—	5d
$4\frac{1}{4} \times 3\frac{1}{4}$ ins.	1/6	1/8	7d
$5\frac{1}{2} \times 3\frac{1}{2}$ ins.	1/9	2/3	8d
$6\frac{1}{2} \times 4\frac{3}{4}$ ins.	2/6	2/6	1/-
$8\frac{1}{2} \times 6\frac{1}{2}$ ins.	4/-	3/6	1/4
10×8 ins.	4/9	4/6	2/6
12×10 ins.	7/-	5/6	8/-
15×12 ins.	15/6	9/-	9/6

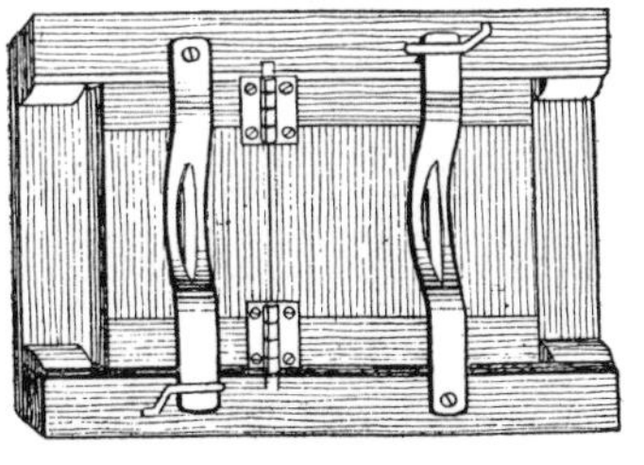

THE 'JAYNAY' PRINTING FRAME

The safest and most reliable of all printing frames
Guaranteed not to slip

			Prices
$2\frac{1}{4} \times 2\frac{1}{4}$ ins. each	1/-	$5\frac{1}{2} \times 3\frac{1}{2}$ ins. each	1/6
3×2 ins. „	1/-	5×4 ins. „	2/-
$3\frac{1}{2} \times 2\frac{1}{2}$ ins. „	1/2	$6\frac{1}{2} \times 4\frac{3}{4}$ ins. „	2/3
$3\frac{1}{4} \times 4\frac{1}{4}$ ins. „	1/3	$8\frac{1}{2} \times 6\frac{1}{2}$ ins. „	5/-
$4\frac{1}{2} \times 2\frac{3}{4}$ ins. „	1/3		

All Frames glazed up to $5\frac{1}{2} \times 3\frac{1}{2}$ ins.

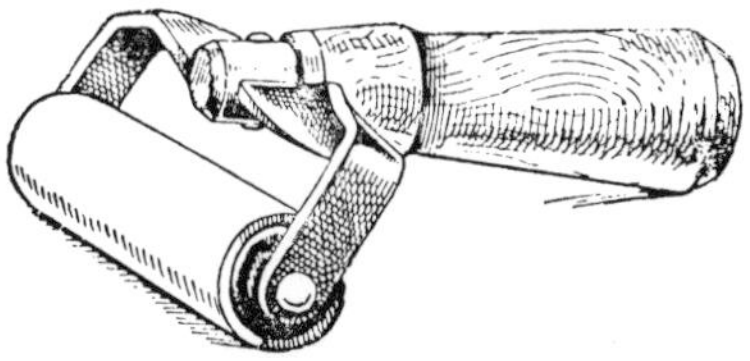

'JAYNAY' ROLLER SQUEEGEE

Prices

4 ins. 2/3	5 ins. 2/6	6 ins. 3/-	7 ins. 3/6
8 ins. 4/-	9 ins. 4/3	10 ins. 4/9	12 ins. 6/-

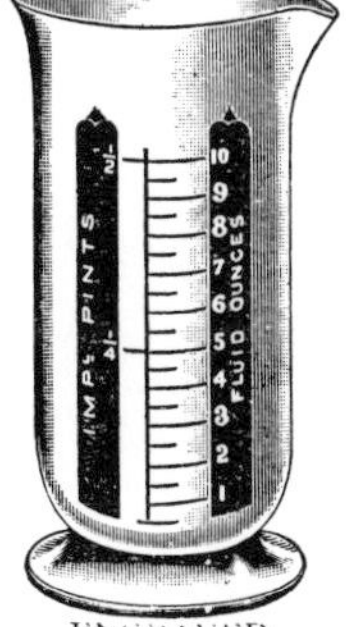

ENGRAVED LETTER MEASURE

1 dr.	9d
2 dr.	9d
1 oz.	1/-
2 oz.	1/2
4 oz.	1/6
10 oz.	2/6
20 oz.	3/6

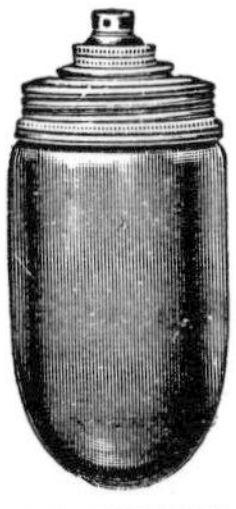

NON-ACTINIC GLOBES

A glass cover for converting ordinary filament lamps into safelights.
Ruby or Orange
Each 3/-

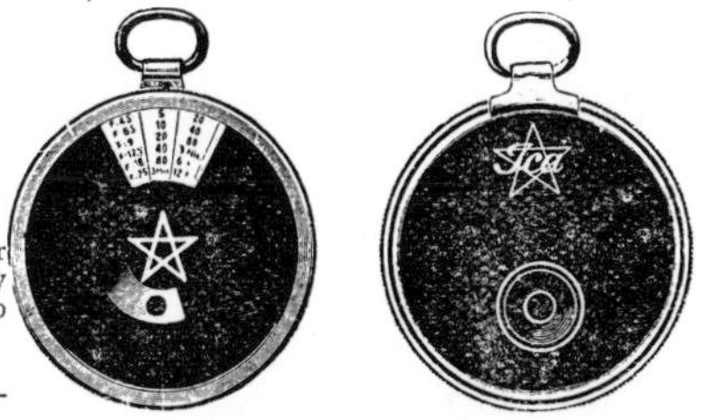

ICA DIOPHOT EXPOSURE METER
4/-

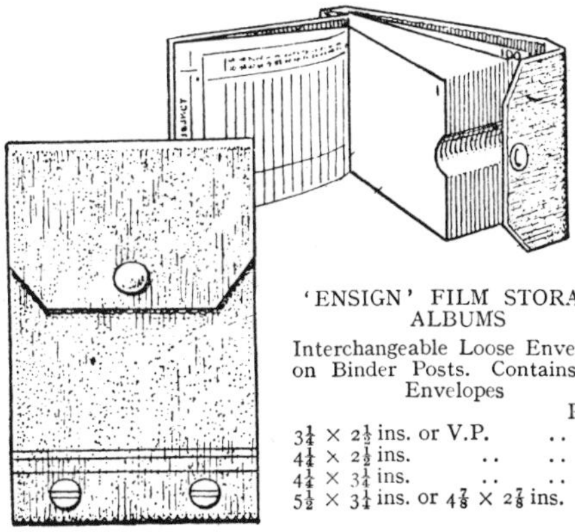

'ENSIGN' FILM STORAGE ALBUMS

Interchangeable Loose Envelopes on Binder Posts. Contains 100 Envelopes

	Prices
$3\frac{1}{4} \times 2\frac{1}{4}$ ins. or V.P.	2/6
$4\frac{1}{4} \times 2\frac{1}{2}$ ins.	3/-
$4\frac{1}{4} \times 3\frac{1}{4}$ ins.	3/-
$5\frac{1}{2} \times 3\frac{1}{4}$ ins. or $4\frac{7}{8} \times 2\frac{7}{8}$ ins.	4/-

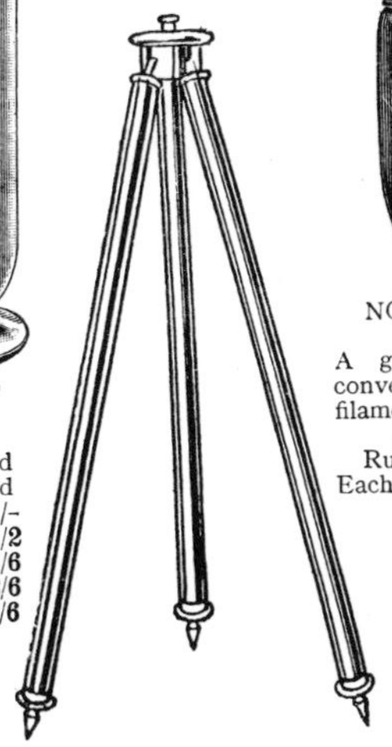

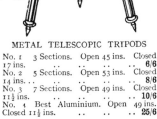

METAL TELESCOPIC TRIPODS

No. 1 3 Sections. Open 45 ins. Closed 17 ins. .. 6/6
No. 2 5 Sections. Open 53 ins. Closed 14 ins. .. 8/6
No. 3 7 Sections. Open 49 ins. Closed $11\frac{1}{2}$ ins. .. 10/6
No. 4 Best Aluminium. Open 49 ins. Closed $11\frac{1}{2}$ ins. .. 25/6

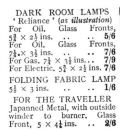

DARK ROOM LAMPS

'Reliance' (*as illustration*)

For Oil. Glass Fronts, $5\frac{3}{4} \times 2\frac{1}{2}$ ins. .. 5/6
For Oil. Glass Fronts, $7\frac{1}{4} \times 3\frac{1}{2}$ ins. .. 7/6
For Gas. $7\frac{1}{4} \times 3\frac{1}{2}$ ins. .. 7/9
For Electric. $5\frac{3}{4} \times 2\frac{1}{2}$ ins. 7/6

FOLDING FABRIC LAMP
$5\frac{1}{2} \times 3$ ins. .. 1/6

FOR THE TRAVELLER
Japanned Metal, with outside winder to burner. Glass Front, $5 \times 4\frac{1}{4}$ ins. .. 2/6

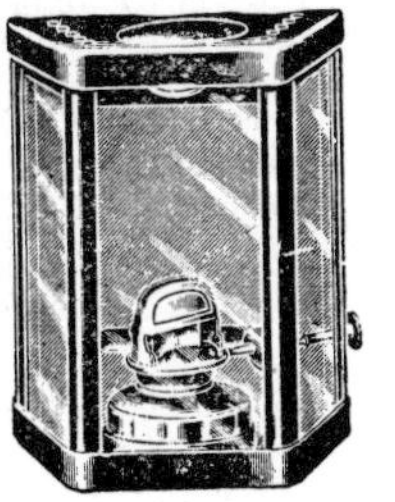

ALL PRICES ARE SUBJECT TO MARKET FLUCTUATIONS

HARRODS LTD

Telephone SLOANE 1234
Telegrams 'EVERYTHING HARRODS LONDON'

LONDON S W 1

PHOTOGRAPHIC DEPARTMENT

Harrods Undertake every kind of Photographic Work

FILMS DEVELOPED IN 24 HOURS AND FINISHED PRINTS SUPPLIED IN 2 DAYS

An Augmented Staff of Experts and New and Enlarged Developing and Printing Rooms enable Harrods to offer the best Photographic Service for Amateurs in London

DRY PLATES AND ROLL FILMS

BARNET ILLINGWORTH PAGET ILFORD IMPERIAL WELLINGTON — *All makes at the same prices* — **KODAK ILLINGWORTH IMPERIAL ENSIGN WELLINGTON PATHE**

PLATES

Size	Except Panchromatic and X-Ray		Panchromatic	Backing Extra
Inches.	½-doz.	1 doz.	1 doz.	1 doz.
2 5/16 × 1¾	—	1/4	—	4d
3¼ × 2¼	—	1/8	—	4d
3¼ × 3¼	—	2/3	—	4d
3½ × 2½	11d	1/8	—	4d
4¼ × 3¼	1/4	2/6	—	4d
5 × 4	2/2	4/2	5/-	6d
5½ × 3¼	2/2	4/2	5/-	6d
5½ × 3½	2/2	4/2	5/-	6d
6½ × 4¾	2/10	5/6	—	9d
6¾ × 3¼	—	4/8	—	9d
7 × 5	—	6/8	8/4	1/-
7½ × 5	—	7/8	9/6	1/-
8½ × 6½	5/2	10/4	12/6	1/-
10 × 8	8/6	17/-	21/6	1/3
12 × 10	12/6	25/-	31/3	1/9
15 × 12	22/1	44/2	57/6	2/6
Cm.				
4½ × 6	—	1/4	2/-	4d
4½ × 10·7	—	1/8	2/6	4d
6 × 9	—	1/8	3/-	4d
6½ × 9	11d	1/8	2/6	4d
8 × 12	1/7	3/-	3/9	4d
9 × 12	1/7	3/-	4/2	6d
10 × 15	2/2	4/2	5/10	9d
13 × 18	—	6/8	8/9	1/-
18 × 24	—	12/6	15/-	1/3

Prices of other sizes on application

FILM PACKS

Kodak Klicam — Imperial Agfa — Imperial Wellington 12 Exposures

4½ × 6 cm.	1/8
3¼ × 2¼	2/4
4¼ × 2½	2/9
4¼ × 3¼	4/-
5¼ × 3	4/8
9 × 12 cm.	4/8
5 × 4	5/-
10 × 15	6/4

LANTERN PLATES 3¼ × 3¼

Barnet. C.G., Black tone; Cold tone

Ilford. Alpha, Warm tone; Special, Black or Sepia tone

Illingworth. Slogas, gaslight; Special, Black tone

Imperial. Special, Black tone Gaslight, Warm tone

Paget. Gravura, Black to Red tone; Rapid, Black; Slow Warm tone

Wellington. S.C.P., Black to Red tone; Lantern, Black tone

Per dozen **2/3**

TRANSPARENCY PLATES

45 × 107 mm.

Ilford, Imperial, Wellington

Per dozen **1/8**

Extra Thin Per dozen **2/-**

FILMS

For Cameras	Six Exposure Spools
Ensignette No. 1	11d
Ensignette No. 2	1/3
Brownie No. 0, Vest Pocket Kodak Ensign Cadet Sportie Carbine Vest Pocket Ensign (6 Exposures 1/-)	1/2 (8 Exp.)
Ensignette Junior 2J	1/5 (7 Exp.)
Pocket Kodak	1/6 (12 Exp.)
F.P.K. No. 0	11d
Brownie No. 1 Box Ensign 2¼A	11d
Brownies, No. 2 Kodaks, No. 1 All Distance Ensign All Ensigns 2¼B Box Ensign 2¼B Ensign Carbine, Nos. 4 and 6 Ensign Cupid Ensign Junior, Model B Ensign Roll Film Reflex (6 Exposures 1/-)	1/2
F.P.K. No. 1	1/2
Brownies, No. 2A Kodaks, No. 1A All Ensigns 2½ Box Ensign 2½ Ensign Carbine, Nos. 10 and 12	1/5
Popular Ensign 2⅞ Brownies and Kodaks, No. 2C	2/-
Kodak No. 3 All Ensigns 3¼	2/-
All Ensigns 3¼A Brownies and Kodaks, No. 3A	2/6
Brownie No. 3	2/-
Stereo Brownie No. 2	2/6
Bull's Eye No. 2 and F.P.K. No. 2	1/8
Bull's Eye No. 4	2/6
F.P.K. No. 4	2/6
Cartridge Kodak No. 3	2/-
Kodaks, No. 4A	3/6
Cartridge Kodak No. 4	2/6
Cartridge Kodak No. 5	4/4

DEVELOPING

ROLL FILMS, FILM PACKS AND PLATES

	Size	6 Exposures
V.P.K.	2½ × 1⅝	8d (8x)
No. 1 Brownie	2¼ × 2¼	8d
No. 2 Brownie	2¼ × 3¼	8d
No. 1 F.P.K.	2¼ × 3¼	8d
No. 1A „	4¼ × 2½	1/3
No. 2 Bullseye	3½ × 3½	1/3
No. 2C „	4⅞ × 2⅞	1/3
¼ plate or No. 3 F.P.K.	3¼ × 4¼	1/3
No. 3A F.P.K.	5½ × 3¼	1/6
No. 4 Cartridge	5 × 4	1/6
No. 4A or ½ plates	6½ × 4¼	2/-

PRINTING

VELOX PRINTS FROM NEGATIVES AS FOLLOWS:—

No. 1 Brownie	2/- per dozen
No. 2 „	2/- „
V.P.K.	1/6 „
No. 1 F.P.K.	2/- „
No. 1A „	2/6 „
No. 2 Bullseye	2/6 „
No. 2C „	3/- „
¼ plate or No. 3 F.P.K.	3/- „
No. 3A F.P.K.	3/6 „
No. 4 Cartridge	3/6 „
No. 5 Cartridge or ½ plates	4/6 „
POSTCARDS, by contact	3/6 „

ENLARGING

ENLARGEMENTS FROM AMATEURS NEGATIVES AS FOLLOWS

Sizes	Unmounted: Black & White Bromide	Unmounted: Sepia-toned Bromide	On Art Mounts: Black & White Bromide	On Art Mounts: Sepia toned Bromide
6½ × 4¾	1/6	1/9	2/6	2/9
8½ × 6½	2/0	2/9	3/6	4/6
10 × 8	2/6	3/6	4/6	5/6
12½ × 7½	2/9	4/3	4/6	6/0
12 × 10	3/6	4/6	5/6	6/6
15 × 12	4/-	5/-	6/6	8/6
17 × 10½	5/-	6/9	8/-	9/9
18 × 15	6/-	7/6	10/6	12/6
20 × 16	6/9	7/9	12/6	14/-
23 × 17	7/6	8/9	14/-	15/9
24 × 18	8/6	10/-	16/9	18/9
30 × 22	15/-	22/6	25/6	33/-

If negatives are not available, Harrods can enlarge from suitable photographs, at a slightly increased charge

Postcards enlarged from any size negatives

Per dozen **6/-**

Camera Cases, Tripods and all Photographic Accessories at moderate prices

ALL PRICES ARE SUBJECT TO MARKET FLUCTUATIONS

HARRODS LTD — *Telephone SLOANE 1234* — *Telegrams 'EVERYTHING HARRODS LONDON'* — LONDON S W 1

ARTISTS' MATERIALS DEPARTMENT

Specially Selected Oil Colours and Varnishes

Harrods Artists' Materials Section not only has the Finest Selection of Paints for Water Colour and Oil Painting, but also every accessory for Fine Art Work

Series 1

Single 4 in. Tube **5**d   Studio Size **1/2**

Brown Ochre
Burnt Sienna
Burnt Umber
Caledonian Brown
Copal Megilp, No. 1
Flake White, No. 1
Indian Red
Ivory Black
Lamp Black
Light Red
Medium (Copal Megilp) [No. 1
Megilp
Raw Sienna
Raw Umber
Terra Rosa
Terre Verte
Vandyke Brown
Venetian Red
Yellow Ochre

Series 1a

Single 2 in. Tube **5**d   Studio size **2/3**

Crimson Lake
Emerald Green
Indigo
Mauve
New Blue
Permanent Blue
Permanent Yellow
Purple Lake
Sap Green
Scarlet Lake
Ultramarine Deep
Ultramarine Light

Series 2a

Single 2 in. Tube **9**d   Studio Size **3/6**

Brown Madder   Rembrandt Madder
Rubens Madder

FLAKE WHITE AND ZINC WHITE

Four-inch Tubes, **5**d each. Double Tubes, **10**d each. Studio Tubes, **1/2** each. ½ lb. Tubes, **2/-** each. 1 lb. Tubes **4/-** each

Size of Studio Tube

Series 1b

Single 3 in. Tube **5**d   Studio Size **1/6**

Antwerp Blue
Blue Black
Brown Pink
Chrome Deep
Chrome Green, No. 1
Chrome Green, No. 2
Chrome Green, No. 3
Chrome Lemon
Chrome Orange
Chrome Yellow
Cinnabar Green, Deep
Cinnabar Green, Middle
Italian Pink
Naples Yellow
Neutral Tint
Payne's Gray
Prussian Blue

Series 2

Single 2 in. Tube **6**d
Studio Size **2/6**

Alizarin Crimson
Alizarin Green
Gamboge
Geranium Lake
Olive Green
Sepia

Series 4

Single 2 in. Tube **1/6**
Studio Size **6/9**

Aureolin
Cadmium Orange
Cadmium Yellow
Cadmium Yellow, Deep
Cadmium Yellow, Pale
Carmine

Series 3

Single 2 in. Tube **1/-**   Studio Size **4/6**

Carmine No. 2
Cobalt Blue
Emerald Ox. of Chromium
French Ultramarine
Indian Yellow
Leitch's Blue
Lemon Yellow
Oxide of Chromium
Oxide of Chromium Trans.
Pink Madder
Rose Madder (Pink Shade)
Vermilion
Vermilion, Chinese
Vermilion, Scarlet
Viridian

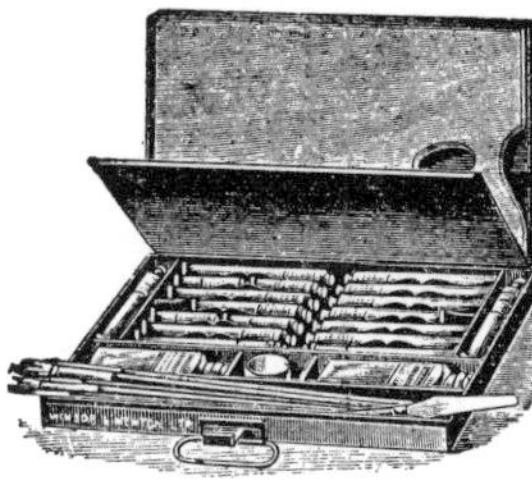

'THE COMPACT BOX'
Size 10⅜ × 7¼ × 1½ ins. deep

Contains 17 colours and Megilp. Also Brushes, Linseed Oil and Turpentine Palette Knife and Mahogany Palette **24/3**

'COLLEGE' SERIES OF BOXES OF OIL COLOURS

		each
No. 11	9 Colours, etc.	**11/6**
No. 12	12 Colours, etc.	**12/6**
No. 13	16 Colours, etc.	**15/6**

WINSOR & NEWTON'S OIL AND VARNISHES

VARNISHES

	Glass Bottles each	¼-pint Tin, or Glass each
Amber Varnish	**1/6**	**3/2**
Amber Varnish, Light ..	**1/9**	**3/9**
Chinese or Map Varnish..	**1/6**	**3/2**
Crystal Varnish	**1/6**	**3/2**
Mastic Varnish	**2/-**	**4/4**
Oil Copal Varnish ..	**1/6**	**3/3**
Picture Copal Varnish ..	**1/9**	**3/9**
Picture Mastic Varnish ..	**1/9**	**3/9**
White Spirit Varnish ..	**1/4**	**2/10**

OILS AND MEDIUMS

Fat Oil	**1/6**	**3/2**
Manganesed Linseed Oil..	**1/-**	**2/2**
Oil of Spike Lavender ..	**2/8**	**5/8**
Pale Drying Oil	**1/-**	**2/2**
Poppy Oil, Purified ..	**1/-**	**2/2**
Linseed Oil, Purified ..	**9d**	**1/6**
Spirits of Turpentine ..	**9d**	**1/6**
Strong Drying Oil ..	**1/2**	**2/6**
Walnut Oil	**1/1**	**2/4**
Copal Oil Medium ..	**1/6**	**3/2**
Japan Gold Size	**1/2**	**2/6**
Florentine Medium ..	**1/6**	—

OIL COLOUR SKETCHING BOXES
(Tin lined)

Polished Oak, Walnut or Mahogany Fitted with Colours, Brushes, etc.

No. 3	11 × 8½ ins.	..	**£2 15 0**
No. 4	13 × 10¼ ins.	..	**£3 10 0**
No. 5	15 × 11¼ ins.	..	**£3 14 6**
No. 6	17 × 13¼ ins.	..	**£4 10 0**

Without Colours or Brushes, etc.

No. 3	11 × 8½ ins.	..	**£2 1 6**
No. 4	13 × 10¼ ins.	..	**£2 9 0**
No. 5	15 × 11¼ ins.	..	**£2 12 0**
No. 6	17 × 13¼ ins.	..	**£3 0 0**

SKETCHING BOX

For oil painting. Made of Walnut wood lined Tin to take canvas board (14 × 10 ins.). Complete with Palette .. **32/6**

ALL PRICES ARE SUBJECT TO MARKET FLUCTUATIONS

ARTISTS' MATERIALS DEPARTMENT

Outfits and Materials for Lacquer Work, Fabric Painting and Sketching

CHINESE LACQUER WORK OUTFITS AND MATERIALS

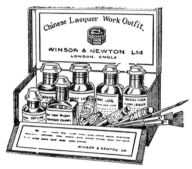

Illustration of No. 1 Outfit

Bottles of Coloured Lacquer in Red, Black, Green, Blue, Cream, Yellow, White, Mauve, Apricot, Orange, Buff, Heliotrope, Brown, Almond Green, Jade Green and Dull Black Each **1/-**

No. 0—Outfit containing all necessary materials **10/-**

No. 1—Outfit containing all necessary materials **15/-**

'BARBOLA' WORK
(THE NEW GESSO WORK)

No. 1—Outfit containing 8 'Barbola' Colours in tubes, tin of 'Barbola' Paste, Bottle of 'Barbola' Varnish, Brush and two modelling Tools **7/6**
Also larger Outfits at **12/6, 15/6, 22/6, 28/6**

'BARBOLA' PASTE

Small Tins, as in No. 1 Outfit .. Each **8d**
Large Tins, as in No. 2 Outfit .. „ **1/3**
Tins containing about 1 lb. .. „ **2/6**
Tins containing about 2 lbs. .. „ **4/3**
Boxwood Modelling Tools
6-in., each **4d.**, 7-in., each **5d**

'BARBOLA' VARNISH

Small size, as in No. 1 Outfit Per bot. **6d**
Large size, as in No. 2 Outfit „ **10d**

'VENUS' SET

Beautifully padded box in Green and Gold, fitted with 'Venus' full length and pocket Pencils, Pencil Lengthener and Ink and Pencil Erasers **7/6**
Other sets .. .. .. **5/- and 3/-**

'RENASCO'

For Italian Renaissance work. Can be used on any kind of woodwork, pulpware, papier maché or thick cardboard
Complete outfit .. **10/6**

SKETCHING UMBRELLAS

Good strong umbrellas exceptionally practicable and serviceable. Plain Cream covers fitted at the top with an adjustable fan joint, centre joint and spike .. **35/-**
With Green lining .. **40/-**

STENCILLING OUTFITS

ARTISTS' LIQUID OIL COLOURS IN BOTTLES

No. 9—Outfit containing 5 Colours in bottles, 2 Brushes, 4 English Cut Stencils, 4 Drawing Pins and Manilla Paper .. **5/-**

No. 10—Outfit containing 6 Colours in bottles, 3 Brushes, 3 English Hand-Cut Stencils, Stirring Rod, 6 Drawing Pins and 3 pieces of Oiled Manilla Paper for Stencil Cutting **7/6**

Also in larger sizes .. **10/6 and 15/-**

'DARGEENA' PAINTING ON FABRIC

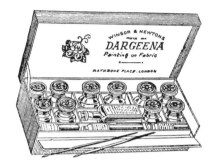

No. 1—Outfit containing
5 Bottles of 'Dargeena' Colour, 1 Tube of Enamel, 1 Bottle Medium, 1 Glass Tube of each Silver Flake and Gold Bronze Powder, 2 Brushes and 2 Tin Nozzles **8/6**

Larger outfits .. .. **10/6 and 12/-**

WATER BOTTLE AND CUP
Made in strong Japanned tin
Complete .. **1/6**

PENCILS
The 'Royal Sovereign' all degrees
4d each, **3/9** doz.
The 'Venus'
4d each, **3/9** doz.
The 'Kandahar'
4d each, **3/9** doz.
The 'Kohinoor'
4d each, **3/9** doz.
The 'Eversharp' Pencil
5/- to **21/-**

SKETCHING STOOLS

No. 1—21 ins. Loose Seat **5/-**

No. 1A—21 ins. Fixed Seat **6/-**

SKETCHING EASELS
(*On right*)
In Whitewood, measuring 50 ins. when open and 27 ins. closed
5/6

ALL PRICES ARE SUBJECT TO MARKET FLUCTUATIONS

PICTURE DEPARTMENT
Oil and Water Colour Paintings, Artists Signed Proof Engravings, Etchings and Mezzo Tints in Colour

RESTORATION AND PRESERVATION

The most valuable pictures may be entrusted to Harrods with full confidence, for none but experts are entrusted with this highly specialized work

Regilding of every description undertaken. Collections of Pictures arranged and maintained

FINE FLOWER STUDY BY VAN HUYSEN
Finely printed in colour and varnished as old piece
Size 38 × 30 ins. In Old Gold frame with Dutch
Motif in Red **£6 15 0**

ARTISTIC FRAMING OF EVERY DESCRIPTION

Special attention is given to all classes of framing. Harrods have a large stock of mouldings and sample frames of recent designs for selection. A special feature of the framing by Harrods is the high standard of quality and workmanship maintained and the reasonable prices charged

FINE LACQUER PHOTO FRAMES
In Black, Blue, Red, Gold, etc. Fitted with strong Covered Strut Backs

14 × 10 ins., **30/-**		12 × 9 ins., **23/-**
11 × 8 ins., **22/-**		8 × 6 ins., **13/6**
10 × 7 ins., **20/-**		Cabt. size, **8/9**
7 × 5 ins., **10/-**		

'THE JAPANESE ROOM'
By L. Campbell Taylor, A.R.A. Size 22½ × 19ins.
Framed in Old Gold and Antique Blue with Japanese Motif
Prints only .. **£2 0 0** Complete .. **£3 5 0**

Series 418

BLUE AND GILT PHOTO FRAMES

Post card	**2/3**	Cabt. size,	**2/9**
8 × 6 ins.,	**4/9**	10 × 7 ins.,	**6/9**
11 × 8 ins.,	**7/9**	12 × 9 ins.,	**8/6**
14 × 10 ins.,	**9/11**	15 × 12 ins.,	**10/9**

SOLID-FLAT BLACK AND MAHOGANY POLISHED FRAMES

	Polished Wood Backs	Strong Cloth Covered Backs
Post card ..	**2/3**	**2/6**
Cabinet size ..	**2/3**	**3/-**
7 × 5 ins. ..	**3/3**	**3/9**
8 × 6 ins. ..	**4/3**	**4/9**
10 × 7 ins. ..	**5/-**	**5/6**
11 × 8 ins. ..	**6/3**	**7/6**
12 × 9 ins. ..	**7/3**	**8/6**
14 × 10 ins. ..	**8/-**	**9/6**
15 × 11 ins. ..	**8/6**	**10/9**

Walnut and Black	Mahogany and Black	Rosewood and Satinwood

ASSORTED INLAID PHOTO FRAMES

Post card	.. **1/9**	Cabt. size	.. **2/0**
8 × 6 ins.	.. **3/6**	10 × 7 ins.	.. **4/6**
11 × 8 ins.	.. **4/11**	12 × 9 ins.	.. **5/6**
14 × 10 ins.	.. **6/9**	15 × 11 ins.	.. **7/9**

Series 343

SHAPED TOP CHINESE LACQUER FRAMES
In Red, Blue, Black, Gilt, etc.

Sight	Outside Size	Each
5¼ × 4 ins.	8 × 6 ins.	**15/-**
7 × 5 ins.	10 × 7 ins.	**18/6**
8 × 6 ins.	11 × 8 ins.	**21/-**
10 × 7 ins.	13 × 10 ins.	**27/6**
11 × 8 ins.	14 × 11 ins.	**28/9**
12 × 9 ins.	15 × 12 ins.	**30/-**
14 × 10 ins.	17 × 13 ins.	**32/-**

All frames fitted with glass and strong strut backs, hang and stand

ALL PRICES ARE SUBJECT TO MARKET FLUCTUATIONS

HARRODS LTD   *Telephone SLOANE 1234*   **LONDON S W 1**
Telegrams 'EVERYTHING HARRODS LONDON'

Harrods Portrait Studio

Interior showing Reception Room of the Portrait Studio

HARRODS Photographic Studio with its beautifully appointed Reception and Dressing Rooms in the Georgian Lounge is equipped with every Modern Process for the perfecting of art and technique, whilst a new and thoroughly efficient lighting installation enables results to be obtained that would be altogether impossible in an ordinary photographic studio

Their Majesties' Courts and Levées

Ladies and Gentlemen attending Courts and Levées may have special sittings at any hour of the day or night. Appointments should be made in advance, so that the necessary special arrangements may be made

Portraits

Oils, Water Colours, Pastels, Miniatures and enlargements in Monochrome at moderate charges. Complete list on application

Social Events

Weddings, Family Groups and every form of social function taken at Clients' residences

Children's Portraiture

Delightfully natural photographs are obtained of children at the studio or in the home

HARRODS LTD

Telephone SLOANE 1234
Telegrams 'EVERYTHING HARRODS LONDON'

LONDON S W 1

PIANOFORTE DEPARTMENT

The Finest Selection of Musical Instruments in the Kingdom

Spacious Showrooms and a magnificent range of instruments enable Harrods to offer a selection of models by the most famous English and Continental makers. You are cordially invited to visit the Piano Salon and judge—under perfect acoustic conditions—the tonal merits of the different instruments. If a personal visit is impossible send a brief description of your requirements : you may rely on a satisfactory selection being made by Harrods

Sir Landon Ronald writes :—
' You cannot do better, it seems to me, than to place yourself in the hands of a firm like Harrods and avail yourself of the tremendous advantages attaching to a collection of instruments and a service of experts which, so far as my knowledge takes me, cannot be bettered in Britain '

Writing on ' How to Choose a Piano,' Mark Hambourg says :—
' . . . it takes real knowledge to judge of such things oneself. If one has not had the opportunity of experience, the next best thing is to go to a first-class firm where only first-class instruments are kept and are looked after by experts. Harrods are always ready to place their experience at your disposal, to determine the superiority of construction, and the durability of the various instruments submitted to you, points which are only properly understood by experts '

HARRODS GUARANTEE

Harrods guarantee every new and second-hand pianoforte to give entire satisfaction. Should any defect arise through faulty material or workmanship within five years from the date of purchase, the instrument will be exchanged or repaired free of charge

DEFERRED PAYMENTS

Under this plan Pianos may be purchased by quarterly instalments extending over a period of from one to three years. Delivery is made on payment of the first quarterly instalment, the balance being payable in further quarterly instalments as agreed

	£	s.	d	
EXAMPLE				
Harrods Cash Price, 36 gns.	37	16	0	Payable by 12 quarterly instalments of **£3 9 4**
Interest for 3 years	3	16	0	
	£41	**12**	**0**	

TUNING SERVICE

Harrods send experienced tuners to all parts of London, the Suburbs and the Country at frequent intervals. Quotations for special visits or contract work will be gladly furnished on request, and customers may rely on their instruments being maintained in the best possible condition

REPAIRS

Old or worn Pianofortes sent to Harrods refinishing factory will be restored to a perfect condition. An expert will be sent, free of charge, to give an estimate of the cost

HIRE

Horizontal Grand Pianos from **4** gns. a month
Upright Grand Pianos from **2** gns. a month
Delivery each way is an extra charge, according to distance
Should any hired Piano be purchased within three months from the date of delivery, the hire already paid will be allowed towards the purchase

PIANOFORTES FOR TROPICAL CLIMATES

These Pianofortes are specially prepared instruments designed to give the greatest possible resistance against the injurious effects of extreme humidity and heat

EXCHANGE

Pianofortes, irrespective of age and condition, are taken in part payment and the utmost value is allowed for them. This applies to purchases for Cash and by Deferred Payments. Harrods will gladly send an expert to value the pianoforte

RETURNED HIRE PIANOS AT REDUCED PRICES

In consequence of the extensive hiring business done by Harrods, it is possible to offer at most times a wonderful range of slightly-used instruments

These comprise models by the most famous makers, and having been on hire only to the best houses, are for all practical purposes as useful as new instruments and carry the same guarantee

ALL PRICES ARE SUBJECT TO MARKET FLUCTUATIONS

PIANO DEPARTMENT

These Instruments may be Seen and Tested in Harrods Piano Salon

BROADWOOD

MODEL 7
(As illustration)

Height 4 ft. 1 in., complete iron frame, braceless back. Overstrung scale, compass $7\frac{1}{4}$ octaves, ivory keys, underdamper action, Studded Bridge. Polished Mahogany or Rosewood colour

Net cash price
64 guineas

12 quarterly payments of **£6 3 3**

MODEL 21

Height 4 ft. $2\frac{1}{2}$ ins., complete iron frame. Overstrung, braceless back, underdamper action, compass $7\frac{1}{4}$ octaves, ivory keys. Polished Mahogany or Rosewood colour

Net cash price .. .. .. 85 guineas

12 quarterly payments of £8 3 9

ROGERS

MODEL 1

(As illustration) In Jacobean style, true to period. Height 4 ft., width 5 ft. Overstrung, underdamper tape check action, compass $7\frac{1}{4}$ octaves, ivory keys Dark Oak case

Net cash price
75 guineas

12 quarterly payments of **£7 4 6**

'VOCALIST' MODEL 1
(Illustrated below)

Height 4 ft., width 5 ft. Overstrung, underdamper tape check action, compass $7\frac{1}{4}$ octaves, ivory keys. Rosewood or Mahogany

Net cash price .. .. .. 75 guineas

12 quarterly payments of £7 4 6

MODEL 4

Height 4 ft. 3 ins., width 5 ft. 1 in. Overstrung, underdamper tape check action, metal standards, compass $7\frac{1}{4}$ octaves, ivory keys. Rosewood Mahogany or Oak case

Net cash price
84 guineas

12 quarterly payments of **£8 1 9**

BUNGALOW PIANO

Compass 6 octaves, with folding keyboard. Also manufactured with special construction for the Tropics and ship use. Height 3 ft. 10 ins., width 3 ft. 11 ins., depth closed 1 ft. $4\frac{1}{2}$ ins., or can be made with 7 octaves, height 3 ft. 10 ins., width 4 ft. 6 ins., depth closed 1 ft. $4\frac{1}{2}$ ins.

Net cash price
54 guineas

12 quarterly payments of **£5 4 0**

STROHMENGER

CHAPPELL

'RUBY'
(As illustration)
Height 4 ft. $\frac{1}{2}$ in., $7\frac{1}{4}$ octaves. Overstrung, Mahogany case
Net cash price
76 guineas
12 quarterly payments of **£7 6 6**

A Standard of excellence and value

'EMERALD'

Height 4 ft. 2 ins., width 5 ft., compass $7\frac{1}{4}$ octaves, ivory keys, Overstrung. Mahogany case

Net cash price .. .. .. 85 guineas

12 quarterly payments of £8 3 9

'DIAMOND'

Height 4 ft. 3 ins., width 5 ft., compass $7\frac{1}{4}$ octaves, ivory keys. Overstrung, underdamper tape check action, fitted with extra large sound board

Net cash price .. .. .. 94 guineas

12 quarterly payments of £9 1 0

'STUDENT'
(As illustration)

Mahogany case, height 4 ft. 3 ins. Overstrung, underdamper tape check action, compass $7\frac{1}{4}$ octaves.

Net cash price
€5 guineas

12 quarterly payments of **£6 5 3**

ALL PRICES ARE SUBJECT TO MARKET FLUCTUATIONS

HARRODS LTD

Telephone SLOANE 1234
Telegrams 'EVERYTHING HARRODS LONDON'

LONDON S W 1

PIANO DEPARTMENT
Payment of the First Instalment Secures Delivery

BLUTHNER

NEW MINIATURE GRAND

(*as illustrated*)

Model 4 Length 5 ft. 5 ins., width 4 ft. 11 ins., compass 7¼ octaves, ivory keys, Mahogany or Rosewood case

Net cash price
217 guineas

12 quarterly payments of **£20 17 9**

Ebonized case
Net cash price
207 guineas

12 quarterly payments of **£19 18 6**

MINIATURE GRAND

Style VI Length 5 ft. 7 ins., width 4 ft. 11 ins. Fitted with Aliquot Scaling which is based upon recent discoveries as to the composite nature of musical tone and is a practical application of the Acoustic Law of Sympathetic Vibration, whereby the pianoforte gains additional richness and singing quality of tone. Rosewood case.
Net cash price **248** guineas   12 quarterly payments of **£23 17 6**

BOUDOIR GRAND

Style VIII Length 6 ft. 3 ins., width 5 ft., compass 7¼ octaves, three square legs, Rosewood case and Aliquot Scaling

Net cash price .. .. .. **288** guineas
12 quarterly payments of **£27 14 3**

BECHSTEIN

'LILLIPUT' GRAND

(*as illustrated*)

Model 'L' Length 5 ft. 6 ins., width 4 ft. 10 ins., compass 7¼ octaves, three square legs. Mahogany case
Net cash price
212 guineas

12 quarterly payments of **£20 8 1**

Ebonized case
Net cash price
204 guineas

12 quarterly payments of **£19 12 9**

MINIATURE GRAND

Model 'M' Length 5 ft. 10 ins., compass 7¼ octaves. Rosewood or Mahogany case

Net cash price **228** guineas   12 quarterly payments of **£21 18 9**
Ebonized case
Net cash price **220** guineas   12 quarterly payments of **£21 3 6**

BOUDOIR GRAND

Model 'B' Length 6 ft. 8 ins., width 4 ft. 11 ins., compass 7¼ octaves A-C, three square legs or double square legs at a slightly increased charge. Rosewood or Mahogany case
Net cash price **248** guineas   12 quarterly payments of **£23 17 6**
Ebonized case
Net cash price **240** guineas   12 quarterly payments of **£23 2 0**

STEINWAY

MINIATURE GRAND

(*as illustrated*)

Style 'M' The smallest Steinway Grand. Length 5 ft. 6 ins., width 4 ft. 9½ ins., compass 7¼ octaves. Rosewood, Mahogany or Ebonized case

Net cash price
In Rosewood Case
253 guineas

12 quarterly payments of **£24 7 0**

In Ebonized case
238 guineas
12 quarterly payments of **£22 18 3**

MINIATURE GRAND

Style 'O' Length 5 ft. 10 ins., width 4 ft. 10½ ins., compass 7¼ octaves. Rosewood or Mahogany case

Net cash price **276** guineas   12 quarterly payments of **£26 11 6**
Ebonized case
Net cash price **262** guineas   12 quarterly payments of **£25 4 6**

GROTRIAN-STEINWEG

MIGNON GRAND

(*As illustrated*)

Style 160 Length 5 ft. 3 ins., width 4 ft. 10 ins., compass 7¼ octaves, three square tapered legs. Rosewood or Mahogany case, dull finish
Net cash price
212 guineas

12 quarterly payments of **£20 8 1**

Ebonized case
Net cash price
200 guineas

12 quarterly payments of **£19 5 0**

GROTRIAN-STEINWEG BOUDOIR GRAND

Style 185. On three square tapered legs, length 6 ft. 1 in., width 4 ft. 11 ins. In Rosewood or Mahogany case
Net cash price .. .. .. **243** guineas
12 quarterly payments of **£23 8 0**

ALL PRICES ARE SUBJECT TO MARKET FLUCTUATIONS

HARRODS LTD

Telephone SLOANE 1234
Telegrams 'EVERYTHING HARRODS LONDON'

LONDON S W 1

PIANO DEPARTMENT

Library System Available for Music Roll Supply

ROGERS

PLAYER PIANO
In Rosewood or Mahogany case. Height 4 ft. 4 ins., width 5 ft. 2 ins. depth 2 ft. 4 ins., compass 7¼ octaves. Fitted with all the latest expression devices including Divided Treble and Bass, Automatic Solo, Tracking and Transposing devices
Net cash price
157 guineas
12 quarterly payments of **£15 2 3**

PLAYER PIANO
Height 4 ft. 1½ ins. width 4 ft. 9½ ins., depth 2 ft. Dark Mahogany case, compass 7 octaves. Overstrung, full iron frame, metal standard tape check action. Fitted with Aeolian Co.'s player action, comprising Expression Controls, Bass and Treble Automatic Solo and Tracking devices together with Silent, Tempo and Re-roll levers
Net cash price
86 guineas
12 quarterly payments of **£8 5 9**

UNIVERSAL

HARWOOD

PLAYER PIANETTE
In Mahogany case. Height 4 ft., depth 1 ft. 11 ins., width 4 ft. 3 ins., compass 6 octaves, overstrung. Fitted with full-scale Triumph-Auto action, Automatic Solo, Bass and Treble Levers
Price, 75 guineas.   £7 4 6 per quarter.

PLAYER PIANO
Dark Mahogany case. Height 4 ft. 3 ins., width 5 ft. 1 in., full scale 'Standard' Player action, Divided Treble and Bass, Solo, Accenting, Bass and Treble levers, Silent stop, Retard, Accel.

Net cash price
84 guineas

12 quarterly payments of **£8 1 9**

PLAYER GRAND
In Rosewood case, Aliquot scaling. Length 6 ft. 3 ins. Fitted with the Hupfeld Solophonola player action with Transposing, Auto Tracking, Auto Solo, Auto Pedal, and device for graduating accompaniment
Net cash price
540 guineas
12 quarterly payments of **£51 19 6**

BLUTHNER-HUPFELD

CRAMER

PLAYER PIANO
In Mahogany case. Height 4 ft. 4 ins., width 5 ft. 2 ins., depth, 2 ft. 5 ins., full scale 7¼ octaves. Automatic tracking, Transposing device, etc.
Net cash price
103 guineas
12 quarterly payments of **£9 18 3**

CHALLEN-ANGELUS

PLAYER GRAND
In Mahogany case. Length 5 ft. Fitted with the Angelus player action with Auto Solo, Transposing and other expression devices including the Registered Phrasing Lever
Net cash price
275 guineas
12 quarterly payments of
£26 9 6

ALL PRICES ARE SUBJECT TO MARKET FLUCTUATIONS

HARRODS LTD

Telephone SLOANE 1234
Telegrams 'EVERYTHING HARRODS LONDON'

LONDON S W1

PIANO DEPARTMENT

Harrods Piano Salon Displays all the Newest Models

AMPICO ELECTRIC RE-ENACTING PIANOS

THE AMPICO is the most highly perfected re-producing piano in the world. It is found only in fine pianos of quality and recognised reputation—MARSHALL & ROSE, JOHN BROADWOOD & SON, COLLARD & COLLARD, CHAPPELL, ROGERS, HOPKINSON and CHALLEN, GROTRIAN-STEINWEG

A piano containing the AMPICO brings the living art of the great pianists into the home, and all the music of which the piano is capable

The device is so skilfully incorporated into the piano, that when played by hand a pianist could not possibly detect its presence, for it in no way interferes with the action or touch of the instrument

Only when a roll is inserted, a button pressed, and the strings sing under the unmistakable touch of a great artist do the wonderful tones of the AMPICO become believable

Almost every great pianist of modern times may be heard. Rachmaninoff, Moiseiwitsch, and many of the greatest artists have recorded their playing exclusively for the AMPICO

Only on the AMPICO can be heard dance music played by Vincent Lopez himself, and the stars of the Paul Whiteman Orchestra

The AMPICO may be supplied foot blown and electric reproducing, and may be installed on any voltage, D.C. or A.C. private or district circuit. The AMPICO is also adapted to play all standard 88-note music rolls and they can be operated according to one's individual ideas of expression

BROADWOOD AMPICO

Upright in Dark Rosewood or Mahogany case, height 4 ft. 4½ ins. width 5 ft. 2½ ins. Overstrung, ivory keys, compass 7¼ octaves

Net cash price .. **306** guineas

12 quarterly payments of

£29 9 3

ROGERS AMPICO
REPRODUCING
PLAYER-GRAND

Length 5 ft., width 4 ft. 10 ins. Compass 7¼ octaves, ivory keys Mahogany or Rosewood case, on twin legs

Net cash price .. **476** guineas

12 quarterly payments of

£45 16 6

MARQUE AMPICO

Foot-power Upright Model in finely figured Mahogany case, height 4 ft. 4½ ins., width 5 ft. 1 in. This instrument has been specially designed for those who prefer a foot-power model, and besides being an Ampico Reproducing piano, it is a piano on which any Standard full-scale rolls can be used

Net cash price .. **178** guineas
12 quarterly payments of
£17 2 9

Electric or foot operated, as desired, Upright model
Net cash price .. **225** guineas
12 quarterly payments of
£21 13 3

ALL PRICES ARE SUBJECT TO MARKET FLUCTUATIONS

HARRODS LTD

Telephone SLOANE 1234
Telegrams 'EVERYTHING HARRODS LONDON

LONDON S W 1

MUSICAL INSTRUMENTS AND SHEET MUSIC

Instruments Value £5 or over Supplied on Deferred Terms

UKULELES

MI 364

MI 377

	£	s.	d.
MI 360 Blue on Black or Yellow on Black with gut strings		6	0
MI 361 Italian model, Rosewood finish		12	6
MI 362 Spanish model with non-slip pegs		14	0
MI 363 Spanish model, better quality		18	0
MI 364 (as illustrated) Concert model, extra large, genuine American	1	0	0
MI 365 'Martin,' stained Mahogany body top and neck, dull finish	4	10	0
MI 366 'Martin' as above, with best patent pegs	5	5	0
MI 377 'Martin' (as illustrated) in Koa wood	7	7	0
MI 368 'Martin,' stained Mahogany, 17 frets, pearl position marks. Best patent pegs, Satin finish	9	0	0
MI 369 'Martin,' as above in Koa wood	10	10	0
MI 370 'Kumalae,' in Koa wood, genuine Hawaiian			
MI 371 Model A	1	15	0
„ B	2	5	0
„ C	2	15	0
„ D	3	17	6

Cases for Ukuleles 2/6, 4/-, 7/-, 8/6, 22/6

ORDINARY BANJOS

MI 453

	£	s.	d.
MI 450 10½ ins. plated loop, 10 brackets, peg head	2	5	0
MI 451 10½ ins. plated double spun loop, 12 brackets	2	17	6
MI 452 10½ ins. plated double spun loop, 18 brackets	3	5	0
MI 453 (as illustrated) 10½ ins. plated double spun loop, heavy bezel, 24 brackets	4	17	6

Cases 15/-, 21/-, 30/-

TENOR BANJOS

	£	s.	d.
MI 454 (as illustrated) 10½ ins. Walnut veneered rim, heavy strained bezel, 24 brackets, 3 geared pegs, walnut box resonator ..	7	15	0
MI 455 As above, but fitted with tone chamber and best Roger vellum. A high class instrument	14	0	0

Cases 25/- and 35/-

MI 454

Back view of
MI 454

TAROPATCH

	£	s.	d.
MI 400 Polished Mahogany body and neck, best patent pegs ..	4	7	6
Case for Taropatch		15	6
'Leis' as illustrated, or Taropatch in Light and Dark Orange, Purple, Red and Blue, each		1	2

UKULELE BANJOS

	£	s.	d.
MI 350 Ebonized body, White Wood neck. With case	1	10	0
MI 351 White neck, grip pegs metal, embossed resonator Nickel-plated, with case	1	17	6
MI 352 Mahogany neck, grip pegs, Rosewood rim in case ..	2	5	0
MI 353 White neck, grip pegs, extended box resonator, 10-in. vellum, wood rim with case ..	3	0	0
MI 354 10-in. polished Maple hoop, with inlay, selected Maple resonator, Ebony fingerboard with case	4	1	0

THE FLEXATONE

A fascinating musical novelty for the home band, in four sizes

1/6, 2/6, 5/9, 12/6

Any instrument not in stock can be procured to order

METRONOMES

MI 491

French make (System Maezel)

	£	s.	d.
MI 490 Mahogany finish, without bell, loose door ..		14	6
MI 491 Mahogany finish with bell, loose door	1	3	6
MI 492 Real Mahogany, without bell, loose door ..		15	6
Real Mahogany with bell, fixed door	1	6	6

JAP FIDDLES

MI 480 Home model 'Stroh' as illustrated **£1 14 0**

MI 481 Concert model 'Stroh' .. **£2 17 0**

Harrods guarantee every instrument to give satisfaction, and should any fail to do so they will readily exchange it

ALL PRICES ARE SUBJECT TO MARKET FLUCTUATIONS

HARRODS LTD

Telephone SLOANE 1234
Telegrams 'EVERYTHING HARRODS LONDON'

LONDON S W 1

MUSICAL INSTRUMENTS AND SHEET MUSIC
Saxophones, Clarionets, Portable Organs and Jazz Outfits

MUSIC STANDS

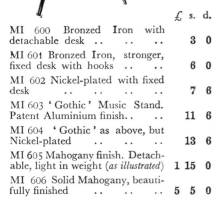

MI 605

		£	s.	d.
MI 600	Bronzed Iron with detachable desk		3	0
MI 601	Bronzed Iron, stronger, fixed desk with hooks		6	0
MI 602	Nickel-plated with fixed desk		7	6
MI 603	'Gothic' Music Stand. Patent Aluminium finish.. ..		11	6
MI 604	'Gothic' as above, but Nickel-plated		13	6
MI 605	Mahogany finish. Detachable, light in weight (*as illustrated*)	1	15	0
MI 606	Solid Mahogany, beautifully finished	5	5	0

VIOLONCELLOS
Full, Three-Quarter and Half Sizes

	£	s.	d.
1464A Stradivarius model, red brown varnish, purfled	5	10	0
1469 Guarnerius model, by Ignaz Thomas, gold yellow varnish, fire flamed wood, ebony fittings, rosewood pegs with gilt mounts. French finish	12	12	0
1472A Stradivarius model by Robert Dolling. Very fine imitation old. Choicest matched woods of fine figure, best quality fittings throughout	16	16	0

And many others at prices of
£3 3 0 upwards

VIOLONCELLO BAGS

	£	s.	d.
1499 Twill, leather bound with bow pocket, leather handles, etc.	1	5	0
1501 Mail Canvas, leather bound, with bow pocket. Guaranteed pitch proofed	1	19	0

CLARIONETS

Clarionets in B flat, A.C. or E flat, high **or** low pitch

		£	s.	d.
MI 500	8 key in C or B flat only	1	5	0
MI 501	13 key as above	1	15	0
MI 502	14 Nickel-Silver keys, 2 rings in ebony, patent C sharp key	4	17	6
MI 503	15 Nickel-Silver keys, 4 rings, Barrett system ..	6	15	0
MI 504	Boehm system, by Rampore and Cazzani, Milan	17	17	0

Repairs undertaken and estimates given free of charge

PORTABLE ORGANS

MI 801

MI 800 One row of reeds G—C, 4 octaves, with folding case. Dimensions closed, 2 ft. 6 ins. × 11 ins. × 11 ins. .. **£11 11 0**

MI 801 As 800, but 2 sets of reeds, 2 knee swells **£15 15 0**

JAZZ OUTFITS

	£	s.	d.
MI 520 Small Portable, 12 pieces		12	6
MI 521 Small Portable, larger drums, 13 pieces ..		16	6
MI 522 Small Portable larger drums, 15 pieces ..	1	5	0
MI 523 Robin Hood set, finished in Red, with small foot pedal arrangement. With case	1	10	0
MI 524 Portable set with adjustable drums, 17 pieces	1	13	0
MI 525 Gong drum outfit, 17-in. and 10-in. drums, foot pedal, etc., and case ..	3	10	0
MI 527 Gong drum outfit, 24-in. and 14-in. drums with all accessories. Genuine Chinese Tom-tom and cymbal, etc. ..	5	18	0
Cover extra	1	2	6

PROFESSIONAL OUTFITS
£10 15 0, **£12 15 0** and upwards

THE 'SWANEE SAX'

The 'Swanee Sax' is a perfect reed instrument with a range of two complete chromatic octaves. All the Saxophone effects are obtainable with very little practice. Learn this effective instrument and accompany your Gramophone or Piano

MI 510 Silver-plated Brass **£2 10 0**

Case, Cloth covered **6/9**

Book of instructions free

Best quality strings sold for every kind of instrument

MI 526 Gong Drum Outfit, 20-in. and 12-in. drums. All accessories with Waterproof Canvas cover **£4 15 0**

ALL PRICES ARE SUBJECT TO MARKET FLUCTUATIONS

GRAMOPHONE DEPARTMENT

Any Instrument may be obtained under Harrods System of Easy Payments

Harrods Gramophone Showrooms contain a wonderful selection of the world's finest instruments and records. A complete range of His Master's Voice and Columbia Instruments are always on view as well as many other celebrated instruments including Academy, Dulcetto, Itonia, Decca, etc. Twenty-four Audition Rooms each differing in size enable customers to judge the merits of the various instruments and records under similar conditions to those obtaining in their own homes

Repairs executed in Harrods own workshops by skilled mechanics

---

═══ HIRE PURCHASE SYSTEM ═══

Any purchases over £5 can be had on Hire Purchase subject to the following terms

Purchases over £5 and not above £20 at 2½ per cent. per annum. The Instrument is delivered on the first of 12 monthly payments

Purchases over £20 and not exceeding £40 at 2¼ per cent. per annum. The Instrument is delivered on the first of 24 monthly instalments

Purchases over £40 at 2½ per cent. Interest per annum. The Instrument is delivered on the first of 36 monthly instalments

Shorter periods with a corresponding rebate of interest can be arranged for the convenience of customers

---

THE WONDER PORTABLE CLIFTOPHONE

This perfectly constructed instrument, finished in Black Leatherette, is fitted with an automatic brake, internal horn and plays with lid closed. The 10-in. turntable plays 12-in. records; Cliftophone Sound Box with new type tone arm **£5 15 0**
Or delivered on first payment of **9/10** and 11 monthly payments of **9/10**

┌─ RECORD CARRIERS ─┐

To hold 50 Records, 12 ins. In best Rexine. Black or Brown .. **22/6**
To hold 50 Records, 10 ins. In best Rexine. Black or Brown .. **19/6**
To hold 25 Records, 12 ins. In best Cow Hide **23/-**
To hold 25 Records, 10 ins. In Cow Hide **21/-**
To hold 12 Records, 12 ins. In best Cow Hide **15/6**
To hold 12 Records, 10 ins. In best Cow Hide **13/6**
To hold 25 Records, 12 ins. In best Rexine **10/6**
To hold 25 Records, 10 ins. In best Rexine **9/6**
To hold 25 Records, 12 ins. In best Leatherette **7/6**
To hold 25 Records, 10 ins. In best Leatherette **6/6**
All the above with Locks

To hold 25 Records, 12 ins. In Leatherette **5/6**
To hold 25 Records, 10 ins. In Leatherette **4/6**
Above without Locks

ALBUMS

To hold 12 Records, 12 ins.
H.M.V., Best Grade **10/-**
H.M.V., 2nd Grade **5/6**
To hold 12 Records, 10 ins.
H.M.V., Best Grade **7/6**
H.M.V., 2nd Grade **4/6**

PIXIE GRIPPA GRAMOPHONE

The 'Pixie' weighs approximately 6½ lbs., measures 10½ × 7½ × 4¾ ins., and is made in a strong dovetailed box covered with Dark Waterproof Leatherette. Fitted with powerful single spring motor and tone arm of entirely new design. The Sound Box is encased in metal to prevent damage
Plays 10-in. or 12-in. Records
£2 15 0

ALL PRICES ARE SUBJECT TO MARKET FLUCTUATIONS

GRAMOPHONE DEPARTMENT
The New 'His Master's Voice' Gramophone

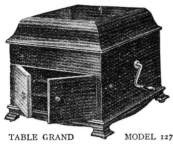

TABLE GRAND   MODEL 127

Height 14½ ins.   Width   17 ins.   Depth   20½ ins.
New 'His Master's Voice' internal horn and No. 4 Sound
Box. Best Satin finish Mahogany Cabinet. Double
spring motor, automatic brake, and speed regulator,
automatic speed indicator. Also made in Oak

Oak £15 0 0
Or delivered on first payment of £1 5 8 and 11
     monthly instalments of £1 5 8
Mahogany £17 0 0
Or delivered on first payment of £1 9 1 and 11
     monthly payments of £1 9 1

TABLE GRAND   MODEL 103

Height 12½ ins.   Width   15½ ins.   Depth 18½ ins.
New 'His Master's Voice' internal horn and No. 4
Sound Box. Wax finish Oak Cabinet, graduated
     speed regulator. Single spring motor

Oak £7 10 0
Or delivered on first payment of £0 12 10 and 11
     monthly payments of £0 12 10
Mahogany £8 10 0
Or delivered on first payment of £0 14 7 and 11
     monthly instalments of £0 14 7

**MODEL 157
(OAK)
UPRIGHT
GRAND**

Height   36¼ ins.   Width   18¼ ins.   Depth   20 ins.
Fitted with new 'His Master's Voice' patented tone
chamber and No. 5A Sound Box. Finest wax finish Oak
Cabinet. Double spring motor, self-releasing automatic
brake, speed regulator and automatic speed indicator
          £22 0 0
Or delivered on first payment of 19/3 and 23 monthly
          instalments of 19/3
Similar design in Mahogany £25 0 0
Or delivered on first payment of £1 1 11 and 23
     monthly instalments of £1 1 11

UPRIGHT GRAND MODEL 193 (OAK)

Height   44¼ ins.   Width   25¼ ins.   Depth   22¾ ins.
Fitted with the new 'His Master's Voice' re-entrant
tone chamber, and No. 5A Sound Box. Lid lock.
Quadruple spring motor.   Self-releasing automatic
brake, speed regulator and automatic speed indicator
          £45 0 0
Or delivered on first payment of £1 6 11 and 35
     monthly instalments of £1 6 11
Similar design in Mahogany £52 10 0
Or delivered on first payment of £1 11 4 and 35
     monthly instalments of £1 11 4

UPRIGHT GRAND MODEL 202 (OAK)

Height   40½ ins.   Width   28½ ins.   Depth   23½ ins.
Fitted re-entrant tone chamber and No. 5A Sound Box.
Oak Cabinet with lid lock.   Quadruple spring motor,
     and self-releasing automatic brake
          £60 0 0
Or delivered on first payment of £1 15 10 and
     35 monthly payments of £1 15 10
Similar design in Mahogany £75 0 0
Or delivered on first payment of £2 4 10 and 35
     monthly payments of £2 4 10

**MODEL 101
PORTABLE**

Height (closed) 11½ ins.   Width 5⅝ ins.   Length 16¼ in.
New 'His Master's Voice' internal horn and No. 4
Sound Box. Cabinet of light construction, covered
with Black Leather Waterproof Cloth, fitted with
leather carrying handle. Equipped with improved
single spring motor, and graduated speed regulator
Provision is made for carrying 6 records in lid
          £7 0 0
Or delivered on first payment of £0 12 0 and 11
     monthly payments of £0 12 0

TABLE GRAND   MODEL 109

Height 13½ ins. Width   15½ ins. Depth 18½ ins.
New 'His Master's Voice' internal horn, and No. 4
Sound Box. Satin finish Mahogany Cabinet. Double
spring motor, automatic brake, speed indicators and
          regulator

Oak £10 10 0
Or delivered on first payment of £0 18 0 and 11
     monthly payments of £0 18 0
Mahogany £12 0 0
Or delivered on first payment of £1 0 6 and 11
     monthly payments of £1 0 6

**MODEL 163
(OAK)
UPRIGHT
GRAND**

Height   39¾ ins. Width   22 ins.   Depth   21½ ins.
Fitted with the new 'His Master's Voice' tone chamber
and No. 5A Sound Box. Finest wax finished Cabinet.
Double spring motor and self-releasing automatic brake
          £30 0 0
Or delivered on first payment of £1 6 3 and 23
          monthly payments of £1 6 3
Similar design in Mahogany £35 0 0
Or delivered on first payment of £1 10 8 and 23
     monthly payments of £1 10 8

ALL PRICES ARE SUBJECT TO MARKET FLUCTUATIONS

HARRODS LTD   *Telephone SLOANE* 1234   LONDON S W 1
                    Telegrams 'EVERYTHING HARRODS LONDON'

GRAMOPHONE DEPARTMENT
Every 'Columbia' Model always in Stock

No. 153A OAK CONSOLE
Cabinet. Oak or Mahogany satin finish. Size 34 × 36¼ × 20 ins. Fitted with tone control shutters, and two side cupboards for storing records. Plano-Reflex tone arm. Double-spring motor to play two 12-in. records
£14 10 0
Or delivered on first of 12 monthly payments of **£1 4 10**
No. 154. MAHOGANY £15 15 0
Or delivered on first of 12 monthly payments of **£1 6 11**

No. 125A OAK CABINET
Size 37½ × 17⅝ × 19 ins. Fitted with tone control shutters and cupboard in lower section for storing records. Double-spring motor to play two 12-in. records. Plano-Reflex tone arm **£14 10 0**
Or delivered on first of 12 monthly payments of **£1 4 10**

No. 126 Mahogany £15 15 0
Or delivered on first of 12 monthly payments of **£1 6 11**

No. 131A MAHOGANY CABINET

Fitted with the new Plano-Reflex tone chamber which purifies and mellows the tone volume to a degree hitherto unknown. Size 41¾ × 22 × 24 ins. Piano hinged top. Triple-spring motor to play three 12-in. records **50 Gns.**
Or delivered on first of 36 monthly payments of **£1 11 5**

No. 123A BOUDOIR OAK
Size 34 ins.; width 16¾ ins; depth 18 ins. Fitted with tone control shutters, and cupboard in lower section for storing records. Plano-Reflex tone arm. Double-spring motor to play two 12-in. records
£11 10 0
Or delivered on first of 12 monthly payments of **19/8**
MAHOGANY .. £12 15 0
Or delivered on first of 12 monthly payments of **£1 1 10**

No. 117A OAK TABLE GRAND
Size 12½ × 17¼ × 19 ins. Single-spring motor to play 10-in. and 12-in. records. Plano-Reflex tone arm **£6 10 0**
Or delivered on first of 12 monthly payments of **11/1**
No. 118A Mahogany £7 10 0
Or delivered on first of 12 monthly payments of **12/10**

No. 119A OAK TABLE GRAND
Superior quality of tone to the smaller model on left of page (No. 117A). Size 14 × 17¼ × 19 ins. Double-spring motor to play two 12-in. records .. **£8 10 0**
Or delivered on first of 12 monthly payments of **14/7**
MAHOGANY £9 10 0
Or delivered on first of 12 monthly payments of **16/3**

The New Columbia Portable

No. 109—'Junior' Model £3 10 0
Standard Model No. 112A £4 15 0 or delivered on 1st of 12 monthly payments of **8/2**
No. 111NA—Brown Cowhide (Nickel-plated fittings) £7 10 0
No. 111GP—Brown Cowhide (Gold-plated fittings), carrier in lid for eight 10-in. records .. £9 9 0

Model 113 (*above*)
A New '*Viva-tonal*' Columbia portable that possesses the most phenomenal tone ever obtained in a Portable machine **£10 10 0**
Or delivered on 1st of 12 monthly payments of **18/-**
Size
17½ × 13¼ × 8

STANDARD MODEL
Will play 10-inch and 12-inch Records

No. 155A OAK CONSOLE
Cabinet. Jacobean style in Oak. Fitted with new Plano-Reflex tone chamber. Latest sound box. Height 36¼ ins ; width 33 ins ; depth 22½ ins. Two side sections for storing records. British made triple-spring motor to play three 12-in. records .. **£25 0 0**
Or delivered on first of 24 monthly payments of **£1 1 11**

No. 156A MAHOGANY CONSOLE
Satin finish. Fitted with Plano-Reflex tone chamber which overcomes distortion. Latest sound box. Height 34 ins. ; width 31½ ins. ; depth 21½ ins. Two side cupboards for storing records. Triple-spring motor to play three 12-in. records .. **£27 10 0**
Or delivered on first of 24 monthly payments of **£1 4 1**

ALL PRICES ARE SUBJECT TO MARKET FLUCTUATIONS

HARRODS LTD

Telephone SLOANE 1234
Telegrams 'EVERYTHING HARRODS LONDON'

LONDON SW1

WIRELESS DEPARTMENT

You'll Find Everything You Need in Wireless Accessories at Harrods

THE 'ULTRA'
AIR COLUMN SPEAKER
Standard Model 130.

Gives the world a new appreciation of radio reproduction. It is scientifically and acoustically correct and reproduces faithfully every tone, from a whisper to a full orchestra. It will enhance the tonal qualities of any radio set

Finished in Brown Cellulose. Size: 15 ins. high, 13 ins. wide, 7 ins. deep **£4 10 0**

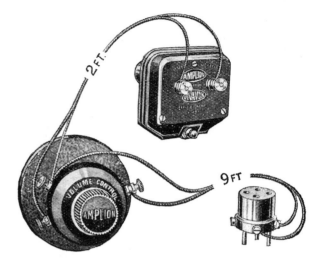

THE AMPLION VIVAVOX
(Gramophone Pick-up)

Enables gramophone records to be played electrically. Remarkably sensitive yet very stable and capable of giving pure distortionless reproduction. The volume control is a very useful feature, whilst the plug adaptor permits the Vivavox being connected to a wireless receiver without alteration or disconnection of the wiring

VIVAVOX with volume control, adaptor and connecting leads **£2 10 0**
VIVAVOX with adaptor and connecting leads **£1 15 0**
VIVAVOX with volume control and connecting leads .. **£2 7 6**

THE 'ULTRA'
ACOUSTIC FILTER

This Unit is contained within the 'Ultra' Speaker above and is designed to meet the rigid requirements of reproducing not only the low tones, now so much in demand, but also the high frequencies which aid in definition and clarity. The tone range as well as the sensitivity is thus greatly increased Complete with 'Ultra' Air Column Speaker above.

SPRING BALANCE FOR
GRAMOPHONE 'PICK UP'
Constructed to prevent the wearing of records by distributing the weight evenly throughout the tone arm. Gilt finish Complete with 'Pick Up' .. **£2 10 0**

PHILIPS
LIGHTNING
ARRESTER

◆

Protect your Wireless
and Home against
Lightning

◆

The danger of lightning striking an aerial is by no means imaginary. In order to prevent such an accident Philips have constructed a special apparatus which is entirely automatic and does not require any operation such as switching. Absolutely reliable and safe

Instal one now!

Complete **9/6**

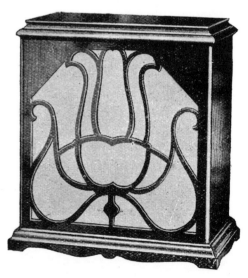

THE 'ULTRA'
AIR COLUMN SPEAKER

This Model incorporates Model 130 (*illustrated top left corner*) in a handsome oak cabinet. Size: 16 ins. high, 15 ins. wide, 8 ins. deep **£6 6 0**

Ditto in Mahogany. Cabinet Model No. 134.
£6 10 0

ALL PRICES ARE SUBJECT TO MARKET FLUCTUATIONS

WIRELESS . DEPARTMENT
Harrods Representative Selection of Well Known Loud Speakers

PHILIPS LOUD SPEAKER

This loud speaker is wonderfully responsive to a very wide range of frequencies and maintains a very natural tone throughout **£5 5 0**

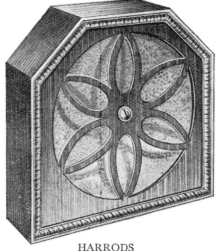

HARRODS CABINET CONE LOUD SPEAKER

No longer need a 'Loud Speaker' be considered an expensive item. Hear Harrods wonderful new model and you will be amazed that such volume, pure reproduction and clarity of tone can be obtained at so low a cost.

In Handsome Mahogany Cabinet 12 ins. high **£1 12 6**

MODEL C 10

Resistance 2000 ohms. Size 12 × 12 × 5 ins. Oak **£5 10 0**

Mahogany   .. **£5 12 6**

CELESTION MODEL C 12

Resistance 2000 ohms. Size 14 × 14 × 6 ins. Oak **£7 5 0**

Mahogany **£7 10 0**

PHILIPS BATTERY CHARGER

(*not illustrated*)

The new improved model for A.C. Mains High Tension and Low Tension Charger **£5 10 0**

MARCONI MODEL 75

(*Illustrated on Left*)

Gives ideal reception and surpasses in every way that of the Horn type. Adjustment is at the front and the cone is protected at the back.

Brown finish   ─   **£3 15 0**

MARCONI OCTAGON LOUD SPEAKER

(*Illustrated on Right*)

This speaker can be placed on a table or on the receiver at two angles according to requirements; it can be also suspended on a wall in such a position as to project the sound evenly over maximum area .. **£1 19 6**

CELESTION MODEL C 14

Resistance 750 ohms

Size 20½ × 20½ × 9½ ins. Mahogany **£14 0 0**

ALL PRICES ARE SUBJECT TO MARKET FLUCTUATIONS

HARRODS LTD

Telephone SLOANE 1234
Telegrams 'EVERYTHING HARRODS LONDON'

LONDON S W 1

STATIONERY DEPARTMENT
Household Necessities and Sundries

COLLAPSIBLE BOXES

Butter Boxes, 1 lb. .. 3/9 per 50
,, ,, 2 lb. .. 4/3 ,, ,,
,, ,, 3 lb. .. 5/9 ,, ,,
Game Boxes, 1 brace size .. 2/9 per doz.
,, ,, 2 ,, ,, .. 3/3 ,, ,,
,, ,, 3 ,, ,, .. 3/9 ,, ,,

BLOTTING PAPERS

Blotting paper, White or Pink, 22 ins. × 17 ins.	24	sheets	1/6
,, ,, ,, ,, ,,	120	,,	6/6
,, ,, ,, ,, ,,	480	,,	24/6
,, ,, ,, Cadogan	24	,,	2/6
,, ,, ,, ,,	480	,,	46/-
,, ,, ,, Extra thick	24	,,	3/3
,, ,, ,, ,,	480	,,	60/-

Blotting paper, Fords Prize Medal. White, Pink, Buff, Purple, Mauve, Violet, Black, Blue, Scarlet, Orange, Green
24 sheets .. 3/3
480 sheets .. 60/-

Blotting Book refills, white watered, paper covers (limp)
Size 10 ins. × 8 ins. .. 8d
,, 11 ins. × 9 ins. .. 9d
,, 13 ins. × 8 ins. .. 1/2
Blotterettes 10½ × 4½, 24 sheets .. 9d

LUGGAGE LABELS

Denisons Patent with string attached

Size 4¼ ins. × 2⅛ ins.	per 100	2/3
,, 4¾ ins. × 2⅜ ins.	,,	2/6
,, 5¼ ins. × 2⅝ ins.	,,	2/9
,, 5⅞ ins. × 2⅞ ins.	,,	3/3
Manilla Labels—Size 4¾ ins. × 2⅜ ins.	,,	1/2
,, ,, 5¼ ins. × 2⅝ ins.	,,	1/4
,, ,, 5⅞ ins. × 2⅞ ins.	,,	1/6
Adhesive labels in books of 24		2d per book
,, ,, ,, 36		3d per book

Books of Labels perforated to tear out. Stock colours, Red, Blue, Green or Buff
36 tie on and 36 adhesive labels .. Per book 6d

HOUSEKEEPERS' ACCOUNT BOOKS

Mrs. Sykes Simplified Account Book showing on one page Expenses for each week, month, quarter, half year, and year .. 3/-
Household Account Book showing 1 month's expenses per page .. 6/9
Housekeeper safeguard book. A simple means of checking tradesmen's charges .. 1/3
Handy Books of Forms each containing 100 Forms, viz.: Rent, Receipts, Please Receive, Statement, Invoices, Memorandum, Received of, Please supply, General Receipts .. 1/-

CLOAK ROOM TICKETS

Gummed 1—500	per 100	10d
Ungummed 1—500	,, ,,	10½d
,, 1—500	,, ,,	3d
,, 1—300	per 300	8½d

MARKING INK

John Bonds. Non-heating or requiring heat .. 6d and 1/- per bottle
Melanyl, non-heating .. 7½d and 1/- per bottle
Harrods Marking Ink, non-heating .. 1/-, 1/6, 2/6 and 3/6 per bottle

STENCIL PLATES

New Improved Linen Markers .. from 2/6

KITCHEN PAPERS

Cartridge Paper, 21 ins. × 26 ins.	24	sheets	10d
,, ,, ,,	120	,,	4/-
,, ,, ,,	480	,,	15/-
Whitey Brown, 20 ins. × 30 ins.	24	,,	4d
,, ,, ,,	120	,,	1/6
,, ,, ,,	480	,,	4/9
Tissue Paper, 20 ins. × 30 ins.	24	sheets	3½d
,, ,, ,,	120	,,	1/3
,, ,, ,,	480	,,	4/3
Tissue Paper, Superfine quality, 20 ins. × 30 ins.	24	,,	5d
,, ,, ,, ,,	120	,,	1/11
,, ,, ,, ,,	480	,,	6/9
Butter Paper, Grease proof, 20 ins. × 30 ins.	24	,,	5d
,, ,, ,, ,,	120	,,	1/11
,, ,, ,, ,,	480	,,	7/3
Brown Paper, strong Kraff Brown, 29 ins. × 45 ins.	24	,,	1/4
,, ,, ,, ,, ,,	120	,,	6/6
,, ,, ,, ,, ,,	480	,,	24/6
Thick White Drawer Paper, Double Crown, 20 ins. × 30 ins.	24	,,	8d
,, ,, ,, ,, ,,	120	,,	3/-
,, ,, ,, ,, ,,	480	,,	11/-

TOILET ROLLS AND TOILET PAPERS

See page 153

ASSORTED INKS

Stephens Blue Black, Stone Bottles .. 7d, 1/-, 2/3, 3/9
,, ,, ,, Glass Bottles .. 2d and 4d
,, Stone Jars .. Per gall. 11/- Jar 2/-
Half gall. 5/6 ,, 1/3
Jars returnable
Stephens Scarlet Ink in bottles .. 1/-, 2/3, 3/6, 5/3
Stephens Copying .. 1/-, 2/3, 3/6, 5/-
Glass bottles .. 3d and 6d

Fields Non-corrosive Blue Black, Glass bottle .. 3d, 4½d, 7½d, 1/3, 2/-, 3/9
Coloured Ink: Red, Blue, Violet, Green .. 3d, 6d, 1/-
Walkdens Coloured Inks: Scarlet, Green, Blue, Violet and Purple, per bottle .. 1/3 and 1/9
Onoto Blue-Black Ink .. 6d, 1/-, 2/-, 3/-, 4/-

FOUNTAIN PEN INKS

Waterman's Travelling Inkbottles with Filler .. 2/6
Onoto .. 1/6
Swan .. 1/9

INDIA RUBBER BANDS

Perry's Round Red or Grey, assorted per box .. 6d, 1/-, 1/6, 2/-, 3/-
Perry's Thread Bands, size 12 .. 9d
,, ,, ,, ,, 14 .. 10d
,, ,, ,, ,, 16 .. 1/-
Sloans' Grey Rubber bands, flat, in assorted sizes, per half gross box .. 2/-
Small sizes, per quarter gross box .. 1/6
Thread, assorted per gross .. 9d

GLUE, GUMS AND PASTES

Seccotine, per tube .. 4½ and 9d
Durofix, ,, .. 6d and 1/-
Lion's Cement, per bottle .. 6d and 1/-
Le Page's glue, ,, .. 6d and 1/-
Croid glue, ,, .. 2d and 6d
Dennisons Mucilage, per tube .. 9d
,, Glue, ,, .. 6d
Stephens Gum .. 1/- and 1/6
,, ,, sponge top .. 1/6
Samuel Jones Eveready Gum with rubber distributing top, per bottle .. 1/-
Stickfast Complete with cap and brush, per bottle .. 11d and 1/4
Gloy with cap and brush, per bottle .. 11d and 1/4
Grip-fix with brush, per tin .. 1/6

PAPER FASTENERS AND CLIPS

Paper Fasteners and Clips, spear pointed in 1 gross boxes—
S. 52, 5d; S. 53, 7d; S. 54, 8d; S. 56, 10d per box.
Wire paper clips .. 3d per box of 100
Large size 3½d

STRING

Fine White Cotton .. per ball 5½d
White Hemp best quality. Fine and medium .. ½ lb. ball 10½d
Thick .. 1 lb. ball, 1/6
,, .. ½ lb. ball, 9d

MISCELLANEOUS

Moth bags. *See* Page 153
Picnic plates. *See* Table Stationery, Page 158
Toothpicks .. per bundle of 25, 2d
Sterilized quill toothpicks .. 100 for 1/3
Cutlet Frills, White or Pink .. per box of 3 doz. 5½d
Ham Frills, White or Pink .. per box of 2 doz. 4d
Crepe Paper, 50 colours .. per fold of 10 feet 9d
Dessert Papers, *See* Table Stationery, Dish Papers, Page 158
Dress Shirt Envelopes .. 4 for 2/-

SEALING WAX

Red or Black, per ¼ lb. box .. 1/9
Perfumed Sealing Wax in coloured tones, per stick .. 8d
Per box, three sticks .. 1/9
Taper Wax, three sticks in box, assorted colours .. 1/6

ALL PRICES ARE SUBJECT TO MARKET FLUCTUATIONS

STATIONERY DEPARTMENT

Harrods will gladly forward on application, estimates and samples of :—

WEDDING AND AT HOME INVITATIONS, BALL PROGRAMMES,
MENU AND NAME CARDS, RETURN THANKS CARDS, HYMN
SHEETS, ETC., PRINTED IN THEIR OWN FACTORIES

VISITING CARDS—PLATE SPECIMENS

Mr Clarence Bannering SD 1	SIR REGINALD & LADY STAPLETON SD 2	*Miss Beatrice Kean* SD 3
Mr Henry J. Vernon. SD 4	*Mrs Brandon Thomson.* SD 5	SIR GEORGE & LADY DRUMMOND. SD 6
Lady Henry Macdonald. SD 7	*Sir Charles Macredy.* SD 8	*Charles G. Kearton.* SD 9

WEDDING INVITATIONS

Printed from Copper Plate	Per 100	*Printed from Type (no Plate required)*	Per 100
Printed Black	From £2 2 6	Printed Black	From £1 5 0
Additional quantities	,, 17 6	Additional quantities	,, 12 6
Printed Silver	,, 2 15 0	Printed Silver	,, 1 10 0
Additional quantities	,, 1 7 6	Additional quantities	,, 15 0

Envelopes are included in the above prices

INVITATION CARDS (in stock)

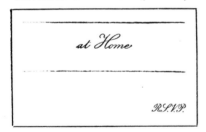

at Home

R.S.V.P.

Ivory Wove Cards, square corners, 50 for **2/-**
100 for **3/9**

ST 051 AT HOME.
ST 052 AT HOME. R.S.V.P.
ST 053 AT HOME. Dancing R.S.V.P.
ST 054 AT HOME. Bridge R.S.V.P.
ST 057 Much regret not being able to accept kind invitation for . . .
ST 055 Request the pleasure of Company at Dinner on . . .
ST 056 Request the pleasure of Company R.S.V.P.
ST 058 Have much pleasure in accepting kind invitation for . . .
ST 059 Has much pleasure in accepting kind invitation for . . .

RETURN THANKS FOR SYMPATHY CARDS, BLACK BORDERED

25 for **7/6** including envelopes
50 for **8/9** including envelopes
100 for **10/9** including envelopes

WEDDING-CAKE BOXES

Postal, size 3½ × 2½ Wedge shape ..		2/6 dozen
,, ,, 3¼ × 2¼ × 1		1/4 ,,

ENGRAVING VISITING CARD PLATE

Name only in Script (Men's)	2/6 per line
,, ,, ,, (Ladies)	3/- per line
Address in Script	..... 1/2 per line
Name, Block or Roman letters	4/6 per line
Address ,, ,, ,,	3/6 per line
Name, Old English	..... 5/- per line
Address ,. ,, ...	..... 4/- per line

CARDS PRINTED FROM COPPER PLATE

De la Rue's finest quality Ivory boxed—

Men's cards, thick quality ..	.. 50 for 2/3		
,, ,, ,, ,, ..	.. 100 ,, 3/6		Black
,, ,, thin ,, ..	.. 50 ,, 2/1		Bordered
,, ,, ,, ,, ..	.. 100 ,, 3/3		Cards,
Ladies' cards, thick quality ..	.. 50 ,, 2/9		9d
,, ,, ,, ,, ..	.. 100 ,, 4/-		per 100
,, ,, thin ,, ..	.. 50 ,, 2/7		extra
,, ,, ,, ,, ..	.. 100 ,, 3/9		

Deepening engraving on worn plates, per line, **9d**

Plates that are worn or scratched and require touching up will be cleaned and re-engraved without giving notice and charged accordingly. Plates are retained and registered for future use unless instructions are received to the contrary

PRIVATE GREETING CARDS

Albums of Specimen Greeting Cards by the leading publishers will be sent on request during October, November and December

CHILDREN'S TEA INVITATIONS

10 cards, assorted designs, and envelopes, per box 1/-

CHILDREN'S PARTY INVITATIONS

10 leaflets, assorted designs and envelopes, per box 1/-

BIRTH ANNOUNCEMENT CARDS

With Baby's card attached by ribbon

Printed from Copper Plate

	Silver		Black
25	27/-	25	19/6
50	34/-	50	25/-
75	39/-	75	29/-
100	44/-	100	34/-

Printed from Type (no Plate required)

	Silver		Black
25	12/6	25	8/6
50	16/6	50	10/6
75	20/6	75	12/6
100	24/6	100	14/6

ALL PRICES ARE SUBJECT TO MARKET FLUCTUATIONS

STATIONERY DEPARTMENT
Relief Stamping and Illuminating

CUSTOMERS are requested to forward impressions of their Dies when ordering, also to state colour and position of Die. When a new address Die is required care should be taken to write the address in Block Letters to prevent mistakes. Specimens of Address, Crest and Monogram Dies free on application

FROM CUSTOMERS' OWN DIES

	¼ ream	½ ream	1 ream
Plain Relief	9d	10d	1/-
Colour	1/2	2/-	3/6
Gold, Silver or Bronze, any tint	5/-	8/6	16/-
Illuminating two letter Monogram or Crest, and Motto Die in one colour and Gold, Silver or Bronze	6/-	11/-	21/-

The aforementioned prices are for Ordinary Dies. Deeply sunk or extra large Dies will be charged at special rates

If proofs are required from Dies they will be charged 6d each
Press for private use, fitted with ordinary address, up to 24 letters 8/6 Longer addresses, etc., at special prices
Company Seals or Dies supplied on the shortest notice from 18/6 Estimates and sketches forwarded on application
If envelopes are to be stamped with address Die, instructions should be given; otherwise they will be sent unstamped
Colour relief stamping in large quantities :—
   Note paper, one size .. (4 reams) 2/9 per ream per Die
   Envelopes .. .. 5/6 per 1,000
Dies are registered under names and it is necessary to quote the correct name when ordering

Special Notice—All Dies and Plates are kept for registration unless requested to be returned

SPECIMENS OF STEEL DIES

Please observe that the style number is shewn above specimen in each case. Cost of Die (no charge for steel) 1/3 per dozen letters, minimum 2/6. Additional charge for extra large Dies, hand cut and fancy styles. Crest Dies from 7/6. Crest Die and Motto from 10/-

D 1

D 2
33, NEW PARK DRIVE, KINGS NORTON.

D 3
MILBOROUGH GRANGE TROWBRIDGE

D 4
NORTON CRESCENT, NEW TREDEGAR.

D 6
COLLEGE PARK, BOURNEMOUTH.

D 8
GRAFORD TOWERS CHICHESTER.

D 9
3ᴱ CLANRICARDE GARDENS W. 2.

D 11

D 12
BROAD SANCTUARY, WESTMINSTER, S.W.

D 13
DRAKEFIELD GARDENS, CHORLTON-CUM-HARDY.

D 14
Courtfield Mansion, West Kensington, W.

SPECIMENS OF PRINTED ADDRESSES (no Die required)

L.3.
HIGH VIEW, SANDGATE, KENT.

L.10.
THE LODGE, DOWN STREET, PICCADILLY.

L.11.
"The Firs," Liphook.

L.20.
2, THE BOLTONS, LONDON, S.W.10.

L.21.
AVENUE HOUSE, BEAR WOOD, WOKINGHAM, BERKS.

L.13.
THE ELMS, EWELL, SURREY.

L.14.
3, The Hill, Cardiff, S. Wales.

L.22.
ASH HALL, SUNBURY.

These type specimens represent styles for notepaper addresses where no die is used, *i.e.*, for temporary use

Particulars of Printing	5 quires 120 sheets	10 quires 240 sheets	15 quires 360 sheets	1 ream 480 sheets	1½ reams 720 sheets	2 reams 960 sheets	3 reams 1,440 sheets	4 reams 1,920 sheets	5 reams 2,400 sheets
Address only (printed in black) ..	2/6	3/3	4/-	4/6	6/3	7/6	10/6	13/6	16/6
Address and Telephone, etc. (1 or 2 lines only) ..	3/9	4/6	5/3	5/9	7/6	8/9	11/9	14/9	17/9
Printed in any colour	Up to 2 reams, 6d extra				Over 2 reams, 9d extra			Over 5 reams, 1/- extra	

ALL PRICES ARE SUBJECT TO MARKET FLUCTUATIONS

HARRODS LTD

Telephone SLOANE 1234
Telegrams 'EVERYTHING HARRODS LONDON'

LONDON S W 1

STATIONERY DEPARTMENT
Toilet Requisites, Perforated Rolls, Fixtures, Packets, etc.

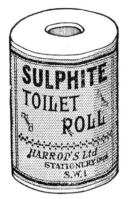

SULPHITE TOILET PAPER
Thin smooth paper of excellent quality

Per gross rolls ..	48/-
Per dozen rolls ..	4/3
Per roll	4½d

SANITINE TOILET PAPERS
SULPHITE PAPER
480 sheets in packet

Doz. packets ..	3/6
Per packet ..	4d

MANILLA
480 sheets in packet

Per doz. packets ..	4/9
Per packet ..	5d

BRONCO TOILET PAPER

Per dozen rolls	7/3
Per roll	7½d

MANILLA TOILET PAPER
Pure Manilla paper, best thin quality

Per gross rolls ..	60/-
Per dozen rolls ..	5/3
Per roll	5½d

M. G. TOILET PAPER
Good quality paper

Per gross rolls ..	43/-
Per dozen rolls ..	3/9
Per roll	4d

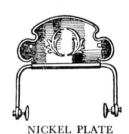

BRASS TOILET FIXTURES
1/- each
Fixed on Mahogany back
9d extra

BRASS TOILET FIXTURES
1/4 each
Mounted on Mahogany
9d extra

NICKEL PLATE FIXTURES
3/- each
Mounted on Mahogany back
9d extra

FINEST MANILLA TOILET PAPERS. Large size 8 × 5¼ ins. In carton containing 500 sheets 8½d per dozen **8/3**

NOVIO SANITARY PAPER
Packet of 500 sheets with hook to hang

8d each	**7/6** per dozen

NOVIO SANITARY PAPER
500 sheets per Carton 1/- each
11/6 per dozen

'MOTHEX' MOTH BAG

Airtight—Dust Proof—
Moth Proof and
DAMP PROOF

This light convenient Moth Proof Bag is sold in three distinct sizes and closes securely, thus preventing moths from getting to the clothes
It may be had either odourless or impregnated with a Pine Tar or Cedar Odour

No. 1   24 × 40 ins.
For Men's Suits, Women's Blouses, Furs and Children's garments

Odourless or Pine Tar ..	2/11
Cedar	3/-

No. 2   26 × 60 ins.
For Men's Overcoats, Women's Suits and Furs

Odourless or Pine Tar ..	3/3
Cedar	3/6

No. 3   28 × 65 ins.
For Larger Garments, Fur Coats, etc.

Odourless or Pine Tar ..	3/9
Cedar	3/11

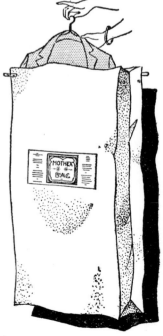

NOVIO TOILET ROLL
A thin soft paper

10d per roll	**9/6** per dozen

'VIRILLA' TOILET PAPER
'Virilla' packets are medicated

Packet 1/1	Dozen 12/9

ALL PRICES ARE SUBJECT TO MARKET FLUCTUATIONS

HARRODS LTD

Telephone SLOANE 1234
Telegrams 'EVERYTHING HARRODS LONDON'

LONDON S W 1

STATIONERY DEPARTMENT

Fountain Pens of Every Famous Make

ST 3 WATERMAN SELF FILLING

Fountain Pen	..	..	17/6	Larger Model	..	.. 22/6	With Gold band ..	.. 21/-
With Clip ..	..	..	18/6	With Clip ..	..	.. 23/6	Wider band ..	.. 25/-
				With two Gold bands	..	.. 25/- and 30/-		

ST 1 ONOTO SELF-FILLING SAFETY PEN

Long or short model	..	..	.. 17/6	Gold Body and Cap	..	..	.. £4 10 0
Fitted with Gold band	..	..	.. 25/-	Fully covered Gold	..	..	.. £6 6 0
Two Gold bands	..	..	.. 32/6				

ST 8 CAMERON LEVER FILLING PEN

Fitted with Hindoo, Waverley, 'J,' or Normal nibs .. 10/6

ST 10 THE DRAKE LEVER FILLING PEN

In all colours 5/6

ST 5 SWAN LEVER FILLING PENS

With Gold band .. .. 22/6 and 30/-   Plain Model without band .. .. 15/- and 17/6

ST 4 WATERMAN PEN. SELF FILLER

Silver Body and Cap .. .. 45/-   Rolled Gold Body and Cap .. 55/-   9-ct. Gold Body and Cap **£5 0 0**

ST 2 ONOTO PEN. STREAMLINE MODEL

Long or short .. .. 15/-   Larger size .. .. 21/-   Grand Model 35/-

ST 7 PARKER DUOFOLD PEN

Ladies' Model in Red, Blue, Jade Green or Black .. **21/-**

ST 6 PARKER DUOFOLD PEN

Senior Model in Red, Jade Green, Blue or Black .. **30/-**   Medium size .. **25/-**   Junior .. **21/-**

ALL PRICES ARE SUBJECT TO MARKET FLUCTUATIONS

HARRODS LTD   *Telephone SLOANE* 1234
Telegrams 'EVERYTHING HARRODS LONDON'   **LONDON S W** 1

STATIONERY DEPARTMENT

Harrods Stationery Requisites for the Table

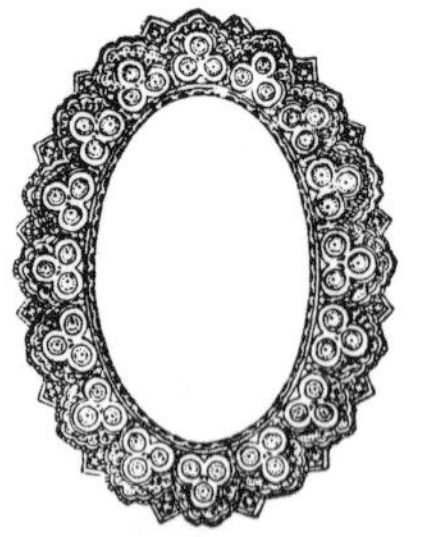

LACE DISH PAPERS
Per pkt. of 3 doz.
8½×6¼ ins. ... **9d**
10½×8¼ „ ... **1/-**
12½×9 „ ... **1/7**

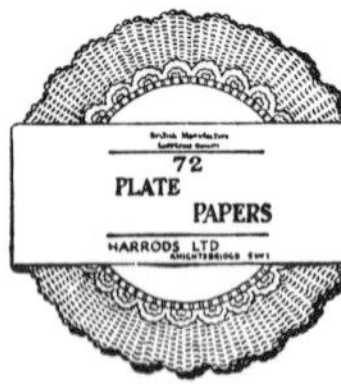

PLATE PAPERS
Per pkt. of 6 doz.
5½ ins. diam. ... **3½d**
6½ „ „ ... **4½d**
7½ „ „ ... **5½d**
8½ „ „ ... **6½d**

MENU CARDS

Gilt Edges, Embossed Gold

No. 1 size, 4½×2, 50 for **2/9**; 100 for **5/-**

No. 2 size, 5⅛×2¾, with strut at back, 50 for **5/-**; 100 for **9/6**

No. 3 size, 4½×3, round corners, 50 for **3/-**; 100 for **5/9**

No. 4 size, 5×3¼, 50 for **3/3**; 100 for **6/3**

MENU CARDS FOR HOTELS

Thin for typing purposes, size 6×4 ins., Including Die and Embossing of address in any colour.

1,000 for **15/6**; 5,000 for **67/6**

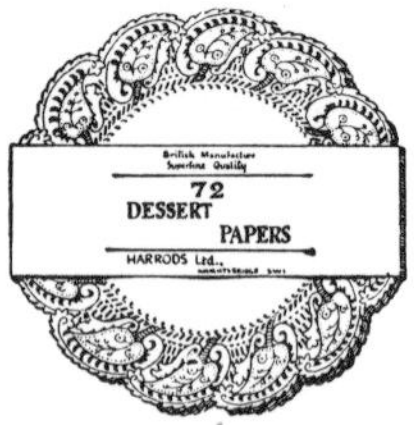

DESSERT PAPERS
Per pkt. of 6 doz.
5½ ins. diam. ... **4d**
6½ „ „ ... **5d**
7½ „ „ ... **6d**
8½ „ „ ... **7d**
9½ „ „ ... **8d**

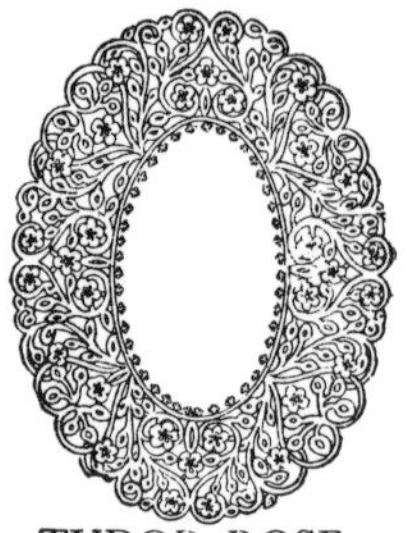

TUDOR ROSE DISH PAPERS
Per pkt. of 3 doz.
8½×6¼ ins. ... **11d**
10½×8¼ „ ... **1/4**
12½×9½ „ ... **1/8**

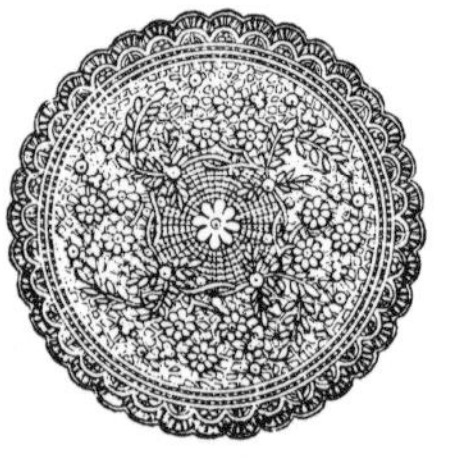

BABY IRISH D'OYLEYS
Per pkt. of 3 doz.
6 ins. diam. ... **11d**
7 „ „ ... **1/-**
8 „ „ ... **1/1**
9 „ „ ... **1/4**

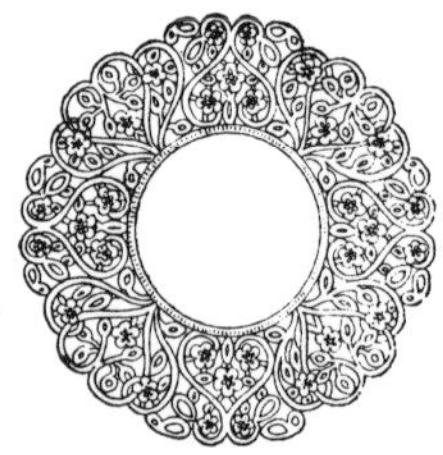

ENGLISH ROSE D'OYLEYS
Per pkt. of 3 doz.
6 ins. diam. ... **11d**
7 „ „ ... **1/-**
8 „ „ ... **1/1**
9 „ „ ... **1/4**

KITCHEN REQUIREMENTS
Refillable Tablets with pencil attached for recording requirements **1/6**
Refill Blocks **1/-**

KITCHEN ORDERS
Refillable Tablets for Kitchen Orders **1/6**
Refills **1/-**

HOUSEHOLD WANTS INDICATOR
128 'Wants' shown, with signal at side. Size of Indicator 13 ins. × 11 ins. **3/6**

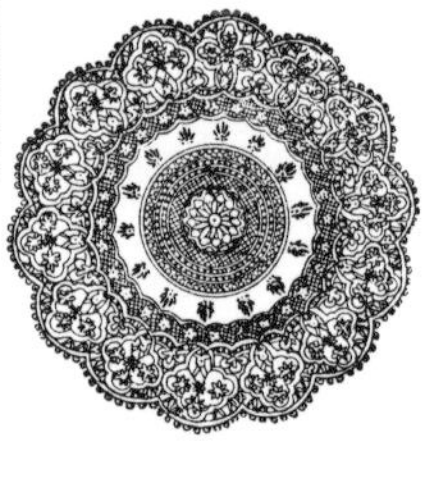

IVINGHOE D'OYLEYS
Per pkt. of 3 doz.
6 ins. diam. ... **11d**
7 „ „ ... **1/-**
8 „ „ ... **1/1**
9 „ „ ... **1/4**

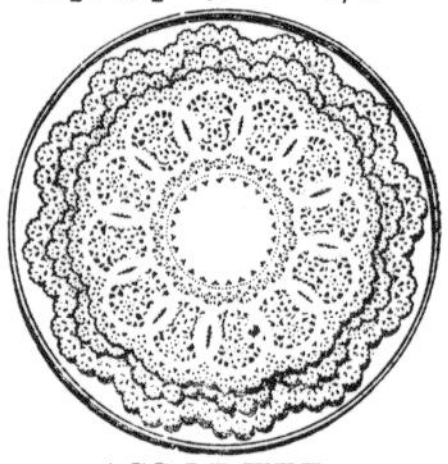

ASSORTED D'OYLEYS
144 assorted sizes in box **1/10**

PICNIC PLATES
Meat Plates, 9″ diam. per pkt. of 1 doz. **9½d**
Pudding Plates, 7″ diam. per pkt. of 1 doz. **7½d**
Cheese Plates, 6″ diam. per pkt. of 1 doz. **6d**
With greaseproof linings

TRAY CLOTHS
Dainty patterns with Lace edges
Size 15×10″ .. 36 for **1/6**
„ 16½×11½″ .. 36 for **1/8**
„ 18½×12½″ .. 36 for **2/-**

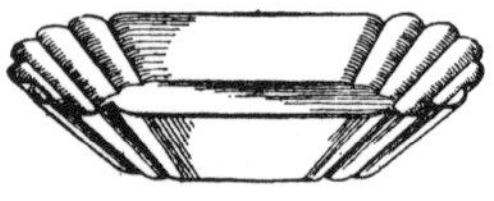

WOOD PULP TRAYS
7¾×5×1¼″ per pkt. of 1 doz. **5d**
8¾×5½×1¾″ „ „ „ **6d**
9×6×2″ „ „ „ **7d**
10×7×2″ „ „ „ **8d**

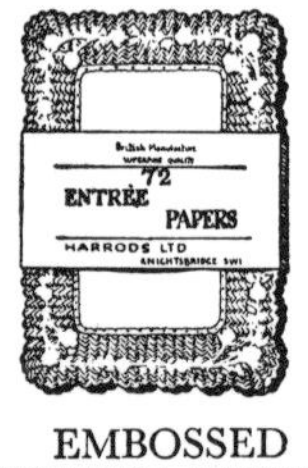

EMBOSSED ENTREE PAPERS
8½×6″ per pkt. of 6 doz. **5d**
9½×6½″ „ „ „ **6d**
11 ×7″ „ „ „ **7d**

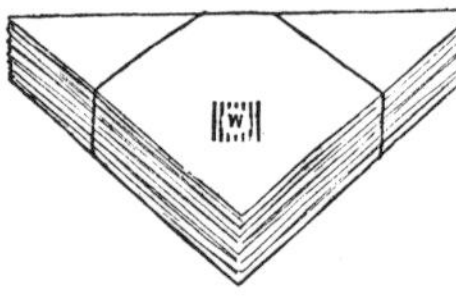

SERVIETTES
Initial embossed in Mauve
Per 25 .. .. .. **1/-**
„ 100 .. .. .. **3/9**

SERVIETTES
White Crepe Paper, per 100 **9d**
White Crepe Paper with Gold and Floral Border, per 100 **1/1**

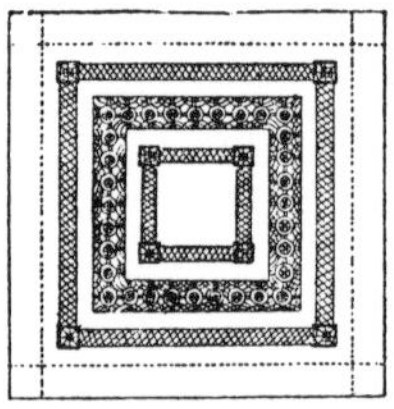

TENERIFFE D'OYLEYS
5″ diam., per pkt. of 3 doz. **7d**
6″ „ „ „ „ **8d**
7″ „ „ „ „ **10d**
8″ „ „ „ „ **11d**

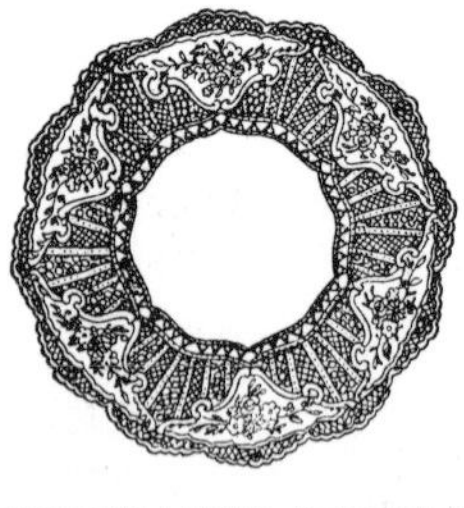

RENAISSANCE D'OYLEYS
6½″ diam., per pkt. of 6 doz. **1/3**
7½″ „ „ „ „ **1/6**
8½″ „ „ „ „ **1/9**
9½″ „ „ „ „ **2/-**

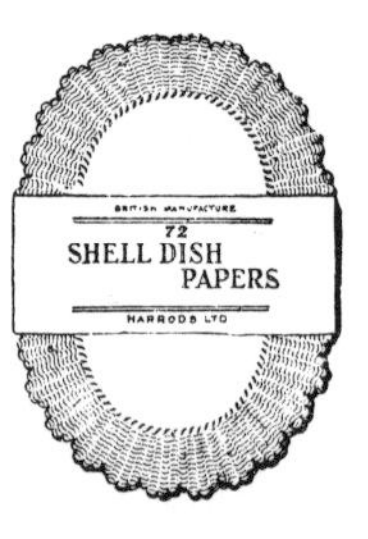

SHELL OR LACE PATTERN DISH PAPERS
8×6″ per pkt. of 6 doz. **4d**
10×8″ „ „ „ **5d**
12×10″ „ „ „ **7d**

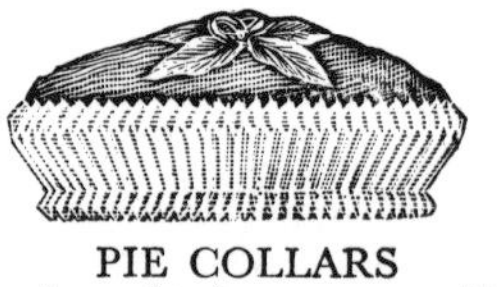

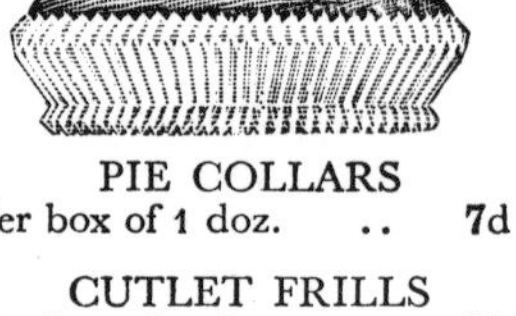

PIE COLLARS
Per box of 1 doz. .. **7d**

CUTLET FRILLS
Per box of 3 doz. .. **5½d**

CUTLET SKEWERS
Per box of 3 doz. .. **1/4**

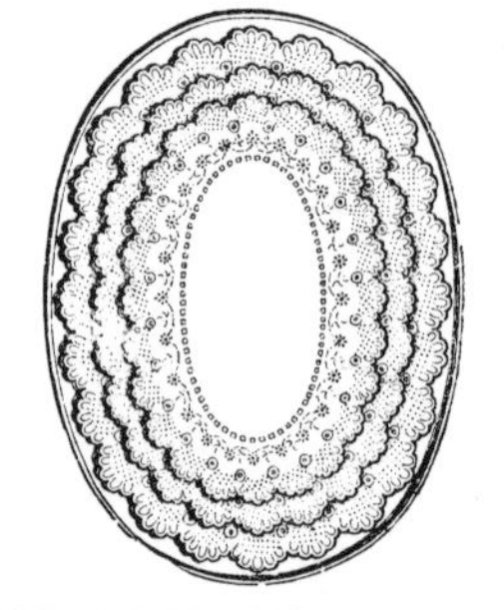

ASSORTED DISH PAPERS
Shell or Lace patterns
144 assorted sizes in box **1/10**

ALL PRICES ARE SUBJECT TO MARKET FLUCTUATIONS

FANCY LEATHER DEPARTMENT
Ladies' Handbags in New Designs and Fascinating Colours

FL 399
METAL BEAD BAGS
In great variety, on Silver Gold and Pastel shade grounds. Various designs **14/9, 18/9**
Other prices **25/6, 32/6 to 97/6**

FL 403 DAINTY POCHETTE
With imitation Point de Beauvais front on Black, Navy or Beige ground .. **21/-**

FL 49
MOROCCO POCHETTE
with 'Zip' Fastener. Red Beige, Snuff, Light Navy or Black **21/-**

FL 402 POCHETTE
Of Silver or Gold Brocade. Lined White Silk **21/6**

FL 1712
EMBROIDERED POCHETTE
in tasteful Colours on Black ground. Lined Moire Silk
Size 9¾ × 5 ins. **45/9**

FL 400
METAL BEAD HANDBAGS
Attractively made on frames. Various delightful patterns
29/6, 35/6, 42/-, 57/6, 65/6, 73/6, 85/6

FL 3383
A THOROUGHLY PRACTICAL HANDBAG
Beautifully finished in attractive coloured Leathers Imitation Shell frame. Colours, Red, Black, Navy and Beige **11/6**
Large size **25/6**

FL 32 FLAT 'ZIP' FASTENING POUCHETTE
9½ ins. This new-design bag opens quite square and has fixed purse and hanging mirror which can be taken out of the bag
Snuff Morocco **36/9** Brown Box Calf **48/9**

FL 28/12
ROOMY POUCH SHAPE HANDBAGS
With lightning fastener and double handles. Fixed purse and mirror. Black, Snuff and Light Navy
40/6

FL 836 MOROCCO HANDBAG
With inner division divided into two pockets. Good quality lining and mirror Colours, Black Snuff, Light Navy, Red and Beige. Size 9 × 7 ins **21/-**

FL 3352
SOFT LEATHER HANDBAG
Imitation Shell frame. Colours, Navy, Black, Red, Beige **34/9**

FL 397 FINE HANDBAG
Of Antique Moire Silk with handsome Silver Marcassite mount. Roomy interior **97/6**

ALL PRICES ARE SUBJECT TO MARKET FLUCTUATIONS

HARRODS LTD

Telephone SLOANE 1234
Telegrams 'EVERYTHING HARRODS LONDON'

LONDON SW1

FANCY GOODS DEPARTMENT
Fine Work and Writing Tables in Lacquer and Polished Woods

Orders value 20/- and over post free in England and Wales

FL 2320 AUTOMATIC COMBINATION SEWING AND WRITING TABLE
in Chinese Lacquer. Superior quality fittings

Black Lacquer	£26 15 0
Coloured lacquer	£27 15 0
Plain Mahogany	£24 15 0

Orders by post accurately and promptly executed

FL 202 TUCKAWAY FOLDING WRITING TABLE
With Leather cover, fitted as illustration

Size of top 18 × 14 ins.	.. ..	67/6
,, ,, 18½ × 18 ins.	.. ..	97/6
,, ,, 21 × 18 ins.	.. ..	105/-

FL 2 FOLDING WRITING TABLE
Lined pockets and fittings, spring lock and catches

Jacobean Oak	..	£10 19 6
Polished Mahogany	..	£12 17 6
Chinese Lacquer Black	..	£14 10 0

FL6120 REFERENCE BOOK CABINETS.
Shaped front, size 13 × 10 × 11 ins. Five book covers and drawer for telegram pad. In Jacobean or Fumed Oak **94/6**

Polished Mahogany	..	97/6
Inlaid Mahogany	..	105/-

FL 1224 WORK TABLE
Size 14 × 14 × 24 ins. high. Single lid, lined Moirette, with fitted drawer. Black Lacquer with long pocket in well **£6 7 6**

Coloured Lacquer	..	£6 15 0
In Jacobean or Fumed Oak		75/6
Polished Mahogany	..	84/6

FL 1316 DORIS WORK TABLE
With Cabriole shaped legs in Quarter Burr Walnut, Fine figured Mahogany or Black Chinese Lacquer .. **£9 15 0**

FL 640 LETTER BOX
With hinged slanted lid. 10 ins. long, lock and key bevelled glass panel
In Jacobean or Fumed Oak 57/6
Polished Mahogany .. 59/6

FL 116/136 LADY'S FOLDING SEWING TIDY
With catch. 16 ins. long, 27 ins. high. Broche Silk bag lined to tone and two large pockets

Polished Mahogany	..	67/6
Black Chinese Lacquer ..		79/6

FL 138 PARTY CASE
With beautiful enamelled fittings and large mirror inside lid. Most useful for Parties and Dances. In Beige, Brown, Blue or Pink Crushed Calf, 8 ins. long **73/6**

FL 1219 AUTO-GRAPHIC COMBINED SEWING AND WRITING TABLE
19 × 19 ins., 29 ins. high. Deep well for sewing and smaller one for correspondence Lined Leather and Moire Silk to tone. Two ink bottles, sewing and writing fittings. In Black Lacquer .. £19 15 0

Coloured Lacquer	..	£20 7 6
Polished Mahogany ..	..	£17 10 0

ALL PRICES ARE SUBJECT TO MARKET FLUCTUATIONS

HARRODS LTD

Telephone SLOANE 1234
Telegrams 'EVERYTHING HARRODS LONDON'

LONDON S W 1

FANCY GOODS DEPARTMENT
Beautiful Models of Ships Famous in History

THE COLUMBUS FLEET

'Santa Maria' Flagship *(as illustrated)* (XV Century)

33 ins. long, 21 ins. high
£9 12 6

21 ins. long, 21 ins. high
£4 15 6

Miniature Size

17 ins. long, 15 ins. high
£2 19 6

'La Pinta'

33 × 30 ins. .. **£9 12 6**

'La Nina'

33 × 30 ins. .. **£9 12 6**

THE 'GOLDEN HIND'

(Drake's Flagship)

40 ins. long, 38 ins. high
£13 10 0

26 ins. long, 26 ins. high
£6 6 0

21 ins. long, 21 ins. high
£4 10 0

Miniature Size

17 ins. long, 15 ins. high
£2 19 6

Columbus' Flagship, The 'Santa Maria'

THE 'MAYFLOWER'

(XVII Century)

29 ins. long, 29 ins. high
£9 12 6

26 ins. long, 26 ins. high
£5 15 6

21 ins. long, 21 ins. high
£4 9 6

THE 'GREAT HARRY'

(Exhibition Model)

A.D. 1514—1533

A superb Model

Length 47 ins., height 40 ins.
£27 10 0

THE 'VICTORY'

(Nelson's Flagship)

29 ins. long, 28 ins. high
£14 17 6

Modelled after the recent restoration of this famous ship

Smaller Model **£9 17 6**

HAND-PAINTED BARBOLA WORK

FL 517 PANEL MIRROR
With fine Barbola decoration in floral cluster. 13 × 9 ins.
29/6

FL 520 BARBOLA HAND MIRROR
Prettily decorated on Gilt ground .. **12/6**

FL 519 ROUND MIRROR
With floral cluster and ribbon surround. Size over all 11 × 9½ ins. **16/6**

FL 515 HANDSOME OVAL MIRROR
Rose cluster at top with decorative border. In bright, tasteful colouring, 16 × 9½ ins.
29/6

FL 516 BARBOLA POWDER BOWL
Decorated in choice colours on Black ground
14/9

FL 522 CUPID
Beautifully hand painted with Silver or Gold Wings .. **57/6**
Barbola stand **18/9**

FL 521 BARBOLA WASTE PAPER BASKET
On Gilt ground with floral cluster in bright colouring **16/6**

FL 518 BARBOLA BOOK ENDS
Grape and Flower design in tasteful colours .. Per pair **28/6**

ALL PRICES ARE SUBJECT TO MARKET FLUCTUATIONS

HARRODS LTD

Telephone SLOANE 1234
Telegrams '*EVERYTHING HARRODS LONDON*'

LONDON S W 1

TRUNK DEPARTMENT

Harrods Guaranteed Pukka Luggage is the finest Canvas-Covered Luggage on the Market

The reliability of 'Pukka' Luggage is guaranteed to all purchasers by the issue, with every article purchased, of a 'Pukka' Guarantee Bond. Every article of 'Pukka' luggage is kept in repair free of charge *for a period of five years from date of purchase.* All 'Pukka' luggage not lasting five years, or damaged beyond repairs, will be replaced free of charge

'PUKKA' IMPERIAL TRUNK (Registered design)   Fitted air-tight, waterproof and dustproof adjustment. Covered Brown or Green Flax Canvas, fitted with tray 4½ inches deep. Two web straps in tray and body of trunk

30 × 19 × 17 ins.	33 × 20 × 18 ins.	36 × 21 × 19 ins.
£9 4 0	**£10 2 0**	**£11 0 0**

39 × 22 × 20 ins.	42 × 23 × 21 ins.
£11 19 0	**£12 19 0**

'PUKKA' HAT BOX (Registered design)   Fitted dustproof and waterproof adjustment. Covered Brown or Green Flax Canvas, fitted with removable wire fittings

20 × 16 × 16 ins.	22 × 18 × 18 ins.	24 × 20 × 20 ins.
£5 19 0	**£6 9 0**	**£7 2 0**

'PUKKA' SUIT CASE
(Registered design)

Fitted dustproof and waterproof adjustment. Covered Brown or Green Flax Canvas ; fitted with leather inside

22 × 15 × 7½ ins.	..	75/-
24 × 15½ × 8 ins.	..	82/-
26 × 16 × 8½ ins.	..	89/-
27 × 16½ × 9 ins.	..	99/-

30 × 17 × 9½ ins.
£5 10 0

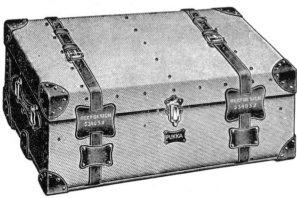

'PUKKA' CABIN TRUNK (Registered design)   Fitted waterproof adjustment, covered Brown or Green Flax Canvas, tray 4 inches deep and two web straps in tray and body of trunk

30 × 19 × 14 ins.	33 × 20 × 14 ins.	36 × 21 × 14 ins.
£7 7 6	**£8 2 6**	**£8 17 0**

30 × 22 × 14 ins.	42 × 22 × 14 ins.
£9 12 0	**£10 6 6**

'PUKKA' WARDROBE TRUNK (Registered design) Fitted dustproof and waterproof adjustment, covered Brown Vulcanized Fibre, five drawers, garment hangers, shoe box and linen bag

37½ × 21 × 14 ins.	40 × 21 × 14 ins.	40 × 21 × 16 ins.	42 × 21 × 21 ins.
£13 14 6	**£13 18 6**	**£14 5 6**	**£16 18 6**

ALL PRICES ARE SUBJECT TO MARKET FLUCTUATIONS

HARRODS LTD

Telephone SLOANE 1234
Telegrams 'EVERYTHING HARRODS LONDON'

LONDON S W 1

MOTOR TRUNK DEPARTMENT
Motor Trunks Strongly Made for the Light or Big Car

'THE INDUSTRIA' MOTOR TRUNK
Similar to the 'Chested' Motor Trunk
(*on right*) In Black with nickel fittings

Length 28 ins., width at top 15½ ins.,
width at bottom 18 ins., vertical depth
17 ins. **£6 15 0**

Length 32 ins., width at top 16 ins.,
width at bottom 17 ins., vertical depth
16 ins. **£7 17 6**

CHESTED MOTOR TRUNK
Superior quality throughout. Made with dome top,
fitted with dust proof embushment and rubber
cushion—rendering it absolutely watertight and
dust proof. The top suit case is lined throughout
with moirette, and is designed especially for ladies'
use. Eminently sound and practical trunk.
Particularly suitable for a large touring car
Size 33 × 18 × 17—22 ins. high
Price **£14 5 0**

HARRODS IMPROVED MOTOR TRUNK
Exclusive design, watertight and dustproof
Very practical for the touring car. Covered and lined Black Rexine, edges bound Vulcanized
Fibre, with strengthening corners; front and sides fitted lever clips, dustproof English lock
Size 30 ins. long, 18 ins. high, 18½ ins. wide at bottom and 17 ins. at top. Inside fitted with
two full-size Suit Cases covered Black.
Rexine, strengthened with fibre binding
Size 29 × 16 × 8 ins. each

SET COMPLETE **£8 8 0**

HARRODS INEXPENSIVE TRUNK
Specially suitable for the Light Car
Strongly made outer case, covered with Rexine. Fitted with two Fibre
inner cases. Length 28 ins., width 17 ins., vertical depth 15½ ins. **£2 5 0**
Complete with grid straps

HARRODS POPULAR MOTOR TRUNK
Soundly constructed of three and five ply foundation, covered black leather cloth
Closing is of improved design, rendering it thoroughly dust proof and watertight
The two inner cases are strongly made on three ply foundation, covered black Rexine
Size 30 × 17½ × 16 ins. **£7 7 0**
33 × 18 × 16½ ins. **£8 2 6**
A similar trunk of cheaper make but thoroughly practical. 30 × 17 × 16 ins... **£5 5 0**

ALL PRICES ARE SUBJECT TO MARKET FLUCTUATIONS

HARRODS LTD   *Telephone SLOANE 1234*
Telegrams 'EVERYTHING HARRODS LONDON'   **LONDON SW1**

WARDROBE TRUNK DEPARTMENT
The Popular 'Oshkosh' Travelling Wardrobe Trunks

THE 'CHIEF' OSHKOSH

The finest model of the Oshkosh range. An exceptionally strong and attractive trunk, fitted with laundry bag and shoe holder, ironing board, electric iron carrier and convertible hat box. Covered with Oshkosh Cord

Duck with interwoven Red and Yellow bands

43 × 22½ × 25 ins. 12 hangers **£41 10 0**
Fitted with combination dust door, laundry bag and shoe holder
43 × 22½ × 22½ ins. 10 hangers **£40 10 0**

THE 'OSHKOSH' No. 606

A model of guaranteed durability The outside is of Black Vulcanized Fibre lined strong Fabrikoid. Fitted with shoe box, laundry bag, ironing board electric iron carrier, convertible hat box and Art Silk dust curtain

43 × 22½ × 22½ ins. 10 hangers **£24 15 0**
43 × 22½ × 20 ins. 8 hangers **£24 0 0**
No. 489 Another model on similar lines to the above, covered in Blue Fibre,
43 × 22½ × 22½ ins. 10 hangers **£19 5 0**
43 × 22½ × 20 ins. 8 hangers **£18 7 6**
43 × 22½ × 14½ ins. 5 hangers **£16 5 0**

'OSHKOSH' WARDROBE TRUNK No. 444J

Covered with Mulberry Brown Vulcanized fibre, bound Black; lined Fabrikoid. Fitted solid Brass Yale lock, four drawers (two of which are adaptable for hats), six hangers and clothes retainer, shoe box, linen bag and dust curtain. Size 43 × 22½ × 16 ins. **£13 13 0**

MODEL No. 4440C
Similar to above, but with eight hangers. Size 43 × 22½ × 20 ins. **£14 14 0**

> An Enormous Range of 'OSHKOSH' MODELS always in Stock from **£8 17 6**

THE 'OSHKOSH' No. 1105

Specially light in weight yet exceptionally durable. Finished in Fawn Fibre with Brown binding. Lined Fabrikoid and fitted with shoe carrier, laundry bag and convertible hat box. Suitable for men or women

38 × 22½ × 20 ins. 8 hangers **£16 16 0**
38 × 22½ × 16 ins. 7 hangers **£15 17 6**

ALL PRICES ARE SUBJECT TO MARKET FLUCTUATIONS

HARRODS LTD

Telephone SLOANE 1234
Telegrams 'EVERYTHING HARRODS LONDON'

LONDON S W 1

TRUNK DEPARTMENT
School Travelling Needs must be Strong and Well Made

SCHOOL SATCHEL

In superior quality Tan Basil Leather
Very serviceable. Length 14 ins. .. **10/9**

SCHOOL 'FIRST NIGHT' BAG

In stout Tan colour Hide. Leather
covered frame, Hide piping and
strong lining

Length 18 ins. ..	..	..	**24/9**
,, 16 ins. ..	..	..	**22/-**
,, 14 ins. ..	..	..	**19/6**
,, 12 ins. ..	..	..	**16/6**

Superior quality, fuller shape

12 ins. .. **27/-**	14 ins. .. **31/6**
16 ins. .. **36/-**	

ATTACHE CASES

In stout Brown polished Cowhide, hand sewn;
reliable locks.   Lined cloth

Length 18 ins...	..	..	..	**16/6**
,, 16 ins...	..	..	..	**14/6**
,, 14 ins...	..	..	..	**12/6**
,, 12 ins...	..	..	..	**10/9**

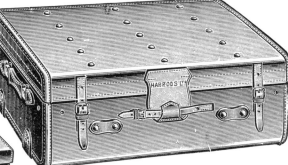

SCHOOL TRUNK

Brown Japanned Waterproof Canvas, stiffened on genuine 'Flaxite'
Fibre fitted with tray, Leather straps, Brass Clips and Solid Leather
moulded corners.   This trunk is also fitted with the new improved
steel frame.   Size 30 × 19 × 14 ins... .. .. **81/6**

SCHOOL TRUNK

Covered fine quality polished Brown Cowhide, stiffened on genuine
fibre, lined Holland.   Inside steel frame ; all hand-welted, specially
recommended.   Size 30 × 20 × 12½ ins. **£6 2 6**

Similar Trunk, covered Black Japanned Canvas, stiffened on
genuine 'Flaxite' foundation, four Leather corners, Leather back
joint, double action lock, and good quality lining.   Complete with
tray.   Size 30 × 20 × 12 ins. **63/-**

SCHOOL SATCHELS

Superior quality Brown Waterproof
Canvas, with leather gusset ; made with
shoulder strap

13 ins. .. **6/9**	14 ins. .. **7/6**

Similar to above, with canvas gusset

13 ins. .. **5/9**	14 ins. .. **6/6**

KIT BAGS

In good quality English Cowhide ; strong Leather
covered frame, hide piping, and lining
Lengths 16 ins., **40/-**   18 ins., **45/-**   20 ins., **50/-**

LEATHER HAT CASES

Oblong shape, in polished Brown Cowhide, hand
sewn.   For one hat **57/6**   No. 2 Quality **33/6**
A similar case, covered Rexine .. **15/-**

SCHOOL TRUNKS

Made from extra strong vulcanized Fibre, lined with good
quality striped cotton.   Fitted with solid Leather corners
and inside tray.   Light, roomy and reliable

Size 30 × 19 × 13 ins. **£4 0 0**

EXTRA STRONG SCHOOL PLAY BOX

Stout plain Deal, metal clamped
Fitted with till inside

18 × 13 × 12 ins.	..	..	..	**14/3**
20 × 13 × 12 ins.	..	..	..	**15/6**
22 × 13 × 12 ins.	..	..	..	**16/9**
24 × 14 × 12 ins.	..	..	..	**18/-**
26 × 14 × 12 ins.	..	..	..	**19/3**
28 × 14 × 12 ins.	..	..	..	**21/6**

SCHOOL PLAY BOXES

Extra strong.   Made with 3-ply top and bottom,
much stronger and more durable than the
ordinary type of Play Box.   Polished all over,
metal clamped

26 × 15 × 12½ ins.	..	..	..	**24/6**
24 × 14½ × 12½ ins.	..	..	..	**23/-**
22 × 14½ × 12½ ins.	..	..	..	**21/6**
20 × 14½ × 12 ins.	..	..	..	**20/-**
18 × 13½ × 12 ins.	..	..	..	**18/6**

ALL PRICES ARE SUBJECT TO MARKET FLUCTUATIONS

HARRODS LTD

Telephone SLOANE 1234
Telegrams 'EVERYTHING HARRODS LONDON'

LONDON SW1

TRUNK DEPARTMENT
Hat Cases that afford Complete Protection

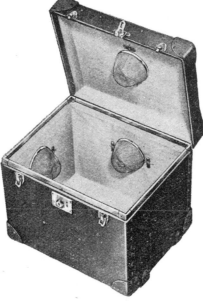

LADY'S COMBINED WEEK-END HAT CASE

Brown Japanned Canvas, stiffened on Fibre foundation with eight leather corners, and inside steel frame. Complete with two hat cones and web straps in bottom

22×17×11 ins. **42/-**   20×16×11 ins. **38/6**
18×15×11 ins. **35/-**

Similar case in superior quality. On genuine 'Flaxite' fibre foundation

20×18×12 ins. **50/-**   22×20×13 ins. **53/6**

LADY'S HAT BOX

Superior quality Green Rotproof or Brown Japanned Canvas on genuine 'Flaxite' fibre foundation. Edges turned over and riveted. Eight solid blocked leather corners, improved steel frame, lever lock, complete with six wire cones

18×16×14 ins. **55/6** 20×18×15½ ins. **62/6**
22×18×18 ins. **67/6**

Similar Case in No. 2 quality.

18×16×14 ins. **46/6** 20×16×15½ ins. **54/-**
22×18×18 ins. **58/6**

HAT CASE

In Brown Vulcanized Fibre, hand-welted Brown leather. Fitted with inside cone and straps. Very light and strong

20×10 ins. deep **52/6** 22×10 ins. deep **57/6**

Similar case covered with real Hide

18×10 ins. deep **81/-**   20×10 ins. deep **90/-**

Similar Hat Case covered Black Enamelled Leather-cloth on Fibre foundation

20×10 ins. deep **52/6** 22×10 ins. deep **57/6**

LADY'S HAT BOX

A wonderfully light yet remarkably strong bag in all Black Enamelled Leather-cloth piped with Red or Blue or in all Red, Blue, Green, and Beige. Note the wide stiff opening at the top which allows the easy removal of hats. Complete with lock and key

Size 14 in.	..	..	**11/-**
16 in.	..	..	**13/6**
18 in.	..	..	**15/-**

CIRCULAR HAT BAG

Light weight, can be carried on the arm Good quality Black Enamelled Leather-cloth. Lined fancy Cretonne, fitted with inside pocket in all Black or Black with Blue or Red piping.

14×7 ins. .. **10/-**   16×7 ins. .. **11/6**
18×7 ins. .. **13/-**

LADY'S HAT BOX
(Not illustrated)

In polished Brown Hide, lined Brown Moirette. Fitted with cones and tray

18×17½×12 .. **80/-**

LADY'S LEATHER HAT CASE

Fine quality Brown polished Hide Case, lined quilted Sateen. Fitted with inside hat cone, straps and drawn pocket at back

18×10 ins. deep **75/-** 20×10 ins. deep **83/6**

ALL PRICES ARE SUBJECT TO MARKET FLUCTUATIONS

HARRODS LTD

Telephone SLOANE 1234
Telegrams 'EVERYTHING HARRODS LONDON'

LONDON S W 1

TRUNK DEPARTMENT
Compact Travelling Gear in Mail Canvas

Manufactured
in Harrods
own
Workshops

SERVICEABLE HOLDALL Superior quality Brown Waterproof Mail Canvas, stout Brown Leather along top ; long Bridle Leather straps and strong handle. Lined waterproof Wigan. Large pocket at bottom, divided pockets for umbrellas and two large waterproof flaps inside. Waterproof pocket with gusset outside. All sizes 60 inches long
27 ins. wide **72/-** ; 30 ins. wide **77/-** ; 33 ins. wide **80/-** ; 36 ins. wide **84/-** ; 39 ins. wide **87/6**

WATERPROOF HOLDALL Brown Mail Canvas, long Bridle Leather straps with long handle plate. Lined waterproof Twill. Large bottom pocket and two large flaps inside. All sizes 60 inches long
27 ins. wide **54/-** ; 30 ins. wide **57/-** ; 33 ins. wide **59/6** ; 36 ins. wide **61/6** ; 39 ins. wide **63/6**

USEFUL HOLDALL Superior quality Brown Waterproof Mail Canvas, long Bridle Leather straps. Long handle plate, strengthened with tempered steel bar, covered with stout Brown Cowhide, the whole width of holdall. Lined waterproof Wigan. Large bottom pocket, and two large flaps inside. All sizes 60 inches long
27 ins. wide **66/9** ; 30 ins. wide **71/6** ; 33 ins. wide **75/-** ; 36 ins. wide **78/6** ; 39 ins. wide **81/9**

'VICTORIA' HOLDALL In Brown Waterproof Canvas, lined Brown Twill; fitted inside with pocket at bottom, and two flaps fastened with tapes. Good quality outside straps, with long bar handle and outside pocket
27 × 42 ins. **26/3** ; 30 × 48 ins. **38/6** ; 33 × 54 ins. **40/-** ; 36 × 60 ins. **42/6**

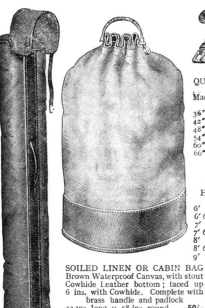

RUG STRAPS WITH RIVETTED HANDLE

SUPERIOR QUALITY BRIDLE LEATHER
Made in Harrods own workshops

	Per pair
36″ × ¾″	6/9
42″ × ¾″	7/6
48″ × ⅞″	8/3
54″ × 1″	8/9
60″ × 1⅛″	9/6
66″ × 1⅛″	10/6

	Per pair
36″ × ¾″	4/9
42″ × ¾″	5/-
48″ × ⅞″	5/6
54″ × ¾″	7/6
60″ × ⅞″	8/9
66″ × 1″	9/9

RUG STRAPS WITH ROUND HANDLE

	Per pair
24″ × ⅞″	2/-
30″ × ⅞″	2/6
36″ × ⅞″	3/-

LUGGAGE OR TRUNK STRAPS

LUGGAGE OR TRUNK STRAPS Superior quality, Harrods own make.	Price	GOOD QUALITY LEATHER STRAPS	Price	WEB LUGGAGE STRAPS	Price
6′ × 1½″	7/9 each	6′ × 1¼″	5/3 each	4′	2/6 each
6′ 6″ × 1¼″	8/6 ,,	6′ 6″ × 1¼″	5/9 ,,	5′	2/6 ,,
7′ × 1¼″	9/- ,,	7′ × 1¼″	6/6 ,,	6′	3/- ,,
7′ 6″ × 1¼″	9/9 ,,	7′ 6″ × 1¼″	6/9 ,,	7′	3/- ,,
8′ × 1¼″	10/6 ,,	8′ × 1¼″	7/- ,,	8′	3/9 ,,
8′ 6″ × 1¼″	11/3 ,,	8′ 6″ × 1¼″	7/6 ,,	9′	3/9 ,,
9′ × 1½″	12/- ,,	9′ × 1½″	8/- ,,	10′	4/6 ,,

SOILED LINEN OR CABIN BAG Brown Waterproof Canvas, with stout Cowhide Leather bottom ; laced up 6 ins. with Cowhide. Complete with brass handle and padlock
33 ins. long × 58 ins. round .. **50/-**
42 ins. long × 58 ins. round .. **55/-**

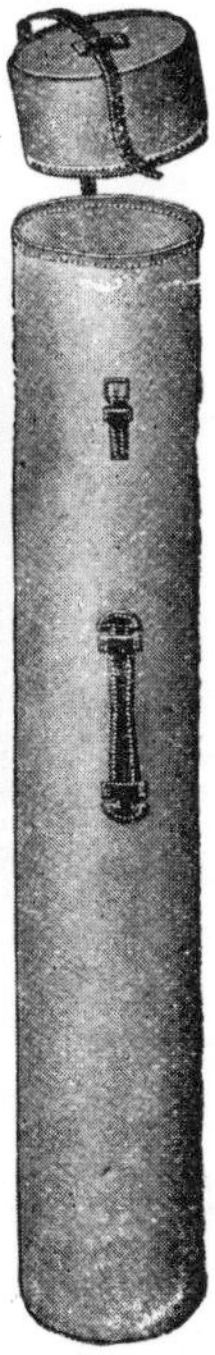

SOILED LINEN OR CABIN BAG Made in Brown Waterproof Canvas, complete with brass bar handle and lever padlock
33 ins. long × 58 ins. round .. **25/-**
36 ins. long × 45 ins. round .. **21/-**
42 ins. long × 58 ins. round .. **28/-**
42 ins. long × 45 ins. round .. **22/6**

UMBRELLA CASE
New improved pattern having a light rod running the whole length of case. Is protected and strengthened with a lay-on of Brown Cowhide. Cap is attached to the case and cannot be mislaid. Made in Harrods workshops, from superior quality Brown Waterproof Canvas, with leather bottom
42 ins. long × 15½ ins. round, **25/9** ; 46 ins. long × 19½ ins. round **29/6**

LIGHT WEIGHT HOLDALL TRAVELLING BAG
In good quality Waterproof twill, with strap fastening
Length 24 in. Price **21/** each
,, 27 in. ,, **23/6** ,,
If fitted with Zip fastener as illustration
Length 24 in. Price **28/6** each

UMBRELLA CASE
In Brown Waterproof, bound and welted leather round top and bottom. Complete with strap, buckle and handle
Also supplied in Green Willesden Canvas to order
42 ins. long × 14 ins. round **11/6**
42 ins. long × 16 ins. round **12/9**
42 ins. long × 18 ins. round **14/6**

ALL PRICES ARE SUBJECT TO MARKET FLUCTUATIONS

HARRODS LTD

Telephone SLOANE 1234
Telegrams 'EVERYTHING HARRODS LONDON

LONDON S W 1

DRESSING BAG DEPARTMENT
Ladies' Handbags chosen from Harrods
Remarkable Collection

COLLAPSIBLE HAND KIT BAG

No. 20   In finest quality polished Pigskin lined Moire Silk.   Also Morocco in various colours

12 ins. ..	£4 17 6
14 ins. ..	£5 12 6
16 ins. ..	£6 7 6

A NEW 'ZIP' BAG   A practical and easy-to-carry Bag that will be greeted with approval.   In London colour grained Baghide, lined strong Holland.   Fitted with stout leather handles, handy 'zip' fastener and padlock

Size 18 ins.	£3 15 0
Size 20 ins.	£4 4 0
Size 22 ins.	£4 12 6

MONITOR BAG

No. 13   In fine quality Morocco Leather lined Moire Silk;   drawn pockets as illustration.   Blue, Green or Purple

12 ins. ..	..	..	£7 0 0
14 ins. ..	..	..	£8 5 0
16 ins. ..			£9 9 0

STEAMER BAG

Polished 'Russia' Leather, lined with soft Suede

14 ins. ..	..	..	£10 10 0

Also in Pigskin and Crocodile

'LAST MINUTE' BAG
Fine quality Morocco Leather, lined with Art Silk.   Improved lightning fastener.   A good variety of colours from which to choose

12 ins. ..	£2 15 0	14 ins. ..	£3 5 0
	16 ins. ..	£3 15 0	

Similar bag in real Pigskin

12 ins. ..	£3 4 0	14 ins. ..	£3 14 0
	16 ins. ..	£4 4 0	

'LAST MINUTE' BAG
Made of good hard wearing Baghide and lined with Drill.   Improved lightning fastener

18 ins. ..	£3 7 6
20 ins. ..	£3 15 0
22 ins. ..	£4 4 0
24 ins. ..	£4 15 0

AN INEXPENSIVE MODEL

A strong useful bag.   Brown Waterproof Canvas, leather handles and piping.   Lining which includes two pockets, is of Moirette Lightning fastener

14 ins. ..	£1 6 0	18 ins. ..	£1 12 6
16 ins. ..	£1 9 6	20 ins. ..	£1 17 6

NEW BOLSTER BAG

Stout grained Cowhide Leather.   A light capacious bag conveniently fitted with lightning fastener

18 ins. ..	£2 15 0	24 ins. ..	£3 10 0
20 ins. ..	£3 0 0	26 ins. ..	£3 15 0
22 ins. ..	£3 5 0	28 ins. ..	£4 1 0

STEAMER BAG OF NEW DESIGN

In Morocco Leather.   Most useful for Continental travel, fitted with two large outside pockets, inner pocket fitted with 'zip' fastening, lined throughout with art silk, supplied in Black, Brown, Beige, Royal Blue, Dark Blue and Green

Size 14 ins. ..	52/6	Size 16 ins. ..	60/-

ALL PRICES ARE SUBJECT TO MARKET FLUCTUATIONS

HARRODS LTD

Telephone SLOANE 1234
Telegrams 'EVERYTHING HARRODS LONDON'

LONDON S W 1

SADDLERY AND TRUNK DEPARTMENT
Men's Hat Cases and a Selection of Useful Accessories in Fine Quality Leather

COLLAR BAG
Best quality Pigskin lined Art. Silk **13/6**
Second quality Pigskin lined
Moirette **10/6**
Morocco Leather in various colours **8/6**

POST BAG
(Post Office Regulation Pattern)
Superior quality Brown Cowhide, with Leather flap which tucks into lid, making it impossible to extract letters when bag is closed. Fitted spring lock and three keys .. **39/6**
Fitted with Hobb's Unpickable lock **62/6**

HANDKERCHIEF CASE
With expanding gusset. Blue or Purple Hide **10/6**
Pigskin but without gusset **10/6**

BROWN HIDE COLLAR BOX
7½ ins. dia. **7/6** 8 ins. dia. **8/6** Best Quality
Hand-sewn, lined Leather 7½ ins. .. **17/6**
Real Pigskin lined Leather 8 ins. .. **19/6**
7½ ins. dia. **11/9** 8 ins. dia. **12/9**
Finest quality Pigskin Lined Silk .. **26/6**

HIDE DOCUMENT CASE
16 × 10 ins. Fitted with lock and two straps with 4 inside pockets **56/6**

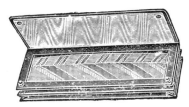

TIE CASE WITH GUSSET
In real Pigskin **15/6**
Many other qualities in various leathers from **7/6 to 42/-**

DOCUMENT CASES
Cheaper Quality. Similar in construction to the one illustrated on right
With one pocket **28/6**
" two pockets .. **32/6**
" three pockets .. **36/6**

COLLAPSIBLE SHIRT CASE
Made in best quality Pigskin (No. 17) **£3 13 0**
Second quality Pigskin **£3 3 0**
Imitation Pigskin **£2 8 0**

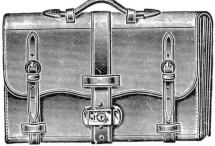

SUPERHIDE DOCUMENT CASE
With 7 inside pockets and leather blotter. Fitted with Bramah pattern lock Size 16 × 10 ins... **£6 15 0**

FINEST QUALITY PIGSKIN DOCUMENT CASE
Leather lined and fitted 4 inside pockets, with Bramah lock. Size 16 × 10 ins. **£5 17 6**
In Hide **£4 14 6**

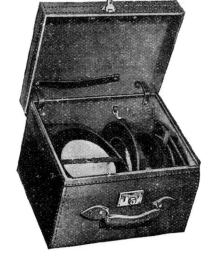

MAN'S HAT CASE In finest quality Cowhide
Hand-sewn throughout **£10 2 6**
Also in best quality Solid Butt Leather .. **£11 0 0**
MAN'S HAT CASE of fine quality Cowhide. (*Not illustrated*) Hand-sewn throughout and fitted with two Nickel lever locks **£6 0 0**

MAN'S HAT CASE THE 'REPLEX'
Made from finest quality unbuffed Hide, lined polished Red Leather. Specially designed to take soft felt, silk, bowler and opera hats, with loop for Panama and cap. Complete with brush and pad .. **£8 5 0**
Smaller size **£7 7 0**
Green Rot-Proof Canvas **£5 10 0**

MAN'S HAT CASE Oblong shape. Polished Brown
Hide, hand-sewn. For one hat only .. **£7/6**
No. 2 quality **33/6**
MAN'S HAT CASE. (*Not illustrated*) Good quality Brown Hide. To hold silk hat, bowler, straw, opera and panama **£3 15 0**
Better quality, hand-sewn throughout .. **£4 15 6**
Brown Japanned Canvas on fibre foundation **£2 17 6**

ALL PRICES ARE SUBJECT TO MARKET FLUCTUATIONS

Telephone SLOANE 1234
Telegrams 'EVERYTHING HARRODS LONDON'

HARRODS LTD   LONDON S W 1

DRESSING BAG DEPARTMENT
Tortoiseshell Dressing Table Requisites

FINEST QUALITY VENEER TORTOISESHELL DRESSING-TABLE SET
Comprising mirror, two hair brushes, hat brush clothes brush and comb **£7 7 0**
Similar set, superior quality, London made.. .. .. .. **£13 10 0**
Attractive Presentation Case, in leather cloth, lined with velvet .. **£1 10 0**

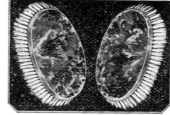

GENTLEMEN'S VENEER TORTOISESHELL HAIR BRUSHES
With fine quality bristles
Per pair **£4 4 0**
Do. in Case complete with Comb **£5 5 0**

FINE QUALITY SOLID TORTOISESHELL DRESSING-TABLE SET
Comprising mirror, two hair brushes, hat brush cloth brush and comb **£14 14 0**
Other qualities .. **£22 10 0** **£27 10 0** **£30 0 0**
£39 10 0 **£40 0 0** **£47 10 0** and **£55 0 0**

Repairs of every description to Ivory and Tortoiseshell.
Brushes re-bristled. *Estimates free.*
Solid gold, silver or engraved monograms of any design

EXTRA FINE DEMI BLONDE TORTOISESHELL DRESSING-TABLE SET
£59 10 0
Blonde .. **£95 0 0** **£67 0 0** **£110 0 0**

OVAL TORTOISESHELL TRINKET BOX
£9 15 0 **£8 15 0**

TORTOISESHELL TRINKET BOX
Prices 50/-, 60/-, 70/-
Light Colour 110/-, 120/-

REAL TORTOISESHELL TAIL COMBS
8 inch 10/6, 12/6, 15/6 and 17/6

REAL TORTOISESHELL PAPER KNIFE
12/6, 15/-, 21/-, 30/- to 50/-

TORTOISESHELL SHOE LIFT
Each 19/6, 42/-, 50/-, 55/-

FINE CUT GLASS POWDER BOWL
With real Tortoiseshell lid
39/-, 47/6, 52/6, 75/-, 105/-

REAL TORTOISESHELL POWDER BOX
45/-, 55/-, 60/- to £7 7 0
Other qualities and sizes from 21/-

REAL TORTOISESHELL DRESSING COMBS
7¼ inch .. 12/3, 15/-, 17/6, 21/-
24/6, 27/6 to 5/-
Demi Blonde Shell 30/-, 35/-, 40/-

REAL TORTOISESHELL DRESSING TABLE CLOCK
Various Designs
30-hour 19/6
8-day .. 50/-, 55/-, 63/-

Not Illustrated
FOLDING CLOCK IN REAL TORTOISESHELL
30 hour .. **£5 5 0**
8 day .. **£6 15 0**
and **£7 7 0**

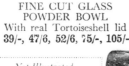

REAL TORTOISESHELL HOOK AND LIFT
Combined. 10 inch
30/-, 39/6, 45/-, 63/-

REAL TORTOISESHELL BUTTONHOOKS
20/-, 23/6, 27/6, 32/6
Light Colour 35/-, 47/6, 50/-

REAL TORTOISESHELL GLOVE STRETCHERS
35/-, 42/-
Light Colour 62/-, 70/-, 75/-

FINE DRESSING-TABLE MIRROR
With bevelled glass, real Tortoiseshell frame, inlaid Ivory. Size 10¾ × 7¼ ins.
46/6, 57/6, 65/6

ALL PRICES ARE SUBJECT TO MARKET FLUCTUATIONS

HARRODS LTD
Telephone SLOANE 1234
Telegrams 'EVERYTHING HARRODS LONDON'
LONDON S W 1

FITTED DRESSING CASE DEPARTMENT
Harrods Roll-Up Dressing Cases

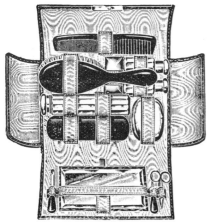

LADY'S ROLL-UP DRESSING CASE in Crocodile-grained Velvet Calf, lined Moirette, completely fitted *as illustration*, Ebony hair brush. Size when closed, 9¾ × 7 × 1¾ ins. **32/6**

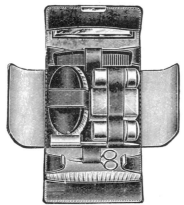

MAN'S ROLL-UP DRESSING CASE in polished real Hide. Fitted *as illustration* Size when **closed** 9 × 4½ × 2½ ins **19/6**

MAN'S ROLL-UP DRESSING CASE in superior quality polished Pigskin, lined Brown Suede. Fitted with Ebony brushes, solid silver-topped bottles, shaving brush in metal case, genuine Gillette razor, leather back mirror, manicure instruments .. **£10 17 6**
Size closed 12 × 8½ × 2½ ins.
Ditto, real Ivory brushes .. **£15 15 0**

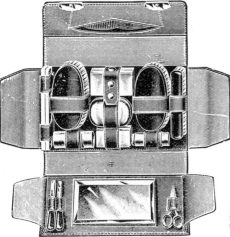

MAN'S FOLDING DRESSING CASE in fine quality polished Cowhide, fitted with real ebony brushes **65/-**
Ditto in real Pigskin or polished Hide, lined Suede Leather throughout **75/-**
Size when closed 12½ × 7 × 2½ ins.

MAN'S FITTED DRESSING CASE good quality real Hide, fitted *as illustration*. Complete with safety razor **30/-**
Size when closed 9½ × 6 × 2 ins.

MAN'S ROLL-UP DRESSING CASE in finest quality London Velour Hide, lined Brown Suede, fitted Ebony brushes, best quality nickel fittings, safety razor, mirror and manicure instruments, *as illustration*
Size closed 10¾ × 8 × 2½ ins. **£4 12 6**
In Real Pigskin **£6 10 0**

Set of CUT GLASS TOILET BOTTLES Silver mounted, with solid Ivory tops. Complete in polished Crushed Morocco or real Pigskin case.
Two bottles, *as illustration* .. **84/-**
Three bottles **£5 5 0**

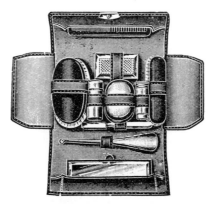

MAN'S ROLL-UP DRESSING CASE Real Pigskin, lined Suede Leather real Ebony brushes, complete with safety razor **45/-**
Size when closed 10 × 7½ × 2 ins.

Set of FOUR SQUARE BOTTLES with nickel screw tops and inside glass stoppers. Complete in solid Leather case, hand-made, lined Leather **30/-**
A variety of other shapes and sizes
26/6, 33/6, 39/6, 42/6

ALL PRICES ARE SUBJECT TO MARKET FLUCTUATIONS

HARRODS LTD

Telephone SLOANE 1234
Telegrams 'EVERYTHING HARRODS LONDON'

LONDON S W 1

FITTED DRESSING CASE DEPARTMENT

Ladies' Motor Cases Neatly Designed and Fitted

FITTED MOTOR CASE. London made. In polished Morocco leather. Shades of Blue, Brown or Black. Fitted with solid silver brushes and bottle tops.
Size 11¾ × 7¾ × 4 in. **£5 15 0**
Size 14 × 9 × 4 in. **£5 19 0**

LADY'S FITTED MOTOR CASE Polished Morocco Leather, lined Silk, fitted with solid silver brushes and silver-topped glass bottles, comb, mirror, trinket box, scissors. Size 10½ × 6½ × 4½ ins. **£8 17 6**
Similar Case in Real Crocodile Leather .. **£11 10 0**

LADY'S MOTOR CASE in Crushed Morocco with enamel fittings. Size 13 × 9 × 4⅞ ins. .. **£9 15 0**
Polished Persian Leather. Size 13 × 9 × 4⅞ ins.
£8 5 0

MOTOR CASE in Morocco Leather with Gilt fittings. Size 10 × 7½ × 4½ ins. **65/-**
Size 10 × 7½ × 4½ ins. in Velvet Crocodile-grained Leather **65/-**
Larger size 14 × 9½ × 4½ in. **£4 4 0**

BLONDE HORN TUMBLER
(SD 307) Set of six, each with solid silver rim, in Leather case **£5 15 0**
Unmounted. In leather case .. **50/-**

LADY'S FITTED MOTOR CASE in polished Persian Leather, completely fitted, *as illustration* **43/6**
Similar case in real Crushed Morocco, with enamel fittings **85/-**

TRAVELLING FLASK
Glass flask with screw top forming cup. In solid Hide Leather case
Small **8/6**
Medium .. **10/-**
Large **11/6**

LADY'S FITTED MOTOR CASE in real Morocco, lined Silk. Fitted with mirror in lid, three glass bottles with plain gilt tops, fancy cigarette and match case, pin cushion, instrument board and memo tablet. Size 7 × 5½ × 3½ ins. .. **57/6**

Goods are delivered free within the radius of Harrods Motor Vans

In addition to the examples illustrated, Harrods have a splendid selection of Fitted Motor Cases at prices ranging from 29/6

FITTED MOTOR CASE In finest quality Morocco, lined Silk, and fitted with Leather-back mirror, best enamel-back or engine-turned silver-gilt hair brush, cloth brush, five enamel-topped glass toilet bottles
Size 11 × 7 × 4 ins. **£18 18 0**

FITTED MOTOR CASE In polished Crushed Calf, lined Moire Antique Silk, fitted with silver hair brush, cloth brush, five silver-topped bottles and comb, Leather jewel box, mirror and scissors. Size 12 × 7½ × 4½ ins. **£12 17 6**

A NOVEL DESIGN Fitted Hand Bag. Finest quality polished Crushed Calf Leather, lined rich Silk, fitted with silver-topped glass bottles, real ivory hair brush and ivory cloth brush, mirror in lid, complete with patent safety handle. Size 6½ × 7 × 2¾ ins.
£13 10 0

ALL PRICES ARE SUBJECT TO MARKET FLUCTUATIONS

SADDLERY DEPARTMENT
Bridles and Saddlery made from the Finest Quality Leather

THE 'WEYMOUTH' BRIDLE
Superior quality double-rein bridle, sewn on to super quality, hand forged steel, LONG CHEEK HACKNEY bit, or SHORT CHEEK POLO BIT and bridoon, complete with plain wide caveson noseband .. **75/-**
If supplied with fixed mouth Hackney bit .. **75/-**

DOUBLE-REIN SNAFFLE BRIDLE, WITH FLAT RING BRIDOON BIT
Superior quality double-rein snaffle bridle, sewn on to super quality, hand-forged steel, plain jointed, flat ring bridoon, complete with plain wide caveson noseband **57/6**

SINGLE-REIN SNAFFLE BRIDLE
Superior quality single-rein snaffle bridle, sewn on to super quality, hand-forged steel, plain jointed, flat ring bridoon, complete with plain wide caveson noseband **52/6**

CHILD'S SINGLE CHAIR SADDLE
To face front as illustration. Fitted with Red leather Cushion and Waist Belt. Complete with Crupper and Girths **67/6**

BRIDLE FOR DONKEY OR PONY UP TO 12 HANDS
Single-rein snaffle with bit sewn on, best quality.. **18/6**

THE 'BANBURY-PELHAM' BRIDLE
Bit made with sliding, revolving mouth. Superior quality double-rein bridle, sewn on to super quality, hand-forged steel 'Banbury-Pelham' Bit, as illustration, complete with plain wide caveson noseband **72/6**

THE 'RUGBY POLO PELHAM' BRIDLE
Superior quality double-rein bridle sewn on to super quality hand-forged steel 'RUGBY POLO PELHAM' BIT, as illustration, complete with plain wide caveson noseband **75/-**

THE 'PELHAM' BRIDLE.
Superior quality double-rein bridle, sewn on to super quality hand-forged steel SNAFFLE JOINTED PELHAM BIT, complete with plain wide caveson noseband **70/-**
Sewn on to super hand-forged steel PELHAM BIT with plain HALF-MOON MOUTH. Complete with plain wide caveson noseband **70/-**

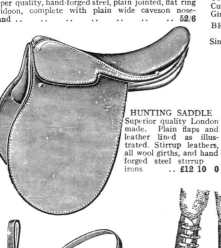

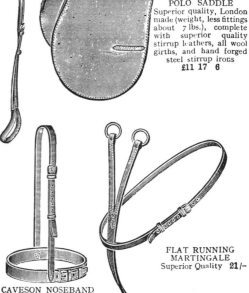

HUNTING SADDLE
Superior quality London made. Plain flaps and leather lined as illustrated. Stirrup leathers, all wool girths, and hand forged steel stirrup irons .. **£12 10 0**

CHILD'S FELT RIDING PAD
Best London make Complete with stirrup irons, leathers and crupper .. **£2 15 0**

POLO SADDLE
Superior quality, London made (weight, less fittings about 7 lbs.), complete with superior quality stirrup leathers, all wool girths, and hand forged steel stirrup irons **£11 17 6**

FLAT STANDING MARTINGALE
Superior quality **13/6**

POLO BOOTS 'THE RANELAGH'
made in best quality Felt and stout Elastic Web, with 4 straps. Fawn or Blue, per pair .. **22/6**
Superior quality, made extra deep to cover fetlocks
Per pair **30/-**

WITHER PAD
Knitted Wool made in White, Fawn, Blue and Grey. Superior quality **6/-**

CAVESON NOSEBAND
As illustrated
Plain .. each **12/6**
Lined .. ,, **18/6**

FLAT RUNNING MARTINGALE
Superior Quality **21/-**

ALL PRICES ARE SUBJECT TO MARKET FLUCTUATIONS

HARRODS LTD

Telephone SLOANE 1234
Telegrams 'EVERYTHING HARRODS LONDON'

LONDON S W 1

SADDLERY DEPARTMENT
Whips, Riding Crops, Hunting Canteens and Sandwich Cases

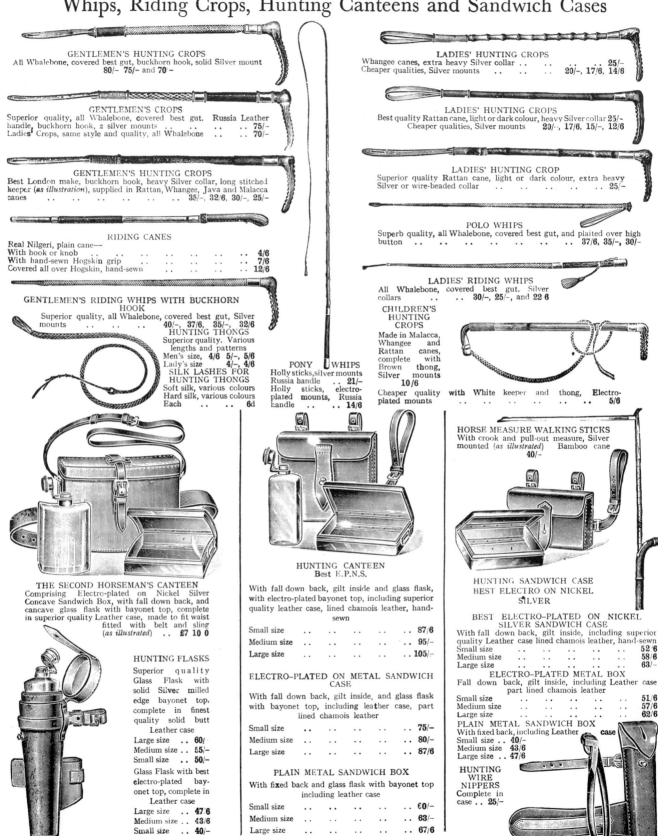

GENTLEMEN'S HUNTING CROPS
All Whalebone, covered best gut, buckhorn hook, solid Silver mount
80/- 75/- and 70 -

GENTLEMEN'S CROPS
Superior quality, all Whalebone, covered best gut. Russia Leather
handle, buckhorn hook, 2 silver mounts 75/-
Ladies' Crops, same style and quality, all Whalebone 70/-

GENTLEMEN'S HUNTING CROPS
Best London make, buckhorn hook, heavy Silver collar, long stitched
keeper (as illustration), supplied in Rattan, Whangee, Java and Malacca
canes 35/-, 32/6, 30/-, 25/-

RIDING CANES
Real Nilgeri, plain cane—
With hook or knob 4/6
With hand-sewn Hogskin grip 7/6
Covered all over Hogskin, hand-sewn 12/6

GENTLEMEN'S RIDING WHIPS WITH BUCKHORN HOOK
Superior quality, all Whalebone, covered best gut, Silver
mounts 40/-, 37/6, 35/-, 32/6

HUNTING THONGS
Superior quality. Various lengths and patterns
Men's size, 4/6 5/-, 5/6
Lady's size 4/-, 4/6

SILK LASHES FOR HUNTING THONGS
Soft silk, various colours
Hard silk, various colours
Each 6d

LADIES' HUNTING CROPS
Whangee canes, extra heavy Silver collar 25/-
Cheaper qualities, Silver mounts 20/-, 17/6, 14/6

LADIES' HUNTING CROPS
Best quality Rattan cane, light or dark colour, heavy Silver collar 25/-
Cheaper qualities, Silver mounts 20/-, 17/6, 15/-, 12/6

LADIES' HUNTING CROP
Superior quality Rattan cane, light or dark colour, extra heavy
Silver or wire-beaded collar 25/-

POLO WHIPS
Superb quality, all Whalebone, covered best gut, and plaited over high
button 37/6, 35/-, 30/-

LADIES' RIDING WHIPS
All Whalebone, covered best gut. Silver
collars .. .. 30/-, 25/-, and 22 6

CHILDREN'S HUNTING CROPS
Made in Malacca, Whangee and Rattan canes, complete with Brown thong, Silver mounts
10/6
Cheaper quality, Electro-plated mounts

with White keeper and thong, Electro-
5/6

PONY WHIPS
Holly sticks, silver mounts
Russia handle .. 21/-
Holly sticks, electro-plated mounts, Russia handle .. 14/6

THE SECOND HORSEMAN'S CANTEEN
Comprising Electro-plated on Nickel Silver Concave Sandwich Box, with fall down back, and cancave glass flask with bayonet top, complete in superior quality Leather case, made to fit waist fitted with belt and sling (as illustrated) .. £7 10 0

HUNTING FLASKS
Superior quality Glass Flask with solid Silver milled edge bayonet top, complete in finest quality solid butt Leather case
Large size .. 60/-
Medium size .. 55/-
Small size .. 50/-
Glass Flask with best electro-plated bayonet top, complete in Leather case
Large size .. 47/6
Medium size .. 43/6
Small size .. 40/-

HUNTING CANTEEN
Best E.P.N.S.

With fall down back, gilt inside and glass flask, with electro-plated bayonet top, including superior quality leather case, lined chamois leather, hand-sewn

Small size	87/6
Medium size	95/-
Large size	105/-

ELECTRO-PLATED ON METAL SANDWICH CASE
With fall down back, gilt inside, and glass flask with bayonet top, including leather case, part lined chamois leather

Small size	75/-
Medium size	80/-
Large size	87/6

PLAIN METAL SANDWICH BOX
With fixed back and glass flask with bayonet top including leather case

Small size	60/-
Medium size	63/-
Large size	67/6

HORSE MEASURE WALKING STICKS
With crook and pull-out measure, Silver mounted (as illustrated) Bamboo cane
40/-

HUNTING SANDWICH CASE
BEST ELECTRO ON NICKEL SILVER

BEST ELECTRO-PLATED ON NICKEL SILVER SANDWICH CASE
With fall down back, gilt inside, including superior quality Leather case lined chamois leather, hand-sewn
Small size 52/6
Medium size 58/6
Large size 63/-

ELECTRO-PLATED METAL BOX
Fall down back, gilt inside, including Leather case part lined chamois leather
Small size 51/6
Medium size 57/6
Large size 62/6

PLAIN METAL SANDWICH BOX
With fixed back, including Leather case
Small size .. 40/-
Medium size 43/6
Large size .. 47/6

HUNTING WIRE NIPPERS
Complete in case .. 25/-

ALL PRICES ARE SUBJECT TO MARKET FLUCTUATIONS

Telephone SLOANE 1234
Telegrams 'EVERYTHING HARRODS LONDON'

HARRODS LTD   LONDON S W 1

DOG ACCESSORIES DEPARTMENT
A Further Selection of Dog Leads, Whips, Chains, Brushes, etc.

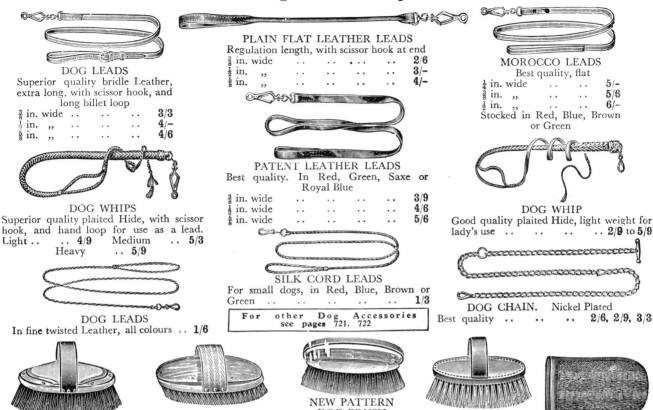

DOG LEADS
Superior quality bridle Leather, extra long, with scissor hook, and long billet loop

$\frac{3}{8}$ in. wide	.. .. ..	3/3
$\frac{1}{2}$ in. „	.. .. ..	4/-
$\frac{5}{8}$ in. „	.. .. ..	4/6

DOG WHIPS
Superior quality plaited Hide, with scissor hook, and hand loop for use as a lead.
Light .. .. 4/9 Medium .. 5/3
Heavy .. 5/9

DOG LEADS
In fine twisted Leather, all colours .. 1/6

PLAIN FLAT LEATHER LEADS
Regulation length, with scissor hook at end

$\frac{3}{8}$ in. wide	.. ..	2/6
$\frac{1}{2}$ in. „	.. .. ..	3/-
$\frac{5}{8}$ in. „	.. .. ..	4/-

PATENT LEATHER LEADS
Best quality. In Red, Green, Saxe **or** Royal Blue

$\frac{3}{8}$ in. wide	.. .. ..	3/9
$\frac{1}{2}$ in. wide	.. .. ..	4/6
$\frac{5}{8}$ in. wide	.. .. ..	5/6

SILK CORD LEADS
For small dogs, in Red, Blue, Brown or Green 1/3

> For other Dog Accessories see pages 721, 722

MOROCCO LEADS
Best quality, flat

$\frac{1}{4}$ in. wide	.. ..	5/-
$\frac{3}{8}$ in. „	.. ..	5/6
$\frac{1}{2}$ in. „	.. ..	6/-

Stocked in Red, Blue, Brown or Green

DOG WHIP
Good quality plaited Hide, light weight for lady's use .. .. 2/9 to 5/9

DOG CHAIN. Nickel Plated
Best quality 2/6, 2/9, 3/3

BLACK SPLIT WHALE-BONE DOG BRUSH
For large dogs .. 3/6
Whisk Dog Dandy Brush 1/6

DOG BRUSH
With slanting bristles penetrating when brushed one way, soft when brushed the reverse way .. 3/-

NEW PATTERN DOG BRUSH
Whalebone and Bristle mixture, with Leather hand loop, suitable for Terriers 3/6

DOG BRUSH
Leather back, medium stiffness, with hand loop 3/6

HOUND GLOVE
Each 3/6 & 6/-

HORN WHISTLE
Large size 2/6
Small „ 2/-

NICKEL DOG WHISTLE
The 'Acme' 1/6

FLAT DOG WHISTLE FOR VEST POCKET
With double note 2/-

TRIMMING COMBS Each **1/9**

ADJUSTABLE STRIPPING COMBS Each **3/-**
Better qualities at 3/6, 4/6, 5/6

BROWN'S POODLE CLIPPERS
Small or large sizes **13/6**
POODLE CLIPPERS
New improved design, running on ball bearings, warranted not to drag the hair when clipping .. .. .. Per pair **13/6**

METAL DOG COMBS
Fine, medium or coarse
Each **1/6 & 1/9**

HANDLE DOG COMBS
Suitable for all small dogs .. **2/6**

DOUBLE NIT COMB
Two grades of teeth **2/3 & 3/6**

METAL DOG COMBS
Two grades of teeth (fine and coarse) 7 ins. .. **2/6**

DOUBLE DOG RAKE
For removing dead hair .. 1/6

HINDES WIRE OR RUBBER DOG BRUSH
For Chows, Poodles, etc. .. 7/6

SCISSOR CLIPS
Small 1/-
Large 1/6

SHORT ROUND ALSATIAN DOG LEADS
Bridle Leather .. **6/-**   Coloured Morocco .. **7/6**
LONG ROUND BULLDOG LEADS
Bridle Leather .. **7/6**   Coloured Morocco (to order) **10/6**

DOUBLE SWIVELS
Brass or Steel 2/3

Everything for Dogs is supplied in this Section including Kennels, Baskets, Rugs, India Rubber Bones, and Medicines, etc.

ALL PRICES ARE SUBJECT TO MARKET FLUCTUATIONS

HARRODS LTD

Telephone SLOANE 1234
Telegrams 'EVERYTHING HARRODS LONDON'

LONDON S W 1

SPORTS AND GAMES DEPARTMENT
Come to Harrods and be advised by Golfing Experts

A few helpful notes for the beginner

WEIGHT OF CLUBS   This depends to a great extent upon the strength of the individual, but one must always remember that it is essential to good Golf to have complete control of the Clubs at the end of a Round as at the beginning.   Harrods always advise medium weight Clubs, especially in the driving Clubs

LIE   A very important item.   This term means the angle which the sole of the Club makes with the shaft Inconsistent form is invariably due to players having the incorrect 'Lie' of Club

QUALITY AND SPRING OF SHAFT   All Harrods Shafts are selected by experts and we can thoroughly guarantee their quality.   The athletic player will find that the stiffer Shafts will render the better service, but the lightly built or elderly player will find that a little spring in the Shaft will help considerably

THE LARGEST AND BEST SELECTION OF GOLF CLUBS IN THE UNITED KINGDOM
EVERY CLUB SELECTED BY AN EXPERT GOLFER
HARRODS SPECIALISE IN COPYING CLUBS TO CUSTOMER'S REQUIREMENTS

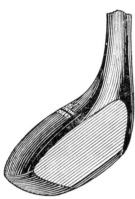

J. H. TAYLOR'S CLUBS
Drivers, Brassies, Niblicks and Putters, Medium Irons, Mashies
12/6

OTHER CLUBS

W. HAGEN'S Cleeks, Driving Irons, Mid Irons, Mashie Irons, Mashies, Driving Mashies, Mashie Niblicks, Jiggers, Sammy's Niblicks and Putters	16/6
ALEX. HERD'S	16/6
E. RAY'S	15/6
J. SHERLOCK'S	15/6
F. ROBSON'S	15/6
ABE MITCHELL'S..	15/6
H. VARDON'S	13/6
TOM STEWART'S Pipe Brand	15/6
H. LOGAN'S Genii	13/6
STAR SMITH, Non-socketing	14/-
JAMES BRAID'S	14/-
STAR MAXWELL'S	13/6
GEO. DUNCAN'S All Models Akros ..	14/-
THE 'STELLA' Model Irons	13/6
W. L. RITCHIE'S Model Irons	18/6
MAMMOTH Niblick	16/6
R. H. de MONTMORENCY'S Push Cleek, Push Iron and Jigger	13/6
J. H. TAYLOR'S All Autograph Models	12/6
RANGEFINDER IRONS in Rustless Iron	21/-
MAXWELL IRONS in Rustless Iron ..	17/6

Harrods are Sole West End Agents for all W. L. Ritchie's and W. G. Oke's Golf Clubs

A Large Selection always in stock

PRACTICE BALLS

CORK PRACTICE BALLS
Painted White.   Each **8d**

WOOL PRACTICE BALLS
Each **4½d**

FELT-COVERED PRACTICE BALLS
Each **1/3**

POLITA for cleaning Golf Clubs or any steel article. Per block **6d**

W. G. OKE'S
CHAMPIONSHIP IRONS
18/6

'JACK WHITE' CLUBS
'Bobby Jones' models
21/-

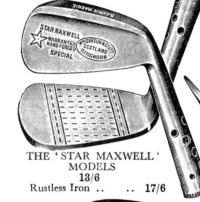

THE 'STAR MAXWELL' MODELS
13/6
Rustless Iron **17/6**

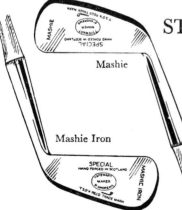

Mashie

Mashie Iron

STEWART'S FAMOUS CLUBS

THE 'PIPE' BRAND

These Clubs are some of the finest models procurable and are fitted with superfine shafts For Ladies or Gentlemen.   The following Clubs are in Stock :—

No. 1 Irons	Mashie Niblicks
No. 2 Irons	Niblicks
No. 3 Irons	Jiggers
Deep-faced Mashies	Mashie Irons
Shallow-faced Mashies	Putting Cleeks
Spade Mashies	

ALL CLUBS ONE PRICE .. **15/6**

Niblick

No. 2 Iron

ALL PRICES ARE SUBJECT TO MARKET FLUCTUATIONS

SPORTS AND GAMES DEPARTMENT
Everything for the Golfer at Harrods

OWING to the innumerable differences in the build of individuals, it is impossible to lay down any hard and fast rules of guidance for those about to begin Golf; but the general principles which are given here will be of great assistance to intending purchasers of Golf Clubs. Harrods do not advise the purchasing of a complete set of Clubs at the outset, but simply the following necessary Clubs :—Brassie (which can be used from the Tee and through the Green), Mid Iron, Mashie, Putter and Niblick. When one is acquainted with these, one will then know what other Clubs are necessary

Free Instruction in Harrods Golf Practice Nets

Purchases value 20/- or over sent post paid to any address in England and Wales

The 'Ritchie' Clubs Drivers, Brassies and Spoons Each 21/-

WOODEN CLUBS
DRIVERS, BRASSIES AND SPOONS

W. L. RITCHIE'S	21/-	ABE MITCHELL'S	21/-
RANGE FINDER	21/-	G. OKE'S	22/6, 18/6
SHERLOCK'S (Montmorency Model)	21/-	FORGAN'S Gold Medal	17/6
ALEX HERD'S	18/6	J. H. TAYLOR'S 12/6, 18/6	
W. HAGEN'S	21/-	G. DUNCAN'S	21/-
F. ROBSON'S	21/-	A. PATRICK'S	15/6
		A. COMPSTON	21/-

PUTTERS

THE 'HUNTLY'	18/6	The 'GEO. OKE'	15/6
THE 'F. G. TAIT' Putting Cleek	11/6	MILL'S 'ALUM' (Various Models)	13/6
THE 'ORION'	14/-	HARRODS ALUMINIUM (Various Models)	11/6
THE 'BROWN VARDON'	15/-	COMPSTON'S 100 per cent.	16/6
TRAVERS	20/-	TOLLEY PUTTER	15/6
H. B. PUTTER	21/-		

Harrods Special Models in Drivers, Brassies and Spoons each 15/6

THE 'HUNTLY' PUTTER

For accuracy this Putter is absolutely unique because of its rectangular handle with special groove for thumbs. The head is made of aluminium, slightly bombed to obviate fluffed puts. Very neat and workmanlike .. .. Each **18/6**

ACCESSORIES

GRIPOLIN In Tubes
Each **1/-**
BRITONIA GRIP WAX .. Each **3d**
ROUGH RUBBER STRIP GRIPS .. **9d**
TUBULAR TAPERED RUBBER GRIPS **1/3**
GOLF GRIPS. Best Basil .. Per strip **1/-**
BLACK AMERICAN CLOTH (Rubbered) Fitted **9d**
GOLF BALL PAINT Per Tin **1/-**
LONDON GRIP WAX **6d**
LAUDER'S WAX **6d**
'KADDISHELP' With handle. Each **7½d**
FULFORD GRIP **2/3**

GOLF PORTMANTEAU

Best quality in Green Willesden or Brown Canvas. Size 50 × 7¾ × 7¾ ins., fitted with spring lock, two trunk clips, pair Leather straps and strong Leather handle **£4 17 6**

'MILLS'
ALUMINIUM CLUBS
NEW SERIES OF ALUMINIUM PUTTERS

(*Shown below*) Retains the superior and well-known features of the 'MILLS' Putter with the added advantage that the centre of gravity is placed at the point of impact, thus enabling the player to place his long approach putts accurately

Each **13/6**

GOLF PRACTICE NETS

Golf Practice Nets have been installed for the convenience of customers, who may there test Clubs, Balls or various Practice Devices before deciding on their purchase. Needless to say, there are no charges for this Service

10 × 10 × 8 ft. high Complete
£6 15 0

10 × 10 × 9 ft. high Complete
£7 11 0

10 × 10 × 10 ft. high Complete
£8 5 0

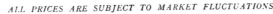

ALL PRICES ARE SUBJECT TO MARKET FLUCTUATIONS

HARRODS LTD

Telephone SLOANE 1234
Telegrams 'EVERYTHING HARRODS LONDON'

LONDON SW 1

SPORTS AND GAMES DEPARTMENT
All Tennis Rackets are Selected by Harrods own Experts

THE 'COLLEGE' LAWN TENNIS RACKET

(*On right*) A well made Racket, slightly under full size. Strung with English Green and White gut. Weights from 9 to 11½ ozs. .. 17/6
Peter Pan 13/9
The Gem 13/6
Weights as above

THE H.B.

THE 'ROEHAMPTON' LAWN TENNIS RACKET

(*On left*) Superior quality Racket. Rounded frame, strung with good quality English gut with double centre mains. Shoulders bound vellum and gut 30/-

HARRODS SUPER RACKET

The last word in Tennis Racket construction Guaranteed for one Season

The most perfect Racket ever produced

Made from the best English Rent Ash Guaranteed strung with Tracey's White gut.

Double centre mains Shoulders strengthened.

Double bound at shoulders with Green and White gut
72/6

'LAMBERT CHAMBERS'

(Slazenger's, Ltd.) (*Below*) Made from seasoned wood and finest gut to the instructions of Mrs Lambert Chambers, winner of the World's Championship

1919	65/-
V.V.V.	67/6
Anderson	68/6

THE 'CARLTON'

(*On left*) Frame made of finest English Rent Ash. Concave wedge with Ash insertion. Shoulders double bound with gut and surgical binding. Strung with finest English Green and White gut. Made by F. H. Ayres Ltd.
45/-

'HURLINGHAM' LAWN TENNIS RACKET

(*Below*) Frame is of finest Rent Ash. Concave wedge with Ash insertion at top of wedge. Shoulders double bound with gut and surgical binding. Strung with good quality Black and White English gut 35/-

THE 'QUEEN'
(*On left*)
Guaranteed strung with English gut. Two double centre mains and concave wedge
25/-

THE 'WILTON' RACKET

(*Above*) Excellent English Ash frame with hollow wedge and bound shoulders. Strung with English gut with double mains 25/-

THE 'WINDSOR' LAWN TENNIS RACKET

(*On left*) Frame is of English Rent Ash with concave wedge. Shoulders bound with gut and surgical binding. Strung with good quality Red and White English gut
21/-

Every RACKET sold by HARRODS GUARANTEED for one Season

THE 'RUTLAND' LAWN TENNIS RACKET

(*On right*) Made from best English Rent Ash. Frame slightly rounded on the inside. Strung with good quality English gut (all White) and double bound with Purple gut at shoulders 45/-

THE 'FRINTON'

(*On left*) Made specially for Harrods by Messrs. Slazenger's, Ltd. Frame of finest English Rent Ash with concave wedge strengthened by a cane insertion on top of wedge. Shoulders treble bound with surgical gut. Strung with good quality White English gut 45/-

Any of these Rackets are sent post free

ALL PRICES ARE SUBJECT TO MARKET FLUCTUATIONS

HARRODS LTD

Telephone SLOANE 1234
Telegrams 'EVERYTHING HARRODS LONDON'

LONDON S W 1

SPORTS AND GAMES DEPARTMENT
Order any of these By Post if you cannot visit Harrods

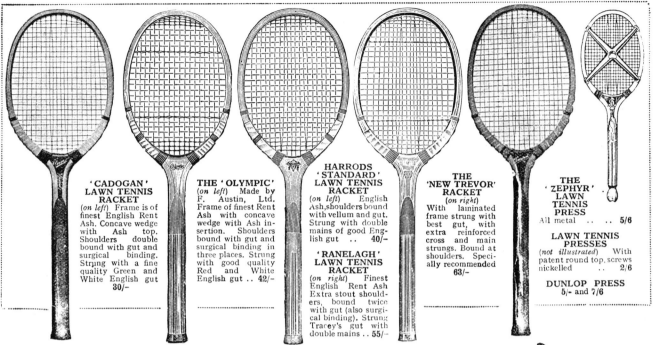

'CADOGAN' LAWN TENNIS RACKET

(*on left*) Frame is of finest English Rent Ash. Concave wedge with Ash top. Shoulders double bound with gut and surgical binding. Strung with a fine quality Green and White English gut. **30/-**

THE 'OLYMPIC'

(*on left*) Made by F. Austin, Ltd. Frame of finest Rent Ash with concave wedge with Ash insertion. Shoulders bound with gut and surgical binding in three places. Strung with good quality Red and White English gut .. **42/-**

HARRODS 'STANDARD' LAWN TENNIS RACKET

(*on left*) English Ash, shoulders bound with vellum and gut. Strung with double mains of good English gut .. **40/-**

'RANELAGH' LAWN TENNIS RACKET

(*on right*) Finest English Rent Ash Extra stout shoulders, bound twice with gut (also surgical binding). Strung Tracey's gut with double mains .. **55/-**

THE 'NEW TREVOR' RACKET

(*on right*) With laminated frame strung with best gut, with extra reinforced cross and main strungs. Bound at shoulders. Specially recommended **63/-**

THE 'ZEPHYR' LAWN TENNIS PRESS

All metal **5/6**

LAWN TENNIS PRESSES

(*not illustrated*) With patent round top, screws nickelled .. **2/6**

DUNLOP PRESS
5/- and **7/6**

THE 'LEADER' MARKER (Patent)

Tank is of Cast Iron, marking wheel at front, small wheel and centre wheel secured by a hinged bracket which can be lifted clear of the tank when the marker is not required or to facilitate cleaning, refilling or emptying. Self scraping. No loose wheels. No. 1 size (Capacity ½ gallon) **22/6**

No. 3 size (Capacity 1 gallon) **26/6**

THE 'CADOGAN' LAWN MARKER

(Capacity 6 pints) **17/6**

THE 'KLEENBALL' TENNIS BALL CLEANER

With tin of powder **12/6**

Extra tins .. .. each **6d**

'LAWNYTE'

A special preparation for marking lawns. Saves all trouble of mixing 28-lb. tin **7/-**, 14-lb. tin **3/9**, 7-lb. tin **2/3**

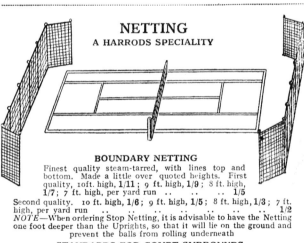

NETTING
A HARRODS SPECIALITY

BOUNDARY NETTING

Finest quality steam-tarred, with lines top and bottom. Made a little over quoted heights. First quality, 10ft. high, **1/11**; 9 ft. high, **1/9**; 8 ft. high, **1/7**; 7 ft. high, per yard run **1/5**

Second quality. 10 ft. high, **1/6**; 9 ft. high, **1/5**; 8 ft. high, **1/3**; 7 ft. high, per yard run **1/2**

NOTE—When ordering Stop Netting, it is advisable to have the Netting one foot deeper than the Uprights, so that it will lie on the ground and prevent the balls from rolling underneath

STANDARDS FOR COURT SURROUNDS

Tubular pattern of Steel, painted Green. 9 ft. high, **2/6**; 8 ft. high **2/2**; 7 ft. high **2/-**

Top Rods, complete with hooks, 9 ft. long **1/3**

Above measurements are lengths out of ground

NETTING in lengths of 21 yards and 24 yards. Best quality always in stock. 21 yards × 9 ft. .. .. .. Per piece **£1 16 9**

24 yards × 9 ft. .. .. .. " **£2 2 0**

All netting is steam tarred and made from good quality Italian Hemp, fitted to tarred hemp lines in top and bottom selvedges

The quantity of standards and top rods, etc., required to cover the ends of a court is as follows :—16 standards, 14 top rods and 2 pieces 21 yards netting. Cost as follows :

		£ s. d.
With 7 ft. Standards and 8 ft. Netting		£5 16 0
With 8 ft. Standards and 9 ft. Netting		£6 5 9
With 9 ft. Standards and 10 ft. Netting		£6 18 0

To cover ends and sides of court, the quantity required is as follows : 34 Standards, 30 Top Rods and 2 pieces Netting each 21 yards × 24 yards Cost as follows :

		£ s. d.
With 7 ft. Standards and 8 ft. Netting		£12 8 0
With 8 ft. Standards and 9 ft. Netting		£13 8 8
With 9 ft. Standards and 10 ft. Netting		£14 15 0

All the above are of the best quality netting

THE 'SIMPLEX' TENNIS COURT MARKER The tank is of Cast Iron and constructed with dished bottom. Self scraping. An inexpensive and reliable marker Capacity approx. 5 pints Each **18/-**

TENNIS EYE-SHADE Strongly made in White with peaks lined in Green Each

With elastic band **2/-**

" full head covering **3/-** and **4/6**

" full head covering of White or Brown net **3/6** and **5/-**

ALL PRICES ARE SUBJECT TO MARKET FLUCTUATIONS

HARRODS LTD

Telephone SLOANE 1234
Telegrams 'EVERYTHING HARRODS LONDON'

LONDON S W 1

SPORTS AND GAMES DEPARTMENT
Offers for the Cricketer—Amateur or Professional

HARRODS BATS

H. B. BATS

Three strips of Rubber have been inserted (on a new principle) in the handle of this bat, and by this means greater resilience is obtained, with a total absence of jarring. It adds greatly to the driving power of the bat. Every blade is of selected English Close Bark Willow .. **40/-**

HARRODS 'RANELAGH' BAT

Double rubber handle with selected Close Bark English Willow blade. Full size .. **21/-**

YOUTHS' BATS
Double Rubber

Size 3	.. ..	.. **10/-**
Size 4	.. ..	.. **11/6**
Size 5	.. ..	.. **12/6**
Size 6	.. ..	.. **13/6**

'FORCE' BAT

Tension rubber ring handle, most resilient, giving great driving power. A powerful 'Cutter' without jar. Perfectly balanced

25/-, 30/-, 35/-, 38/6, 42/-

HARROW SIZE
22/6, 26/-, 30/-, 34/-

YOUTHS' SIZE

4	5	6
18/6,	21/-,	22/6

GRADIDGE'S IMPERIAL DRIVER CRICKET BATS

MEN'S

Each **42/-, 35/-; 30/-, 27/6**

Short handle bats same price

Size 3	..	..	**12/6**
Size 4	..	**21/-, 16/-**
Size 5	..	**25/-, 17/6**
Size 6	..	**27/6, 21/-**

INSTRUCTIONS FOR SEASONING AND USING BATS

Oil the blade of the bat with raw linseed oil, and when rubbed in, stand it upright, to prevent the oil getting to the handle

This process will have to be repeated daily for about a fortnight. Bats that have become soiled or dirty can be cleaned as follows:
Well oil with raw linseed oil; after soaking for about twenty minutes, rub off with very fine glass paper; now apply another coat of oil and rub off with a dry cloth

Great care should be taken in first using a new bat. Until it gets seasoned and hardened it should not be too much used at rough practice and an old ball should be used

CRICKET BALLS

HARRODS SPECIAL MATCH BALL
5½ ozs. Guaranteed .. .. .. Each **12/6**

HARRODS SPECIAL PRACTICE BALL
Each **10/6**

HARRODS SPECIAL COLLEGE BALL
4¾ ozs., as used in most public schools. Each **11/6**

Cheaper Quality
Club Practice Ball
Each **8/6**
Youth's Ball
Each **6/6**
HARLEQUIN CRICKET BALL
Full size .. **13/6**
Youths' size .. **12/6**
Boys' 4 oz. .. **9/-**
ABDOMINAL PADS
Aluminium Shield covered Cape leather. The lightest Pad made .. **5/6, 7/6**

WICKET KEEPING GAUNTLETS

THE 'STEDMAN' GAUNTLET
Made to the instructions of F. Stedman, the noted Surrey Wicket-keeper

Per pair, including undergloves .. **25/-, 30/-**

Best Gold Cap., blocked finger-tips, black rubber palms Per pair **19/6**

Men's Best Tan Cape, with black rubber palms, padded finger tips
Per pair **17/6**

Men's Stout Tan Cape, with black rubber palms
Per pair **13/6**

Men's White Mock Buck with ventilated finger tips
Per pair **10/-**

Youths' Wicket Keeping Gauntlets 6d. per pair less than above prices.

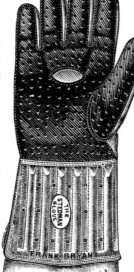

JACK HOBBS 'THE OVAL' CRICKET BATS

Full Size .. **42/-**

Harrow Size .. **32/6**

GUNN & MOORE'S BATS

'AUTOGRAPH' BATS
These are specially selected by William Gunn .. **33/-, 37/6, 42/-**

'CANNON' BATS
Treble Spring Handles **28/6**

PUBLIC SCHOOL BATS
As supplied to Eton and Harrow season after season, G. and M.'s Eton and Harrow 'Autograph' Bat, Perfect balance and finish, stamped Extra Special facsimile of W. Gunn's autograph. Warranted
Each **27/-, 31/-**

YOUTHS' BATS
No. 4 'The Autograph'. .**16/- 21/-**
No. 5 'The Autograph'. .**18/6 23/6**
No. 6 'The Autograph'. .**21/- 26/6**

ACCESSORIES

CRICKET BAT COVERS
Green Baize **2/-**

BAT HANDLE COVERS
Indiarubber **1/-**

CRICKET MEASURING TAPES
66 feet. In Brass Case. Each **7/6**
In Leather Case .. .. Each **10/6**

THE COUNTY TAPE
Unstretchable Steel, marked at wicket and crease lines only **7/6**

UMPIRES' COATS
Each **15/6**

LAWS OF CRICKET
Per copy **6d**

CRICKET BAT OIL
Per tin **1/-**

CRICKET BAT BINDING
Per roll **1/-**

NEW BLADES
Each .. .. .. **10/6 to 30/-**

NEW HANDLES
Each .. .. **7/6 to 15/-**

Repairs executed by skilled workmen promptly at lowest possible prices

CRICKET STUMPS

WITH BAILS
30 ins. long. In Ash polished and steel shoes

Per set				**6/6**
30 ins. long. Brass bound .. .. Per set				**7/6**
30 ins. long. Brass bound, with iron shoes .. .. Per set				**8/6**
30 ins. long. Ash polished with solid brass revolving tops and steel shoes				
Per set				**11/6**

BOYS' SUPERIOR POLISHED STUMPS

24 ins.	Per set	**3/6**
26 ins.	Per set	**4/6**
28 ins.	Per set	**5/6**

BAILS

In Polished Ash ..	Per set	**9d**
In Boxwood	Per set	**1/6**
In Ebony	Per set	**2/-**

REPAIRS
Repairs of all descriptions carefully carried out
Special quotations given to Clubs

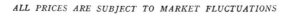

ALL PRICES ARE SUBJECT TO MARKET FLUCTUATIONS

SPORTS AND GAMES DEPARTMENT
Complete Equipment for the Bowling Green

TAYLOR ROLPH LAWN BOWLS

'The Empire'	..	..	per pair	**40/-**
'The Drake'	..	..	,,	**30/-**

JAQUES SPECIAL QUALITY LAWN BOWLS

Made from extra heavy wood of the finest growth and quality. Fitted with real Ivory Mounts Richly ornamented

Any size and Bias	..	..	per pair	**42/6**
Extra quality	..	..	,,	**40/-**
Special Club	..	..	,,	**34/-**
Club Quality	..	..	,,	**32/6**

BOWLER'S BAG
Finest grained Cowhide leather

Round pattern	..	each	**7/6**
Brown or Green Canvas	..	,,	**4/6**

BOWLING SETS
'TOURNAMENT' SET

Containing four pairs of $5\frac{3}{16}$ ins. Match Bowls, black with Ivory number plates, each Bowl of standard size, weight and bias, and bearing the official stamp of the English Bowling Association. Complete with two China Jacks and Books of Laws In Iron-bound case .. **£7 15 0**

THE 'ASSOCIATION' SET

Consisting of eight Bowls. French polished, two Jacks. Complete with Rules in box **£5 10 0**
THE 'CLUB' SET, similar to above **63/-**

WIRE BOUNDARY NETTING

(Improved pattern) consisting 2 each 30 yards and 37 yard lengths, 6 ins. deep, with sufficient stout galvanised detachable iron supports for fixing Set complete **115/-**

SLAZENGER'S BOWLS

The Stadium	..	per pair	**40/-**
Extra Quality Match	..	,,	**35/-**
Club Quality, pair	..	,,	**32/6**

MISCELLANEOUS

Bowling Green Overshoes, per pair			**5/6**
Rubber Mats, each	..	..	**6/3**
Bowl Measures, each	..	**2/6 & 3/6**
Rules of Bowls	..	..	**6d**

ARCHERY NEEDS FROM HARRODS

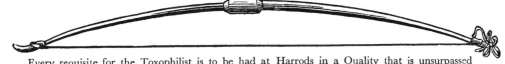

Every requisite for the Toxophilist is to be had at Harrods in a Quality that is unsurpassed

BOWS

4 ft. 6 ins.	Best Lancewood	..	..	**8/-**
4 ft. 6 ins.	Best Lancewood	..	..	**8/6**
5 ft. 0 ins.	Best Lancewood	..	..	**9/-**
5 ft. 3 ins.	Ladies'	..	..	**16/-**
6 ft. 0 ins.	Men's ..	..	..	**18/6**
5 ft. 3 ins.	Ladies' Lemonwood	..		**18/-**
6 ft. 0 ins.	Men's Lemonwood	..		**20/3**
5 ft. 3 ins.	Ladies' Lance and Hickory			**24/6**
6 ft. 0 ins.	Men's Lance and Hickory	..		**31/6**
5 ft. 3 ins.	Ladies' Fancy Wood backed			**36/-**
6 ft. 0 ins.	Men's Fancy Wood backed	..		**38/-**
5 ft. 3 ins.	Ladies' three-piece	..		**37/-**
6 ft. 0 ins.	Men's three-piece	..		**39/6**
5 ft. 3 ins.	Ladies' Self Yew	..		**62/-**
6 ft. 0 ins.	Men's Self Yew	..		**84/-**
5 ft. 3 ins.	Ladies' Spanish and Italian Yew		**79/-**
6 ft. 0 ins.	Men's Spanish and Italian Yew	..	**94/-**

TO STRING BOWS

Warning—The flat part of the bow is the outside and should be kept nearest the body in the act of stringing, or bow will in all probability be broken
To String—Hold the bow in the centre by either hand (whichever is more suitable to the archer), place the end on which the string is made a fixture in the hollow of the foot (not resting the bow on the ground), and pull strongly with the hand holding the centre of bow and press the string forward with the other until it reaches the nock made for it in the horn tip

TARGET STANDS New and improved pattern Iron, 5 ft., pair **21/3**, 5 ft. 6 ins., pair **22/6**, 6 ft., pair **23/6**
The strength of the pull of the ladies' bows is between 20 and 30 lbs.
The strength and pull of the men's bows is between 35 and 55 lbs.
TARGETS Superior painted canvas faces, mounted on stout straw bosses, and produced by experienced workmen

24 inch .. per pair **34/-**		42 inch .. per pair **67/6**
30 inch .. ,, **43/-**		48 inch .. ,, **90/-**
36 inch .. ,, **56/-**		

........ARCHERY ACCESSORIES........

ARM GUARDS. Men's	..	..	**4/-**
Ladies', plain Green, lined	..	..	**2/10**

CHILDREN'S ARCHERY SETS Bow and Arrows on cardboard with target face, 3 ft. 3 ins. Bow **11/3**

QUIVER BELTS	Ladies' **5/6**;	Men's **5/9**,	**6/6**
IVORY TABLETS	..	..	**2/3**
WOOD-SPRING PRICKERS	..	..	**1/3**
Green Tassels to wipe the dirt from the arrows when drawn from the ground ..	..	**2/3**
Ladies' Bow Strings, best whipped Flemish	..	**2/6**
Men's Bow Strings, best whipped Flemish	..	**2/10**
Baize Bow Bags, Men's	..	..	**4/-**
Baize Bow Bags, Ladies'	..	..	**3/9**
Scoring Cards	..	per doz.	**1/3**
Instruction Book	..	,,	**1/-**

ARROWS

21 in.	Painted and polished	..	per doz.	**5/9**
24 in.	Painted and polished	..	,,	**6/-**
25 in.	¼-Knocks, polished	..	,,	**8/6**
21 in.	½-Knocks, polished	..	,,	**8/9**
28 in.	¼-Knocks, polished	..	,,	**9/-**
25 in.	¾-Knocks, polished	..	,,	**10/-**
28 in.	¾-Knocks, polished	..	,,	**10/6**
22 in.	Youth's best Pine painted	..	,,	**12/6**
25 in.	Ladies' best painted and Gilt		,,	**16/-**
28 in.	Men's	..	,,	**16/6**
28 in.	Men's painted between feathers		,,	**29/-**
25 in.	Ladies' Pine footed	..	,,	**39/-**
25 in.	Ladies' best	..	,,	**45/-**
28 in.	Men's best	..	,,	**46/-**

ARROW BOXES To hold 12 Ladies' or Men's full size arrows **6/6**

WOOD GREASE CUPS **1/3**

TO UNSTRING BOWS

The same attitude to be observed as when stringing, only pulling with the one hand and pressing with the other, so as to slacken the string, which should then be slipped out of the nock by the forefinger. When the shooting is over, the bow should be unstrung. The bow must not be left or kept in a damp situation and when not in use should always be kept in a bag

---

ALL PRICES ARE SUBJECT TO MARKET FLUCTUATIONS

HARRODS LTD

Telephone SLOANE 1234
Telegrams '*EVERYTHING HARRODS LONDON*'

LONDON S W 1

SPORTS AND GAMES DEPARTMENT
Polo Kit and all Accessories can Always be Obtained from Harrods

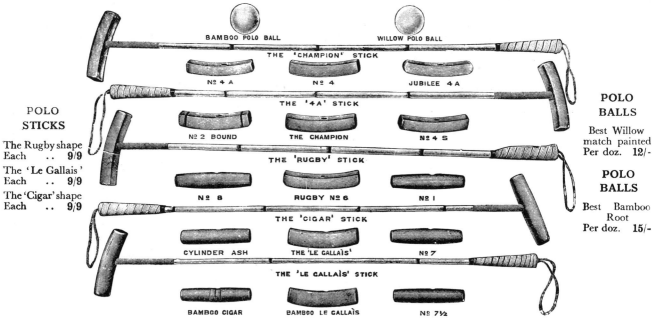

BAMBOO POLO BALL   WILLOW POLO BALL

THE 'CHAMPION' STICK

Nº 4 A   Nº 4   JUBILEE 4 A

THE '4A' STICK

Nº 2 BOUND   THE CHAMPION   Nº 4 S

THE 'RUGBY' STICK

Nº 8   RUGBY Nº 6   Nº 1

THE 'CIGAR' STICK

CYLINDER ASH   THE 'LE GALLAIS'   Nº 7

THE 'LE GALLAIS' STICK

BAMBOO CIGAR   BAMBOO LE GALLAIS   Nº 7½

POLO STICKS

The Rugby shape
Each .. 9/9

The 'Le Gallais'
Each .. 9/9

The 'Cigar' shape
Each .. 9/9

POLO BALLS

Best Willow
match painted
Per doz. 12/-

POLO BALLS

Best Bamboo
Root
Per doz. 15/-

POLO STICKS made from the finest Rattan Canes. Well shaped handles fitted with strong wrist thongs. Heads of specially selected Sycamore, Willow or Ash

Prices of all accessories will gladly be quoted on request

RELIABLE KITES OF EVERY DESCRIPTION

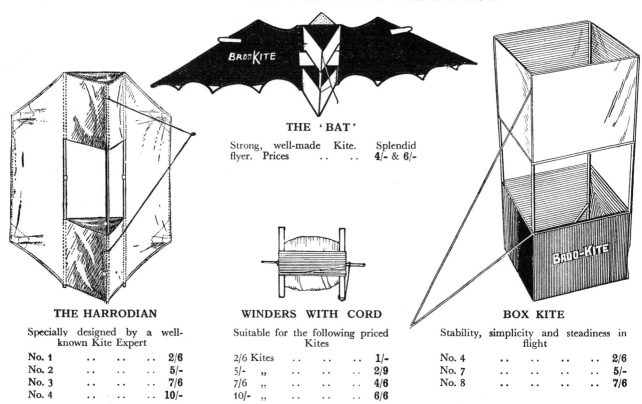

THE 'BAT'

Strong, well-made Kite. Splendid flyer. Prices .. .. 4/- & 6/-

THE HARRODIAN

Specially designed by a well-known Kite Expert

No. 1	..	..	.. 2/6
No. 2	..	..	.. 5/-
No. 3	..	..	.. 7/6
No. 4	..	..	.. 10/-

WINDERS WITH CORD

Suitable for the following priced Kites

2/6 Kites	..	..	.. 1/-
5/- ,,	..	..	.. 2/9
7/6 ,,	..	..	.. 4/6
10/- ,,	..	..	.. 6/6

BOX KITE

Stability, simplicity and steadiness in flight

No. 4	..	..	.. .. 2/6
No. 7	..	..	.. .. 5/-
No. 8	..	..	.. .. 7/6

ALL PRICES ARE SUBJECT TO MARKET FLUCTUATIONS

HARRODS LTD   *Telephone SLOANE 1234*
Telegrams 'EVERYTHING HARRODS LONDON'   LONDON S W 1

SPORTS AND GAMES DEPARTMENT
Healthy Outdoor Games for Limited Spaces

SPORTS AND GAMES DEPARTMENT

Every Croquet Player should be Interested in these Splendid Sets

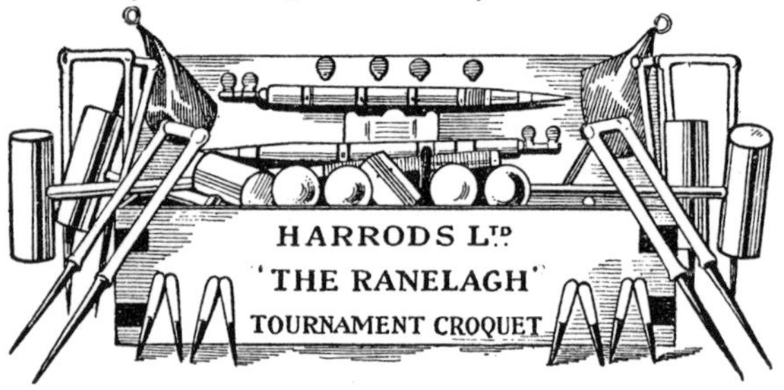

HARRODS 'RANELAGH' TOURNAMENT CROQUET SET

Containing four superior Boxwood Mallets, with Whipcord bound cane, spliced octagon handles, 9 × 3-inch heads, six Hoops, 3⅞ × ⅝-inch, the latest Turning and Winning Posts, four Spring Clips, four Corner Flags, eight Boundary Pegs, Hoop Gauge, Drill Hammer, Book of Association Laws, and all requisites for setting out Match Croquet Grounds. Complete in stout box, fitted with Composition Balls **£7 19 6**

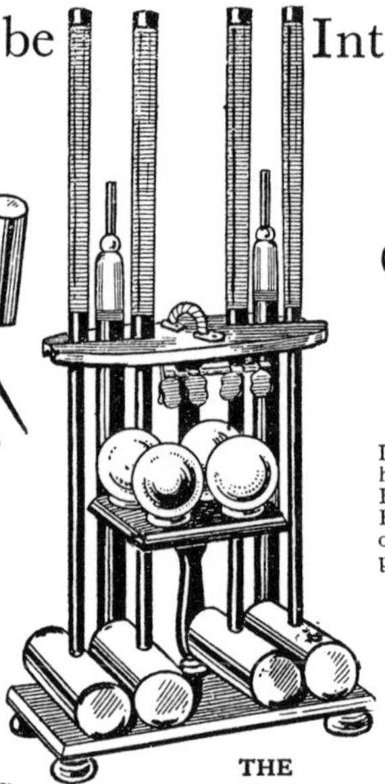

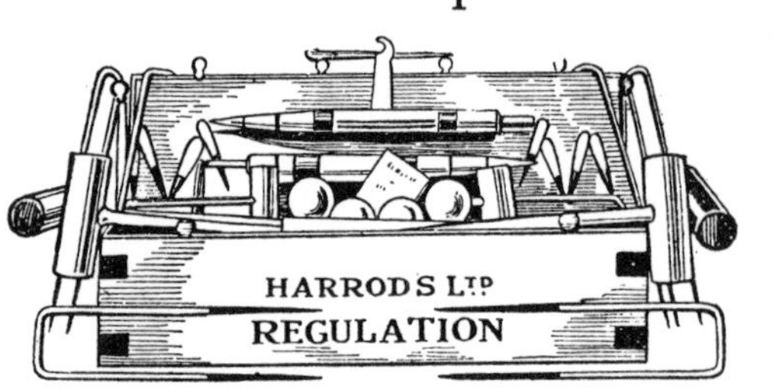

HARRODS REGULATION CROQUET SET

Including four superior French polished Boxwood Mallets, 9 × 3 ins. heads, with English Ash octagonal handles; four best Composition Balls 3⅝ ins. diameter; six enamelled Hoops, ⅝ in. iron, 3¾ ins. wide; Boxwood Hammer, Iron Drill, Starting and Turning Pins, and a copy of Laws of Croquet, in strong iron-clamped box. All implements painted regulation colours **£4 10 0**

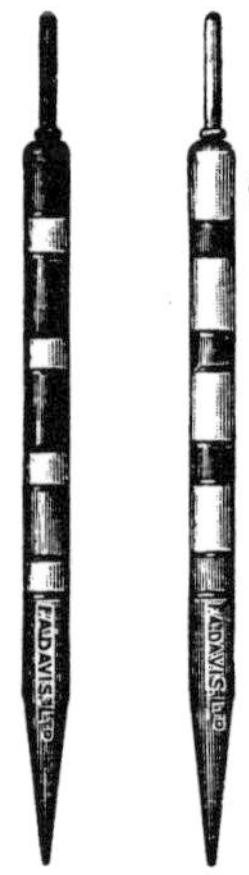

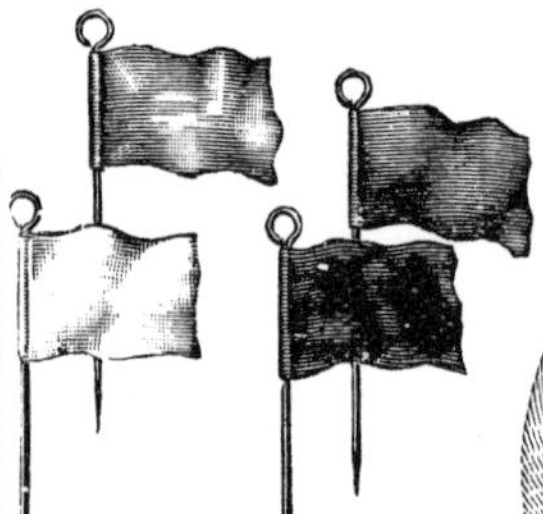

IRON STANDARDS

With best bunting flags in Association colours
The set **3/6**

CROQUET CLIPS

Composition .. **5/6**

CROQUET TURNING AND WINNING POSTS

Best finish, Association colours: fitted removable Clip Pegs **5/6**
With steel shoes **6/9**

THE 'SIMPLEX' CROQUET COURT MARKER

The tank is of Cast Iron and constructed with dished bottom. Self scraping. Capacity approx. 5 pints .. .. .. Each **18/-**

THE 'ECLIPSE' BOUNDARY NETTING

Two lengths each of 7 ins. Tarred Cord Netting, fitted with top and bottom straining lines, thumb-screws at ends, patent holding-down pins and slides. Four corner ground sockets and removable uprights, eight removable bracket arms to carry the wire straining lines Price, complete for one full-sized Croquet Court **110/-**

WIRE NETTING BOUNDARY

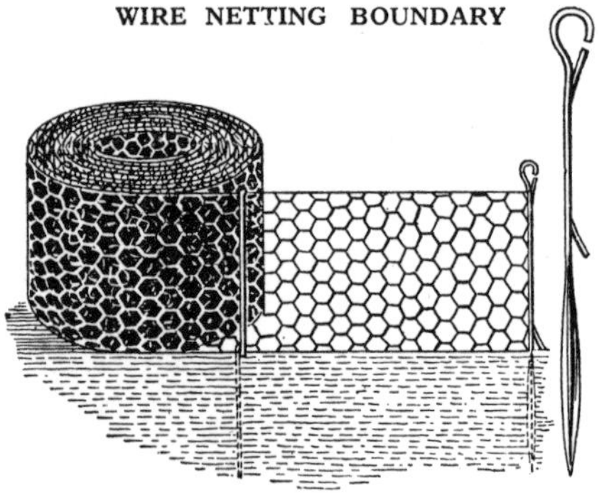

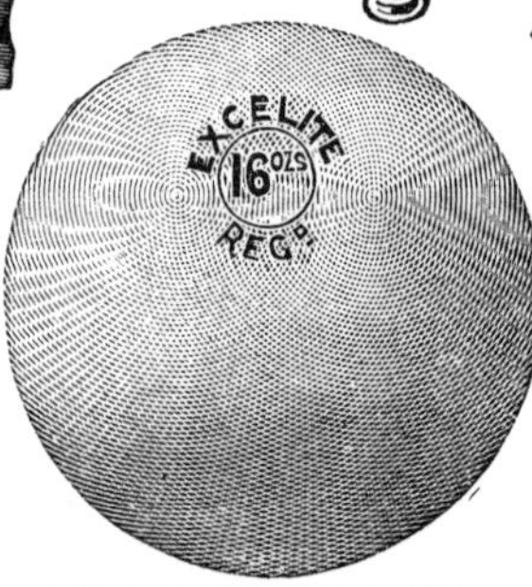

'EXCELITE' CROQUET BALL

The new composition ball, guaranteed perfect in every way, conforming to the rules and regulations of the Croquet Association.
The 'Tournament' Ball .. **37/6**
The 'Practice' **32/-**

'CHAMPIONSHIP' COMPOSITION CROQUET BALLS

F. H. Ayres' .. Set **45/-**
Slazenger's Stadium Composition Balls .. .. Set **36/-**

COMPOSITION CROQUET BALLS

Regulation colours. Impervious to damp. The set **21/-**

'F. H. AYRES'

Once used. Championship Balls. Set **27/6**

WIRE NETTING BOUNDARY

The netting is now supplied with detachable wire supports, which renders it more portable, and in case of damage can be more easily straightened or renewed than hitherto. The supports are easily pressed into the ground with the hand, consequently the netting can be quickly set up and packed away after play, without leaving any holes in lawn

Prices: WIRE NETTING (improved pattern) consisting each of 30 yard and 37 yard lengths, 6 ins. deep, with the necessary number of stout detachable iron supports **100/-**

THE 'WIMBLEDON' CROQUET STAND

To hold four Mallets, four Balls, Starting and Turning posts as illustration .. **40/6**

THE 'CARLTON' CROQUET STAND

In Birch .. **25/-**

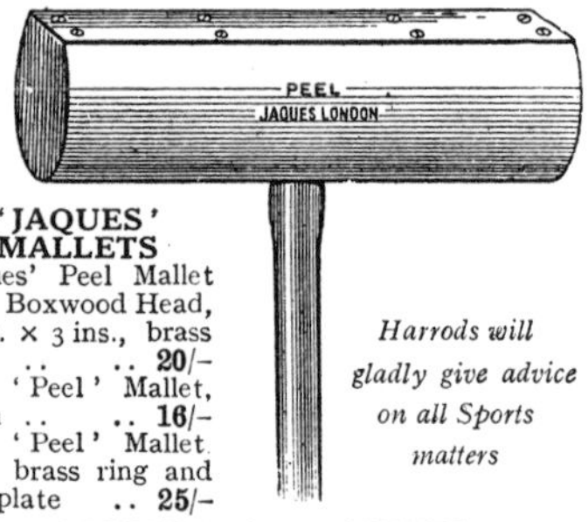

'JAQUES' MALLETS

Jaques' Peel Mallet with Boxwood Head, 9 ins. × 3 ins., brass base **20/-**
The 'Peel' Mallet, plain **16/-**
The 'Peel' Mallet with brass ring and sole plate .. **25/-**

Harrods will gladly give advice on all Sports matters

ASSOCIATION MALLETS

Slazenger's 'Corbally' with Lignum Head **17/6**
Slazenger's 'Corbally' with Boxwood Head **15/-**
Slazenger's 'Corbally' with Lignum Head and Brass Rings **23/6**
Slazenger's 'Corbally' with Boxwood Head and Brass Rings **21/-**
'WIMBLEDON' MALLET .. **13/6**

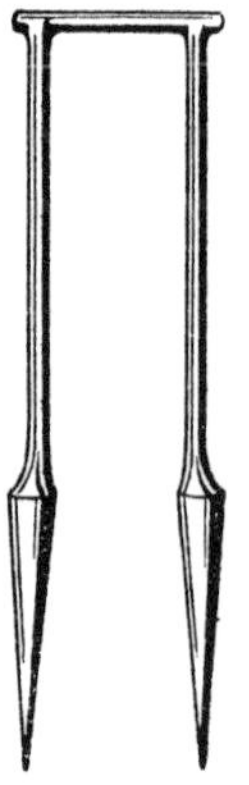

'DAVIDSON' CROQUET HOOPS

As used in the Championship Meetings and the principal Tournaments throughout the Kingdom for twelve seasons.
3¾ ins. wide × ⅝ in. thick **51/-**
3¾ ins. wide × ½ in. thick **39/6**

'WIMBLEDON' HOOPS

3¾ ins. × ⅝ ins. Set .. **12/6**

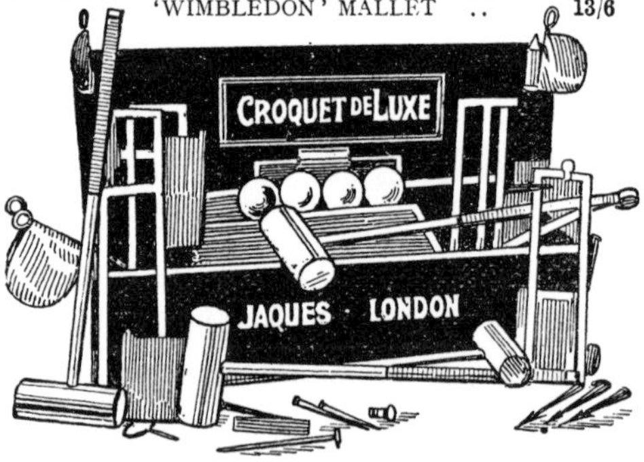

CROQUET DE LUXE

No. 101

The materials contained in this set are of the very finest quality and finish, and of the latest Regulation pattern. Containing four Mallets, brass bound, of the famous Snell type, set of four 3⅝ ins. 'Eclipse' Composition Balls, set of six 3¾ ins. or 4 ins. by ⅝ ins. Association Hoops with Twin Drill and Hammer, pair of Association Starting and Turning Pegs with vertical clip Rests, set of 'Midget' Composition Clips, Bunting Corner Flags, Boundary Pegs, Ball marking Pegs and Rules, the whole being enclosed in a Superior Box .. **£10 0 0**

JUVENILE CROQUET

15/9, 18/6, 22/6, 31/6 per set

MALLET CASE

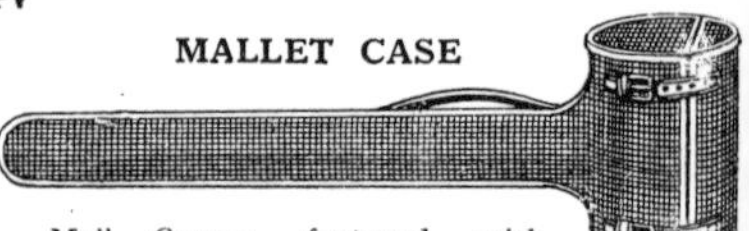

Mail Canvas, fastened with leather straps **9/-**

'RULES OF CROQUET' **6d**

CROQUET BALL STAND

In Mahogany or Walnut, with brass fittings, to hold four balls and four clips **11/6**

CROQUET PAINTING COMPENDIUMS

The proper treatment of Croquet Balls is a most important matter, and well worth the attention of players. An essential point towards their preservation is to keep them covered with paint to prevent the action of the air or sun from affecting the wood. They should, as soon as the paint shows any sign of wear, be retouched. This Compendium contains sufficient paint to entirely repaint one set of balls Each **10/6**

ALL PRICES ARE SUBJECT TO MARKET FLUCTUATIONS

SPORTS AND GAMES DEPARTMENT
Offers from the Well-Equipped Boating Section
Samples of boats as under usually on show

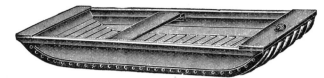

ROWING DINGHIES Strongly built with elm keel, oak stem and stern post, elm transome, elm or larch planking, ash timbers. English oak gunwale, yellow pine thwarts. Fully copper fastened throughout; one galvanized ring bolt in bow galvanized keel and stern band; one pair galvanized rowlocks; one pair sculls
Finished four coats of varnish inside and out

7 ft.	..	£13 10 0	8 ft...	.. £14 15 0	9 ft...	.. £16 10 0
10 ft.	..	£18 5 0	11 ft.	.. £19 15 0	12 ft.	.. £21 10 6

SAILING DINGHIES £10 extra on above prices.
PRAM DINGHIES Same specification as above.

7 ft.	..	£11 12 6	8 ft...	.. £13 2 6	9 ft...	.. £14 12 6

STEEL PUNTS (To Order)
Green painted Galvanized Steel. The gunwales, false bottom and seat are of wood. The bottom being of corrugated steel, it is wonderfully strong, and the corrugations running longitudinally do not retard the progress of the craft, but tend to keep it straight. Sides and bottom are rivetted in galvanized angle steel, which also adds to the rigidity. Sides constructed of one piece galvanized sheet steel, the bottom of two pieces, and consequently there are few joints—these are closely rivetted and doubly seamed. The false bottom is of strong laths fixed in four sections. The middle seat is portable so that it can be removed if the punt is required for weed cutting or netting fish £18 18 0
Extra Rowlocks. Pair 7/–   Ash Oars .. Pair 37/6   Punt Poles Each 20/-

---

CANOES

DOUBLE-HEADED SHOOTING PUNT
(To Order)
For Wild Fowling. 10 ft. × 3 ft. 2 ins. beam, depth 14 ins. Built to row either way, portable thwart and removable floor boards, one pair sculls, one pair rowlocks, deck each end £19 10 0

When writing for particulars of Second-hand Boats and Punts please state full requirements.

CANADIAN CANOES Specially imported. Built of Bass Wood and supplied with two paddles

	14 ft. ..	.. £17 10 0	14½ ft. ..	.. £17 15 0	
15 ft. ..	£18 0 0	15½ ft. ..	£18 10 0	16 ft. ..	£19 0 0

Canoe Fittings extra on above prices See below

CUSHIONS Per set of three .. 40/–		**BACK RESTS** Hinged .. Each 10/–	
CARPETS FOR FLOOR From 50/–		**MATTING** 17/6	
SAIL AND MAST 60/–		**DUST COVERS..** 30/–	

THAMES PUNTS (*not illustrated*)   24 ft. long, complete with pole, paddle, set of large cushions for floor and back £47 10 0

ROB ROY CANOES
(To Order)
Strongly built to take one person. 9 ft. long by 2 ft. 10 ins. beam
With Paddle **£10 15 0**
Better quality **£15 15 0**

SAND YACHTS
To order only
Suitable for boys up to 8 stone in weight
£18 0 0
For adults
£25 0 0
All Boats are sent Carriage Forward Customers when ordering should give the nearest Station

POND PUNT (To Order) Strongly made. Of Pine, painted, with square ends. Complete with one pair rowlocks and one pair sculls.

8 ft.	..	£12 0 0	9 ft.	..	£13 10 0
10 ft.	..	£18 18 0	12 ft.	..	£24 0 0

CORK CUSHIONS
Covered with White or Green Canvas
Oblong

12 × 8 ins.	12 × 10 ins.
6/–	7/–
14 × 10 ins.	16 × 12 ins.
9/6	12/–

NURSERY PUNT Specially designed for children's use. Very safe and strong, copper fastened. Length 8 ft. Beam 3 ft. 4 ins. Complete with pair of sculls, rowlocks Varnished four coats inside and out (or painted if desired) £14 14 0

PADDLING AND ROWING PUNT
(To Order)

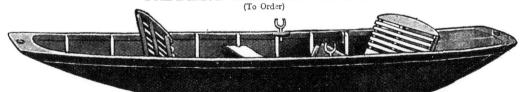

POLES, HOOKS etc.

PUNT POLES Shod complete and varnished

Length 14 ft.	..	22/6
Length 16 ft.	..	24/–

SPRUCE PADDLE BOAT HOOKS

Each	..	15/6

SPRUCE CANADIAN CANOE PADDLES

Varnished	.. Each	10/6
Beech Punt Paddles Each		12/–

Mahogany Sides, Deck and Seats; Oak Floor and Side Timbers; Larch or similar wood Bottom; Gratings throughout and two Backs. The arrangement of Backs provides comfortable seats similar to a Pleasure Punt. Complete with 2 Backs, 4 Cushions, 1 pair Rowlocks, 1 pair of Sculls, Stretcher, Rowing Seat and Paddle
This Punt is stocked in two sizes

14 ft. long by 34 ins. beam	..	..	..	..	..	..	..	..	..	..	£24

This small Punt is much safer than a Canadian Cance, and is very suitable for Children

17 ft. long by 38 ins. beam	..	..	..	..	..	..	..	..	..	..	£28
20 ft.	..	..	..	..	..	..	..	..	..	..	£32

This size is most suitable for adults

SCULLS
Best quality

6 ft. 0 ins.	..	..	32/–
7 ft. 0 ins.	..	..	33/6
7 ft. 6 ins.	..	..	34/6
8 ft. 0 ins.	..	..	35/6
9 ft. 0 ins.	..	..	37/6
9 ft. 6 ins.	..	..	40/–
10 ft. 0 ins.	..	..	42/6

When ordering, please state if required for square or round Rowlocks

ALL PRICES ARE SUBJECT TO MARKET FLUCTUATIONS

HARRODS LTD

Telephone SLOANE 1234
Telegrams 'EVERYTHING HARRODS LONDON'

LONDON SW1

SPORTS AND GAMES DEPARTMENT
Enjoy the Delights of the River Economically

STARBOARD OR PORT LAMPS
Plain lens

Lens	Back	Galvanised	Copper
4 × 3 in.	5½ × 4½ in.	18/6	26/-
5 × 3½ in.	6 × 5 in.	28/-	31/-
6 × 4½ in.	7½ × 5¾ in.	27/6	35/-
7 × 4½ in.	7¾ × 6½ in.	34/6	43/6

ANCHOR LAMPS
Fitted cone chimney

6 ins. plain, Galvanised	19/-
7 ins.	21/-
6 ins. dioptric	32/6
7 ins.	38/6

BLOCKS
Solid galvanised malleable iron pulley blocks, measured by length
Exclusive of all fittings

Size of Block	1½	1¾	2	2¼	2½ ins.
Dia. of Sheave	⅝	⅞	1	1⅛	1¼ ins.
No. 1 Single with eye	9d	9d	1/-	1/3	1/9
No. 2 Single with eye and becket (oval)	9d	1/-	1/3	1/6	2/-
No. 3 Double with eye only (oval)	1/-	1/4	1/6	2/-	2/6
No. 4 Single with eye and tackle hook (oval)	1/-	1/3	1/6	1/10	2/3
No. 5 Single with eye, tackle hook and becket	1/3	1/6	1/9	2/-	2/3
No. 6 Double with eye and tackle hook	1/6	1/9	2/-	2/6	2/9

THE STOWAWAY FOLDING BOAT

This watercraft can be ready for use in 30 seconds and can be dismantled as quickly. A boat that can be carried on any car or even by hand—a punt that will stow away in a minimum of space—flat against a wall if necessary. No boathouse required. A serviceable folding craft for sea or river, for duck shooting, fishing, etc. Complete with paddle £10 10 0   In Dinghy style   £17 17 0

ANCHOR GLOBE LAMP
Galvanised Copper

6 ins.	..	6 6	8/6
7 ins.	..	7/-	9/-
8 ins.	..	8 3	12/-
9 ins.	..	10 6	14/6

TRICOLOUR LAUNCH LAMP WITH BRACKET

Plain front lens, 5½ × 4 ins. Galvanised	..	22/-
Ditto 6½ ins.	..	30/-
Copper, 5½ ins.	..	28/6
Ditto 6½ ins.	..	36/-

MASTHEAD LAMPS
Plain lens

Lens	Back	Galvanised	Copper
4 × 3½ in.	5½ × 4½ in.	16/-	21/-
5½ × 4 in.	6¼ × 5½ in.	19/-	24/6

PATENT STOCKLESS ANCHORS
Galvanised

4½	7	14	21 lbs.
8/-	12/-	21/6	30/-

GALVANISED ORDINARY ANCHORS

6	10	14	21	28 lbs.
7/6	8/6	12/-	14/6	19/6

Larger sizes to order

DOUBLE-ACTING BAILER OR BILGE PUMP

For Launches, Motor and other Boats. An improved Brass hand pump for quickly and cleanly pumping out bilge water

With Rose at bottom, 18 × 1 ins.					12/6
20 × 1⅜ ins.	..				20/-
27 × 1¾ ins.	..				24/-

With Nozzle to connect Suction Hose

18 × 1 ins.	..	..	..	..	13/6
20 × 1⅜ ins.	..	..	..	..	22/6
21 × 1¾ ins.	..	..	..	..	27/6

With stirrup for foot and Nozzle to connect suction hose

18 × 1 ins.	..	..	..	..	17/6
20 × 1⅝ ins.	..	..	..	..	27/6
27 × 1¾ ins.	..	..	..	..	34/-

Suction Hose, per foot

18 × 1 ins.	..	..	..	..	1/6
20 × 1⅜ ins.	..	..	..	..	1/8
27 × 1¾ ins.	..	..	..	..	2/-

Delivery Hose, per foot

18 × 1 ins.	..	..	..	..	6d
20 × 1⅜ ins.	..	..	..	..	8d
27 × 1¾ ins.	..	..	..	..	1/-

CARROL'S 'WONDER' LIFEBUOYS
Adopted by the Royal Humane Society and approved by the Board of Trade. Weights, in 24-in. size, 6¾ lbs., will support 5 men

24 ins.	..	..	..	19/6
30 ins.	..	..	..	32/6

ORDINARY CORK LIFEBUOYS

18 ins.	..	..	..	10/6
21 ins.	..	..	..	11/6
24 ins.	..	..	..	12/6
27 ins.	..	..	..	13/6
30 ins.	..	..	..	15/-

CARROL'S WONDERFUL WATER WINGS
No inflating required .. 6/-

BRASS BOWL SPIRIT COMPASSES
Brass Bowls in strong dovetailed Hardwood. Splendidly finished

6 ins. box, 3 ins. card	..	34/-
7 ins. box, 3½ ins. card	..	40/-

MEGAPHONE
(Patented and Patents applied for. Registered No. 396,893.) With patent mouthpiece, made of special Fibre Board

No. 00   7 ins. long, fitted with straps 8/6
10 ins. long, fitted with handle in place of strap. Will carry about 200 ft. 8/-
No. 0   15 ins., handle in place of straps. Will carry about 500 ft. 10/-
No. 1   18 ins., handle in place of straps. Will carry about 750 ft. 12/-
No. 2   24 ins., handle in place of straps. Will carry about 1,000 ft. 16/-
No. 3   30 ins., handle in place of straps. Will carry about 1,600 ft. 22/-

SKIFF-HEAD PRAM DINGHY (To order)

CHILDREN'S PADDLE BOATS (To order)

6 ft. × 2 ft. 9 ins. × 15 ins.
Strongly built with Wych, Elm, Oak, or other Hardwood Planking or Oak Frames with Steel Paddle Wheels £10 10 0

Wych, Elm, Oak or other Hardwood Planking on Oak Frames. 7 ft. long 3 ft. beam, 12 ins. deep, with one pair of Sculls, one pair of Rowlocks, and Rudder £12 12 0

ALL PRICES ARE SUBJECT TO MARKET FLUCTUATIONS

HARRODS LTD

Telephone SLOANE 1234
Telegrams 'EVERYTHING HARRODS LONDON'

LONDON S W 1

SPORTS AND GAMES DEPARTMENT
Hammerless Guns—Ejector and Non-Ejector

'WEBLEY' HAMMERLESS EJECTOR GUNS

Proprietary Hammerless Ejector

12 and 16 Bore	£22	0 0
20, 28 and ·410 Bore	£24	0 0

Proprietary Hammerless Non-Ejector

12 and 16 Bore	£16 16	0
20, 28 and ·410 Bore	£18 16	0

'WEBLEY' AIR PISTOL, MARK I
·177 and ·22 calibre

Mark I Air Pistol, ·177
or ·22 .. .. .. £1 10 0
Extra Interchangeable Barrel 10 0

B.S.A. SHOT GUNS

Ejector Model .. **£16 16 0**   Non-Ejector .. **£13 13 0**

B.S.A. AIR RIFLES
·177 Bore .. £4 0 0   ·22 Bore .. £4 10 0
Pellets per 1,000 2 6   Pellets per 1,000 5 0

DOUBLE BARREL HAMMERLESS GUNS. BELGIAN MAKE
Ejector Model, ·12, ·16, ·20 and ·410 £10 10 0   Non Ejector £7 10 0
·410 Single Barrel, Hammer, Folding Gun 45/-   Hammerless 63/-

Shot-Gun Cartridges

The following brands, made at the 'Eley' and 'Kynoch' Factories of Nobel Industries Limited, can be supplied in 12, 16 and 20 gauge. Loaded with standard loads and any size of shot and packed in boxes of twenty-five each

FREE CARRIAGE Quantities of 500 of any Cartridges, 12 to 28 bore, per goods train Carriage Paid to any Station in England and Wales

'ZENITH' Steel lined, Metal lined Cartridge, loaded with 'Smokeless Diamond' or 'E.C.' Powder Per 100 .. **19/6**

'ELEY GRAND PRIX' Smokeless Diamond Loaded with 'Smokeless Diamond' Powder Per 100 .. **15/-**

'PRIMAX' Smokeless Diamond Loaded with 'Smokeless Diamond' Powder Per 100 .. **17/6**

'BONAX' E.C. Powder Loaded with 'E.C.' Powder Per 100 .. **15/-**

ALL PRICES ARE SUBJECT TO MARKET FLUCTUATIONS

HARRODS LTD

Telephone SLOANE 1234
Telegrams 'EVERYTHING HARRODS LONDON'

LONDON S W 1

SPORTS AND GAMES DEPARTMENT

Offers from Harrods Fishing Rod and Tackle Section

This Section is exceptionally well stocked with all requirements for the Angler. Those who cannot come to Harrods should send their orders by post; all enquiries are dealt with by an expert, and customers are assured of a practical interpretation of their needs. When ordering Rods, customers are requested to state length required. *Harrods build rods to order if desired. Time required for Greenhearts about ten days; Split Cane one month*

'THE SPECIAL FLY ROD' Made in Three Pieces, varying in length from 8 feet to 12 feet. Two best Whipped Tops, Snake Rings, Cork Stoppers, Butt Spear, Cane Landing Handle to hold Tops; in Partitioned Bag

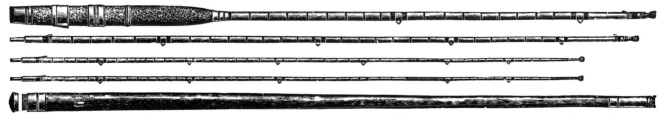

Rods, etc., in the following list are generally in stock, but supply of all patterns cannot be guaranteed at all times

SPLIT CANE SALMON AND GRILSE RODS

Best Quality and Finish

Split Cane, 3 joints, 2 tops in landing handle, double cork handle, best lock joints, rubber button. FT 898

13 feet	14 feet	15 feet	16 feet
175/-	180/-	190/-	200/- each

GREENHEART SALMON AND GRILSE RODS

Best quality, solid winch fittings, rubber button, cork handle lock joints, revolving butt and end rings. FT 353

13 feet	14 feet	15 feet	16 feet
85/-	90/-	95/-	105/- each

SALMON SPINNING AND PRAWNING RODS

Three Joint Greenheart, double cork handle, rubber button, bridge rings throughout, lock joints, 2 tops making 11 ft and 12 ft. FT 5569 .. .. .. **70/-**

Two Joint Best Split Cane Salmon Spinning Rod, best lock joints, agate rings throughout, cork handle, one top, 10 feet Steel centre. Best quality and finish. FT 556.. .. **90/-**

'The Climax' Three Joint Split Cane, double cork handle, agate rings throughout, 2 tops, making 11 ft. and 12 ft. FT 5570
195/-

DAPPING RODS FOR MAY-FLY FISHING

WHOLE CANE DAPPING RODS

Three-Joint Whole Cane Dapping Rod, 2 lancewood tops, single brazed. FT 893 .. .. .. 16 ft. **30/-** ; 17 ft. **40/-**

Three Joint Whole Cane Dapping Rod, 2 Greenheart tops double brazed. FT 894 .. .. 16 ft. **45/-** ; 17 ft. **70/-**

60 yards Undressed Plaited Silk Line **6/-**

Special Pattern Hooks on finest long gut .. per doz. **2/6**

Floating May Flies on Eyed Hooks .. .. ,, **4/-**

All Tackle suitable for May Fly Fishing stocked

BOTTOM AND TROLLING RODS

Four Joint Hickory, brazed and winch fitted, 2 tops, 11 feet FT 690cc **12/6**

Ditto, very superior, 12 ft. FT 690b **25/-**

Three Joint Mottled Cane, extra short top for minnow. 10 feet FT 327d **15/6**

SPLIT CANE TROUT RODS

Three Joint, Best Split Cane, with cork handle, standard bridge rings, agate butt and end rings, rubber button, 2 tops, lock joints, 9, 10 and 10½ ft. FT 1345 .. .. .. **120/-**

TWO-PIECE SPLIT CANE FLY RODS

Two Joint, Best Split Cane, 1 top, agate butt ring and end ring, standard bridge rings, lock joints, 9 ft. and 10 ft. FT 7636 .. .. **120/-**

Three Joint, Greenheart, cork handle, extra short top, superior finish, 10 ft. and 11 ft. FT 5 .. .. **82/6**

GREENHEART FLY RODS

Extra good quality and finish, three joint with cork grip, 2 fly tops, lock joints, 10 ft., 10½ ft., 11 ft. and 12 ft. FT 99 .. .. **82/6**

TROUT SPINNING AND FLY ROD

Harrods Special Rod, selected Greenheart, corkie grip, one fly top and one short top for spinning, 3 joints, snake rings, 10 ft. with lock joints. FT 367 .. .. **50/-**

THE JOHN BICKERDYKE ROD

This Rod has been produced with a view to covering most styles of fishing. It is made of Cane, with Greenheart tops, and is fitted with an interchangeable butt which admits the rod being used in a number of lengths from 7 ft. 6 ins. to 14 ft. A practical Rod for Roach, Perch, Bream, Pike and Sea Fishing; well-balanced and light, and the cheapest Rod yet produced. Revolving rings, best cork handle, superior fittings .. **45/-**

ASH BOTTOM RODS

Three Joints, Snake Rings, Stained, Brazed, in bag. FT.B 94a

9 feet	10 feet	11 feet	12 feet
7/6	9/6	11/6	12/- each

Four Joints, Ringed, Stained, Brazed, 2 tops in bag, 12 ft. FT.B 109 .. .. **15/-**

MOTTLED CANE BOTTOM RODS

With Balance Handles in Bags

Three Joints, Snake Rings, Brazed, 2 tops. FT.B 319a
10 feet **14/6** ; 12 feet **17/6**

Harrods undertake Repairs of all kinds to Rods, Reels, etc. Full estimates given free

ALL PRICES ARE SUBJECT TO MARKET FLUCTUATIONS

HARRODS LTD

Telephone SLOANE 1234
Telegrams 'EVERYTHING HARRODS LONDON'

LONDON S W 1

SPORTS AND GAMES DEPARTMENT
Naturalists', Taxidermists' and Entomologists' Section

Harrods retain a staff of competent and skilful Taxidermists and are prepared to undertake the Modelling of Big Game Heads and the artistic mounting of Animals, Birds, Fish, and Reptiles as Trophies, Museum Specimens or Ornaments, at moderate prices. Experts will gladly be sent to Customers' own residences (town or country) to examine and report upon Trophies, the arrangement of Collections, or upon the periodical attention which is absolutely necessary with Stuffed Birds, Heads, Rugs, etc. Fullest Estimates given on request

HEADS and HORNS, also FOX, HARE, BADGER or OTTER MASKS mounted on Oak Shields
HORSES' HOOFS, DEER SLOTS, FOX, HARE or OTTER PADS cured and mounted in various styles

FOX BRUSHES and OTTER RUDDERS cured and mounted
BIRDS and ANIMALS of all descriptions preserved and artistically mounted for decorative purposes
SKINS cured and mounted as Rugs or for Wall Decoration.

EVERY DESCRIPTION OF TAXIDERMIST WORK undertaken

Note—Customers are particularly requested to ask for written estimates, as verbal ones are necessarily only approximate, and cannot be recognised as final under any circumstances. When sending specimen Birds or Animals in the flesh, or Fish, intended for preservation or mounting, please address to Naturalist Department, Harrods Ltd., Brompton Road, S.W.1

HINTS TO NATURALISTS

If the following simple directions are observed in sending specimens for preparation it will ensure the latter reaching us in good condition. Animal Skins, if freshly taken off, should be laid out in the open air (not in the sun) skin side up, until they can be despatched to us, which should be done as quickly as possible. Fold up the skin, hair outwards; use some straw or shavings to prevent parts of the skin coming together. If the weather is very hot, sprinkle some salt on the skin as soon as it is taken off the animal. Always keep skins, heads, etc., as dry as possible. As many which have been partly dressed by natives do not always turn out so satisfactorily as might be desired after dressing and softening, Customers are informed that Harrods *cannot take any responsibility in this respect.* ALL SKINS DRESSED BY US GO THROUGH EXACTLY THE SAME PROCESS Fox Brushes should have a tapered piece of wood inserted into them after the tail is drawn out

DRESSING AND CURING. Nearly all work in Natural History must be allowed a considerable time for drying, so that it is in most cases impossible to return specimens in a few days

A SELECTION OF NATURALISTS' REQUISITES

Harrods can supply every need of the Naturalist and every item is of trustworthy Quality. British and Exotic Lepidoptera supplied, and Cabinets of every description made to order if desired

STORE BOXES
Deal. With Camphor cells. Best make, papered and corked

10 × 8 ins. ..	**4/6**
13 × 9 ins. ..	**6/-**
14 × 10 ins. ..	**7/6**
16 × 11 ins. ..	**9/-**
17½ × 12 ins. ..	**10/6**

CLIMBING IRONS
For Bird Nesting, with straps complete
Per pair .. **7/6**

SETTING HOUSES
Plain Deal drying house with ten corked setting boards (various sizes), drawers for pins, perforated zinc door, brass handles at top (12 × 9 × 5 ins.) Each **18 6**

Larger size (14 × 10 × 5 ins.) .. Each **21/-**

Corked at back and answering as store box. (To order) Each **25/6**

INSECT & BUTTERFLY CABINETS
NH 22 Corked, glazed and papered
Suitable for beginners

Drawers	Height	Width	
4	12 ins.	13 ins.	.. **25/6**
6	16½ ins.	15 ins.	.. **33/6**
8	22 ins.	18 ins.	.. **62/6**
10	27½ ins.	19½ ins.	.. **90/-**

INSECT CASES
(To hang)

NH 32 Corked and papered, glass frame top. In polished Deal to imitate Mahogany. The following sizes usually in stock; outside measurements given

10 × 8 ins. ..	**4/6**	16 × 12 ins. ..	**9/6**
13 × 9 ins. ..	**6/-**	18 × 14 ins. ..	**11/-**
14 × 10 ins. ..	**7/6**	18 × 18 ins. ..	**12/6**
16 × 10 ins. ..	**9/-**		

CABINETS FOR BIRDS' EGGS
NH 20 Suitable for beginners. Made in Deal, polished and stained

Drawers	Height	Width		Price
4	13 ins.	12 ins.	.. ..	**25/6**
6	18 ins.	15 ins.	.. ..	**33/6**
8	25 ins.	19 ins.	.. ..	**62/6**
10	33 ins.	22 ins.	.. ..	**90/-**

NH 24 Glazed Cases with Wooden Partitions for Birds' Eggs. Made to hang up. In polished Imitation Mahogany

10 × 8 ins. ..	**4/6**	16 × 12 ins. ..	**9/6**
13 × 9 ins. ..	**6/-**	18 × 14 ins. ..	**11/-**
14 × 10 ins. ..	**7/6**	18 × 18 ins. ..	**12/6**
16 × 10 ins. ..	**9/-**		

BUTTERFLY NETS
All splendidly made and finished. Plain Cane with net and stick and brass Y

Small size .. .. Each	**4/6**
Large size .. .. ,,	**5/6**

Three-piece, Folding Ring, brass Y, net and stick

Small size .. .. Each	**5 6**
Large size .. .. ,,	**7/6**
Kite or Balloon Net .. .. ,,	**9 6**

SETTING BOARDS
These are available in various sizes; corked
All are 1 ft. 2 ins. long

½ in. ..	..	**9d**	2¼ ins. ..	.. **1/9**
¾ in. ..	..	**9d**	2½ ins. ..	.. **1 9**
1 in. ..	..	**1/-**	3 ins. ..	.. **2/-**
1¼ ins. ..	..	**1/4**	3½ ins. ..	.. **2/-**
1½ ins. ..	..	**1/4**	4 ins. ..	.. **2/-**
1¾ ins. ..	..	**1/6**	4½ ins. ..	.. **2/-**
2 ins. ..	..	**1/6**	5 ins. ..	.. **2 6**

ENTOMOLOGICAL PINS
Mixed Pins, four sizes (white) .. per oz. **3/-**

CABINETS
Corked, glazed and papered. For Minerals, Shells, Fossils, etc.

4 Drawers, 13 × 12 × 9 ins.	**25/6**
6 ,, 18 × 15 × 9½ ins.	**33/6**
8 ,, 25 × 19 × 11 ins.	**60/-**

Any size made to order

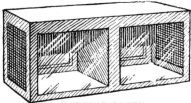

BREEDING CAGES

Larva breeding cages .. .. .. Each	**4/6**
Two compartments .. .. .. ,,	**9/6**
On new principle, one door .. .. ,,	**6/6**
Larger (to order only) .. .. ,,	**12/6**

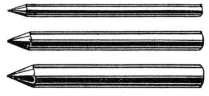

EGG COLLECTORS' REQUISITES

EGG DRILLS All sizes .. .. .. Each	**3d**
Rose Top Egg Drills with wood handles .. ,,	**1/-**
EGG BLOW PIPES Brass or glass Each **6d** and	**1/-**

EGG LIFTERS, OR OOLOGISTS' FORCEPS
Each **6d**

ALL PRICES ARE SUBJECT TO MARKET FLUCTUATIONS

SPORTS AND GAMES DEPARTMENT
Installation of any Gymnasia Estimated for on Application

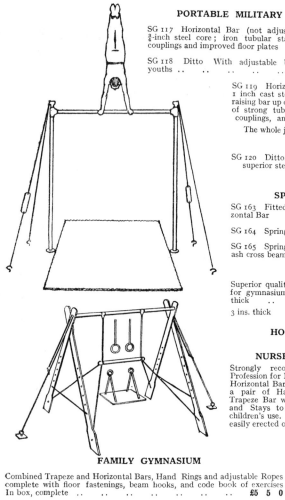

PORTABLE MILITARY HORIZONTAL BAR

SG 117 Horizontal Bar (not adjustable) of best Ash, fitted with ¾-inch steel core; iron tubular standards, japanned; iron stays, couplings and improved floor plates **£4 17 0**

SG 118 Ditto With adjustable bar for vaulting. Suitable for youths **£6 0 0**

SG 119 Horizontal Bar of best Ash, covering 1 inch cast steel core, with arrangement for raising bar up or down for vaulting. Standards of strong tubular iron, iron stays, screw couplings, and improved floor fastenings

The whole japanned any colour to order

£6 8 0

SG 120 Ditto. With tubular standards of superior steel, the whole highly finished

£6 15 0

SPRING BOARDS

SG 163 Fitted with hooks to fix to Horizontal Bar **26/6**

SG 164 Spring Board **28/6**

SG 165 Spring Board of Ash or Hickory with ash cross beam and blocks **36/6**

MATS

Superior quality Fibre Mats, expressly made for gymnasium use, 6 ft. × 4 ft. × 2½ ins. thick **60/-**

3 ins. thick **68/-**

HORIZONTAL BAR
WITH
NURSERY ATTACHMENT

Strongly recommended by the Medical Profession for Nursery use. This comprises a Horizontal Bar with steel core for adult use, a pair of Hand Rings (leather covered), Trapeze Bar with steel core, Sitting Swing, and Stays to form a Horizontal Bar for children's use. Indoor and outdoor. Can be easily erected or taken down in a few minutes

£8 15 0

FAMILY GYMNASIUM

Combined Trapeze and Horizontal Bars, Hand Rings and adjustable Ropes complete with floor fastenings, beam hooks, and code book of exercises In box, complete **£5 5 0**

TRAPEZE BARS

Trapeze Bar only, Iron Core and Iron ends .. Each **8/6**

Trapeze Bar, Steel Core Each **10/-**

Trapeze Bar, Steel Core and Brass ends .. Each **16/6**

Special prices are quoted to Clubs and Institutions

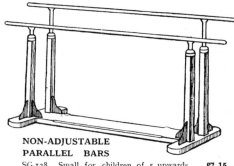

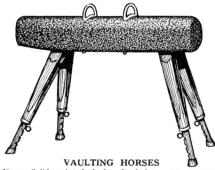

NON-ADJUSTABLE PARALLEL BARS

SG 128 Small, for children of 5 upwards		**£7 15 0**
SG 130 Suitable for School use		**£8 13 0**
SG 131 Full size		**£9 4 0**
SG 132 With platform		**£11 10 0**
SG 136 Adjustable Bars, with platform ..		**£13 15 0**

VAULTING HORSES

No. 1 Solid painted body, fixed legs, no pommels **£7 14 0**

No. 2 Solid painted body, adjustable legs, no pommels **£8 11 6**

No. 3 Leather covered body, 4 ft. long, fixed legs, no pommels, adjustable legs **£9 6 0**

No. 4 Leather covered body, 5 ft. long, adjustable legs, covered pommels **£12 10 0**

No. 5 The 'Military,' 6 ft. long, leather covered body, adjustable legs, complete with leather-covered pommels **£17 10 0**

MATTRESSES

Mattresses of best Canvas, stuffed with best cocoa fibre, quilted and fitted with canvas handles, 6 ft. × 4 ft. × 4 ins. thick **58/6**

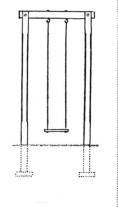

JUMPING STANDS

SG 174 Jumping Stand, Varnished Deal. 6 ft. high **30/-**

SG 176 7 ft. high. Cast Iron bases **29/6**

SG 177 8 ft. high. Heavy bases **54/-**

SG 178 10 ft. high. Heavy bases **75/6**

STRONG SWING FRAME

Frame 8 ft. above ground, complete with swing, beam hooks and ropes **£9 17 6**

Frame 10 ft. above ground, complete with swing, beam hooks and ropes **£10 0 0**

Frame 12 ft. above ground, complete with swing, extra strong **£10 12 6**

HAND RINGS

253 Hand Rings only, plain iron (round) .. .. .. Per pair **3/-**

254 Hand Rings only, leather covered .. .. .. ,, **14/-**

255 Hand Rings only, leather covered, stouter .. .. ,, **16/-**

ROPES FOR HAND RINGS AND TRAPEZE BARS

Ropes of best quality Russian Hemp, 2 ins. circumference, as supplied to War Office. 9 ft. over all, fitted with scissor hooks, rings and thimbles **16/6**

As above, adjustable **18/6**

Adult's strong polished hardwood seat Swing with 10 ft. adjustable ropes and hooks and thimbles **26/6**

PLAIN CLIMBING ROPES

3 ins. circumference .. .. .. Per foot run **2/3**

3½ ins. ,, ... ,, ,, **2/9**

4½ ins. ,, ... ,, ,, **3/6**

ALL PRICES ARE SUBJECT TO MARKET FLUCTUATIONS

HARRODS LTD

Telephone SLOANE 1234
Telegrams 'EVERYTHING HARRODS LONDON'

LONDON S W 1

Visit the Sports Salon and Consult the Experts in Attendance

FULL SIZE BILLIARD TABLE

(*Right*) This full size fine Billiard Table has a thick bolted slate bed on a stand and eight massive turned and ornamented legs with raised panels to knees. It is fitted with the latest low and fast frost-proof built up strip 'Resilient' indiarubber cushions, with invisible pocket plates, and is covered with the new superfine West of England Billiard Cloth. In Mahogany or Oak. Complete with:—Twelve Cues, Cue Rest, Long Butt, Half Butt, and Rest, Marking Board, Rules in Frame, Cue Rack, Brush, Iron, Cover, Chalks, Tips, Wafers, and three full size Ivory or guaranteed Composition Billiard Balls .. **£75 0 0**

COMBINED BILLIARD DINING TABLE

Polished Oak or Mahogany, highly finished, with thick slate bed and built up strip low and fast frost-proof indiarubber cushions. Covered with an extra fine Billiard cloth. The loose dining leaves and carved legs are of solid Oak or Mahogany. Fine finish throughout. The simplicity of the construction of the COMBINED BILLIARD DINING TABLE is its chief recommendation. Fitted with screw adjusters so that a perfect level is assured

ACCESSORIES: Four Cues, Brass Headed X Rest, Oak Marking Board, Rules in frame and glazed, Spirit Level and three Ivory or Bonzoline Balls

5 ft. 5 ins. × 2 ft. 11 ins., as Billiard and Dining Table **£22 0 0**
6 ft. 6 ins. × 3 ft. 6 ins., as Billiard and Dining Table **£25 4 0**
7 ft. 4 ins. × 4 ft. 0 ins., as Billiard and Dining Table **£32 10 0**
8 ft. 6 ins. × 4 ft. 6 ins., as Billiard and Dining Table **£42 10 0**

MINIATURE BILLIARD TABLE

(*Not illustrated*) To stand on ordinary table. Supplied complete with two Cues, Billiard Balls, Marking Board. Strongly made, good cushions, covered fine quality green cloth and fitted with adjustable screw feet for levelling. Ideal for children
5 ft. 0 ins. × 2 ft. 6 ins. **£5 15 0**

MINIATURE BILLIARD TABLE

(Lower Priced Quality)

4 ft. × 2 ft. Complete with 2 Cues, Set of Balls and Marking Board .. **63/-**

MINIATURE BILLIARD TABLE

To stand on ordinary dining table. Supplied complete, with two Cues, Ivory Billiard Balls, Marking Board, Rules and Chalk

The above tables are of superior make, correct in every particular, fitted with best slate beds, the latest 'Rapide' cushions and screw adjusting toes for levelling, which can be fitted to suit almost any size dining table

Sets of pyramid and pool balls suitable for the 6 ft. miniature billiard tables can be purchased

5 ft. × 2 ft. 6 ins. .. **£10 14 0** 6 ft. × 3 ft. **£12 0 0**
7 ft. × 3 ft. 6 ins. **£16 10 0**
Stands for above: 5 ft. **£4 0 0** 6 ft. **£4 10 0** 7 ft. **£5 15 0**

BILLIARD REQUISITES

BILLIARD CUES The 'Champion' Ebony butted, full size Each **27/6**
The 'Match' Ebony butted, full size .. .. ,, **22/6**
The 'Joe Davis' .. .. ,, **28/-**
The [illegible] Record .. .. ,, **17/6**
Butted, full size .. .. Each **10/6, 14/6, 16/6**
Best plain Ash .. .. Each **4/6**
Best Ash, 4 ft. .. .. ,, **2/6**
3 ft. 6 ins. .. .. ,, **2/-**
Butted, 4 ft. .. .. ,, **10/6**
CUE CASES Japanned Tin .. .. Each **4/3**
RACK FOR CUES Mahogany, superior make, to hold 6 cues Each **10/6**
9 cues .. .. ,, **22/6**
12 cues .. .. ,, **30/-**
CUE CLIPS For affixing to the wall .. .. Each **5d**
SILK SPOTS .. .. Per box **6d**
STRAIGHT EDGE AND HALF CIRCLE Mahogany **9/6**
SPIRIT LEVEL 6-in. **13/6**, 8-in. **16/6**

CUE TIP FASTENERS

Improved Brass screw top .. .. Each **2/3**
Boxwood, with file and brass ring .. .. ,, **3/9**

CIRCULAR CUE STANDS

For 24 Cues **£8 10 0**
For 18 Cues **£7 0 0**
For 12 Cues **£6 0 0**
For 9 Cues **£4 10 0**
BILLIARD BRUSHES special large size .. .. .. Each **13/6**
Cheaper quality .. .. ,, **9/9**

CRYSTALATE OR BONZOLINE BILLIARD BALLS

Per set .. .. $2\frac{1}{16}$-in. **37/6** .. $2\frac{1}{8}$-in. **42/-** .. .. $1\frac{7}{8}$-in. **13/6**
Best quality $2\frac{1}{8}$-in. Ivory, Per set of three **£5 12 6**
Second quality, to weight, match **£4 5 0**
Best quality, $2\frac{1}{16}$-in. Ivory **£5 12 6**
Second quality, $2\frac{1}{16}$-in. Ivory **£4 5 0**

PYRAMID OR POOL BALLS

First quality, Ivory, $2\frac{1}{16}$-in. .. .. Per ball **22/6**
Second quality, Ivory, $2\frac{1}{16}$-in. .. .. ,, **16/6**
Bonzoline, $2\frac{1}{16}$-in. .. .. ,, **12/6**
Crystalate .. .. ,, **12/6**
BAGATELLE BALLS Crystalate or Bonzoline, set of 9, 1-in. **8/-**, $1\frac{1}{4}$-in. **10/6**, $1\frac{1}{4}$-in. **15/-**, $1\frac{3}{8}$-in. **19/-**, $1\frac{1}{2}$-in. **23/-**, $1\frac{5}{8}$-in. **29/6**, $1\frac{3}{4}$-in. .. **31/6**
FOLDING BAGATELLE BOARDS Indiarubber cushions and complete Balls, Cue, Mace, Bridge and Rules. Superior quality, 6 ft. × 19 ins. **£5 15 0** 7 ft. × 21 ins. **£7 2 6** 8 ft. × 24 ins. **£8 10 0** 9 ft. × 27 ins. **£10 7 6**
TELESCOPIC STANDS (*for above*) 6 ft. **£3 0 0**, 7 ft. **£6 5 0**, 8 ft. **£7 10 0**, 9 ft. **£9 0 0.**
RULES, BILLIARDS, POOL OR PYRAMID Billiards, Pool, Pyramid and Snooker Pool .. .. Each **2/6**
BILLIARD MARKER **22/6**
With Brass rails and runners **60/-**

BILLIARD WATERPROOF COVERS

Waterproof table covers, full size, 15 × 9 ft. **46/6, 72/-, 95/-**
POOL SKITTLES Per set of 10 Boxwood and 2 Ebony **3/6**
Numbered balls for above .. .. Per set **2/9**
Rules with diagram .. .. Each **6d**

TIPPING REQUISITES

CUE TIPS .. .. Per box **1/9**
CUE CEMENT Kay's **7d**
CUE TIP WAFERS .. .. Per box **6d**
FULL SIZE POCKETS Best White Cord .. .. Per set **12/9, 17/6**
RESTS Cross Brass model, fibre tips **7/9**
Spider Brass head, fibre tips **8/6**
REST HEADS Cross Brass model **3/3**
Spider Brass model **3/3**
Shafts to fit heads **4/-**
BILLIARD SHOE AND IRON .. .. .. Small **11/6**; large **16/6**

ALL PRICES ARE SUBJECT TO MARKET FLUCTUATIONS

SPORTS AND GAMES DEPARTMENT

Offers from the Extensive Winter Sports Section

SHAPED SKI

FLAT SKI

Persons of 5 ft. 3 ins. require 6¼ ft. Skis	Persons of 5 ft. 7 ins. require 7 to 7¼ ft. Skis
,, 5 ft. 4 ins. ,, 6¼ to 6½ ft. Skis	,, 5 ft. 9 ins. ,, 7¼ to 7½ ft. ,,
,, 5 ft. 5 ins. ,, 6½ to 6¾ ft. ,,	,, 5 ft. 11 ins. ,, 7½ ft. ,,
,, 5 ft. 6 ins. ,, 6¾ to 7 ft. ,,	,, 6 ft. ,, 7½ ft. ,,

Hickory Ski with shaped top. Best Norwegian make. Extra wide and perfectly balanced. Specially selected sizes from 6 ft. to 7 ft. 6 ins.

Blades .. .. per pair £2 12 6
Bindings fitted to Blades .. .. per pair 2/-
Huitfeldt Bindings fitted, free of charge.

Juvenile Ski complete with Huitfeldt Bindings (Ash Ski Blades). Best quality

48 ins. (120 cm)	.. .. 15/6	65 ins. (165 cm)	.. .. 21/-
52 ins. (130 cm)	.. .. 16/6	70 ins. (175 cm)	.. .. 23/6
56 ins. (140 cm)	.. .. 17/6	74 ins. (185 cm)	.. .. 25/6
62 ins. (155 cm)	.. .. 18/6		

SKI BINDINGS

	Complete
B.B.B. Binding	19/6
ALPINA Binding	18/6
ERIKSON Binding	14/6
GRESVIGS LOIPE Binding	14/6
HAUG Binding	15/6
HUITFELDT Binding with Patent Fram Irons	11/6

SKI WAX

	Per tin
OSTBY KLISTER	1/9
,, SKARE	2/-
,, MIX	1/-
,, MEDIUM	1/-
SOHMS WAX	9d.
PARA-SKI WAX IRONS .. each	7/6

SKI GLOVES

(Sizes for Men and Women)	Per pair
Waterproof Grey Canvas	5/-
,, Sheepskin with Green tops ..	8/6
,, White Kid	13/6
,, Black Horse Hide with Gabardine Cuff	13/6
,, Black Horse Hide, very strong ..	18/6

TOBOGGANS AND SLEDGES

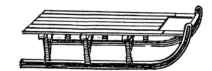

'DAVOS' LUGES Swiss pattern specially imported for

Harrods .. .. each 25/-, 29/-, 34/-, 36/-

When ordering Skis by Post, please give height and weight.

'DIRIGIBLE' FLYER Flexible or Dirigible Fliers, lightly but firmly constructed. Slight pressure of hand or foot on the steering bar is sufficient to guide perfectly. Lengths: 36 ins., 23/-; 40 ins. 26/-; 45 ins., 30/-; 50 ins. 39/-; 62 ins., 45/-

'STAR' TOBOGGANS. Toboggans of regulation Canadian pattern. Lengths: 4 ft., 21/-; 5 ft., 23/-; 6 ft., 27/-; 7 ft., 32/-

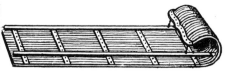

SKI STICKS

Patent 'Caulfield' Metal Ski Sticks, indestructible—
The newest Stick on the market .. per pair 30/-
Bamboo Ski Sticks .. per pair 10/6 and 12/6

SUNDRIES

SKI SCRAPERS	1/-
ALU SKI POINTS .. .. each 5/- 6/-	7/6
SKI SLINGS .. .. .. each	3/6
CAULFIELD TOE IRONS .. .. pair	8/6
CLAMPS & BLOCK with Top Stretcher for keeping Ski when not in use .. .. set	3/9

SKI SKINS

SOHMS SKI SKINS .. per pair	£1 0 0
SKINS with Lever and Hooks per pair	£1 5 0

SNOW SHOES

Women's	per pair	8/6
Men's	per pair	10/6

SKATES

All the latest improvements are embodied in Harrods Roller and Ice Skates. The wide range of different designs provides for individual preference and ensures an accurate fit for every foot

When ordering Ice Skates give length of boot from heel to toe to ensure correct size

'STILLE' SKATE used by many leading Skaters Per pair 63/-

'BORUSSIA' SKATE with pointed and serrated toe
Welded and tempered blades £1 2 6
Ditto with welded tops .. £1 12 6
'Astor' Continental pattern £1 1 0

'Skedskor' Serrated Toe, made in Sweden, with tempered, fine polished hollow ground blades, nickel-plated
per pair £2 2 0

ENGLISH MADE SKATES

'MOUNT CHARLES' Aluminium fittings, polished nickel-plated Acme pattern blades per pair 21/-

'MONIER WILLIAMS' Polished nickel-plated blades and aluminium fittings, 7 ft. radius
per pair 25/-

THE CONTINENTAL FIGURE SKATE
'Continental' Skate, with welded and tempered blades, nickel-plated
per pair £1 2 6
Ditto with welded footplates .. .. per pair £1 12 6

ALL PRICES ARE SUBJECT TO MARKET FLUCTUATIONS

HARRODS LTD

Telephone SLOANE 1234
Telegrams 'EVERYTHING HARRODS LONDON'

LONDON S W 1

SPORTS AND GAMES DEPARTMENT
Fascinating Games that will delight Children of all Ages

TUMBLETTE
A game requiring much skill, endeavouring to manipulate the tumbling men into the best position .. **3/6**

PETER RABBIT'S RACE GAME
Introducing Beatrix Potter's world-famed characters, Peter Rabbit, etc. .. .. .. Each **3/6 and 6/-**

LOTO
Or the great Family Game of 'House.' An old established Christmas favourite .. **2/6, 3/6, 4/-**

BRITISH EMPIRE
This game has a decided educational basis as it familiarises the Players with the positions of the various British Possessions and their products. Board and Pieces in box **3/9, 4/9**

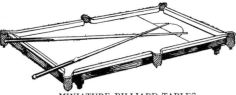

MINIATURE BILLIARD TABLES
Beautifully made with non-warping base oak rails, adjustable legs, good billiard cloth, rubber cushions, etc. Complete with three balls, 2 cues, marker, chalk and rules.
3 ft. × 1 ft. 6 ins. .. **21/-**   3 ft. 6 ins. × 1 ft. 9 ins. **32/-**
4 ft. × 2 ft. .. .. **42/6**   5 ft. × 2 ft. 6 ins. **£4 17 6**

FOLDING BAGATELLE BOARDS
Indiarubber cushions and complete balls, cue, mace, bridge and rules. Superior quality
6 ft. × 19 ins. .. **£6 0 0**   7 ft. × 21 ins. .. **£7 5 0**
8 ft. × 24 ins. .. **£9 0 0**   9 ft. × 27 ins. ..**£10 10 0**

TELESCOPIC STANDS (for above)
6 ft., **80/-**; 7 ft., **96/-**; 8 ft., **110/-**; 9 ft., **130/-**

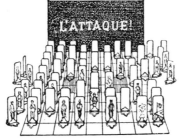

'L'ATTAQUE'
Famous game of military tactics. A fascinating and amusing game for two players. Each player has 36 pieces. Rivals chess in popularity
Each .. .. **4/6, 6/6 and 10/6**

> The newest games always in stock

> Orders by Post promptly executed

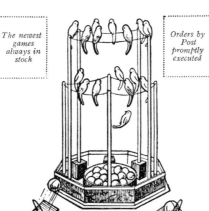

BOM BIRD
A new game. Birds perch on the cords in a life-like manner and fall off when hit, scoring accordingly. Two sizes .. .. **4/6 and 8/6**

WHIRLETTO
(The Original)
An exciting game of chance, played with a top spinning in the centre sending coloured balls flying about the track, and into the corner goals, Full of life from start to finish. A number of different games can be played. Complete with cover and rules.
Retail at .. .. .. each **3/6 and 5/6**

> Purchases value 10/- and over are sent Post Free in England and Wales.

DOVER PATROL
A thrilling game similar to L'Attaque, but using naval warfare .. .. **4/6, 6/6 and 10/6**

THE 'TEST MATCH'
An exciting indoor game. Simple mechanism to operate, giving endless thrills and pleasure as in the real outdoor game. Complete set of instructions with every box
Three sizes **5/6, 7/6, 10/6**

AUTO-GO
The new Motor Race Game for two to six players. A road race with all the advantages and mishaps encountered in real racing. Complete with six cars **3/-**

'WELL QUOITS'
The game to train the straight eye! Suitable for use in clubs and institutes, as well as the home .. .. per set **16/-**

ST. FRANK'S FOOTBALL
An excellent home game closely reproducing the actual game of Football. Can be played on any size table **7/6**

ALL PRICES ARE SUBJECT TO MARKET FLUCTUATIONS

HARRODS LTD

Telephone SLOANE 1234
Telegrams 'EVERYTHING HARRODS LONDON'

LONDON S W 1

SPORTS AND GAMES DEPARTMENT
Always a Splendid Selection of Indoor Games from which to Choose

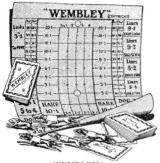

'WEMBLEY'

A most exciting Dog Racing Game in which any number of players can take part **7/6**

SPILLI-WOBBLE

A tantalising yet entrancing ' magnetic ' game, causing a good deal of fun. The more you laugh the more you wobble

For 2 Players **4/6**
,, 4 ,, ... **8/6**

WHIRLIGIG

A simple and amusing game for any number of players **2/6**

MAGNETIC FISHING

The popular outdoor sport adapted to the drawing-room. All the thrills of an Angling Competition without any of its discomforts!

No. 2 .. .. **2/9**
No. 3 .. .. **4/6**

The PRINCES' QUEST
A FASCINATING INSTRUCTIVE FAIRY-TALE GAME.

THE ' PRINCES'' QUEST

There are six different paths by which the Princes set out to seek the Princess: these paths recross one another, and the various experiences that the Princes meet with on their journey embody the chief events culled from all the well-known fairy tales. The board is a work of art, and will, independently of the game, be interesting to children **5/9 and 8/9**

MIDGET GOLF

Golf enthusiasts to whom this game has been submitted pronounce it as near the outdoor game as possible. The ball, which is light, cannot damage ornaments. Can be hit with great precision by the practised hand **3/9, 7/9, 11/6**

FAVOURITE RACE GAME

An exciting game of skill, racing horses along the table **3/-**

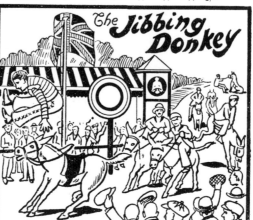

JIBBING DONKEY. One of the very best shooting games. The marksman shoots through the centre hole, releasing the donkey, which springs up and throws the rider over his head **3/3**

A NEW GAME
SPIN-JENNY
A SCORING GAME OF ABSORBING INTEREST

SPIN-JENNY

A top is spun amongst the balls and knocks them into the holes, which are numbered.. .. **10/6**

POP-SHOTS

An amusing game of skill for young and old, played with a small, harmless air-gun The set, **5/6**

'SPINGOFF'

A new form of Table Golf which provides all the thrills of the older game yet allows every player to play with an equal chance of success **15/6 and 21/-**

HUMPTY DUMPTY

Players endeavour to get Humpty to travel down strings and to seat him securely on a wall by an ingenious method. Four players **3/9**

ALL PRICES ARE SUBJECT TO MARKET FLUCTUATIONS

HARRODS LTD

Telephone SLOANE 1234
Telegrams ' EVERYTHING HARRODS LONDON '

LONDON S W 1

SPORTS AND GAMES DEPARTMENT

All New Games are Demonstrated in Harrods Sports Section

ROULETTE CLOTHS

Green with Yellow marking

No. 1 size, 2 ft. 3 ins. × 1 ft. 8 ins.
Single **9/6**

No. 2 size, 2 ft. 11 ins. × 1 ft. 11 ins.
Single **14/6**

No. 3 size, 3 ft. 6 ins. × 2 ft. 6 ins.
Single **22/6**

Above quality in double size

Nos. 1 and 3 sizes only **19/-, 45/-**

ROULETTE WHEELS

Best French make

Outside measurements of Bowl

8 ins.	..	..	..	**15/-**
10 ins.	..	..	..	**20/-**
11½ ins.	..	..	..	**32/-**
14 ins.	..	..	..	**45/-**

COUNTERS FOR ROULETTE, ETC

Spade Guinea	..	.. Per gross	**5/6**
Spade ½ Guinea	..	.. ,,	**4/6**
Galalith Counters	..	.. Per box	**4/6**

POKER CHIP STANDS

Polished Wood, with divisions for different colours

Holding about 15 doz. chips	..	**37/6**
Holding about 20 doz. chips	..	**47/6**
Holding about 25 doz. chips	..	**65/-**

ROULETTE RAKES

Size 18 ins.	.. .. ..	**7/6**
Size 26 ins.	.. .. ..	**8/6**

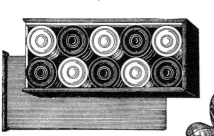

DRAUGHTS SETS

In attractive Leatherette box

Size 1 in., 30 men ..	..		**1/6**
,, 1¼ ins., ,,			**2/-**
,, 1½ ins., ..	..		**2/6**

BILLIARDS NICHOLAS

This popular game is arranged for four players, and consists of a large round board with nickel fittings and best rubber inflators, handsomely finished

Price for four players, 30 ins.	.. ..	**47/6**
Extra blowers ..	.. ..	Each **5/6**
Extra cork balls	.. ..	Per dozen **2/-**

BACKGAMMON BOARDS

Including Dice Cups

	13 ins.	15 ins.	18 ins
Superior Leather	**8/6**	**11/9**	**15/9**
Best Bark Leather	**12/6**	**17/-**	**22/-**

PLOPITIN

Quite a new idea, and should be very popular with those who favour Table Tennis. Players play against a board to get captive ball into one or other of the holes   Price **7/6**

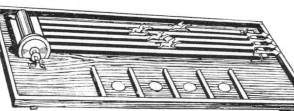

GAME OF SANDOWN

The most exciting race game ever produced. By Finch Mason and C. Welman. (Regd. and Copyright)

Medium size, disc 8½ ins. ..	.. ..	Each **112/-**
Small size, disc 3½ ins.	.. ..	,, **56/-**
Cloth, for either large or medium sizes ..		Each **6/6, 13/6**

All the above have glass tops, and are fitted in Mahogany cases. Pocket Sandown, metal disc 3½ ins., with cards and counters .. .. Each **29/-**

SPRING-O

An attractive game whereby players flip counters by means of springs into various rings
1/9

GREYHOUND RACE GAME

Racing dogs along the table

An exciting game of skill
3/-

TILTING THE BUCKET

A good and amusing game for children calling for a certain amount of skill
Price **3/6**

GEE-WHIZ

Absolutely new and original

Popular Model, 22 × 12 ins., four horses ..	Each	**21/-**
Derby Model, 31 × 12½ ins., six horses ..	,,	**35/-**
Aintree Model, stamped steel ware, six horses		**7/6**
Better Clockwork Models	.. Each	**£7 10 0**

ALL PRICES ARE SUBJECT TO MARKET FLUCTUATIONS

HARRODS LTD

Telephone SLOANE 1234
Telegrams 'EVERYTHING HARRODS LONDON'

LONDON S W 1

TOY DEPARTMENT
Harrods Immense Stock of Toys provide Ample Choice for Children of every Age

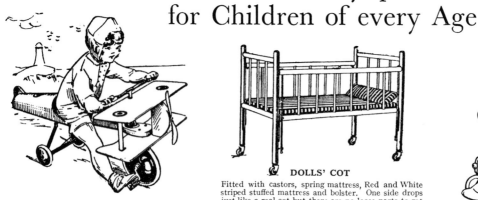

PEDAL PLANE
Beautifully finished White, with Red wheels, plated handlebars, and rubber tyres. Propellor revolves in the wind. Overall length 39 ins. packed in a box 19/6

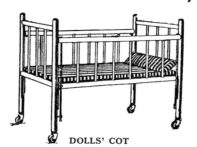

DOLLS' COT
Fitted with castors, spring mattress, Red and White striped stuffed mattress and bolster. One side drops just like a real cot but there are no loose parts to get lost. Finished in White Washable Enamel. Length 25 ins. As illustrated 19/6

TODDLEKAR
A splendid nursery toy that keeps baby out of mischief and teaches him to use his feet. Finished in Washable White Enamel with tray and coloured beads 15/-

DOLLS' PRAMS
Silver Steel panels give a hard glossy finish that wears really well. Bodies upholstered
Model D, with laced hood spring chassis and plated folding handles. Height to handles 24 ins.
34/6
Model C, as illustrated 25/6

Purchases value £1 and over are sent post free in England and Wales

Orders by Post promptly and satisfactorily executed

STRONGLY CONSTRUCTED DOLLS' BEDS
Splendid models with wire springs and stuffed mattress and bolster. Frame finished White Enamel. Three sizes, all folding models and packed in boxes
13/6 10/6 7/6

BUNGALOWS
Complete with imitation front garden full of beautifully coloured flowers. White Rough Cast finish to walls
Model Q with three rooms 11/3
Model P with two rooms 7/6

STEEL BARROW
Every gardener uses a barrow so the kiddies, too, must have one. This is a folding model painted Red with varnished wood shafts and steel disc wheel with rubber tyre. Packed in a box. 26 ins. overall 5/-

DOLLS' PRAMS
The new Tri-ang dolls prams with bodies built like motor car bodies from Silver Steel panels
Beautifully finished and really hard wearing
Model M.E. illustrated has folding handles, apron, laced hood, etc. Height to handle 27 ins. 45/-

DOLLS' PRAMS
Moulded model with Black enamelled folding handles, cushion tyred wheels, etc.
Model B., 23 ins. high to handle 19/6
Model A., 20 ins. high to handle, as illustrated.. 15/9

DOLLS' HOUSES
Dolly must have somewhere to live in and some are not just content with a small cottage. The fine model illustrated has six rooms fitted with curtains, fireplaces, etc. 150/-
Other models range from 6/9 up to £18 15 0

ALL PRICES ARE SUBJECT TO MARKET FLUCTUATIONS

HARRODS LTD

Telephone SLOANE 1234
Telegrams 'EVERYTHING HARRODS LONDON'

LONDON S W 1

TOY DEPARTMENT

A Visit to Harrods Toy Department will prove a Real Entertainment for the Children

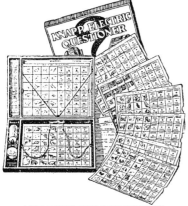

THE ELECTRIC QUESTIONER
TY 99
A most interesting game in which questions are asked—and answered—by means of Electricity. This is a new game with a decided educational value. When the buzz is sounded the question is answered, correctly! Complete with battery **18/6**

LOTT'S BRICKS
TY 103

Box	0	6	Models..			2/-
,,	OA	12	,,			3/3
,,	I	30	,,			5/-
,,	IA	12	,,			5/6
,,	2	48	,,			19/-
,,	2A	18	,,			10/6
,,	3	72	,,			17/6
,,	3A	6	,,			7/6
,,	4	84	,,			30/-
,,	4A	6	,,			7/6
,,	5	100	,,	Made of Stone		42/-

TY 109
THE FOX TOY GUN
The cartridges are removable as in a real gun, but a strong spring supplies the power. Absolutely harmless, but will shoot with sufficient force and accuracy for target practice **17/6**

TY 101
SUNBEAM RACER
Fitted with strong clockwork and rubber tyres. A model approved by Major H. O. D. Seagrave, the famous motorist **15/-**

TY 102
BUDDY 'L' AERIAL FIRE ESCAPE
This is a true working model, with apparatus which automatically raises ladders and a windlass which extends them to a height of 4½ ft. A handwheel enables the ladders to be rotated. The Escape is enamelled in bright red. Ladders are nickel-plated. A brass bell adds realism. Weight 15 lbs. .. **75/-**

TY 104
ALFA-ROMEO RACING CAR
Fitted with steering gear and balloon tyres. A first-class reproduction of a wonderful Italian Racing Car with numerous successes to its credit **25/-**

TY 108
MECCANO
The very word, to a boy, conjures up the prospect of unlimited hours of sheer ecstasy. Give your boy Meccano and watch his face !

MECCANO PRICE LIST

MECCANO OUTFIT	Price	ACCESSORY OUTFIT	Price
No. 00	3/6	No. 00A	1/6
No. 0	5/-	No. 0A	5/6
No. 1	10/-	No. 1A	7/-
No. 2	16/-	No. 2A	12/6
No. 3	27/6	No. 3A	23/6
No. 4	50/-	No. 4A	15/-
No. 5 Carton	65/-	No. 5A Carton	50/-
No. 5 Wood	95/-	No. 5A Wood	80/-
No. 6 Carton	115/-	No. 6A Wood	215/-
No. 6 Wood	150/-		
No. 7 Wood	380/-		

Each Outfit contains a beautifully illustrated Book of Instructions

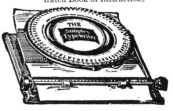

TY 105
SIMPLEX TYPEWRITERS
Special Demonstrated Models. Each model prints all characters shown on its dial on paper or card of any length.

Size E	..	5/-	Size F	..	10/-
Size G	..	15/-	Size H	..	20/-

TY 106
THE ZULU BLOW-GUN
The Novelty of the Year. The latest and most original game for boys and girls. Harmless, and can be played outdoors and in the house; it develops the children's lungs and provides fun for everyone. The outfit contains six indoor and outdoor arrows, four targets, blow-gun and book of instructions.. **5/11**

JOKE ROLLS	..	.. 1/- each
JOKE LEMONS	..	.. 1/- ,,
BALLOONS	..	2d 4d 6d 9d ,,

TY 107
AEROPLANES
Guaranteed to fly. Illustration shows tractor type, which will

rise from the ground					21/-
Pusher types, Model 0	..				5/6
With under carriage—No. 0A	..	..	..		6/6
No. 1A		..	..		8/6
No. 2A		..	..		14/6
Without under carriage, No. 1	..	..	..		7/6

ALL PRICES ARE SUBJECT TO MARKET FLUCTUATIONS

HARRODS LTD

Telephone SLOANE 1234
Telegrams 'EVERYTHING HARRODS LONDON'

LONDON S W 1

TOY DEPARTMENT
No more Acceptable Gift for Children than One of These Handsome Model Cars

Harrods have an exceptionally fine range of Model Cars embodying all the newest designs. Just the kind the youthful motorist will be proud to own, and more important still, there's a range of prices which brings healthy outdoor enjoyment within the means of the most modest purse

LIZZIE
Built entirely of Steel and finished Black with Red bands over bonnet Double crank drive makes it easy to pedal. A most reliable little 'Bus.' 31 ins. long **15/-**

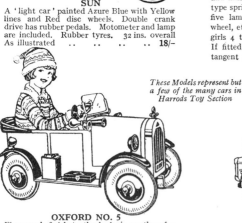

SUN
A 'light car' painted Azure Blue with Yellow lines and Red disc wheels. Double crank drive has rubber pedals. Motometer and lamp are included. Rubber tyres. 32 ins. overall As illustrated **18/-**

'ROLLS ROYCE'
Like its namesake, this fine car is the last word in style, comfort and finish. Body has curved panels and is mounted on car type springs. Accessories include bumper, detachable wheels, five lamps, starter, buzzer, mechanical horn, trunk, spare wheel, etc. Brake operates on back axle. Fine for boys or girls 4 to 9 years. As illustrated **£10 0 0**
If fitted with DUNLOP cord pneumatic balloon tyres and tangent spoke wheels **£11 13 9**

These Models represent but a few of the many cars in Harrods Toy Section

Carriage paid on all purchases value **20/-** *and over in England and Wales*

OXFORD NO. 5
Fine coach finish to the body is worthy of a real car. Plated radiator is pressed out just like real ones. Mudguards, 5 lamps, luggage grid, etc., included. As illustrated, 42 ins. long **81/-**

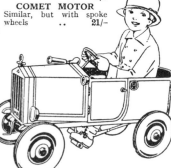

L.B. NO. 5
Kiddies just love this fine little runabout with its complete equipment. Radiator is modelled on the lines of a real one and accessories include luggage grid with trunk, 5 lamps, starter buzzer, bulb horn, bumper, dummy hood, etc. As illustrated **93/9**

PRINCE NO. 5
(on left)
Fitted with dummy hood, luggage grid and trunk, cycle chain drive. 43 ins. long **94/6**

DARRACQ NO. 5
(on right)
Side door model with cycle chain drive, plated radiator, adjustable seat, large balloon disc wheels, etc. Suits kiddies 4 to 8 years. Length overall 41 ins. **57/9**

SPEEDY NO. 4
The plated radiator on this car looks just like a real one and has a number plate attached Lamp, motometer and starting handle are fitted Balloon wheels are most realistic and have rubber tyres. Length 35 ins. overall **39/9**

ORB NO. 4
Quite inexpensive, but strongly made and really well finished. Balloon disc wheels make it up-to-date and very smart. Painted bright Red with contrasting lines. Length overall 35 ins. As illustrated .. **25/6**
COMET MOTOR
Similar, but with spoke wheels .. **21/-**

PLANET NO. 4
The side door on this model opens and is fitted with a neat plated handle. Wood body is comfortable and well finished. Upholstered seat is adjustable. Bulb horn and 4 lamps are included **49/6**

ALL PRICES ARE SUBJECT TO MARKET FLUCTUATIONS

HARRODS LTD

Telephone SLOANE 1234
Telegrams 'EVERYTHING HARRODS LONDON'

LONDON S W 1

TOY DEPARTMENT
'Hornby' Trains are British made and Guaranteed

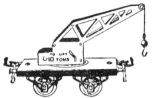

CRANE TRUCK .. Price 3/6

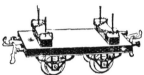

No. 1 LUMBER WAGON, 2/-

HOPPER WAGON   4/-

GAS CYLINDER WAGON 2/6

BRAKE VAN 3/6

No. 1 TIMBER TRUCK, 1/9

TRAIN ACCESSORIES
The Hornby System includes a complete range of Rolling Stock, Train Accessories, Rails, Points and Crossings—everything with which boys may build up a comprehensive Miniature Railway

No. M3 GOODS SET
Strongly built with reliable clockwork mechanism. This set comprises Loco, Tender, two Goods Wagons and set of Rails. A brake rail is included by means of which the train may be braked from the track. The set is printed in imitation of the colours of the principal British Railway Companies' rolling stock. Each Loco is fitted with brake mechanism. Gauge 0. Non-reversing **15/-**

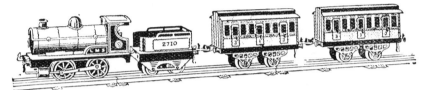

HORNBY No. 1 PASSENGER SET
Each set contains Loco, Tender, and two Coaches, with rails to form either a circle 2 ft. in diameter or an oval 2 ft. in width by 2 ft. 10 ins. in length. One of the rails is a brake rail by means of which the train may be braked from the track. The Loco is fitted with reversing gear and brake mechanism. In colours to represent the L.M.S., L.N.E. or G.W. Railway Companies' Passenger Trains. The doors of the Coaches open. Gauge 0 .. .. **25/-**

HORNBY No. 1 TANK GOODS SET
This Set contains a Hornby No. 1 Tank Loco, Hornby Wagon, Petrol Tank Wagon, Brake Van and set of Rails to form either a circle 2 ft. in diameter or an oval 2 ft. in width by 2 ft. 10 ins. in length. One of the rails is a brake rail by means of which the train may be braked from the track. The set is supplied with Red or Black loco and tender, lettered L.M.S., or with Green or Black loco and tender, lettered L.N.E.R., or with Green loco and tender, lettered G.W. Gauge 0 .. .. .. **22/6**

HORNBY No. 2 PULLMAN SET
This handsome Clockwork Train is fitted with a superior mechanism that is exceptionally powerful and efficient in operation It is altogether a most attractive and satisfactory train. Each set includes Loco, Tender, and two Pullman Coaches with set of Rails. The rails include one brake rail by means of which the train may be both braked and reversed from the track. In colours to represent the L.M.S., L.N.E. or G.W. Railway Companies' Passenger Trains. The Loco. is fitted with reversing gear and brake mechanism

Gauge 0					
No. M 1 Passenger Set	7/6	Hornby No. 1	Tank Goods Set fitted for Hornby		
„ M 2 Passenger Set	9/-		Control		26/-
„ M 3 Goods Set	15/-	„ „ 2	Tank Goods Set		37/6
Hornby No. 0 Goods Set	17/6	„ „ 2	Tank Goods Set fitted for Hornby		
„ „ 0 Passenger Set	22/6		Control		42/6
„ „ 1 Goods Set	20/-	„ „ 2	Tank Goods Set		40/-
„ „ 1 Goods Set fitted for Hornby Control	23/6	„ „ 2	Tank Passenger Set fitted for Hornby		
„ „ 1 Passenger Set	25/-		Control		45/-
„ „ 2 Goods Set	32/6	„ Metropolitan Train Set No. 1 (100-250 Volt)			110/-
„ „ 2 Goods Set fitted for Hornby Control	37/6	„ Metropolitan Train Set No. 2 (4 Volt) ..			95/-
„ „ 2 Pullman Set	50/-	„ Metropolitan Train Set No. 3 (Clockwork)..			55/-
„ „ 2 Pullman Set fitted for Hornby Control	55/-	Riviera 'Blue' Train Set No. 1 (4 Volt) ..			85/-
„ „ 1 Tank Goods Set	22/6	„ „ „ „ 2 (Clockwork) ..			70/-

No. 2 Pullman Set 50/-

THE HORNBY CONTROL SYSTEM
All boys who make a hobby of Hornby Miniature Railway construction will welcome the latest development—the Hornby Control System. This system enables you to manipulate the Signals and Points, and to control the starting and stopping of the train entirely by the levers in the Signal Cabin. A booklet is now available entitled 'The Hornby Control System' which gives full details, and a copy can be obtained free on request

ALL PRICES ARE SUBJECT TO MARKET FLUCTUATIONS

Telephone SLOANE 1234
Telegrams 'EVERYTHING HARRODS LONDON'

HARRODS LTD   **LONDON S W 1**

TOY DEPARTMENT

Harrods have a Wonderful Selection of Dolls and Dolls' Accessories

DOLL'S HAT BOX. Strongly constructed and covered with a light cloth covering. In Red and Blue. (TY 208). Size 8 ins. **4/6**   10 ins. **5/9**

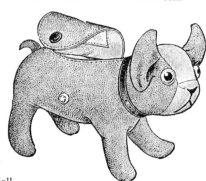

DOLL'S WEEK-END CASE. Gay floral lining and a soft lid fastening with snaps. In Red or Blue. (TY 208). 12 ins. **6/11**   10 ins. **5/11**

LUCY ATTWELL DOLL. An exceptionally well made doll dressed in coloured felt and velvet (TY 211) **15/6**

AN ITALIAN DOLL dressed in dainty crisp Organdie. Made from soft fabric she is an ideal toy for the little girl. In Blue, Orange and Jade. (TY 202) .. **16/11**

VELVET DOLL. Dressed in lovely velvet coat and cap, trimmed with fur. In Jade, Blue and Pink. (TY 227) .. **8/11**

FABRIC DOLL. A beautifully dressed doll made from soft fabric. (TY 212). **35/6**

KNOCKABOUT DOLL. Specially designed for hard wear. Made from soft felt in Jade, Blue and Pink. (TY225). **5/9**

' HUSHABYE DOLLY.' This quaint doll made in deep pile Plush has the quaintest squeak imaginable when squeezed. (TY 210) .. **3/9**

TOY DOG. Made of soft Leather in Harrods own Factory and fitted inside with lots of useful pockets. (TY 217) **10/6**

BABY DOLL. With sleeping eyes and lovely long clothes beautifully made and finished. (TY 214) .. **15/6**

KNOCKABOUT DOLL. Will stand all the 'falls' and 'accidents' that are inevitable in every doll's life. (TY 212). **15/6**

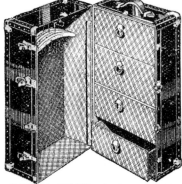

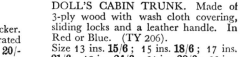

DOLL'S WARDROBE TRUNK. Strong 3-ply foundation with a washable cloth covering bound with fibre. Strong locks. (TY 209). Size 24 ins. .. **49/6**

' PRINCESS ' PRAM. Made of Wicker. This pram has muslin lined hood and is decorated with painted flowers **20/-**

BABY DOLL inside the pram **7/6**

DOLL'S CABIN TRUNK. Made of 3-ply wood with wash cloth covering, sliding locks and a leather handle. In Red or Blue. (TY 206). Size 13 ins. **15/6**; 15 ins. **18/6**; 17 ins. **21/6**; 19 ins. **24/6**; 21 ins. **28/6**; 23 ins. **31/6**

ALL PRICES ARE SUBJECT TO MARKET FLUCTUATIONS

HARRODS LTD

Telephone SLOANE 1234
Telegrams 'EVERYTHING HARRODS LONDON'

LONDON SW1

MOTOR ACCESSORIES AND CYCLES

Accessories and Cycles from the Leading Manufacturers

'Superbe' Cycles

THESE Cycles are specially constructed to HARRODS own Specifications by one of the leading Cycle makers. They are highly recommended by HARRODS and will give ease, comfort and smooth running. Every detail—from the bell to the mudguards—is the best obtainable

MAN'S 'SUPERBE' MODEL

SPECIFICATION OF MAN'S 'SUPERBE' MODEL

Frame—Built of best quality steel tubing
Sizes—22, 24 and 26 ins.
Tyres—Dunlop Magnum
Wheels—28 × 1½ ins.
Chain—½ × ⅛ in. Hans Renold
Gear—Sturmey Archer Three speeds
Brakes—Front and rear
Handlebars—Raised, with roller levers

Mudguards—Enamelled steel, with front extension
Saddle—Brock's B.75, three coil
Pedals—Rubber
Gearcase—Oilbath
Finish—Enamelled Black and lined. All bright parts plated
Fittings—Tools, Toolbag, Bluemel's Pump, Bell and Rear Reflector

All Black Finish. No extra charge

COMPLETE
Or 12 Monthly Payments of **12/11**
CASH PRICE **£7 7 0**

SPECIFICATION OF LADY'S 'SUPERBE' MODEL

Frame—Built of best quality steel tubing
Sizes—22 and 24 ins.
Tyres—Dunlop Magnum
Wheels—28 × 1½ ins.
Chain—½ × ⅛ in. Hans Renold
Gear—Sturmey Archer Three speeds
Brakes—Front and rear
Handlebars—Raised, with roller levers

Mudguards—Enamelled steel, with front extension
Saddle—Brooks B.75, three coil
Pedals—Rubber
Gearcase—Oilbath
Finish—Enamelled Black and lined. All bright parts plated
Fittings—Tools, Toolbag, Bluemel's Pump, Bell and Rear Reflector

All Black Finish. No extra charge

COMPLETE
Or 12 Monthly Payments of **12/11**
CASH PRICE **£7 7 0**

```
···············A NOTE ON DELIVERY···············
Cycles are delivered free in the radius of Harrods Motor Service
Country orders are sent Carriage Paid to the nearest Goods Station,
or to any port in the Channel Isles having direct steamer communica-
tion with London. Purchases of cycle accessories value 20/- or over
              Carriage Paid to any address in Britain
```

LADY'S 'SUPERBE' MODEL

A De Luxe machine in the truest sense of the word

ALL PRICES ARE SUBJECT TO MARKET FLUCTUATIONS

HARRODS LTD

Telephone SLOANE 1234
Telegrams 'EVERYTHING HARRODS LONDON'

LONDON S W 1

HARRODS 'SPECIAL' MODEL CYCLES

Man's
'SPECIAL'
Model

SPECIFICATION OF MAN'S MODEL

Frames—Manufactured from best quality steel tubing. Guaranteed Sizes 22, 24 or 26 inches

Wheels—28 × 1½ inches

Tyres—'Dunlop Roadsters'

Brakes—Roller lever, front and rear

Handlebars—Upturned

Pedals—Rubber

Free Wheel—Ball bearing

Chain—Renolds

Mudguards—Enamelled steel with front extension

Saddle—Three-coil springs

Accessories— Tool - bag, Oilcan, Spanners, Lucas Bell, Bluemel's Pump and Rear Reflector

Finish—Black Enamelled and lined. All bright parts plated

All Black Finish—No extra charge

COMPLETE
Cash Price **£4 19 6**
Or 12 Monthly Payments of **8/9**
With three-speed gear, **18/-** extra

If you cannot possibly call, order by post with full confidence

SPECIFICATION OF LADY'S MODEL

Frames—Manufactured from best quality steel tubing. Thoroughly guaranteed. Sizes 22 or 24 ins.

Wheels—28 × 1½ inches

Tyres—'Dunlop Roadsters'

Brakes— Roller lever front and rear

Handlebars—Upturned

Pedals—Rubber

Free Wheel—Ball bearing

Chain—Renolds

Mudguards—Enamelled steel with front extension.

Saddle—Three-coil springs

Gearcase—Leatherette

Accessories— Tool-bag, Oilcan, Spanners, Lucas Bell, Bluemel's Pump and Rear Reflector

Finish—Black Enamelled and lined All bright parts plated

All Black Finish—No extra charge

COMPLETE
Cash Price **£5 5 0**
Or 12 Monthly Payments of **9/3**
With three-speed gear, **20/-** extra

Lady's
'SPECIAL'
Model

HARRODS
'ALL WEATHER'
Model

DELIVERY TERMS
Cycles are delivered free in the radius of Harrods Motor Service. Country orders are sent Carriage Paid to the nearest Goods Station, or to any port in the Channel Isles having direct communication with London

SPECIFICATION OF HARRODS 'ALL-WEATHER' MODEL

Frames—22, 24, 26 inches Ladies' 22, 24 inches.

Wheels—28 × 1½ ins.

Tyres—'Dunlop Roadsters'

Brakes—Roller Lever, Front and rear

Handlebars—Upturned

Gearcase—Oil Bath

Gear—Sturmey Archer three speeds

Saddle—Dunlop

Chain—Renolds

Accessories—Tool - bag, Tools, Pump, Lucas Bell, and Rear Reflector

COMPLETE
Cash Price .. **£6 10 0**
Or 12 Monthly Payments of **11/5**

ALL PRICES ARE SUBJECT TO MARKET FLUCTUATIONS

HARRODS LTD

Telephone SLOANE 1234
Telegrams 'EVERYTHING HARRODS LONDON'

LONDON S W 1

MOTOR ACCESSORIES & CYCLE DEPARTMENT
Models of all Leading Makes on Show

HUMBER

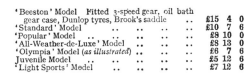

'Beeston' Model Fitted 3-speed gear, Dunlop tyres, oil bath gear case, Brook's saddle .. £14 14 0
'Standard' Model £10 0 0
'Popular' Model £9 0 0
'All-Weather-de-Luxe' Model (as illustrated) .. £8 8 0
'Olympia' Model £5 17 6
'Light Roadster' Model £5 19 6
Road Racer Model £7 5 0
'Cob' Model £5 19 6
Boy's Juvenile Model £5 12 6

'Beeston' Model Fitted 3-speed gear, oil bath gear case, Dunlop tyres, Brook's saddle .. £15 4 0
'Standard' Model £10 7 6
'Popular' Model £8 10 0
'All-Weather-de-Luxe' Model £8 13 0
'Olympia' Model (as illustrated) £6 7 6
Juvenile Model £5 12 6
'Light Sports' Model £7 12 6

RALEIGH

Model 'Superbe' Fitted 3-speed gear, oil bath gear case, Dunlop tyres.. .. .. .. £15 0 0
'Special' Model Fitted 3-speed gear, oil bath gear case .. £11 0 0
'Standard' Model Dunlop tyres, gear case £7 19 6
'Popular' Model (as illustrated) .. £5 19 6
'Club' Model £7 5 0
'Popular' Light Roadster £5 19 6

Model 'Superbe' Fitted 3-speed gear, oil bath gear case, Dunlop tyres £15 0 0
'Special' Model Fitted 3-speed gear, oil bath gear case £11 0 0
'Standard' Model Dunlop tyres. Gear case £7 19 6
'Popular' Model (as illustrated) .. £6 9 6
'Junior' Models. Boys' and Girls'.. £5 19 6

SWIFT

'Club' Tourist Model Fitted 3-speed gear and oil bath gear case (as illustrated) £8 8 0
'Club' Sports Model £7 7 0
'All-Weather' Model £6 15 0
'Imperial' Model £5 19 6
'Imperial' Light Roadster Model £5 19 6

'Club' Tourist Fitted 3-speed gear and oil bath gear case (as illustrated) £8 8 0
'Club' Sports Model £7 7 0
'All-Weather' Model £7 0 0
'Imperial' Model £6 5 6
Juniors' Models
Boys' £4 15 0
Girls' £4 17 6

Selections of Models Always on View

Harrods also undertake any repairs to bicycles

ALL PRICES ARE SUBJECT TO MARKET FLUCTUATIONS

MOTOR ACCESSORIES & CYCLE DEPARTMENT

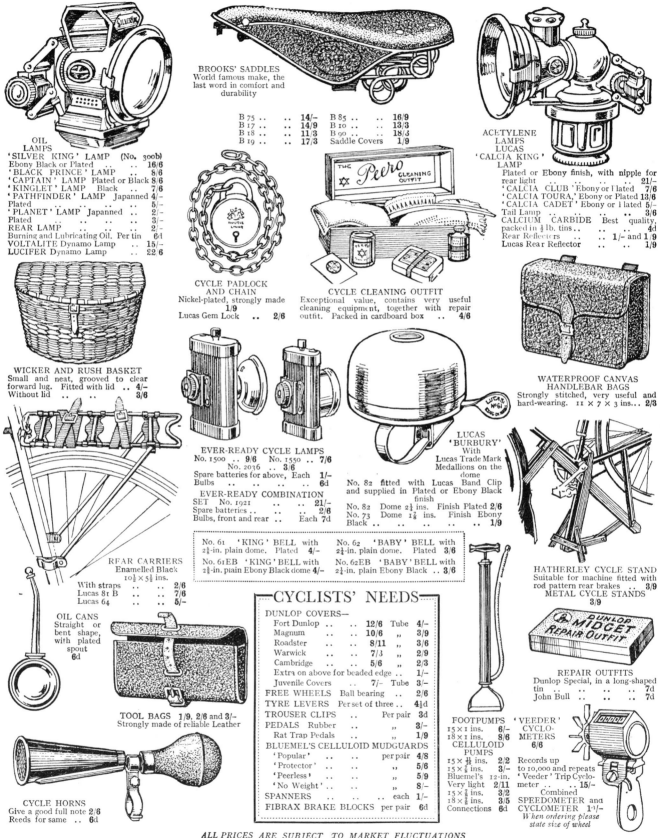

OIL LAMPS
'SILVER KING' LAMP (No. 300b)
Ebony Black or Plated 16/6
'BLACK PRINCE' LAMP .. 8/6
'CAPTAIN' LAMP Plated or Black 8/6
'KINGLET' LAMP Black .. 7/6
'PATHFINDER' LAMP Japanned 4/-
Plated 5/-
'PLANET' LAMP Japanned .. 2/-
Plated 3/-
REAR LAMP 2/-
Burning and Lubricating Oil. Per tin 6d
VOLTALITE Dynamo Lamp .. 15/-
LUCIFER Dynamo Lamp .. 22/6

BROOKS' SADDLES
World famous make, the last word in comfort and durability

B 75 ..	.. 14/-	B 85 ..	.. 16/9	
B 17 ..	.. 14/9	B 10 ..	.. 13/3	
B 18 ..	.. 11/3	B 90 ..	.. 18/3	
B 19 ..	.. 17/3	Saddle Covers	1/9	

ACETYLENE LAMPS LUCAS 'CALCIA KING' LAMP
Plated or Ebony finish, with nipple for rear light 21/-
'CALCIA CLUB' Ebony or Plated 7/6
'CALCIA TOURA,' Ebony or Plated 13/6
'CALCIA CADET' Ebony or Plated 5/-
Tail Lamp 4d
CALCIUM CARBIDE Best quality, packed in ½ lb. tins 4d
Rear Reflectors .. .. 1/- and 1/9
Lucas Rear Reflector 1/9

WICKER AND RUSH BASKET
Small and neat, grooved to clear forward lug. Fitted with lid .. 4/-
Without lid 3/6

CYCLE PADLOCK AND CHAIN
Nickel-plated, strongly made 1/9
Lucas Gem Lock .. 2/6

CYCLE CLEANING OUTFIT
Exceptional value, contains very useful cleaning equipment, together with repair outfit. Packed in cardboard box .. 4/6

WATERPROOF CANVAS HANDLEBAR BAGS
Strongly stitched, very useful and hard-wearing. 11 × 7 × 3 ins... 2/3

EVER-READY CYCLE LAMPS
No. 1500 .. 9/6 No. 1550 .. 7/6
No. 2036 .. 3/6
Spare batteries for above, Each 1/-
Bulbs 6d
EVER-READY COMBINATION
SET No. 1921 .. .. 21/-
Spare batteries 2/6
Bulbs, front and rear .. Each 7d

LUCAS 'BURBURY'
With Lucas Trade Mark Medallions on the dome
No. 82 fitted with Lucas Band Clip and supplied in Plated or Ebony Black finish
No. 82 Dome 2¼ ins. Finish Plated 2/6
No. 73 Dome 1⅞ ins. Finish Ebony Black 1/9

No. 61 'KING' BELL with 2⅜-in. plain dome. Plated 4/-	No. 62 'BABY' BELL with 2¼-in. plain dome. Plated 3/6
No. 61EB 'KING' BELL with 2⅜-in. plain Ebony Black dome 4/-	No. 62EB 'BABY' BELL with 2¼-in. plain Ebony Black .. 3/6

REAR CARRIERS
Enamelled Black 10½ × 5¼ ins.
With straps 2/6
Lucas 81 B 7/6
Lucas 64 .. .. 5/-

OIL CANS
Straight or bent shape, with plated spout 6d

TOOL BAGS 1/9, 2/6 and 3/-
Strongly made of reliable Leather

HATHERLEY CYCLE STAND
Suitable for machine fitted with rod pattern rear brakes .. 3/9
METAL CYCLE STANDS
3/9

REPAIR OUTFITS
Dunlop Special, in a long-shaped tin 7d
John Bull 7d

CYCLISTS' NEEDS

DUNLOP COVERS—

Fort Dunlop ..	.. 12/6	Tube	4/-	
Magnum ..	.. 10/6	„	3/9	
Roadster ..	.. 8/11	„	3/6	
Warwick ..	.. 7/3	„	2/9	
Cambridge ..	.. 5/6	„	2/3	
Extra on above for beaded edge ..			1/-	
Juvenile Covers ..	7/-	Tube	3/-	

FREE WHEELS Ball bearing .. 2/6
TYRE LEVERS Per set of three .. 4½d
TROUSER CLIPS .. Per pair 3d
PEDALS Rubber .. „ 3/-
Rat Trap Pedals .. „ 1/9
BLUEMEL'S CELLULOID MUDGUARDS
'Popular' .. .. per pair 4/8
'Protector' .. .. „ 5/6
'Peerless' .. .. „ 5/9
'No Weight' .. .. „ 8/-
SPANNERS .. .. .. each 1/-
FIBRAX BRAKE BLOCKS per pair 6d

FOOTPUMPS
15 × 1 ins. 6/-
18 × 1 ins. 8/6
CELLULOID PUMPS
15 × 1½ ins. 2/2
15 × ⅞ ins. 3/-
Bluemel's 12-in. Very light 2/11
15 × ¾ ins. 3/2
18 × ⅞ ins. 3/5
Connections 6d

'VEEDER' CYCLOMETERS 6/6
Records up to 10,000 and repeats
'Veeder' Trip Cyclometer .. 15/-
Combined SPEEDOMETER and CYCLOMETER 1·¹/-
When ordering please state size of wheel

OIL CANS

CYCLE HORNS
Give a good full note 2/6
Reeds for same .. 6d

ALL PRICES ARE SUBJECT TO MARKET FLUCTUATIONS

MOTOR CYCLE & ACCESSORIES DEPARTMENT

If You Have Never Owned a Motor-cycle You Have Missed one of the Thrills of Life

GET YOUR MACHINE AT HARRODS !

A selection of 1929 Models

A.J.S.

	£	s.	d.
248 s.v. (M.12)	39	17	6
349 s.v. (M.5)	45	0	0
349 s.v. de luxe (M.3 and M.4)	48	10	0
349 o.h.v. (M.6)	52	0	0
349 o.h.v. two-port (M.6) ..	54	10	0
349 o.h.c. (M.7)	62	0	0
498 s.v. de luxe (M.9) ..	54	0	0
498 o.h.v. (M.8)	59	10	0
498 o.h.v. two-port (M.8) ..	62	0	0
498 o.h.c. (M.10)	72	0	0
996 (M.2)	66	0	0
996 (M.1) de luxe	76	10	0

ARIEL.

	£	s.	d.
250 s.v. de luxe	36	0	0
250 o.h.v. two-port.. ..	38	10	0
500 o.h.v. two-port standard	47	10	0
500 o.h.v. two-port de luxe	50	0	0
557 s.v. standard	44	0	0
557 s.v. de luxe	46	10	0

ASCOT-PULLIN.

	£	s.	d.
500 sports utility	73	0	0
500 utility de luxe ..	75	0	0

B.S.A.

	£	s.	d.
174 two-stroke	26	5	0
174 two-stroke de luxe ..	28	0	0
249 s.v. de luxe	36	0	0
349 s.v.	43	0	0
349 o.h.v. standard ..	47	10	0
349 o.h.c. two-port ..	54	15	0
493 s.v.	44	0	0
493 o.h.v. light two-port ..	49	10	0
493 s.v. de luxe	52	15	0
493 o.h.v. standard ..	55	10	0
493 o.h.v. two-port.. ..	57	10	0
557 s.v. standard	46	0	0
557 s.v. de luxe	53	15	0
770 s.v. light twin	58	15	0
770 s.v. de luxe	65	0	0
986 s.v. de luxe	66	0	0
986 s.v. " World Tour " twin	69	0	0

COTTON.

	£	s.	d.
250 two-stroke (1)	42	0	0
300 s.v. (3)	44	10	0
350 s.v. (7)	46	10	0
350 o.h.v. single-port (9)	58	15	0
350 o.h.v. two-port (29)	64	10	0
496 s.v. (8)	56	10	0
496 o.h.v. single-port (5) ..	64	10	0
496 o.h.v. two-port (25) ..	69	10	0

DOUGLAS.

	£	s.	d.
350 s.v. (A.29)	41	0	0
350 s.v. (B.29)	45	0	0
350 o.h.v. (D.29)	49	10	0
350 o.h.v. T.T.	92	10	0
500 dirt-track model ..	85	0	0
500 o.h.v. T.T.	95	0	0
600 s.v. (E.29)	49	10	0
600 s.v. sports (F.29) ..	52	10	0
600 o.h.v. (G.29)	68	0	0
600 o.h.v. sports (H.29) ..	70	0	0

DUNELT.

	£	s.	d.
250 sports (K.)	35	10	0
250 Royal (K.)	39	0	0
250 Royal de luxe (K.) ..	41	0	0
350 o.h.v. two-port, Majestic	51	5	0

EXCELSIOR.

	£	s.	d.
147 utility	21	0	0
250 two-stroke	34	13	0
250 o.h.v. two-port.. ..	41	10	0
250 o.h.v. T.T.	79	10	0
300 s.v.	36	10	0
350 o.h.v.	50	15	0
350 o.h.v. T.T.	81	10	0
500 s.v.	47	10	0
500 o.h.v.	60	15	0

FRANCIS-BARNETT.

	£	s.	d.
147 two-speed (3)	26	0	0
147 two-speed (4)	29	0	0
172 three-speed sports (5)..	32	10	0
172 three-speed super-sports (9)	36	0	0
247 three-speed (12) ..	39	10	0

LEVIS.

	£	s.	d.
247 (R)	33	10	0
247 (Z)	36	10	0
247 six-port, standard ..	39	10	0
247 electric (Z)	42	5	0
247 six-port electric ..	47	5	0
346 o.h.v. (A)	52	10	0
346 o.h.v. electric (A) ..	57	15	0

MATCHLESS.

	£	s.	d.
246 s.v. (R/S)	36	0	0
246 o.h.v. two-port (R/3) ..	39	10	0
347 s.v. (T/4)	43	0	0
347 o.h.v. two-port (T/S) ..	46	10	0
347 o.h.c. (LR/2)	53	10	0
347 o.h.v. two-port racing (T/R)	51	10	0
498 s.v. (T/3)	44	0	0
495 o.h.v. two-port (V/2) ..	53	10	0
495 o.h.v. two-port racing (V/2)	58	10	0
586 s.v. (V/5)	49	10	0
990 s.v. touring (X) ..	60	0	0
990 s.v. sports (X/R) ..	62	0	0

HARRODS DEFERRED PAYMENTS

AN EXAMPLE

Harrods supply every known make of Motor Cycles or Sidecar Combinations on their Deferred Payment System

	£	s.	d.
3.49 H.P. B.S.A. Model L28. O.H.V. Cash Price	47	10	0
Comprehensive Insurance	3	15	0
	51	5	0
25 per cent. Deposit	12	16	0
	38	9	0
8 per cent. on Balance	3	2	0
	41	11	0
Payable in 12 monthly instalments	3	9	3

NEW IMPERIAL.

	£	s.	d.
250 o.h.v. two-port (B9) ..	42	10	0
250 o.h.v. two-port racing (9A)	60	0	0
350 s.v. (2)	37	15	0
350 s.v. de luxe (DL2) ..	43	15	0
350 o.h.v. two-port (10) ..	48	15	0
350 o.h.v. two-port racing (10A)	65	0	0
500 s.v. (7)	48	15	0
500 o.h.v. two-port (7B) ..	52	10	0

NORTON.

	£	s.	d.
350 o.h.v.	68	0	0
350 o.h.c.	77	0	0
490 s.v. (16H)	56	0	0
490 o.h.v. (18)	63	10	0
490 o.h.v. semi-dry sump (21)	67	0	0
490 o.h.v. cradle frame (ES2)	73	10	0
490 o.h.c. (CS1)	82	10	0
588 o.h.v. (19)	66	0	0
588 s.v. four-speed (24) ..	71	0	0
633 s.v.	60	5	0
633 s.v. four-speed (14) ..	65	10	0

P. AND M.

	£	s.	d.
147 two-stroke	24	18	6
246 o.h.v. Panthette ..	60	0	0
250 Villiers	37	10	0
499 o.h.v. Panther	59	10	0
600 o.h.v. Panther	60	10	0
600 o.h.v. Panther (85 m.p.h.)	63	0	0

RUDGE-WHITWORTH.

	£	s.	d.
250 s.v.	39	10	0
250 o.h.v.	43	0	0
350 o.h.v.	49	0	0
500 special	55	0	0
500 Ulster	69	0	0
500 dirt-track model ..	70	0	0

SUNBEAM.

	£	s.	d.
347 s.v. touring (1) ..	69	6	0
347 s.v. sports (2)	66	3	0
347 o.h.v. single-port (8) ..	69	6	0
347 o.h.v. two-port.. ..	74	11	0
347 T.T. two-port	89	5	0
492 s.v. light tourist (5) ..	78	15	0
492 s.v. long-stroke (6) ..	75	12	0
493 o.h.v. single-port (9) ..	78	15	0
493 o.h.v. two-port.. ..	84	0	0
493 two-port T.T.	105	0	0
599 **s.v.** four-speed (7) ..	84	0	0

TRIUMPH.

	£	s.	d.
277 s.v. (W)	36	0	0
277 s.v. (WS)	37	17	6
348 o.h.v. (CO)	52	17	6
494 (NL)	44	10	0
498 **s.v.** (CN)	46	17	6
549 s.v. (NSD)	46	17	6
549 s.v. (CSD)	47	17	6
498 o.h.v. (ST)	59	17	6

ALL PRICES ARE SUBJECT TO MARKET FLUCTUATIONS

HARRODS LTD

Telephone SLOANE 1234
Telegrams 'EVERYTHING HARRODS LONDON'

LONDON S W 1

MOTOR ACCESSORIES & CYCLE DEPARTMENT

A Large Variety of Mascots always in Stock

'PETER PAN'
Bright Silver-plated,
or Oxidised Silver
Finish
6 ins. high £2 **15** 0

**'MODERN
WITCH'**
Bright Silver-plated,
or Oxidised Silver
Finish
7 ins. high
£3 **3** 0

'FLYING STORK'
Height 4½ ins. × 6 ins.
(11 cm. × 15 cm.)
Silver-plated finish .. £2 **2** 0
Larger Model.. .. £3 **3** 0

'FUTURIST'
'RACING GREYHOUND'
Bright Silver-plated, or Oxidised Silver
Finish
Length, 6¾ ins. £2 **10** 0

'NINETTE'
Bright Silver-plated, or
Oxidised Silver Finish
5½ ins. high .. £2 **5** 0

'L'AIGLE'
Height 3 ins. × 6 ins. (7 cm. × 15 cm.)
Silver-plated finish £2 **2** 0
Polished Bronze finish **2** 0 0
Height 4 ins. × 8 ins. (10 cm. × 20 cm.)
Silver-plated finish **3** 3 0
Polished Bronze finish **3** 0 0
Height 5 ins. × 10 ins. (12 cm. × 25 cm.)
Silver-plated finish **4** 10 0
Polished Bronze finish **4** 5 0

'CONQUEROR OF THE ROAD'
Silver-plated finish .. £2 **10** 0
Polished Bronze finish .. **2** 8 0

'FLYING MAN'
Height 3 ins. by 6½ ins. (7 cm. by 16 cm.)
Silver plated finish £3 **3** 0
Polished Bronze finish .. £3 **0** 0

'WILD DUCK'
Height 4 ins. × 4 ins. (10 cm. × 10 cm.)
Silver-plated finish .. £2 **15** 0
Polished Bronze finish .. **2** 13 0

'THE LEADER'
Bright Silver-plated, or Oxidised
Silver Finish
Height 5½ ins. × 6½ ins. £4 **4** 0

ALL PRICES ARE SUBJECT TO MARKET FLUCTUATIONS

HARRODS LTD

Telephone SLOANE 1234
Telegrams 'EVERYTHING HARRODS LONDON'

LONDON S W 1

MOTOR ACCESSORIES & CYCLE DEPARTMENT
A Wide Choice of Every Conceivable Need for Motorists

CLEANING BRUSHES

Water Brush	7/6
Wire Wheel and Hub Brush ..	5/9
Cheaper quality	4/-
Artillery Wheel Spoke Brushes ..	7/-
All round Model { Triangle	6/6
{ Flat ..	5/9
Bent Wing Brush	6/-, 7/-
Upholstery Brushes	5/6, 6/11
Engine Cleaning Brushes ..	1/6, 2/6

POLISHING CLOTH

Harrods Stockinette Ideal Polishing
Cloth (*as illustrated*). 25 yd. roll — 3/-
50 yd. roll 5/10
Approximate width 22 ins.
THE 'POLI' CLOTH, 26 × 26
ins. Ideal Polishing Cloth for
Bodywork 1/-

CAR BODY POLISHES

SIMONIZ CLEANER	5/-
SIMONIZ POLISHER	5/-
RECKITT'S 'KARPOL' ..	1/-, 2/-
WONDERMIST	3/6, 5/6
ATOMIST	3/6, 5/6
LIQUID VENEER	1/6, 3/-
SPRAYER for above	2/9
JOHNSON'S WAX Liquid or Solid	2/6
JOHNSON'S CLEANER ..	2/-
CHEMICO CAR POLISH ..	2/-, 3/9
FURMOTO BODY POLISH	2/-, 5/-
'STADIUM' FABRIC BODY CLEANER	2/6

METAL POLISHES

'GLITTERIT'	8d
'GLITTERIT'	1/3
BLUEBELL	1/3
GODDARD'S DOUBLE TRIANGLE	1/3
MIRROR METAL POLISH ..	1/3

TYRE PAINT

Black Nitrex	3/6
Black, Dullite	1/9
Black, Dullite	3/4
Black, Goodyear	1/6
Farmiloe's Grey and White ..	1/6
Farmiloe's Grey and White ..	3/-
Harding's 'Ringol' in Black ..	1/9
Larger size	3/6

SCREEN WIPERS

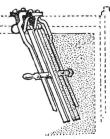

THE 'DESMO'
Screen Wiper .. 6/-
(*as illustrated*)
LUCAS AUTOMATIC
Screen Wiper, all
Nickel-plated .. 21/-
'LUCAS'
Electric Screen Wiper,
6 or 12 volt 21/-
THE 'DESMO'
Electric Wiper .. 29/6
THE 'BERKSHIRE'
Electric Wiper .. 42/-

STEP MATS

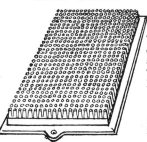

BRISTLE RUBBER
In Aluminium Frame (*as
illustrated*) 11½ × 7½ ins.
7/6, 9/6
FIBRE STEP MATS
THE 'SLIP ON'
15 × 9 ins. .. 10/6
12 × 8 ins. .. 8/6
'DUNLOP' STEP MAT
without Frame
12 × 7½ ins. .. 5/6
'UCEERITE'
Glass Polish .. 3/-
Ensures clear vision in
the heaviest rain

CAR COMPANION SETS

In Mahogany, Walnut or Morocco Leather, lined
throughout to match the car linings
£4 15 0 per pair (*as illustrated below*)
Any colour can be made to order

*Contains two Travelling Bottles, Note Book and Pencil,
Card Case and Mirror*

*Contains Ash Tray and Match Box, Electro Plated on
Nickel Silver*

**Smith's Wireless Electric
Cigarette Lighter**

In Grey, Black or Brown
6 or 12 volts **15/6**

With Ash Tray attached **21/-**

PETROL AND OIL CONTAINER

The 'STADIUM' Petrol and Oil
container. Enamelled steel with lock
and key 22/6
The 'STADIUM' Tool Box. Steel,
Black enamelled. With lock and key

Height	Length	Width		
6½ ins.	13 ins.	1 in.		12/6
18 ,,	18 ,,	7¼ ,,		19/6
22 ,,	9 ,,	10¼ ,,		22/6

GOGGLES

Non-Inflammable Talc Face Masks 1/9
A large selection of Goggles always in
stock in Plain, White or Coloured Glass
2/6, 3/6, 5/9
'STADIUM' Safety Glass Goggles
7/6 and 12/6

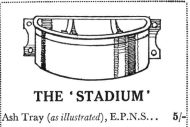

THE 'STADIUM'

Ash Tray (*as illustrated*), E.P.N.S... 5/-

NICKEL SILVER ASH TRAYS

Ash Tray Electro-plated on Nickel Silver
8/6

Nickel-plated Ash Tray ..	3/6, 6/9
Oxidized Silver Plated ..	5/6, 8/6
Polished Mahogany ..	12/6, 17/6
Greywood	13/6, 19/6

CAR FOOT PUMPS

The 'HANDY' Very powerful	50/-
The 'WOOD MILNE'	40/-
The 'KISMET'	40/-, 58/6
'DUNLOP'	21/-, 4?/-
'STADIUM'	25/-
,, with Gauge ..	27/6

Above are all fitted with pressure gauges
Strong Brass Hand Pumps .. 10/6

IRISH LINEN CAR DUST SHEETS

12 × 9 ft.	19/6	15 × 9 ft.	25/-
18 × 9 ft.	29/6	18 × 12 ft.	38/-
21 × 15 ft.	57/6		

These Dust Sheets are fitted with tapes
for tying, in same materials

Write for prices and particulars of
Lighting and Starting Batteries, Sparking
Plugs and all Motor Accessories

ALL PRICES ARE SUBJECT TO MARKET FLUCTUATIONS

HARRODS LTD

Telephone SLOANE 1234
Telegrams 'EVERYTHING HARRODS LONDON'

LONDON S W 1

HARRODS
CHINA AND EARTHENWARE SECTION

At Harrods will be found a selection of China and Earthenware which, for sheer beauty and variety of design, is without equal in the Kingdom. Harrods urge all who can to pay a visit of inspection to the Department

SERVICES Harrods offer an exceptional choice of Services by such famous manufacturers as Minton, Copeland, Crown Derby, Cauldon, Doulton, Wedgwood, Worcester and Limoges

ORNAMENTAL CHINA An unparalleled selection of all the newest and best shapes is available, representative of all the most noted makers

MATCHINGS Careful attention is given to this important section, and every effort is made to secure speedy delivery. To avoid misunderstanding, please secure an estimate in writing

REPAIRS Harrods undertake China repairs of every kind. Best materials are used and expert workmen execute the work in the shortest possible time

NOTE.—Pieces for matching or repairs are only sent for, and returned, at customers' own risk ; but every care will be taken to ensure safety

CRESTS OR BADGES Harrods give special attention to the supplying of crested or badged China Estimates gladly sent free on application

PRICES In the event of any fall in prices between time of ordering and delivery, Harrods give their customers full benefit

PACKING While the greatest possible care is exercised in packing goods, Harrods cannot hold themselves responsible for damage to purchases after they have been despatched from Harrods. Experienced and skilful packers are employed for export orders, and no allowance for breakage in transit can be made. Goods for Export are packed in Casks or Barrels, and only in Cases when specially stipulated

BREAKAGES IN TRANSIT Purchaser should advise Carriers—as well as Harrods—of breakages, immediately on receipt of goods. If goods are sent by Post or Rail, packing case and materials must be retained for inspection

COMPOSITION OF SERVICES SHOWN IN FOLLOWING PAGES

DINNER SERVICE
26 Pieces

6 Meat Plates
6 Pie ,,
6 Cheese ,,
3 Meat Dishes, various sizes
2 Vegetable Dishes and Covers
1 Sauce Boat

DINNER SERVICE
52 Pieces

12 Meat Plates
12 Pie ,,
12 Cheese ,,
6 Dishes : two 9 inch, one 10 inch, one 12 inch, one 14 inch, one 16 inch
2 Vegetable Dishes and Covers
2 Sauce Tureens and Stands

DINNER SERVICE
67 Pieces

12 Meat Plates
12 Pie ,,
12 Cheese ,,
12 Soup ,,
6 Dishes : two 9 inch, one 10 inch, one 12 inch, one 14 inch, one 16 inch

67 Pieces—continued

1 Soup Tureen and Stand
2 Sauce Tureens and Stands
2 Vegetable Dishes and Covers

Size of Dishes—These vary according to maker. Sizes given here are in every case less than actual measurements, which are from 1 to 2 inches more than quoted

TEA SERVICE
21 Pieces

6 Cups and Saucers
6 Tea Plates
1 Slop Basin
1 Cream Jug
1 Cake Plate

(If 23 Pieces, add covered Sugar Box)

TEA SERVICE
40 Pieces

12 Cups and Saucers
12 Tea Plates
1 Slop Basin
1 Cream Jug
2 Cake Plates

(If 42 Pieces, add covered Sugar Box)

BREAKFAST SERVICE
29 Pieces

6 Cups and Saucers
6 Plates
2 Bread and Butter Plates
1 Slop Basin
1 Sugar ,,
1 Milk Jug
6 Egg Cups

(If 30 Pieces, covered Sugar Box instead of Sugar Basin)

BREAKFAST SERVICE
51 Pieces

12 Cups and Saucers
12 Plates
2 Bread and Butter Plates
1 Slop Basin
1 Sugar ,,
1 Milk Jug
2 Dishes : one 10 inch, one 12 inch
1 Covered Muffin Dish
6 Egg Cups

(If 52 Pieces, covered Sugar Box instead of Sugar Basin)

TOILET SERVICE

5 Pieces	*10 Pieces*
1 Ewer	2 Ewers
1 Basin	2 Basins
1 Soap Dish	1 Soap Dish
1 Brush Vase	1 Brush Vase
1 Chamber	2 Chambers
	1 Sponge Bowl
	1 Toilet Pail

12 Pieces
Two 5-Piece Sets and Toilet Pail and Sponge Bowl

DESSERT SERVICE
18 Pieces

12 Plates
6 Comportiers or Fruit Dishes

TEA AND BREAKFAST
48 Pieces

6 Teas and Saucers
6 Breakfasts and Saucers
6 Tea Plates
6 Breakfast Plates
2 Bread and Butter Plates
6 Egg Cups
1 Slop Basin
1 Sugar ,,
1 Cream Jug
1 Milk ,,

(If 49 Pieces, covered Sugar Box instead of Sugar Basin)

ALL PRICES ARE SUBJECT TO MARKET FLUCTUATIONS

CHINA DEPARTMENT
New Designs in Harrods Quality Dinner Services

Harrods exclusive designs

For Tea and Breakfast Services to match these patterns see pages 277 and 278

' ROCOCO ' SERVICE
A striking design in rich tones of Green, Chinese Red, Fawn and Ebony. Gold edge lines and traced handles

'DEVON ' SERVICE
A charming Blue border with Marbled effect and White flowers. Edges and handles are finished with Gilt lines

' WILDFLOWERS ' SERVICE
Gracefully shaped basket, filled with flowers, leaves and grasses in natural colours. A beautiful under-glaze design and therefore unfadable. Rose-Pink lines at edges and handles

For Tea and Breakfast Services to match these patterns see page 278

These Services are Harrods regular stocks and replenishments are always available

' VIGO ' SERVICE
A most dainty and beautifully executed Lavender border with scrolls in Hair-Brown, panelled with birds and flowers in colours. The centre has a finely coloured spray. All edges and handles finished Gold lines

' ORLEANS ' SERVICE
Fine vase and flower design in natural colours. Elegant shapes throughout. All edges and handles finished with Gilt lines

' MADRAS ' SERVICE
Best Staffordshire Pottery. Coloured design of exotic birds and flowers. Gilt edges

' SAPPHIRE ' SERVICE
Neat design of deep Blue border, broken by baskets of fruit naturally coloured. Edges and handles finished with Gilt lines

' HARROW ' SERVICE
A wide border of rich Ivory with sprays of mixed flowers in natural tints. Edges and handles finished with gilt lines

' ROSINA ' SERVICE
Effective design of wide Turquoise border with panels of roses finished Hair-Brown tracings. Edges and handles finished Gilt lines

		Rococo			Devon			Wildflowers			Vigo			Orleans			Madras			Sapphire			Harrow			Rosina		
		£	s.	d.	£	s.	d.	£	s.	d.	£	s.	d.	£	s.	d.	£	s.	d.	£	s.	d.	£	s.	d.	£	s.	d.
Meat Plates	Dozen		19	0	1	0	0		19	0		17	9		18	0		15	0		17	9	1	3	0		15	0
Soup Plates	"	1	1	0	1	2	0	1	1	0		18	9	1	0	0		16	0		19	9	1	5	6		16	0
Pudding Plates	"		16	0		16	9		16	0		15	6		15	0		13	6		15	0		19	6		13	0
Cheese Plates	"		10	0		10	6		10	0		10	0		9	6		9	6		9	3		12	6		8	6
Dish, 9 inch	Each		2	6		2	6		2	6		2	6		2	6		2	3		2	3		2	11		2	3
Dish 10 inch	"		3	0		3	3		3	0		3	3		2	11		2	11		2	9		3	9		2	9
Dish 12 inch	"		5	0		5	3		5	0		5	0		5	6		4	9		4	9		6	0		4	6
Dish 14 inch	"		6	11		7	3		6	11		6	11		7	9		6	9		6	6		8	6		6	6
Dish 16 inch	"		11	0		11	6		11	0		11	0		12	0		10	6		10	3		13	6		10	3
Dish 18 inch	"		—			16	9		—			—			18	0		15	0		15	0		—			15	0
Vegetable Dish	"		10	0		10	6		10	0		10	0		11	0		9	6		9	3		12	6		9	3
Sauce Tureen and Stand	"		9	0		9	6		9	0		9	0		10	0		8	9		8	6		11	0		8	6
Sauce Boat	"		3	3		3	6		3	3		3	3		3	9		3	3		3	0		4	3		3	0
Soup Tureen and Stand	"	1	10	0	1	11	6	1	10	0	1	10	0	1	13	0	1	8	6	1	8	0	1	16	6	1	8	0
Salad Bowl	"		4	0		4	3		4	0		4	0		4	3		3	11		3	9		3	9		3	9
Salad Plate	Dozen	1	16	0		12	9	1	16	0	1	16	0		13	0		11	6	1	16	0	2	5	0		11	3
Dinner Service, 26 pieces	Each	2	16	0	2	19	3	2	16	0	2	16	0	2	13	6	2	11	0	2	10	0	3	4	6	2	7	0
Dinner Service, 52 pieces	"	5	12	6	5	19	0	5	12	6	5	12	0	5	7	6	4	17	0	5	0	0	6	10	0	4	15	0
Dinner Service, 67 pieces	"	8	3	6	8	12	6	8	3	6	8	3	6	7	16	0	6	18	0	7	5	0	9	7	6	6	15	0

For composition of Services, see page 272

ALL PRICES ARE SUBJECT TO MARKET FLUCTUATIONS
Telephone SLOANE 1234
Telegrams 'EVERYTHING HARRODS LONDON'

HARRODS LTD **LONDON S W 1**

'OLD BOW' SERVICE
This elegant pattern will appeal to all lovers of the beautiful. Soft colourings on exquisitely modelled shapes. Handles finished with finest Gilt

These designs are all exclusive to Harrods and unobtainable elsewhere

'CHELSEA' SERVICE
Copeland's reproduction of a famous design. The coloured hand-decorations are charming and retain the eighteenth century softness of unfadable colourings

'PEPLOW' SERVICE
A Copeland reproduction of Spode's famous design, made about 1770-1880. The fine hand colourings and the delicate modelling of each piece lend a special charm to the service

'COBRIDGE' SERVICE
A distinctive service with hand decorated design in Dark Blue, Puce, Red and Green, with Blue lines. A faithful reproduction of the original design

For Tea and Breakfast Services to match these patterns see page 281

'BATTERSEA' SERVICE
Fruit border on Dark Blue ground. (Period 1800-1810) Painted in original colours. Reproduced faithfully from Spode's design book in their old shapes

Harrods will gladly supply any single item separately and will effect replacements at once

'ROCKINGHAM' SERVICE
This reproduction dates from 1770-1790. Another example of Spode's original faultlessly reproduced by Copeland's for Harrods. Beautifully coloured fruit design

'BUXTON' SERVICE
Copeland Fine China. Rich Mazarine Blue band and Gilt design, superimposed. Grey lace design below. Best burnished Gold throughout

Any piece from these Copeland Services may be purchased separately

'GEORGE III' SERVICE
(Reg. No. 677526). Famous about 1790. A grand piece of underglaze colouring. Birds and fruit design on Light Blue printed ground, finished Dark Blue edges. Fruit knobs form handle

Come if possible and see these Services for yourself

'TRENTHAM' SERVICE
Copeland Fine China. Wide Powder Blue with classical gilt design. A very charming and elegant service. Best burnished gold throughout

		Old Bow £ s. d.	Chelsea £ s. d.	Peplow £ s. d.	Cobridge £ s. d.	Battersea £ s. d.	Rockingham £ s. d.	Buxton £ s. d.	George III £ s. d.	Trentham £ s. d.
Dinner Plates	Dozen	1 7 6	1 6 6	1 6 6	1 6 6	1 7 6	1 9 0	8 0 0	1 10 9	9 18 0
Soup Flates	,,	1 8 0	1 7 6	1 7 6	1 7 6	1 8 0	1 10 0	8 13 0	1 12 0	10 10 0
Pudding Plates	,,	1 3 0	1 3 0	1 3 0	1 3 0	1 3 0	1 5 0	6 19 0	1 7 6	8 12 0
Cheese Plates	,,	1 1 0	1 1 0	1 1 0	1 1 0	1 1 0	1 1 3	6 0 0	1 3 0	7 9 0
Meat Dish, 9 inch	Each	4 11	4 9	4 9	4 9	4 11	5 8	16 6	6 0	19 9
Meat Dish, 10 inch	,,	6 6	6 6	6 6	6 6	6 6	7 3	18 3	7 9	1 1 6
Meat Dish, 12 inch	,,	9 6	9 6	9 6	9 6	9 6	9 11	1 6 6	10 9	1 11 6
Meat Dish, 14 inch	,,	13 3	13 3	13 3	13 3	13 3	13 9	1 16 6	15 0	2 3 0
Meat Dish, 16 inch	,,	17 6	17 6	17 6	17 6	17 6	18 0	2 10 0	1 0 3	2 18 0
Meat Dish, 18 inch	,,	1 5 6	1 5 0	1 5 0	1 5 0	1 5 6	1 8 0	4 3 0	1 9 9	4 16 0
Vegetable Dish	,,	1 4 6	17 0	17 0	1 0 6	18 6	19 3	3 5 0	1 0 3	3 18 0
Sauce Tureen and Stand	,,	1 2 0	14 9	14 9	1 0 0	15 9	13 3	2 18 0	13 9	3 8 0
Soup Tureen and Stand	,,	3 0 0	2 5 0	2 5 0	2 19 0	2 11 0	2 3 9	6 19 0	2 5 9	8 2 0
Salad Bowl	,,	1 3 6	17 0	17 0	17 0	18 6	19 3	3 0 0	1 0 3	3 10 0
Salad Plates	Dozen	1 16 0	1 17 6	1 17 6	1 17 6	1 16 0	2 0 6	9 5 0	2 2 6	11 1 0
Dinner Service, 52 pieces	Each	10 3 6	8 11 9	8 11 9	9 10 0	9 1 0	9 6 6	39 15 6	9 18 6	48 12 6
Dinner Service, 67 pieces	,,	14 5 6	11 17 6	11 17 6	13 10 0	12 14 6	12 15 3	54 15 6	13 11 3	66 12 6

For composition of Services, see page 272
ALL PRICES ARE SUBJECT TO MARKET FLUCTUATIONS

HARRODS LTD

Telephone SLOANE 1234
Telegrams 'EVERYTHING HARRODS LONDON'

LONDON SW1

CHINA DEPARTMENT
English-made Tea and Breakfast Services

Any piece sold separately

Reproducing the beautiful XVIII Spode services

'OLD BOW' SERVICE
A most beautiful and pleasing design. Soft colourings on exquisitely modelled shapes. Handles and edges finished with best Gilt

'CHELSEA' SERVICE
Copeland's reproduction of a famous design. The coloured hand-decorations are charming and retain the eighteenth century softness of unfadable colourings

'PEPLOW' SERVICE
Copeland's China, reproduction of old Spode from originals, in their fine old colourings. Best burnished Gold edges

For Dinner Services to match these Patterns see page 276

HARRODS Exclusive Designs

'COBRIDGE' SERVICE
Copeland's China. Hand-coloured design in **Dark Blue**, Puce, Red and Green. **Blue lines**

'BATTERSEA' SERVICE
Fruit border on Dark Blue ground. Period 1800-1810. **Painted** in original colours. Reproduced from Spode's design book in their old shape

'ROCKINGHAM' SERVICE
This reproduction of beautifully coloured fruits dates from 1770-1790. Copeland's have here adopted the original shapes designed by Spode and the most charming effects are obtained

No. CC 2451 Royal Crown Derby China, famous Witches Japan. Red, Blue, and rich Gilding in best burnished Gold

'BOSTON' SERVICE
Charming Tuscan china, artistic design. Bird on floral branch, beautifully hand-enamelled and richly Gilt

No. CC 3111 Doulton's China, sprays of naturally coloured Pink roses, with Gilt edges

Any piece sold separately

Replenishments always available

'POMONA' SERVICE
Finest Staffordshire China. Charming coloured **fruit** border with foliage and branch, naturally **coloured** Edges and handles finished with **Black**

'CONWAY' SERVICE
Finest Staffordshire China. Exotic bird in artistic **natural colours**, on floral branch. Solid Black handles and Black lines at edges

'SYLVAN' SERVICE
Finest Staffordshire China. Woodland scene in Black with early English dancing figures. Canary art ground below. Black lines at edges and handles

		Old Bow, Chelsea (£ s. d.)	Peplow, Rockingham (£ s. d.)	Cobridge (£ s. d.)	Battersea (£ s. d.)	No. 2451 (£ s. d.)	Boston (£ s. d.)	No. 3111 (£ s. d.)	Pomona (£ s. d.)	Conway (£ s. d.)	Sylvan (£ s. d.)
Tea Cups and Saucers	Dozen	4 3 0	4 3 0	3 12 0	4 11 0	10 15 0	1 5 6	1 14 0	1 8 9	1 7 0	1 9 0
Coffee Cups and Saucers	"	4 3 0	4 3 0	3 12 0	4 11 0	10 15 0	1 5 6	1 14 0	1 8 9	1 7 0	1 9 0
Breakfast Cups and Saucers	"	5 14 0	5 14 0	5 4 6	6 5 6	13 17 0	1 18 0	2 11 0	2 2 6	2 1 0	2 6 0
Breakfast Plates, 7 inch	"	3 12 0	3 12 0	3 8 6	3 19 9	9 18 0	1 5 6	1 14 0	1 8 9	1 7 0	1 7 0
Tea Plates, 6 inch	"	3 1 0	3 1 0	2 17 0	3 4 6	7 18 0	19 0	1 5 6	1 5 6	1 0 6	1 3 9
Tea Plates, 5 inch	"	2 11 0	2 11 0	2 5 6	2 17 0	6 18 6	16 6	1 1 6	1 0 3	17 6	1 1 0
Milk Jug	Each	11 3	11 3	10 6	12 3	1 3 0	4 6	5 3	5 9	4 9	5 3
Cream Jug	"	7 3	7 3	6 9	8 3	18 0	3 3	3 9	3 9	3 6	3 11
Slop Basin	"	6 3	6 3	5 9	6 11	1 4 0	3 3	4 3	3 9	3 6	3 11
Sugar Basin	"	4 9	4 9	4 3	5 3	17 3	3 3	3 3	3 3	3 6	3 11
Cake Plate	"	9 6	9 6	8 6	10 9	1 4 0	3 3	4 9	4 9	3 9	3 11
Covered Muffin Dish	"	19 0	19 0	18 0	1 0 0	1 19 6	8 9	10 6	9 3	9 0	9 3
Egg Cups	Dozen	2 2 0	2 2 0	1 18 0	2 5 6	4 19 0	12 0	13 0	13 6	12 9	13 3
Breakfast Dish, 10 inch	Each	17 9	17 9	17 0	18 0	2 4 6	10 6	7 6	9 3	9 0	9 3
Breakfast Dish, 12 inch	"	1 4 9	1 4 9	1 3 0	1 6 6	2 12 9	10 6	10 6	12 9	10 9	11 0
Tea Service, 40 pieces	"	7 19 9	7 19 9	6 19 9	8 16 9	21 2 6	2 13 6	3 12 9	3 5 0	2 17 6	3 4 6
Breakfast Service, 29 pieces	"	7 9 6	7 9 6	6 17 9	8 5 6	19 5 6	2 11 9	3 8 0	2 19 6	2 15 6	3 1 0
Breakfast Service, 51 pieces	"	14 19 6	14 19 6	13 19 0	16 7 9	37 5 6	5 7 9	6 15 0	6 2 6	5 14 6	6 4 0
Combined Tea and Breakfast Service, 48 pieces	"	10 18 6	10 18 6	10 2 6	12 10 6	28 14 6	3 15 9	4 19 0	4 8 6	4 1 6	4 9 6

For composition of Services, see page 272

ALL PRICES ARE SUBJECT TO MARKET FLUCTUATIONS

HARRODS LTD

Telephone SLOANE 1234
Telegrams 'EVERYTHING, HARRODS LONDON'

LONDON SW1

CHINA DEPARTMENT
Beautiful English Stone Ware of Finest English Manufacture

PLANT POT (CH 7)
(below)
5½ 6¼ 7½ 8¾ ins. high
6/3 7/- 8/9 11/6 each

Cleverly fashioned in a subtle shade of Electric Blue with a charming powdered effect

WATER JUG (CH 9)
(below)
1½ 2 3 pints
4/6 5/3 6/3 each

VASE (CH 27)
each
6 ins. high 2/6
8 ins. „ 3/9
10 ins. „ 6/-

FLOATING FLOWER BOWL (CH 17)
11 ins. diameter .. 9/9 each

VASE (CH 8)
each
5 ins. high .. 3/11
6 ins. „ .. 4/9
7 ins. „ .. 5/6
8 ins. „ .. 6/9
10 ins. „ .. 9/3

VASE (CH 2)
each
8 ins. high 8/-
10½ ins. „ 10/6
12 ins. „ 16/-

VASE (CH 3)
5 ins. high 2/4
7 ins. „ 3/3
8 ins. „ 4/6
11 ins. „ 9/9

BEDROOM CANDLESTICK (CH 26)
each
Small size 2/6
Large size 3/3

GOBLET CANDLESTICK (CH 24) *(on left)*
4½ ins. high .. 3/- each

PILLAR CANDLESTICK (CH 23) *(on right)*
7 ins. .. 4/6 each

ASH TRAY (CH 21)
1/9 each

Order by Post with confidence
Harrods guarantee your satisfaction

PEMBROKE ART POT
Green
6 7½ 8¼ 9 in. dia.
3/3 3/9 6/3 7/3 each
Pink or Heather bloom
6 7½ 8¼ 9 in. dia.
3/9 4/3 5/11 7/3 each

CH 2147 Art colours: Green, Crimson Saxe Blue or Gold
6 ins. 7 ins. 8 ins.
2/9 3/11 4/9

BULB BOWL No. CC 2156 Art Colours: Green, Crimson, Saxe Blue or Old Gold
8 × 3in. 2/- 9½ × 4in. 3/3 11 × 5in. 5/6 each
Also Troughs for Gas Stoves, 10 × 3 in. 2/6

BASKET SHAPE ART POT Art Colours: Bronze, Green, Red, Pink or Heliotrope
3¾ 5 6 7 8½ 10 12 13½ in. dia.
10d. 1/5 2/6 3/6 5/- 7/3 11/- 17/- each

BEAUTIFULLY DECORATED ENGLISH CHINA FOR THE NURSERY

'GEORGE AND THE DRAGON'
Design of humorous prehistoric figures beautifully enamelled

The **'BROWNIE' Design** Finely coloured subjects. Edges finished with Grass Green lines

Milk Tumblers
½ pint .. Each 1/11
⅜ „ .. 1/8
With handle, ½ pint, 2/6 each

Plates
6 in. 6¾ in. 7¾ in.
Each 1/3 1/5 1/9

Porridge Plate
7½ in. .. 2 3 each

Tea Cup and Saucer
Each 1 9
Coffee Cup and Saucer 1/7

Oatmeal Saucers
Each 1/9

The China Department is on the Second Floor

Mugs
Large size .. Each 1/9
Medium size „ 1/7
Small size .. „ 1/6

Baby Plates
Oval, 8½ in. .. 2/6 each
Round, 7¼ in., 2/6 ; 6½ in., 1/10 „

Teapot
¾ pint .. .. Each 6/11
1 pint .. .. „ 8/6

Milk Tumbler
Small size Each 2/6
Large size „ 3/3

Tea Cup and Saucer
Each 2/9
Mug to match .. Each 2/6

Plates
6 in. 7 in. 8 in.
Each .. 1/8 1/11 2/9
Can also supply to match :—
S/s L/s
Pair Pair
Sugar & Cream 4/5 5/3

ALL PRICES ARE SUBJECT TO MARKET FLUCTUATIONS

HARRODS LTD
Telephone SLOANE 1234
Telegrams 'EVERYTHING HARRODS LONDON'
LONDON S W 1

CHINA DEPARTMENT
Wonderful Values in Toilet Services from Harrods

Small Toilet Sets for Antique Washstands

No. CH 2560 Cetem Ware. Reproduction for Antique Corner Stands. Enamelled coloured floral sprays with Blue printed border
Set 5 pieces ... 19/6

The 'COBRIDGE' Small antique set, Copeland hand-coloured design in Dark Blue, Puce, Red and Green 5 pieces, £2 12 6

'OXFORD' TOILET SET
Simple design in White or White & Gold.

			White	White & Gold	Better quality White & Gold
Ewer or Basin	..	Each	4/6	5/11	8/3
Chamber	..	,,	2/11	3/3	4/9
Soap Dish	..	,,	1/6	2/1	2/9
Brush Vase..	..	,,	1/0	1/3	1/9
Sponge Bowl	..	,,	3/0	4/6	5/9
Set 5 pieces..	..	,,	13/9	18/0	25/6
Slop Pail	..	,,	7/3	10/9	18/0

'DENMARK' TOILET SET
A charming conventional floral design Printed in Blue.

	Each
Ewer or Basin	7/6
Chamber	3/11
Soap Dish	2/6
Brush Vase	1/6
Sponge Bowl	5/3
Set 5 pieces	22/6
Slop Pail	16/6

No. CH 2559 Best Staffordshire manufacture. The favourite Willow design in Blue, finished with Gilt edges and handles, Gilt lined

Ewer or Basin	..	..	..	..	Each	9/0
Chamber	..	..	..	..	,,	4/3
Soap Dish	..	..	..	..	,,	3 3
Brush Vase ..	..	..	..	..	,,	2/0
Sponge Bowl	..	..	..	..	,,	6/6
Set 5 pieces..	..	..	..	..	,,	£1 7 6
Slop Pail	..	..	..	..	,,	16/0

No. CH 2437 Best English Ware. Oriental design with birds and flowers enamelled in bright colours Gilt edges

			£	s.	d.
Single Service, 5 pieces	..	..	2	3	0
Double Service, 10 pieces	..	..	5	14	9
Double Service, 12 pieces	..	..	6	1	3
Slop Pail	..	..	1	5	3
Sponge Bowl				10	0

No. CH 525 Crown Devon Ware. Art shades in Yellow, Pink, Dark Green or Mauve. Edges and handles finished with Black lines

		£	s.	d.
Single Service, 5 pieces	..	1	9	6
Double Service, 10 pieces	..	4	0	0
Double Service, 12 pieces	..	4	4	6
Slop Pail	..		18	0
Sponge Bowl	..		7	6

COLOURED WILLOW
Fine Staffordshire manufacture. Simple Willow design, in bright blue, terra-cotta and green foliage, gilt lines and traced handles.

			£	s.	d.
Single Service, 5 pieces	..	..	1	1	9
Double Service, 10 pieces	..	..	2	19	0
Double Service, 12 pieces	..	..	3	3	0
Slop Pail	..	..		13	6
Sponge Bowl	..	..		6	0

No. CH 6376 Artistic fruit and foliage border in natural colours, with Black top; handles and edges are attractively finished in Black. This design can also be supplied with Yellow or Pale Mauve top

			£	s.	d.
Single Service, 5 pieces	..	..	2	2	0
Double Service, 10 pieces	..	..	5	14	9
Double Service, 12 pieces	..	..	6	3	9
Slop Pail	..	..	1	10	0
Sponge Bowl	..	..		9	9

For Composition of Services see page 272

No. CH 28416 Crescent China. Artistic design of pink ribbon and basket of roses. Edges and handles are finished with grass green lines

		£	s.	d.
Single Service, 5 pieces	..	3	10	6
Double Service, 10 pieces	..	9	5	0
Double Service, 12 pieces	..	9	18	0
Slop Pail..	..	2	1	6
Sponge Bowl	..		15	6

'CHELSEA' SERVICE
(By Copeland) Reproduction of Old Spode from the originals, in their fine underglaze colourings

			£	s.	d.
Single Service, 5 pieces	..	..	3	10	0
Double Service, 10 pieces	..	..	9	8	6
Double Service, 12 pieces	..	..	10	2	6
Slop Pail	..	..	2	4	0
Sponge Bowl	..	..		18	0

ALL PRICES ARE SUBJECT TO MARKET FLUCTUATIONS

Telephone SLOANE 1234
Telegrams 'EVERYTHING HARRODS LONDON'

HARRODS LTD

LONDON SW 1

CHINA DEPARTMENT
Morning Tea and Coffee Sets on Attractive Trays

Harrods have an unrivalled selection of Coffee and Tea Sets in every imaginable colour and design. These are always on view in the China Department on the Second Floor

Every one of these Coffee and Tea Services is of the finest British Manufacture. Replacements are therefore easily effected

'KNIGHTSBRIDGE' COFFEE SET
Fine Staffordshire manufacture. Pink, Yellow, or Blue ground, with Black edges. On Wicker edged tray with glass base 29/-

'KNIGHTSBRIDGE' EARLY MORNING TEA SET
Fine Staffordshire manufacture. Pink, Yellow or Blue ground, with Black edges. Two-cup size. On Wicker-edged tray with glass-lined base 25/-

'BASIL' MORNING TEA SET
Cetem Ware. Black lace border with Scarlet ground. On Wicker-edged tray. Can also be supplied in Yellow or Apple Green grounds at same price 29/-

THE 'TUDOR' BREAKFAST-IN-BED SERVICE
Fine Staffordshire manufacture. Hand-coloured floral design in Red, Green and Dark Blue, with hair-brown lace band broken by panels of flowers. Edges and handles finished with Gilt lines. Complete on Wooden tray with Wicker edge 47/3

THE 'CONWAY' MORNING TEA SET
Finest Staffordshire China. Exotic bird, in artistic natural colours, on floral branch. Solid Black handles and Black lines at edges. Complete on Wicker-edged tray, glass base.
33/6

'WESTMINSTER' EARLY MORNING TEA SERVICE
Finest Staffordshire manufacture. Ivory border and beautifully coloured floral sprays, Cane-coloured edges. Complete on Wicker-edged tray with glass base 29/-

'HARROW' EARLY MORNING TEA SERVICE
English China. Ivory border, coloured sprays and burnished Gold edges. Complete on Wicker-edged tray with glass base .. 40/6

'BOSTON' EARLY MORNING TEA SERVICE
Charming Tuscan China, artistic design. Bird on floral branch, beautifully hand-enamelled and richly gilt. Complete on Wicker-edged tray with glass base 33/6

'POMONA' MORNING TEA SET
Finest Staffordshire China. Coloured fruit design; Black lines at edges and handles. On Wicker-edged tray 35/3

THE 'COBRIDGE' EARLY MORNING TEA SERVICE
Copeland China. A superb reproduction. Hand-coloured design in Dark Blue, Puce, Red and Green-Blue lines. On Wicker-edged tray, glass base .. .. Complete 59/6

THE 'CHELSEA'
Morning Tea Set. Mahogany tray. Copeland (Spode) China. A faithful reproduction of an old design on original shapes .. .. .. Complete £5/6

Tea, Breakfast and Dinner Services are available to match the majority of these services. All are Harrods exclusive designs

THE 'PEPLOW'
Copeland's China Two-cup Morning Set. Reproduction of old Spode from the originals, in their fine underglaze colourings, with best burnished Gilt edges. On Mahogany tray .. .. .. Complete 64/3

ALL PRICES ARE SUBJECT TO MARKET FLUCTUATIONS

HARRODS LTD

Telephone SLOANE 1234
Telegrams 'EVERYTHING HARRODS LONDON'

LONDON S W 1

CHINA DEPARTMENT

Further Offers of Domestic Utensils in Earthenware

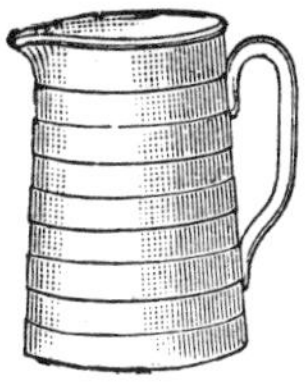

JUGS
Tankard Shape (White)

½ pt.	¾ pt.	1 pt.
11d	**1/-**	**1/1**
1½ pt.	2 pts.	3 pts.
1/3	**1/7**	**2/1**
4 pts.	6 pts.	8 pts.
3/-	**6/3**	**8/-**

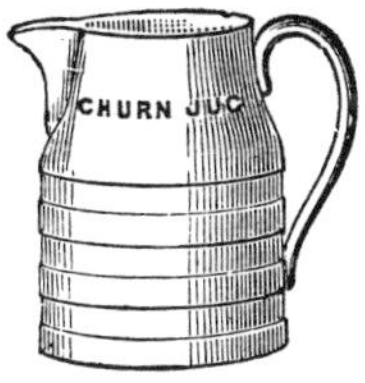

JUGS
Churn Shape (White)

¾ pt.	1 pt.	1½ pts.
10d	**1/-**	**1/3**
2 pts.	3 pts.	4 pts.
1/6	**2/-**	**2/11**
6 pts.	8 pts.	
4/3	**5/9**	

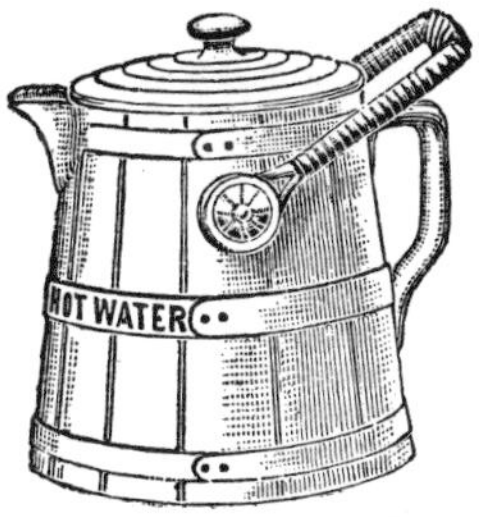

HOTWATER CARRIER
Lock Lid and Cane Handle
White, lettered in Black

	1 qt.	2 qts.	3 qts.	4 qts.	6 qts.
White	**4/3**	**5/6**	**6/9**	**8/6**	**11/-**
White and Gold	**5/11**	**7/6**	**9/3**	**11/9**	**14/3**

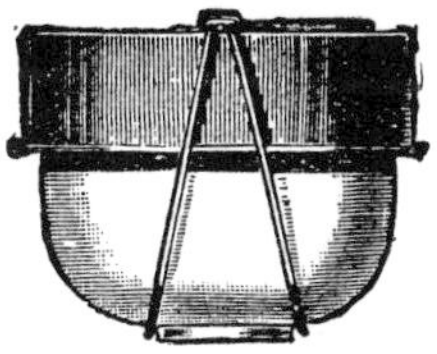

QUEEN'S
PUDDING BASIN

1 pt.	**1/9**	3 pts.	**3/9**
1½ pts.	**2/3**	4½ pts.	**4/9**
2 pts.	**2/9**	6 pts.	**6/11**

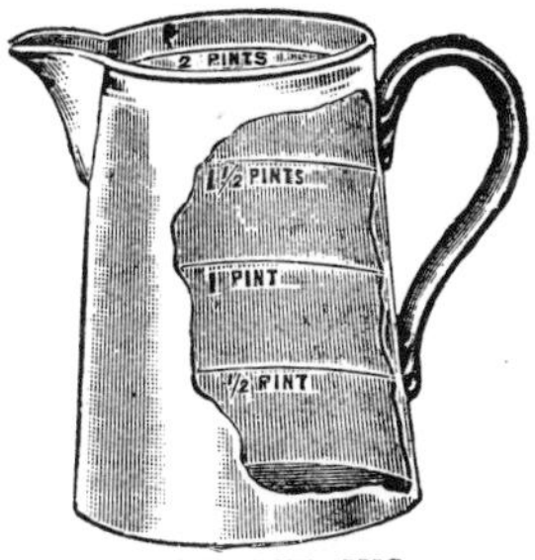

GRADUATED JUG
Average capacity

1 pt.	2 pts.	4 pts.
1/9	**2/11**	**5/-**

Lettered Jars are not stocked but can be supplied to order

Order by Post with confidence.
Satisfaction guaranteed

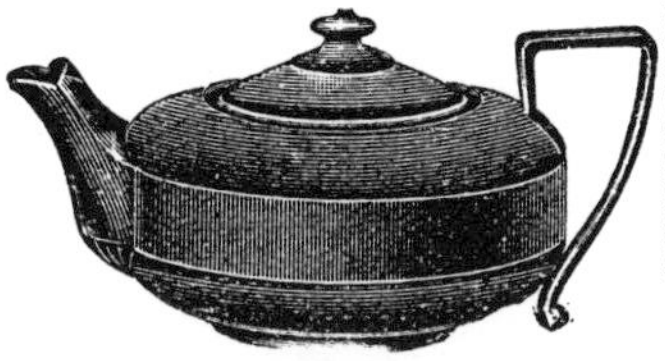

TEAPOT
'Super' Shape Brown Rockingham

Pints	⅓	½	¾	1⅓	1½	2
Each	**1/2**	**1/4**	**1/6**	**1/10**	**2/6**	**3/9**

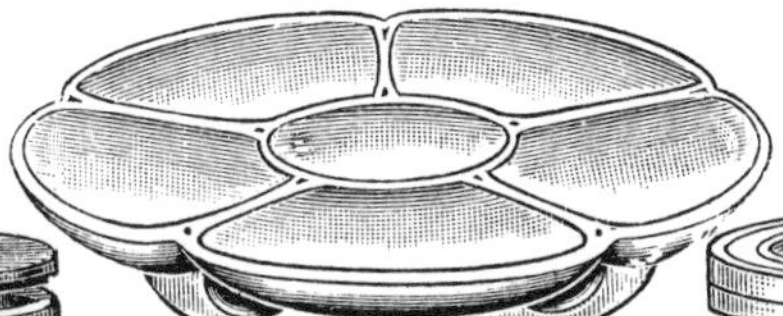

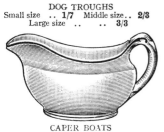

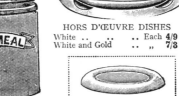

HORS D'ŒUVRE DISHES
White .. .. .. Each **4/9**
White and Gold .. „ **7/3**

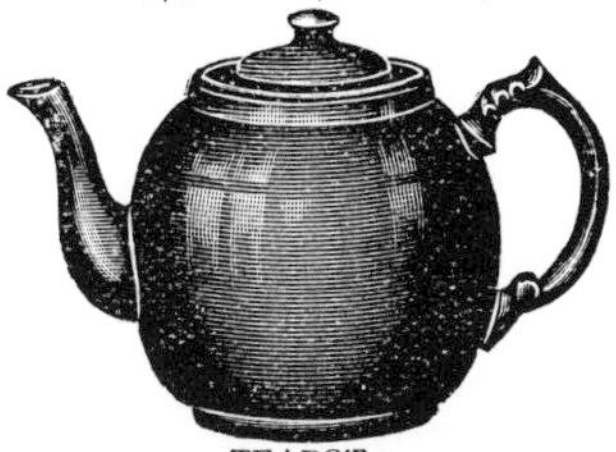

TEAPOT
Plain Black Rockingham

½ pt. ..	**1/0½**	1½ pts. ..	**1/6**
¾ pt. ..	**1/2**	2 pts. ..	**1/10**
1 pt. ..	**1/4**	2½ pts. ..	**2/6**
		3 pts. ..	**3/9**

PATENT NON-DRIP TEAPOT
In Brown Rockingham Ware

1 pt. ..	**1/4**	2½ pts. ..	**2/-**
1½ pts. ..	**1/6**	3 pts. ..	**2/9**
2 pts. ..	**1/9**	4 pts. ..	**3/11**

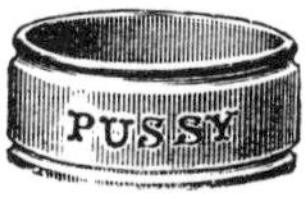

DRINKING TROUGH
Stamped either 'Pussy' or 'Doggie' **1/7**

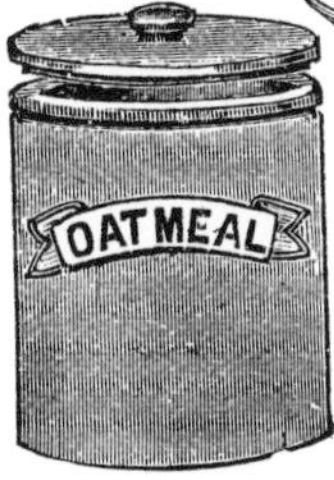

STONEWARE JARS

Liquid capacity	Plain White	With any Name
½ pt.	**10d**	**1/3**
1 pt.	**1/4**	**1/10**
2 pts.	**2/1**	**2/11**
3 pts.	**2/6**	**3/6**
4 pts.	**3/1**	**4/3**
6 pts.	**4/3**	**5/6**

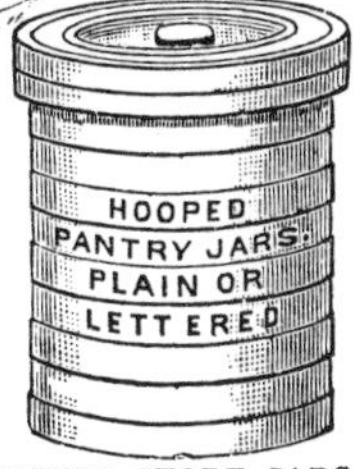

WHITE STORE JARS

Liquid Capacity	Plain White	With any Name
½ pt.	**10d**	**1/-**
1 pt.	**1/1**	**1/3**
1½ pts.	**1/10**	**2/1**
2 pts.	**2/6**	**2/9**
3 pts.	**3/3**	**3/9**
5 pts.	**5/-**	**5/6**
8 pts.	**6/3**	**6/9**
11 pts.	**7/6**	**8/6**
15 pts.	**10/-**	**11/-**

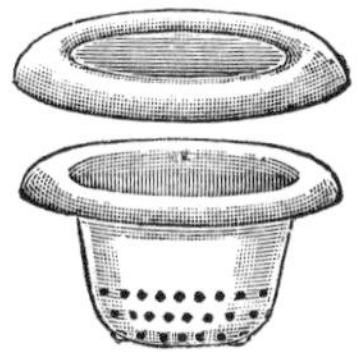

Patent Tea Infuser
(*above*) White
Earthenware .. **1/11**
White China .. **2/3**

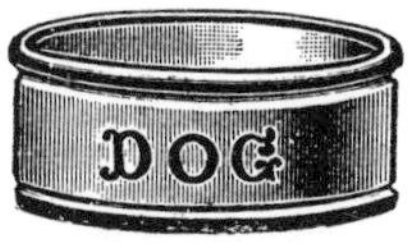

DOG TROUGHS
Small size .. **1/7** Middle size .. **2/3**
Large size **3/3**

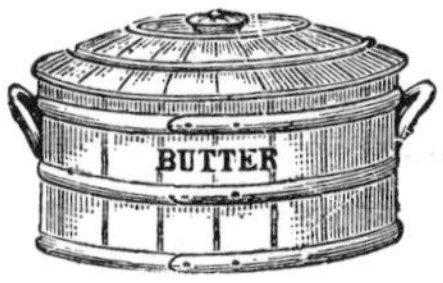

BUTTER TUB
White Earthenware. Lettered in Black

6 ins. ..	**1/9**	8 ins. ..	**3/-**
7 ins. ..	**2/3**	9 ins. ..	**3/6**

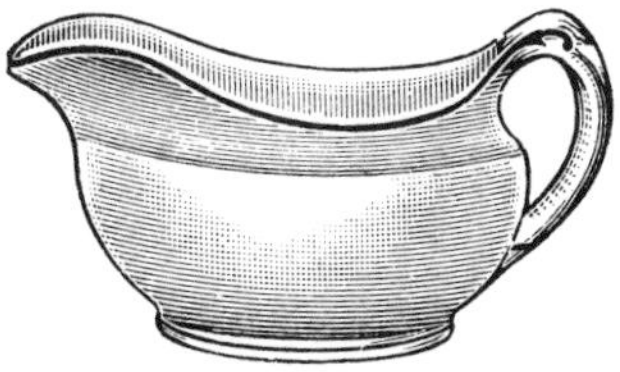

CAPER BOATS
Earthenware

	Small	Medium	Large
White	**1/7**	**1/9**	**1/10**
White and Gold ..	**1/9**	**1/10**	**2/-**

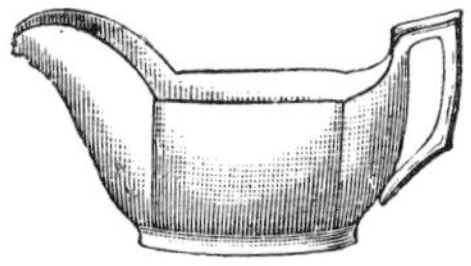

CAPER BOATS
Best China

No.	4	3	2	1
White	**2/4**	**2/9**	**3/-**	**3/6**
White and Gold	**3/6**	**4/-**	**5/3**	**6/-**

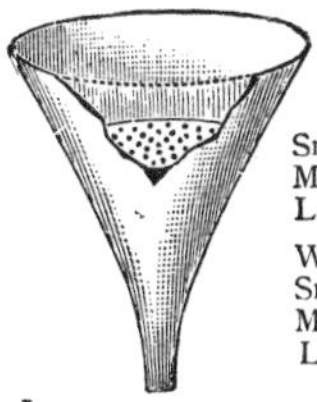

FUNNELS
White

Small size	**2/6**
Medium size ..	**3/1**
Large size	**3/6**
With strainer, as above	
Small size	**3/6**
Medium size ..	**4/6**
Large size	**5/6**

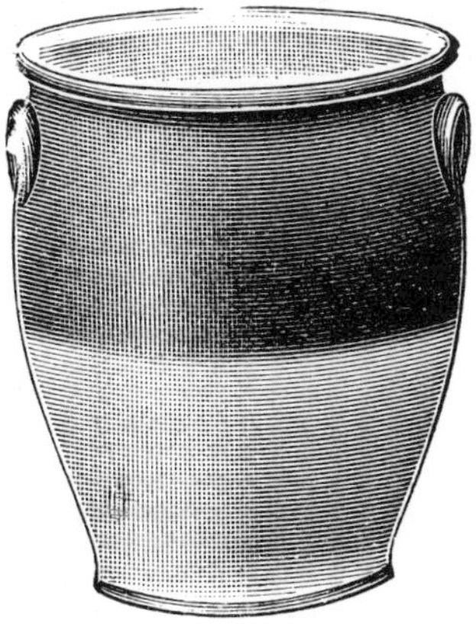

SUNDERLAND EGG CROCK
Approximate capacity

Sizes	Eggs	Each
7 quarts	72	**3/1**
10 „	108	**4/-**
15 „	165	**6/3**
17 „	190	**8/3**
22 „	250	**10/3**
26 „	280	**12/6**
30 „	340	**15/6**
40 „	450	**18/6**

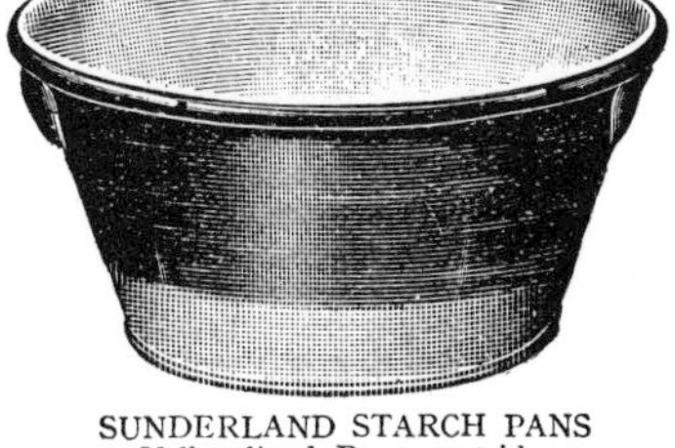

SUNDERLAND STARCH PANS
Yellow lined, Brown outside

9½ ins. ..	**1/6**	15 ins. ..	**5/9**
10½ ins. ..	**2/-**	16½ ins. ..	**8/3**
12 ins. ..	**2/11**	18 ins. ..	**9/3**
13½ ins. ..	**4/3**	20 ins. ..	**11/3**
		22 ins. ..	**13/6**

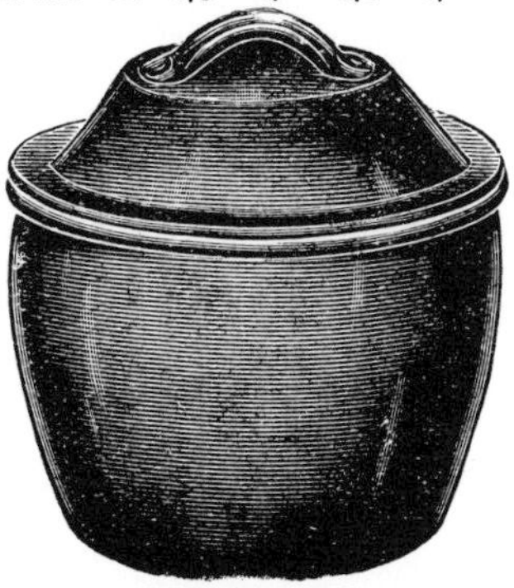

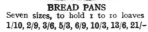

BREAD PANS
Seven sizes, to hold 1 to 10 loaves
1/10, 2/9, 3/6, 5/3, 6/9, 10/3, 13/6, 21/-

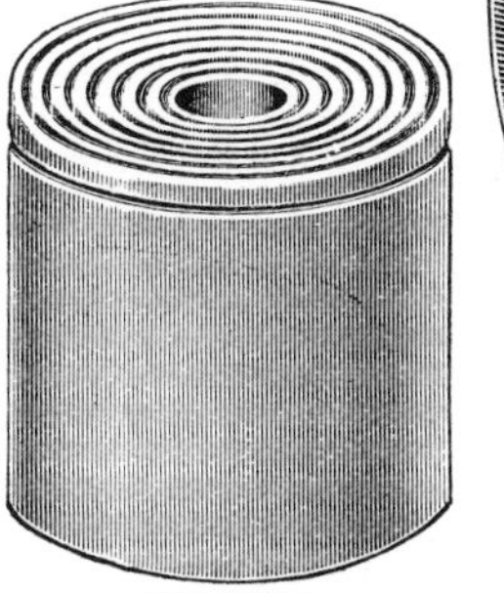

JAM POTS
For Preserving. Approximate capacity in liquid ozs.

	Dozen		Dozen
3 ozs. ..	**3/6**	15 ozs. ..	**5/6**
5 ozs. ..	**3/9**	24 ozs. ..	**7/-**
9 ozs. ..	**4/3**	40 ozs. ..	**10/9**
		60 ozs. ..	**14/9**

ALL PRICES ARE SUBJECT TO MARKET FLUCTUATIONS

CHINA DEPARTMENT
Splendid Values in Toilet Ware

THE 'KYROP'
The New Foot Bath, in White Earthenware
18½ × 14½ × 8½ ins. high **£1 14 0**

FOOT BATH (White)
16 ins. .. **£1 0 6**   18 ins. .. **£1 5 6**

SLOP PAIL
With Patent Non-splashable Cover. White .. **8/-**
White and Gold **12/-**
Harrods specially recommend this Pail. The hard body and non-crazing glaze guarantee it being permanently sanitary
Cheaper make. White **7/6**
White and Gold **11/6**

DOULTON'S IMPROVED STONE FOOT WARMER

1½ pts.	2 pts.	3 pts.	4 pts.	6 pts.
2/9	3/3	3/11	4/6	5/3

THE ADAPTABLE FOOT WARMER

1 pt.	2 pts.	3 pts.	4 pts.
2/3	2/11	3/6	4/3

THE 'LITTLE FOLKS' FOOT WARMER
An ideal gift for a child. In Cream glazed Stone-ware
6 ins. wide .. Each **2/1**

SPITTING MUGS
(Bisto China) White China

Small size	Med. size	Large size
2/6	2/9	3/6

White and Gold

3/6	3/11	4/9

THE BUNGALOW FOOT WARMER
In Cream-glazed Stone-ware

2 pts.	3 pts.	4 pts.
3/3	3/11	4/9

Enquiries by Post receive careful and prompt attention

IMPROVED SHAVING MUG
Specially adapted for Safety Razors
White **1/5**
White and Gold **1/9**

COMMODE PAN
Complete with metal handle. White
Small size .. **7/9**
Large size .. **8/11**

MILK TUMBLERS
White China, with handle **1/8**
White China, without handle **1/3½**
White Earthenware without handle **4¾d**

CC 115 SHADED CANDLESTICK
In Plain Art Colours
Each **2/6**

NIGHT LIGHT STANDS
White .. **10½d**
White and Gold **1/4**

'BEATRICE' SHAVING MUG
Ivory **2/3**
Ivory and Gold **3/1**

CC 113 PILLAR CANDLESTICK
7 ins. **2/3**
8 ins. **2/11**
In Plain Art Colours

CC 114 BEDROOM CANDLESTICK
In Plain Art Colours
Each .. **1/11**

ROUND BED PAN

9 ins.	10 ins.	11 ins.	12 ins.
6/6	7/-	7/6	8/11
Covered			
8/6	9/3	10/-	11/9

HYGIENIC SICK FEEDER CC 4
Practical in every way. Easily cleansed. Established its superiority over all others in the late war

	3½ ins.	4 ins.	4½ ins.
White Earthenware	1/2½	1/3½	1/5
White & Gold	1/8	1/10	2/1

THE 'COMFORTABLE'
(Reg. No. 246628) The New Sanitary Bed Pan

	Small size	Medium size	Large size
Uncovered ..	10/-	11/9	14/3
Covered ..	13/6	15/9	19/-

SLIPPER BED PAN AND COVER

	10 ins.	11 ins.	12 ins.
Uncovered ..	7/11	9/3	10/9
Covered ..	10/9	12/3	14/-

GAS-PROOF SLIPPER
Patent Air-tight cover (white) .. **14/3**

CHAIR PANS
Diameter

6 ins.	7 ins.	8 ins.	9 ins.	10 ins.	11 ins.	12 ins.
1/6	2/3	2/11	3/3	3/9	4/6	4/11

CHAMBERS
Round Rim

Approx. Dia.	White	White and Gold
4¾ ins. ..	11d	1/6
5¼ ins. ..	1/1	1/10
5¾ ins. ..	1/5	2/3
6¼ ins. ..	2/-	2/6
7¼ ins	2/3	3/6

REGD. IMPROVED "ABERDEEN" MALE URINAL.
URINALS (White)
Male **3/4**
Female **3/9**

SECTION ON A·B

ALL PRICES ARE SUBJECT TO MARKET FLUCTUATIONS

Telephone SLOANE 1234
Telegrams 'EVERYTHING HARRODS LONDON'

HARRODS LTD   **LONDON SW 1**

CHINA DEPARTMENT

A Further Choice of Fireproof China

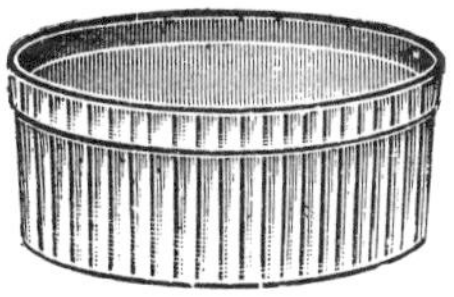

WHITE SOUFFLE DISH

7⅞ ins.	3/3	Extra deep	3/9
6¾ ins.	2/9	,, ,,	3/-
6 ins.	2/6	,, ,,	2/9
5¼ ins.	2/3	,, ,,	2/6
4¾ ins.	1/9	,, ,,	2/-

'LONDON' RAMEKIN

Diam.	Dozen
2 ins.	5/6
2¼ ins.	6/-
2½ ins.	7/-
2¾ ins.	7/6

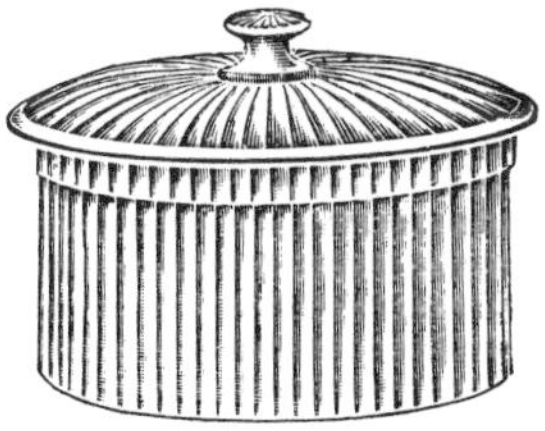

ROUND COVERED DEEP SOUFFLE

6¾ ins. diam.	4/6
6 ins. ,,	3/9
5¼ ins. ,,	3/6
4¾ ins. ,,	2/9

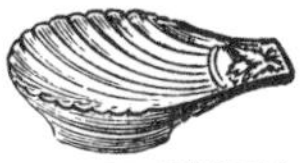

SCALLOP SHELLS

White

3¾ ins.	6d
4¼ ins.	8d
4¾ ins.	10d
6 ins.	1/2

WHITE RIBBED STEWPOT

5½ ins. diam.	4/-
6¾ ins. ,,	5/6
7¼ ins. ,,	6/3
7¾ ins. ,,	7/9

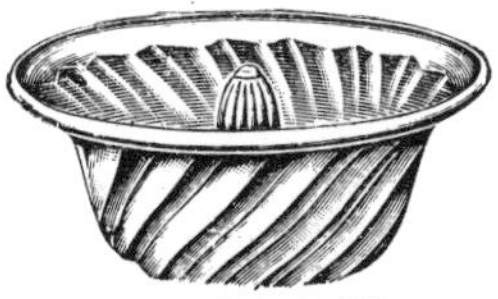

JELLY MOULD

White

1½ pints	4/-
1 pint	3/9
½ pint	2/6

SALAD BOWL

White china

6¾ ins. diam.	2/3
7¾ ins. ,,	2/9
8¾ ins. ,,	3/3
10 ins. ,,	4/-

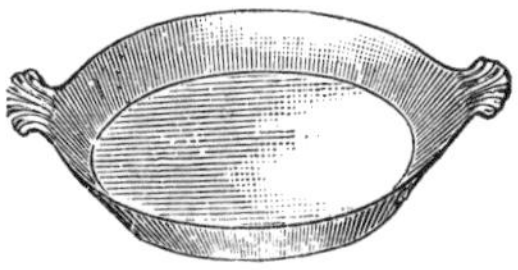

EARED DISH

Round, White

Diam.	4″	4½″	5″	5¾″	6¼″
Each	10d	11d	1/-	1/1	1/4
Diam.	7″	7½″	8″	8½″	9″
Each	1/5	1/7	1/9	2/-	2/3

Oval, White

Diam.	5½″	6⅝″	7¾″	9″	10¼″
Each	9d	11d	1/1	1/3	1/7
Diam.	11¼″	12½″	13½″	14″	15½″
Each	2/-	3/-	3/6	4/6	5/11

The sizes given above are approximate, the dishes actually measuring ½ to 1½ ins. larger than quoted

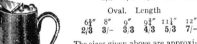

PIE DISHES

Fluted, White. Round

Diam.	5¼″	6¼″	7¼″	8¼″	9½″
	1/2	1/4	1/9	2/6	3/3

Oval. Length

6¾″	8″	9″	9¾″	11¼″	12″
2/3	3/-	3/3	4/3	5/3	7/-

The sizes given above are approximate, the dishes actually measuring ½ to 1½ ins. larger than quoted

COVERED SOUP TUREEN

White china

5 ins. diam.	1 pint	3/11
6 ins. ,,	2 pints	5/3
7¼ ins. ,,	3 pints	6/9
8½ ins. ,,	5 pints	9/6

HOT WATER JUG B

With metal cover

½ pint	3/6
1 pint	4/3
1½ pints	5/6
2 pints	6/3

Write for Special Book, 'Casserole Cookery,' by C. Herman Senn, M.B.E., G.C.A. Price 9d nett

HOT WATER JUG

With metal cover

Brown or Green

½ pint	4/-
¾ pint	4/9
1 pint	5/6
1½ pints	6/6
2 pints	7/3

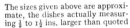

EGG POACHERS

Diam.	3″	3⅜″	4″
	11d	1/-	1/3

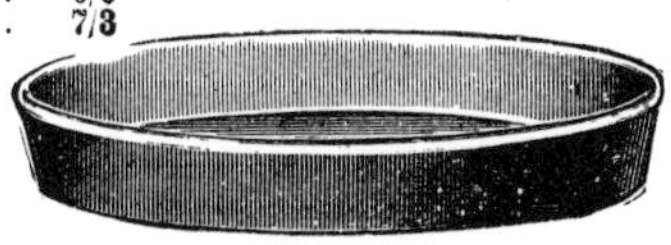

OVAL FISH DISH

Green or Brown

8 ins.	1/3	11½ ins.	2/6
9¼ ins.	1/9	12½ ins.	3/3
10¼ ins.	2/-	13¾ ins.	4/6
		14½ ins.	5/9

OVAL COVERED POTTING

Green

Diam.	5¼″	4½″	4″
	2/6	1/11	1/6

ROUND CHINA TART DISH

In natural crust colour

7 ins.	6/6
8 ins.	8/9

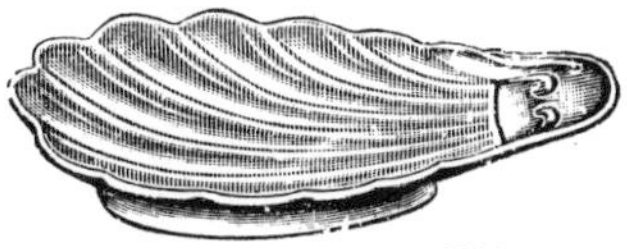

RADISH SHELLS White

5¼″	5¾″	6⅝″	7½″	8½″	9″
7d	8d	10d	11d	1/-	1/2

FINEST FRENCH FIREPROOF CHINA IN NICKEL-PLATED FRAMES

CC 9 PETITE MARMITES

Set of 6 (size 2¾ ins. diameter) in nickel-plated frame

Complete £1 9 9

CC 4 PETITE SAUCEPANS

Set of 6 (size 2¾ ins. diameter) in nickel-plated frame

Complete £1 4 9

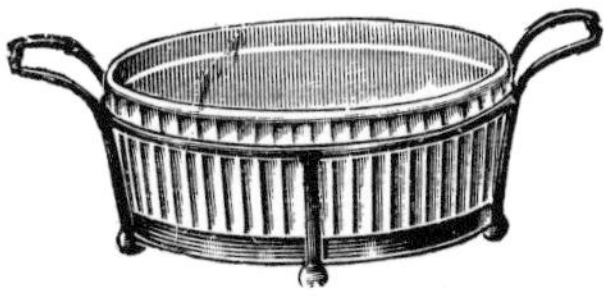

CC 6 WHITE CHINA SOUFFLE

In nickel-plated frame

6 ins... 16/- 7¼ ins... 19/6

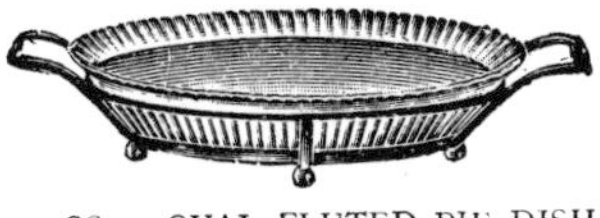

CC 7 OVAL FLUTED PIE DISH

White. In nickel-plated frame

9 ins.	17/-
9¾ ins.	18/6
11¼ ins.	£1 0 9

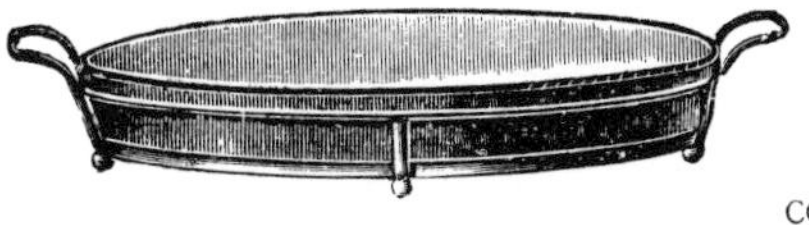

CC 2 OVAL SOLE DISH

Green or Brown, 12½ ins., in nickel-plated frame £1 1 0

CC 8 OVAL COVERED PIE DISH

Green or Brown in nickel-plated frame

9¼ ins.	19/9
9¾ ins.	£1 5 0

CC 3 OVAL BREAKFAST DISH

Green or Brown on nickel-plated frame With lamp

9¾ ins... £1 13 0 10½ ins... £1 19 0

CC 1 MILK BOILER

1½ pints. Green or Brown on nickel-plated frame. With lamp

£1 10 0

ALL PRICES ARE SUBJECT TO MARKET FLUCTUATIONS

GLASS DEPARTMENT
Latest Designs in Finest English Crystal Dessert Services

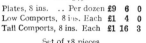

CG 22684

Plates	.. Per dozen	**£13 13 0**
Dessert Centre, 9½ ins.		
Each	.. .. ..	**£2 4 0**
Set of 14 pieces		
Complete	.. ..	**£18 1 0**

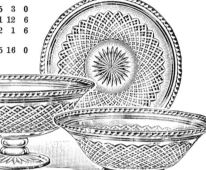

CH 19374

Plates	.. Per dozen	**£15 3 0**
Low Comports	.. Each	**£1 12 6**
Tall Comports	.. ,,	**£2 1 6**
Set of 18 pieces		
Complete	.. ..	**£25 16 0**

DESSERT SERVICES
18 pieces consists of
12 Dessert Plates
4 Low Comports
2 Tall Comports

CG 23498

Plates, 8 ins.	.. Per dozen	**£9 6 0**
Low Comports, 8 ins.	Each	**£1 4 0**
Tall Comports, 8 ins.	Each	**£1 16 3**
Set of 18 pieces		
Complete **£17 14 6**		

CH 19373

Plates	.. Per dozen	**£18 9 0**
Low Comports	.. Each	**£1 18 0**
Tall Comports	.. ,,	**£2 8 9**
Set of 18 pieces		
Complete **£30 18 6**		

FINEST ENGLISH CRYSTAL LIQUEUR SETS ON TRAY

CG 22328
Finest English
Crystal Bread Plate
Richly cut
5 ins. diameter
Each **8/–**

No. 23112
English Crystal
Cigarette or Cigar
Holder, with Ash
Tray
Richly cut
Small size .. **8/9**
Large size .. **11/3**

CH 17925 Etched English Crystal Liqueur Set
on Mahogany Tray. Complete .. **£1 15 3**

THE LATEST INNOVATION

CH 17928 Cut English Crystal Liqueur Set on
Mahogany Tray. Complete **£4 2 0**

Finest English Crystal Pastry, Dessert or Cracker Tray. Handle ensures freedom while serving, and the whole
piece is beautifully balanced

THE IDEAL TRAY
For sandwiches, afternoon tea pastries, sweets, fruit,
etc. Finest 'Stuart' English Crystal, beautifully
hand-made and richly cut

CG 23094

10½ ins. diameter	.. .. Each	**£1 16 0**
12 ins. ,,	.. .. .. ,,	**£2 12 6**

CG 23899

6 ins. diameter	.. .. .. Each	**12/9**
7 ins. ,,	.. .. .. ,,	**15/6**

CG 23902

10½ ins. diameter	.. .. .. Each	**£2 6 0**
12 ins. ,,	.. .. .. ,,	**£3 6 0**

ALL PRICES ARE SUBJECT TO MARKET FLUCTUATIONS

HARRODS LTD

Telephone SLOANE 1234
Telegrams 'EVERYTHING HARRODS LONDON'

LONDON S W I

GLASS DEPARTMENT
Table Services—all in Finest English Crystal
Harrods offer a superb selection of the newest designs in plain, etched, intaglio, engraved or heavily cut

TABLE SERVICE
CH 430 Plain throughout, of fine quality. Specially suitable where monograms or crests are required

TABLE SERVICE
CH 14048 Slight optic flute. Decanters cut at neck

'CLUB' TABLE SERVICE
Plain and serviceable. Decanters have cut neck and with cut lapidary stoppers

TABLE SERVICE
CH 13834 Etched key border design

TABLE SERVICE
CH 13833 Etched circles border design. Shapes as CH 13834

TABLE SERVICE
CH 774 Plain, with cut leg and cut star base. Decanters cut at neck and stopper

Any piece sold separately

Shop by Post with confidence

TABLE SERVICE
CH 21699 Splendid reproduction. Plain with effectively moulded bands giving effect of silver

TABLE SERVICE
CH 21700 Finely engraved border with moulded bands, giving silver effect

TABLE SERVICE
CH 21694 Cut row of hollows with moulded bands giving effect of silver

TABLE SERVICE
CH 21693 Engraved grape vine design, with moulded bands giving silver effect

		430 £ s. d.	14048 £ s. d.	Club £ s. d.	13834 £ s. d.	13833 £ s. d.	774 £ s. d.	21699 £ s. d.	21700 £ s. d.	21694 £ s. d.	21693 £ s. d.
Port Glasses	Dozen	11 0	10 3	11 0	12 9	12 9	17 0	15 6	1 2 9	1 6 0	1 14 9
Sherry Glasses	,,	11 0	10 3	11 0	12 9	12 9	17 0	15 6	1 2 9	1 6 0	1 14 9
Claret Glasses	,,	12 6	12 0	12 6	17 3	17 3	1 2 0	1 0 6	1 9 3	1 13 0	2 3 3
Champagne Glasses	,,	15 3	14 6	15 3	1 2 3	1 2 3	1 7 0	1 5 9	1 16 6	2 1 6	2 15 6
Liqueur Glasses	,,	11 0	10 3	11 0	12 9	12 9	16 0	14 9	1 1 9	1 5 0	1 13 9
Tumblers, ½ pint	,,	11 0	10 3	11 0	15 6	15 6	17 0	1 1 9	1 12 0	1 15 3	2 2 6
Tumblers, Soda	,,	1 2 0	1 0 6	1 2 0	1 10 6	1 10 6	1 7 0	1 18 0	2 13 6	2 19 0	3 9 9
Finger Bowls	,,	1 2 0	1 5 6	1 2 0	1 10 9	1 10 9	1 7 0	1 11 0	2 10 6	2 12 0	3 9 9
Ice Plates	,,	17 6	1 9 6	17 6	17 6	17 6	1 4 0	1 11 0	2 10 6	2 12 0	3 9 9
Custard Glasses	,,	17 6	15 6	17 6	17 3	17 3	1 9 0	1 0 6	1 9 3	1 13 0	2 3 0
Decanters, Quart	Each	12 0	11 3	16 9	14 6	14 6	16 0	1 0 6	1 4 0	1 9 6	1 8 9
Decanters, Claret	,,	18 9	16 0	1 2 0	19 9	19 9	1 2 6	1 10 9	1 14 6	1 19 9	1 17 9
Water Set (Jug and two Tumblers)	,,	7 3	6 0	7 3	14 6	14 6	10 0	8 6	12 9	17 9	15 6
Suite of 87 pieces	,,	7 4 6	6 18 6	7 17 6	9 12 9	9 12 9	10 7 6	11 6 6	15 12 0	17 19 6	21 5 0

For composition of Suite see page 295

ALL PRICES ARE SUBJECT TO MARKET FLUCTUATIONS

HARRODS LTD

Telephone SLOANE 1234
Telegrams 'EVERYTHING HARRODS LONDON'

LONDON S W 1

GLASS DEPARTMENT
The Latest Designs in Cocktail Glasses and Shakers, All of Finest English Crystal

CG 23495 English Crystal Cocktail Glass Per doz. **£1 13 6**

CG 23784 English Crystal Cocktail Glass Per doz. **£3 15 0**

CG 23914 English Crystal Cocktail Glass Per doz. **£2 14 0**

CG 22207 English Crystal Cocktail Glasses with engraved Cock Per doz. **£1 16 0**

CG 23926 English Crystal Cocktail Shaker. Beautifully hand made .. .. Each **18/-**

CG 22202 English Crystal Cocktail Glasses with engraved Cock Per doz. **£1 12 9**

CG 23914 English Crystal Cocktail Shaker. Beautifully hand made Richly cut. Each **£1 9 6**

CG 23671 English Crystal Cocktail Glass Per doz. **£2 11 0**

CG 23494 English Crystal Cocktail Glass Per doz. **£2 7 0**

FINEST ENGLISH CRYSTAL—GRAPE FRUIT GLASSES

CG 23562 Fruit Glass. Cut laurel design. 4 ins. diameter Each **10/-**

CG 23492 Fruit Glass. Plain with bands below giving effect of silver. 4¾ ins. diameter. Each **2/3**

CG 23506 Fruit Glass. Cut diamonds and flat flute 5 ins. diameter .. Each **13/-**

CG 23432 Fruit Glass. Engraved fruit design. Each **6/-**

CG 23573 Fruit Glass. Design of cut leaves and berries 4 ins. diameter .. Each **3/9**

HOCK GLASSES   ENGLISH CRYSTAL FRUIT SERVICE   HOCK GLASSES

CG 10446 Hock Glasses Continental make. Fine quality Flint bowl and Green leg Per doz. .. **15/6**

CG 10455 Hock Glasses Continental make. Fine quality Flint bowl and Green leg Per doz. .. **14/6**

CG 23737 Fruit Service of finest English Crystal. Hand made and effectively decorated Fruit Bowl. Individual Fruit Glasses. Set complete, 7 pieces (*as shown*) .. **£1 8 9**
Other richer designs (*not shown*)
CG 23738 Complete set .. **£1 10 9**   **CG 23735** Complete set .. **£1 15 0**

CG 10318 Hock Glasses Continental make. Finely cut coloured bowl Crystal leg Each **11/6**

CG 55505 Hock Glasses English Crystal Plain Flint bow with coloured leg Amber or Jade Each **3 6**

LIQUEUR GLASSES FOR THE CONNOISSEUR

Finest hand-made English Crystal

Sipped from these paper-thin crystal glasses, the value of a good liqueur is enhanced ten-fold—its aroma, bouquet and character wonderfully emphasized. They are gracefully fashioned in the favoured shapes, but are many times larger than ordinary liqueur glasses. Connoisseurs everywhere have adopted them

No.	Height	Diam. at top	Each
52433	5 ins.	2 ins.	2/-
39846	8 ins.	3½ ins.	7/6
52842	5⅝ ins.	2⅜ ins.	2/9
46301	6 ins.	2⅝ ins.	4/6
53248	5 ins.	1¾ ins.	2/-
51256	7 ins.	5½ ins.	8/9
35999	4¾ ins.	2¾ ins.	2/9
43498	5½ ins.	3 ins.	2/9

ALL PRICES ARE SUBJECT TO MARKET FLUCTUATIONS
Telephone SLOANE 1234
Telegrams 'EVERYTHING HARRODS LONDON'

HARRODS LTD   **LONDON S W 1**

GLASS DEPARTMENT
Beautiful Table Decorations in Finest English Crystal

FLOATING FLOWER BOWLS

CG 21811 New Floating Flower Bowl, English Cut Crystal. Cut laurel band, and optic bands below giving a silver effect

11½ ins. diameter	.. ..	Each £1 10 0
13½ ins. ,,	.. ..	,, £2 6 6
15½ ins. ,,	.. ..	,, £3 3 0

CG 21780 New Floating Flower Bowl, English Cut Crystal. Cut Diamond Band and optic bands below giving silver effect

11½ ins. diameter	.. ..	Each £1 11 0
13½ ins. ,,	.. ..	,, £2 6 6
15½ ins. ,,	.. ..	,, £3 3 0

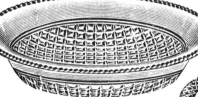

CG 21300 Richly Cut Floating Flower Bowl. Finest English Crystal

12 ins. diameter	..	Each £2 16 6
13 ins. ,,	..	,, £3 13 6
14 ins. ,,	..	,, £4 14 6

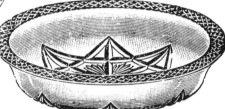

CG 21683 New Floating Flower Bowl. Finest English Crystal. Richly cut base with fine intaglio border

12 ins. diameter	..	Each £3 3 0
13 ins. ,,	..	,, £3 19 0
14 ins. ,,	..	,, £5 0 0

WHISKY SETS IN FINEST ENGLISH CRYSTAL

CG 21366 New Floating Flower Bowl, Finest English Cut Crystal

12 ins. diameter	.. ..	Each £2 16 6
13 ins. ,,	.. ..	,, £3 13 6
14 ins. ,,	.. ..	,, £4 14 6

CG 21729 Whisky Set. Finest English Cut Crystal. Cut hollow flute with moulded rings below giving silver effect
Decanters, Each **£1 4 6** Jug 1½ pints each **15/-** Goblets per doz. **£3 6 0**
Complete with Tray .. **£4 11 6**

CG 20298 Cut Laurel-wreath English Crystal Whisky Set

Decanters	.. .. ..	.. Each **19/-**
Jug, 1½ pints	.. ..	.. **10/-**
Tumblers	.. ..	Per doz. **£2 5 0**
Complete with Tray	.. ..	.. **£3 9 6**

CG 21730 Whisky Set. Finest English Crystal. Cut band and star base. With moulded rings below giving effect of silver
Decanters, Each **£1 10 9** Jug 1½ pints each **£1 5 9** Goblets per doz. **£4 1 0**
Complete with Tray .. **£5 15 0**

CG 20766 Whisky Set. Finest English Cut Crystal, on Mahogany Tray with brass handles

Decanters	.. ..	.. Each **£1 8 0**
Jug, 1½ pints	.. ..	,, **£1 2 6**
Goblets ..	.. ..	Per doz. **£4 16 0**
	Complete with Tray ..	**£5 16 6**

GLASS DEPARTMENT
Fine Collection of English Cut Crystal Salad Bowls

CG 2 Glass Salad Plates. Flat fluted sides
Polished edges, star base .. .. Each 2/-

RICHLY CUT SALAD BOWLS

CG 18060 Richly Cut English Crystal
7 ins.   8 ins.   9 ins.
£1 11 0   £1 17 0   £2 4 0 each

CG 11758
8 ins.   9 ins.   10 ins.
£1 0 6   £1 5 0   £1 10 9 each

CG 12945 Richly Cut English Crystal
7 ins.   8 ins.   9 ins.   10 ins.
17/-   £1 3 6   £1 9 9   £1 18 0 each

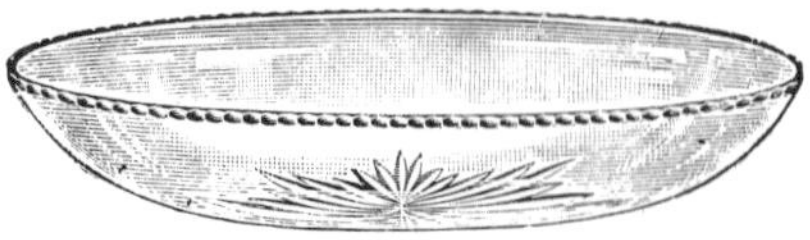

CG 118
Glass Dishes. Cut Star base and cut notched edge

	4 ins.	4½ ins.	5 ins.	5½ ins.	6 ins.	7 ins.
Oval	11d	1/1	1/4	1/6	2/-	2/6
Round	1/-	1/2	1/5	1/9	2/3	2/9

	8 ins.	9 ins.	10 ins.	11 ins.	12 ins.
Oval	2/11	3/6	4/6	5/3	6/6
Round	3/1	3/9	4/11	5/9	6 11

CG 354 Salad Bowl Finely Moulded
8½ ins. Dia. 4/- each

No. 5334 Glass Spoons. 4¾ ins. 5½d ; 5½ ins. 6½d
7 ins. 9d ; 8 ins. 1/3 ; 9½ ins. 1/6 each
No. 5360 Glass Servers. 9½-in. Spoons, each 1/9
No. 5361   „   9½-in. Forks   „   2/3
Glass Knives „ Kitchen Fruit. 9 ins.   „   2/11
     „   „ Butter or Fruit 6¾ ins.   „   2/6

CG. 15713A Richly Cut English Crystal
8 ins. £2 14 0   9 ins. £3 5 0 each

CG 11782 Richly Cut English Crystal
8 ins. £1 16 9   9 ins. £2 2 0   10 ins. £2 11 0 each

CG 6326 English Crystal. Cut star base and
notched edge
7 ins.   8 ins.   9 ins.   10 ins.
5/9   8/3   12/-   15/6 each

FINELY MOULDED GLASS DISHES

CG 341 Oval Dish
5½ ins. 6½ ins. 7½ ins. 8½ ins. 9½ ins.
10½d   1/1   1/6   1/11 2/3 each
10½ ins. 2/9 each

CG 1122
Sweet or Jam Dish, with
handle. Width of dish 5 ins.
Each 10d

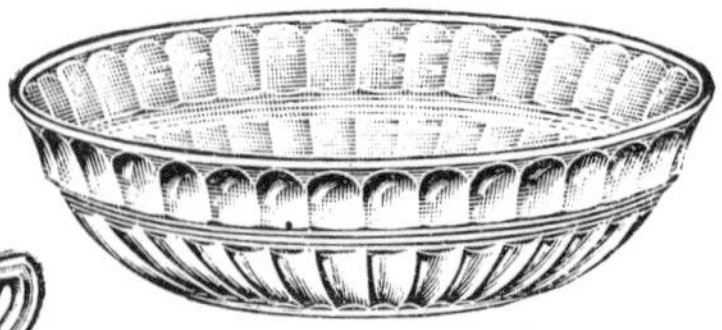

CG 1122 Glass Dishes. Finely Moulded. Excellent
quality

Inches	4	4½	5½	6½	7½	8½	9½	10½
Oval			8d	9½d	1/2	18	2/-	29
Round	7½d	8d	9½d	11½d	13	1/9	2/6	3/6

CG 99 Glass Salad Plate, with Cut Star bottom
Each 4/6
Also in Plain Glass 3/6

FINEST ENGLISH CRYSTAL

CG 18355
8 ins. £2 13 0   9 ins. £3 1 6 each

CG 18064 Richly Cut English Crystal
7 ins.   8 ins.   9 ins.
£1 1 6   £1 6 3   £1 13 6 each

CG 22654
7 ins.   8 ins.   9 ins.
£1 2 9   £1 11 6   £2 1 6 each

CG 1426 Glass Dishes

Inches	4½	5½	6½	7½	8½	9½	10¼
Round	6½d	7d	8d	10½d	1/4	1/10	2/6
Inches	5½	6½	7½	8½	9½	10¼	
Oval	6½d	7d	10d	1/2	1/7	1/11	

CG 283 Moulded Flat Panels with polished edge and
star bottom

	4½	5½	6½	7½	8½	9½	10½ ins. dia.
Round	1/-	1/3	1/6	2/3	3/6	4/6	5/9 each
Oval	1/-	1/4	2-	3/-	3/11	5/3 each	

ALL PRICES ARE SUBJECT TO MARKET FLUCTUATIONS

Telephone SLOANE 1234
Telegrams 'EVERYTHING HARRODS LONDON'

HARRODS LTD   LONDON S W 1

GLASS DEPARTMENT
Fine Selection of Inexpensive Jugs, Richly Cut

Jugs. Tankard shape, English
Crystal

	Plain	Cut Star Base
¼ pint ..	2/6	3/3
½ pint ..	2/9	3/6
¾ pint ..	3/-	4/-
1 pint ..	3/6	4/6
1½ pints ..	4/6	5/6
2 pints ..	5/6	6/9
3 pints ..	8/-	10/-
4 pints ..	10/9	12/9

CG 16357
Plain English Jug, with
Optic Rib

1 pint ..	.. Each 6/-
1½ pints ..	.. ,, 7/9
2 pints ..	.. ,, 9/3

Iced Champagne Jugs
Separate Cylinder, prevents
ice-water mixing with contents of jugs

4 pints .. Each £1 4 9

CG 2770
Fluted English Glass with
Cut Star Bottom

½ pint ..	.. Each 6/3
1 pint ..	.. ,, 7/6
1½ pints ..	.. ,, 8/6
2 pints ..	.. ,, 9/6
3 pints ..	.. ,, 13/9
4 pints ..	.. ,, 18/-

CG 16282
Finely Cut English Glass

1 pint ..	.. Each 11/9
1½ pints ..	.. ,, 15/-
2 pints ..	.. ,, 18/-

CG 19853

1 pint ..	Each 19/6
1½ pints ..	,, £1 4 3
2 pints ..	,, £1 8 9

CG 14009
Finely Cut English Glass

| 1 pint .. | .. Each 12/9 |
| 2 pints .. | .. ,, 19/- |

CG 21699
English Crystal, with moulded
bands giving silver effect

1½ pints .. . Each 6/6

CG 12512
Finely Cut English Glass

| 1 pint .. | .. Each 12/6 |
| 2 pints .. | .. ,, 18/9 |

CG 19396
English Crystal. Richly cut
facets

| 1½ pints .. | .. Each 15/3 |
| 2 pints .. | .. ,, 18/6 |

CG 15066
Finely Cut English Glass

| 1 pint .. | .. Each 12/6 |
| 2 pints .. | .. ,, 18/9 |

CG 15663
English Crystal, with fine Cut
Diamond band

	1 pt.	1½ pts.	2 pts.
Cut ..	8/-	10/-	12/-
S.B. only	5/-	6/-	7/9
Plain ..	4/6	5/3	6/3

CG 15065
Richly Cut English Jug

1 pint ..	.. Each 15/9
1½ pints ..	.. ,, 20/-
2 pints ..	Each £1 3 9

CG 21693
English Crystal

1 pint ..	.. Each 10/6
1½ pints ..	.. ,, 11/9
2 pints ..	.. ,, 13/9

CG 23108
English Crystal. Beautiful Antique
reproduction. 2 pints Each £2 9 0

PEG OR SODA WATER JUGS (ABOUT ONE PINT)

CG 18515

| 1½ pints .. | .. Each £1 10 9 |
| 2 pints .. | .. ,, £1 17 0 |

CG 13087
English Glass, Venetian
Flute

Each 5/3

The 'Grecian'
Without Lip

| Plain .. | .. 3/3 |
| Star Bottom .. | 4/- |

CG 12973
English Glass, Venetian
Flute

Each 3/11

CG 20047

1 pint ..	.. Each 17/6
1½ pints ..	.. ,, £1 1 6
2 pints ..	.. ,, £1 6 3

ALL PRICES ARE SUBJECT TO MARKET FLUCTUATIONS

HARRODS LTD

Telephone SLOANE 1234
Telegrams 'EVERYTHING HARRODS LONDON'

LONDON S W 1

GLASS DEPARTMENT
An Attractive Variety of Items in Richly Cut Glass

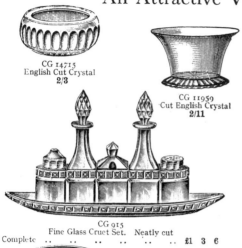

CG 14715
English Cut Crystal
2/3

CG 11959
Cut English Crystal
2/11

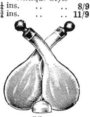

CG 21844
English Cut Crystal
Antique Style

3¼ ins.	..	8/9
3¾ ins.	..	11/9

CG 5485
English Cut Glass

Small size	..	..	1/9
Large size	..	..	2/3

CG 4022
Cut English Crystal

Small size	..	..	5/-
Large size	..	..	6/3

CG 915
Fine Glass Cruet Set. Neatly cut
Complete £1 3 6

CG 59
Twin Oil and Vinegar Bottle

Plain Glass	..	..	3/-
Smaller size	..	..	2/9

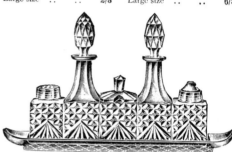

CG 209
Fine Glass Cruet Set. Richly Cut
Complete £1 2 0

CG 14841
Sweet Dish. Cut English Glass

3 ins. 3/6, 3½ ins. 3/9, 4 ins. 4/3
5 ins. 5/11, 6 ins. 8/3

CG 18083
Handled Sweet, Cut English
Glass

4 ins.	..	..	5/3
5 ins.	..	..	6/6

Plain, Handled Sweet, English
Glass

4 ins.	..	..	2/3
5 ins.	..	..	2/6
6 ins.	..	..	3/3

Plain, Unhandled

4 ins.	..	..	1/9
5 ins.	..	..	1/11
6 ins.	..	..	2/3

CH 643
Glass Luncheon Tray
Finely moulded, with handle
3/3

CG 6140
New Butter or Preserve
Baskets. Handled, Cut
English Glass

3 ins.	..	..	2/9
4 ins.	..	..	4/-
5 ins.	..	..	5/-

CG 18084
New Footed Sweet. Cut
English Glass

4 ins.	..	..	3/9
5 ins.	..	..	5/6

Plain

4 ins.	..	..	1/11
5 ins.	..	..	2/6

CG 12982
Sweet Dish. English Glass

3 ins.	1/9	4 ins.	2/6
5 ins.	3/3	6 ins.	4/6

CG 5
Lemon Squeezers
In moulded Glass
Hygienic and easily cleaned
6d
Cheaper make 4d

ENGLISH CRYSTAL BUTTER DISHES

CG 1
The Hygienic Glass Cheese Preserver
Keeps cheese fresh for long periods
Directions :—Place one-third pint
Vinegar and one tablespoonful of Salt
in bottom. The cheese rests on the
glass supports above. Each .. 7/9
Also smaller size. Square, 5 inches
across .. .. Each .. 3/6

CG 13012
Butter Dish 12/6

CG 3911 Butter Dish 10/-
Also small size. Plain
Each .. 1/6

CG 15092 Butter Dish
12/9

CG 234
Covered Honey Box and Stand. Fine
English Glass. Polished edges. To
take section of Honey 5/9

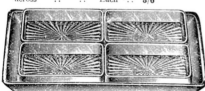

CH 2399
Hors D'Œuvre or Relish Set. Glass tray and four
sections. Fine quality. Star base .. 10/6
Also available in six sections. CG 2400 .. 17/9

CG 2404
Luncheon Set. Fine English Glass. Polished edges
For Biscuits, Butter and Cheese with three sections .. 12/-

CG 2401
Hors D'Œuvre. Fine English Glass. Polished
edges. Complete £1 0 0

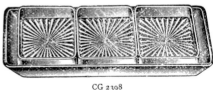

CG 2398
Hors D'Œuvre or Relish Set .. 7/3
Extra Sections 1/- each

ALL PRICES ARE SUBJECT TO MARKET FLUCTUATIONS

HARRODS LTD

Telephone SLOANE 1234
Telegrams 'EVERYTHING HARRODS LONDON'

LONDON SW1

GLASS DEPARTMENT
English Crystal Toilet and Bedroom Requisites

CG 22646
English Crystal Candlestick. Richly cut. With fitting, can also be used for electric light
8 ins. .. Each £1 12 0
12 ins. .. ,, £2 5 0
16 ins. .. ,, £3 4 9

CG 766
Finely Moulded Flint Candlestick
4 ins. .. Each 1/3
6 ins. .. ,, 2/9
7½ ins. .. ,, 3/9

CG 23328
English Crystal Candlestick. Hand made. Richly cut
5 ins. .. Each 14/6
6 ins. .. ,, 17/3

CG 20413
English Crystal. Richly Cut
6 ins. .. Each £1 0 6
8 ins. .. ,, £1 12 6
10 ins. .. ,, £2 19 0

CG 22534
English Crystal Candlestick. Hand made. Richly cut
Each .. £1 1 9

CG 51
Finely Moulded Flint Candlestick
8½ ins. .. Each 5/11

CG 10454 English Crystal. Splendid reproduction of Jacobean Twist
8 ins. Each 12/6   10 ins. Each 15/6
12 ins. Ea. £1 0 9   14 ins. Ea. £1 7 0

CG 23426 English Crystal Powder Bowl. Richly cut
4½ ins. Ea. £1 2 0   5½ ins. Ea. £1 8 6

CG 22697 English Crystal Powder Bowl. Richly cut
5 ins. .. .. Each 11/-

CG 17707 Bath Powder Box. Richly cut English Glass
5½ ins. £1 11 6   7 ins. £2 1 6
8 ins. £2 11 0   9 ins. £3 3 0

CG 17717 Bath Powder Boxes, Each
5½ in., £1 2 6 ;   7 in., £1 10 0
8 in., £1 15 6 ;   9 in., £2 3 6

CG 21289 Richly Cut English Crystal Trinket Set. Fine illuminated design
Tray 11½ ins., £2 19 6 ; Tray 10 ins., £2 3 0 ; Powder, £1 1 6
Pomade, 17/3 ; Ring Stand, 11/9 ; Pin Tray, 10/- ; Candlestick 6 ins., £1 1 6
Scent Bottles, Capacity 4 ozs., £1 7 0 ; Hair-Tidy, £1 5 9 each

These Services do not include a Chamber

CG 24462 English Crystal Toilet Services. Plain with optic rings below giving effect of silver
Ewer .. .. Each £1 10 6
Basin .. .. ,, £1 11 6
Sponge Bowl 6 6
Soap Dish 5 6
(See next column)

CG 2800 Glass Toilet Service, with wide flat flutes and star base. Finely moulded
Service of 5 pieces £1 18 6

CG 24462 (continued)
Brush Vase .. .. Each 2 3
Service, 5 pieces £3 16 0
Bedroom Bottle and Glass to match Each 2 6

CG 23210 English Crystal Toilet Service. Richly cut. Beautifully hand made
Ewer .. .. Each £2 10 0
Basin .. .. ,, £2 19 6
Sponge Bowl .. .. ,, 12 6
Soap Dish .. .. ,, 10 0
Brush Vase .. .. ,, 9 3
Service, 5 pieces £7 1 0
Bedroom Bottle and Glass to match .. 10 3

ALL PRICES ARE SUBJECT TO MARKET FLUCTUATIONS

HARRODS LTD

Telephone SLOANE 1234
Telegrams 'EVERYTHING HARRODS LONDON'

LONDON S W 1

GLASS DEPARTMENT

'PYREX' the Wonderful Transparent Ovenware. Guaranteed against Breakage in the Oven for Six Months from Date of Purchase

CASSEROLE—ROUND

Ref. No.	Cap.	Outside Measurements ins.	Price Each
267	1½ pt.	7½ × 2⅞	6/6
268	2½ pt.	8¼ × 3	7/6
269	3¼ pt.	9¼ × 3¼	9/-
270	4 pt.	9¾ × 3¼	10/9

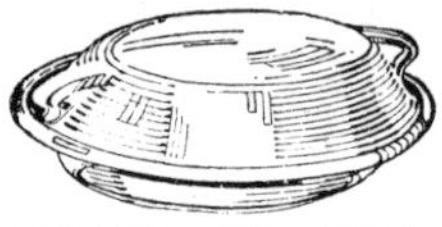

ENTREE DISH—OVAL
Reversible Cover

Ref. No.	Outside Measurements ins.	Price Each
110	10⅝ × 8 × 2⅞	8/9

PYREX BLUE RIBBON GIFT SET

Each Set contains:—
- 1 No. 268 Round Casserole
- 1 No. 212 Bread Pan
- 1 No. 404 Pudding Dish
- 1 No. 231 Utility Dish

Per Set .. 19/6

RAMEKIN—ROUND

Ref. No.	Cap.	Outside Measurements ins.	Price Per doz.
432	3½ oz.	3¼ × 1⅞	9/3
442	4 oz.	3¾ × 1⅞	12/-

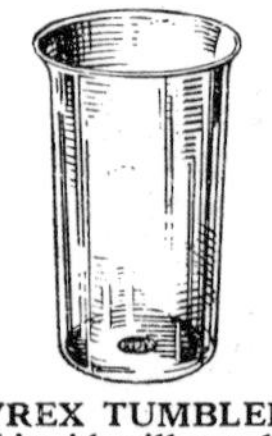

PYREX TUMBLERS
Hot Liquid will not break them

No. 2 Capacity ½ pint. Flanged top Per dozen .. 15/-

PUDDING DISH—ROUND—WIDE RIM

Ref. No.	Cap.	Outside Measurements ins.	Price Each
464	1½ pt.	7½ × 2¼	3/6
465	2½ pt.	8½ × 2¾	4/6
466	3¼ pt.	9½ × 3	5/6
467	4 pt.	9¾ × 3¼	6/-

ENTREE DISH—ROUND—SHALLOW

Ref. No.	Cap.	Outside Measurements ins.	Price Each
112	1½ pt.	7⅞ × 2¼	6/6
113	2 pt.	8½ × 2¼	7/6

PIE DISH—OBLONG

Ref. No.	Cap.	Outside Measurements ins.	Price Each
145	1 pt.	7¾ × 5¾ × 2	3/6
146	1½ pt.	8½ × 6⅛ × 2¼	4/6
147	2½ pt.	9¾ × 7½ × 2½	5/6

PIE DISH—OVAL—SHALLOW

Ref. No.	Cap.	Outside Measurements ins.	Price Each
183B	1½ pt.	9 × 6½ × 2⅜	3/9
184B	2½ pt.	10⅝ × 7¾ × 2¾	4/6
185B	3¼ pt.	12 × 8¼ × 2½	5/6

PIE DISH—OVAL—DEEP

Ref. No.	Cap.	Outside Measurements ins.	Price Each
193B	1¾ pt.	8½ × 6¼ × 3	3/9
197B	2¼ pt.	8¾ × 6½ × 3⅜	4/6
194B	3 pt.	9½ × 6⅞ × 3⅞	5/6
190B	4½ pt.	10¼ × 8 × 4⅞	8/-

DIVIDED DISH

Ref. No.	Outside Measurements	Price Each
130	9¾ in. × 1⅞ in. without Cover	6/6
134	9¾ in. × 1⅞ in. with Cover	9/9

PIE DISH—OVAL—DEEP

Ref. No.	Cap.	Outside Measurements ins.	Price Each
403	¾ pt.	8½ × 6 × 1⅞	2/9
404	1¼ pt.	9 × 6¾ × 2	3/6
405	1½ pt.	9¾ × 7⅞ × 2¼	4/3
406	2 pt.	10¾ × 8¼ × 2¼	5/-
407	2½ pt.	11¾ × 8⅞ × 2¼	6/-

BISCUIT PAN—OBLONG

Ref. No.	Outside Measurements ins.	Price Each
234	9¾ × 7¾ × 1¼	3/9

STEW POT—ROUND

Ref. No.	Cap.	Outside Measurements ins.	Price Each
504	1¾ pt.	5¾ × 4¼	7/6
506	3¼ pt.	7¼ × 5¼	11/-

BREAD OR CAKE PAN—OBLONG

Ref. No.	Outside Measurements ins.	Price Each
212	9¾ × 5¼ × 2⅜	4/-
214	10⅜ × 5⅝ × 3⅜	6/6

INDIVIDUAL SOUP POT

Ref. No.	Cap.	Outside Measurements ins.	Price Each
500	7 oz.	3 × 2⅝	3/-

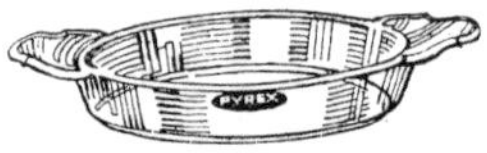

EARED DISH—OVAL

Ref. No.	Outside Measurements Each (including ears) ins.	Price
331	11⅜ × 5¾ × 1⅛	4/6
332	12½ × 6½ × 1⅛	5/9

FISH OR MEAT PLATTER

Ref. No.	Outside Measurements ins.	Price Each
313	13¾ × 8¼ × 1⅜	6/9

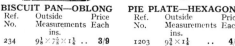

PIE PLATE—HEXAGONAL

Ref. No.	Outside Measurements ins.	Price Each
1203	9¾ × 1¼	4/6

CASSEROLE—OVAL—DEEP

Ref. No.	Cap.	Outside Measurements ins.	Price Each
293	1¾ pt.	8¾ × 6¼ × 3	6/6
297	2½ pt.	8¾ × 6⅛ × 3⅜	7/6
294	3 pt.	9¼ × 6¾ × 3¾	9/-
290	4½ pt.	10⅝ × 8 × 4¾	13/6

UTILITY DISH—OBLONG

Ref. No.	Outside Measurements ins.	Price Each
231	10⅜ × 6⅞ × 2	4/6
232	12⅜ × 8¼ × 2	7/6

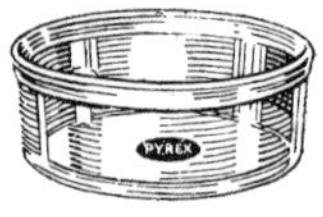

SOUFFLE DISH (Shallow).

Ref. No.	Cap.	Outside Measurements ins.	Price Each
350	1 pt.	5⅞ × 2¼	2/6
351	1⅜ pt.	6 × 2½	3/6
352	1¾ pt.	6¾ × 2¾	4/6
353	2½ pt.	7¾ × 3	5/6

CUSTARD CUPS—FRENCH PATTERN
For Custards, Junket and Mousse

Ref. No.	Cap.	Outside Measurements ins.	Price Doz.
424	4 oz.	3¼ × 2⅝ ins.	12/3
426	6 oz.	3⅜ × 2⅝ ,,	15/-

PYREX TUMBLERS WITH HANDLES
Useful for Hot Milk or Water

No. 4 Capacity ½ pint. Flanged top Per dozen .. 24/-

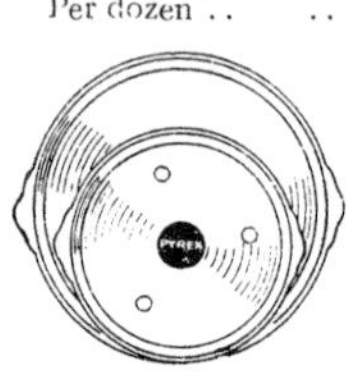

SERVING TRAYS

Ref. No.	Outside Measurements Each (not including ears) ins.	Price
706	6 × ⅝	2/3

ENTREE DISH—OVAL—SHALLOW

Ref. No.	Cap.	Outside Measurements ins.	Price Each
283	1½ pt.	9 × 6½ × 2⅞	6/6
284	2½ pt.	10⅝ × 7½ × 2¾	7/6
285	3½ pt.	12 × 8¾ × 2½	9/-

CASSEROLE—SQUARE

Ref. No.	Cap.	Outside Measurements ins.	Price Each
800	2½ pt.	7½ × 2¾ ins.	9/9

SOUFFLE DISH (Deep).

Ref. No.	Cap.	Outside Measurements ins.	Price Each
360	1¼ pt.	5½ × 2¾	3/-
361	1¾ pt.	6 × 3½	4/-
362	2¼ pt.	6½ × 3¾	5/-
363	3 pt.	7½ × 5¼	6/-

PUDDING OR BAKING DISH—ROUND—SHALLOW

Ref. No.	Cap.	Outside Measurements ins.	Price Each
132	1½ pt.	7¾ × 2¼	3/6
155	2½ pt.	8¼ × 2¼	4/6

PIE PLATES—ROUND—WIDE RIM

Ref. No.	Outside Measurements ins.	Price Each
207	7½ × 1¼	2/9
208	8¼ × 1⅜	3/6
209	9½ × 1½	3/9
210	10½ × 1½	4/6

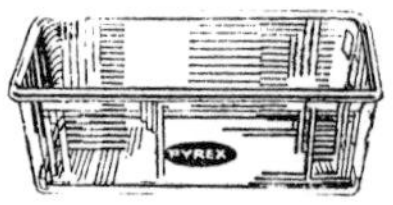

PUDDING DISH—SQUARE

Ref. No.	Cap.	Outside Measurements ins.	Price Each
800B	2½ pt.	7½ × 2¾ ins.	5/6

ALL PRICES ARE SUBJECT TO MARKET FLUCTUATIONS

HARRODS LTD

Telephone SLOANE 1234
Telegrams 'EVERYTHING HARRODS LONDON'

LONDON S W 1

GLASS DEPARTMENT
Pasteur (Chamberland) and Non-Pressure Filters

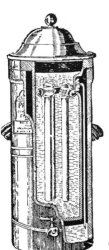

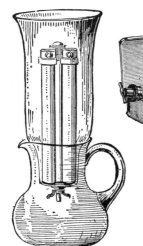

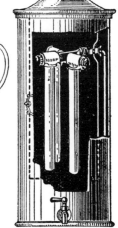

STONEWARE

No. 202			
No.	Capacity	Output per day	Price
202 A	2 gallons	3 gallons £2 2 0
202 B	3 ,,	5 ,,	£3 0 0
202 C	4 ,,	6 ,,	£4 0 0
202 D	5 ,,	7 ,,	£4 13 4
202 E	6 ,,	8 ,,	£5 13 4
202 F	8 ,,	10 ,,	£7 6 8
202 G	10 ,,	12 ,,	£10 6 8
Extra Filtering Candles		Each	6/9

CH 200 Crystal Filter with filtered water vase. Capacity, 3 pints. Output per day, from 4 pints upwards, according to number of times refilled £1 16 9 complete

TRAVELLERS' POCKET FILTERS
These filters are designed to yield in the smallest compass a rapid supply of pure water. The conical india-rubber plug will fit the service water bottle or any other ordinary water bottle which may be handy. By means of the small air pump a partial vacuum is created in the bottle, and water begins to flow. After the flow has started, the pump need not be continuously worked. In this way, with one filter tube a pint of water is obtained in a few minutes

CH 212 1 tube, in Japanned **case**
Output 6 pints per hour .. **£1 8 0**

CH 213 3 tubes, in Japanned **case**
Output 18 pints per hour .. **£2 16 0**

ENAMELLED IRON
No. 234

No.	Capacity	Output per day	Price
234 A	2 galls.	3 galls.	£2 15 0
234 B	3 ,,	5 ,,	£3 18 9
234 C	4 ,,	6 ,,	£5 5 0

Extra Filtering Candles 6/9 each
Also supplied in larger sizes
Prices on application

PASTEUR-CHAMBERLAND FILTERS

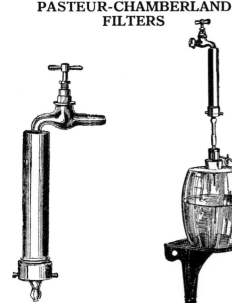

No. CH 215   No. CH 216A

CH 215 Nickel-plated **Filter** with screw-down tap for attachment to water service. Output per day, 10 gallons
£1 8 0

CH 216 With Stoneware filtered water reservoir, overflow and nickel-plated draw-off tap .. **£2 16 3**

CH 216A. With Crystal filtered water reservoir
£3 13 6

Bracket for above **8/9**

Cheavin's English Made Filters, Berkfeld Model
Combining rapidity of action with perfect filtration

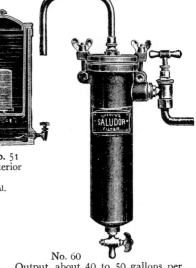

An entirely new design in beautifully white glazed Ironstone China

No. 51 Exterior   No. 51 Interior

	No. 50	51	52	53	54
Capacity	1-gal.	1½-gal.	2½-gal.	3½-gal.	4½-gal.
No. of Filtering Blocks	1	1	2	3	4
Yield per day Gallons	5	6	12	18	24
Price	28/-	35/-	47/-	60/-	75/-

Spare Filtering Candles **6/6** each
Size of Blocks, 5½ ins. high × 3 ins. diameter

Order by post with confidence if you cannot call. All orders are filled in strict rotation

No. 60
Output about 40 to 50 gallons per hour with the ordinary main pressure of 35 to 45 lbs. per square inch
Where main pressure is not available, the filter can be fixed to the house supply pipe from cistern, but in this case it should be fixed not less than 12 feet below the cistern
Complete in box with full instructions for fitting and cleaning
Price **£1 17 6**
Spare Filtering Candles 5/- each

*ALL PRICES ARE **SUBJECT** TO MARKET FLUCTUATIONS*

TURNERY DEPARTMENT
Long-Handled Brushes make Housework Easier

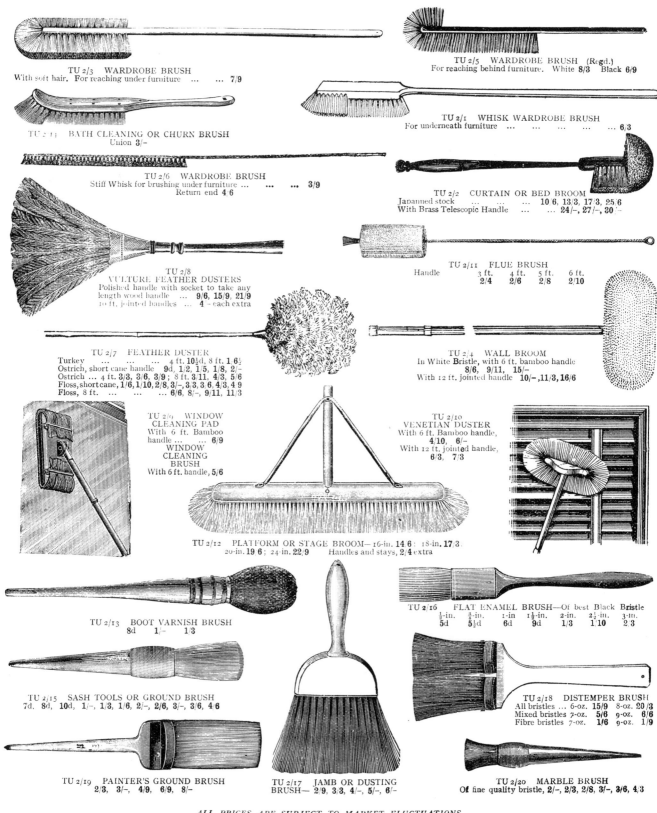

TU 2/3   WARDROBE BRUSH
With soft hair. For reaching under furniture 7/9

TU 2/5   WARDROBE BRUSH   (Regd.)
For reaching behind furniture.   White **8/3**   Black **6/9**

TU 2/14   BATH CLEANING OR CHURN BRUSH
Union **3/-**

TU 2/1   WHISK WARDROBE BRUSH
For underneath furniture **6/3**

TU 2/6   WARDROBE BRUSH
Stiff Whisk for brushing under furniture **3/9**
Return end **4/6**

TU 2/2   CURTAIN OR BED BROOM
Japanned stock **10/6, 13/3, 17/3, 25/6**
With Brass Telescopic Handle **24/-, 27/-, 30/-**

TU 2/8   VULTURE FEATHER DUSTERS
Polished handle with socket to take any
length wood handle   ...   **9/6, 15/9, 21/9**
10 ft. jointed handles   ...   **4/-** each extra

TU 2/11   FLUE BRUSH
Handle   3 ft.   4 ft.   5 ft.   6 ft.
                2/4   **2/6**   **2/8**   **2/10**

TU 2/7   FEATHER DUSTER
Turkey   ...   . 4 ft. **10½d**, 8 ft. **1/6½**
Ostrich, short cane handle   **9d, 1/2, 1/5, 1/8, 2/-**
Ostrich ... 4 ft. **3/3, 3/6, 3/9**; 8 ft. **3/11, 4/3, 5/6**
Floss, short cane, **1/6, 1/10, 2/8, 3/-, 3/3, 3/6, 4/3, 4/9**
Floss, 8 ft. **6/6, 8/-, 9/11, 11/3**

TU 2/4   WALL BROOM
In White Bristle, with 6 ft. bamboo handle
8/6, 9/11, 15/-
With 12 ft. jointed handle   **10/-, 11/3, 16/6**

TU 2/9   WINDOW CLEANING PAD
With 6 ft. Bamboo
handle **6/9**
WINDOW CLEANING BRUSH
With 6 ft. handle, **5/6**

TU 2/10   VENETIAN DUSTER
With 6 ft. Bamboo handle,
4/10, 6/-
With 12 ft. jointed handle,
6/3, 7/3

TU 2/12   PLATFORM OR STAGE BROOM—16-in. **14/6**; 18-in. **17/3**;
20-in. **19/6**; 24-in. **22/9**   Handles and stays, **2/4** extra

TU 2/13   BOOT VARNISH BRUSH
8d   1/-   1/3

TU 2/16   FLAT ENAMEL BRUSH—Of best Black Bristle

½-in.	¾-in.	1-in.	1½-in.	2-in.	2½-in.	3-in.
5d	**5½d**	**6d**	**9d**	**1/3**	**1/10**	**2/3**

TU 2/15   SASH TOOLS OR GROUND BRUSH
7d. 8d, 10d, 1/-, 1/3, 1/6, 2/-, 2/6, 3/-, 3/6, 4/6

TU 2/18   DISTEMPER BRUSH
All bristles ... 6-oz. **15/9**   8-oz. **20/3**
Mixed bristles 7-oz. **5/6**   9-oz. **6/6**
Fibre bristles 7-oz. **1/6**   9-oz. **1/9**

TU 2/19   PAINTER'S GROUND BRUSH
2/3, 3/-, 4/9, 6/9, 8/-

TU 2/17   JAMB OR DUSTING BRUSH— **2/9, 3/3, 4/-, 5/-, 6/-**

TU 2/20   MARBLE BRUSH
Of fine quality bristle, **2/-, 2/3, 2/8, 3/-, 3/6, 4/3**

ALL PRICES ARE SUBJECT TO MARKET FLUCTUATIONS

HARRODS LTD
Telephone SLOANE 1234
Telegrams 'EVERYTHING HARRODS LONDON'
LONDON SW1

TURNERY DEPARTMENT
Exceptional Variety of Brooms and Carpet Sweepers

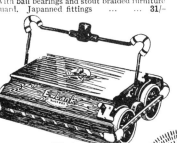

TU 3/2
'GRAND RAPIDS' CARPET SWEEPER
With ball bearings and stout braided furniture guard. Japanned fittings **31/-**

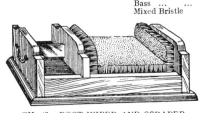

TU 3/1
'SUCCESS' CARPET SWEEPER
With heavy rubber corner buffers, ball bearing wheels and patent brush cleaner. Japanned fittings ... **34/3**
Similar machine with nickelled fittings... ... ... **40/6**

TU 3/10   BOOT WIPER
With Iron Pole
Bass **30/3**
Mixed Bristle ... **38/6**

TU 3/6   O'CEDAR WAXIT
On the one side of the O'Cedar Waxit is a brush which applies the wax thoroughly and evenly while on the reverse side is a sheepskin polisher. Both pad and handle are interchangeable... ... ... **7/6**
O'Cedar Wax to use with above
7½d, 1/-, 1/10, 3/6, 6/6

Applying Wax with an O-Cedar Waxit

TU 3/5
'GRAND RAPIDS'
Combined Carpet Sweeper and Vacuum Cleaner embodying all the latest improvements **63/-**

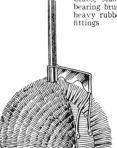

TU 3/9
BOOT WIPER AND
SCRAPER
With Iron Pole
Bass **34/6**
Mixed Bristle ... **43/6**

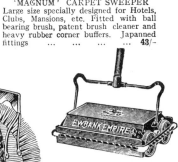

TU 3/4
'MAGNUM' CARPET SWEEPER
Large size specially designed for Hotels, Clubs, Mansions, etc. Fitted with ball bearing brush, patent brush cleaner and heavy rubber corner buffers. Japanned fittings **43/-**

TU 3/3
'EMPIRE' CARPET
SWEEPER
With armoured brush ends
Japanned fittings... ... **28/9**

TU 3/8   BOOT WIPER AND SCRAPER
In solid Oak
Size of base, 21 × 14 ins. **45/-**
Without scraper, 15½ × 14 ins. **37/6**

TU 3/14   FLOOR POLISHING BRUSH
Best bristles, with cast iron top, swivel handle and wings all round. Weight 24 lbs. **34/-**
Weight 14 lbs. **27/-**
As above with padded sides. Weight 14 lbs. **23/6**

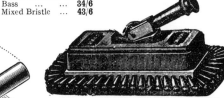

REPAIRS
All kinds of Carpet Sweepers Repaired at short notice. Estimates are sent if desired

MASON

TU 3/17   FLOOR POLISHER
With swivel handle and stout wood block weighted with lead
Best grey bristle. Weight 18 lbs. **41/6**

TU 3/13   DECK OR BOAT SCRUBBER
With double wings
Hair ... ... **6/3**   Bass or Union ... **2/9**
Smaller size without wings **2/2**

TU 3/15
FLOOR POLISHING BRUSH
For hand use. Stiff grey bristles **16/6**

TU 3/7
PARQUET FLOOR BROOM
Made of White Wool **7/9**
TU 3/18   FLOOR POLISHER
For small spaces. Iron base with bristle brush
Weight about 6 lbs. **11/3**

TU 3/12
O'CEDAR POLISH MOP
Battleship model ... **5/-**
Smaller size **4/-**
O'Cedar Oil in tins
5/2, 7/6, 12/6
O'Cedar Oil in bottles, **1/3, 2/6**

TU 3/16
MOP AND SCRUBBER
For use with 'Do-all' Pail.   Handled scrubber **2/8**
TU 3/19
Handled Mop **2/-**
TU 3/20
Superior quality... ... ... **2/6**

TU 3/11
THE RONUK HOME POLISHER
Invaluable for polishing wood floors, lino, etc. The brush is used to remove the dirt, after which the duster is placed in position for polishing and rubbing. Fitted long handle with swivel joint to move in any direction **7/6**
Liquid floor dressing for use with above, 1 pint, **2/9**; 1 quart, **4/6**; ½-gallon, **8/6**

ALL PRICES ARE SUBJECT TO MARKET FLUCTUATIONS

HARRODS LTD
Telephone SLOANE 1234
Telegrams 'EVERYTHING HARRODS LONDON'
LONDON SW1

TURNERY DEPARTMENT
Household Requisites that Repay with Lasting Service

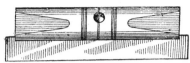

TU 5/11 SQUEEGEE WITH HANDLE
Width ... 12 ins. 15 ins. 18 ins. 24 ins.
           3/7   4/3   5/11 - 7/6

TU 5/4 CHAMOIS LEATHER
First quality. Very soft finish. Free from sewings.

13 × 13 ins. ...	1/6	21 × 21 ins. ...	5/3
15 × 15 ins. ...	2/3	24 × 24 ins. ...	6/6
17 × 17 ins. ...	3/6	26 × 26 ins. ...	8/-
19 × 19 ins. ...	4/3	28 × 28 ins. ...	9/6

TU 5/30 RUBBER BLOCKS FOR PLATE CLEANING
Size 3 × 2 ins. ... 3/3
  ,,   4 × 2 ins. ... 4/3
  ,,   4 × 3 ins. ... 5/3

Orders value 20/- and over Post Free in England and Wales

TU 5/12 'DUSMO' SWEEPING POWDER
Cleans and disinfects the carpet while sweeping
In cartons ... 9d each
In tins ... 3/6 ,,

TU 5/9 NAIL BRUSH
In strong Fibre, 9d each

TU 5/20 FRENCH LAVATORY WHISK 1/6
Superior quality 2/11

TU 5/26 THE 'GOSO' SELF-WRINGING MOP
It will wash and dry your floors with ease and thoroughness in a third of the time, and with half the effort usually taken
Price complete 7/11
Refills 2/11 each

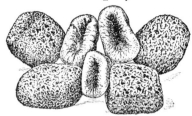

TU 5/13 SPONGES
A large assortment of selected Turkey and Honeycomb Sponges for all purposes always in stock

Honeycomb Bath Sponges ...	7/6, 8/6, 10/6, 15/-, 18/6
TU 5/14 Turkey Bath Sponges ...	8/9, 10/6, 12/6 to 21/-
TU 5/15 'Honeycomb' Toilet Sponges	2/6, 3/6, 5/6, 8/6
TU 5/16 'Turkey' Toilet Sponges	3/6, 5/6, 7/6, 10/6
TU 5/17 Motor or Stable Sponges	2/6, 4/6, 6/6, 8/6
TU 5/18 Pantry or Paint Sponges	1/-, 1/6, 2/6, 3/-, 4/3, 5/3

When ordering Sponges, please quote the Reference Number of the quality required

TU 5/10 TANNED LEATHER GARDENING GLOVES
For Ladies 3/-
TANNED LEATHER GARDENING GAUNTLETS
For Ladies 3/6

TU 5/5 HOUSEMAIDS' GLOVES
Chamois Leather	1/11, 2/6
Chamois Gauntlets	3/3, 3/6
Soft Cotton Gloves ...	1/-
White Fabric Gloves ...	1/8

TU 5/30 MOP HEADS
For water. In Wool, 14-oz., 2/3, 16-oz., 2/9, 18-oz., 3/-
In Cotton ... 16-oz., 2/6
Handles with ferrules 1/- each extra

TU 5/3 SELVYT BOOT PADS
Black or brown ... 6d each

TU 5/21 CHIMNEY SWEEPING AND DRAIN CLEANING SET
Comprising best quality canes in 3 ft. lengths, 16-in. bass head, cloth, shovel, double worm screw, cup, cap, scraper and rubber plunger

30 ft.	40 ft.	50 ft.	60 ft.	80 ft.	100 ft.
67/9	79/-	84/6	94/-	112/9	131/6

TU 5/22 CHIMNEY SWEEPING MACHINE
Best quality canes, complete with 18-inch whalebone head, cloth, brass cup and wheel

30 ft.	40 ft.	50 ft.	60 ft.	80 ft.
39/6	46/9	51/6	58/9	70/9

TU 5/24 THE 'CRUMBER'
Specially designed for removing crumbs on polished tables. Handsome Lacquer decoration 12/6
Solid Mahogany or Oak 10/6

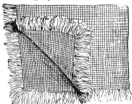

TU 5/6 SWABS OR DISH CLOTHS
22 × 20 ins. ... ... 2/3 per doz.
28 × 28 ins. ... ... 3/11 ,, ,,

TU 5/7 FLOOR CLOTHS OR SCOURERS
20 × 20 ins. ... 5/11 and 7/6 per doz.
23 × 24 ins. ... ... 8/11 ,, ,,

TU 5/8 FLOOR FLANNEL
24 ins. wide.

	per yd.	Doz. yds.	Roll (45 yds.)
Superfine quality	1/3	14/-	49/3
	1/5	15/9	55/6

TU 5/1 SELVYT POLISHING CLOTHS

	Single	Double
10 × 10 ins. ...	8d	—
14 × 14 ins. ...	1/-	1/9
17 × 14 ins. ...	1/3	2/3
21 × 17 ins. ...	1/9	3/3
21 × 20 ins. ...	2/3	4/-
21 × 25 ins. ...	2/9	5/-
28 × 28 ins. ...	4/-	7/6

TU 5/2 YELLOW POLISHING CLOTHS OR DUSTERS
Very soft, 6d each, 5/11 per dozen
Redio Polishing Cloths for Brass or Silver, 7½d each

TU 5/23 NAIL BRUSH
Grey Bristle
4-row 1/8, 5-row 1/10, 6-row 2/2
Superior quality, 4-row 3/3, 5-row 4/3, 6-row 5/1, 8-row 7/2
Yellow Bristle, 4-row 3/6, 5-row 4/4, 6-row 5/6, 8-row 7/11
Superior quality, 4-row 4/10, 5-row 6/3, 6-row 7/9, 8-row 10/9, 10-row 14/3

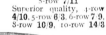

TU 5/31 FLESH BRUSH
Bent Handle ...					11/3
Straight Handle	...	...	...	...	10/9
Web Handle ...	...	...	...		10/6

TU 5/29 DECANTER BRUSH
½-pint 1/3, ½-pint 1/8, 1-pint 2/2, 2-pint 2/8

TU 5/28 DECANTER BRUSH
(Registered) 1/8

TU 5/27 CRUMB BRUSH AND TRAY
Polished Wood ... 7/6, 10/6, 15/-

ALL PRICES ARE SUBJECT TO MARKET FLUCTUATIONS

HARRODS LTD

Telephone SLOANE 1234
Telegrams 'EVERYTHING HARRODS LONDON'

LONDON S W 1

TURNERY DEPARTMENT
Harrods Supply Every Conceivable Need in the Domestic Sphere

TU 10/1 SANDWICH TRAY
Polished Mahogany. Sides fall flat as required

	26"	28"	30"
	104/9	107/3	111/6
Stands	26"	28"	30"
	15/9	16/3	17/3

TU 10/22 THE 'BESWAY' TABLE WAGON
A new type of Wagon which can be easily and safely converted into a rigid table. Cellulose finished to resist heat marks or stains

		Oak
Size of Wagon 15 × 24 × 34 ins. high.	Size of Table 30 × 24 × 26 ins. high ..	£4 14 6
Size of Wagon 18 × 30 × 37 ins. high.	Size of Table 30 × 30 × 28 ins. high ..	£5 5 0
Size of Wagon 18 × 36 × 37½ ins. high.	Size of Table 36 × 36 × 28½ ins. high ..	£6 6 0

	Mahogany or Teak .. £4 19 6	£5 12 6	£6 16 6
	Walnut .. £5 5 0	£5 15 6	£7 7 0

TU 10/16 BUTLER'S TRAY AND STAND
Solid Mahogany
Trays only

	26"	28"	30"	32"
Plain	18/9	20/9	23/-	24/6
Polished..	24/6	26/6	28/9	32/3

Stands only

	16"	17"	19"	21"
Plain	10/6	11/-	12/3	13/3
Polished..	15/9	16/3	17/3	19/6

TU 10/5 KNIFE BOXES
Solid Mahogany
Single division

	Plain	Lined Green Baize
	9/9	13/6
Polished	13/6	17/3

Double division

	Plain	Lined Green Baize
	11/-	15/-
Polished	15/-	18/6

TU 10/12 PLATE TRAY
Polished Mahogany, Baize lining and cover. 3 ins. deep

20 × 15 ins.	..	33/9
22 × 16½ ins.	..	37/6
24 × 18 ins.	..	42/9
26 × 19 ins.	..	46/6
28 × 20 ins.	..	52/6

TU 10/3 HOUSEMAID'S BOX
Improved square shape

12"	14"	16"
5/9	6/-	6/6

TU 10/9 BUTLER'S PLATE TRAY
Polished Mahogany, Baize lined. Specially made for removing cutlery, glass, etc.
20½ × 12½ × 3 ins. deep 24/6

TU 10/18 JELLY BAG STAND

Height	30"	33"	36"
	8/6	9/-	9/6

TU 10/19 JELLY BAGS
Best seamless felt

Pints	3½	4½	7	9	14
	2/3	2/6	3/-	3/6	4/6

TU 10/6 LEMON SQUEEZER
In Wood, with china cup .. 1/3

TU 10/10 FLOUR BARREL

½ stone	..	..	4/9
1 stone	..	..	7/-
5 stones	..	..	24/-
10 stones	..	..	37/6
20 stones	..	..	54/-

TU 10/20 EGG STANDS
(not illustrated)
These stands can be used in tiers of two, three or more

To hold 12 eggs	..	1/-
,, 24 eggs	..	2/-

TU 10/4 'BESWAY' COLLAPSIBLE TRAY
The 'Besway' Tray is light and rigid. Enables one hand to do easily and safely the work of two. Leaves one hand free to open doors. Folds flat when not in use. Collapsible 2-tier Tray. All in dark Jacobean Oak finish All other finishes to order

	Size of Tray		
No. 4	10 × 18 ins.	..	17/6
,, 5	12 × 20 ins.	..	21/-
,, 6	12 × 24 ins.	..	25/6

TU 10/7 CHOPPING BOARDS
1 in. thick

12"	14"	16"	18"	20"
3/9	4/6	5/8	7/6	10/6

1½ ins. thick

		16"	18"	20"
		5/8	7/-	9/3	12/9

TU 10/15 THE 'BESWAY' KNIFE CLEANER
Handsomely finished in polished Oak with Oxidized Copper fittings Can be clamped to the dresser or table for use
Price .. 8/11
(One year guarantee given with every machine)

TU 10/8 PASTRY BOARD
Best quality White Wood

	18"	21"	24"	27"	30"
Solid	7/3	8/9	10/3	12/3	14/8
Jointed	6/-	6/9	7/6	8/9	9/9

TU 10/21 DECANTER DRAINER

2 hole	4 hole	6 hole
4/6	7/6	9/9

TU 10/11 COOKS' SIEVES
Tinned Wire
Medium or Coarse

8"	9"	10"	11"	12"
1/11	2/1	2/5	2/10	3/4
13"	14"	15"	16"	
3/10	4/6	5/-	5/8	

Fine

8"	9"	10"	11"	12"
2/-	2/2	2/6	3/-	3/6
13"	14"	15"	16"	
4/-	4/8	5/4	6/-	

Best Hair. Fine or Coarse

8"	9"	10"	11"	12"
3/3	3/9	4/4	4/10	5/6
13"	14"	15"	16"	
6/4	7/3	8/3	9/3	

Orders value 20/- and over Post free in England and Wales

TU 10/2 WOOD SPOONS
Best quality

8"	10"	12"
3¼d	4¼d	5¼d
14"	16"	18"
6½d	8¼d	10½d

TU 10/13 SHOE BRUSH BOX
(not illustrated)
Hardwood .. 1/10

TU 10/17 PASTRY ROLLER
16 ins. .. .. 8d   18 ins. 9d
Revolving 1/-

TU 10/23 HARDWOOD SALT BOX
(not illustrated)

8"	10"	12"	14"
2/2	2/11	3/3	4/-

ALL PRICES ARE SUBJECT TO MARKET FLUCTUATIONS

HARRODS LTD

Telephone SLOANE 1234
Telegrams 'EVERYTHING HARRODS LONDON'

LONDON SW1

TURNERY DEPARTMENT
Cupboards, Fittings and Shelves of Finest Workmanship

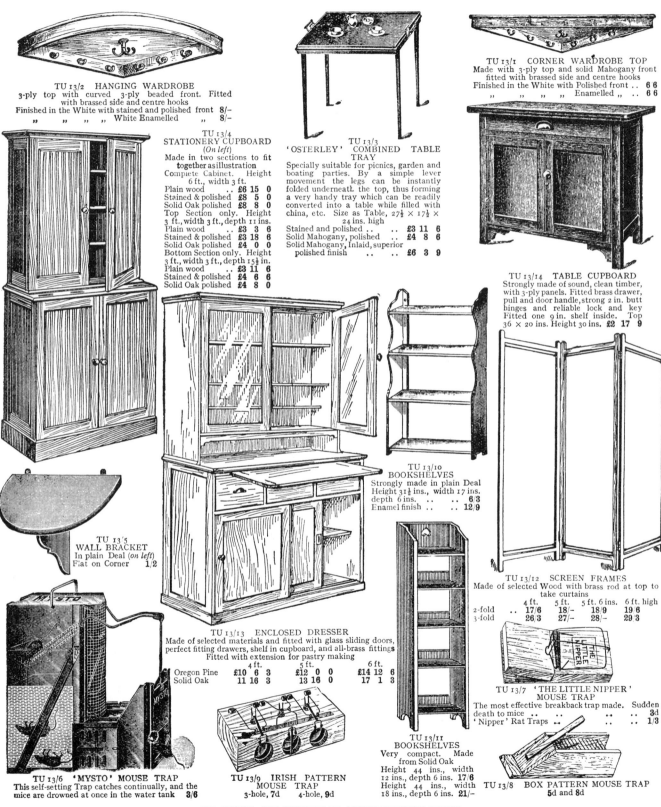

TU 13/2 HANGING WARDROBE
3-ply top with curved 3-ply beaded front. Fitted with brassed side and centre hooks
Finished in the White with stained and polished front 8/-
„   „   „   „ White Enamelled   „   8/-

TU 13/4
STATIONERY CUPBOARD
(On left)
Made in two sections to fit together as illustration
Complete Cabinet. Height 6 ft., width 3 ft.
Plain wood   .. £6 15 0
Stained & polished £8 5 0
Solid Oak polished £8 8 0
Top Section only. Height 3 ft., width 3 ft., depth 11 ins.
Plain wood   .. £3 3 6
Stained & polished £3 18 6
Solid Oak polished £4 0 0
Bottom Section only. Height 3 ft., width 3 ft., depth 15½ in.
Plain wood   .. £3 11 6
Stained & polished £4 6 6
Solid Oak polished £4 8 0

TU 13/3
'OSTERLEY' COMBINED TABLE TRAY
Specially suitable for picnics, garden and boating parties. By a simple lever movement the legs can be instantly folded underneath the top, thus forming a very handy tray which can be readily converted into a table while filled with china, etc. Size as Table, 27½ × 17½ × 24 ins. high
Stained and polished £3 11 6
Solid Mahogany, polished .. £4 8 6
Solid Mahogany, Inlaid, superior polished finish £6 3 9

TU 13/1 CORNER WARDROBE TOP
Made with 3-ply top and solid Mahogany front fitted with brassed side and centre hooks
Finished in the White with Polished front .. 6 6
„   „   „   „ Enamelled „ .. 6 6

TU 13/14 TABLE CUPBOARD
Strongly made of sound, clean timber, with 3-ply panels. Fitted brass drawer, pull and door handle, strong 2 in. butt hinges and reliable lock and key Fitted one 9 in. shelf inside.   Top 36 × 20 ins. Height 30 ins. £2 17 9

TU 13/10
BOOKSHELVES
Strongly made in plain Deal Height 31½ ins., width 17 ins. depth 6 ins. 6/3
Enamel finish 12/9

TU 13/5
WALL BRACKET
In plain Deal (on left)
Flat on Corner 1/2

TU 13/12 SCREEN FRAMES
Made of selected Wood with brass rod at top to take curtains

	4 ft.	5 ft.	5 ft. 6 ins.	6 ft. high
2-fold ..	17/6	18/-	18/9	19/6
3-fold ..	26/3	27/-	28/-	29/3

TU 13/13 ENCLOSED DRESSER
Made of selected materials and fitted with glass sliding doors, perfect fitting drawers, shelf in cupboard, and all-brass fittings Fitted with extension for pastry making

	4 ft.	5 ft.	6 ft.
Oregon Pine	£10 6 3	£12 0 0	£14 12 6
Solid Oak	11 16 3	13 16 0	17 1 3

TU 13/7 'THE LITTLE NIPPER' MOUSE TRAP
The most effective breakback trap made. Sudden death to mice 3d
'Nipper' Rat Traps 1/3

TU 13/6 'MYSTO' MOUSE TRAP
This self-setting Trap catches continually, and the mice are drowned at once in the water tank 3/6

TU 13/9 IRISH PATTERN MOUSE TRAP
3-hole, 7d   4-hole, 9d

TU 13/11
BOOKSHELVES
Very compact. Made from Solid Oak
Height 44 ins., width 12 ins., depth 6 ins. 17/6
Height 44 ins., width 18 ins., depth 6 ins. 21/-

TU 13/8 BOX PATTERN MOUSE TRAP
5d and 8d

ALL PRICES ARE SUBJECT TO MARKET FLUCTUATIONS

HARRODS LTD

Telephone SLOANE 1234
Telegrams 'EVERYTHING HARRODS LONDON'

LONDON SW 1

TURNERY DEPARTMENT
Bamboo Furniture—Useful Trays, Tables and Screens

TU 18/2
TILED TOP BAMBOO TABLE
With undershelf. Size of Top
16 × 16 ins. **26/3**
19 × 19 ins. **33/9**

TU 18/17
BAMBOO BOOT STAND
Shelves covered fine Matting. 38 ins. high
18/9

TU 18/16
JAPANESE LACQUERED TRAYS
Oblong shape. Green or Black. Best quality

17″	18″	20″	21″	23″	24″	26″	27″
7/6	8/6	11/6	12/6	15/6	17/3	22/6	25/-

Medium quality

17″	18″	20″	21″	23″	24″	26″	27″
3/6	4/-	5/6	6/9	8/3	9/3	11/3	12/6

ROUND OR SQUARE SHAPE
Best quality. Black or Green

9″	9½″	11″	12″	14″	15″	17″	18″
3/6	4/3	5/6	6/9	8/3	10/9	12/9	14/9

Medium quality

9″	9½″	11″	12″	14″	15″	17″	18″
2/-	2/3	2/9	3/6	4/6	5/6	6/9	7/9

TU 18/11
CAKE STAND
(On left) Bamboo frame with Lacquer panels **12/-**
With plain Matting panels. Square **9/-**
With plain Matting panels. Round **7/6**

TU 18/1
BAMBOO TABLE
With tiled top. Very strongly made. Size of top
22 × 16 ins. .. **32/3**
16 × 16 ins. .. **27/-**

TU 18/15
BAMBOO STOOL OR TABLE
With tiled top
13 × 13 × 24 ins. .. **13/6**
As above, size 9 × 9 ins. .. **10/6**
With Matting top, 13 × 13 ins. **11/6**

TU 18/6
BEDSIDE CABINET
On castors. A **very** useful and lightweight article
Height 30 ins. Size of top
16 × 13 ins. **45/-**

TU 18/10
ENCLOSED CUPBOARD
Bamboo frame with Matting top
34 × 15 × 36 ins. high .. **49/6**
22 × 15 × 36 ins. ,, .. **38/3**
18 × 15 × 33 ins. ,, .. **30/9**

TU 18/14
FOLDING STAND
Suitable for Japanese or Benares Trays Made of stout Bamboo, well finished
20/3

TU 18/3
KITCHEN OR SERVICE TRAY
Made of well seasoned Hardwood, with screwed bottoms, and dovetailed corners. Light Oak finish.

17⅛″	20″	22½″	24½″	27″
4/9	5/9	7/3	8/6	10/6

TU 18/4 TEA TRAY
With strong Pulp Cane rim and Glass bottom. Painted art colours, also Black and fitted with 3-ply backing boards
16 × 12 ins. **9/3**
18 × 12 ins. **10/6**
20 × 14 ins. **13/6**
As above but with plain Wood bottom
16 ins. **5/9** 18 ins. **6/6** 20 ins. **7/3**

TU 18/7 NEWS RACK
Made throughout of Bamboo
Small size **7/3**
Medium size **8/-**
Large size **12/-**

TU 18/5 BAMBOO TABLE
With Matting-covered top
15 × 15 ins. **9/6**
18 × 18 ins. **12/3**
21 × 21 ins. **13/6**
22 × 14 ins. **9/6**
24 × 16 ins. **12/3**
27 × 18 ins. **14/9**

TU 18/9 SCREEN FRAME
Made throughout of stout Bamboo Specially suited for hospital use as they are so very light
5 ft. high. Per fold .. **9/-**
5 ft. 6 ins. high. Per fold .. **9/9**
6 ft. high. Per fold .. **10/6**

TU 18/8 BOWL STAND
Made of carved Blackwood

2½″	3″	3½″	4½″
2/9	3/6	5/-	6/9
5½″	6½″	7″	7½″
9/9	12/9	15/9	18/9

TU 18/13
BLACKWOOD PLATE STAND
5½ ins. high **3/9**
6½ ins. ,, **4/6**
7½ ins. ,, **5/-**
9½ ins. ,, **5/6**

TU 18/12 WOOD TEA TRAY
Dark Oak, highly polished, with handles carved in rim

16″	18″	20″	22″	24″
8/6	10/6	11/6	13/6	15/6

In Fumed Oak

16″	18″	20″	22″	24″
4/6	7/6	8/9	10/-	11/3

ALL PRICES ARE SUBJECT TO MARKET FLUCTUATIONS

HARRODS LTD

Telephone SLOANE 1234
Telegrams 'EVERYTHING HARRODS LONDON'

LONDON S W 1

TURNERY DEPARTMENT
Luncheon and Tea Baskets Perfectly Made and Fitted

TU 22/1
LUNCH AND TEA BASKET
Lined Ivory-White Celastoid. Removable partitions. Fitted with two thermos flasks, two provision jars, cups, saucers, glasses, milk bottle, sugar box and stainless cutlery

For two persons	16 × 12 × 7 ins.	..	£7 2 6
,, four ,,	26 × 15 × 8 ins.	..	£12 10 0
,, six ,,	33 × 17 × 8 ins.	..	£17 8 0

TU 22/6 TEA BASKET
Metal lined throughout. Fall front to basket, fitted with nickel-plated metal tray. Complete with stove kettle, infuser, etc. Water can be boiled in basket without removing stove and kettle

For two persons	11 × 7 × 8 ins.	..	..	£4 17 6
,, four ,,	13 × 9 × 8 ins.	..	..	£6 6 0
,, six ,,	16 × 10 × 8 ins.	..	..	£7 18 0

Also made with Tin lining
two persons
£3 13 6
four persons
£5 0 0
six persons
£6 12 0

TU 22/9
LUNCH BASKET
With especially ample food accommodation, Wine bottles, glasses, butter and preserve jars and stainless cutlery. Basket lined Ivory-White Celastoid

For two persons	13 × 11 × 7½ ins.	..	£4 16 0
,, four ,,	18 × 13 × 7½ ins.	..	£7 19 0
,, six ,,	27 × 16 × 8 ins.	..	£14 12 6

Order by Post with confidence Harrods guarantee satisfaction

Postage paid on all purchases value 20/- and over

TU 22/8 INEXPENSIVE TEA BASKET
Fitted with cake tin, tea and sugar canister, butter pot, milk bottle, tea kettle and stove, cups and saucers

| For two persons | 12 × 9 × 7 ins. | .. | £0 17 6 |
| ,, four ,, | 15 × 11 × 7 ins. | .. | £1 7 6 |

TU 22/7   TEA BASKET
Fitted with fluted china cups and saucers, thermos flask, sugar box, cake box, milk flask and stainless cutlery. Nickel-plated tray

For two persons
13 × 9 × 6 ins.
£2 15 0
For four persons
18 × 10 × 7 ins.
£3 13 6

TU 22/4 LUNCH BASKET
Lined throughout. Fitted with nickel-plated provision jars, wine bottles, glasses, butter pot, plates and stainless cutlery

| For two persons | 15 × 10 × 7 ins. | .. | £3 16 6 |
| ,, four ,, | 20 × 12 × 7 ins. | .. | £5 18 0 |

TU 22/2 LUNCH AND TEA BASKET
Fitted with food box, wine bottle, milk flask, tea kettle and stove, cups and saucers, beakers, tea and sugar box, plates and stainless cutlery

For two persons	16 × 10 × 8 ins.	..	£3 7 6
,, three ,,	16 × 10 × 8 ins.	..	£3 15 0
,, four ,,	18 × 12 × 9 ins.	..	£4 10 0
,, six ,,	21 × 12 × 9 ins.	..	£6 0 0

TU 22/3 LUNCH AND TEA BASKET
Fitted with food box, wine bottle, milk flask, tea kettle, tea and sugar box, butter pot, cups and saucers, beakers and cutlery

| For two persons | 15 × 11 × 8 ins. | .. | £1 16 0 |
| ,, four ,, | 17 × 12 × 8 ins | .. | £2 11 0 |

TU 22/5
LUNCH AND TEA BASKET
Lined throughout Ivory-White Celastoid. Fitted with copper kettle, food jar, cake box, tea and sugar box, cups and saucers, glasses, milk bottle and stainless cutlery

For two persons	17 × 12 × 8 ins.	..	£7 10 0
,, four ,,	23 × 12 × 8 ins.	..	£11 9 6
,, six ,,	29 × 15 × 9 ins.	..	£16 7 0

ALL PRICES ARE SUBJECT TO MARKET FLUCTUATIONS

HARRODS LTD

Telephone SLOANE 1234
Telegrams 'EVERYTHING HARRODS LONDON'

LONDON S W1

TURNERY DEPARTMENT
Harrods Quality Basket Ware in Many Useful Forms

TU 24/1 DOME TOP KENNEL
Door and hinged top. Best Buff Wicker
Length at bottom

13	15	18	20	22	24 ins.
20/3	23/9	27/-	33/-	36/-	39/-

TU 24/2 JAPANESE PILGRIM BASKETS
Best quality, 20 × 10½ ins., 2/6; 21½ × 12 ins.,
3/6; 23 × 13½ ins., 6/6; 25 × 15½ ins., 8/6
27 × 17 ins., 10/6
Carrying straps for above
2/3, 2/5, 2/7, 2/10, 3/-

TU24/3 VENTILATED DOG HAMPER For travelling. Fitted with iron fastenings and battens at bottom
15½″ 11/3; 17½″ 14/-; 19½″ 17/-; 21½″ 19/6; 24″ 23/3

TU24/8 COTTAGE TOP DOG KENNEL
Best Buff Wicker. 13 ins. bottom,
22/6; 15 ins., 29/3; 18 ins., 31/6
20 ins., 37/6; 22 ins., 39/9; 24 ins., 45/-

TU 24/7 WINE HAMPER
Oval. To hold 3 bottles, 2/9
4 bottles, 3/-; 6 bottles, 3/3
9 bottles, 3/9; 12 bottles, 4/-
18 bottles, 4/9; 24 bottles, 5/6
30 bottles, 6/6; 36 bottles, 6/9

TU 24/6 CAT OR DOG BASKET ON STAND Best Walnut Wicker lined Serge with loose cushion. Diameter at bottom
11 ins., 14/9; 12 ins., 16/3; 13 ins.
18/6; 14 ins., 20/-; 15 ins., 22/3
16 ins., 26/-

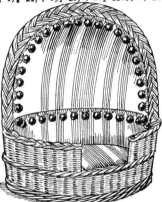

TU 24/4 HOODED DOG BASKET Best Walnut Wicker, lined Serge and fitted with cushion, 15 × 13 ins., 18/-; 17 × 14 ins., 20/3
19 × 15 ins., 23/9; 21 × 16 ins., 28/3
Similar Basket (TU 24/5), fitted on stand, 23/3,
26/-, 29/-, 33/6

TU 24/9 HAMPER Trunk lid for laundry, etc. White Wicker with strong cane handles and hinges, stout battens underneath

Outside sizes	Plain	Lined stout American Cloth
24 × 17 × 16 ins.	21/9	29/9
27 × 19 × 19½ ins.	26/9	37/6
30 × 20 × 20 ins.	35/9	47/9
33 × 21 × 21 ins.	39/6	52/-
36 × 24½ × 24½ ins.	49/9	62/-

Galvanised Padlocks,
two keys 3/11, 5/3

TU24/10 PROVISION HAMPERS Best London make
White Wicker with galvanized hasp and staple. 14 in., 9/3
16 ins., 9/9; 18 in., 10/6; 20 in.,
12/3; 22 in., 14/-; 24 in., 15/3

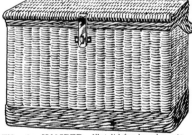

TU 24/11 HAMPER Flat lid for laundry, etc. Best London make. White Wicker with strong cane handle and hinges, stout battens underneath bottom. Galvanised hasp and staple. All hampers above 27 ins. have two hasps and staples. Outside sizes 24 × 17 × 16 ins., plain 21/-, lined 28/6.
27 × 19 × 19½ ins., plain 24/6, lined 35/-. 30 × 20 × 20 ins., plain 32/-, lined 43/9. 33 × 21 × 21 ins., plain 36/3, lined 48/9. 36 × 24½ × 24½ ins., plain 44/9, lined 58/- Galvanised padlocks, two keys 3/11, 5/3

TU 24/15 PICNIC BASKET
Best Buff Wicker
9 in., 5/6; 11 in., 6/6; 13 in., 8/-
15 in., 10/3; 17 in., 13/3; 19 in., 15/3
21 in., 19/9
Lighter Quality
9 in., 3/-; 10 in., 3/9; 11 in., 4/3; 12 in.
4/10; 13 in., 5/9; 14 in., 6/6
*Purchases value 20/- or over
carriage paid in England and Wales*

TU 24/14 DOG BASKETS, round best Walnut Wicker. Diameter at Bottom. 11 in., 3/9; 12 in., 4/3;
13 in., 5/9; 14 in., 6/9; 15 in., 9/-;
16 in., 10/6; 17 in., 11/9; 18 in.,
13/6; 19 in., 18/-; 20 in., 20/6;
22 in., 26/6; 24 in., 29/6; 28 in.,
32/6. Oval ditto, size at top, 17 ×
14 in., 6/9; 19 × 16 in., 7/6; 20 ×
18 in., 10/-; 23 × 19 in., 11/9;
25 × 21 in., 14/-; 27 × 23 in., 15/3

TU 24/13 DOG KENNEL
Made of Fine French Wicker

Size	1	2	3	4
White Buff	19/3	24/-	28/9	35/3
varnished	20/-	25/-	30/-	36/9

Also in White Pulp Cane, 11/9
13/-, 16/6, 20/-

TU 24/12 DRESS BASKETS
Best Buff Wicker

Size 20 × 12 × 8 ins.	..	13/3
„ 22 × 14 × 10 ins.	..	16/3
„ 24 × 16 × 12 ins.	..	21/9

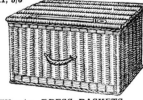

ALL PRICES ARE SUBJECT TO MARKET FLUCTUATIONS

TURNERY DEPARTMENT
'BEATL' WARE   A Light, Durable, Daintily-coloured Table Ware

A delightful Table Ware delicately shaded, which gives a pretty touch of colour to any table.   The fact that it is tastelesss and odourless and does not warp or crack if placed in hot water, gives it a decided advantage over all other forms of table ware, but although it is considerably stronger than Glass or China, it is not offered as unbreakable.   'Beatl' Ware is non-inflammable, but it should not be placed in hot ovens and should only be washed in soap and hot water, otherwise the delicate colouring may be impaired or the surface roughened.   Standard Colours :—Orange, Red, Pink, Yellow, Dark Blue, Light Blue, Green, Natural and Marble

TU 28/9
LARGE BREAKFAST
CREAM JUG
(ML 104) 2/6

TU 28/12 BEAKER
½-pint (165) .. 1/9
Lid for above (166) 9d

TU 28/4 ¾ PINT TEAPOT
(ML 124/125) 9/-

TU 28/23
LARGE DESSERT PLATE
(161) 2/3
TU 28/24
TEA PLATE
6½ ins.(139) .. 2/-

TU 28/8
BUTTER BOWL
(134L) 3/9

TU 28/8
TENNIS SET (T 41)
Cup, Saucer and Plate combined
3/11

TU 28/3 TEAPOT
Will make sufficient tea for two persons (145) 10/6

TU 28/1
½-PINT BREAKFAST
CUP AND SAUCER
(ML 116/7) .. 4/6

TU 28/15 FRUIT BOWL
8 in. diam., on stand (130) 12/6

TU 28/13 BOWL
4 in. (101) .. 2/-
If with lid as Powder Bowl (101/2) .. 3/11

TU 28/27
BREAKFAST CUP
AND SAUCER
(S 10/11) 3/-

TU 28/2¡
CANDLESTICKS
(147) Per Pair .. 7/6

TU 28/8
Afternoon Tea Set
(not illustrated)
21 pieces (T 46a)
36/6

TU 28/21
TEAPOT STAND
(120) 4/6
Smaller size (67) .. 2/6

TU 28/19
PIN TRAY
3¼ in. (129) .. 1/-

TU 28/7   MORNING TEA SET
7 pieces (T 42) 20/-
Tea Cup and Saucer (135/6) .. 2/9
Cream Jug (137) .. 2/6
Small Sugar Bowl, 3¼ ins. (138) .. 1/6
Tray, 13 ins. by 8ins. (143) .. 10/6

TU 28/22
BREAD AND BUTTER PLATE
(158) 4/-

TU 28/10 FRUIT STAND
(E 293) 9/6

TU 28/14
BIRMITE POWDER BOWL
(M 567) 4/-

TU 28/17 FLOATING BOWL
10 in. (131) 8/6

TU 28/6
FRUIT PLATE
(ML 128) 2/3

TU 28/2 CUP AND SAUCER
Unique design
(ML 119/20) 3/3

TU 28/20 BOWL
8½ in. (154) .. 9/6

TU 28/11
BREAKFAST SUGAR BASIN
(134) 2/3

BULB BOWL
6 in. diameter
4 in. high
5/6

TU 28/16
OCTAGONAL BOWL
(ML 115) .. 2/6

TU 28/26 OCTAGONAL BOWL
6 ins. (151) .. 3/11

ALL PRICES ARE SUBJECT TO MARKET FLUCTUATIONS

HARRODS LTD

Telephone SLOANE 1234
Telegrams 'EVERYTHING HARRODS LONDON'

LONDON S W 1

TURNERY DEPARTMENT
Garden Needs that are Proof against All Weather Conditions

TU 30/10 SPAN ROOF CYCLE HOUSE
Boarded and Felt Covered roof. Match boarded sides on good stout framework. Fitted with floor and two doors. Made in sections so that it can be easily fitted together

7 ft. × 3 ft. × 6 ft. high to eaves ..	£11 14	9
Painted three coats ..	£12 5	6
8 ft. × 6 ft. × 7 ft. high to eaves ..	£18 4	3
Painted three coats	£19 15	9

TU 30/3 REVOLVING SUMMER HOUSE
Well made throughout of best selected materials. All joints cleated over, and boarded roof covered 'Pluvex' Sheeting. The house is mounted on revolving platform, to face any desired direction. Interior stained and varnished

6 ft. × 5 ft. × 6 ft. to eaves ..	£15 17	6
With folding doors	£19 18	3
7 ft. × 6 ft. × 6 ft. to eaves ..	£19 15	6
With folding doors	£24 10	9
7 ft. × 7 ft. × 6 ft. 6 ins. to eaves	£21 15	6
With folding doors ..	£26 8	3
8 ft. × 7 ft. × 6 ft. 6 ins. to eaves	£25 0	0
With folding doors	£30 6	3

TU 30/1 NEW REVOLVING SUMMER HOUSE
Outside covered with prepared matching Roof double boarded and interlined with Felt

6 ft. × 5 ft.	£18 12	6
7 ft. × 6 ft.	£22 10	0
7 ft. × 7 ft.	£25 10	6
8 ft. × 7 ft.	£28 19	6

Doors and panels £5 10 6 extra

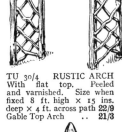

Send for complete list of Garden Furniture

TU 30/4 RUSTIC ARCH
With flat top. Peeled and varnished. Size when fixed 8 ft. high × 15 ins. deep × 4 ft. across path 22/9
Gable Top Arch .. 21/3

TU 30/5 RUSTIC GARDEN CHAIR Without arms. Strongly made .. 13/6

TU 30/14 RUSTIC TABLE With stout Elm top. Size 48 × 24 ins., height 31 ins. .. 58/6

TU 30/7 RUSTIC ARM CHAIR Strongly made and comfortable .. 16/6

TU 30/8 RUSTIC ARCH
Extra strong. Peeled Wood, well varnished. Size when fixed 8 ft. high × 15 ft. deep. × 4 ft. across path 23/6
TU 30/9 FOUR-WAY ARCH
Built in sections. Height when fixed 8 ft. Width of opening 2 ft. 4 ins. .. 92/9

TU 30/2 RUSTIC GARDEN SEAT
Strong and comfortable. Hollow shaped seat of strong Deal Laths.

	4 ft.	5 ft.	6 ft.
	19/3	24/3	29/6
Extra heavy seat	45/-	50/-	55/-

TU 30/11 RUSTIC PIGEON COTE Stained and varnished

6 hole	£2 15	0
12 ,, ...	£4 16	3
18 ,, ...	£6 16	3
24 ,, ...	£9 1	6
Pole and Spurs extra	£1 4	3
Thatched Roof extra	£0 10	6

TU 30/13 RUSTIC SUMMER OR TENNIS HOUSE Very well constructed on good sound framing. Joints cleated over at ends and back. Stout wood floor and well boarded roof. Size 10 ft. × 5 ft. .. £19 17 6

TU 30/6 PORTABLE HEXAGON SUMMER HOUSE Boards cleated over joints.
Inside dimensions
Angle to angle 6 ft. back to front 5 ft. 6 ins., height to eaves 6 ft. .. £12 13 3
6 ft. × 6 ins. × 5 ft. 11 ins. × 6 ft. 0 ins. £15 0 0
7 ft. 0 ins. × 6 ft. 5 ins. × 6 ft. 6 ins. £17 7 6
7 ft. 6 ins. × 6 ft. 11 ins. × 6 ft. 6 ins. £21 8 3
8 ft. 0 ins. × 7 ft. 4 ins. × 6 ft. 6 ins. £25 9 6
A less expensive house of this design can be supplied with felted roof and joints not cleated
£9 10 9; £11 17 6; £14 7 6; £18 5 9; £22 3 9

TU 30/12 PIGEON HOUSE
Made of tongued and grooved boards. Each hole partitioned. Stained and varnished.

5 hole	£1 13	9
8 ,, ...	£2 14	0
11 ,, ...	£3 14	3
14 ,, ...	£4 14	6

ALL PRICES ARE SUBJECT TO MARKET FLUCTUATIONS

HARRODS LTD

Telephone SLOANE 1234
Telegrams 'EVERYTHING HARRODS LONDON'

LONDON S W 1

TURNERY DEPARTMENT
Poultry Houses, Bee Hives and
Reliable Garden Shelters

TU 31/1   GABLE ROOF SHED

5 ft. × 4 ft.	6 ft. × 4 ft.	6 ft. × 5 ft.	8 ft. × 5 ft. 6 ins.
£7 3 9	£7 16 3	£9 1 3	£10 3 6
9 ft. × 6 ft.	10 ft. × 7 ft.	12 ft. × 8 ft.	15 ft. × 10 ft.
£11 17 6	£14 1 3	£17 10 0	£22 3 9

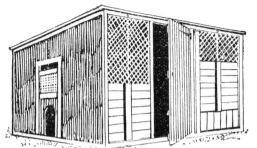

TU 31/2   POULTRY HOUSE

Constructed of well-seasoned framing, covered with best tongued and grooved boards, and divided in sections with sliding ventilating shutters over wire netting. Roof covered Pluvex Felt. Exterior treated with 'Creosotum'

Length	Width		Price	Floor extra
6 ft.	4 ft.	..	£3 10 9	22/-
7 ft.	5 ft.	..	£5 6 3	27/-
8 ft.	6 ft.	..	£7 5 9	35/9

Nest Boxes and Perches are not supplied with this house

TU 31/4   BEE HIVE
W.B.C. Design. The lifts are all the same size and can be tiered up to any height. There are no plinths used in the construction of the outer cover, therefore stocks are always kept dry. Complete with stock box, ten frames with ends and two dummy shallow-frame boxes, with eight frames **44/-**

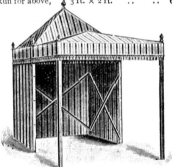

TU 31/6   POULTRY COOP
Creosoted. Strongly made with slide front for removal of birds, and shutter to close up at night.
2 ft. × 1 ft. 9 ins. × 1 ft. 9 ins. high at front   9/9
Shutter for front, extra 1/9
Run for above,   3 ft. × 2 ft. 6/9

TU 31/5   RABBIT HUTCH
Outside—stained and varnished.   Inside—limewhited
Size 3 ft. long × 18 ins. deep × 3 ft. high in front
Price **£2 0 0**

TU 31/3   LEAN-TO SHED

5 ft. × 4 ft.	6 ft. × 4 ft.	6 ft. × 5 ft.	8 ft. × 5 ft. 6 ins.
£7 3 9	£7 16 3	£9 1 3	£10 3 6
9 ft. × 6 ft.	10 ft. × 7 ft.	12 ft. × 8 ft.	15 ft. × 10 ft.
£11 17 6	£14 1 3	£17 10 0	£22 3 9

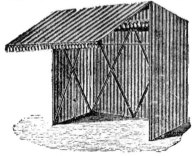

TU 31/7   SUPERIOR LAWN TENT
Size 6 ft. square.   Extension 6 ft. square. Complete as shown in Striped Canvas **175/9**
Extra Curtains in Striped Canvas, size 6 ft. wide, each, extra **14/9**
Green Rot-proof Canvas (flax) **215/9**
Extra Curtains in Green Rot-proof Canvas, 6 ft. wide, each, extra **20/9**

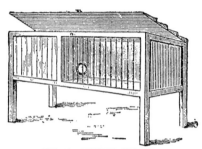

TU 31/8   SUPERIOR LAWN PAVILION
Size 12 ft.× 6 ft. wide. Made of selected materials, with cross folding frame which enables the Tent to be used without guy ropes in sheltered places.   Ropes are provided for additional support in rough weather
Complete as shown in Striped Canvas **205/-**
Extra Curtain in Striped Canvas 6 ft. wide, each, extra **14/9**
Green Rot-proof Canvas (flax) **259/6**
Extra Curtains in Green Rot-proof Canvas 6 ft. wide, each, extra **20/9**

TU 31/11   RUSH GARDEN CUSHION
(not illustrated)
With coloured design, 17 ins. square **2/6**

TU 31/9   THE 'WEMBLEY'
IMPROVED SUN AWNING
Size 6 ft. square.   6 ft. high at sides, The improved frame with cross stays enables the tent to be used without guy ropes, but these are supplied for additional support in rough weather.   Orange or Green Striped Canvas Three separate curtains are supplied, but can be had in one piece if specially ordered
Complete **113/9**   Extra curtain for front **11/3**

TU 31/10   SUPERIOR GARDEN SHELTER
Size 6 ft. × 3 ft. 6 ins. deep × 6 ft. high in front. The frame is of light construction and can be moved from place to place without folding. The cover is of best quality Canvas, in one piece. The whole shelter can be erected or taken down in an instant Folds into bag
Best Striped Canvas **55/-**
In Green Rot-proof Canvas (flax) .. **71/6**

TU 31/13   'SUPERIOR' GARDEN SHELTER WITH EXTENSION
Size 6 ft. × 3 ft. 6 ins. deep × 6 ft. high in front
Extension extra. Guy ropes and pegs are supplied
In Best Striped Canvas **66/-**
In Green Rot-proof Canvas (flax) .. **85/-**
Cheaper quality—
In Striped Canvas **42/6**
In Green Rot-proof Canvas **51/6**

TU 31/12   PUNT OR GARDEN CUSHION
Well filled, covered with gay coloured Cretonne on one side and Rubber on the other. Cushions can be neatly rolled and are fitted with straps for carrying **19/6**
With headrest **27/9**
Double size 6 ft. × 3 ft. 9 ins. **53/3**

ALL PRICES ARE SUBJECT TO MARKET FLUCTUATIONS

Telephone SLOANE 1234
Telegrams 'EVERYTHING HARRODS LONDON'

HARRODS LTD   **LONDON S W 1**

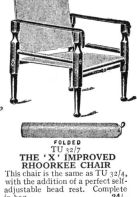

TU 32/3 OCEAN DECK CHAIR

The framework of this chair is made exceptionally heavy, has double-laced Canvas seating, extra long leg rest and broad arms. A cushion is attached to the seat and covers the joint where leg rest and chair meet An adjustable head pillow is also supplied. The strongest and most comfortable chair on the market Made in Green Rot-proof Canvas only

Complete with leg rest 30 ins. long 49/6
Canopy extra 10/-
Fitting Solid Copper Glass Holder, 1/6 each extra

TU 32/1 MILITARY HAMMOCK CHAIR

Made of selected materials throughout. The frames are exceptionally heavy and best quality canvas only is used. Very firm and rigid

	Green Striped Canvas	Black & Rot-proof Canvas	Orange Canvas
Chair with broad arms ..	26/6	27/6	27/6
Chair with broad arms and leg rest ..	34/6	37/-	37/-
Chair with broad arms, leg rest and canopy ..	42/9	47/-	47/-
Fitting Solid Copper Glass Holder, 1/6 each extra			

TU 32/2 THE 'ABYSSINIAN' TABLE

Size of top (open) 36 ins. × 36 ins., size (closed) 36 ins. × 18 ins. × 6 ins. Made of selected Hardwood, with special brass hinges to enable it to be folded in half. Polished self colour 47/6

Purchases value 20/- sent Post free in England and Wales

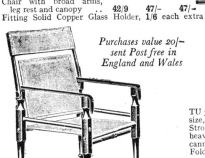

FOLDED

TU 32/4 THE 'X' RHOORKEE CHAIR

This well known Chair is made of selected Hardwood and extra strong Green Rot-proof Canvas is used for the seat and back. Straps are best bridle leather

Complete in bag 42/-
Folding leg rest for same, 10/- extra

TU 32/6 THE 'WEST AFRICAN' TABLE

size, top 43 ins. × 23 ins., height 27 ins. Very Strong and rigid table. Made of selected Hardwood; heavy birch legs of simple construction which cannot get out of order. Polished self colour Folds perfectly flat 35/-

TU 32/5 LATRINE SEAT

Made from Hardwood with a polished seat. Folds flat in bag. Complete in bag .. 20/-

FOLDED
TU 32/7
THE 'X' IMPROVED RHOORKEE CHAIR

This chair is the same as TU 32/4, with the addition of a perfect self-adjustable head rest. Complete in bag 34/-
Folding leg rest for same 10/-extra

TU 32/13 THE 'WEST AFRICAN' CHAIR

Made of selected Hardwood Best quality double Green Rot-proof canvas sewn seats are used. Folds flat. Polished self colour

Bent Arms 18/-
Bent arms with laced seat 19/6

TU 32/9 GARDEN RETREAT

Made of selected Wood and fitted with canvas awning Folds perfectly flat 3 ft. 6 ins. long

In Striped Canvas .. 39/-
In Green Rot-proof Canvas .. 45/-
In best Green Rot-proof Canvas (flax) .. 52/6

TU 32/12 SUPERIOR SWING HAMMOCK CHAIR

Height of stand 6 ft., length of Chair extended 5 ft. 9 ins. Made of selected materials throughout, with tinned weldless chain and fittings. Chair is so well balanced that it adjusts itself to the body Folds flat

In best Striped Canvas .. 63/-
In Black and Orange Canvas 63/-
In Green Rot-proof Canvas 69/6

TU 32/11 THE CAMP FIRE CHAIR

Made of selected Hardwood polished self colour. Seat and back of Green Rot-proof canvas. All fittings coppered. Highly finished

In Green Rot-proof Canvas.. 15/-
In Black and Orange Rot-proof canvas .. 15/-
Cheaper quality
In Green or Orange Striped Canvas .. 9/11
In Green Rot-proof Canvas.. 10/9
If with wide arms 9d extra

TU 32/14 FIRM SEAT HAMMOCK CHAIR

Made of selected Hardwood and best quality Canvas. Is adjustable in the same way as the ordinary Hammock Chair, but is supplied with a firm square seat, and has a canvas band to give support to the back

	Green Striped Canvas	Black & Rot-proof Canvas	Orange Canvas
Chair with broad arms ..	26/6	27/6	27/6
Chair with broad arms and leg rest	34/6	37/-	37/-
Chair with broad arms, leg rest and canopy..	42/9	47/-	47/-
Fitting Solid Copper Glass Holder 1/6 each extra			

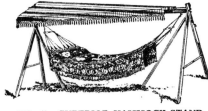

TU 32/8 SUPERIOR HAMMOCK STAND

Length (inside legs) 10 ft. 6 ins., extended length (inside legs) 12 ft. This stand, which is adjustable to take any size hammock, is made from selected Pitch Pine, polished. Will carry any weight. It has a sun awning, sloping at sides, made from best quality Canvas. Fittings are tinned, and the whole folds into small space

In Striped Canvas (without hammock) 65/6
In Green Rot-proof Canvas (without hammock) .. 75/6
Stand only (without hammock or canopy) 44/9

Order by post with confidence, Harrods guarantee satisfaction

TU 32/10 THE 'X' HAMMOCK LOUNGE

Size (open) 6 ft. long by 24½ ins. wide by 30 ins. high

In best Striped Canvas 42/6
In Black and Orange Canvas 42/6
In Green Rot-proof Canvas 47/6

ALL PRICES ARE SUBJECT TO MARKET FLUCTUATIONS

TURNERY DEPARTMENT

Luncheon Baskets, Picnic Case and Garden Furniture

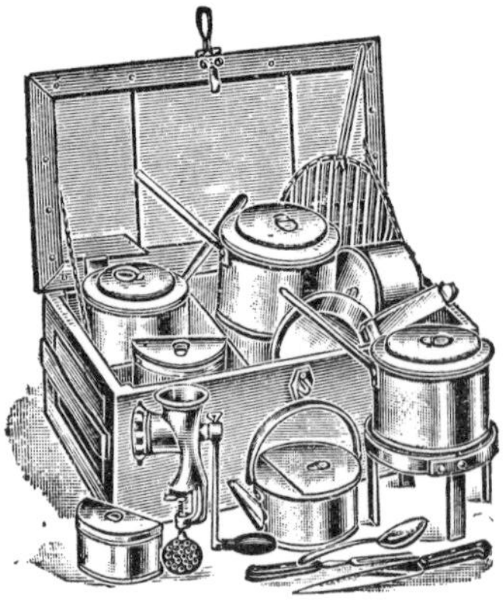

TU 33/4 COOK'S CASE
Size 25 × 13 × 10 ins. Weight 30 lbs.
Contains all necessary utensils. **£7 11 6**

TU 33/5 A SIMILAR CASE
Size 17 × 10 × 10½ ins. Weight 20 lbs.
With the same fittings less mincer and chopping board **£5 4 6**

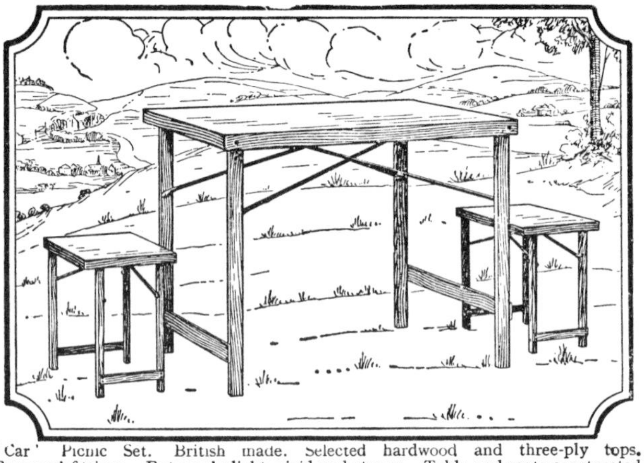

'Car' Picnic Set. British made. Selected hardwood and three-ply tops. Coppered fittings. Extremely light, rigid and strong. Table and seats constructed with new patent interlocking steels. Seats fold into Table when closed and cannot fall out. Opened or closed in a few seconds. Invaluable for Car Picnics, Race Meetings and other outdoor occasions.

For two persons. Consisting of table and two seats ..	Price **21/6**
Approx. sizes, folded 26 × 18½ × 2½ ins.	Total weight 12 lbs.
Table Top 26 × 18½ ins. Height 25 ins.	" " 7 lbs.
Seats, Top 14 × 9½ ins. Height 13 ins. folded, each 14 × 9½ × 1¼ ins.	" " 2½ lbs.
For four persons. Consisting of table and four seats. ..	Price **29/6**
Folded. 29½ × 23½ × 2½ ins.	Total Weight 19 lbs.
Table. 29½ × 23½ ins. Height 25 ins.	" " 9 lbs.
Seats. Top 14 × 9½ ins. Height 13 ins. Folded, each 14 × 9½ × 1¼ ins.	" " 2½ lbs.

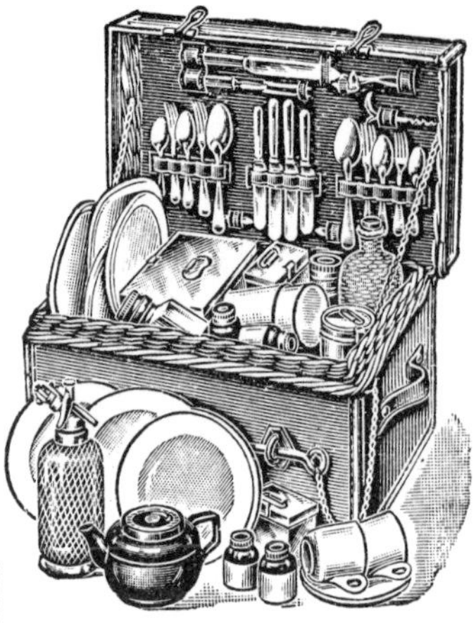

TU 33/6 COOK'S CASE
Size 23 × 15 × 14 ins. Weight 48 lbs. Covered Rot-proof Canvas and bound Raw Hide .. **£10 14 0**

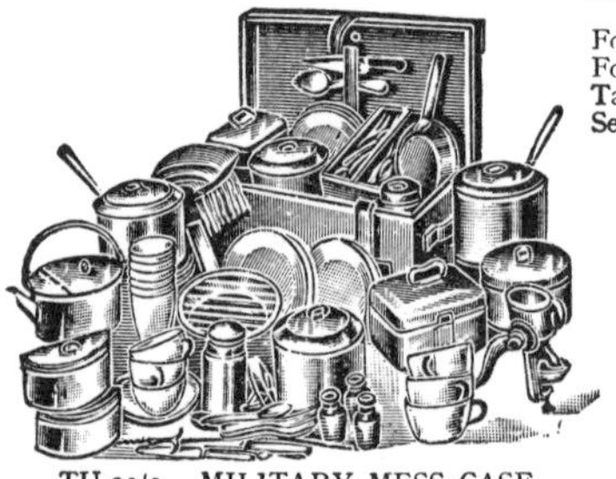

TU 33/3 MILITARY MESS CASE
Size 24 × 13 × 12 ins. Contains all the necessary table and cook's utensils for a mess of six officers. **£13 11 6**

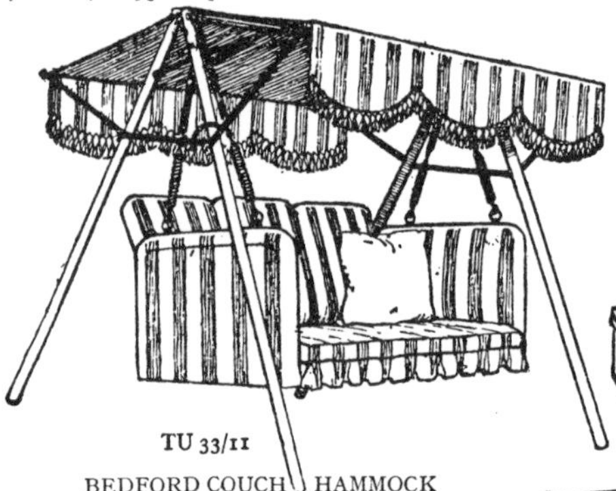

TU 33/11

BEDFORD COUCH HAMMOCK
Supplied with shaped scalloped adjustable back, giving a three cushioned effect. Reversible seat cushion is fitted and buttoned to match the back. Fitted with adjustable canopy sunshade **£12 12 0**

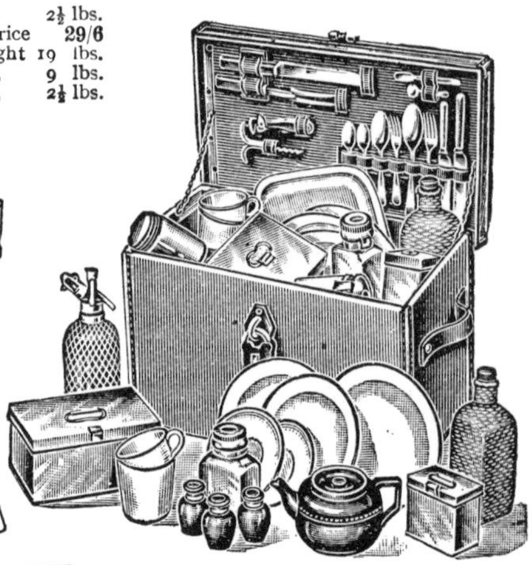

TU 33/1 COOK'S CASE
Size 21 × 12 × 14 ins. Weight 40 lbs. Covered Rot-proof Canvas and bound Raw Hide **£9 5 6**

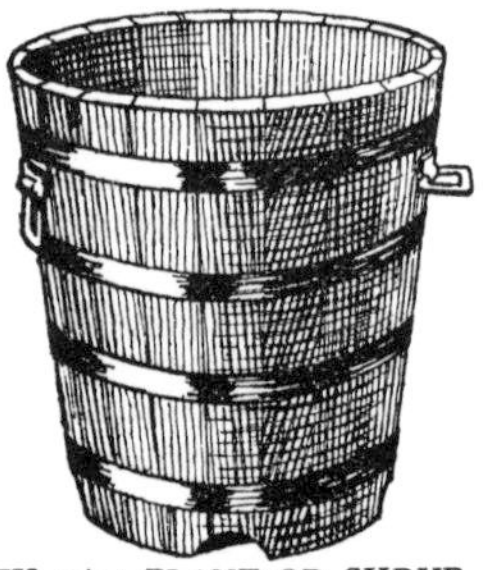

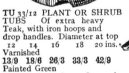

TU 33/12 PLANT OR SHRUB TUBS Of extra heavy Teak, with iron hoops and drop handles. Diameter at top

12	14	16	18	20 ins.
Varnished				
13/9	**18/6**	**26/3**	**33/3**	**42/9**
Painted Green				
12	14	16	18	20 ins.
15/-	**20/6**	**28/6**	**35/3**	**45/9**

TU 33/13 SIMILAR TUBS
Lighter make, in Solid Oak, varnished or painted Green

12	14	16	18	21 ins.
12/6	**14/6**	**15/6**	**19/9**	**23/-**

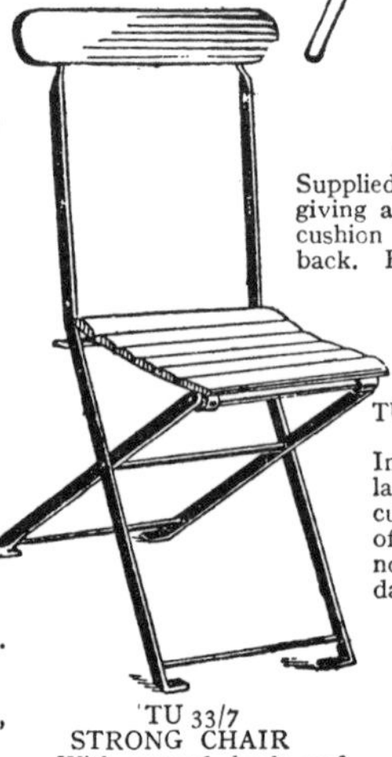

TU 33/7
STRONG CHAIR
With curved back and strong Iron framework As used in the London Parks
Each **8/9**

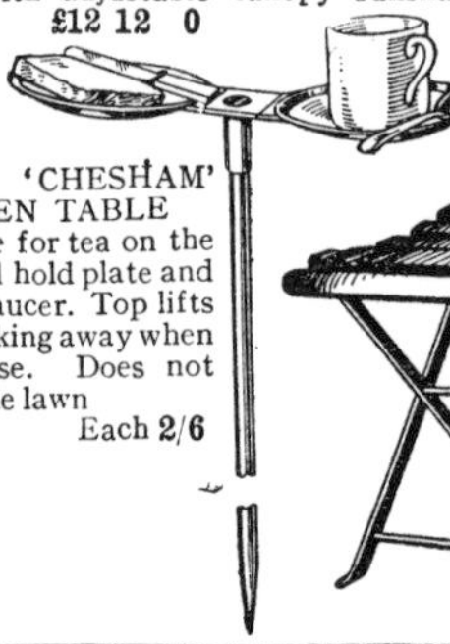

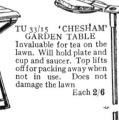

TU 33/15 'CHESHAM' GARDEN TABLE
Invaluable for tea on the lawn. Will hold plate and cup and saucer. Top lifts off for packing away when not in use. Does not damage the lawn
Each **2/6**

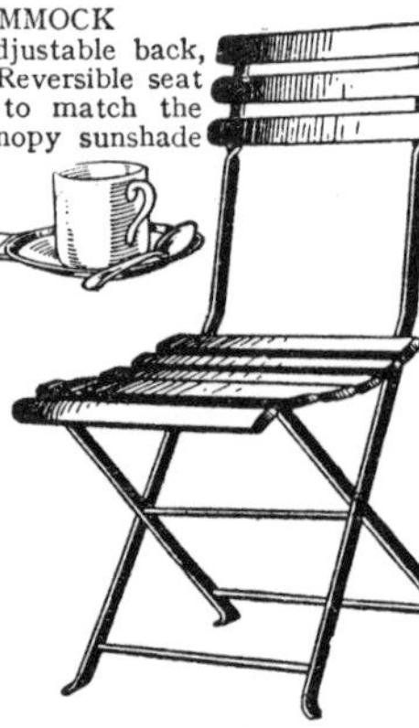

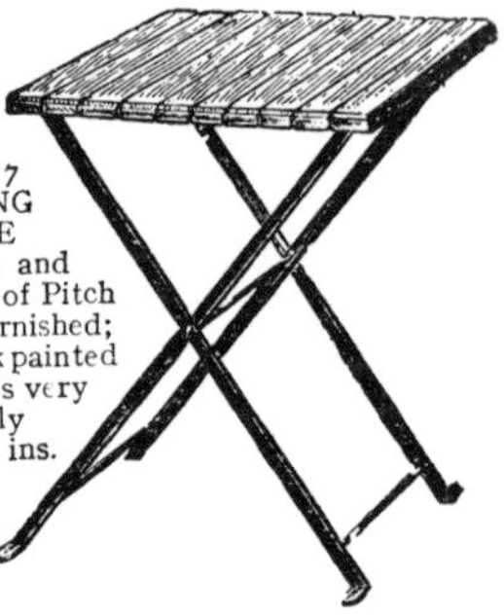

TU 33/17
FOLDING TABLE
Well made and finished. Top of Pitch Pine splines, varnished; Iron framework painted Green. Folds very compactly
Size 30 × 21 ins.
23/6

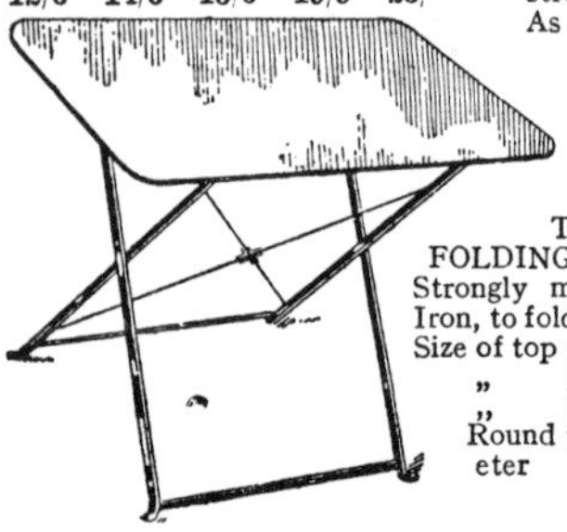

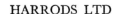

TU 33/14
FOLDING IRON TABLE
Strongly made of Wrought Iron, to fold up flat; painted
Size of top 34 × 22 ins. **17/6**
" 30 × 30 ins. **15/-**
" 23 × 23 ins. **14/-**
Round top 23 ins. diameter **12/-**

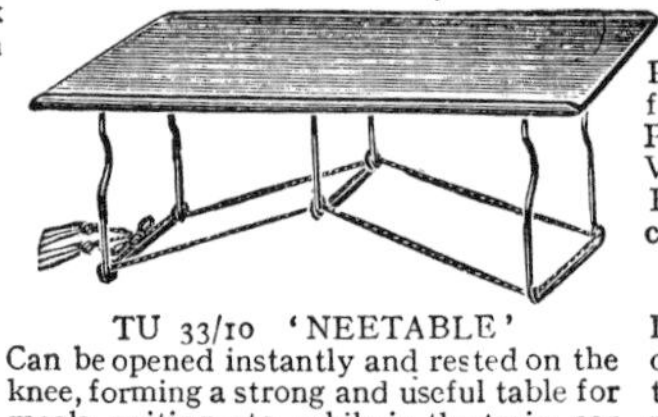

TU 33/10 'NEETABLE'
Can be opened instantly and rested on the knee, forming a strong and useful table for meals, writing, etc., while in the train, car or for picnic. Size of top 17½ × 10 ins.
In Oak or Mahogany **7/6**
Walnut with plated wire supports .. **13/6**

TU 33/8
CHAIR
Painted Iron frame, Pitch Pine splines Varnished. Folds quite compactly
8/3 each

TU 33/9
Lighter quality with two Black rails. Painted Green all over
Each **7/3**

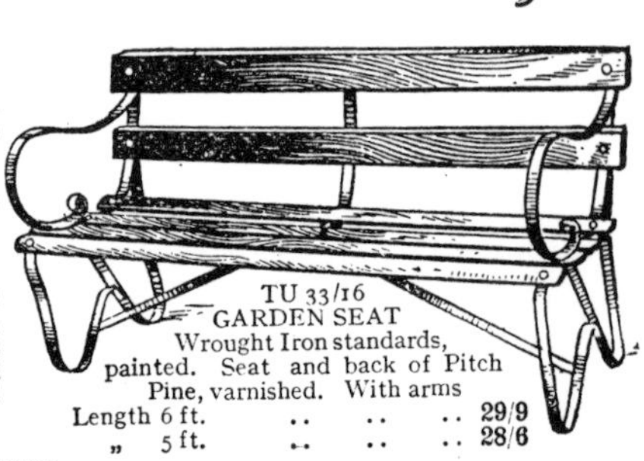

TU 33/16
GARDEN SEAT
Wrought Iron standards, painted. Seat and back of Pitch Pine, varnished. With arms
Length 6 ft. **29/9**
" 5 ft. **28/6**

ALL PRICES ARE SUBJECT TO MARKET FLUCTUATIONS

TURNERY DEPARTMENT
Harrods Serviceable Camp Equipment

TU 34/1
THE SENIOR PATROL TENT

Doorway one end, ventilator on side of roof. Complete with jointed poles, guy and bracing lines, pegs, mallet and bag

	No.	1	2	3	4
		ft. ins.	ft. ins.	ft. ins.	ft. ins.
Length	..	7 0	8 0	10 0	10 0
Width	..	6 0	7 0	7 0	8 0
Height	..	5 6	6 0	6 0	6 0
Walls	..	2 0	2 6	2 6	2 6
No. 904 White Cotton		£5 9 6	£5 16 6	£7 17 9	£8 9 3
No. 904G G.R.P. Cotton		£6 9 3	£8 1 3	£9 7 9	£10 1 6
Ground Sheets G.R.P. Cotton		19/9	26/-	32/9	36/9

Above prices include Fly Sheet and Canopy as illustrated

TU 34/2
THE 'X' IMPROVED COMPACTUM BED
Size (open) 6 ft. 6 ins. long × 2 ft. 6 ins. wide
Size (closed) 3 ft. long × 5 ins. × 5 ins.
This bed is fitted with our new malleable hook joint in place of the old pattern tube socket. This prevents the side sticks in the canvas top coming apart when the Canvas becomes worn and stretched. Green Rotproof Flax Canvas only used for these beds

Bed, with Green Rotproof Canvas top	58/-
Valise, Green Rotproof Canvas	5/6
Pillow, Green Rotproof Canvas, filled hair, 21½ × 15½ ins. ..	8/3
Mattress, striped Canvas, filled cork	21/-
Mattress, Green Rotproof Canvas, filled cork ..	31/-
Mattress, Green Rotproof Canvas, filled hair ..	42/6

TU 34/3 THE SQUATTERS' TENT
Complete with jointed poles, ventilators, guy and bracing lines, pegs and mallet. Fitted with pockets on each wall. Doorway and shuttered window each end. All 7 ft. high to ridge of Tent, with walls 3 ft. deep

No.	Size	719G Green Rotproof Cotton	391G Flax	Ground Sheets G.R.P. Cotton
1	8 × 6 ft.	£11 6 3	£12 18 3	£1 2 6
2	9 × 7 ft.	12 14 6	14 11 3	1 9 6
3	10 × 8 ft.	14 18 9	16 16 0	1 16 9
4	11 × 9 ft.	16 11 3	18 17 0	2 4 9
5	13 × 10 ft.	20 3 6	23 7 0	2 18 6

The Squatters' Tent prices include Valises and can also be supplied with bathroom and verandah

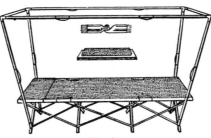

TU 34/5
THE 'X' BED WITH WOODEN MOSQUITO RODS
The mosquito frame is made of half-inch hardwood rods, jointed so that no part is longer than the bed when folded. The parts are linked together by strong chain, the sockets being of solid brass

Complete set of wooden rods	14/6
White Mosquito Curtain	27/6
Green " "	30/-

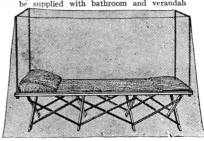

TU 34/4
THE 'X' BED SHOWING BRASSED MOSQUITO RODS
These rods are of Brass Cased Tube, and fit into special sockets in top part of bed. Cord at top to support net

Complete set of Brass Rods	9/-
White Mosquito Curtain	23/-
Green " "	25/6

TU 34/6
THE 'XL' BED
Size (open) 6 ft. 3 ins. × 2 ft. 4 ins. wide × 1 ft. 5 ins. high. Size (folded) 3 ft. 2 ins. × 8 ins. × 5 ins. Made from selected Hardwood, with japanned iron fittings, covered best Green Rotproof Canvas

Complete, with handle for carrying ..	33/-
Wooden Mosquito Rods	4/-
White Mosquito Curtain	23/-
Green Mosquito Curtain	25/6
Valise, Green Rotproof Canvas	7/-

TU 34/7
KITBAG
Green Rotproof Canvas

32 × 12 ins. dia. ..	6/3
36 × 14 ins. dia. ..	8/-

Complete with bar and padlock, 2/6 each extra

TU 34/8
THE 'X' CHAIR
Size (folded) 23 × 6 × 2 ins. In Green Rotproof Canvas (Flax) .. **11/6**

TU 34/9
THE 'X' TABLE
Small size (open) 25 × 19 ins. Whole (folded) 29 ins. long by 4½ ins. diameter .. **25/-**
Large size. Top (open) 32 × 26 ins. Whole (folded) 34 ins. long by 5 ins. diameter . **39/-**
Tops covered Green Rotproof Canvas

Carriage paid on Purchases value 20/- and over to any part of England and Wales

TU 34/13
'JAEGER' SLEEPING BAG
Made of Camel Hair and Wool. 6 ft. long × 3 ft. wide
Three layers **80/-**

TU 34/10 SOILED LINEN OR BEDDING BAG
In Green Rotproof Canvas
38 × 18 ins. dia. (without lock) **13/9**
49 × 18 ins. dia. (without lock) **16/6**
Brass handle lock for same **6/-**

TU 34/11 BUCKET
These buckets are made of extra stout Green Rotproof Flax Canvas, with rope handle .. **4/-**

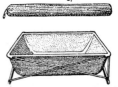

TU 34/12 THE 'X' COMBINED BATH AND WASHSTAND
Size of whole folded in valise 2 ft. 10 ins. × 4 ins. dia.
Size of bath open, 2 ft. 6 ins. × 2 ft. 6 ins. × 11 ins. deep. 'X' Combined Bath and Washstand (all in Green Rotproof Canvas) in valise **33/-**
'X' Bath (Green Rotproof Canvas with frame in bag) **29/-**
'X' Washstand (Green Rotproof Canvas basin Frame only) **15/-**

TU 34/14
BATH
Heavy Green Rotproof Cotton Canvas. 24 ins. dia. **11/9**
27 ins. dia. **12/9**
30 ins. dia. **14/9**
In case complete

ALL PRICES ARE SUBJECT TO MARKET FLUCTUATIONS

Telephone SLOANE 1234
Telegrams 'EVERYTHING HARRODS LONDON'

HARRODS LTD   LONDON S W 1

TURNERY DEPARTMENT

SPRATT'S Famous Appliances for Poultrymen and Dog Breeders

TU 35/1 HEARSON'S 'CHAMPION' INCUBATOR

Fitted with all the latest improvements in these famous incubators

Capacity	Price
50/60 eggs	£8 10 0
100/120 ,,	£12 15 0
200/240 ,,	£19 15 0

Carriage forward

TU 35/2 Fitted with Copper tank, wind proof lamp, feeding troughs and drinking fountains. Provided with three chambers, a sleeping compartment, a glass covered run and a wire covered run, making it a very efficient rearer for winter or summer

No.	To rear		Approx. size	Price
3	25 chicks		5' 10" × 1' 8"	£6 6 0
7	50 ,,		8' 0" × 2' 6"	£9 10 0
13	100 ,,		11' 2" × 3' 7"	£13 13 0
21	200 ,,		16' 0" × 5' 0"	£24 10 0

Carriage forward

HEARSON'S 'HYDROTHERMIC' FOSTER MOTHER

TU 35/3 HEARSON'S 'CHAMPION' FOSTER MOTHER

Complete with copper tank, wind proof lamp, feeding troughs and drinking fountains. One size only, 7 ft. 6 ins. × 2 ft. 6 ins., for 50/75 chicks
£8 10 0

Order by Post with confidence Harrods guarantee your satisfaction

TU 35/4 HEARSON'S COAL BURNING BROODERS

No. 1	500 chick capacity ..	£5 0 0
No. 2	1,000 ,, ,, ..	£6 15 0

10 feet of 4-in. diameter Galvanised Sheet Iron smoke pipe, with cap and damper to regulate draught 18/-
Galvanised Flange for roof 5/-
2 ft. lengths of extra piping .. .. per ft. 1/4
Elbows .. .. Each 2/-
These Brooders are highly recommended where it is desired to rear birds in large flocks, being constructed of solid Grey Iron castings, with Galvanised Steel hovers and double thermostat regulators. Carriage paid to nearest Railway Station

TU 35/6 HEARSON'S PATENT EGG-TESTING LAMP
15/9

TU 35/7 POSTAL EGG BOXES
Strong cardboard with case lids, corrugated linings, and felt pad at top and bottom

To hold		Price
6 eggs ..	..	11d
12 ,,	..	1/2
24 ,,	..	1/10

THE HAMMOCK PARCEL POST EGG-BOX

TU 35/5 HEARSON'S COLD BROODER
(No artificial heating) Consists of two compartments. One, serving as the sleeping chamber is thickly insulated with non-conducting material to prevent loss of heat, and the other chamber is covered with glass to afford shelter when Brooder is out of doors. The nursery floor is removable for cleaning

25 Chick capacity	..	..	..	£3 0 0
50 ,, ,,	..	..	..	£4 0 0
100 ,, ,,	..	..	..	£6 0 0

Carriage paid to nearest Railway Station

TU 35/10 IMPROVED EGG-TESTING LAMP
The most simple and ingenious egg tester invented. By placing the egg over the opening the electric bulb is immediately lit up 10/6
Extra batteries .. .. Each 9d

POCOCKS PATENT

TU 35/8 'HAMMOCK' PARCEL POST EGG BOX
Very light, strong and safe
Made of 3-ply Wood

To hold		Price
6 eggs	..	1 9
12 ,,	..	2 3
18 ,,	..	3/-
24 ,,	..	3/3

TU 35/9 'POCOCK' FELT LINED EGG BOX
Made of 3-ply Wood with metal corners

	To hold		
3 doz.	4 doz.	5 doz.	6 doz.
12/6	13/-	14/-	16,6
8 doz.	10 doz.	12 doz.	
20/-	22/-	23/6	

TU 35/11 SPRATT'S 'UNIVERSAL' BREEDING KENNEL

	Length Overall	Height Front	Height Back	Depth	Sleeping Compart.	Run
Terriers	4' 6"	3' 0"	2' 6"	2' 0"	2' 0" × 2' 0"	2' 6"
Airedales	6' 0"	3' 6"	3' 0"	2' 6"	2' 6" × 2' 6"	3' 6"
Alsatians	9' 0"	4' 6"	4' 0"	3' 0"	3' 0" × 3' 0"	6' 0"
St. Bernards	12' 0"	6' 0"	5' 6"	4' 6"	4' 6" × 4' 6"	7' 6"
Prices—	£5 0 0	£6 0 0		£9 10 0	£16 16 0	

ALL PRICES ARE SUBJECT TO MARKET FLUCTUATIONS

HARRODS LTD

Telephone SLOANE 1234
Telegrams 'EVERYTHING HARRODS LONDON'

LONDON S W 1

TURNERY DEPARTMENT

Comfortable Well Made Cane Lounge Chairs for House or Garden

TU 36/7
COMBINED FOLDING CANE LOUNGE
With adjustable back and striped Canvas awning; the leg-rest slides beneath seat when not required **70/-**

TU 36/1   CANE LOUNGE
With adjustable back and pull-out leg rest, best quality glossy Cane, with glass holder at side.. .. .. **37/9**

TU 36/2
CANE LOUNGE WITH EXTRA LONG ARM RESTS
Adjustable back, pull-out leg rest, of natural pulp Cane. Fitted with glass holder and pocket for books, etc. **89/9**

TU 36/3   CANE LOUNGE
With adjustable back, fixed leg rest and tumbler holder at side. Very strong.
Made of Glossy Cane **56/6**
With fixed back rest.. .. .. **51/6**

TU 36/4   CANE LOUNGE
Superior quality, Whole Pulp Cane with adjustable back, pull-out leg rest and two pockets for books, etc. This is a first-class lounge made to stand hard wear **£5 0 0**

TU 36/12
HORSE SHOE SHAPED CHAIR
Made of Rod Cane, with sunk seat **24/3**

TU 36/6   GARDEN CHAIR
Made of best White English Willow and fitted with thick cushion Seat and shoulders covered in Red Leather cloth.. .. **17/9**

TU 36/5
INVALID CARRYING CHAIR
Made throughout Cane with stout Bamboo poles. Very strong and perfectly safe **29/3**
With detachable poles .. **32/3**

TU 36/10
THE 'PICKWICK' GARDEN CHAIR
Improved design. **Tub** shape with well shaped back and arm rests. Strongly made of best English Wicker in Light Brown finish, well varnished. Complete with cushion **17/6**
Without cushion **13/9**

TU 36/8
GARDEN CHAIR
Made with strong Malacca Cane frame covered with selected Cane. Specially suitable for outdoor use, with a patent hoop foot to prevent legs sinking into turf .. **42/6**

TU 36/13
ROD CANE GARDEN CHAIR
The sunk seat makes this chair exceedingly comfortable .. **23/6**
Extra strong **27/6**

TU 36/14   THE 'WESTWARD HO!' PULP CANE LOUNGE
The back is adjustable and the leg rest slides underneath. Glass holder on one side and book holder on the other
Price **£7 5 0**

TU 36/9
DOME GARDEN SEAT OR ARBOUR
Strongly made of best Buff Wicker
Height 5 ft., width 24 ins., depth 21 ins.
.. **35/6**
Lighter quality **25/9**
Seat Cushion, covered Green Casement Cloth **13/6**

ALL PRICES ARE SUBJECT TO MARKET FLUCTUATIONS

HARRODS LTD

Telephone SLOANE 1234
Telegrams 'EVERYTHING HARRODS LONDON'

LONDON S W I

TURNERY DEPARTMENT

'Lloyd Loom' Products in Seventeen Standard Colours

All Models may be obtained in any of the Seventeen Standard Colours, or in Gold or Silver, or any of the colours may be frosted either with Silver or Gold. In the event of any of these colours being unsuitable we will match customers' own special colours

STANDARD COLOUR SHADES

White	Natural	Old Rose
Orange	Red	Rose-du-Barry
Mauve	Mahogany	Pale Blue
Middle Blue	Royal Blue	Deep Smoke Grey
Brown	Jacobean	Green
Black	Primrose	

TU 37/3 TUB CHAIR
Total Height 34 ins. Total Width 23 ins. Size of Seat 17 × 17 ins. Height of Seat from ground 17 ins.
Standard Colours .. 42/-
Gold or Special .. 45/-
Frosted Colours .. 46/-

TU 37/1 ARM CHAIR
Total Height 34 ins. Total Width 20 ins. Size of Seat 17 × 17 ins. Height of Seat from ground 15 ins.
Standard Colours .. 39/-
Gold or Special .. 42/-
Frosted Colours .. 43/-

TU 37/2 TABLE
Height 27 ins. Size of Top 22 ins. With plain glass top and fabric undershelf
Without glass tops
Standard Colours 40/6
Gold or Special 43/6
Frosted Colours 44/6
With plain or coloured glass tops
Standard Colours 68/6
Gold or Special 71/6
Frosted Colours 72/6

TU 37/5 SHIRT BOX
Height 17 ins. Length 27 ins. Width 16½ ins.

	Unlined	Lined
Standard Colours ..	39/-	51/-
Gold or Special ..	42/-	54/-
Frosted Colours ..	43/-	55/-

TU 37/4 OTTOMAN BOX
Height 16 ins. Length 36 ins. Width 21 ins.
Standard Colours
Lined 73/6 Unlined 56/6
Gold or Special
Lined 77/6 Unlined 60/6
Frosted Colours
Lined 78/6 Unlined 61/6

TU 37/6 SOILED LINEN BASKET
Oblong Shape. Height 23 ins. Length 16½ ins. Width 11½ ins.
Without Glass Top
Standard Colours .. 27/9
Gold or Special .. 30/3
Frosted Colours .. 31/3
With Glass Top
Standard Colours .. 41/3
Gold or Special .. 43/9
Frosted Colours .. 44/9

TU 37/7 SOILED LINEN BASKET
With dome shaped lid. Height 29 ins. Length 18 ins. Width 13½ ins.
Standard Colours 33/6
Gold or Special 36/-
Frosted Colours 37/-

TU 37/8 ARM CHAIR
Total Height 33 ins. Total Width 28 ins. Size of Seat 17 × 17 ins. Height of Seat from ground 16 ins.
Standard Colours .. 43/6
Gold or Special .. 46/6
Frosted Colours .. 47/6

TU 37/10 CORNER LINEN BASKET
Height 23 ins. Angle 15½ ins.

	Without glass top	With glass top
Standard Colours	27/9	45/9
Gold or Special	30/3	48/3
Frosted Colours	31/3	49/3

TU 37/9 SOILED LINEN BASKET
Round shape Height 28 ins. Diameter 15 ins.
Standard Colours 24/9
Gold or Special 27/3
Frosted Colours 28/3

ALL PRICES ARE SUBJECT TO MARKET FLUCTUATIONS

HARRODS LTD

Telephone SLOANE 1234
Telegrams 'EVERYTHING HARRODS LONDON'

LONDON S W 1

TURNERY DEPARTMENT
Comfort and Durability in Harrods Wicker Chairs

Attractive Upholstery in Cretonne, Tapestry or Corduroy

TU 40/1 CLUB CHAIR
A very comfortable chair with spring stuffed seat and loose kapoc seat cushion. Well upholstered in Tapestry .. 92/9

TU 40/2 'GLASGOW' CHAIR
Walnut Wicker with seat and shoulders upholstered in Cretonne
Seat 18 ins. 20 ins.
26/9 30/9

TU 40/4 'REGAL' CHAIR
Walnut Wicker with peak top and arm rests, fully upholstered
Cretonne Corduroy Tapestry
43/3 53/3 54/6

'CAMBRIDGE' CHAIR
Walnut frame. Fully upholstered in Cretonne 60/9

TU 40/9 DERBY CHAIR
As used in all the Universities. An exceedingly comfortable chair, made in various sizes, to suit tall or short people. Best Walnut Wicker with close work base, and fully upholstered in Cretonne

Depth of seat	22	24	27	30 ins.
	48/-	51/6	57/9	66/6
in Tapestry	59/3	63/9	72/-	81/6

TU 40/3 'NORWICH' CHAIR
In Walnut Wicker fully upholstered
Cretonne .. 44/-

Harrods undertake the re-upholstering of Wicker Chairs

Chairs can be upholstered with customer's own Materials if desired. Estimates sent free in every case

TU 40/8 CROQUET CHAIR
Walnut Wicker. Seat and shoulders upholstered in Cretonne
Seat 18 ins. 20 ins.
17/11 19/11

TU 40/10 'MANCHESTER' CHAIR
In best Walnut Wicker
Upholstered in Corduroy 53/-
" Cretonne 44/-

TU 40/7 HIGH BACK LIBRARY CHAIR
In best Walnut Wicker fully upholstered
Cretonne 47/3
Corduroy 59/3
Tapestry 60/-

The Material used in stuffing these Chairs is specially prepared for Harrods; guaranteed and thoroughly purified

'COULSDON' CHAIR
In Walnut Wicker. Fully upholstered in Cretonne .. 62/-

TU 40/12 SUNK SEAT CHAIR
With spring stuffed seat and head pillow. Fully upholstered in Tapestry and mounted on castors. Walnut Wicker frame .. £5 11 0
Without spring seat and no castors
96/6

TU 40/11 'PEAKTOP' CHAIR
In best Walnut Wicker. Fully upholstered in Cretonne
Seat 18 ins. 20 ins.
23,3 27/9

TU 40/15 STUDENT CHAIR
Walnut Wicker. Fully upholstered
Cretonne, 40/9 Tapestry 64/9

TU 40/16 ROLL BORDER CHAIR
Best Walnut Wicker, with close wicker base. With spring stuffed seat and back
22 in. seats
Corduroy, 100/6 Tapestry, 102/3

TU 40/14 'REIGATE' CHAIR
Walnut Wicker, fully upholstered in Cretonne.. .. .. .. 50/3

TU 40/13 TUB CHAIR
Walnut Wicker. Seat and back upholstered. Seat 20 ins.
Cretonne, 36/- Tapestry, 45/9

ALL PRICES ARE SUBJECT TO MARKET FLUCTUATIONS

HARRODS LTD

Telephone SLOANE 1234
Telegrams 'EVERYTHING HARRODS LONDON'

LONDON SW1

IRONMONGERY DEPARTMENT

HARRODS for Every Household Requisite and Hardware of Every Description

DEPENDABLE QUALITY—ENDURING SERVICE—REAL ECONOMY

WILL it last? Almost without exception this is the deciding factor in the purchase of any Domestic Requisite and herein lies the true test of its value

Harrods unswerving guarantee ensures the trustworthiness of every item offered, and their vast resources enable them to offer all articles at prices which they believe to be the lowest possible consistent with the highest quality obtainable Lack of space prevents the inclusion of many important items in this list, but customers may order with confidence, any article not shewn, in the full knowledge that their order will be satisfactorily fulfilled

HARRODS KITCHEN CABINETS

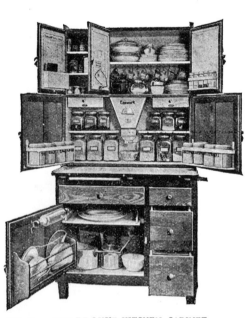

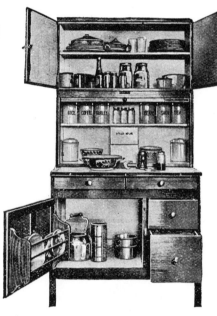

IR 1274   THE DE LUXE KITCHEN CABINET
Canadian Ash, Varnished Golden Oak and White Enamel Exterior

Height	Width	Depth of bottom section
6 ft. 7 ins.	3 ft. 6½ ins.	1 ft. 10 ins.

Depth of top section, 12 ins.
With extending White Vitreous Porcelain Table extends 2 ft. × 3 ft. 6 ins. Complete with Flour Bin and Rotary Sifter and 5 glass Spice Jars
6 2-lb. Glass Food Containers with aluminium screw tops.

6	4 lb.	,,	,,	,,	,,
8	2-lb. Japanned Canisters				
1	Glass Rolling Pin	..	..	Price	**£19 19 0**

Dark Oak finish.   Price 20s 6d extra
The Kitchenette Model, similar to above **£15 15 0**
Dark Oak finish. Price 10s 6d extra

IR 1276   THE COOKS KITCHEN CABINET
Varnished Golden Oak

Height	Width	Depth of top section
6 ft. 2 ins.	2 ft. 5½ ins.	12 ins.

Depth of bottom section, 22 ins. Flap down enamel table, 2 ft. 1½ ins. × 1 ft. 8 ins. Full depth with Table down, 2 ft. 8 ins.
Complete with 5 Glass Spice Jars
1 Flour Box and Scoop
2 1 lb. Glass Food Containers

| 5 | 2 lb. | ,, | ,, | ,, |
| 2 | 4 lb. | ,, | ,, | ,, | Price **£9 9 0** |

Dark Oak finish, 10s 6d extra

IR 1275   THE LONDON KITCHENETTE CABINET. Varnished Golden Oak

Height	Width	Depth of Top Section
5 ft. 11 ins.	3 ft.	12 ins.

Depth of bottom section, 25 ins.
White enamelled interior. Roller Shutter Front and extending Porcelain Table, 36 ins. × 25 ins.
Complete with Flour Box and scoop
6 1-lb. Glass Jars
4 2-lb.   do.
6 2-lb. Japanned Canisters
Price **£12 12 0**
Dark Oak finish   10s 6d extra

ALL PRICES ARE SUBJECT TO MARKET FLUCTUATIONS

HARRODS LTD

Telephone SLOANE 1234
Telegrams 'EVERYTHING HARRODS LONDON'

LONDON S W 1

IRONMONGERY DEPARTMENT
Aluminium Utensils for Cleanliness and Durability

IR 1   DOUBLE MILK OR PORRIDGE SAUCEPAN
Capacity of inner lining

Pints	1¾	2¾	4
	3/6	4/9	5/6

EXTRA STRONG QUALITY

Pints	2	3½	4¾	8
	10/-	13/-	16/-	20/9

IR 169   FLOUR OR SUGAR DREDGER
With handle .. 1/1
Without handle .. 11d

IR 1090   COLANDER
Made in one piece. Solid handles
Diameter 10½ ins. 6/3, 9½ ins. 5/9
IR 518   Lighter quality
8 ins. 2/3, 9 ins. 2/9, 10 ins. 3/-

IR 31   ALUMINIUM BAIN MARIE SET
14 gauge, highly polished. With removeable top plate, fitted with three loose vessels and covers. Size of bottom vessel 12 × 4¾ ins., size of three loose vessels 5 ins. diameter Approximate capacity 2 pints each 30/6

IR 640   TEA URN
With Tea Infuser and Brass Tap

Gallons	2	3	4	5
	38/-	41/-	47/9	53/6

Without Tea Infuser

	32/9	35/6	41/6	46/6

Goods valued at 20/- and over are sent Carriage Free to any address in England and Wales

Goods are delivered free within the radius of Harrods Motor Vans. See District List on pages 9, 10, 11

IR 12   SINK BASKET
Frosted finish. 10-in. 1/5

BAKING DISHES
(Frosted finish). Complete with grid
11 × 9 ins. 3/-   13 × 10 ins. 3/9

IR 4   FISH KETTLE
Complete with Drainer

	13-in.	15-in.	17-in.	19-in.	21-in.
	25/6	30/-	34/-	39/6	50/6

Lighter quality

	18/-	21/-	25/6

IR 21   ALUMINIUM FISH FRYERS
With Strong Tinned Wire Drainers
13 × 8½ × 4½ ins. deep 12/-
15 × 9¼ × 5   „   „ 14/3

IR 7012   ALUMINIUM FISH SLICER
12-in. 2/6
Cheaper quality, 8d & 1/1

IR 1105 ALUMINIUM EGG STEAMERS
With Black Wood Knob

	3	4	7	12 Eggs
	5/-	6/3	11/3	19/9

IR 13   DISH COVERS

9-in.	10-in.	11-in.	12-in.	14-in.	16-in.
5/6	6/-	7/-	7/9	9/6	12/6

The Ironmongery Department is on the Second Floor

IR 18   ALUMINIUM MIXING BOWLS

Diameter ..	13-in.	14-in.
Depth ..	4¾ ins.	5 ins.
	6/11	8/-
Lighter quality	4/3	4/9

IR 271   GRADUATED BOWL
Capacity, ¼ to 2 pints, 1/3
¼ to 4 pints, 1/11

IR 107   PLATE COVERS
Ebonized Knob
7-in. 1/1   8-in. 1/3   9-in. 1/5
Extra strong quality, 8-in., 2/7, 9-in., 3/1

IR 190   ALUMINIUM LADLE
3-in. .. 7d   4-in. .. 11d

IR 505   EGG STEAMER

1	2	3	4	6 Eggs
1/-	2/9	3/3	4/3	8/9

IR 11   ALUMINIUM FISH TROWEL
7d each

IR 2301   STEAM COOKER
Bronze fittings. Complete with three steamers and one boiler. Diameter, 8 ins. 26/6, 9 ins. 30/-, 10 ins. 37/-.
Lighter quality, 8 ins. 19/6, 9 ins. 24/9

IR 1388   POTATO MASHER
5/6

IR 1080   ALUMINIUM GRAVY STRAINERS
Fine, Medium or Coarse
4¾ ins. 1/9   5¼ ins. 2/3

IR 71   ALUMINIUM CAKE PAN

4-in.	5-in.	6-in.	7-in.
10d	1/1	1/5	1/9

IR 1081   ALUMINIUM CONICAL GRAVY STRAINER
Fine, Medium or Coarse

4¾-in.	5¾-in.
2/9	3/3

Lighter quality

5-in.	6-in.
1/9	2/2

IR 2   ALUMINIUM SELF-BASTING HOUSEHOLD ROASTER
Roasts, Boils, Steams, Fries, may be used with Gas, Oil, or Electric Stoves either in or on top of the Oven size 12¼ × 9½ × 7 ins. for Chicken or Joint up to 3 lbs. 12/9
14 × 10½ × 8 for a large Fowl or Joint up to 8 lbs. 14/3

ALL PRICES ARE SUBJECT TO MARKET FLUCTUATIONS

IRONMONGERY DEPARTMENT
Aluminium Ware Halves the Work and Doubles the Service

IR 271 ALUMINIUM YORK PUDDING PANS

10½″ × 6½″	.. 1/2
11½″ × 7½″	.. 1/4
12½″ × 8¾″	.. 1/6
14½″ × 10″	.. 1/9

IR 111 ALUMINIUM HOT WATER JUG

Pints	1	2	3
With lid	2/10	3/9	4/8
Without lid	2/3	3/2	4/-

IR 327 COCKTAIL SHAKER
With strainer
1 pint .. 2/3

IR 45 ALUMINIUM DINNER PLATES
Folished

6″	7″	8″	9″	10″
6d	7d	9d	1/-	1/1

each

IR 60 SOUP PLATES
9½″ 1/1 10″ 1/3 each

IR 507 ALUMINIUM TEAPOTS
With wood grip handles

Cups	4	6	8	10	12	14
	4/6	5/-	5/3	5/6	6/9	8/9

ALUMINIUM PICNIC KETTLE
Fitted with Tea Infuser which enables Kettle to be used as a Tea-pot

Pints	1½	2½
	3/-	3/9

Kettles only

Pints	¾	1½	2
	2/-	2/3	2/9

IR 21 ALUMINIUM FISH OR POTATO FRYER
Complete with tinned wire basket

Diameter	8½	9½	10½ ins.
	3/4	3/9	4/9

Oval shape
10½″ × 8½″ 7/-

IR 122 ALUMINIUM TEA STRAINETTE
Frosted finish with side supports for resting on cup
Each 4d

IR 165 MUFFIN DISH
With hot water container
8-in. .. 4/6 9-in. .. 5/9

IR 40 EGG POACHER

Eggs	3	4	6
	2/9	3/3	4/6

IR 123 ALUMINIUM TEA STRAINER
Perforated Strainer .. Each 3d
Gauze ,, .. ,, 6d

IR 600 ALUMINIUM TUMBLERS

Pts.	¼	½	¾	
	6d	7d	9d	1/1

IR 333 ALUMINIUM HOT WATER CAN

Pints	3	4	6
	12/3	13/6	14/6

IR 5 CANDLESTICK
Diameter 5½ ins. 1/9

EGG SLICE
Of Aluminium. Cuts clean
Simple to use .. Each 6½d

IR 29 HOT WATER JUG

Cups	4	6	8	10
	4/6	5/3	6/3	7/-

IR 30 COFFEE POT TO MATCH
(Not shown)

Cups	4	6	8	10
	5/3	6/-	7/-	8/-

IR 465 TRAVELLING SPIRIT STOVE

Pints	1	1½
	6/3	7/-

IR 35 CUPS AND SAUCERS
Breakfast size. With wicker handle 1/-
Tea Cup and Saucer .. 8d

IR 123 COFFEE PERCOLATOR
Attractive shape; black wood handle

Cups	4	6	8	10
	7/3	8/-	9/-	10/-

IR 23 TEA-POT
With ebonised handle

Cups	3	5	7	9
	3/9	4/3	4/6	5/-

If with red handle and knob

Cups	3	5	7	9
	5/-	5/9	6/-	6/6

IR 127 EGG CUP
Each 10d
Lighter quality, Each 3d

IR 124 THE 'UNIQUE' ALUMINIUM COFFEE PERCOLATOR
Black ebonised handle

Pints	2	3
	6/-	6/6

IR 5 ALUMINIUM KETTLES
Best quality aluminium. Quick boiling

Pints	3	4	6
	5/3	5/9	6/6

IR 3 KETTLE
Stamped body, quick boiling

Pints	3	4	6
	3/6	4/-	5/9

IR 50 ALUMINIUM TEA-SET
Comprising 3-cup Tea-pot, Cream Jug, Sugar Basin and 10-in. Round Tray 7/-

IR 30 ALUMINIUM KETTLE
Heavy quality. Wood grip handle. With non-welded spout.

Pints	4	6	8
	10/6	12/6	17/-

IR 250 ALUMINIUM BREAKFAST CRUET
Pepper, Mustard and Salt
2/-

ALL PRICES ARE SUBJECT TO MARKET FLUCTUATIONS

HARRODS LTD

Telephone SLOANE 1234
Telegrams 'EVERYTHING HARRODS LONDON'

LONDON SW1

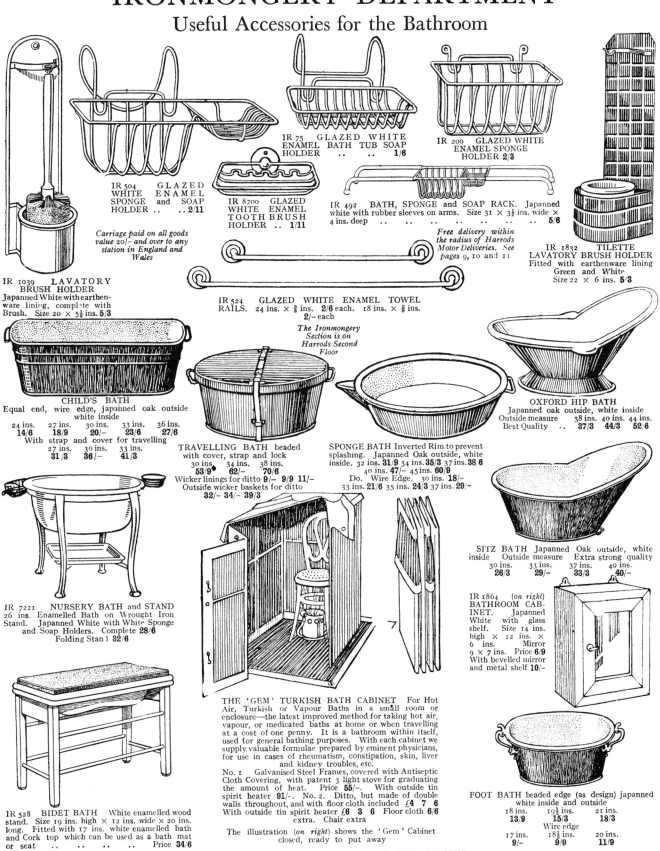

IRONMONGERY DEPARTMENT
Useful Accessories for the Bathroom

IR 75 GLAZED WHITE ENAMEL BATH TUB SOAP HOLDER 1/6

IR 200 GLAZED WHITE ENAMEL SPONGE HOLDER 2/3

IR 504 GLAZED WHITE ENAMEL SPONGE and SOAP HOLDER 2/11

IR 8700 GLAZED WHITE ENAMEL TOOTH BRUSH HOLDER .. 1/11

IR 492 BATH, SPONGE and SOAP RACK. Japanned white with rubber sleeves on arms. Size 31 × 3½ ins. wide × 4 ins. deep 5/6

IR 1832 TILETTE LAVATORY BRUSH HOLDER Fitted with earthenware lining Green and White Size 22 × 6 ins. 5/3

Carriage paid on all goods value 20/- and over to any station in England and Wales

IR 1039 LAVATORY BRUSH HOLDER Japanned White with earthenware lining, complete with Brush. Size 20 × 5½ ins. 5/3

Free delivery within the radius of Harrods Motor Deliveries. See pages 9, 10 and 11

IR 524 GLAZED WHITE ENAMEL TOWEL RAILS. 24 ins. × ⅜ ins. 2/6 each. 18 ins. × ⅜ ins. 2/- each.

The Ironmongery Section is on Harrods Second Floor

CHILD'S BATH
Equal end, wire edge, japanned oak outside white inside

24 ins.	27 ins.	30 ins.	33 ins.	36 ins.
14/6	18/9	20/-	23/6	27/6

With strap and cover for travelling

27 ins.	30 ins.	33 ins.
31/3	36/-	41/3

TRAVELLING BATH
beaded with cover, strap and lock

30 ins.	34 ins.	38 ins.
53/9	62/-	70/6

Wicker linings for ditto 9/- 9/9 11/-
Outside wicker baskets for ditto 32/- 34/- 39/3

SPONGE BATH
Inverted Rim to prevent splashing. Japanned Oak outside, white inside.

32 ins.	34 ins.	37 ins.
31/9	35/3	38/6

40 ins.	45 ins.
47/-	60/9

Do. Wire Edge. 30 ins. 18/-
33 ins. 21/6 35 ins. 24/3 37 ins. 29/-

OXFORD HIP BATH
Japanned oak outside, white inside
Outside measure 38 ins. 40 ins. 44 ins.
Best Quality .. 37/3 44/3 52/6

SITZ BATH
Japanned Oak outside, white inside Outside measure Extra strong quality

30 ins.	33 ins.	37 ins.	40 ins.
26/3	29/-	33/3	40/-

IR 7221 NURSERY BATH and STAND
26 ins. Enamelled Bath on Wrought Iron Stand. Japanned White with White Sponge and Soap Holders. Complete 28/6
Folding Stand 32/6

IR 1864 (on right) BATHROOM CABINET. Japanned White with glass shelf. Size 14 ins. high × 12 ins. × 6 ins. Mirror 9 × 7 ins. Price 6/9 With bevelled mirror and metal shelf 10/-

THE 'GEM' TURKISH BATH CABINET
For Hot Air, Turkish or Vapour Baths in a small room or enclosure—the latest improved method for taking hot air, vapour, or medicated baths at home or when travelling at a cost of one penny. It is a bathroom within itself, used for general bathing purposes. With each cabinet we supply valuable formulae prepared by eminent physicians, for use in cases of rheumatism, constipation, skin, liver and kidney troubles, etc.
No. 1 Galvanised Steel Frames, covered with Antiseptic Cloth Covering, with patent 3 light stove for graduating the amount of heat. Price 55/-. With outside tin spirit heater 91/-. No. 2. Ditto, but made of double walls throughout, and with floor cloth included £4 7 6 With outside tin spirit heater £6 3 6 Floor cloth 6/6 extra. Chair extra

The illustration (on right) shows the 'Gem' Cabinet closed, ready to put away

IR 528 BIDET BATH
White enamelled wood stand. Size 19 ins. high × 12 ins. wide × 20 ins. long. Fitted with 17 ins. white enamelled bath and Cork top which can be used as a bath mat or seat .. .. Price 34/6

FOOT BATH
beaded edge (as design) japanned white inside and outside

18 ins.	19½ ins.	21 ins.
13/9	15/3	18/3

Wire edge

17 ins.	18½ ins.	20 ins.
9/-	9/9	11/9

ALL PRICES ARE SUBJECT TO MARKET FLUCTUATIONS

HARRODS LTD

Telephone SLOANE 1234
Telegrams 'EVERYTHING HARRODS LONDON'

LONDON SW1

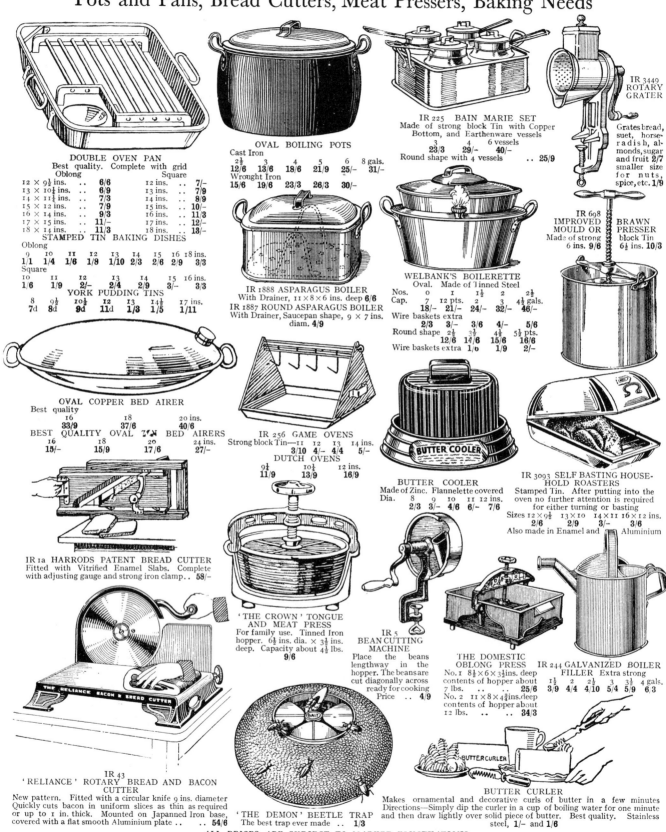

IRONMONGERY DEPARTMENT

Pots and Pans, Bread Cutters, Meat Pressers, Baking Needs

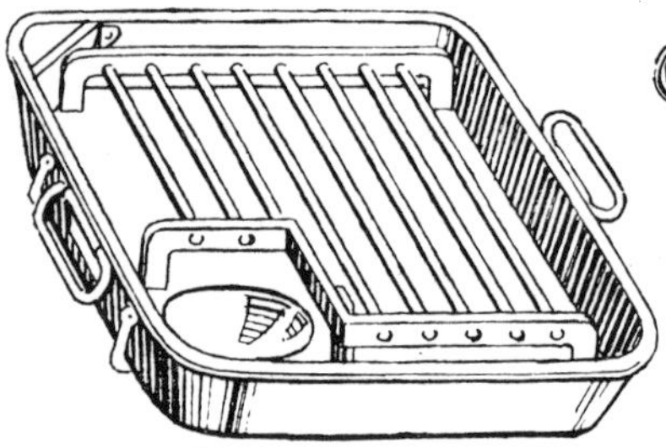

DOUBLE OVEN PAN

Best quality. Complete with grid

Oblong		Square	
12 × 9½ ins. ..	6/6	12 ins. ..	7/-
13 × 10¼ ins. ..	6/9	13 ins. ..	7/9
14 × 11¼ ins. ..	7/3	14 ins. ..	8/9
15 × 12 ins. ..	7/9	15 ins. ..	10/-
16 × 14 ins. ..	9/3	16 ins. ..	11/3
17 × 15 ins. ..	11/-	17 ins. ..	12/-
18 × 14 ins. ..	11/3	18 ins. ..	13/-

STAMPED TIN BAKING DISHES

Oblong

9	10	11	12	13	14	15	16	18 ins.
1/1	1/4	1/6	1/8	1/10	2/3	2/6	2/9	3/3

Square

10	11	12	13	14	15	16 ins.
1/6	1/9	2/-	2/4	2/9	3/-	3/3

YORK PUDDING TINS

8	9½	10½	12	13	14½	17 ins.
7d	8d	9d	11d	1/3	1/5	1/11

OVAL BOILING POTS

Cast Iron

2½	3	4	5	6	8 gals.
12/6	13/6	18/6	21/9	25/-	31/-

Wrought Iron

15/6	19/6	23/3	26/3	30/-

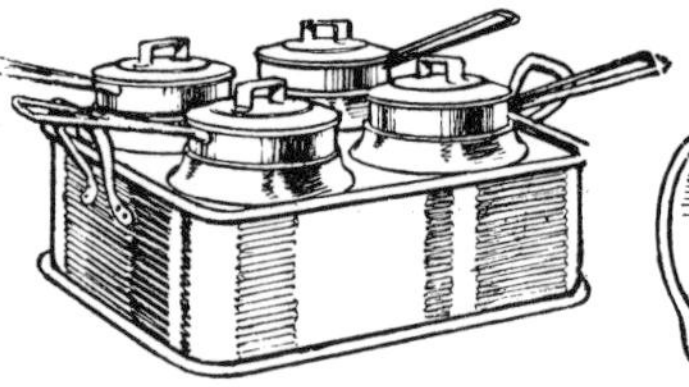

IR 225 BAIN MARIE SET

Made of strong block Tin with Copper Bottom, and Earthenware vessels

3	4	6 vessels
23/3	29/-	40/-

Round shape with 4 vessels .. 25/9

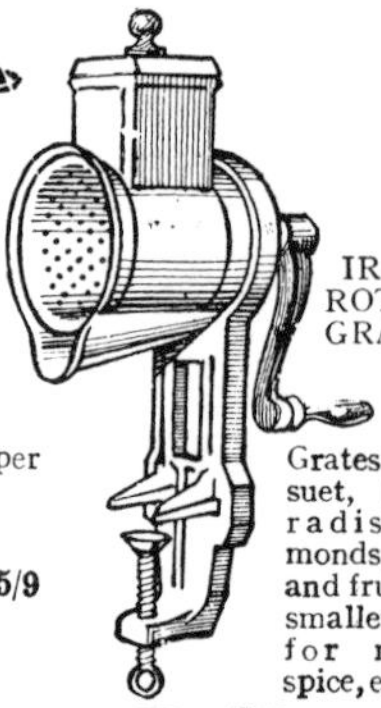

IR 3449 ROTARY GRATER

Grates bread, suet, horse-radish, almonds, sugar and fruit 2/7 smaller size for nuts, spice, etc. 1/9

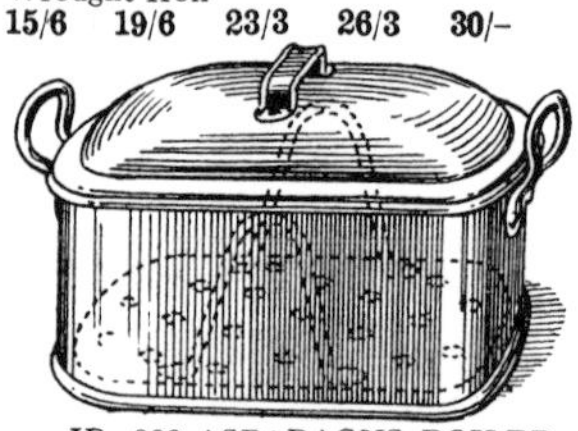

IR 1888 ASPARAGUS BOILER

With Drainer, 11 × 8 × 6 ins. deep 6/6

IR 1887 ROUND ASPARAGUS BOILER

With Drainer, Saucepan shape, 9 × 7 ins. diam. 4/9

WELBANK'S BOILERETTE

Oval. Made of Tinned Steel

Nos.	0	1	1½	2	2½
Cap.	7	12 pts.	2	3	4½ gals.
	18/-	21/-	24/-	32/-	46/-
Wire baskets extra	2/3	3/-	3/6	4/-	5/6

Round shape	2½	3½	4½	5½ pts.
	12/6	14/6	15/6	16/6
Wire baskets extra	1/6		1/9	2/-

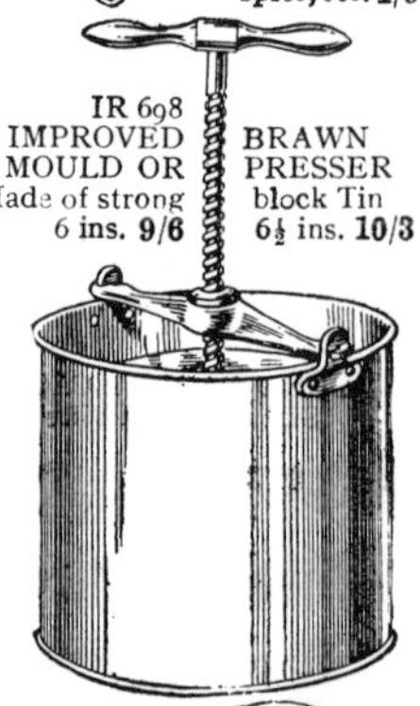

IR 698 IMPROVED MOULD OR BRAWN PRESSER

Made of strong block Tin

6 ins. 9/6 6½ ins. 10/3

OVAL COPPER BED AIRER

Best quality

16	18	20 ins.
33/9	37/6	40/6

BEST QUALITY OVAL [illegible] BED AIRERS

16	18	20	24 ins.
15/-	15/9	17/6	27/-

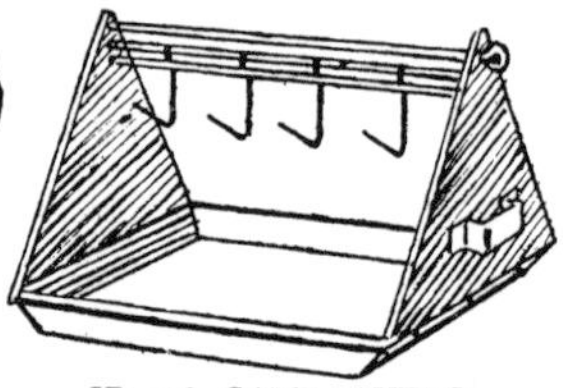

IR 256 GAME OVENS

Strong block Tin—11 12 13 14 ins.
3/10 4/- 4/4 5/-

DUTCH OVENS

9¼	10½	12 ins.
11/9	13/9	16/9

BUTTER COOLER

Made of Zinc. Flannelette covered

Dia.	8	9	10	11	12 ins.
	2/3	3/-	4/6	6/-	7/6

IR 3093 SELF BASTING HOUSEHOLD ROASTERS

Stamped Tin. After putting into the oven no further attention is required for either turning or basting

Sizes	12 × 9½	13 × 10	14 × 11	16 × 12 ins.
	2/6	2/9	3/-	3/6

Also made in Enamel and Aluminium

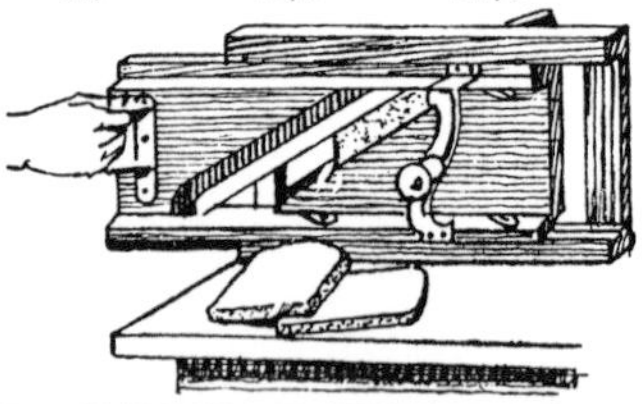

IR 1a HARRODS PATENT BREAD CUTTER

Fitted with Vitrified Enamel Slabs. Complete with adjusting gauge and strong iron clamp .. 58/-

'THE CROWN' TONGUE AND MEAT PRESS

For family use. Tinned Iron hopper. 6½ ins. dia. × 3½ ins. deep. Capacity about 4½ lbs. 9/6

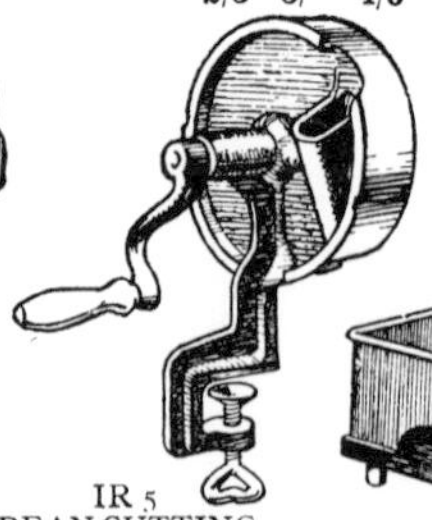

IR 5 BEAN CUTTING MACHINE

Place the beans lengthway in the hopper. The beans are cut diagonally across ready for cooking

Price .. 4/9

THE DOMESTIC OBLONG PRESS

No. 1 8½ × 6 × 3½ ins. deep contents of hopper about 7 lbs. .. 25/6

No. 2 11 × 8 × 4¾ ins. deep contents of hopper about 12 lbs. 34/3

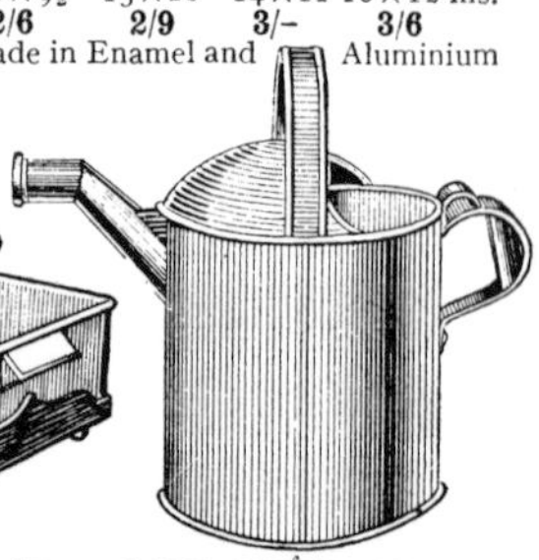

IR 244 GALVANIZED BOILER FILLER Extra strong

1½	2	2½	3	3½	4 gals.
3/9	4/4	4/10	5/4	5/9	6/3

IR 43

'RELIANCE' ROTARY BREAD AND BACON CUTTER

New pattern. Fitted with a circular knife 9 ins. diameter Quickly cuts bacon in uniform slices as thin as required or up to 1 in. thick. Mounted on Japanned Iron base, covered with a flat smooth Aluminium plate 54/6

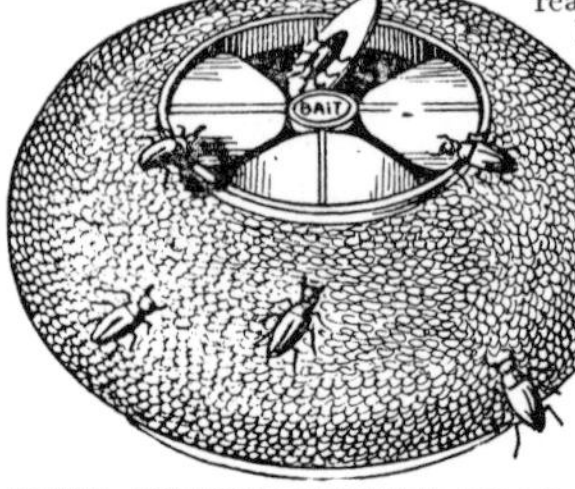

'THE DEMON' BEETLE TRAP

The best trap ever made .. 1/3

BUTTER CURLER

Makes ornamental and decorative curls of butter in a few minutes Directions—Simply dip the curler in a cup of boiling water for one minute and then draw lightly over solid piece of butter. Best quality. Stainless steel, 1/- and 1/6

ALL PRICES ARE SUBJECT TO MARKET FLUCTUATIONS

IRONMONGERY DEPARTMENT
Well Made and Attractively Designed Cages, Perches and Aviaries

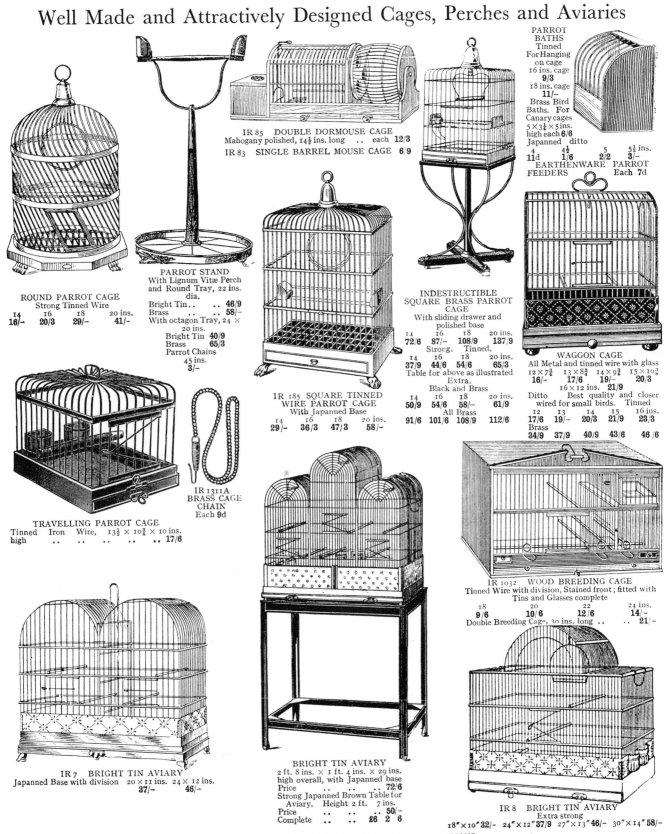

IR 85   DOUBLE DORMOUSE CAGE
Mahogany polished, 14½ ins. long   ..   each 12/3
IR 83   SINGLE BARREL MOUSE CAGE   6/9

PARROT BATHS
Tinned
For Hanging
on cage
16 ins. cage
9/3
18 ins. cage
11/-
Brass Bird
Baths. For
Canary cages
5 × 3½ × 5 ins.
high each **6/6**
Japanned ditto

4	4½	5	5½ ins.
11d	1/6	2/2	3/-

EARTHENWARE PARROT FEEDERS   Each **7d**

ROUND PARROT CAGE
Strong Tinned Wire

14	16	18	20 ins.
16/-	20/3	29/-	41/-

PARROT STAND
With Lignum Vitæ Perch
and Round Tray, 22 ins.
dia.
Bright Tin **46/9**
Brass **58/-**
With octagon Tray, 24 ×
20 ins.
Bright Tin **40/9**
Brass **65/3**
Parrot Chains
45 ins.
3/-

IR 185   SQUARE TINNED WIRE PARROT CAGE
With Japanned Base

14	16	18	20 ins.
29/-	36/3	47/3	58/-

INDESTRUCTIBLE SQUARE BRASS PARROT CAGE
With sliding drawer and
polished base

14	16	18	20 ins.
72/6	87/-	108/9	137/9

Strong.   Tinned.

14	16	18	20 ins.
37/9	44/6	54/6	65/3

Table for above as illustrated
Extra.
Black and Brass

14	16	18	20 ins.
50/9	54/6	58/-	61/9

All Brass

14	16	18	20 ins.
91/6	101/6	108/9	112/6

WAGGON CAGE
All Metal and tinned wire with glass

12 × 7¾	13 × 8¾	14 × 9¾	15 × 10¾
16/-	17/6	19/-	20/3
		16 × 12 ins.	21/9

Ditto   Best quality and closer
wired for small birds.   Tinned

12	13	14	15	16 ins.
17/6	19/-	20/3	21/9	23/3

Brass

34/9	37/9	40/9	43/6	46 /6

IR 1311A   BRASS CAGE CHAIN
Each **9d**

TRAVELLING PARROT CAGE
Tinned   Iron   Wire,   13½ × 10¾ × 10 ins.
high **17/6**

IR 1032   WOOD BREEDING CAGE
Tinned Wire with division, Stained front; fitted with
Tins and Glasses complete

18	20	22	24 ins.
9/6	10/6	12/6	14/-

Double Breeding Cage, 30 ins. long   ..   **21/-**

BRIGHT TIN AVIARY
2 ft. 8 ins. × 1 ft. 4 ins. × 29 ins.
high overall, with Japanned base
Price **72/6**
Strong Japanned Brown Table for
Aviary.   Height 2 ft.   7 ins.
Price **50/-**
Complete **£6   2   6**

IR 7   BRIGHT TIN AVIARY
Japanned Base with division   20 × 11 ins.   24 × 12 ins.
37/-   **46/-**

IR 8   BRIGHT TIN AVIARY
Extra strong
18″ × 10″ **32/-**   24″ × 12″ **37/9**   27″ × 13″ **46/-**   30″ × 14″ **58/-**

IRONMONGERY DEPARTMENT
Attractive and Useful Brass Reproductions of Antique Designs

IR 11564 Antique Brass BOOK ENDS
Ye Olde Coaching Days. Size 4¼ ins. × 5 ins.
Pair **20/3**
Book Rests Same design Pair **14/3**

IR 3948 The VICTORY INK STAND. Solid
Brass Antique Finish 5½ ins. long **15/-**

IR 3595
Brass BEDROOM
DOOR KNOCKER
'Rheims' **4/6.** Also
supplied in 'Brussels'
4/6, 'Malines' **4/6,**
'Antwerp' **4/6**

IR 11711 BRASS JARDINIERE
10 ins. diameter × 10 ins. high. Polished
Brass or Special Old Colour Brass **20/3**

**IR 14738 Outside BRASS
DOOR KNOCKER.** 7 ins.
long 16th Century Galleon.
Antique finish **12/9**

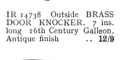

**IR 2193 Brass DOOR
KNOCKER** Shakes-
peare's House
Size 3 × 3 ins. **3/-**

**IR 11640H
BOOK
MARKERS**
Antique Brass
Lincoln Imp **2/9**
Winchester Imp
2/9
Dickens .. **3/-**

**IR 14982 Antique Brass
ASH TRAY.** Sealyham
design. 4½ ins. diameter, **4/6**
Can be supplied in **various**
other designs

**IR 3665 BRASS JAR-
DINIERE.** 8 ins. dia-
meter × 7 ins. high.
Polished Brass or Spe-
cial Old Colour finish **23/3**

IR 2890
Antique, BRASS TABLE
BELL, The 'Crinoline'
4¾ ins. high .. **9/9**

IR 2483
Antique BRASS
CANDLESTICK
6 ins. high
Per pair .. **9/9**

**IR 15300 BED-
ROOM DOOR
KNOCKER.** Pek-
ingese. 1¾ ins.
long. Antique
Brass .. **1/9**

**IR 15301 BED-
ROOM DOOR
KNOCKER**
Bulldog. 1¾ ins.
long. Antique
Brass .. **1/9**

**IR 1735
BEDROOM
DOOR KNOC-
KER.** Cheshire
Cat. 3¼ ins. An-
tique Brass **1/5**

IR 1620
Lincoln Imp
BEDROOM
DOOR
KNOCKER
Antique
Brass.. **1/2**

**IR 11821
SIR FRANCIS
DRAKE**
Antique Brass Paper
Weight or Ornament
3 ins. high **3/9**

**IR 2601
ANTIQUE BRASS STICK
OR UMBRELLA STAND**
32 ins. high **97/6**

**IR 1754
BELL
CANDLE-
STICK**
In Antique
Brass. 13 ins.
Per pair **37/6**

**IR 10533
The GRAND-
FATHER'S
CLOCK**
Brass Nutcracks
6/-

**IR 2549 BRASS
HAND BELL**
The Elizabeth
4¾ ins. high .. **6/9**

**IR 2035
CHAMBER
CANDLESTICK**
In brass
Each .. **7/3**

**IK 2522
BRASS
NUT-
CRACKERS**
Fagin and
Sykes **5/3**

**IR 1881
CANDLESTICK**
Per 6 in. 8 in. 10 in. 12 in.
pair **11/3 12/- 13/6 16/6**
Polished Brass or Special
Old Colour

**IR 14592
BRASS
CRUMB SCOOP**
(On right) De-
sign Dartmoor
Pixie in Antique
finish .. **6/6**

**IR 11056
BRASS PAPER
KNIVES**
(On left)
Cheshire Cat
7¾ ins. long
Each .. **3/-**

ALL PRICES ARE SUBJECT TO MARKET FLUCTUATIONS

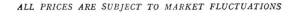

HARRODS LTD

· Telephone SLOANE 1234
Telegrams 'EVERYTHING HARRODS LONDON'

LONDON S W 1

IRONMONGERY DEPARTMENT
Grind Your Own Coffee and Use a Percolator

IR 706
COFFEE ROASTER
For use with methylated spirit
¼ lb. to ½ lb. 7/6

IR 4
COFFEE ROASTER
With spring movement
To stand on stove
holds ¾ lb. .. 65/-

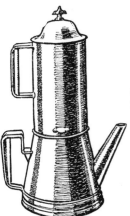

IR 150
ECONOMICAL COFFEE POT
Hutchinson's pattern, made of best block tin with nickel-plated brass centre tap. Two cloth strainers supplied with each cafetiere

Pints	1	1½	2
	12/6	13/6	15/-
Pints	2½	3	4
	16/3	18/3	20/9

IR 413
THE 'PLATOW' COFFEE MAKER
A simple and perfect way of making coffee. Can be used on the range or gas stove
Copper Bottom

Pts.	1	1½	2	3	4
	17/-	17/6	19/-	20/6	27/-

All copper

| | 22/6 | 25/6 | 28/3 | 31/3 | 37/9 |

IR 74
THE UNIVERSAL COFFEE PERCOLATOR
Aluminium with ebonized handle. Can be used on any range, stove or gas ring

Pts.	1½	2	3	4½
	22/-	23/6	28/-	31/-

IR 0 BOX COFFEE MILLS

No. 0	1	2	3
8/-	8/9	10/-	12/-

IR 385
ABRAIZO STEEL WOOD
An ideal cleaner for household uses, such as aluminium, wood, glass, tiles, sinks, etc.
Per packet with 1 cake of soap
7½d and 1/6

CARRIAGE
Carriage Paid on all Goods value £0/- and over to any Station in England and Wales.

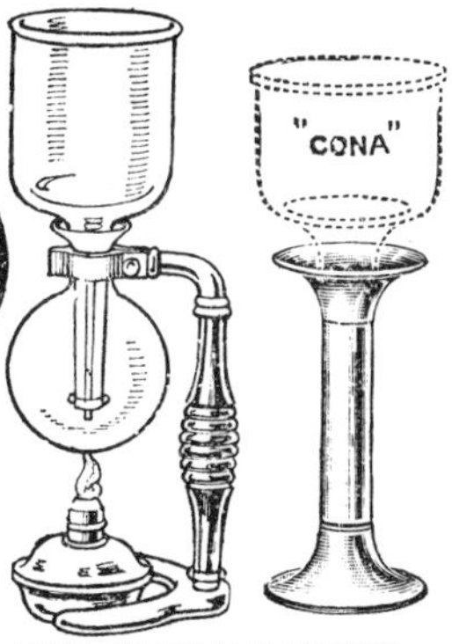

CONA COFFEE MACHINE
Makes excellent coffee, retains all the flavour and aroma. Approximate contents

Pts.	¼	½	1	1½	2
Nos. 0	1	2	2A	3	
10/6	18/-	21/-	25/-	30/-

THE CONA COFFEE MACHINE FUNNEL HOLDER
Seven inches high, holds all sizes of funnels, and will be found a great boon. Silver plated
Each 7/6

REPLACEMENTS:

	Sizes 0	1	2	2A	3
Bowls ..	2/-	2/9	3/-	3/6	4/-
Funnels ..	3/6	4/3	4/9	6/3	7/6
Lamps ..	1/6	2/-	2/-	2/-	3/-
Metal Drainers	1/-	1/-	1/-	1/2	1/6
Cloth Strainers	3d	3d	3d	3d	4d

IR 64—THE UNIVERSAL COFFEE PERCOLATOR
Made of pure aluminium ebonized handle. Operates successfully on any range, stove or gas stove

Pts.	1½	2	3	4½
	19/6	22/-	25/6	29/-

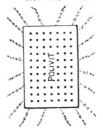

IR 6012 THE 'LIGHTNING POLIVIT'
Unequalled for cleaning and polishing silver, electro plate etc. The patent cleaner is placed in a basin with a solution of boiling water and ordinary washing soda, when after a few seconds all tarnish disappears

Small, 6 × 4 ins.	..	1/9
Medium, 9 × 6 ins.	..	3/-
Large, 12 × 9 ins.	..	5/6
3½ × 2¼ ins.	..	1/-

IR 3183
BON AMI
For all the finer kinds of polishing and cleaning Windows, baths, mirrors, kitchen utensils, tin, paint, tiles, aluminium, etc. 12 oz. tin, powder form .. 9d
9½ oz. cake form .. 6½d

IR 151 FRENCH PATTERN CAFETIERE
Best quality. Made of best block tin complete with plunger and perforation

	3	4	6	8	10	12 Cups
	4/9	5/6	6/-	7/9	8/3	9/9

TURKISH COFFEE POT
Plain Brass or Copper
Superior quality

Cups		2	3	4
		3/9	4/-	4/9
Cups	5	6	7	8
	5/9	6/9	7/-	8/6

QUICK GRINDING COFFEE MILL
As illustration
Capacity of Hopper

1¾ ozs.	2¼ ozs.	4 ozs.
8/-	10/-	13/-

THE SOLAR CLEANING COMPOSITION
Also suitable for all kinds of kitchen utensils
7 lb. tin 3/9   1 lb. bag. 6d

GLOBE METAL POLISH
MADE IN ENGLAND
TRADE MARK
GLOBE The KING of POLISHES imparts a DAZZLING BRILLIANCY to METAL

THE GLOBE BRASS PASTE
Per tin 4½d
MATCHLESS METAL PASTE
Per tin 4½d
Liquid, per tin 7½d

IR 4002
THE UNIVERSAL COFFEE MACHINE
Nickel-plated on copper
Coated inside with pure tin

Pts.	1	1½	2½	4
	36/-	40/-	43/-	52/-

IR 1403
Initial Plated Individual
COFFEE FILTER
For placing over the top of a cup or tumbler .. 3/9

IR 152
'SIMPLEX' CAFETIERE
Of best block tin

Cups 4	6	8	10	12
5/6	6/6	7/9	8/3	9/6

IR 26645
INDIVIDUAL COFFEE MAKER
For one person

Aluminium	..	..	..	5/6
Tin	..	..	..	2/3

ALL PRICES ARE SUBJECT TO MARKET FLUCTUATIONS

HARRODS LTD

Telephone SLOANE 1234
Telegrams 'EVERYTHING HARRODS LONDON'

LONDON SW1

IRONMONGERY DEPARTMENT
Coal Boxes and Scuttles—Hard Wearing and of Good Appearance

THE HELMET COAL VASE
Best heavy quality, in Polished Brass or Copper
Antique Brass or Antique Copper finish
16 in. .. **52/3** 17 in. .. **56/9** 18 in. .. **63/-**

IR 58
POLISHED BRASS or COPPER COAL SCOOP
Complete with Hand Scoop   Price **90/-**

COAL SCOOP
Extra strong Polished Brass or Copper
complete with hand scoop
16 in. **74/-**   17 in. **79/-**   18 in. **86/-**

IR 3+3   WOOD LOG OR COAL BOX
Solid Oak. Fitted with a loose Galvanised Lining
19 ins   21 ins.   23 ins.
76/3   **86/3**   **95/-**

IR 217   COAL CABINET
Jacobean Oak. Galvanised Lining
Price **68/-**

IR 72   WOOD COAL BOX
Solid Jacobean Oak with
Wood Handle
Galvanised lining **31/6**

IR 67   WOOD COAL BOX
Inlaid Mahogany. Polished Brass Fittings
Galvanised Lining **33/6**

**THE CONQUEST
WOOD COAL BOX**
Brass fittings and strong Galvanised Linings
No. 0 No. 1 No. 2   If with brass reeded
Solid Oak   strips on front to
46/6   56/-   67/6 protect box when the
Mahogany   lining is being
48/6   58/-   74/9 put in—**3/-** extra
Walnut
54/6   69/-   86/3

IR 223   COAL CABINET
Solid Mahogany, with Galvanised
Lining **91/9**
Solid Walnut **103/9**

IR 45   WOOD COAL BOX
(On left)
Solid Fumed or Jacobean Oak,
Antique Copper Fittings, Japan-
ned Iron Lining .. **22/6**

**IR 195
COAL CABINET**
Fumed Oak, Walnut or
Mahogany **78/-**
Inlaid Mahogany, Galvanised
Lining **91/6**
IR 14   WOOD COAL BOX
(On right)
In Solid Oak or Mahogany,
with Brass Fittings. Gal-
vanised Lining **37/-**
With Antique Coppered
Fittings **39/3**
With Oxidized Silver Fittings
43/6

ALL PRICES ARE SUBJECT TO MARKET FLUCTUATIONS

HARRODS LTD

Telephone SLOANE 1234
Telegrams 'EVERYTHING HARRODS LONDON'

LONDON SW 1

IRONMONGERY DEPARTMENT
Indispensable Household Needs of Harrods Quality

IR 48 GALVANISED GAR-BAGE OR DUSTBIN Suitable for small houses, flats, etc. Lid cannot become detached. Drops into position automatically

13 × 14 ins	14 × 16 ins	15 × 18 ins
6/9	7/9	8/6

IR 330 AUTOMATIC CLOTHES WASHER
Does not injure the clothes. The boiling water is forced up the central tube and then sprayed over the clothes. Can be used on Gas Ring, Frimus Stove, or Range. Made of strong galvanised iron.

3	4	6 gallons
5/3	6/3	7/9

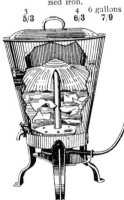

IR 333 THE HARROD AUTO-MATIC CLOTHES WASHER
A simple washer, no rubbing or scrubbing. A great labour saver. Strong Galvanised boiler with Brass tap. Capacity 10 gallons Complete with stand and Gas Ring .. **21/-**

Also supplied with Premier Oil Stove at the same price Stoves extra

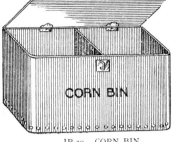

IR 30 CORN BIN
Galvanised Iron, strong quality

Length Bush.	Width ins.	Depth ins.	Price	With partition extra
4	28	18	23	26/3	5/-
6	29	23	29	37/9	5/9
8	34	23	29	43/6	6/6
10	42	23	29	50/9	7/3
12	42	23	35	59/6	8/9

IR 2300 HELICAL DOOR SPRING

	3	4	5	6 ins.
Iron ..	2/6	4/-	5/6	6/9
Brass ..	4/6	6/6	9/-	11/-

IR 700 SPIRAL DOOR SPRING
Can be attached or detached instantaneously Easily adjusted No. 0, 1/8 No. 1, 2/- No. 2, 2/9
No. 700A Special for Iron Gates 1/6

BATHS Galvanised. Oval shape, very strong

16	18	20	22	24	26	28	30 ins.
2/-	2/5	2/8	3/-	3/9	4/6	5/3	5/9

Equal End Galvanised Baths

36	39	42	45	48	51	54 ins.
12/6	13/-	14/6	15/3	16/9	19/-	21/-

IR 214 NEW IMPROVED CORRUGATED GALVAN-ISED BINS With cinder sifters. Very strong

Sizes 16	17	18	20 ins.
14/-	15/-	15/6	20/6

IR 268 BRIGHT TIN HOODED DUST PAN (*as illustration*)
With improved wedge edge, being more effective to use

Size 13	14½	16 ins.
2/3	2/6	3/-

With wood handle, same price Japanned Art Colours, Red, Blue, or Green. Heavy quality similar to illustration 14 ins. **1/6**

IR 1066 BEST QUALITY CIRCULAR DUST BINS
With outside rainproof cover

Dia. ..	14	15	16 ins.
Height ..	16	18	20 ins.
Extra Strong	7/3	8/-	8/9

Fitted with 2 mild steel straps up each side **11/9 12/6 13/3**

Dia. ..	17	18	20 ins.
Height ..	22	24	28 ins.
Extra Strong	9/6	10/-	15/-

Fitted with 2 mild steel straps up each side **14/- 15/- 18/3**

IR 55 GALVANISED CINDER SIFTER
12 ins. dia., 11 ins. high. A real coal saver. Quick and effective .. **7/6**

GARBAGE PAIL OF GALVANISED IRON
12 ins. dia. at top, 11 ins. deep .. **3/6**
Lighter quality .. **2/3**

IR 22 GALVANISED GARBAGE OR REFUSE HOLDER
With strainer and lid. To stand near sink and hold daily rubbish, wet or dry 12 ins. dia. by 9 ins. deep **4/6**

IR 5552 IMPROVED MOP AND BUCKET (*On right*)
Strong Galvanised bucket with perforated drainer in the top, which enables one to wring the mop with a twisting motion, and without wetting the hands Complete with mop **4/3**

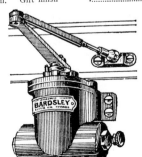

IR 491 DOLLY TUB
Corrugated Galvanised Steel Height 21 ins. Diameter at top 17 ins. **9/-**

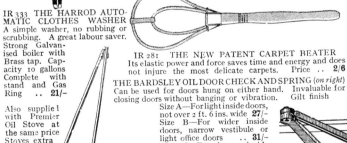

IR 281 THE NEW PATENT CARPET BEATER
Its elastic power and force saves time and energy and does not injure the most delicate carpets. Price .. **2/6**

THE BARDSLEY OIL DOOR CHECK AND SPRING (*on right*)
Can be used for doors hung on either hand. Invaluable for closing doors without banging or vibration. Gilt finish
Size A—For light inside doors, not over 2 ft. 6 ins. wide **27/-**
Size B—For wider inside doors, narrow vestibule or light office doors .. **31/-**
Size C—For larger inside doors. Most suitable size for ordinary office doors up to 3 ft. wide, or narrow outside doors up to 2 ft. 6 ins. wide **40/-**

IR 3000 PERPHECTO PATENT DUST PAN (*on left*)
Japanned Black. Complete with combined hard and soft brush. A great improvement on the ordinary dustpan as no stooping is necessary
5/10

GALVANISED PAILS			
Seamed 11	12	13	14 ins.
1/1	1/2	1/6	1/7
Strong 2/1	2/3	2/5	2/8

GALVANISED BINS
For indoor use. Made of strong Galvanised sheets on good substantial framing. Guaranteed to keep out rats and mice, and will not rust. Each bin is fitted with hasp and staple fastening, and lids are strongly hinged, and fitted with chain to take strain when opening

Size	Approx. Capacity cwts.	Length	Width	Height	No. of Compartments	Prices
B	4½	2′ 9″	1′ 9″	2′ 0″	2	£1 16 6
D	9	5′ 9″	1′ 9″	2′ 0″	4	£2 12 0
I	13	5′ 9″	2′ 3″	2′ 6″	4	£3 18 6
O	22	5′ 9″	2′ 9″	3′ 0″	2	£5 12 6
S	44	11′ 7″	2′ 9″	3′ 0″	4	£10 0 0

ALL PRICES ARE SUBJECT TO MARKET FLUCTUATIONS

HARRODS LTD

Telephone SLOANE 1234
Telegrams 'EVERYTHING HARRODS LONDON'

LONDON S W 1

IRONMONGERY DEPARTMENT
Harrods offer a Selection of Ironmongery unequalled elsewhere

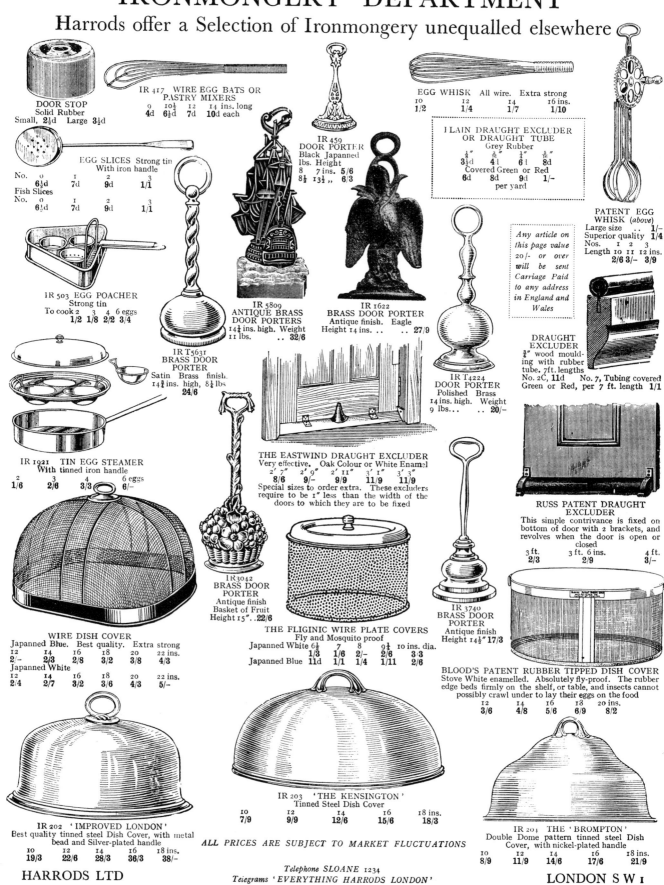

DOOR STOP
Solid Rubber
Small, 2½d   Large 3½d

IR 417   WIRE EGG BATS OR PASTRY MIXERS

9	10½	12	14 ins. long
4d	6½d	7d	10d each

EGG SLICES   Strong tin
With iron handle

No.	0	1	2	3
	6½d	7d	9d	1/1

Fish Slices

No.	0	1	2	3
	6½d	7d	9d	1/3

IR 503   EGG POACHER
Strong tin
To cook 2   3   4   6 eggs
1/2 1/8 2/2 3/4

**IR T5631
BRASS DOOR PORTER**
Satin Brass finish.
14¾ ins. high, 8½ lbs.
24/6

IR 1921   TIN EGG STEAMER
With tinned iron handle

2	3	4	6 eggs
1/6	2/6	3/3	6/-

WIRE DISH COVER
Japanned Blue.   Best quality.   Extra strong

12	14	16	18	20	22 ins.
2/-	2/3	2/8	3/2	3/8	4/3

Japanned White

12	14	16	18	20	22 ins.
2/4	2/7	3/2	3/6	4/3	5/-

**IR 459
DOOR PORTER**
Black Japanned
lbs. Height
8   7 ins.   5/6
8½ 13½ ,,   6/3

**IR 5809
ANTIQUE BRASS
DOOR PORTERS**
14¼ ins. high. Weight
11 lbs.
.. 32/6

**IR 1622
BRASS DOOR PORTER**
Antique finish.   Eagle
Height 14 ins. 27/9

**IR 3042
BRASS DOOR
PORTER**
Antique finish
Basket of Fruit
Height 15".. 22/6

THE EASTWIND DRAUGHT EXCLUDER
Very effective.   Oak Colour or White Enamel

2' 7"	2' 9"	2' 11"	3' 1"	3' 3"
8/6	9/-	9/9	11/9	11/9

Special sizes to order extra.   These excluders
require to be 1" less than the width of the
doors to which they are to be fixed

THE FLIGINIC WIRE PLATE COVERS
Fly and Mosquito proof

Japanned White	6½	7	8	9½	10 ins. dia.
	1/3	1/6	2/-	2/6	3/3
Japanned Blue	11d	1/1	1/4	1/11	2/6

**IR T4224
DOOR PORTER**
Polished Brass
14 ins. high.   Weight
9 lbs... .. 20/-

**IR 3740
BRASS DOOR
PORTER**
Antique finish
Height 14½" 17/3

EGG WHISK   All wire.   Extra strong

10	12	14	16 ins.
1/2	1/4	1/7	1/10

**PLAIN DRAUGHT EXCLUDER
OR DRAUGHT TUBE**
Grey Rubber

⅜"	½"	⅝"	¾"
3½d	4½	6½	8d

Covered Green or Red

6d	8d	9d	1/-

per yard

*Any article on
this page value
20/- or over
will be sent
Carriage Paid
to any address
in England and
Wales*

**PATENT EGG
WHISK** (above)
Large size .. 1/-
Superior quality 1/4
Nos.   1   2   3
Length 10 11 12 ins.
2/6 3/- 3/9

**DRAUGHT
EXCLUDER**
¾" wood mould-
ing with rubber
tube. 7ft. lengths
No. 2C, 11d   No. 7, Tubing covered
Green or Red, per 7 ft. length 1/1

**RUSS PATENT DRAUGHT
EXCLUDER**
This simple contrivance is fixed on
bottom of door with 2 brackets, and
revolves when the door is open or
closed

3 ft.	3 ft. 6 ins.	4 ft.
2/3	2/9	3/-

BLOOD'S PATENT RUBBER TIPPED DISH COVER
Stove White enamelled.   Absolutely fly-proof.   The rubber
edge beds firmly on the shelf, or table, and insects cannot
possibly crawl under to lay their eggs on the food

12	14	16	18	20 ins.
3/6	4/8	5/6	6/9	8/2

IR 203   'THE KENSINGTON'
Tinned Steel Dish Cover

10	12	14	16	18 ins.
7/9	9/9	12/6	15/6	18/3

IR 202   'IMPROVED LONDON'
Best quality tinned steel Dish Cover, with metal
bead and Silver-plated handle

10	12	14	16	18 ins.
19/3	22/6	28/3	36/3	38/-

IR 201   THE 'BROMPTON'
Double Dome pattern tinned steel Dish
Cover, with nickel-plated handle

10	12	14	16	18 ins.
8/9	11/9	14/6	17/6	21/9

ALL PRICES ARE SUBJECT TO MARKET FLUCTUATIONS

HARRODS LTD

IRONMONGERY DEPARTMENT
Fire Screens Attractively Designed and Thoroughly Practical

IR 4246 POLISHED BRASS STANDING GUARD
With strong flat strip panel, ½ in. mesh, 24 ins. wide × 25 ins. high .. **71/9**
Antique Brass .. **76/3** | Antique Copper.. **80/-**
Oxidized Silver .. **86/3** | Polished Steel .. **79/9**

IR 5476 EXTRA STRONG FIRE SCREEN
Fitted with strong spark-proof wire centre panel. Size 30 × 29 ins. high
Polished Brass **£8 2 6** | Antique Brass **£8 6 9**
Oxidized Silver **£9 15 9** | Finer Mesh, Polished Steel **£9 5 0**

IR 3885 FIRE SCREEN
25 ins. wide × 25½ ins. high
Polished Brass .. **85/6** | Antique Brass .. **90/-**
Antique Copper .. **95/9** | Oxidized Silver .. **102/3**

IR 4425 STANDING BRASS FIRE SCREEN
Cast Brass Ornaments, Louis XVI design, French finish. Strong sparkproof wire panel, 18½ ins. wide × 25¼ ins. high **94/3**

IR 4437 BRASS FOLDING GUARD
26 ins. wide when open
Extra strong wirework ⅜ in. mesh, 26 ins. wide × 21½ ins. high .. **61/-** | Antique Brass .. **65/3**
Antique Copper .. **70/6** | Oxidized Silver .. **71/9**

IR 4426 STANDING BRASS FIRE GUARD
With Cast Brass Enrichments
French finish, strong spark-proof wire panel, 24 ins. wide × 25 ins. high **£5 5 3**

IR 5153 FIRE SCREEN (on left)
All polished Brass frame and panel 21 ins. wide × 23½ ins. high **72/6**
Antique Brass **76/3**
Antique Copper **80/-**
Oxidized Silver **92/6**

IR 5152 FIRE SCREEN
All polished Brass Frame, and panel 21 ins. wide × 23½ ins. high ..**72/6** | Antique Brass .. **76/3**
Antique Copper ..**80/-** | Oxidized Silver .. **92/9**

IR 5478 EXTRA STRONG FIRE SCREEN
Fitted with strong spark-proof Wire Centre Panel. Size 30 ins. wide × 28½ ins. high to centre Polished Brass **£7 19 6**
Antique Brass **£8 5 3** | Oxidized Silver **£9 12 3**
Finer Mesh Polished Steel ..**£8 19 6**

IR 4413½ FIRE SCREEN (on left)
Polished Brass Frame, clear cut plate glass panel, in bevelled squares, 18½ ins. wide × 25½ ins. high .. **61/9**
Antique Brass **66/-**
Oxidized Silver **72/6**

IR 2140 HEAVY CAST BRASS LOUIS XV FIRE SCREEN
Blue Gauze wire 29 ins. wide 27½ ins. high ..**£10 3 0**

IR 3998 FIRE SCREEN
Polished Brass Frame. Cut Clear Glass Panel in bevelled strips 22 ins. wide × 23 ins. high **£4 18 9**
Antique Brass **£5 3 9** | Oxidized Silver **£5 13 3**

ALL PRICES ARE SUBJECT TO MARKET FLUCTUATIONS

HARRODS LTD
Telephone SLOANE 1234
Telegrams 'EVERYTHING HARRODS LONDON'
LONDON S W 1

IRONMONGERY DEPARTMENT
Handsomely Constructed Kerbs in a Wide Choice of Designs

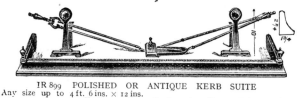

IR 899 POLISHED OR ANTIQUE KERB SUITE
Any size up to 4 ft. 6 ins. × 12 ins.

	Kerb	Dogs	Implements	Stop.	Suite complete
	48/-	19/6	22/3	5/9	£4 15 6
Antique Copper finish	55/3	21/6	24/6	6/6	£5 7 9
Oxidized Silver	65/3	27/3	33/-	7/9	£6 13 3

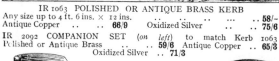

IR 5447 POLISHED BRASS CURB SUITE
Any size up to 4 ft. 6 ins. × 12 ins. inside

	Kerb	Dogs	Implements	Stop	Suite complete
	64/-	41/6	30/6	7/9	£7 3 9
Antique Brass ..	68/3	44/3	32/9	8/6	£7 13 9
Antique Copper ..	73/3	51/6	41/6	10/6	£8 16 9
Oxidized Silver ..	94/3	50/-	39/3	9/9	£9 13 3

IR 5447/5808
POLISHED BRASS CURB
Any size up to 4 ft. 6 ins. × 12 ins. 64/-
Antique Brass .. 68/3
Oxidized Silver .. 94/3

1 PAIR COMPANION SETS
Polished Brass .. 55/3
Antique Brass .. 58/-
Oxidized Silver .. 69/9

Carriage paid on all purchases value **20/-** *and over to any station in England and Wales*

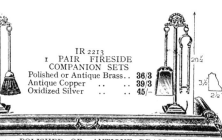

IR 2213
1 PAIR FIRESIDE COMPANION SETS
Polished or Antique Brass .. 36/3
Antique Copper 39/3
Oxidized Silver 45/-

IR 1274 POLISHED OR ANTIQUE BRASS KERB
Any size up to 4 ft. 6 ins. × 12 ins. 40/9
Antique Copper .. .. 43/6 Oxidized Silver .. 56/3

IR 5223 POLISHED BRASS KERB SUITE

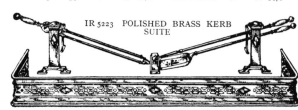

Any size up to 4 ft. 6 ins. × 12 ins.

	Kerb	Dogs	Implements	Stop	Suite complete
	48/9	29/-	21/-	7/-	£5 5 9
Antique Brass ..	52/3	32/-	24/-	7/3	£5 15 6
Antique Copper ..	56/-	35/6	27/-	8/6	£6 7 0
Oxidized Silver ..	73/3	40/-	31/3	9/3	£7 13 9

IR 989
FIRE SCREEN
(on left)
Polished or Antique Brass .. 53/3
Antique Copper .. 58/-
Oxidized Silver .. 65/3

IR 593 POLISHED OR ANTIQUE BRASS KERB SUITE
Any size up to 4 ft. 6 ins. × 12 ins.

	Kerb	Dogs	Implements	Stop	Suite complete
	42/-	18/6	22/3	5/6	£4 8 3
Antique Copper ..	48/3	20/6	24/3	5/9	£4 18 9
Oxidized Silver ..	62/6	26/3	33/-	7/3	£6 9 0

IR 2180
1 PAIR FIRESIDE COMPANION SETS
Polished or Antique
Brass .. 61/-
Antique Copper .. 66/9
Oxidized Silver .. 72/6

IR 1063 POLISHED OR ANTIQUE BRASS KERB
Any size up to 4 ft. 6 ins. × 12 ins. 58/-
Antique Copper .. .. 66/9 Oxidized Silver .. 75/6

IR 2092 COMPANION SET (on *left*) to match Kerb 1063
Polished or Antique Brass .. 59/6 Antique Copper .. 65/3
Oxidized Silver .. 71/3

IR 1206 POLISHED BRASS OR ANTIQUE BRASS KERBS
Any size up to 4 ft. 6 ins. × 12 ins. .. .. 85/- Antique Copper .. 93/-
Oxidized Silver .. 115/6

IR 849
BOX END SEAT KERB

Extending from 2 ft. 11 ins. to 4 ft. 3 ins., inside measurements. Height 16 ins. Size of boxes, 14 × 10 × 12 ins. deep, seats covered Pegamoid, one of the boxes is lined with baize for slippers, the other has a loose lining for Coal. In Antique Brass or Copper or Old Pewter finish. Price .. 55/3

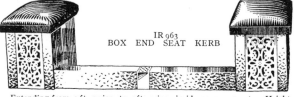

IR 963
BOX END SEAT KERB

Extending from 2 ft. 11 ins. to 4 ft. 3 ins., inside measurements. Height 16 ins. Size of boxes 14 × 10 × 12 ins. deep, seats covered in Pegamoid, one of the boxes is baize lined for slippers, the other has a loose lining for Coal. In Antique Brass or Copper or Old Pewter finish. Price £3 5 3

ALL PRICES ARE SUBJECT TO MARKET FLUCTUATIONS

HARRODS LTD

Telephone SLOANE 1234
Telegrams 'EVERYTHING HARRODS LONDON'

LONDON S W 1

IRONMONGERY DEPARTMENT

Handsomely Designed Brass Kerbs Ensure a Cosy Fireside

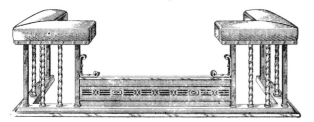

IR 5237   POLISHED BRASS SEAT KERB
With 6-in. Corner Seats upholstered in Pegamoid. Size 4 ft. 6 ins. × 15 ins. inside the base × 18 ins. high

.. ..	£11 8 6
In Antique Brass finish	£11 15 9
In Antique Copper	£12 17 6
In Oxidized Silver	£15 18 6

If seats covered in hide, 35/6 extra

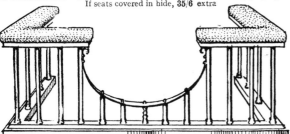

IR 3286½   POLISHED BRASS SEAT KERB
With 6-in. upholstered Pegamoid top.   Stock size 4 ft. 6 ins. × 15 ins. inside base × 21 ins. high.. .. .. .. £9 12 3

Antique Brass finish	£9 15 6
Antique Copper	£10 14 0
Oxidized Silver	£13 1 0

A   A

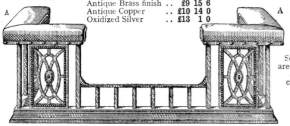

IR 5861   SEAT KERB
Size 4 ins. × 15 ins. inside of base × 18 ins. high overall
6-in. Seats covered in Antique Brown Pegamoid

Polished Brass	£8 15 6
Antique Brass	£9 15 9
Oxidized Silver	£13 1 0

Seat kerbs are measured around cushions A to A

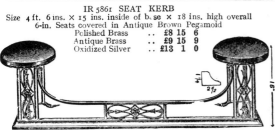

IR 1011   POLISHED OR ANTIQUE BRASS SEAT KERB
Height overall, 16 ins.   Round Seats, 12 ins. diam.   Covered in Pegamoid
£5 10 6

Antique Copper   .. **£6 7 0**   Oxidized Silver   .. **£7 11 0**

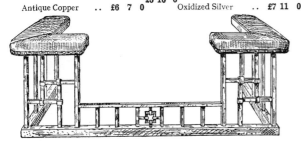

IR 4922   ROUGH ARMOUR BRIGHT SEAT OR CLUB KERB
6-in. Corner Seats upholstered in Pegamoid, 4 ft. 6 ins. × 1 ft. 6 ins. inside base, 21 ins. total height **£10 14 0**

IR 5354   POLISHED BRASS SEAT KERB
With 6-in. Corner Seats upholstered in Pegamoid.   Size 4 ft. 6 ins. × 15 ins. inside base × 18 ins. high

.. ..	£11 12 0
In Antique Brass finish	£11 19 3
Antique Copper	£13 1 9
Oxidized Silver	£15 4 6

If seats covered in hide, 35/6 extra

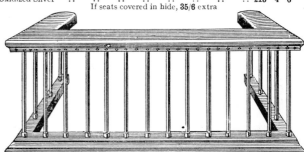

IR 3716   ALL POLISHED BRASS SEAT OR CLUB KERB
Very strong, upholstered 6-in. Pegamoid seats.   Size 4 ft. 6 ins. × 18 ins. × 21 ins. high

.. ..	£10 7 9
Antique Brass finish	£10 15 9
Antique Copper finish	£11 8 6
Oxidized Silver	£14 3 6

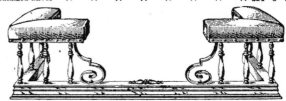

IR 5430   POLISHED BRASS SEAT KERB
With 5-in. Corner Seats upholstered in Pegamoid.   Size 4 ft. × 12 ins. inside base **£7 5 0**

In Antique Brass finish	£7 8 9
Antique Copper	£8 14 6
Oxidized Silver	£9 15 9

If seats covered in hide, 34/3 extra

IR 931   POLISHED OR ANTIQUE BRASS SEAT KERB
Size 4 ft. × 12 ins. inside the base
Height overall, 18 ins.   Seats, 14 × 9 ins., covered in Pegamoid

	£3 5 3
Antique Copper	£3 12 9
Oxidized Silver	£5 1 6

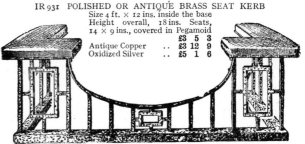

IR 4474   SEAT OR CLUB KERB
Rough Armour Bright.   6-in. Corner Seats upholstered in Pegamoid.   Size 4 ft. 6 ins. × 18 ins. inside base × 21 ins. high **£11 2 0**

ALL PRICES ARE SUBJECT TO MARKET FLUCTUATIONS

HARRODS LTD

Telephone SLOANE 1234
Telegrams 'EVERYTHING HARRODS LONDON'

LONDON S W 1

IRONMONGERY DEPARTMENT
Wheelbarrows, Pumps, Garden Rollers, Etc.

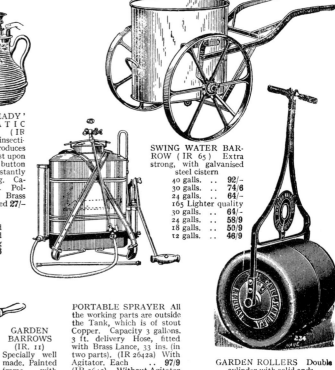

WOOD WHEELBARROWS (IR 698) Made of seasoned Hardwood Strong wood wheel 19 ins. diameter. Painted **Green**. Size of barrow body at top 30 × 24 ins., 16 ins. deep in front, 7 ins. deep at back Complete with top boards **74/3**

(IR 98) With movable backboard, not painted and without top boards. Length at top 36 ins., width at top 24 ins., depth at front 20 ins. .. **49/-**
Lighter quality (IR 90) 32 × 19 × 14 ins., without loose backboard, painted Green **24/9**
Unpainted **22/9**

'EVER - READY' PNEUMATIC SPRAYER (IR 2649) For insecticides, etc. Produces a very fine mist upon pressing the button and stops instantly upon releasing. Capacity 1 pint. Polished Copper, Brass or Nickel Plated **27/-**

GARDEN ENGINE (IR 258) Very strong and durable. Cistern of Galvanised Steel, painted inside and out. The pumps are extremely strong and powerful. 24 gallons **£7 13 6**

SWING WATER BARROW (IR 65) Extra strong, with galvanised steel cistern
40 galls. .. 92/-
30 galls. .. 74/6
24 galls. .. 64/-
165 Lighter quality
30 galls. .. 64/-
24 galls. .. 58/9
18 galls. .. 50/9
12 galls. .. 46/9

IMPROVED PATENT RUBBISH DESTRUCTOR Invaluable for the destruction of all waste Will be found a great boon for burning all refuse of the garden, kitchen, etc. Commended by sanitary authorities on hygienic grounds

No. 681 23 ins. dia. × 40 in. high × 18 gauge **£2 12 6**
No. 682 23 ins. dia. × 46 in. high × 16 gauge **£2 17 6**

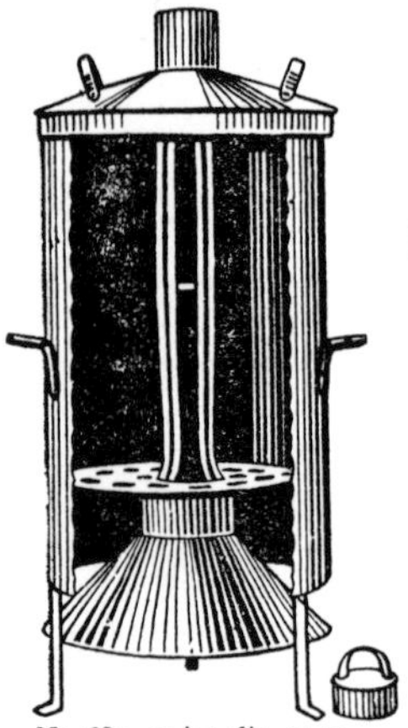

GARDEN BARROWS (IR 11) Specially well made. Painted frame, with galvanised body. Size at top 29 × 32 ins., depth at front 15½ ins., at back 7½ ins. **62/-**
(IR 10) Similar to above, but smaller and lighter make. 24 × 28 ins. at top, depth in front 11 ins., at back 6 ins. **37/-**
(IR 9) For Ladies' and Boy's use 22 × 26 × 10 × 5 ins. .. **33/-**

No. 0679 17 ins. dia. × 24 in. high × 20 gauge **£1 15 0**
No. 679 19 ins. dia. × 32 in. high × 18 gauge **£1 19 6**
No. 680 19 ins. dia. × 38 in. high × 18 gauge **£2 6 0**

PORTABLE SPRAYER All the working parts are outside the Tank, which is of stout Copper. Capacity 3 gallons. 3 ft. delivery Hose, fitted with Brass Lance, 33 ins. (in two parts). (IR 2642a) With Agitator. Each .. 97/9
(IR 2642) Without Agitator Each 89/9

GARDEN ROLLERS Double cylinder with solid ends

Cwts. qrs. lbs.			
14 × 14 ins.	1	3	7	35/6
16 × 16 ins.	2	1	7	43/9
18 × 18 ins.	2	2	14	56/3
20 × 20 ins.	3	0	0	66/6
22 × 22 ins.	3	3	0	83/6
24 × 24 ins.	4	2	0	96/-

Carriage paid to nearest station, England or Wales

IMPROVED BUCKET SPRAYER (IR 79) (left) For spraying and lime-washing of any kind. This sprayer will not clog and is easily cleaned. The bucket is fitted with a strainer for the lime-wash. Capacity four gallons. Complete with 2 ft. Brass delivery lance .. **56/-**

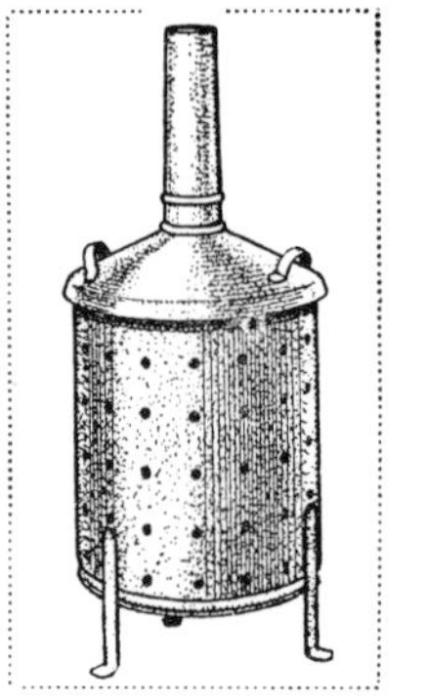

RUBBISH DESTRUCTOR (right) The cheapest, most efficient and sanitary way of destroying your rubbish. Excellent for small as well as large gardens, household, stable, factory, etc. Made of strong Galvanised Iron, corrugated to give extra strength
Sizes 18 ins. diameter × 28 ins. high, excluding lid and chimney **19/6**
Size 16 ins. diameter × 28 ins. high, excluding lid and chimney **16/6**

SEMI-ROTARY LIFT AND FORCE PUMP (IR 951) (below) A new type of Double Acting Lift and Force Pump which is unequalled for simplicity, compactness, and working capacity. It is most durable, very easy to work, and is readily fixed. The handle may be changed to any required position. These Pumps will draw water to about 15 feet vertical, with the aid of a foot valve, and will force water to a height of about 100 or 150 feet

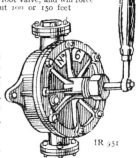

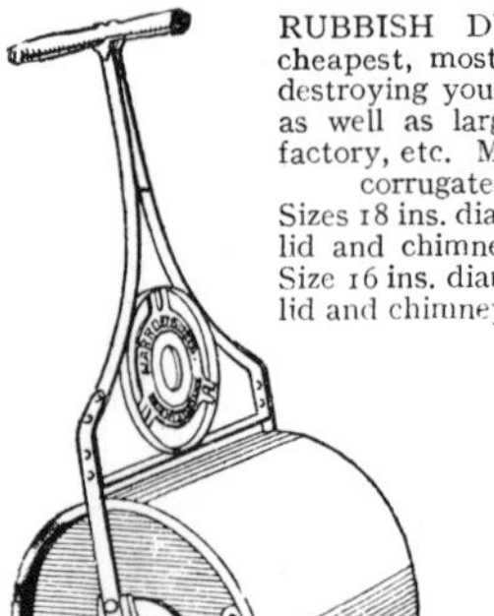

IR 951

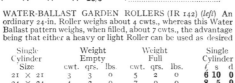

IR 142

WATER-BALLAST GARDEN ROLLERS (IR 142) (left) An ordinary 24-in. Roller weighs about 4 cwts., whereas this Water Ballast pattern weighs, when filled, about 7 cwts., the advantage being that either a heavy or light Roller can be used as desired

Single Cylinder Size	Weight Empty cwt. qrs. lbs.			Weight Full cwt. qrs. lbs.			Single Cylinder £ s d		
21 × 21	3	2	0	5	2	0	6	10	0
24 × 24	4	2	0	7	0	0	8	5	0
27 × 27	6	3	0	10	0	0	11	15	0

Double Cylinder Improved design

	cwt. qrs. lbs.			cwt. qrs. lbs.			£ s d		
20 × 20	3	3	0	4	3	7	6	7	6
22 × 22	4	1	21	5	3	21	7	7	6
24 × 24	5	1	7	7	1	7	8	12	6

No. of Pump

	0	1	2	3	4	5
Outside diam. of Pump Case in.	5¼	6½	7½	9	13	19
Diam. of suction and delivery	½	¾	1	1¼	1¼	1½
Gallons of water raised per minute (approximate)—	4	5	6	9	13	19
	21/9	24/-	29/-	35/-	43/6	48/-

ALL PRICES ARE SUBJECT TO MARKET FLUCTUATIONS

HARRODS LTD

Telephone SLOANE 1234
Telegrams 'EVERYTHING HARRODS LONDON'

LONDON S W 1

IRONMONGERY DEPARTMENT
Harrods for All Your Gardening Needs

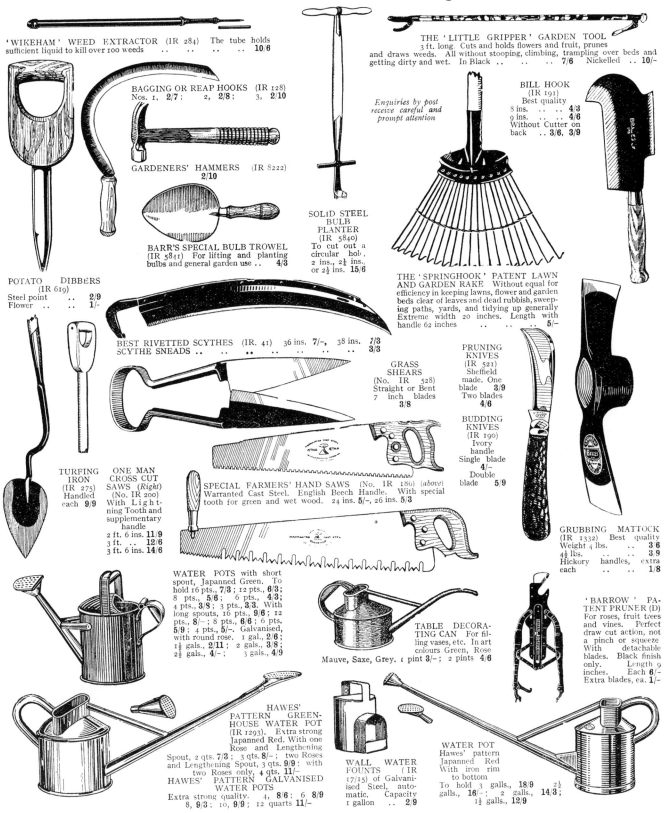

'WIKEHAM' WEED EXTRACTOR (IR 284) The tube holds sufficient liquid to kill over 100 weeds **10/6**

BAGGING OR REAP HOOKS (IR 128) Nos. 1, 2/7; 2, 2/8; 3, 2/10

GARDENERS' HAMMERS (IR 8222) **2/10**

BARR'S SPECIAL BULB TROWEL (IR 5841) For lifting and planting bulbs and general garden use .. **4/3**

POTATO DIBBERS (IR 619)
Steel point .. **2/9**
Flower .. **1/-**

BEST RIVETTED SCYTHES (IR. 41) 36 ins. **7/-**, 38 ins. **7/3**
SCYTHE SNEADS **3/3**

TURFING IRON (IR 275) Handled each **9/9**

ONE MAN CROSS CUT SAWS (Right) (No. IR 200) With Lightning Tooth and supplementary handle
2 ft. 6 ins. **11/9**
3 ft. .. **12/6**
3 ft. 6 ins. **14/6**

SPECIAL FARMERS' HAND SAWS (No. IR 180) (above) Warranted Cast Steel. English Beech Handle. With special tooth for green and wet wood. 24 ins. **5/-**, 26 ins. **5/3**

WATER POTS with short spout, Japanned Green. To hold 16 pts., **7/3**; 12 pts., **6/3**; 8 pts., **5/6**; 6 pts., **4/3**; 4 pts., **3/8**; 3 pts., **3/3**. With long spouts, 16 pts., **9/6**; 12 pts., **8/-**; 8 pts., **6/6**; 6 pts. **5/9**; 4 pts., **5/-**. Galvanised, with round rose. 1 gal., **2/6**; 1½ gals., **2/11**; 2 gals., **3/8**; 2½ gals., **4/-**; 3 gals., **4/9**

HAWES' PATTERN GREEN-HOUSE WATER POT (IR 1293). Extra strong Japanned Red. With one Rose and Lengthening Spout, 2 qts. **7/3**; 3 qts. **8/-**; two Roses and Lengthening Spout, 3 qts. **9/9**; with two Roses only, 4 qts. **11/-**
HAWES' PATTERN GALVANISED WATER POTS Extra strong quality. 4, **8/6**; 6 **8/9** 8, **9/3**; 10, **9/9**; 12 quarts **11/-**

THE 'LITTLE GRIPPER' GARDEN TOOL 3 ft. long. Cuts and holds flowers and fruit, prunes and draws weeds. All without stooping, climbing, trampling over beds and getting dirty and wet. In Black .. .. .. **7/6** Nickelled .. **10/-**

Enquiries by post receive careful and prompt attention

SOLID STEEL BULB PLANTER (IR 5840) To cut out a circular hole, 2 ins., 2¼ ins. or 2½ ins. **15/6**

BILL HOOK (IR 191) Best quality
8 ins. **4/3**
9 ins. **4/6**
Without Cutter on back .. **3/6, 3/9**

THE 'SPRINGHOOK' PATENT LAWN AND GARDEN RAKE Without equal for efficiency in keeping lawns, flower and garden beds clear of leaves and dead rubbish, sweeping paths, yards, and tidying up generally Extreme width 20 inches. Length with handle 62 inches **5/-**

GRASS SHEARS (No. IR 528) Straight or Bent 7 inch blades **3/8**

PRUNING KNIVES (IR 521) Sheffield made. One blade **3/9** Two blades **4/6**

BUDDING KNIVES (IR 190) Ivory handle Single blade **4/-** Double blade **5/9**

GRUBBING MATTOCK (IR 1332) Best quality
Weight 4 lbs. .. **3/6**
4½ lbs. **3/9**
Hickory handles, extra each **1/8**

TABLE DECORATING CAN For filling vases, etc. In art colours Green, Rose Mauve, Saxe, Grey. 1 pint **3/-**; 2 pints **4/6**

'BARROW' PATENT PRUNER (D) For roses, fruit trees and vines. Perfect draw cut action, not a pinch or squeeze With detachable blades. Black finish only. Length 9 inches. Each **6/-** Extra blades, ea. **1/-**

WALL WATER FOUNTS (IR 17/15) of Galvanised Steel, automatic. Capacity 1 gallon .. **2/9**

WATER POT Hawes' pattern Japanned Red With iron rim to bottom To hold 3 galls., **18/9** 2½ galls., **16/-**; 2 galls., **14/3**; 1½ galls., **12/9**

ALL PRICES ARE SUBJECT TO MARKET FLUCTUATIONS

HARRODS LTD

Telephone SLOANE 1234
Telegrams 'EVERYTHING HARRODS LONDON'

LONDON S W 1

IRONMONGERY DEPARTMENT
Everything in Fencing and Decorative Wire Work

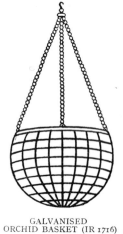

Tennis Court Fencing
Special Quotations
and
Full Specification
for either
Hard or Soft Courts
sent on application

GARDEN ARCH (IR 63)
Galvanised, 7 ft. × 4 ft. × 1 ft.
deep. No. 1 Strong **9/6**
No. 2. Extra strong . . **13/-**
PLAIN ARCH (IR 49)
7 ft. × 4 ft. × 1 ft... **10/3** and **6/6**

THE PATENT TENEFLOS
Makes the arrangement of cut
flowers easy, simple, and artistic
Made entirely of Copper

8	7	6	5	4	3 ins.
3/6	3/-	2/8	2/4	2/-	1/11

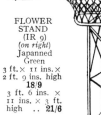

FERN OR FLOWER BASKET
(IR 1368)
New design. Galvanised. 16 ins.
4/9 ; 14 ins., **4/3** ; 12 ins . . **3/9**

GALVANISED
ORCHID BASKET (IR 1716)

15	12	10	8	6 ins.
7/3	4/9	3/8	2/5	1/11

UMBRELLA ROSE TRAINER
(IR 658) (*on right*) Galvanised

Height out of ground.	Diameter across top	
3 ft. 0 ins.	2 ft. 0 ins. . .	12/-
4 ft. 0 ins.	2 ft. 6 ins. . .	15/6
5 ft. 0 ins.	3 ft. 0 ins. . .	21/6
6 ft. 0 ins.	3 ft. 6 ins. . .	25/-
7 ft. 0 ins.	3 ft. 6 ins	28/6

THE 'FLORAL-AID'
Green Lacquered. For
arranging Cut Flowers
naturally in Open
Bowls, Silver Ware,
etc., for the decoration
of Rooms, Tables
etc. 'Floral-Aid'
will not rust nor
affect the water in
the vessels used, and
can be removed with-
out disarranging the
flowers to enable the
water to be changed
day by day
Height 10½ ins., **7/-** ; 9 ins., **5/-** ; 8 ins.,
3/9 ; 6½ ins., **2/3** ; 5 ins., **1/6** ; 3½ ins., **9d**

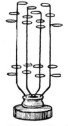

NEW CIRCULAR PEA
TRAINER (*on left*)
Galvanised after being made
4ft. high, 12 ins. in diam.

Each 2/7	Per dozen 27/8
18 ins. diameter . .	Each 3/6
Per dozen . .	. . 36/6

FLOWER STAND
(IR 15)
(*on left*)
Japanned
Green. Best
quality 3 ft.
long × 3 ft. high
36/6
3 ft. 6 ins. long
× 3 ft. 6 ins.
high **42/9**
4 ft. × 3 ft.6 ins.
55/6

GALVANISED LAWN BORDERING (IR 301)
In 3 ft. lengths

15	12	9	6 ins. high
1/10	1/5	1/3	11d per length

FLOWER STAND
(IR 9)
(*on right*)
Japanned
Green
3 ft. × 11 ins. ×
2 ft. 9 ins. high
18/9
3 ft. 6 ins. ×
11 ins. × 3 ft.
high . . **21/6**

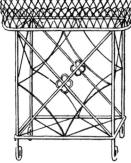

GALVANISED WIRE NETTING
in 50 yard rolls only
Procured to order and
sent direct from Works
Carriage paid only on
purchases over 130/-,
to any Railway Station
in England or Wales,
within 7 days. Wire
netting can only be
returned or the order
cancelled on condition
that a charge be made
for re-galvanising and
cost of carriage. Quota-
tions for any other
widths on application

British made

PEA GUARDS (IR 19a) Galvanised
Wire Netting 3 ft. long × 6 wide ×
¾ inch mesh, with 3 stays. Complete with 2 stop ends to each dozen
Per dozen **3/-** Per gross **34/6**

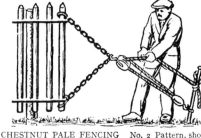

NETTING
(Tanned), for throwing over
Fruit Trees, etc. Made from
Fishing Netting ; Tanned
50 yds. × 2 yds. . . **7/-**
50 yds. × 4 yds. . . **14/-**
This being an old Fishing
Net, no guarantee as to the
quality or exact length can
be given, but it is believed
to be well repaired and full
measure. Supplied in approximately 50 yard lengths only
Measured in the rope and is
in the width stated when
pulled out to extreme width

CHESTNUT PALE FENCING No. 2 Pattern, showing
method of straining and fixing. Prices per yard, without
posts

Height	Approx. Space between Pales. 5ins.	4ins.	3ins.	2ins.	Posts	Inter-mediate Post and Strut
	s d	s d	s d	s d	s d	s d
2ft. 6ins.	0 10	1 0	1 1	1 4	0 8	2 8
3ft. 0ins.	1 0	1 1	1 3	1 7	0 9	3 2
3ft. 6ins.	1 1	1 4	1 6	1 10	0 11	3 8
4ft. 0ins.	1 4	1 6	1 9	2 1	1 1	4 4
4ft. 6ins.	1 6	1 9	2 0	2 4	1 3	5 0
5ft. 0ins.	1 9	2 0	2 3	2 7	1 6	6 0
5ft. 6ins.	2 0	2 3	2 6	3 1	1 9	7 0
6ft. 0ins.	2 3	2 7	3 0	3 6	2 1	8 4

Mesh	Gauge	Width	18	24	30	36	42	48	60	72 ins.
1 in	19	..	10/3	13/-	16/-	18/6	21/6	24/9	30/9	36/9
	18		13/3	16/6	20/9	23/9	27/6	31/6	39/3	47/9
1¼ ins.	19	..	8/3	10/6	12/6	14/-	16/9	19/3	24/9	28/9
	18		10/6	13/3	16/-	18/6	21/6	24/9	30/9	36/9
1½ ins	19	..	7/3	9/-	11/-	12/9	14/9	17/-	21/-	25/3
	18		9/-	11/3	13/9	15/9	18/6	21/3	26/6	31/9
1⅝ ins.	19	..	6/6	8/6	10/-	11/6	13/6	15/6	19/3	23/6
	18		7/9	10/-	12/-	13/9	16/3	18/6	23/-	27/9
2 ins.	19	..	5/3	6/8	8/-	9/-	10/6	12/-	14/10	17/11
	18		7/-	9/-	10/9	12/-	14/3	16/3	20/3	24/3
2½ ins.	19	..	4/9	6/-	7/2	8/-	9/6	10/9	13/6	16/3
	18		6/-	7/9	9/-	10/6	12/-	13/9	17/3	20/9
3 ins.	19	..	4/-	5/3	6/-	7/-	8/-	9/3	11/6	13/9
	18		5/-	6/6	7/9	8/9	10/-	11/6	14/6	17/3

ALL PRICES ARE SUBJECT TO MARKET FLUCTUATIONS

HARRODS LTD

Telephone SLOANE 1234
Telegrams 'EVERYTHING HARRODS LONDON'

LONDON S W 1

IRONMONGERY DEPARTMENT

Mowing Machines with and without Engines Attached

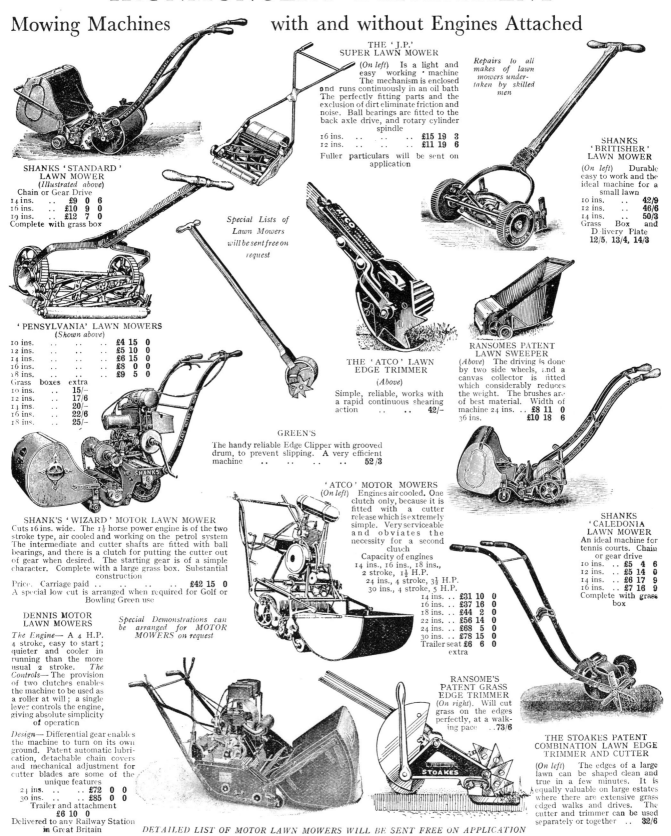

THE 'J.P.' SUPER LAWN MOWER

(*On left*) Is a light and easy working machine The mechanism is enclosed and runs continuously in an oil bath The perfectly fitting parts and the exclusion of dirt eliminate friction and noise. Ball bearings are fitted to the back axle drive, and rotary cylinder spindle

| 16 ins. | .. | .. | £15 19 3 |
| 12 ins. | .. | .. | £11 19 6 |

Fuller particulars will be sent on application

Repairs to all makes of lawn mowers undertaken by skilled men

SHANKS 'BRITISHER' LAWN MOWER

(*On left*) Durable easy to work and the ideal machine for a small lawn

10 ins.	..	..	42/9
12 ins.	..	..	46/6
14 ins.	..	..	50/3

Grass Box and Delivery Plate
12/5, 13/4, 14/3

SHANKS 'STANDARD' LAWN MOWER
(*Illustrated above*)
Chain or Gear Drive

14 ins.	..	£9 0 6
16 ins.	..	£10 9 0
19 ins.	..	£12 7 0

Complete with grass box

Special Lists of Lawn Mowers will be sent free on request

'PENSYLVANIA' LAWN MOWERS
(*Shown above*)

10 ins.	..	..	£4 15 0
12 ins.	..	..	£5 10 0
14 ins.	..	..	£6 15 0
16 ins.	..	..	£8 0 0
18 ins.	..	..	£9 5 0

Grass boxes extra

10 ins.	..	..	15/-
12 ins.	..	..	17/6
14 ins.	..	..	20/-
16 ins.	..	..	22/6
18 ins.	..	..	25/-

THE 'ATCO' LAWN EDGE TRIMMER
(*Above*)

Simple, reliable, works with a rapid continuous shearing action 42/-

GREEN'S
The handy reliable Edge Clipper with grooved drum, to prevent slipping. A very efficient machine 52/3

RANSOMES PATENT LAWN SWEEPER
(*Above*) The driving is done by two side wheels, and a canvas collector is fitted which considerably reduces the weight. The brushes are of best material. Width of machine 24 ins. .. £8 11 0
36 ins. £10 18 6

SHANK'S 'WIZARD' MOTOR LAWN MOWER
Cuts 16 ins. wide. The 1½ horse power engine is of the two stroke type, air cooled and working on the petrol system The intermediate and cutter shafts are fitted with ball bearings, and there is a clutch for putting the cutter out of gear when desired. The starting gear is of a simple character. Complete with a large grass box. Substantial construction
Price. Carriage paid £42 15 0
A special low cut is arranged when required for Golf or Bowling Green use

'ATCO' MOTOR MOWERS
(*On left*) Engines air cooled. One clutch only, because it is fitted with a cutter release which is extremely simple. Very serviceable and obviates the necessity for a second clutch
Capacity of engines
14 ins., 16 ins., 18 ins., 2 stroke, 1½ H.P.
24 ins., 4 stroke, 3½ H.P.
30 ins., 4 stroke, 5 H.P.

14 ins.	..	£31 10 0
16 ins.	..	£37 16 0
18 ins.	..	£44 2 0
22 ins.	..	£56 14 0
24 ins.	..	£68 5 0
30 ins.	..	£78 15 0

Trailer seat £6 6 0 extra

SHANKS 'CALEDONIA' LAWN MOWER
An ideal machine for tennis courts. Chain or gear drive

10 ins.	..	£5 4 6
12 ins.	..	£5 14 0
14 ins.	..	£6 17 9
16 ins.	..	£7 16 9

Complete with grass box

DENNIS MOTOR LAWN MOWERS

The Engine— A 4 H.P. 4 stroke, easy to start; quieter and cooler in running than the more usual 2 stroke. *The Controls—* The provision of two clutches enables the machine to be used as a roller at will; a single lever controls the engine, giving absolute simplicity of operation

Design— Differential gear enables the machine to turn on its own ground. Patent automatic lubrication, detachable chain covers and mechanical adjustment for cutter blades are some of the unique features

| 24 ins. | .. | .. £72 0 0 |
| 30 ins. | .. | .. £85 0 0 |

Trailer and attachment £6 10 0
Delivered to any Railway Station in Great Britain

Special Demonstrations can be arranged for MOTOR MOWERS on request

RANSOME'S PATENT GRASS EDGE TRIMMER
(*On right*). Will cut grass on the edges perfectly, at a walking pace .. 73/6

THE STOAKES PATENT COMBINATION LAWN EDGE TRIMMER AND CUTTER

(*On left*) The edges of a large lawn can be shaped clean and true in a few minutes. It is equally valuable on large estates where there are extensive grass edged walks and drives. The cutter and trimmer can be used separately or together .. 32/6

DETAILED LIST OF MOTOR LAWN MOWERS WILL BE SENT FREE ON APPLICATION

ALL PRICES ARE SUBJECT TO MARKET FLUCTUATIONS

IRONMONGERY DEPARTMENT
Well Chosen Household Utensils Repay Their Value Many Times Over

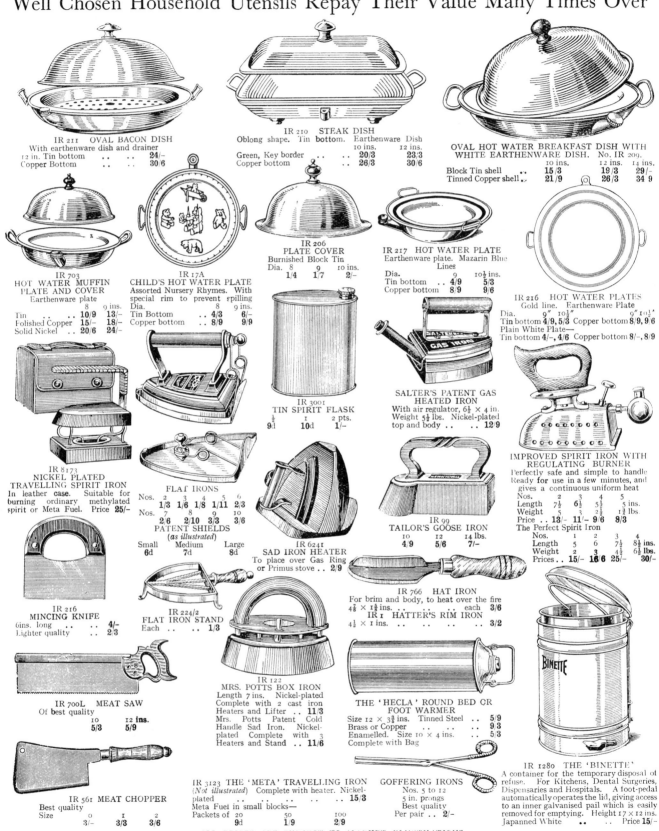

IR 211   OVAL BACON DISH
With earthenware dish and drainer
12 in. Tin bottom 24/-
Copper Bottom 30/6

IR 210   STEAK DISH
Oblong shape. Tin **bottom**. Earthenware Dish
10 ins.   12 ins.
Green, Key border 20/3   23/3
Copper bottom 26/3   30/6

OVAL HOT WATER BREAKFAST DISH WITH WHITE EARTHENWARE DISH. No. IR 209.
	10 ins.	12 ins.	14 ins.
Block Tin shell ..	15/3	19/3	29/-
Tinned Copper shell ..	21/9	26/3	34/9

IR 703
HOT WATER MUFFIN PLATE AND COVER
Earthenware plate
	8	9 ins.
Tin	10/9	13/-
Polished Copper	15/-	18/-
Solid Nickel ..	20/6	24/-

IR 17A
CHILD'S HOT WATER PLATE
Assorted Nursery Rhymes. With special rim to prevent spilling
Dia.	8	9 ins.
Tin Bottom ..	4/3	6/-
Copper bottom ..	8/9	9/9

IR 206
PLATE COVER
Burnished Block Tin
Dia. 8	9	10 ins.
1/4	1/7	2/-

IR 217   HOT WATER PLATE
Earthenware plate. Mazarin Blue Lines
Dia.	9	10½ ins.
Tin bottom ..	4/9	5/3
Copper bottom	8/9	9/6

IR 216   HOT WATER PLATES
Gold line.   Earthenware Plate
Dia.   9″   10½″   9″   10½″
Tin bottom 4/9, 5/3 Copper bottom 8/9, 9/6
Plain White Plate—
Tin bottom 4/-, 4/6 Copper bottom 8/-, 8/9

IR 3001
TIN SPIRIT FLASK
½	1	2 pts.
9d	10d	1/-

SALTER'S PATENT GAS HEATED IRON
With air regulator, 6½ × 4 in. Weight 5½ lbs. Nickel-plated top and body 12/9

IR 8173
NICKEL PLATED TRAVELLING SPIRIT IRON
In leather **case**. Suitable for burning ordinary methylated spirit or Meta Fuel. Price 25/-

FLAT IRONS
Nos.	2	3	4	5	6
	1/3	1/6	1/8	1/11	2/3
Nos.	7	8	9	10	
	2/6	2/10	3/3	3/6	

PATENT SHIELDS
(as illustrated)
Small	Medium	Large
6d	7d	8d

IR 6241
SAD IRON HEATER
To place over Gas Ring or Primus stove .. 2/9

IR 99
TAILOR'S GOOSE IRON
10	12	14 lbs.
4/9	5/6	7/-

IMPROVED SPIRIT IRON WITH REGULATING BURNER
Perfectly safe and simple to handle Ready **for** use in a few minutes, and gives a continuous uniform heat
Nos.	2	3	4	5
Length	7½	6½	5½	5 ins.
Weight	5	3	2½	1½ lbs.
Price ..	13/-	11/-	9/6	8/3

The Perfect Spirit Iron
Nos.	1	2	3	4
Length	5	6	7½	8½ ins.
Weight	2	3	4½	6½ lbs.
Prices ..	15/-	16/6	25/-	30/-

IR 216
MINCING KNIFE
6ins. long	4/-
Lighter quality ..	2/3

IR 224/2
FLAT IRON STAND
Each 1/3

IR 766   HAT IRON
For brim and body, to heat over the fire
4⅞ × 1⅞ ins. .. .. .. each 3/6
IR 1   HATTER'S RIM IRON
4½ × 1 ins. 3/2

IR 700L   MEAT SAW
Of best quality
10	12 ins.
5/3	5/9

IR 122
MRS. POTTS BOX IRON
Length 7 ins.   Nickel-plated Complete with 2 cast iron Heaters and Lifter .. 11/3
Mrs. Potts Patent Cold Handle Sad Iron. Nickel-plated Complete with 3 Heaters and Stand .. 11/6

THE 'HECLA' ROUND BED OR FOOT WARMER
Size 12 × 3¾ ins. Tinned Steel .. 5/9
Brass or Copper 9/3
Enamelled. Size 10 × 4 ins. .. 5/3
Complete with Bag

IR 1280   THE 'BINETTE'
A container for the temporary disposal of refuse. For Kitchens, Dental Surgeries, Dispensaries and Hospitals. A foot-pedal automatically operates the lid, giving access to an inner galvanised pail which is easily removed for emptying. Height 17 × 12 ins.
Japanned White .. .. Price 15/-

IR 561 MEAT CHOPPER
Best quality
Size	0	1	2
	3/-	3/3	3/6

IR 3123 THE 'META' TRAVELLING IRON
(Not illustrated) Complete with heater. Nickel-plated 15/3
Meta Fuel in small blocks—
Packets of	20	50	100
	9d	1/9	2/9

GOFFERING IRONS
Nos. 5 to 12
5 in. prongs
Best quality
Per pair .. 2/-

HARRODS LTD   **LONDON S W 1**

IRONMONGERY DEPARTMENT
Reliable Ice Makers and Ice Cream Freezers

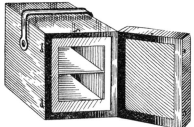

MARSHALL'S PATENT ICE CAVE
No. 2 holds 2 quart mould 105/-
No. 3 holds 4 quart mould 126/-
No. 4 holds 6 large champagne bottles .. 147/-

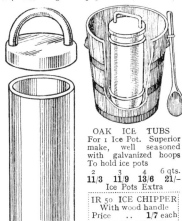

OAK ICE TUBS
For 1 Ice Pot. Superior make, well seasoned with galvanized hoops
To hold ice pots

2	3	4	6 qts.
11/3	11/9	13/6	21/-

Ice Pots Extra

IR 50 ICE CHIPPER
With wood handle
Price .. 1/7 each

ICE SPADDLES
In best pewter, with wood handles

21" 10/9	24" 13/3
30" 15/3	36" long 17/9

IR 255 BEST HARD METAL IMPROVED ICE CREAM FREEZING POTS

2	3	4	6	8 pts.
17/6	21/6	28/9	39/6	47/9

Larger sizes to order

AUTO VACUUM FREEZER
Made of wrought steel, japanned white. Freezes ice cream hard and smooth in 30 minutes. No turning, just fill and set aside. Approximate capacity

1	2	3	4 Qts.
14/-	18/-	24/6	27/6

THE 'RELIANCE' ICE CREAM FREEZER
The tubs are made from selected wood firmly bound with welded steel hoops. All cast parts are well galvanized. Cans are coated with pure tin

1	2	3	4 qts.
12/3	14/-	17/-	20/-
6	8	10 qts.	
27/-	36/-	50/-	

IR 248
Extra strong tin ice mould with loose cover and bottom Solid tinned copper tops fit inside the Auto Freezer
¾ pt., 5/3   1½ pts., 7/3

'WHITE MOUNTAIN' TRIPLE MOTION FREEZER
Very strong and durable

1	2	3	4	6 qts.
18/6	21/9	26/-	31/6	40/-
8	10	12	15 qts.	
51/9	66/9	83/6	100/-	

IR 568   BEST BOXWOOD SPATULES

8"	10"	12"	14"	16"
9d	1/-	1/4	1/6	1/10

BEST QUALITY ICE CAVE
Japanned green outside. White inside

7	8	9	10 in.
29/-	33/-	39/-	45/-

THE ICETTE REFRIGERATOR SAFE
Made of steel plates, stove enamelled in the new granite finish. Easy to clean and absolutely sanitary
Can also be supplied in white
No. 1 13½ × 12 × 20 ins. high **32/9** Stands **8/9** and
No. 2 15½ × 14 × 24 ins. ,, **48/-**   **12/6** extra.

ICE PRICKERS
Strong quality, wood handles, 1/1, 1/3, 1/6

AUTOMATIC ICE CREAM SERVER
Strongly made in nickel-plate. Bowl and knife of solid nickel. Indispensable for the quick serving of a measured quantity. Made in four sizes: 12, 16, 20 and 24 to the quart .. each 7/3

THE 'CRITON' HAND ICE MACHINE

Will make ice in any climate and is designed for obtaining small quantities of ice whenever desired. In hot countries this machine is an undoubted boon. It can always be kept ready for making ice at a minute's notice, and the importance of this can be readily appreciated in cases of illness It is easy to manipulate, and with ordinary care will last an indefinite period Price of machine, including Carafe and Vessel for making Block Ice, Ice Cream, etc., delivered free to Docks, London. Packing extra **£12 0 0**

Waterproof covers to keep the machine clean and dry .. **7/-**	Spare indiarubber rings for ice jar **2/-**	
Spare Acid Containers (absorbers) .. .. each **15/-**	Spare indiarubber rings for Wine Icer **1/6**	
Spare Carafes **3/6**	Spare tin of Compo Grease .. **6d.**	
Spare Ice Jars **6/-**	Spare vapour tubes **1/-**	
Vessel for Icing Wines, etc., in bottles .. .. each **22/-**	For hot climates we can supply a special vessel to hold three large 'Codd's' Soda Water	
Spare charge of special oil .. **1/9**	Bottles to be cooled at one	
Spare indiarubber suction tubes **3/-**	time. Price **48/-**	

The machine weighs about 48 lbs., and when charged with acid about 57 lbs.

MARSHALL'S PATENT FREEZER
Excellently made, and thoroughly reliable

To hold 1 qt.	2 qts.	4 qts.
60/-	**75/-**	**110/-**

IR 514. ICE CONVEYER
Prevents wastage in transit. Saves its cost in a very little time. Specially recommended for carrying ice to the suburbs. Holds 35 lbs. of ice. Inside lined with galvanized iron. Well insulated. Outside grained oak varnished
Size 18 × 9 × 14 ins. deep .. **38/6**

ALL PRICES ARE SUBJECT TO MARKET FLUCTUATIONS

IRONMONGERY DEPARTMENT
Well-made Gongs and Bells in Sounding Brass

IR 4279 BRASS TEA OR CALL BELL
3 ins. Price 5/-

IR 8477 NEWSPAPER RACK
Brass Frame and wirework. Oak base. $12\frac{1}{2} \times 5\frac{1}{2} \times 9\frac{1}{2}$ ins. high Price **12/6**

IR 9678 BRASS TEA OR CALL BELL
$2\frac{1}{2}$ ins. Price **3/9**

IR 1881 TABLE BELL
Brass base, nickel-plated Gong
$2\frac{3}{4}"$ $3"$ $3\frac{1}{2}"$ $4"$
6/-   **7/-**   **10/3**   **12/9**

IR 2234 LETTER RACK
Polished Brass on Oak base $9 \times 5\frac{1}{2}$ ins. overall. Price **17/6**

IR T5653 MUSIC OR PAPER RACKS
Polished Brass Stand with silk cord panels 31 ins. high. Oak board 12×6 ins. Price **22/6**

IR 2005 LETTER CAGES
Best quality Grooved Copper wire
$10"$ $12"$ $14"$
9/9   **11/3**   **13/9**

IR T4489 PIERCED BRASS LETTER RACK
Oak base. $4\frac{5}{8} \times 3\frac{1}{4} \times 4\frac{1}{2}$ ins. high Price **4/3**

IR 51 BRASS HAND BELLS
Sanded finish
3 ins. **3/10**
$3\frac{1}{2}$ ins. **4/6**
4 ins. **4/11**
5 ins. **8/6**
6 ins. **11/3**

IR 62
All polished
3 ins. **4/11**
$3\frac{1}{2}$ ins. **6/-**
4 ins. **6/9**
5 ins. **11/-**
6 ins. **15/3**

IR T5730 LETTER RACK
Polished Brass on Oak Back $11 \times 4\frac{1}{2}$ ins. Price **7/-** each

IR T4272 NEWSPAPER HOLDER
For reading at table. Holds the newspaper without adjustment $4\frac{1}{2} \times 4\frac{1}{2}$ base $\times$ 10 ins. high Price **8/6**

IR T3825 MUSIC OR PAPER RACK
Polished Brass Stand Fumed Oak Board $12\frac{3}{4} \times 7$ ins., height $30\frac{1}{2}$ ins. Price **35/-**

IR 5786 NEW PATTERN GONG (on right)
On Oak base, $5\frac{1}{2} \times 6$ ins. high. 5-in. Gong Brass Satin finish Price **30/-**

IR T5780 THE VICTORY TABLE GONG
Brass Satin Antique Brass finish. 6 ins. diam. On Oak base. $10\frac{1}{2} \times 3\frac{3}{4}$ ins. Height 13 ins. Price **35/-**

IR 4234 TABLE GONG
Polished Brass Frame and 6-in. Gong on Fumed Oak base. $7\frac{3}{4} \times 3\frac{1}{2}$ ins., height $9\frac{3}{4}$ ins. ... Price **21/-**

IR 252 'BURMAH' GONG AND STAND
In Fumed Oak, complete with 16-in. Gong and Beater **£5 3 6**
Plain Stands only, in Fumed or Black Oak
38/3, 45/-, 53/-, 61/9

IR 142
Gongs only, Chinese
12 ins. **16/6**   16 ins. **40/6**
14 ins. **27/-**   18 ins. **60/-**
Gong Beaters **2/6, 3/9, 5/6**

IR 4004 IRON GONG STAND
Rough Armour Bright, with 14-in. Gong and beater **74/3**
With 16-in. Gong and Beater ... **92/9**
With 18-in. Gong and Beater ... **126/-**
Stands only **43/6, 48/6, 60/3**

RESONO-PHONE CHIMES
On Fumed Oak stand. A set of vibrating metal plates, each fitted with resonating chamber of polished brass. Sweet and powerful, 5 notes **61/6**   8 notes **81/-**
Mahogany stand **67/-** and **87/6**

NEW RESONO-PHONE CHIMES
Very sweet and mellow; five notes, on high stand for floor

Fumed Oak 5 notes	**£6 10 3**
8 notes	**£8 13 0**
Mahogany 5 notes	**£7 1 3**
8 notes	**£9 7 6**

IR T5801 TABLE GONG
With 6-in. Polished Brass Gong on Oak Stand. $10\frac{1}{2} \times 3\frac{1}{2} \times 11$ ins. high ... **25/-**
If with 8-in. Gong ... **30/-**

IR T139 BRACKET GONG
6-in. diam. Copper and Brass finish, wood back. $8\frac{1}{2} \times 3\frac{1}{2}$ ins. Price **16/-**

IR 4063 EAGLE HEAD BRACKET GONG (on left)
With 12-in. Gong. Brass Satin Antique finish on Fumed Oak back $16\frac{1}{2} \times 11\frac{1}{2} \times 9$ ins. projection ... Price **125/-**

IR T5417 HANGING GONG
10 ins. diam. Brass Satin finish on Antique Oak Board $14\frac{3}{4} \times 7$ ins. .. Price **50/-**

IR T5787 BRACKET GONG
7 ins. long. Satin Brass finish on Oak back $9\frac{1}{4} \times 4\frac{1}{4}$ ins. Price **27/-**

IR 5723 BRACKET GONG
With 10-in. Gong. Satin Brass finish on Oak back. $15\frac{1}{4} \times 7\frac{1}{2}$ ins. Price **47/6**
Oxidized Silver finish .. **59/3**

IR T661 BRACKET GONG
Polished Reindeer Head and 6-in. Gong on Oak Back $8\frac{1}{4} \times 3\frac{1}{2}$ ins. Price **21/-**

IR 4816 TIGER BRACKET GONG
Brass Head: Satin finished on Polished Fumed Oak Back $12\frac{1}{2} \times 8\frac{1}{2}$ ins. Gong 11 ins. Price **95/-**

ALL PRICES ARE SUBJECT TO MARKET FLUCTUATIONS

HARRODS LTD

Telephone SLOANE 1234
Telegrams 'EVERYTHING HARRODS LONDON'

LONDON SW 1

IRONMONGERY DEPARTMENT
Unsurpassed Quality—Labour Savers for the Kitchen

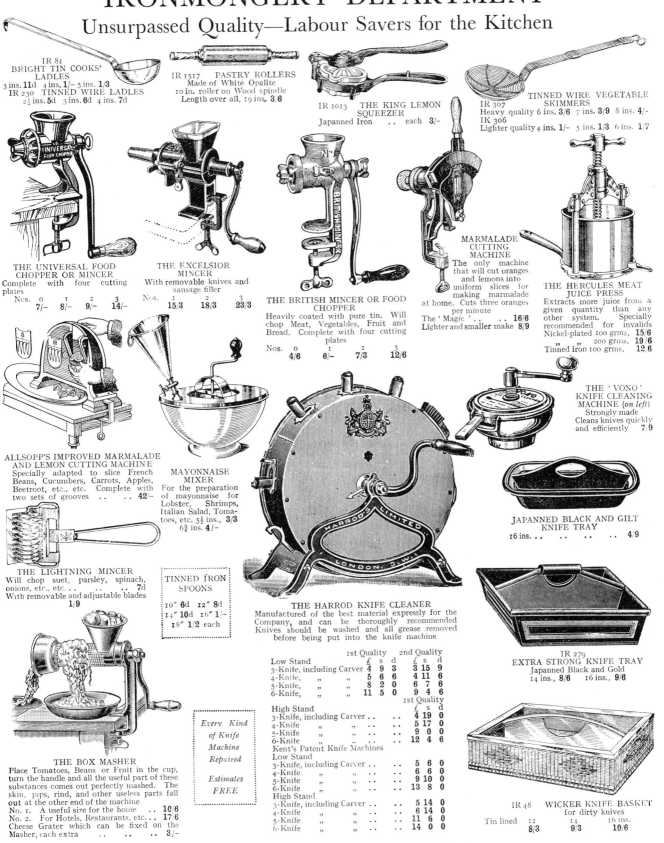

IR 81 BRIGHT TIN COOKS' LADLES
3 ins. **11d** 4 ins. **1/-** 5 ins. **1/3**
IR 230 TINNED WIRE LADLES
2½ ins. **5d** 3 ins. **6d** 4 ins. **7d**

IR 1517 PASTRY ROLLERS
Made of White Opalite
10 in. roller on Wood spindle
Length over all, 19 ins. **3/6**

IR 1013 THE KING LEMON SQUEEZER
Japanned Iron .. each **3/-**

IR 307 TINNED WIRE VEGETABLE SKIMMERS
Heavy quality 6 ins. **3/6** 7 ins. **3/9** 8 ins. **4/-**
IK 306
Lighter quality 4 ins. **1/-** 5 ins. **1/3** 6 ins. **1/7**

THE UNIVERSAL FOOD CHOPPER OR MINCER
Complete with four cutting plates

Nos.	0	1	2	3
	7/-	**8/-**	**9/-**	**14/-**

THE EXCELSIOR MINCER
With removable knives and sausage filler

Nos.	1	2	3
	15/3	**18/3**	**23/3**

THE BRITISH MINCER OR FOOD CHOPPER
Heavily coated with pure tin. Will chop Meat, Vegetables, Fruit and Bread. Complete with four cutting plates

Nos.	0	1	2	3
	4/6	**6/-**	**7/3**	**12/6**

MARMALADE CUTTING MACHINE
The only machine that will cut oranges and lemons into uniform slices for making marmalade at home. Cuts three oranges per minute
The 'Magic' .. **16/6**
Lighter and smaller make **8/9**

THE HERCULES MEAT JUICE PRESS
Extracts more juice from a given quantity than any other system. Specially recommended for invalids
Nickel-plated 100 grms. **15/6**
  " " 200 grms. **19/6**
Tinned iron 100 grms. **12/6**

ALLSOPP'S IMPROVED MARMALADE AND LEMON CUTTING MACHINE
Specially adapted to slice French Beans, Cucumbers, Carrots, Apples, Beetroot, etc., etc. Complete with two sets of grooves .. **42/-**

MAYONNAISE MIXER
For the preparation of mayonnaise for Lobster, Shrimps, Italian Salad, Tomatoes, etc. 5½ ins., **3/3**
6¾ ins. **4/-**

THE 'VONO' KNIFE CLEANING MACHINE (*on left*)
Strongly made
Cleans knives quickly and efficiently **7/9**

JAPANNED BLACK AND GILT KNIFE TRAY
16 ins. **4/9**

THE LIGHTNING MINCER
Will chop suet, parsley, spinach, onions, etc., etc. **7d**
With removable and adjustable blades **1/9**

TINNED IRON SPOONS
10" **6d** 12" **8d**
14" **10d** 16" **1/-**
18" **1/2** each

THE HARROD KNIFE CLEANER
Manufactured of the best material expressly for the Company, and can be thoroughly recommended Knives should be washed and all grease removed before being put into the knife machine

	1st Quality £ s d			2nd Quality £ s d		
Low Stand						
3-Knife, including Carver	4	9	3	3	15	9
4-Knife, " "	5	6	6	4	11	6
5-Knife, " "	8	2	0	6	7	6
6-Knife, " "	11	5	0	9	4	6

	1st Quality £ s d		
High Stand			
3-Knife, including Carver	4	19	0
4-Knife " "	5	17	0
5-Knife " "	9	0	0
6-Knife " "	12	4	6
Kent's Patent Knife Machines			
Low Stand			
3-Knife, including Carver	5	6	0
4-Knife " "	6	6	0
5-Knife " "	9	10	0
6-Knife " "	13	8	0
High Stand			
3-Knife, including Carver	5	14	0
4-Knife " "	6	14	0
5-Knife " "	11	6	0
6-Knife " "	14	0	0

IR 279 EXTRA STRONG KNIFE TRAY
Japanned Black and Gold
14 ins., **8/6** 16 ins., **9/6**

Every Kind of Knife Machine Repaired
Estimates FREE

THE BOX MASHER
Place Tomatoes, Beans or Fruit in the cup, turn the handle and all the useful part of these substances comes out perfectly mashed. The skin, pips, rind, and other useless parts fall out at the other end of the machine
No. 1. A useful size for the home .. **10/6**
No. 2. For Hotels, Restaurants, etc. .. **17/6**
Cheese Grater which can be fixed on the Masher, each extra **3/-**

IR 48 WICKER KNIFE BASKET
for dirty knives

Tin lined	12	14	16 ins.
	8/3	**9/3**	**10/6**

ALL PRICES ARE SUBJECT TO MARKET FLUCTUATIONS

HARRODS LTD

Telephone SLOANE 1234
Telegrams 'EVERYTHING HARRODS LONDON'

LONDON SW1

IRONMONGERY DEPARTMENT
Moulds and Shapes that Make Your Cooking More Interesting

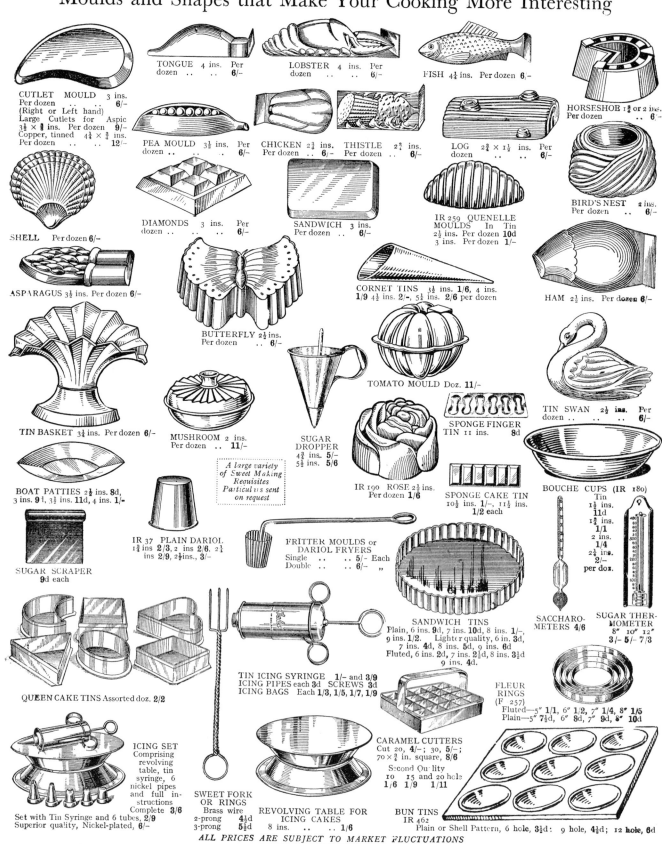

CUTLET MOULD 3 ins.
Per dozen 6/-
(Right or Left hand)
Large Cutlets for Aspic
3½ × ⅞ ins. Per dozen 9/-
Copper, tinned 4¼ × ¾ ins.
Per dozen 12/-

TONGUE 4 ins. Per dozen 6/-

LOBSTER 4 ins. Per dozen 6/-

FISH 4½ ins. Per dozen 6/-

HORSESHOE 1¾ or 2 ins. Per dozen 6/-

PEA MOULD 3½ ins. Per dozen 6/-

CHICKEN 2¾ ins. Per dozen .. 6/-

THISTLE 2¼ ins. Per dozen .. 6/-

LOG 2¾ × 1½ ins. Per dozen 6/-

SHELL Per dozen 6/-

DIAMONDS 3 ins. Per dozen 6/-

SANDWICH 3 ins. Per dozen 6/-

IR 259 QUENELLE MOULDS In Tin
2½ ins. Per dozen 10d
3 ins. Per dozen 1/-

BIRD'S NEST 2 ins. Per dozen 6/-

ASPARAGUS 3½ ins. Per dozen 6/-

BUTTERFLY 2½ ins. Per dozen 6/-

CORNET TINS 3½ ins. 1/6, 4 ins.
1/9 4½ ins. 2/-, 5½ ins. 2/6 per dozen

HAM 2½ ins. Per dozen 6/-

TIN BASKET 3¾ ins. Per dozen 6/-

MUSHROOM 2 ins. Per dozen 11/-

SUGAR DROPPER
4¾ ins. 5/-
5½ ins. 5/6

TOMATO MOULD Doz. 11/-

SPONGE FINGER TIN 11 ins. 8d

TIN SWAN 2½ ins. Per dozen 6/-

BOAT PATTIES 2½ ins. 8d,
3 ins. 9d, 3½ ins. 11d, 4 ins. 1/-

A large variety of Sweet Making Requisites Particulars sent on request

IR 190 ROSE 2½ ins. Per dozen 1/6

SPONGE CAKE TIN
10½ ins. 1/-, 11½ ins.
1/2 each

BOUCHE CUPS (IR 180)
Tin
1½ ins. 11d
1¾ ins. 1/1
2 ins. 1/4
2½ ins. 2/-
per doz.

SUGAR SCRAPER
9d each

IR 37 PLAIN DARIOL
1¾ ins 2/3, 2 ins 2/6, 2¼
ins 2/9, 2½ ins., 3/-

FRITTER MOULDS or DARIOL FRYERS
Single .. .. 5/- Each
Double .. .. 6/- „

SANDWICH TINS
Plain, 6 ins. 9d, 7 ins. 10d, 8 ins. 1/-,
9 ins. 1/2. Lighter quality, 6 in. 3d,
7 ins. 4d, 8 ins. 5d, 9 ins. 6d
Fluted, 6 ins. 2d, 7 ins. 2½d, 8 ins. 3½d
9 ins. 4d.

SACCHARO-METERS 4/6

SUGAR THER-MOMETER
8″ 10″ 12″
3/- 5/- 7/3

QUEEN CAKE TINS Assorted doz. 2/2

TIN ICING SYRINGE 1/- and 3/9
ICING PIPES each 3d SCREWS 3d
ICING BAGS Each 1/3, 1/5, 1/7, 1/9

FLEUR RINGS
(F 257)
Fluted—5″ 1/1, 6″ 1/2, 7″ 1/4, 8″ 1/5
Plain—5″ 7½d, 6″ 8d, 7″ 9d, 8″ 10d

ICING SET
Comprising
revolving
table, tin
syringe, 6
nickel pipes
and full in-
structions
Complete 3/6
Set with Tin Syringe and 6 tubes, 2/9
Superior quality, Nickel-plated, 6/-

SWEET FORK OR RINGS
Brass wire
2-prong 4½d
3-prong 5½d
.. .. 1/6

REVOLVING TABLE FOR ICING CAKES
8 ins. 1/6

CARAMEL CUTTERS
Cut 20, 4/-; 30, 5/-;
70 × ¾ in. square, 8/6
Second Quality
10 15 and 20 hole
1/6 1/9 1/11

BUN TINS
IR 462
Plain or Shell Pattern, 6 hole, 3½d: 9 hole, 4½d; 12 hole, 6d

ALL PRICES ARE SUBJECT TO MARKET FLUCTUATIONS
Telephone SLOANE 1234
Telegrams 'EVERYTHING HARRODS LONDON'

HARRODS LTD   **LONDON S W 1**

IRONMONGERY DEPARTMENT
Moulds and Cutters Attractively Designed

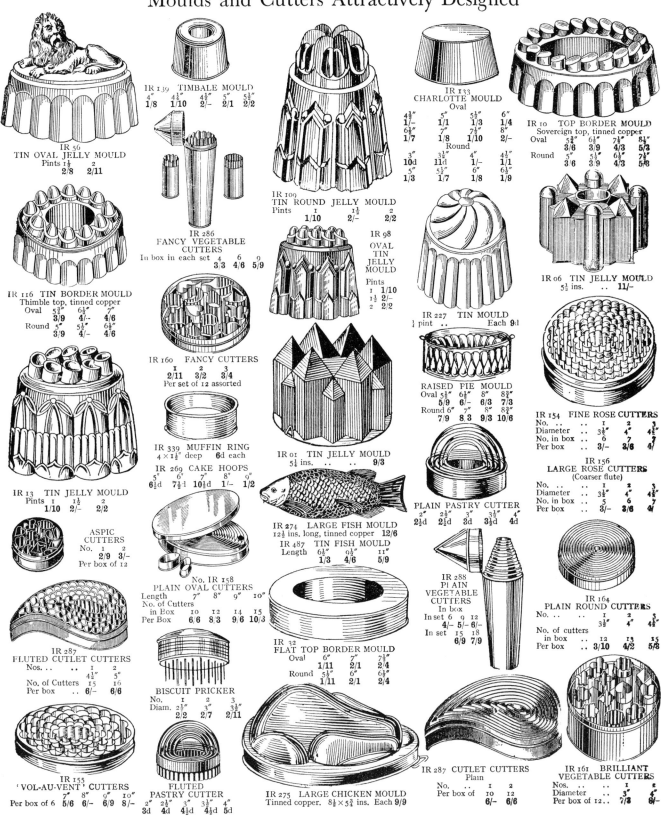

IR 56
TIN OVAL JELLY MOULD
Pints 1½ 2
2/8 2/11

IR 139 TIMBALE MOULD
4″ 4¼″ 4½″ 5″ 5½″
1/8 1/10 2/- 2/1 2/2

IR 286
FANCY VEGETABLE CUTTERS
In box in each set 4 6 9
3/3 4/6 5/9

IR 116 TIN BORDER MOULD
Thimble top, tinned copper
Oval 5¾″ 6½″ 7″
3/9 4/- 4/6
Round 5″ 5½″ 6¼″
3/9 4/- 4/6

IR 160 FANCY CUTTERS
1 2 3
2/11 3/2 3/4
Per set of 12 assorted

IR 339 MUFFIN RING
4 × 1½″ deep 6d each
IR 269 CAKE HOOPS
5″ 6″ 7″ 8″ 9″
6½d 7½d 10½d 1/- 1/2

IR 13 TIN JELLY MOULD
Pints 1 1½ 2
1/10 2/- 2/2

ASPIC CUTTERS
No. 1 2
2/9 3/-
Per box of 12

No. IR 158
PLAIN OVAL CUTTERS
Length 7″ 8″ 9″ 10″
No. of Cutters
in Box 10 12 14 15
Per Box 6/6 8/3 9/6 10/3

IR 287
FLUTED CUTLET CUTTERS
Nos. 1 2
4½″ 5″
No. of Cutters 15 16
Per box 6/- 6/6

BISCUIT PRICKER
No. 1 2 3
Diam. 2½″ 3″ 3½″
2/2 2/7 2/11

FLUTED PASTRY CUTTER
2″ 2½″ 3″ 3½″ 4″
3d 4d 4½d 4½d 5d

IR 155
'VOL-AU-VENT' CUTTERS
7″ 8″ 9″ 10″
Per box of 6 5/6 6/- 6/9 8/6

IR 109
TIN ROUND JELLY MOULD
Pints 1 1½ 2
1/10 2/- 2/2

IR 98
OVAL TIN JELLY MOULD
Pints
1 1/10
1½ 2/-
2 2/2

IR 01 TIN JELLY MOULD
5¼ ins. .. 9/3

IR 274 LARGE FISH MOULD
12½ ins. long, tinned copper 12/6
IR 487 TIN FISH MOULD
Length 6½″ 9½″ 11″
1/3 4/6 5/9

IR 32
FLAT TOP BORDER MOULD
Oval 6″ 7″ 7½″
1/11 2/1 2/4
Round 5½″ 6″ 6½″
1/11 2/1 2/4

IR 275 LARGE CHICKEN MOULD
Tinned copper. 8½ × 5¾ ins. Each 9/9

IR 133
CHARLOTTE MOULD
Oval
4½″ 5″ 5½″ 6″
1/- 1/1 1/3 1/4
6½″ 7″ 7½″ 8″
1/7 1/8 1/10 2/-
Round
3″ 3½″ 4″ 4½″
10d 11d 1/- 1/1
5″ 5½″ 6″ 6½″
1/3 1/7 1/8 1/9

IR 227 TIN MOULD
½ pint .. Each 9d

RAISED PIE MOULD
Oval 5½″ 6½″ 8″ 8½″
5/9 6/- 6/3 7/3
Round 6″ 7″ 8″ 8¾″
7/9 8/3 9/3 10/6

PLAIN PASTRY CUTTER
2″ 2½″ 3″ 3½″ 3½″
2½d 2½d 3d 3½d 4d

IR 288
PLAIN VEGETABLE CUTTERS
In box
In set 6 9 12
4/- 5/- 6/-
In set 15 18
6/9 7/9

IR 287 CUTLET CUTTERS
Plain
No. 1 2
Per box of 10 12
6/- 6/6

IR 10 TOP BORDER MOULD
Sovereign top, tinned copper
Oval 5¾″ 6½″ 7¼″ 8¼″
3/6 3/9 4/3 5/3
Round 5″ 5½″ 6½″ 7½″
3/6 3/9 4/3 5/3

IR 06 TIN JELLY MOULD
5½ ins. .. 11/-

IR 154 FINE ROSE CUTTERS
No. 1 2 3
Diameter .. 3½″ 4″ 4½″
No. in box .. 6 7 7
Per box .. 3/- 3/6 4/-

IR 156
LARGE ROSE CUTTERS
(Coarser flute)
No. 1 2 3
Diameter .. 3½″ 4″ 4½″
No. in box .. 5 6 7
Per box .. 3/- 3/6 4/-

IR 164
PLAIN ROUND CUTTERS
No. 1 2 3
3½″ 4″ 4½″
No. of cutters
in box .. 12 13 15
Per box .. 3/10 4/2 5/8

IR 161 BRILLIANT VEGETABLE CUTTERS
Nos. 1 2
Diameter .. 3″ 4″
Per box of 12.. 7/3 8/-

ALL PRICES ARE SUBJECT TO MARKET FLUCTUATIONS

HARRODS LTD

Telephone SLOANE 1234
Telegrams 'EVERYTHING HARRODS LONDON'

LONDON S W 1

IRONMONGERY DEPARTMENT

Harrods Show a Most Up-To-Date Range of Refrigerators

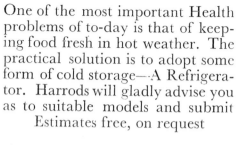

One of the most important Health problems of to-day is that of keeping food fresh in hot weather. The practical solution is to adopt some form of cold storage—A Refrigerator. Harrods will gladly advise you as to suitable models and submit Estimates free, on request

THE DOUBLE HOUSEHOLD REFRIGERATOR

(At right) Made of well-seasoned wood. Heavy insulation, galvanized steel lined throughout. Grained oak and varnished exterior. Superior nickelled hinges and fasteners

No.	Height	Width	Depth	
22	34 ins.	37 ins.	17 ins.	£6 19 6
23	37 ins.	43 ins.	20 ins	£8 15 0

HARRODS CABINET No. 6

Height	Width	Depth	
54 ins.	26 ins.	18 ins.	£13 10 0

For description see foot of Page

Purchases value of £5 and over are sent carriage paid to any goods station in England and Wales

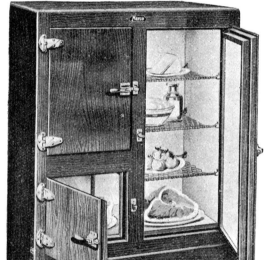

Models 7, 8, 9

THE SINGLE HOUSEHOLD REFRIGERATOR

Lined throughout galvanized iron. Grained oak and varnished oak exterior

No.	Height	Width	Depth	
20	30 ins.	23 ins.	17 ins.	£3 17 6
21	34 ins.	27 ins.	17 ins.	£4 19 6

THE 'HARROD' CABINET REFRIGERATOR

White Enamelled, Lined Food Chambers

The scientific construction of the 'Harrod' Cabinet Refrigerator reduces the consumption of ice to a minimum. A distinct advantage is the completely separate chamber for the ice, which is not exposed to the outside air when putting in or taking out foodstuffs; this obviates waste, and renders these cabinets both economical and efficient. Exterior grained and varnished oak

No.	1	2	3	5
Height	37 ins.	42 ins.	48 ins.	50 ins.
Width	22 ins.	25 ins.	28 ins.	33 ins.
Depth	17 ins.	18 ins.	20 ins.	21 ins.
Prices	£7 15	£9 10	£12 10	£15 10

No.	6	7	8	9
Height	54 ins.	46 ins.	50 ins.	54 ins.
Width	26 ins.	35 ins.	38 ins.	44 ins.
Depth	18 ins.	20 ins.	21 ins.	23 ins.
Prices	£13 10	£17 17	£20 0	£27 0

The insulation consists of best quality compressed cork slabs which renders the Refrigerator impervious to outside changes of temperature. The Ice Containers are so constructed that the larger size from No. 6 upwards can be fitted with any standard automatic electric cooling apparatus

Model No. 5

Models 1, 2, 3

Nos. 1 and 2 have one shelf only

ALL PRICES ARE SUBJECT TO MARKET FLUCTUATIONS

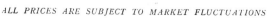
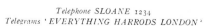

HARRODS LTD

Telephone SLOANE 1234
Telegrams 'EVERYTHING HARRODS LONDON'

LONDON S W 1

IRONMONGERY DEPARTMENT
Automatic Electrical and Gas Refrigerators

HARRODS have a large variety of the most up-to-date models. Customers are invited to see these models actually working in the Ironmongery Department on the Second Floor.

The 'FRIGIDAIRE'

This new type of Refrigerator requires no ice and no attention. It maintains automatically a dry, crisp, cold temperature in which food can be kept in perfect safety for days on end, its purity and freshness assured. And, in addition, it supplies a quantity of ice cubes for drinks

The cabinets have seamless porcelain linings with no corners or crevices to collect dust and germs and are silent in operation, self-starting and stopping, self-oiling and air cooled. They are made in a large range of sizes suitable for the smallest flat or the largest mansion

All these Refrigerators can be secured on Harrods Easy Terms

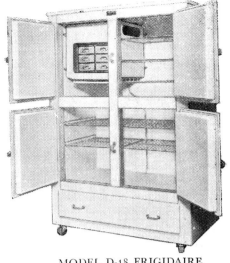

MODEL D-18 FRIGIDAIRE

The Model D-18 is the largest of the Frigidaire household cabinets. The Model D-18 contains twenty-seven square feet of shelf space, and has a capacity of approximately 18 cubic feet

A large drawer for storing vegetables which do not require refrigeration is placed at the bottom. The dimensions of the Model D-18 are : width, 46½ ins. ; depth, 28 ins. ; and height, 67¾ ins.

£160 0 0
(Installation extra)

MODEL D-7 FRIGIDAIRE

This model has available for the storage of food more than eleven square feet of shelf space and has an interior capacity of almost seven cubic feet

The interior of the Model D-7 is of one-piece pure white porcelain with rounded corners and the exterior is finished in enduring white Duco

The Model D-7 is equipped with a Frigidaire cooling coil and the Model A silent air-cooled compressor

The dimensions of the Model D-7 are : width, 33 ins. ; depth 28 ins. ; and height 62 ins.

£92 0 0
(Installation extra)

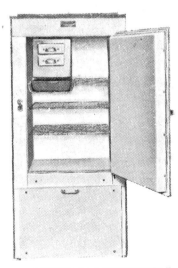

MODEL V-5 FRIGIDAIRE

Model V-5 Frigidaire is particularly adapted to the small household. Inside area is approximately five cubic feet and contains more than eight square feet of shelf space. The Model V-5 Frigidaire occupies a minimum amount of floor space for its capacity. It is 26¾ ins. wide ; 26¼ ins. deep, and 56½ ins. high

£49 10 0
(Installation extra)

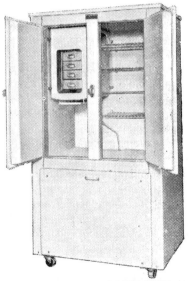

MODEL D-9 FRIGIDAIRE

The Model D-9 Frigidaire contains over fourteen square feet of shelf space for the storage of food, and has an interior capacity of more than nine cubic feet

All the refrigerating equipment as in other Models, is totally enclosed. The dimensions of the Model D-9 are : width, 37¼ ins. ; depth, 28 ins. ; height, 67¾ ins.

£116 0 0
(Installation extra)

ALL PRICES ARE SUBJECT TO MARKET FLUCTUATIONS

PERAMBULATOR DEPARTMENT
Baby Carriages Scientifically Constructed for Smooth Motion

THE 'MAYFAIR' MAIL CAR

A three-position car for all baby's carriage needs. An extension provides a full length bed of 46 ins. for sleeping. Tray when lowered forms an ideal sitting-up car Mounted on flexible strap-hung Cee Steel springs and comfortably upholstered with loose cushions
Grade A Plain coach-built body. Leather-lined hood and coverall apron with storm front. Nickel fittings. Equal size ⅞-in. ribbed tyred wheels £12 12 0
Grade B A superior model with beaded panels as illustrated. ⅞-in. tyred ball-bearing wheels £14 19 6

THE 'SLOANE'

A comfortable and roomy Pram-car mounted on cantilever springs and 12-in. ball-bearing Sorbo-tyred wheels. Upholstered leather cloth, with rubber duck hood and apron with storm flap. Bed length with extension, 43 ins...£11 15 0

THE 'SLOANE'

THE 'MAYFAIR'

> **Baby Carriages cannot be sent out on approval**

THE 'CADOGAN'

An all-purpose carriage which allows an infant to recline at full length (bed measurement is about 32 ins.) and an older child to sit up at the same time in front; or can be used for two children sitting. If required for one child only, front seat can be reversed, giving car the appearance of an ordinary single bed-car. Mounted on strong Steel Cee springs with leather straps and direct spoke ⅞-in. ball-bearing wheels. Rubber duck hood and apron £10 10 0

THE 'STIRLING'

Wonderfully convenient—a car that can be kept under a table or in any odd corner when not in use, yet gives a comfortable, ample bed, with an extension of 32 inches. Hood and apron are lined with washable leather cloth. Folding handle is tubular nickel-plated with celluloid grip. Mounted on Steel Cee springs with leather straps and 10 inch wheels. Measurements, with handle folded: Height 29 ins., length 37 ins., width 24 ins.
£5 10 0

THE 'RUSSELL'

A strongly-made car, upholstered in leather cloth with detachable hood lined with washable leather cloth Mounted on outside Steel Cee springs, with leather straps, nickel-plated fittings, 12-in. wheels and apron Can be supplied with handle levers in front, for child to face the nurse, without extra charge
Fitted direct spoke plain bearing wheels with ⅝-in. white ribbed cushion tyres £6 6 0
Fitted direct spoke plain bearing wheels with ⅞-in. white ribbed cushion tyres £6 17 6
Fitted tangent spoke ball-bearing wheels, rubber duck hood and apron £7 19 6
Larger size, with handles at back only .. £9 19 6

THE 'MARMET'

Models EX & EXR Mounted on Marmet 8-spring underslung chassis. Plated fittings, hood with adjustable joints, apron with storm flap, and safety strap and brake. Tangent spoke wheels, with ⅝-in. white ribbed cushion tyres £5 5 0

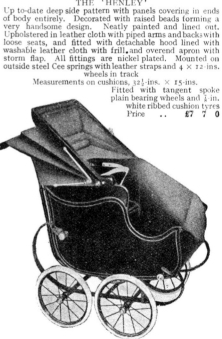

THE 'HENLEY'

Up-to-date deep side pattern with panels covering in ends of body entirely. Decorated with raised beads forming a very handsome design. Neatly painted and lined out. Upholstered in leather cloth with piped arms and backs with loose seats, and fitted with detachable hood lined with washable leather cloth with frill and overend apron with storm flap. All fittings are nickel plated. Mounted on outside steel Cee springs with leather straps and 4 × 12-ins. wheels in track
Measurements on cushions, 32½-ins. × 15-ins.
Fitted with tangent spoke plain bearing wheels and ⅞-in. white ribbed cushion tyres
Price .. £7 7 0

THE 'MARMET'

THE 'RUSSELL'

ALL PRICES ARE SUBJECT TO MARKET FLUCTUATIONS

HARRODS LTD

Telephone SLOANE 1234
Telegrams 'EVERYTHING HARRODS LONDON'

LONDON S W 1

PERAMBULATOR DEPARTMENT

Harrods Perambulators are not only Smart in Appearance but they Afford the Utmost Comfort

MARMET MODEL 'F'

Mounted on patent, underslung, shock-absorbing buffer chassis, with 8-spring suspension. Complete with plated fittings, piped arms and backs, loose cushions, frilled hood with adjustable joints, over-end apron with storm flap, safety strap and safety brake. Measurements 29 × 14 ins. on cushions. Marmet tangent spoke cycle wheels, with plated hubs, beaded rims, adjustable bearings, and ⅞-in. white ribbed cushion tyres .. **£7 7 0**

Model F. de Luxe. Plated handle levers and springs, Marmet ball-bearing wheels and best leather duck hood and apron .. **£9 9 0**

Model FA Specification as Model F. above, but larger. 30 × 15 ins. on cushions **£8 8 0**

Model FA de Luxe. Specification as Model F. de Luxe **£9 19 0**

Model FB Specification as Model FA. above but larger. 33 × 16 ins. on cushions .. **£8 19 6**

Model FB. de Luxe. Specification as Model FA. de Luxe **£10 19 6**

THE 'DOVER'

Attractively cosy carriage; coach built; deep and roomy. Measures 33 × 14 ins. on the bed. Well painted and decorated with mouldings on panels. Upholstered in Crockett's leather cloth, with square piped elbows and loose cushions. Leather cloth hood, lined leather cloth, with lace. Storm apron. Nickel-plated fittings. Mounted on cranked, outside, strap hung, Cee springs, with ⅞-in. white ribbed tangent spoke wheels

£8 8 0

THE 'SIDMOUTH'

Exceptionally deep, broad, model mounted on new patent concealed spring chassis, hidden within the body of the carriage. Nickel-plated folding handles, piped arms and laced hood. Storm apron with rain flap, both lined with sanitary leather cloth. Bed measures 32 × 14 ins. Direct spoke ⅞-in. white ribbed balloon cushion tyres

£5 5 0

Or mounted on strapped Cee springs

£5 5 0

Or Pedigree Tubular chassis **£5 19 6**

Marmet Model 'F'

THE 'PRINCESS'

A smart, serviceable, model mounted upon long flexible flat Cee springs with equal size wheels, as illustrated; fitted with high or low wheels if desired. Upholstered leather cloth, with loose cushions and square piping. Rubber duck hood with lace and coverall apron with storm front. ⅞-in. ribbed lace spoke ball-bearing wheels Size 34 × 15 ins. on bed

£14 14 0

THE 'MELTON'

Newest design in a deep and roomy carriage, upholstered in leather cloth, with loose seat cushions. Detachable rubber duck hood lined with washable leather cloth and finished with frill, over-end apron and storm flap. Mounted on outside Cee springs. Fitted with tangent spoke ball-bearing wheels, ⅞-in. white ribbed cushion tyres. Measurements on cushions 33 × 15 ins.

£10 19 6

THE 'EXMOUTH'

Specially designed to allow twin infants to recline comfortably, or one child to sit and one to recline. Hoods are lined with washable leather cloth and equipped with adjustable joints. Loose seat cushions and nickel-plated fittings. Mounted on outside Steel Cee springs with leather straps. Tangent spoke ball-bearing wheels with ⅞-inch white ribbed cushion tyres and rubber duck hoods and apron. Bed measurements, 38 × 17 ins.

£17 17 0

The 'Princess'

ALL PRICES ARE SUBJECT TO MARKET FLUCTUATIONS

HARRODS LTD

Telephone SLOANE 1234
Telegrams 'EVERYTHING HARRODS LONDON'

LONDON S W 1

PERAMBULATOR DEPARTMENT
Invalid Carriages that are Unequalled for Comfort and Durability

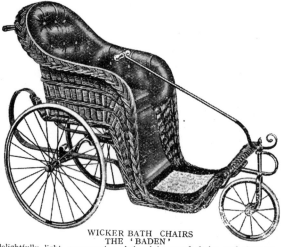

WICKER BATH CHAIRS
THE 'BADEN'

A delightfully light, easy-running chair of improved design and distinguished character. Suspended on flexible Cee springs with leather braces, and mounted on superior quality cycle wheels, with wired-on rubber tyres, complete with self-guiding front wheel. The front wheel fork is mounted in a new type of socket which prevents any possibility of rattle and which is adjustable for wear. Fitted with a firm foot-board close to the ground, affording ease of access

	Small size	Medium size	Large size
Price (exclusive of cushions or upholstery) ..	£11 0 0	£12 15 0	£13 10 0
Padded and Upholstered Back and Sides, and loose Seat Cushion, covered in superior quality leather-cloth, Apron of same material, lined with cloth, and Coco-nut Mat	£3 2 6	£3 10 0	£4 10 0

NOTE—Upholstery for Back and Sides can be supplied loose if required

THE FOLLOWING ARE SUPPLIED AS REQUIRED, EXTRA :—

Hood, double carriage-jointed, covered in extra quality stout leather-cloth	£7 12 6	
Hood, adjustable to any position by quadrant fitting, covered in superior leather-cloth and lined with cloth	4 15 0	
Swivel, for holding umbrella or sunshade in any position	15 0	
Leg Rest	1 1 0	
Provision Basket, painted to match body of chair. Complete with straps for fixing ..	10 0	
Ball Bearings to above direct spoke, solid tyred, wheels	3 0 0	
Laced Spoke ball bearing wheels with Clincher Pneumatic Tyres	5 0 0	
With Resilient Cushion Tyres.	7 10 0	
Carters' 'FLEXIBLE' BRAKE can be fitted to the above. price ..	3 15 0	

SPINAL CARRIAGES
THE 'SOUTHSEA' (WICKER)
ADOPTED BY THE BRITISH RED CROSS SOCIETY.
TO ORDER ONLY

The 'Southsea' is an excellent type of Wicker Carriage, of the best materials and workmanship ; light, roomy, easy running, and inexpensive. The body is entirely suspended on flexible and resilient inverted Cee pattern springs, and cycle wheels fitted with wired-on rubber tyres. To those of moderate means this carriage is specially recommended, and it will be found thoroughly satisfactory in Appearance, Durability and Value. The wicker body is carefully strengthened at all necessary points. Well painted and finished throughout

	'Southsea' Carriage	Superior leather-cloth Apron, lined cloth, and Mattress—EXTRA	Special quality Carriage, jointed leather-cloth Hood lined cloth—EXTRA
4 feet	£12 0 0	£2 17 6	£3 10 0
4 feet 6 inches	13 10 0	3 2 6	3 10 0
5 feet	16 0 0	3 7 6	3 10 0
5 feet 6 inches	16 15 0	3 12 6	4 0 0
6 feet	17 10 0	3 17 6	4 0 0

EXTRA

A light framed stretcher, with webbing handles for lifting invalid in and out of carriage	£2 7 6
Ball Bearings to above direct spoke, solid tyred, wheels	4 0 0
Laced Spoke ball bearing wheels with Clincher Pneumatic Tyres ..	7 0 0
With Resilient Cushion Tyres	10 0 0

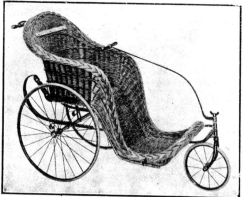

WICKER INVALID CARRIAGE

Cee springs with guide rod. Easy riding and comfortable. Made in sizes as below

Small Size. Width of Seat, inside measurement 14 ins.	£7 2 6
Medium Size ,, ,, ,, ,, 16½ ins.	7 17 6
Large Size ,, ,, ,, ,, 18 ins.	9 5 0

Bath Chair Wheels, 25 ins. × 12 ins. with ¾ in. Grey Wired-on Tyres to medium and large sizes, and 23 ins. × 12 ins. with ⅝ in. Tyres to small sizes

EXTRAS

Cushion only..	17 6
Upholstering..	£1 17 6
Apron	1 11 6
Hood	5 0 0

¾-in. Bath Chair Wheels can be fitted to small size at an extra cost of 10/6

FOLDING INVALID CHAIR

A juvenile Model similar in all details to chair on right, at the same price. Suitable for young persons from 12 years upwards, or an adult of small stature

STANDS SECURE WHEN FOLDED

FOLDING INVALID CHAIR

A perfectly-made model that runs smoothly and encourages patients to take advantage of outdoor air the whole year round The chair is scientifically constructed to enable an average person to wheel and control a full adult patient without strain or fatigue

Standard Model, ⅝-in. solid rubber tyres, either size ..	£2 17 6
,, ,, Balloon Cushion tyres, tangent plated hub wheels	£3 12 6

ALL PRICES ARE SUBJECT TO MARKET FLUCTUATIONS

HARRODS LTD

Telephone SLOANE 1234
Telegrams 'EVERYTHING HARRODS LONDON'

LONDON S W 1

SEWING MACHINE DEPARTMENT

Harrods fine Selection of Hand and Treadle Sewing Machines

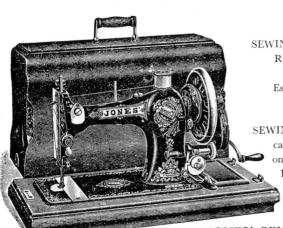

SEWING MACHINES
Repaired and
Cleaned
Estimates free

SEWING MACHINES
cannot be sent
on Approval or
Exchanged

VICKERS SEWING MACHINE
A vibrating Shuttle Sewing Machine of the highest quality and finish throughout, fitted with all the latest improvements, including reversible feed. Full particulars from Harrods
Hand Machine **£5 2 6**

A PERFECT HAND SEWING MACHINE
This is a duplicate of the Lock-stitch model supplied to Her Majesty the Queen. Any sort of sewing can be done on it, no matter how fine or coarse your material is. It can be used by hand or with a treadle. Made with Walnut base and ornamental cover **£6 6 0**

JONES' SEWING MACHINES

LOCKSTITCH SEWING MACHINE
A most reliable Machine at the lowest possible cost Each Machine is supplied with a number of useful labour-saving accessories and full instructions
Price **£2 19 6**

'THREE-DRAWER' DROP HEAD TABLE (CLOSED)
Jones' Drop Head Table has many advantages over any other Machine of this type. The Machine lowers easily and without complication into a dust-proof case below the Table when not required and the large extension leaf folds over the top, making a really useful and beautiful Table
JONES' FAMILY C.S., MEDIUM C.S. AND SPOOL MACHINES
are supplied, as illustrated, in Oak or Walnut
All machines are mounted on New light-running Stand fitted with Adjustable Ball Bearings .. From **£11 11 0**

THE 'WILLCOX & GIBBS' AUTOMATIC CHAINSTITCH SEWING MACHINE
Hand Machine, Automatic **£10 10 0**
Box for Hand Machine **12/6**
The following Accessories, enclosed in a neat box, accompany each Family Sewing Machine :—Guide, Guide-screw, Common Hemmer, Self-sewer, Quilter, Braider (in presser foot), one dozen Needles, Needle-Wrench, Oiler (filled), Stiletto, Gatherer and Instruction Book
To order only

HAND SEWING MACHINE
Perfect in Action. Quick, Durable, Light Running
No. 50 HAND MACHINE, with Cover and Set of Attachments **£5 12 6**
No. 60 Same Machine, with Flush Table and One Drawer, Hand and Treadle .. **£8 19 6**

HARRODIA BRITISH J
Lockstitch vibrating Shuttle Hand and Treadle Sewing Machine and Stand Complete with Cover and attachments
£9 12 6

HARRODIA BRITISH J
Simple, durable and light-running. Makes a perfect Lock-stitch on all materials
With Walnut cover and attachments
£5 5 0

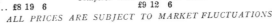

ALL PRICES ARE SUBJECT TO MARKET FLUCTUATIONS

HARRODS LTD

Telephone SLOANE 1234
Telegrams 'EVERYTHING HARRODS LONDON'

LONDON S W 1

IRONMONGERY DEPARTMENT
Potato Peelers, Spice Boxes, and Dish Washers

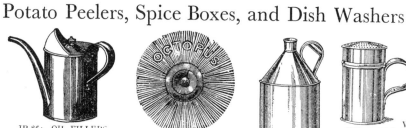

STRONG TIN CHIP POTATO CUTTER
Each 9½

IR 864 OIL FILLERS
Strong tin, for lamp
| 1 | 2 | 3 | pts. |
| 1/6 | 2/- | 2 8 | |

THE 'OCTOPUS' INCRUSTATOR
Prevents the corrosion of pipes and kitchen boilers
No. 0   Small, for kettles 7½d
No. 1   Medium 1/3
No. 2   Size for boilers .. 1/6
Larger sizes to order

OIL BOTTLES—Tin
| 4 | 8 | 16 pts. |
| 2/1 | 3/3 | 4/- |

TIN SUGAR DREDGER
Each
8d, 10d, 1/-

WIRE COOKS' SIEVES
With interchangeable bottoms can be changed instantly from coarse to fine; easy to keep clean. New frames or bottoms can always be obtained
Frames only
| 8 | 10 | 12 | 14 ins. dia. |
| 6/3 | 7/- | 7/9 | 8/3 |
Bottoms only. Prices from 2/- to 5/6 according to dia. and size of mesh
Bottoms stocked in 12, 14, 16, 18, 20, 22, 24, 30 holes to the 1 in. mesh

POTATO MASHER
Strong tinned malleable iron
Can also be used as Fruit Presser
Large size 5/-
Small size 3/9
ALUMINIUM POTATO MASHER
Large size .. .. each 5/6

IR 6 THE 'LIGHTNING' POT SCOURER
A Metal Sponge for cleaning and scouring pots, pans, dishes, tins, etc. .. each 6d

THE WONDER RAT TRAP
(As illustrated) .. each 2/3
GALVANISED WIRE RAT TRAPS
Square pattern
| 12 | 14 | 16 ins. |
| 4/6 | 5/- | 5/9 |

IR 216½ WIRE PLATE STAND
| 3 | 4 | 5 ins. |
| 7d | 7½d | 8d |
WIRE PLATE HOLDERS
4	5	6
4d	4½d	5d
7	8 ins.
5½d	6d
Not illustrated

IR 5 NEW SCOURING CLOTH
Best quality for cleaning all kitchen utensils of wood, tin enamel, etc. Size 6½ × 4½ in.
Each 3d
Larger size, 12 × 9 ins.
Each 4½d

IR 87. SPICE RACK
Japanned Fancy Art Colours. Length 11 ins. Gilt, Pink, Blue and Orange 3/6

IR 2 CHIP POTATO CUTTER
One movement of the lever will convert the potato into chips
Price 12/6
No. 4   Larger size 20/-

THE NOSEY PARKER WIRE BRUSH
IR 390
For cleaning all Gas Ovens .. each 1/-

IR 468   LANCASHIRE POTATO PEELER
Each 6d   Stainless 9d each
IR 1306 STAINLESS POTATO PEELER
With Boxwood handle .. each 1/9

BELGIQUE WIRE SAUCEPAN BRUSH
For cleaning pots and pans
Each 7½d

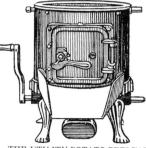

IR 142   SPICE BOXES
Round japanned with gold border
| 6 | 7 | 8 ins. |
| 4/6 | 5/- | 6/- |

IR 87a JAPANNED SQUARE SPICE BOX In art colours, Blue Gilt, Orange & Pink 3/9
IR 245 OPEN SPICE BOX
Japanned Art Colours. Round, Red, Blue or Green .. 5/-

IR 1308 THE DOMESTIC POTATO PEELER
A great labour saver. It peels 3 to 4 lbs. of potatoes in about thirty seconds. No waste. Very hygienic
Galvanised steel metal body
Price 30/-
Rustless Monel Metal Body
Price 42/-

IR 142 OYSTER KNIFE
Horn handle, with guard
1/9
With Beech handle 10d
Without Guard 8½d

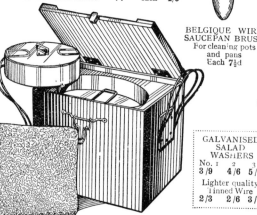

HARRODS KOOKAWAY FIRELESS COOKER
A modern labour saving device whereby cooking may be accomplished without continual burning of coal or gas. Specially recommended for shooting parties, useful for conveying hot lunches. The box is wood and well insulated with aluminium cooking utensils

No.	No. of Cooking Utensils	Size ins.	Size of box in.	Price	No.	No. of Cooking Utensils	Size ins.	Size of box in.	Price
12	One	8 × 7	13 × 13 × 11	53/6	9	Two	9 × 7	14 × 14 × 16	70/6
11	Two	8 × 7	13 × 13 × 15	64/6			9 × 3½		
		8 × 3½			8	One	10 × 7½	15 × 15 × 12½	63/-
10	One	9 × 7	14 × 14 × 11	58/6	7	Two	10 × 7½	15 × 15 × 16	77/6
							10 × 3½		

GALVANISED SALAD WASHERS
| No. 1 | 2 | 3 |
| 3/9 | 4/6 | 5/9 |
Lighter quality Tinned Wire
| 2/3 | 2/6 | 3/- |

THE UTILITY POTATO PEELING MACHINE
Vertical type for hand power
Sheet metal body and top on cast iron bottom with feet or long legs. Lined inside of bottom with carborundum and on sides with stabbed metal. This machine will wash, peel, and deliver 6 to 10 lbs. of potatoes per minute
To work the machine, load with 6 to 10 lbs. of potatoes, turn on water and turn handle of machine for about a minute, and while running, open door and potatoes are delivered
Price £5 5 0
With Long Legs .. £7 10 0

ALL PRICES ARE SUBJECT TO MARKET FLUCTUATIONS

HARRODS LTD

Telephone SLOANE 1234
Telegrams 'EVERYTHING HARRODS LONDON'

LONDON S W 1

IRONMONGERY DEPARTMENT

Harrods Cooking Utensils—Constructed to Give Long Service

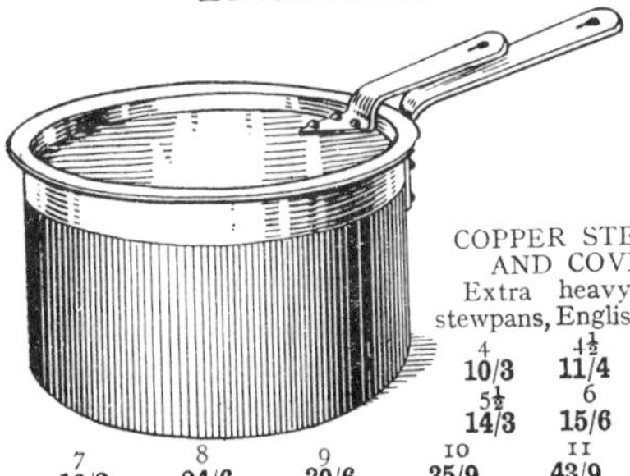

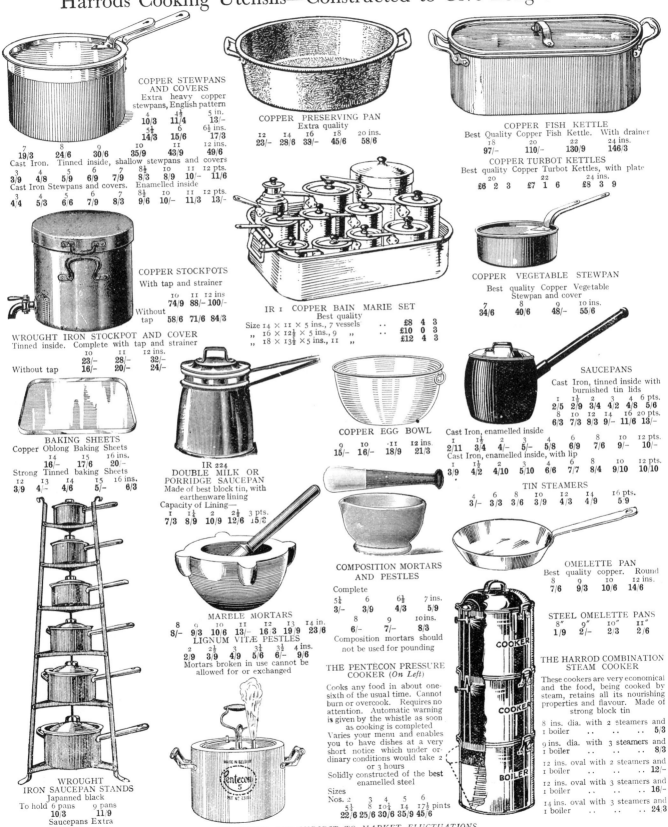

COPPER STEWPANS AND COVERS
Extra heavy copper stewpans, English pattern

4	4½	5 in.
10/3	11/4	13/-
5½	6	6½ ins.
14/3	15/6	17/3

7	8	9	10	11	12 ins.
19/3	24/6	30/6	35/9	43/9	49/6

Cast Iron. Tinned inside, shallow stewpans and covers

3	4	5	6	7	8½	10	11	12 pts.
3/9	4/8	5/9	6/9	7/9	8/3	8/9	10/-	11/6

Cast Iron Stewpans and covers. Enamelled inside

3	4	5	6	7	8½	10	11	12 pts.
4/4	5/3	6/6	7/9	8/3	9/6	10/-	11/3	13/-

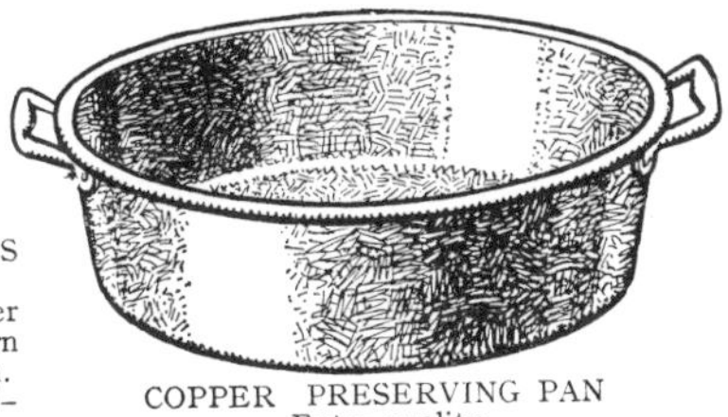

COPPER PRESERVING PAN
Extra quality

12	14	16	18	20 ins.
23/-	28/6	33/-	45/6	58/6

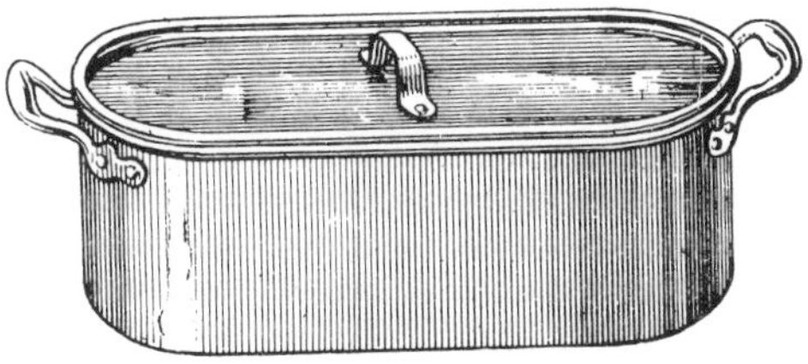

COPPER FISH KETTLE
Best Quality Copper Fish Kettle. With drainer

18	20	22	24 ins.
97/-	110/-	130/9	146/3

COPPER TURBOT KETTLES
Best quality Copper Turbot Kettles, with plate

20	22	24 ins.
£6 2 3	£7 1 6	£8 3 9

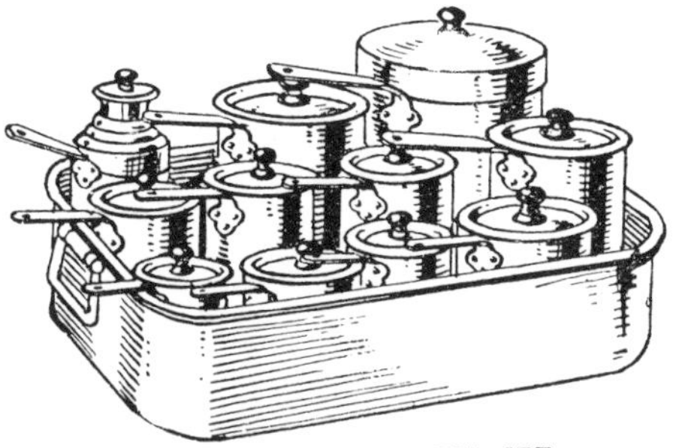

IR 1 COPPER BAIN MARIE SET
Best quality

Size 14 × 11 × 5 ins., 7 vessels .. £8 4 3
„ 16 × 12½ × 5 ins., 9 „ .. £10 0 3
„ 18 × 13½ × 5 ins., 11 „ £12 4 3

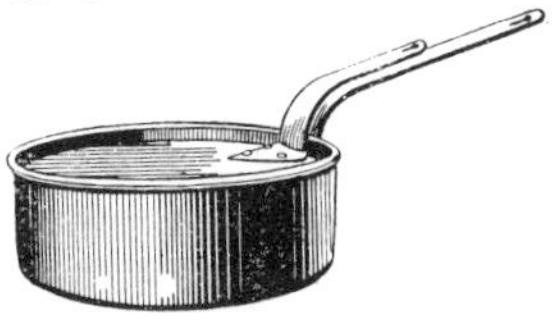

COPPER VEGETABLE STEWPAN
Best quality Copper Vegetable Stewpan and cover

7	8	9	10 ins.
34/6	40/6	48/-	55/6

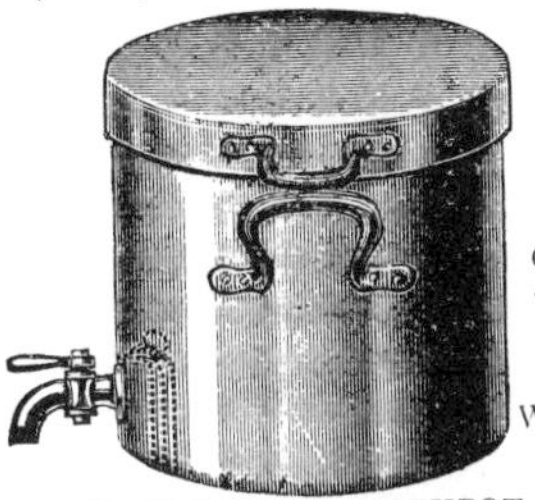

COPPER STOCKPOTS
With tap and strainer

	10	11	12 ins
	74/9	88/-	100/-
Without tap	58/6	71/6	84/3

WROUGHT IRON STOCKPOT AND COVER
Tinned inside. Complete with tap and strainer

	10	11	12 ins.
	23/-	28/-	32/-
Without tap	16/-	20/-	24/-

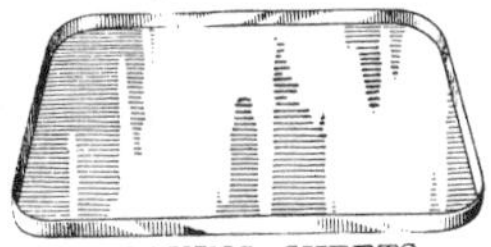

BAKING SHEETS
Copper Oblong Baking Sheets

14	15	16 ins.
16/-	17/6	20/-

Strong Tinned baking Sheets

12	13	14	15	16 ins.
3/9	4/-	4/6	5/-	6/3

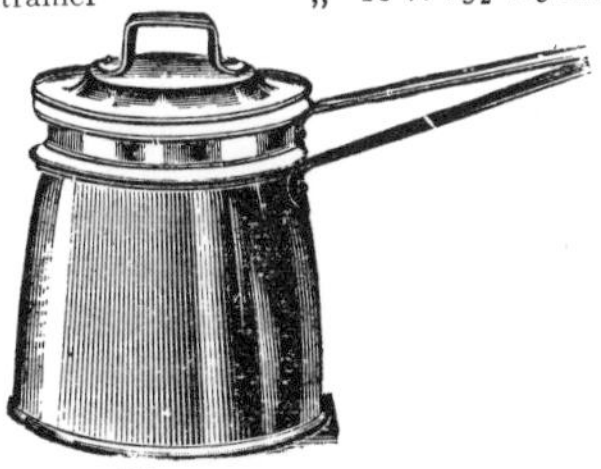

IR 224
DOUBLE MILK OR PORRIDGE SAUCEPAN
Made of best block tin, with earthenware lining
Capacity of Lining—

1	1¼	2	2½	3 pts.
7/3	8/9	10/9	12/6	15/3

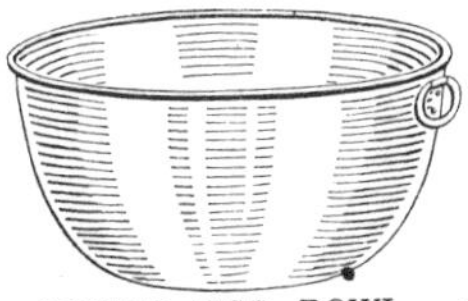

COPPER EGG BOWL

9	10	11	12 ins.
15/-	16/-	18/9	21/3

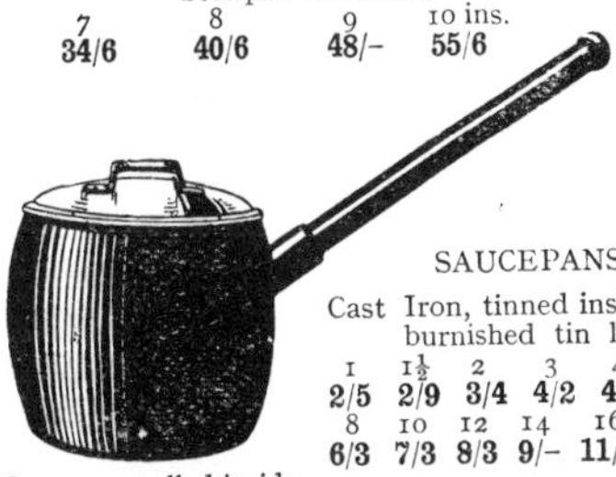

SAUCEPANS
Cast Iron, tinned inside with burnished tin lids

1	1½	2	3	4	6 pts.
2/5	2/9	3/4	4/2	4/8	5/6
8	10	12	14	16	20 pts.
6/3	7/3	8/3	9/-	11/6	13/-

Cast Iron, enamelled inside

1	1½	2	3	4	6	8	10	12 pts.
2/11	3/4	4/-	5/-	5/8	6/9	7/6	9/-	10/-

Cast Iron, enamelled inside, with lip

1	1½	2	3	4	6	8	10	12 pts.
3/9	4/2	4/10	5/10	6/6	7/7	8/4	9/10	10/10

TIN STEAMERS

4	6	8	10	12	14	16 pts.
3/-	3/3	3/6	3/9	4/3	4/9	5/9

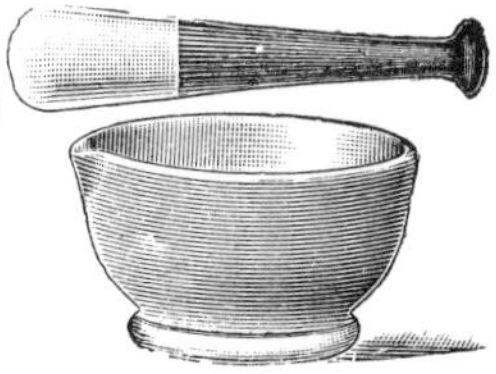

COMPOSITION MORTARS AND PESTLES
Complete

5¼	6	6½	7 ins.
3/-	3/9	4/3	5/9

8	9	10 ins.
6/-	7/-	8/3

Composition mortars should not be used for pounding

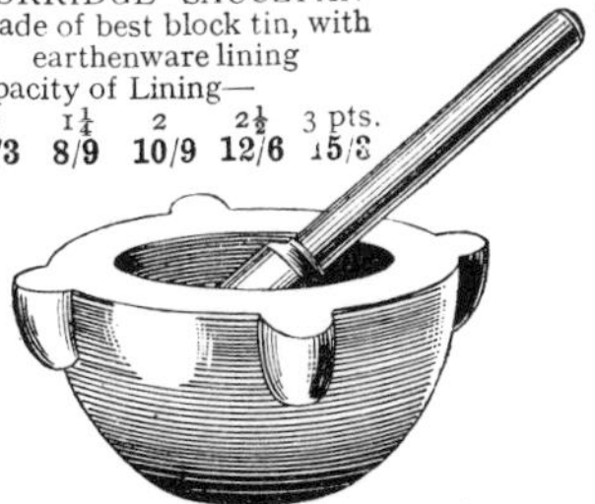

MARBLE MORTARS

8	9	10	11	12	13	14 in.
8/-	9/3	10/6	13/-	16/3	19/9	23/6

LIGNUM VITÆ PESTLES

2	2½	3	3¼	3½	4 ins.
2/9	3/9	4/9	5/6	6/-	9/6

Mortars broken in use cannot be allowed for or exchanged

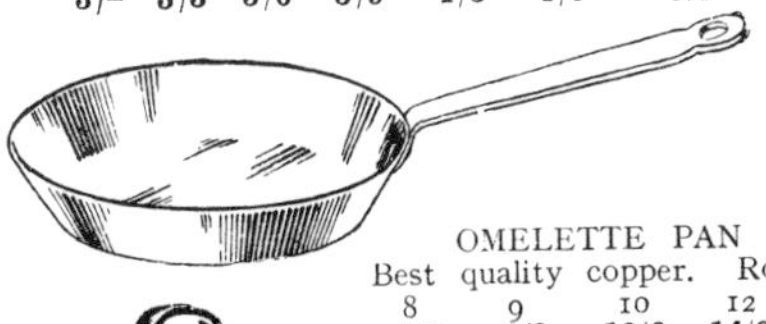

OMELETTE PAN
Best quality copper. Round

8	9	10	12 ins.
7/6	9/3	10/6	14/6

STEEL OMELETTE PANS

8″	9″	10″	11″
1/9	2/-	2/3	2/6

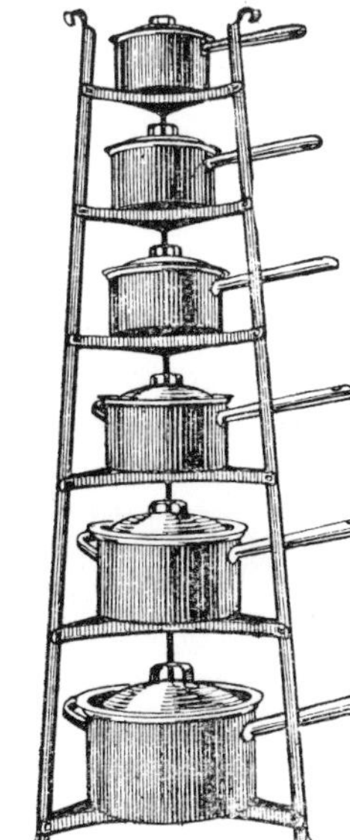

WROUGHT IRON SAUCEPAN STANDS
Japanned black

To hold	6 pans	9 pans
	10/3	11/9

Saucepans Extra

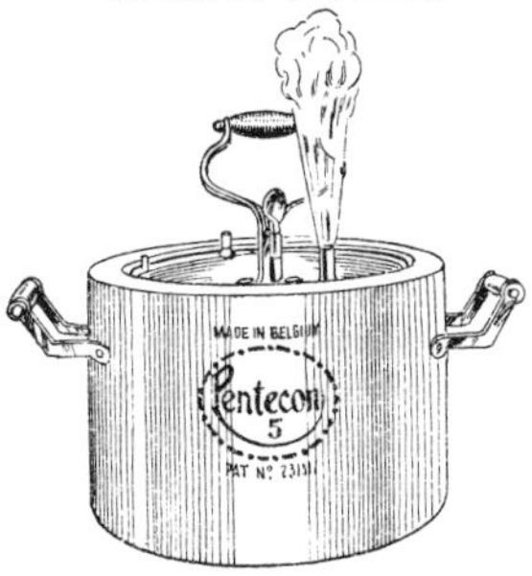

THE PENTECON PRESSURE COOKER (*On Left*)

Cooks any food in about one-sixth of the usual time. Cannot burn or overcook. Requires no attention. Automatic warning is given by the whistle as soon as cooking is completed

Varies your menu and enables you to have dishes at a very short notice which under ordinary conditions would take 2 or 3 hours

Solidly constructed of the best enamelled steel

Sizes Nos.	2	3	4	5	6
	5¼	8	10¼	14	17½ pints
	22/6	25/6	30/6	35/9	45/6

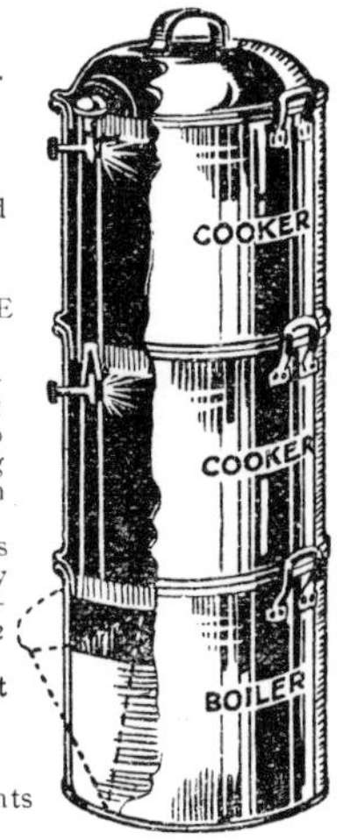

THE HARROD COMBINATION STEAM COOKER

These cookers are very economical and the food, being cooked by steam, retains all its nourishing properties and flavour. Made of strong block tin

8 ins. dia. with 2 steamers and 1 boiler 5/3
9 ins. dia. with 3 steamers and 1 boiler 8/3
12 ins. oval with 2 steamers and 1 boiler 12/-
12 ins. oval with 3 steamers and 1 boiler 16/-
14 ins. oval with 3 steamers and 1 boiler 24/3

ALL PRICES ARE SUBJECT TO MARKET FLUCTUATIONS

IRONMONGERY DEPARTMENT

Quick Cooking Stoves with Low Running Costs

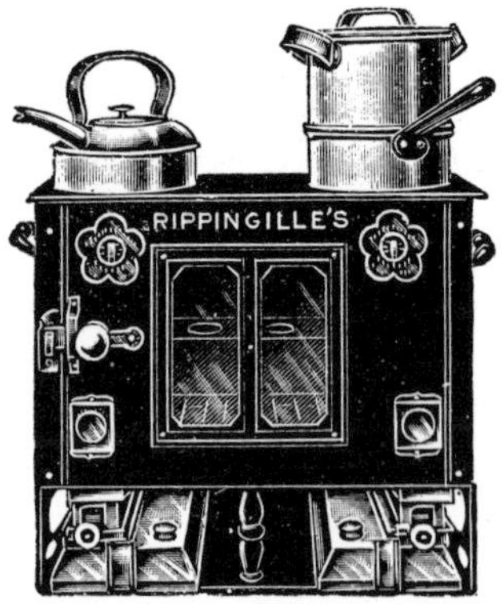

No. 4120 'RALC' DINNER STOVE
Size—Height, $17\frac{1}{4}$ ins.; Width, 20 ins.; Depth, $12\frac{3}{4}$ ins. Oven (available cooking space)—$13\frac{1}{2} \times 12 \times 9\frac{1}{2}$ ins. Burners—Two 6 ins. Movable

Price—No. 4120 Stove, with Shelf, Meat Tray and Grid .. .. each **78/-**
No. 488—As 4120, but with drop-down door .. .. each **81/9**
Price—Utensils. 4-pint Tin Kettle, **3/-**; 4-pint Stewpan, **2/9**; Steamer, **2/9**; Frypan, **2/-**; Toast Hanger, **3/-**

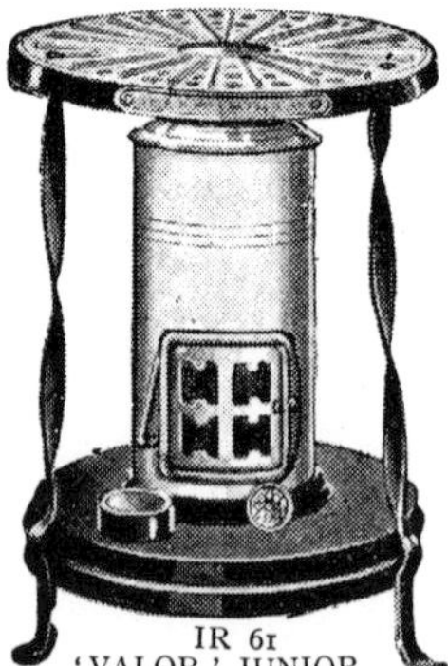

IR 61
'VALOR' JUNIOR
OIL STOVE

This stove is most useful in the house, **always** ready and always reliable. It is fitted with the same burner as the largest perfection cooking stove. Height 17 ins., dia. at top 12 ins. .. **28/-**

IR 62 TWO BURNERS
Height $16\frac{3}{4}$ ins., top 22×12 ins. **50/-**
Oven to fit either of above
Inside dimensions

Length	Depth	Height	
11 ins.	$10\frac{3}{4}$ ins.	$10\frac{1}{2}$ ins. ..	**13/6**

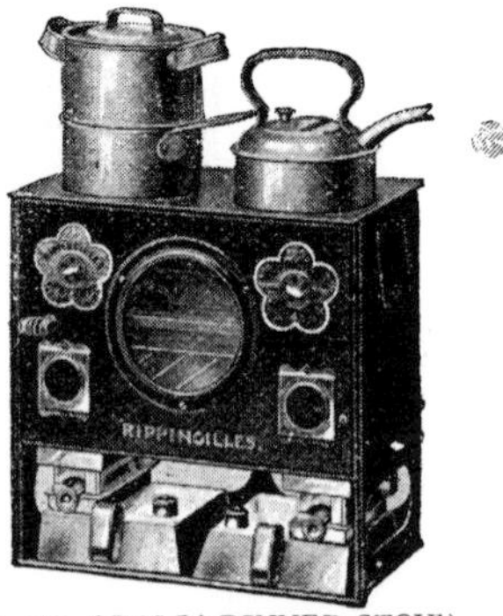

No. 460 'RALC' DINNER STOVE
Inexpensive small Dinner Stove. Allows of four operations being performed at one time, viz.:—Baking, Boiling, Steaming, Frying

Size—Height, 14 ins.; Width, 14 ins.; Depth $8\frac{3}{4}$ ins. Oven (available cooking space)—$9 \times 8 \times 6\frac{1}{2}$ ins. Burners—Two 3 ins. Movable

Price—No. 460 Stove, with Shelf, Meat Tray and Grid .. .. each **36/-**
No. 434—as 460 Stove. But with drop down Door .. .. .. each **37/6**
Price—Utensils. 2-pint Tin Kettle, **2/3**; 2-pint Stewpan, **2/-**; Steamer, **2/-**; Frypan, **1/-**; Toast Hanger, **3/-**

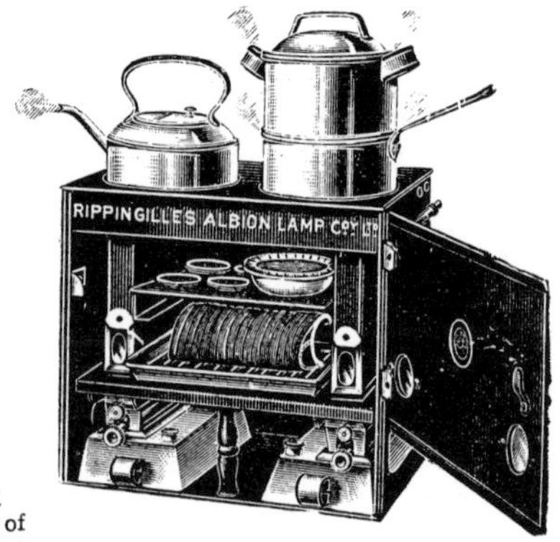

No. 464 'RALC' DINNER STOVE
Medium size Sheet Iron Stove useful for a small family

Size—Height 14 ins.; Width 16 ins.; Depth $10\frac{1}{2}$ ins. Oven (available cooking space)—$10 \times 9\frac{1}{2} \times 7$ ins. Burners—Two $4\frac{1}{2}$ ins. Movable
Price—Stove, with Shelf, Meat Tray and Grid .. .. each **45/9**

No. 490 As 464, but side opening door .. **48/9**
Price — Utensils. 3-pint Tin Kettle, **2/9**; 3-pint Stewpan, **2/9**; Steamer, **2/-**; Frypan **2/-**; Toast Hanger, **3/-**

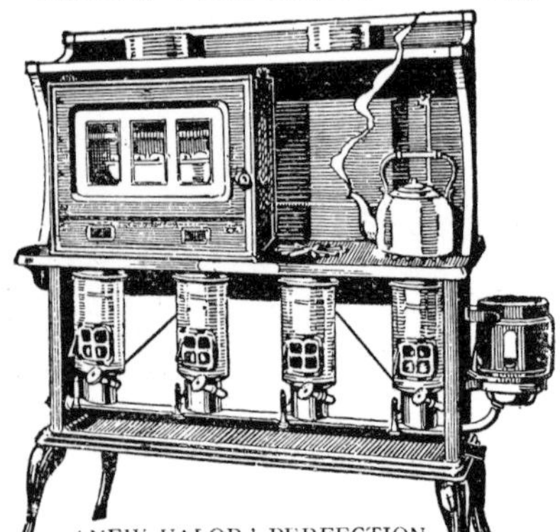

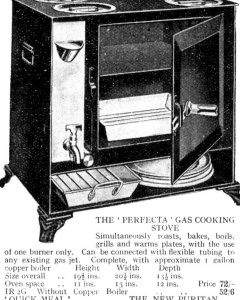

'NEW VALOR' PERFECTION
OIL COOKING RANGE
Showing Stove, with Cabinet top and Oven

No. of Burners	Size of Stove	Price of Stove	Price of Cabinet Top
2	$32\frac{1}{8} \times 17\frac{3}{4} \times 32$ ins. high	**80/-**	**28/-**
3	$42\frac{3}{4} \times 17\frac{3}{4} \times 32$ ins. high	**105/-**	**32/-**
4	$53\frac{3}{8} \times 17\frac{3}{4} \times 32$ ins. high	**130/-**	**42/-**

(*As illustrated*)

Height of Stoves with Cabinet Tops, 56 ins.

Ovens extra
To cover 1 Burner **27/-**
To cover 2 Burners **32/-**

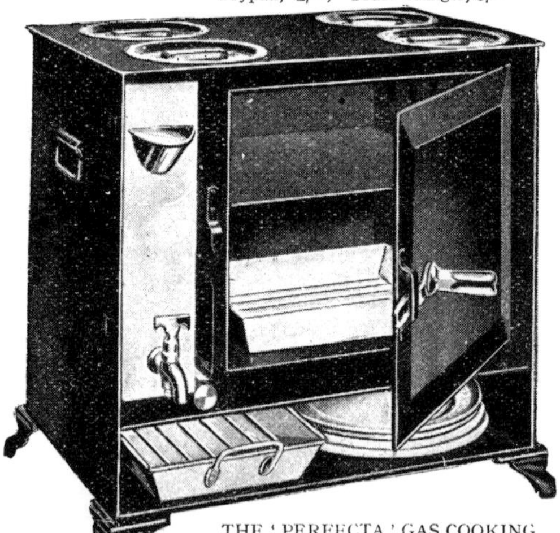

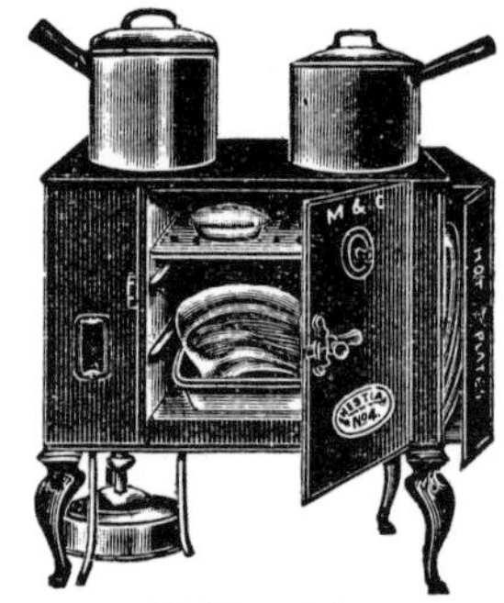

'HESTIA' OVENS
For use with 'Primus' Stoves No. 5, No. 10 (*as illustration*). Most popular size. Inside measure $12\frac{3}{4}$ ins. deep × 11 ins. high × $12\frac{3}{4}$ ins. wide. Will cook a complete dinner for 6 persons .. **60/-**

No. 2 Very useful size. Inside measure, $12\frac{1}{2}$ ins. deep × 10 ins. high × $12\frac{1}{4}$ ins. wide. Without hot plate compartment. Cooks a complete dinner for a small family. For use with Primus No. 4 .. .. **33/-**
Stoves extra

THE 'PERFECTA' GAS COOKING STOVE
Simultaneously roasts, bakes, boils, grills and warms plates, with the use of one burner only. Can be connected with flexible tubing to any existing gas jet. Complete, with approximate 1 gallon copper boiler

	Height	Width	Depth	
Size overall ..	$19\frac{1}{2}$ ins.	$20\frac{1}{2}$ ins.	$13\frac{1}{2}$ ins.	
Oven space ..	11 ins.	13 ins.	12 ins.	Price **72/-**
IR 2G Without Copper Boiler			.. ..	**52/6**

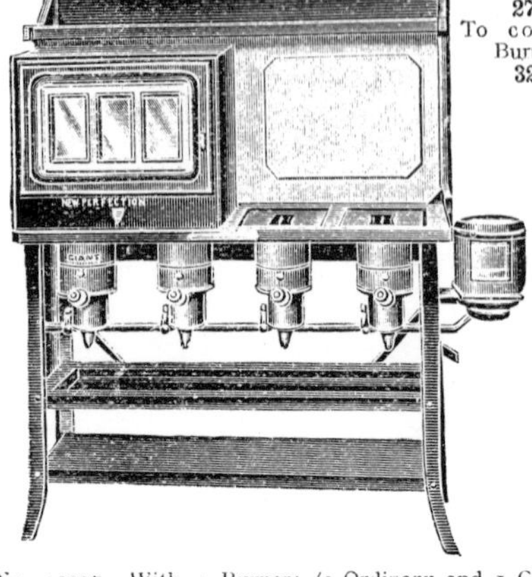

'QUICK MEAL'
OIL COOKING STOVE
Actually burns gas which it makes for itself out of ordinary paraffin oil.

Each Cooker has one Giant Burner giving twice the heat with the same consumption, thus saving 50 per cent. in fuel.
No. 41095 With two burners (1 Ordinary and 1 Giant) **£6 15 0**
With High Shelf and White Vitreous Enamelled Back **£9 3 0**
Top Platform measures $33\frac{1}{2}$ ins. wide by $17\frac{1}{2}$ ins. deep. Height to Platform $32\frac{1}{2}$ ins.
No. 41096 With 3 burners (2 Ordinary and 1 Giant) **£8 12 6**
With High Shelf and White Vitreous Enamelled Back **£11 12 6**
$43\frac{3}{4}$ ins. wide by $17\frac{1}{2}$ ins. deep. Height $32\frac{1}{2}$ ins.

No. 41097 With 4 Burners (3 Ordinary and 1 Giant) **£10 10 0**
With High Shelf and White Vitreous Enamelled Back **£14 1 3**
54 ins. wide by $17\frac{1}{2}$ ins. deep. Height $32\frac{1}{2}$ ins.

THE NEW PURITAN
OIL COOKING STOVE
(*Illustrated on right*)
No trouble in cleaning, no danger of the wick being turned too high and the absolute assurance of a burner that will outlive the life of a stove

Model No. **43** Three Burners (one large and two small)
Stove only **117/-**
With White Enamelled Cabinet Top **159/-**
With Black Japanned Cabinet Top **149/-**
Model No. 42 Two Burners (one large and one small)
Stove only **93/-**
With White Enamelled Cabinet Top **128/-**
With Black Japanned Cabinet Top **121/-**
Ovens Extra. No. 122GE Oven to cover 2 burners .. **32/-**
No. 121GE, to cover burner **27/-**

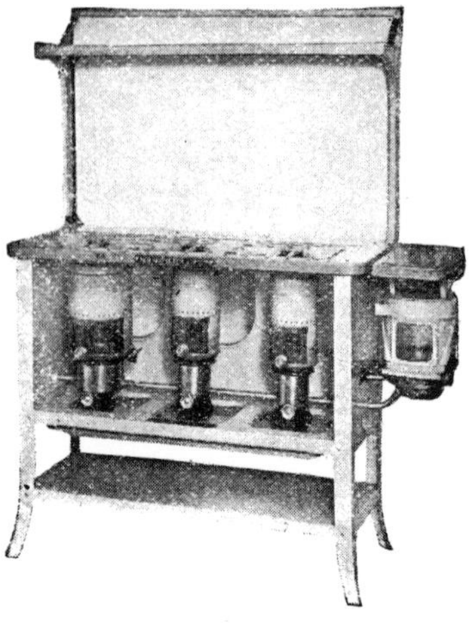

ALL PRICES ARE SUBJECT TO MARKET FLUCTUATIONS

IRONMONGERY DEPARTMENT
Oak Tool Chests and Cabinets Well Made and Finished

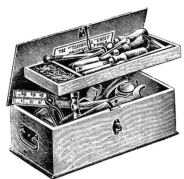

IR 9033   DEAL TOOL CHESTS
'The Technical,' unpolished.   With tray and division for nails, etc.
No. 1   Size 15¼ × 8 × 5 ins.   Containing 11 tools
Price **17/6**
No. 3   Size 16¼ × 9¾ × 5¼ ins.   Containing 16 tools.   Price **27/6**
No. 5   Size 18 × 11 × 6 ins.   Containing 20 tools
Price **37/9**
No. 6   Size 20 × 11 × 7 ins.   Containing 29 tools
Price **52/3**

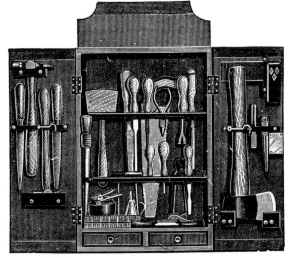

IR 9004   POLISHED OAK TOOL CABINET (*As illustrated*)
Size 21 × 14 × 5½ ins., with Lock and Key.   Complete with 24 tools
Mallet, Chisel, Gouge, Axe, 2 Hammers, Hand Saw, 3 Files, 2 Turnscrews
Square, Tack Claw, Pliers, 2 Gimlets, 2 Bradawls, Pincers, Glue Pot
and Brush, Plane, Compasses, 2 ft. Rule, Cold Chisel, Nails and Screws
Price **81/3**
IR 9006   As above but polished pine **71/-**
IR 9001   18 tools, oak **50/9**
IR 9002   18 tools but polished pine **43/6**

IR 9050   POLISHED DEAL TOOL RACKS
Size   16½ × 10¾ ins.   Containing   8   tools
Price **11/9**
IR 9051
POLISHED DEAL TOOL RACK
Size   16½ × 11¼ ins.   Containing   11 tools
Price **14/6**
IR 9052
Size 23 × 15 ins.   Containing 15 tools
Price **32/6**

IR 9036   BOYS' TOOL SETS
In strong cardboard boxes.   Oak finish, hinged lid
Size 14½ ins. × 4½ ins. × 1½ ins. **6/6**
Contains Hand Saw, Hammer, Turnscrew, Chisel, Rule, Gimlet, Bradawl, Carpenters' Pencil
9037   Size 20 ins. × 5 ins. × 2½ ins.   ..   **10/3**
Contains Hand Saw, Hammer, Turnscrew, Mallet, Chisel, Rule, Pincers, File, 2 Gimlets, Bradawl, Carpenters' Pencil
9038   Size 22¼ ins. × 6 ins. × 2½ ins. **17/-**
Contains Hand Saw, Hammer, Pincers, Turnscrew, Chisel, Gouge, 2 Bradawls, 2 Gimlets, Mallet, Plane, Square, Rule, File, Marking Awl, Carpenters' Pencil

IR 1   GENTLEMEN'S POLISHED OAK TOOL CHESTS
Size 19¼ × 8 × 3¾ ins. **43/6**
Contains Hand Saw, 14 ins. Joiner's Hammer, No. 1, Hatchet No. 0, Pincers, 5½ ins., Turnscrew, 4 ins., Firmer Chisel, Keyhole Saw, Try Square, Spoke Shave, Half-round Bastard File, 6 ins., Saw File, 3½ ins., Nail Punch, 3 Gimlets, 3 Bradawls, Marking Awl, Combination Cutting Pliers, 2 ft. Rule, Cold Chisel, Box Opening Chisel, Nails and Screws
No. 2   21 × 8½ × 4 ins., 27 tools **58/-**
No. 3   23¼ × 9 × 4½ ins., 32 tools **72/6**

IR 9039   SET OF WIRELESS TOOLS
In strong cardboard box.   Oak finish, with hinged lid.   Size 20 in. × 5 in. × 2¾ in.   Contains Hand Drill, 6 Twist Drills, Countersunk Centre Punch, Pliers, Shears, 3 Spanners, Hammer, 2 Screwdrivers, Soldering Iron, Bradawl, File and Tweezers **20/3**

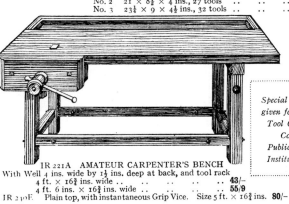

IR 221A   AMATEUR CARPENTER'S BENCH
With Well 4 ins. wide by 1½ ins. deep at back, and tool rack
4 ft. × 16¾ ins. wide **43/-**
4 ft. 6 ins. × 16¾ ins. wide **55/9**
IR 210E.   Plain top, with instantaneous Grip Vice.   Size 5 ft. × 16¾ ins.   **80/-**

Special Quotations given for Complete Tool Outfits for Colleges, Public Schools, Institutions, etc.

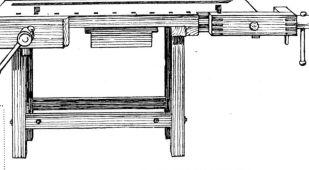

IR 230   IMPROVED CARPENTER'S BENCH
These are heavy and substantially made from Hardwood.   Each Bench is fitted with front and end Vices with hardwood Screws, and also a pair of Iron Bench Stops with well and flush Tool rack at back and draw underneath

4 ft.	5 ft.	6 ft.
£5 10 .0	£6 0 0	£6 12 6

ALL PRICES ARE SUBJECT TO MARKET FLUCTUATIONS

HARRODS LTD
Telephone SLOANE 1234
Telegrams 'EVERYTHING HARRODS LONDON'
LONDON S W 1

IRONMONGERY DEPARTMENT
Harrods Trouser Presses and Stretchers Will Serve You for Years

THE SERVICE TROUSER PRESS AND STRETCHER
Highly polished solid Oak or Mahogany. Antique copper bronze
fittings. Size 30 × 14 ins. **£4 10 0**

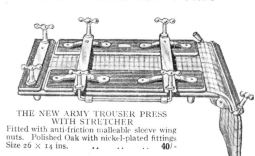

**THE NEW ARMY TROUSER PRESS
WITH STRETCHER**
Fitted with anti-friction malleable sleeve wing
nuts. Polished Oak with nickel-plated fittings
Size 26 × 14 ins. **40/-**

**THE
PREMIER
SCREWLESS
TROUSER
PRESS
WITH
STRETCHER**

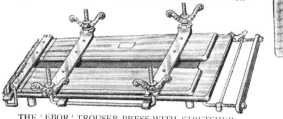

No screws to operate. It combines efficiency with simplicity
Polished Oak with Antique Copper Bronze fittings
Size 30 × 14 ins. .. **42/-** With rustless steel fittings .. **63/-**

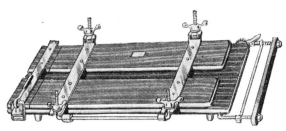

THE 'PRESTO' TROUSER PRESS WITH STRETCHER
Fitted with self locking automatic Ratchet Stretcher and rubber
feet. Anti-friction screw nuts. Polished Oak with nickel-plated
fittings Size 30 × 14 ins. **58/6**

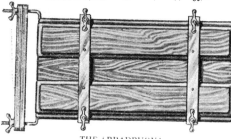

THE 'EBOR' TROUSER PRESS WITH STRETCHER
With self locking Ratchet Stretcher which is an ingenious device
which removes all bagginess from the trousers. In highly polished
Oak or Mahogany. Antique Copper Bronze fittings
Size 30 × 14 ins. **80/-**

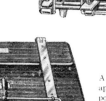

**THE 'CAM' TOURIST
SCREWLESS
TROUSER PRESS**
No screws to operate
A specially light press
designed for travelling
Will fit compactly into a
suit case or trunk. Size
24 ins., approximate
weight, 9 lbs. .. **35/-**
With stretching device
40/-

**THE 'CAM' SCREWLESS
TROUSER PRESS
WITH STRETCHER**
A quick action press which will
appeal to the busy man. Highly
polished Oak with Antique Copper
Bronze fittings. Size 31 × 14 ins.
59/6

**THE 'BRADBURY'
TROUSER PRESS AND STRETCHER**
Highly polished Light or Dark Oak. Nickel-plated fittings
Size 28 × 14 ins. **20/-**
THE 'VICTOR' Similar to above
,, 24 × 12 ins. **16/6**

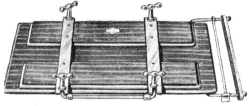

**THE 'NEW CHALLENGE' TROUSER PRESS
WITH STRETCHER**
Polished Oak. Nickel-plated fittings. Size 28 × 14 ins.
25/-

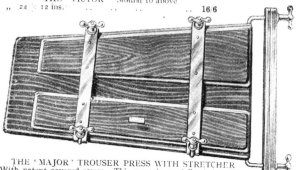

THE 'MAJOR' TROUSER PRESS WITH STRETCHER
With patent covered screw. This press is specially designed for
the man above the average size. Polished Oak with nickel-plated
fittings. Size, width at top 16 ins., width between screws of
stretcher 17½ ins. **36/6**

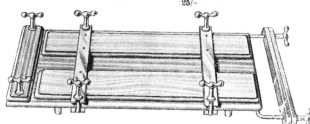

THE 'SUPER' TROUSER PRESS AND STRETCHER
This press has an extra clamp which allows trousers to be stretched
before the top board is put in position. Highly polished Oak with
nickel-plated fittings. Size 28 × 14 ins. **33/6**

ALL PRICES ARE SUBJECT TO MARKET FLUCTUATIONS

HARRODS LTD *Telephone SLOANE 1234* **LONDON S W 1**
Telegrams 'EVERYTHING HARRODS LONDON'

IRONMONGERY DEPARTMENT
Vacuum Cleaners, Portable Wash-Basins, Tables, etc.

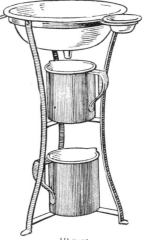

IR C940
PORTABLE WASHSTANDS
With 14 in. Enamel Basin Brass plug and Chain, 11 in. Pail, 6 pint jug and Soap Dish In Blue, Green, Orange, or Cardinal with Black bead .. **42/-**

IR 8026
PORTABLE WASHSTAND
Japanned Blue, Green or White with 14 in. China Basin, Plug and washer **26/6**
With Enamelled basin .. **22/6**

IR 8025
USEFUL WASHSTAND
Japanned Blue, Green or White 15 in. Enamelled Basin with brass plug and chain **23/-**

IR 971
PORTABLE WASHSTAND
A most useful stand and strongly made for the hardest wear. Square shape, enclosed. Japanned Oak colour, fitted with china basin, japanned receiver, and jug **69/9**

Hygienic **VEGETABLE RACK.** Made with four separate compartments, which enables the various kinds of vegetables to be kept apart, and prevents them from being crowded together and becoming stale.
Size 1, 2 Tiers, 3 Bins, Height 24 ins., Width 18 ins., Depth 8 ins.
Price .. **9/9**
Size 2, 3 tiers, 4 bins, Height 30 ins., Width 18 ins., Depth 8½ ins.
Price .. **12/9**
Size 3, 3 tiers, 4 Bins, Height 36 ins., Width 21 ins., Depth 12 ins.
Price .. **18/6**

IR 1
KITCHEN TABLES
Fitted with Porcelain Enamelled Steel top, clean and hygienic. The Ideal Pastry table. Fitted with drawer. Plain wood frame

Length	Width	Height	Price
36 ins.	25 ins.	30 ins.	43/6
41 ,,	25 ,,	30 ,,	47/-
48 ,,	27 ,,	30 ,,	66/9

With Hardwood block at one end for cutting and chopping. Hinged for cleaning. Overall measurements 53 × 25 ins. Size of enamel top 41 × 25 ins. Height 30 ins. Price **75/-**

THE 'STAR' HAND VACUUM CLEANER (on left)
A really efficient single handed Vacuum. Cleans carpets, stairs, furniture, etc.
Complete with improved Aluminium Tubes and Nozzles Price .. **45/-**
Complete with stairs and furniture nozzle Cheaper Model **36/-**

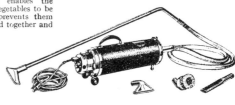

THE 'GOBLIN' ELECTRIC CLEANER
(5 Years' Guarantee.)

The equipment provided with the 'Goblin Electrical' is adequate for all ordinary household cleaning. and lightness and careful design of the attachments ensure its power to penetrate into all the corners of your house.

The motor runs in grease packed ball bearings, which require no oiling and ensure easy running, long life and low running costs, while simplicity of construction is featured in every detail. A triple expansion Turbine Fan revolving at high speed gives unrivalled suction power which effectively withdraws the dust from the thickest fabrics.

Complete with the following equipment:—21 ft. Electric Cable and Lamp Adaptor; 8 ft. Flexible Metallic Suction Hose; Handle in 2 sections; Carpet Nozzle; Dusting Brush; Upholstery Nozzle; Crevice Tool.

(The above equipment is all that is necessary for general use) .. **Cash Price £10 10 0**
Or on first payment of 18/5 and eleven monthly payments of 18/5.
The 'Turbine' Electric Cleaner similar to the 'Goblin' **£15 15 0**
Or on first payment of 27/7 and eleven monthly payments of 27/7

SAFETY WOOD BLOCK WINE BINS
Suitable for cellars or cupboards. Will take ordinary wine or champagne quarts
3 doz. 24 × 24 ins. **11/-**
4 doz. 32 × 24 ins. **12/9**
6 doz. 46½ × 32 ins. **19/-**
8 doz. 46½ × 32 ins. **25/-**
10 doz. 46½ × 38½ ins. **30/-**
Special sizes at a slightly extra cost Measuring and fixing extra

THE 'WHIRLWIND' SUCTION SWEEPER
(on right)
Efficient and easy to manage, yet needs no electricity for working. The 'Whirlwind' marks a further advance in labour saving devices, enabling the house to be kept spick and span without beating and sweeping. Demonstrated daily in Harrods Ironmongery section. Cash price .. **£4 19 6**
Or delivered on a first payment of 8/9 and eleven monthly payments of 8/9

No. IR 7 PASTRY TABLES
Plain Wood Frame fitted with drawer under shelf Enamelled White Porcelain Steel Top Size
24 × 20 ins. **30/-**
30 × 20 ins. **36/3**

THE 'BRIVAC' HAND OPERATED VACUUM CLEANER
(On left)
Weight only 15 lbs. A very efficient machine for all purposes. Made in Polished Oak with metal fittings, Nickel-plated. Demonstrated each day in the Ironmongery Section.
Cash price **£5 5 0**
Or delivered on a first payment of 10/- and eleven monthly payments of **10/-**

ALL PRICES ARE SUBJECT TO MARKET FLUCTUATIONS

IRONMONGERY DEPARTMENT
Harrods Wringers and Mangles to Lighten Home Laundering

THE 'ACME' WRINGER
(On left)
With solid rubber rollers, warranted 5 years. Galvanised iron frame and double cramps for use on tub or table
14 ins. **39 –**   16 ins. **43/-**
THE 'PRESIDENT' similar to above. 12 ins. **33/6**
Warranted 2 years

THE 'QUICKFIX' WRINGER STAND *(on left)*
Can be used with any size Wringer Absolutely rigid and secure. An ample size platform, hinged to fold in the middle, gives space for a bath large enough to catch all draining water
Height of Stand 2 ft. 7 ins. over all. Platform 22 ins. deep × 19 ins. wide. Ground space when open 28 ins. deep × 21½ ins. wide
Price .. **15/9**

THE 'NUGGET' TABLE MANGLE AND WRINGER
With spiral springs, clamps and folding handle. Light and portable 18 × 3½ ins. Rollers **55/9**
20 × 3½ ins. Rollers **57/3**

WRINGER STAND
Will accommodate any size rubber roller wringer. The shelf is removeable to enable a Dolly Tub or Bath to be used underneath
Size height 31 ins., length 26 ins., depth 17 ins.
Shelf 11½ ins.   Price **14/6**
Wringers Extra

THE 'DAINTY' MANGLE
With double spiral springs
Size of rollers
18 × 4 ins. **89/9**   20 × 4 ins. **91/3**

SPECIAL WRINGER & MANGLER
Manufactured expressly for Harrods Ltd., and every one guaranteed

18 ins.	20 ins.	22 ins.	24 ins.
£5 13 0	£5 15 3	£5 17 3	£5 19 6

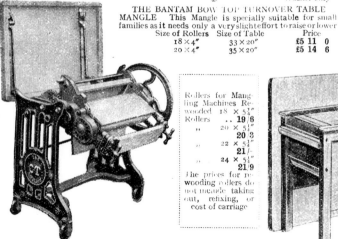

THE 'PILOT' WASHER, WRINGER AND MANGLE COMBINED
The tub of selected hardwood, fitted with brass tap
16 × 3½ ins. wood rollers £7 6 6
18 × 3½ ins. wood rollers £7 7 9
Washer only £4 12 0

THE BANTAM BOW TOP TURNOVER TABLE MANGLE   This Mangle is specially suitable for small families as it needs only a very slight effort to raise or lower

Size of Rollers	Size of Table	Price
18 × 4"	33 × 20"	£5 11 0
20 × 4"	35 × 20"	£5 14 6

Rollers for Mangling Machines Rewooded 18 × 5¼"
Rollers .. **19/6**
  „   20 × 5¼"   **20/3**
  „   22 × 5¼"   **21/-**
  „   24 × 5¼"   **21/9**
The prices for rewooding rollers do not include taking out, refixing, or cost of carriage

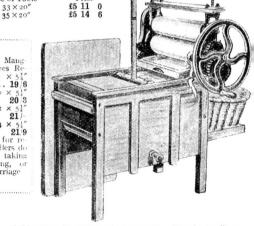

THE 'ACME MAJOR' COMBINED TABLE AND MANGLE
Can be easily raised or lowered. Fitted with patent arrangement for lifting the rollers apart when not in use

Size of Rollers ins.	Size of Table ins.	Price
20 × 5¼	36 × 22	£7 2 0
22 × 5¼	38 × 22	£7 5 6

THE 'SAFELIFT' COMBINED TABLE AND MANGLE
It can be raised or lowered by simply turning the flywheel thus preventing any possible strain when converting the machine. Fitted with Rolax Oil Bath Gear which does away with exposed cog wheels or chains

Size of Rollers ..	4½ × 20"	4½ × 22"
Size of Table	38 × 24"	41 × 24"
Price	£7 5 9	£7 9 3

IMPROVED HOUSEHOLD WASHER   Fitted with Turnover Mangle, Tub Rest, and plain wood top to use as Table when not required for washing purposes. No. 3 Washer with Table and 18 × 4 ins. Turnover Mangle **£9 6 0**
No. 4 Washer with Table and 20 × 5¼ ins. Turnover Mangle
£10 5 0

ALL PRICES ARE SUBJECT TO MARKET FLUCTUATIONS

HARRODS LTD

Telephone SLOANE 1234
Telegrams 'EVERYTHING HARRODS LONDON'

LONDON S W 1

IRONMONGERY DEPARTMENT
Harrods Undertake Repairs to all Ironmongery

Harrods specialise in Repairs to Ironmongery of every description, and customers entrusting such work to Harrods are assured of the fullest measure of satisfaction Only expert workmen are employed and materials of the best quality used Harrods will gladly estimate free for any Repair work not catalogued below

RE-TINNING COPPER UTENSILS WITH PURE TIN (REPAIRS EXTRA)

	4"	5"	6"	7"	8"	9"	10"	11"	12"	13"	14"	15"	16"
STEWPANS Inside only	1/-	1/3	1/6	1/9	2/-	2/3	2/6	2/9	3/-	3/3	3/6	3/9	4/-
„ Over-edge	1/3	1/7	1/10½	2/2	2/6	2/10	3/2	3/5½	3/9	4/1	4/4½	4/8½	5/-
„ Covers	6d	7½d	9d	10½d	1/-	1/1½	1/3	1/4½	1/6	1/8	1/9	1/11	2/-
STOCKPOTS Inside	—	—	—	—	—	—	3/1½	3/5½	3/9	4/1	4/4½	4/8½	5/-
„ Over-edge	—	—	—	—	—	—	3/9	4/1½	4/6	4/10½	5/3	5/7½	6/-
„ Covers	—	—	—	—	—	—	2/6	2/9	3/-	3/3	3/6	3/9	4/-
„ Tap and Grate, extra	—	—	—	—	—	—	3/9	3/9	3/9	3/9	3/9	4/6	4/6
SAUTÉ PANS	—	—	—	—	2/-	—	2/6	—	3/-	—	3/6	—	—
OMELETTE	—	—	—	—	1/6	—	1/10½	—	2/3	—	2/7½	—	—
BAKING SHEETS	—	—	—	—	—	—	2/6	—	3/-	—	—	—	4/-
MOULDS Plain								each 1/5, 1/9, 2/-, according to size
„ Fancy								„ 2/3, 2/9, 3/-, „ „

Fish Kettles and Braize Pans same as Stockpots. Stockpots and Stewpans are measured diagonally from top to bottom

RE-JAPANNING BATHS, CANS, &c. (REPAIRS EXTRA)

HIP BATHS Inside	7/9	9/-	—	—	TRAVELLING BATHS In and out	12/9	15/-
„ In and out	12/9	15/-	—	—	„ With Covers	19/6	21/9
SITZ BATHS Inside	7/9	9/-	—	—	FOOT BATHS Inside	3/9	4/3
„ In and out	12/9	15/-	—	—	„ In and out	6/-	7/-
SPONGE BATHS Inside	7/9	9/-	9/9	12/-	TOILET CANS	4/6	5/3
„ In and out	12/9	15/-	16/6	19/6	„ Inside	3/-	3/9
TRAVELLING BATHS Inside	8/-	9/-	—	—	HOT WATER CANS Inside	1/6	—
„ With Covers	9/9	11/3	—	—	„ „ In and out	3/6	—

COOKS' KNIVES Ground and Set   Small size, 4d ;   Large size, 6d each   MEAT CHOPPERS, SAWS, AXES, etc., Ground and Set
From 6d each

RE-LACQUERING AND RE-POLISHING

This is a special feature of Harrods Repair Department. Harrods employ the newest and best known method of re-lacquering with Zapon for Brass, Steel or Copper goods. This Zapon lacquer ensures a durability and brilliancy of finish unattainable by the ordinary process.   Estimates free

REPAIRS TO PERAMBULATORS
RE-TYRING PERAMBULATOR WHEELS
(Taking off and re-fixing wheels extra)

		12 ins.	14 ins.	16 ins.	18 ins.
⅞-in.White Rubber wired-on	Per pair	11/6	11/6	13/6	13/6
⅝-in. „ „ „	„	7/6	7/6	11/6	11/6

Re-painting and renovating any make of Perambulators a speciality.   Estimates free

The prices quoted for Repairs to Perambulators, etc., do not include the cost of hire for one which may be required whilst repairs are being done. For prices apply to Department

ALL PRICES ARE SUBJECT TO MARKET FLUCTUATIONS

HARRODS SAFE DEPOSIT

DAMP-PROOF ✦ FIRE-PROOF ✦ BURGLAR PROOF

Interior of Strong Room

HARRODS SAFE DEPOSIT PRICES

Section.	Height. ins.	Width. ins.	Depth. ins.	Rent per ann. £ s. d.
A	4¼	4¾	17½	0 15 6
B	4¼	6¾	17½	1 11 0
C	7	6¾	17½	2 5 0
D	8¾	10½	17½	3 3 0
E	13¼	10	17½	3 15 0
F	24	17½	17½	6 6 0

PLATE CHESTS

Per month, 2/6 each ; per annum, small, £1 5 0 ; per annum, large size, £1 10 0

Safes and Strong Rooms can be rented for shorter periods by arrangement

Annual Rent of Burglar-proof and Fire-proof Strong Rooms up to £30. Keys registered, 2/6 for life

Access to Trunks or Chests arranged on the shortest notice. Wedding Presents (other than furniture) stored

CALL AND INSPECT THESE MODERN SAFETY VAULTS

Absolute Security

SAFEGUARD YOUR VALUABLES

Why run the risk of loss by fire or theft when you can be assured of absolute security if your valuables are placed in Harrods Safe Deposit ?

Once entrusted to the Safe Deposit you are relieved from any further anxiety concerning them

THE IDEAL SAFE DEPOSIT FOR JEWELLERY

An even temperature is absolutely essential for the safe keeping of Jewellery and Precious Stones. The fact that Harrods Safety Vaults keep the same temperature all the year round prevents the lustre of the stones being dimmed, no matter how long they are kept in security

A MODEL SAFE DEPOSIT

A Visitor seeing these vaults for the first time would be amazed at the wonderful mechanical devices for resisting the dangers of theft and fire

Steel doors, reinforced concrete walls, electrical fire and burglar alarms, assure every Renter a protection which is the last word in mechanical ingenuity

VALUABLES REMOVED IN SECRECY

The very fact that the Safety Deposit Vaults are built within the building has decided advantages over an isolated establishment outside which undesirables may be watching to waylay those coming out with valuables in their possession. At Harrods it is impossible to distinguish whether the customer leaving the establishment is taking away a purchase after shopping or valuable jewellery from the Safe Deposit

FURNITURE DEPARTMENT
Furnish Your Home at Harrods

FURNITURE AND FURNISHINGS FOR EVERY ROOM AND EVERY HOME

HARRODS Furniture and Upholstery commend themselves to the careful buyer as much for merits that are hidden from view as for outward and visible signs of excellence. To the wide experience of those who design this Furniture is added a thoroughness of execution which produces pieces whose beauty and usefulness are retained through many years. The following pages are intended as a guide in the selection of furniture to suit varying tastes and purses ; of necessity they are representative rather than comprehensive. And for this reason Harrods would urge a personal visit to their showrooms

Those, however, who are unable to come to Harrods need have no hesitation in making their needs known by post, since the reputation which Harrods possess for courteous and intelligent service, for fine merchandise, and for absolute integrity, is a guarantee of complete satisfaction always

HOW TO ORDER

Readers of this Book are advised to study the following points closely when ordering

TERMS

Cash with order, unless an Account has been opened

DEPOSIT ORDER ACCOUNTS

These Accounts are opened upon receipt of £5 and upwards, to be renewed as exhausted. *An immediate Bonus of 6d. in the £ is allowed on sums of £5 and upwards deposited in prepayment for goods. A Deposit Order Account therefore saves Money, Time and Trouble. Fuller details free*

CREDIT ACCOUNTS

Credit Accounts can be opened on receipt of a satisfactory Trade or Banker's reference. These accounts are rendered and payable weekly in Town and monthly in the Country

DEFERRED PAYMENTS

Harrods Furnishing Service is designed to be of the widest possible usefulness, and those desirous of furnishing without disturbance of capital may do so on exceptionally attractive terms. Furnishing purchases as low as £20 in value may be secured on Harrods System of Deferred Payments, and £50 worth of Furnishings may be obtained by payment of £5 only as deposit, the balance (plus interest at 2½ per cent.) being payable in twelve monthly instalments. £100 worth calls for a deposit of £10, the balance (plus 2½ per cent. per annum) being extended over two or even three years

DELIVERY

Goods are delivered free within the radius of Harrods Motor Vans. A list of districts covered will be found on pages 9, 10, 11

CARRIAGE TERMS

Purchases of £5 value or over are sent Carriage Paid to any Goods Station in England and Wales. Purchases of £10 value or over are sent Carriage Paid to any Goods Station in Scotland, or to any Port in the Channel Islands having direct steamer communication with London. Furniture and Furnishings are delivered by Harrods Vans as follows :—£50, 50 miles ; £100, 120 miles ; £200, 150 miles ; £300, 200 miles

PASSENGER TRAIN

Carriage on heavy goods ordered by Passenger Train cannot be paid where the amount of carriage exceeds the Goods Train rates, but an allowance will be made equivalent to the cost of transit by Goods Train

PACKING CASES

Cases and Crates are charged at cost but credited in full if returned Carriage Paid and received in good condition

ORDERS BY POST

Patrons may order by post, telegraph, or telephone with the same assurance of satisfaction as if they shopped personally at Harrods. Books of Order Forms are supplied to all customers opening an account, and orders sent on these Forms facilitate prompt despatch

ALL PRICES ARE SUBJECT TO MARKET FLUCTUATIONS

UPHOLSTERY DEPARTMENT
Easy Chairs of Simple Design Well Stuffed and Covered with Tasteful Fabrics

94/508

Furnishing Purchases value £5 and over sent carriage paid to any Goods Station in England and Wales

The 'ALCESTER' (*on the left*), (94/508) A most luxurious spoon-back Easy Chair stuffed with best horsehair; its cushion filled with down; in every respect a first class chair
£24 0 0

The 'CONNAUGHT' (*shown on the right*) A deep seated and deeply sprung upholstered Easy Chair (94/3850). Delightfully comfortable.   Covered with a 50 in. material
£5 5 0

94/3850

The 'BRAMLEIGH' Chair (94/7372), illustrated here on the right, is a large Divan Easy Chair covered with best quality Cowhide. The upholstery is of fibre and hair, the seat and back are deeply sprung and the loose seat cushion is of Velveteen Width over all 2 ft. 9 ins., depth over all 3 ft. 3 ins.
£15 15 0

The ' Bramleigh '

The 'BURTON' Chair (94/7330) shown on the left. A luxurious Easy Chair in Hide. The springing is most resilient and is placed where it ensures complete comfort. Loose Velveteen cushion is provided for the seat. Width over all 3 ft. 3 ins., depth over all 3 ft. 4 ins.
£25 5 0

The ' Burton '

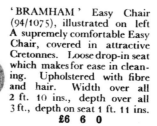

'BRAMHAM' Easy Chair (94/1075), illustrated on left A supremely comfortable Easy Chair, covered in attractive Cretonnes. Loose drop-in seat which makes for ease in cleaning. Upholstered with fibre and hair. Width over all 2 ft. 10 ins., depth over all 3 ft., depth on seat 1 ft. 11 ins.
£6 6 0

The 'SAVOY' Easy Chair, illustrated on the right, is handsome in appearance and comfortable in use. The chair is stuffed with pure hair only, and is entirely covered with Goathide. The cushion seat, too, is of Goathide, filled with down. Width over all 3 ft., depth on seat 1 ft. 11 ins.
£22 10 0

The ' Bramham '

' Savoy '

ALL PRICES ARE SUBJECT TO MARKET FLUCTUATIONS

HARRODS LTD

Telephone SLOANE 1234
Telegrams 'EVERYTHING HARRODS LONDON'

LONDON S W 1

CARPET & LINOLEUM DEPARTMENT

A Wonderful Selection of Oriental and British Made Carpets and Every Conceivable Kind of Floor Covering from the Smallest to the Largest Room Sizes

The illustration shows part of Harrods spacious Carpet Galleries, giving some idea of the wonderful furnishing possibilities which such a vast collection of floor coverings present

Experienced Representative sent to any part of the Town or Country to advise and estimate. Patterns sent to any railway station in the United Kingdom. Carriage paid

Carpets taken up, beaten and relaid at moderate charges. Houses cleaned throughout by vacuum process. Carpet repairs are carried out by skilled Oriental weavers specially engaged for this purpose

ALL ESTIMATES FREE

HARRODS BRITISH-MADE SEAMLESS AXMINSTER CARPETS

Inexpensive Carpets recommended for Rooms in which the wear is not excessive

Size	Price		Size	Price
9 ft. 0 ins. × 7 ft. 6 ins.	£4 16 11		10 ft. 6 ins. × 10 ft. 6 ins.	£7 18 3
10 ft. 6 ins. × 7 ft. 6 ins.	£5 13 0		12 ft. 0 ins. × 10 ft. 6 ins.	£9 1 0
12 ft. 0 ins. × 7 ft. 6 ins.	£6 9 3		13 ft. 6 ins. × 10 ft. 6 ins.	£10 3 6
9 ft. 0 ins. × 9 ft. 0 ins.	£5 16 3		15 ft. 0 ins. × 10 ft. 6 ins.	£11 6 0
10 ft. 6 ins. × 9 ft. 0 ins.	£6 15 9		12 ft. 0 ins. × 12 ft. 0 ins.	£10 6 9
12 ft. 0 ins. × 9 ft. 0 ins.	£7 15 0		13 ft. 6 ins. × 12 ft. 0 ins.	£11 12 6
13 ft. 6 ins. × 9 ft. 0 ins.	£8 14 6		15 ft. 0 ins. × 12 ft. 0 ins.	£12 18 6

These Carpets can also be supplied 7 ft. 6 ins., 9 ft. 0 ins., 10 ft. 6 ins. and 12 ft. 0 ins. wide, by any length which is **a** multiple of eighteen inches ; prices are proportionate to those quoted above. Coloured illustrations sent on request

Rugs are made to match most of the designs on Heavy Wool Backs

5 ft. 3 ins. × 2 ft. 8 ins.		**30/6**	6 ft. 0 ins. × 3 ft. 0 ins.	**40/-**

[There is a Floor Covering in Harrods to suit every part of your House or Flat]

ALL PRICES ARE SUBJECT TO MARKET FLUCTUATIONS

HARRODS LTD

Telephone SLOANE 1234
Telegrams 'EVERYTHING HARRODS LONDON'

LONDON S W 1

CARPET AND LINOLEUM DEPARTMENT

The Greatest Care is Taken in Choosing, Only the Finest Weavings Being Selected

PERSIAN CARPETS AND RUGS

Harrods have a wonderful variety of Persian Carpets and Rugs in all the finest weavings. It is impossible to give a detailed list of this stock which is constantly changing, but a few examples of the various makes are quoted below

FINE OLD KIRMAN CARPETS

10 ft. 4 ins. × 9 ft. 1 in.	£70 10	0
11 ft. 2 ins. × 9 ft. 3 ins.	£77 10	0
13 ft. 3 ins. × 10 ft. 6 ins.	£139 5	0

OLD HEREZ CARPETS

14 ft. 6 ins. × 10 ft. 5 ins.	£92 10	0
15 ft. 5 ins. × 11 ft. 2 ins.	£105 0	0
17 ft. 5 ins. × 12 ft. 5 ins.	£132 10	0

FINE KIRMAN CARPET

26 ft. 9 ins. × 17 ft. 2 ins.	£500 0	0

MESHED CARPET

28 ft. 8 ins. × 19 ft. 8 ins.	£575 0	0

FINE TEBRIZ CARPET

28 ft. 0 ins. × 18 ft. 3 ins.	£700 0	0

OLD SOUMAC RUGS

7 ft. 3 ins. × 5 ft. 3 ins.	£13 0	0
7 ft. 10 ins. × 6 ft. 3 ins.	£16 15	0
10 ft. 11 ins. × 7 ft. 9 ins.	£27 0	0

FINEST QUALITY BOKHARA RUGS

5 ft. 1 in. × 2 ft. 9 ins.	£9 19	6
6 ft. 11 ins. × 4 ft. 9 ins.	£22 10	0
8 ft. 5 ins. × 5 ft. 10 ins.	£37 0	0
12 ft. 10 ins. × 8 ft. 6 ins.	£86 10	0

FINE AFGHAN RUGS

6 ft. 9 ins. × 3 ft. 6 ins.	£7 2	6
7 ft. 8 ins. × 3 ft. 8 ins.	£8 10	0
9 ft. 11 ins. × 7 ft. 3 ins.	£21 11	6

HEREZ RUGS

Renowned for their remarkable wearing qualities as well as their striking colourings, these Rugs are readily adaptable to almost any furnishing scheme. Approximate size 6 ft. × 3 ft., from **£5 0 0** each

KELIM RUGS AND CURTAINS

Harrods always hold a comprehensive stock of Kelims. Rugs, both new and old, from **30/-** each. Curtains from **£6 0 0**

In addition to the above, Harrods have a large and varied stock of all Persian Rugs—Kashan, Sarouk, Kurdistan, Bidjar, Sennah, Feraghan, Khorassan, Cabistan, Saraband Meshed, Shirvan, Baluchistan, Mosouls, etc. Prices according to quality and condition

ALL PRICES ARE SUBJECT TO MARKET FLUCTUATIONS

FURNISHING DRAPERIES DEPARTMENT
A Beautiful Bedspread Adds Much to the Charm and Restfulness of a Bedroom

Harrods remarkable display of beautifully coloured bedspreads offers a selection providing for every kind of setting

B 301
BEAUTIFUL BEDSPREAD
This is an exclusive design of Harrods. Natural coloured flower motifs exquisitely worked on a silver grey repp
3 yds. × 2½ yds. .. £13 17 6
3 yds. × 3 yds. .. £15 15 0

B 299   LOVELY
TAFFETA BEDSPREAD
A wonderful array of colourings include Petunia, Jade and Rose
Size 3 yds. × 2½ yds.. .. £5 15 0
" 3 yds. × 2½ yds. £4 17 6

BED OR COUCH COVERS
Can also be used as curtains. Portuguese design with metal trimmings. Colours :—Blue, Green and Terras on Camel ground frenzies, Cream coloured border
Size 8 ft. × 6 ft. 6 ins. .. .. Each **69/6**

B 293   CHINTZ BEDSPREAD
Daintily worked fabric. Six delightful chintz colourings from which to choose
Size 3 yds. × 2½ yds. £3 5 0
" 3 yds. × 2 yds. £3 0 0

CUSHIONS
Lovely Cushions ' made up ' from superior cretonnes and linens with ' Kapoc ' filling
Size 24 ins. square.   Each 4/11, 5/11, 6/11
Plain Boat Cushions 20 ins. sq.,   each **2/11**

POUFFE OTTOMAN
In Printed Linen or Cretonne.   Good serviceable make. Size 16 ins. square and 10 ins. high **7/6**

B 306   ARTIFICIAL SILK BEDSPREAD
Six beautifully tone colourings worked in self colours
Size 3 yds. × 2½ yds... .. .. .. £2 5 0
" 3 yds. × 2½ yds... .. .. .. £1 19 6

TABLE RUNNERS
OR SIDEBOARD TOPS
In Velour, fringed ends. In shades of Green, Rose or Brown with motif and trimming in Gold
15 ins. wide × 54 ins. long **19/11**
Others at **25/-, 29/11, 35/-, 45/-**

ALL PRICES ARE SUBJECT TO MARKET FLUCTUATIONS

HARRODS LTD
Telephone SLOANE 1234
Telegrams ' EVERYTHING HARRODS LONDON'
LONDON S W 1

FURNISHING DRAPERIES DEPARTMENT

Increase the Value of Your Car by Fitting It Out with Loose Covers of Harrods dependable Quality

Just as the exterior of a car needs re-painting or re-touching from time to time so the interior needs re-decorating or re-covering. Harrods selection of covers are beautifully tailored to cover seats, sides, and doors, and the range of prices enables every car owner to select a set which will not only add to its attractiveness, but will so preserve the interior that its selling value will be considerably increased

Full particulars and prices will be furnished on request

Bridge Covers, Travelling and Motor Cushions

A beautiful collection of Cushions are always on view in Harrods Furnishing Drapery Salon and a visit when in Town will solve many a cherished decorative scheme

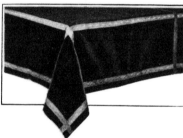

No. 1
BRIDGE COVERS
OR TABLE CENTRES
In Gold Krinkle Satin, trimmed galon, lined Sateen. 50 ins. square
49/6 Lined Silk .. **65/-, 79/6**

No. 5
BRIDGE COVERS
In soft Green shade of Velour, trimmed galon and lined Sateen
50 ins. square **39/6**

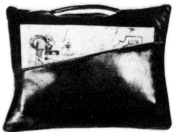

1   2   3

TRAVELLING CUSHION
In Chrome Leather, filled Kapoc. In charming shades of Brown, Blue, Green, Rose, etc. Size 16 × 12 ins. .. **15/9**
Also in cases with detachable cushions filled with Down and Vegetable Down
25/6

No. 1. CUSHION
In Damask of Chinese design filled down. Charming and serviceable gift. 22 ins. square **25/-**
No. 2. MOTOR CUSHION
In Suede Leather, filled Kapoc. In shades of Brown, Crimson, Grey, Blue, Green, etc. ; with fringe. 18 ins. square **21/-**
No. 3. CUSHION
In multi-coloured stripe, filled Kapoc. In bright cheerful colours. 24 ins. square **14/9**

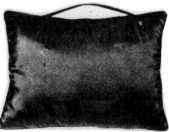

JAP SILK CUSHIONS
Down filled Cushion covered in Jap silk in shades of Blue, Green, Rose, Gold and Wine
16 × 12 ins. **6/6**

ALL PRICES ARE SUBJECT TO MARKET FLUCTUATIONS

HARRODS LTD

Telephone SLOANE 1234
Telegrams 'EVERYTHING HARRODS LONDON'

LONDON S W 1

SECOND-HAND FURNITURE DEPARTMENT

A Large Collection of Handsome Second-Hand Furniture Always on View in Harrods Furniture Galleries

One of our many Show-Rooms of Second-Hand Furniture

HANDSOME FURNITURE GROWS MORE BEAUTIFUL WITH AGE

Good furniture suffers no harm from discriminating use. In the Second-hand Department there is a large collection of handsome furniture in perfect condition, which Harrods are able to offer at prices showing a heavy reduction on the original prices. This reduction may enable a purchaser to whom price is an important consideration to acquire the particular piece on which his heart is set rather than the best new piece that he can afford. While, altogether apart from the question of price, a tour of this department may at any time be rewarded by the most attractive and unexpected 'find'

Harrods are prepared to consider the purchase of approved furniture second-hand from their customers. Communications on this subject should be addressed to the Manager, Second-hand Furniture Department

ANTIQUE FURNITURE DEPARTMENT

Filled with Treasures for the Connoisseur and the Collector

A Corner of Harrods Spacious Department for Antique Furniture

A LARGE SELECTION OF OLD ENGLISH AND CONTINENTAL ANTIQUES

The graceful designs of bygone artists, the patient labour of bygone craftsmen, the character which comes with long use and the deep polish that only time can apply—it is these that give charm to the genuine Antique. In Harrods Antique Furniture Department there is as much to interest the serious collector as there is to interest the amateur who relies on his own good taste and instinct for beauty. The pieces are not crowded —they are displayed in spacious showrooms where they can be inspected in comfort and at leisure

Day by day the collection changes—pieces are sold and are replaced by others as beautiful—but at all times it is a rich and varied collection well worthy the consideration of every lover of fine furniture

Harrods are always prepared to consider the purchase of Genuine Antiques suitable for inclusion in their collection

HARRODS LTD
    Telephone SLOANE 1234
Telegrams 'EVERYTHING HARRODS LONDON'
    LONDON S W 1

CHURCH FURNISHING DEPARTMENT

MEMORIAL CROSS
(*As illustrated*). New design in Marble, well-proportioned and excellently carved. Mounted on three plinths. Over all height, 5 ft. 6 ins. **£42 10 0**

BRASS VASES (*below*)
In good quality cast and lacquered brass, 8 ins. high
Per pair **35/-**
Or in hand-wrought and hammered brass, unlacquered 7½ ins. high. Per pair **£2 19 6**

OAK PULPIT
With straight staircase. Finely carved panels and mouldings. Over all height, 6 ft. .. from **£113 10 0**

SILVER CHALICE (*below*)
Replica of the Trinity College Chalice, A.D. 1527. 7½ ins. high. Stem pierced and enriched with twisted Silver wires. The inside of bowl is Gilt **£23 5 0**

SILVER PATEN
Scale shape, Gilt inside
£3 5 0
Chalice in Electro-Gilt
£29 5 0
Paten in Electro-Gilt
£3 17 6
Leatherette Case .. **25/-**

PROCESSIONAL CROSS
In hand-beaten Brass on wood core, ornament and emblems in relief, modified back, carefully chiselled figure, price including Oak pole **£76 0 0**
Without Figure **£72 0 0**

GRANITE MEMORIALS IN CELTIC DESIGN (*Not illustrated*)
With kerbing for plot 6 ft. 6 ins. × 2 ft. 6 ins., 5 ft. 6 ins. high. Erected complete on regulation York Stone Landing, from **£32 7 6**

MARBLE MEMORIALS
Simple Latin Cross with kerb for ordinary single plot. Height 5 ft. Erected complete on Landing
From **£28 9 6**
Portland Stone Memorial Kerb and Corner Posts for single plot. Erected with overhead and foot resters
From **£12 10 0**
Inscriptions extra

FRONTAL
Panelled and richly embroidered with floss and gold thread, finished silk braid and fringe, lined silk
Estimates, patterns and suggestions for Frontals, Vestments, etc., will be gladly sent free on request

WHITE BIRCHWOOD CHAIR
Strong and reliable make with rush or wood seat **6/9**

DAMASK STOLE
Rich all-silk. Handsomely embroidered by hand in untarnishable gold thread and floss silk, lined silk, and finished with a deep silk fringe .. From **£3 3 0**

ALTAR LINEN
All Irish Linen, hand-embroidered and hemstitched Fair Linen Cloth (*as illustrated*) Sizes—
2 ft. × 9 ft. Embroidered with five crosses **86/3**
2 ft. 3 ins. × 9 ft. Embroidered with five crosses **90/6**
2 ft. × 10 ft. 6 ins. Embroidered with five crosses **90/6**
2 ft. 3 ins. × 10 ft. Embroidered with five crosses **95/6**
A Selection of Altar Linen always in stock. Special sizes made to order

LECTERN
In best quality London-make lacquered Brass, with claw feet and conventional Eagle Gilt finished, 5 ft. high **£39 10 0**
Inscriptions can be engraved on Lecterns from **3/6** doz. letters according to size required

ALL PRICES ARE SUBJECT TO MARKET FLUCTUATIONS

REMOVALS AND WAREHOUSE DEPARTMENT
REMOVALS BY LAND OR SEA
To and from all Parts of the World

Harrods Depository at Barnes stands in its own grounds of 10 acres and is the largest organisation of its kind in the World
This magnificent building has been designed and erected on the most modern and scientific principles for the sole purpose of storing furniture and valuables at the lowest possible rates consistent with the finest service in the country

HARRODS REMOVALS SERVICE

Removals of every kind are undertaken to or from any part of the world. Goods are carefully handled and packed by skilled packers, and their transportation effected with the utmost speed and security. All vans are sent out with clean sheets and matting to provide against any possibility of soiling, and customers may rely implicitly on Harrods guarantee that their goods will be packed, transported, and delivered in perfect condition

LOWEST RATES—BEST SERVICE—ABSOLUTE SECURITY

Harrods Warehousing and Removals service is something more than the mere transportation and storage of goods. It is a highly organised service, equipped on scientific lines, and possessing exceptional resources both in space and in means of transportation. The insurance rates for the depositories are the lowest in the trade—a sufficient testimony as to its suitability and security against loss by fire

Estimates Gladly Given for the Smallest or Largest Contracts

HARRODS LTD   *Telephone SLOANE 1234*
Telegrams 'EVERYTHING HARRODS LONDON'   **LONDON S W 1**

REMOVALS AND WAREHOUSE DEPARTMENT

Furniture, Pictures, and Valuables of Every Description Carefully Packed and Stored

The illustration shows the four elevated roadways at the depository which are a special feature of the building. Along each roadway are tracks stretching the full length of the building and on these tracks, vans are drawn and carefully unloaded exactly opposite the particular storage compartment assigned to them

HOW UNNECESSARY HANDLING IS ELIMINATED

When the loaded van reaches the Depository, a specially constructed lift takes the entire van up to the actual floor upon which the goods are to be deposited. This eliminating of unnecessary handling on staircases and so forth together with the expert care taken over packing, brings the risk of damage to an absolute minimum

Section showing a small part of one of Harrods many Piano Storage Departments. Pianos are accessible at all times for tuning and repairs

ABSOLUTE SECURITY & PERFECT PRESERVATION

Archangel Mats are used for wrapping, cases are used when necessary, and the utmost precautions are taken against damp, dust, and moth. Harrods claim that no matter how long the period of storage lasts, the goods will be in as perfect condition when they are removed as when they were deposited

Section showing how Motor Cars are stored at Harrods Depository Storage. Charges which are extremely moderate forwarded on request

REMOVALS AND WAREHOUSE DEPARTMENT
Removals Undertaken to or from All Parts of the World

This picturesque scene gives some idea of the service which Harrods Depositories offer. The removal in this instance was from Crawley, Sussex, to Venice, and the illustration shows one of Harrods Vans being delivered by Gondola in Venice

REMOVALS ABROAD

Removals by Van

Harrods have their own workshops where vans are specially constructed for Continental traffic. These vans are constantly in transit and are frequently available on their return journey for our clients, thus saving the carriage expense one way on the empty van Harrods have undertaken removals to and from Australia, India, South Africa, Canada, America and in all parts of Europe and that this service is all that is claimed is fully endorsed by the tribute paid them in hundreds of letters received from grateful clients

Packing Cases

Goods are packed at the Barnes Depository and are shipped direct from the Wharf by our own Lighters which ply between this Wharf and the London Docks. This is a great advantage to clients for the cases are delivered free on board at a much lower rate than by road, and all the heavy Dock charges attached to the ordinary system are completely avoided

When it is impracticable or unadvisable to remove furniture aboard in Harrods Railway Vans, estimates will be submitted for the packing and forwarding of it in cases to any part of the World

THREE GROUPS OF DEPOSITORIES

There are three great groups of Harrods Depositories in England, one at Barnes in London, another at Manchester, and another at Southport, altogether comprising the largest Furniture Warehousing business in the world

ELECTRICAL DEPARTMENT
Every Conceivable Electrical Lighting Fitting is Available at Harrods

EL 10169
WALL BRACKET
Oxidized metal work with flame-coloured panels at the side.
Width 13¼ ins.   Depth 12 ins.
£4 10 0

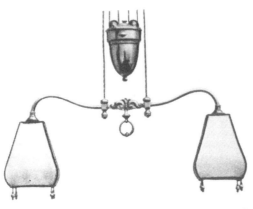

EL 23620   TWO-LIGHT SLIDING PENDANT
For Bedroom Lighting. Width, light to light, 18 ins.
Antique Brass Finish **54/6**
Oxidized Silver **65/6**
Silk Shades, extra ..   ..   ..   Each **12/6**

EL 10307   MODERN ONE-LIGHT
PANEL BRACKET
In Oxidized Silver metalwork, and
glazed with Tango tinted glassware.
Width 12 ins.   Depth 13 ins.
£5 7 6

EL 2122   CEILING LIGHT
Orinula Finish Metalwork. Handsome
Cut Glass Bowl. 9-in. diameter base
£5 10 0

EL 2951
BRASS
FLEXIBLE READING LAMP
Can be focussed in any direction
Polished Brass Finished ..   **17/6**
Oxidized Copper Finish ..   **21/-**

SHELL CRAFT
Bowls can be tinted any colour.
Prices.

No.	Size	Plain	Tinted
137	12½″ × 5½″	58/6	61/6
138	13½″ × 5½″	63/-	66/-
139	16″ × 6″	74/3	78/-
140	19″ × 8″	88/3	92/-

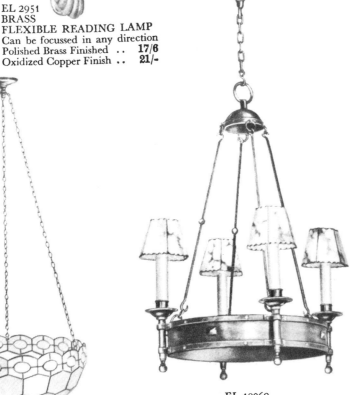

EL 10969
PENDANT
Four-light Rustless Iron Candle Pendant.
16th Century
£10 18 6
Parchment Shades extra.
Each **12/6**

SHELL CRAFT
Made from the shell of the Tropical
Oyster. Artistic and durable, easily
cleaned and unaffected by heat or by
water in washing.

No.	Size	Natural Colour.
133 ..	12½″ × 5½″ ..	60/-
134 ..	14½″ × 5½″ ..	78/6
135 ..	16″ × 6″ ..	87/6
135A	19″ × 8″ ..	102/6

ALL PRICES ARE SUBJECT TO MARKET FLUCTUATIONS

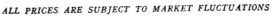

HARRODS LTD

Telephone SLOANE 1234
Telegrams 'EVERYTHING HARRODS LONDON'

LONDON S W 1

ELECTRICAL DEPARTMENT
All the latest Electrical Appliances at Harrods

THE 'THERMEGA' BLANKET
THE NEW ELECTRIC RADIANT BLANKET

No more cold, damp beds. The 'Thermega' Blanket airs, dries and warms the whole of the bed with absolute safety. Can be connected to any Electric Light, and costs less than a farthing an hour for current.

Standard size 'Thermega' Blanket, 44 × 32 ins. .. **£2 2 0**

Universal Type 'Thermega' Blanket, 44 × 32 ins. with adaptor for all voltages and with additional wall plug fitting.. .. .. **£3 3 0**

Covers for use with above :

Cotton, 5/-.   Fadeless Repp **8/6**

VIOLET RAY HIGH FREQUENCY OUTFIT

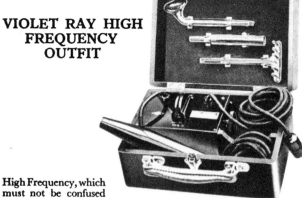

High Frequency, which must not be confused with Artificial Sunlight, has been adopted by Dentists, Doctors, Hospitals and Beauty Specialists throughout the world. This particular set which includes three electrodes will enable you to procure the self same treatment in your own home for nervous affections, reinvigorating the system, and for beautifying the complexion and hair

     Mahogany Case .. **£4 12 6**
     Rexine covered Case .. **£3 17 6**

NICKEL-PLATED HAIR DRYER

Specially designed for home use Hot or cold air with a turn of the switch **£2 18 6**
Cheaper quality .. **£1 10 0**

THE 'THOR 30' FOLDING ELECTRIC IRONER

The operator has merely to sit in a comfortable chair, turn a switch and guide the pieces through. Electricity operates the motor, heats the iron and does all the work economically and quickly. There are no pedals—everything is automatic. When the ironing is finished the ironer can be folded up compactly, for it takes up even less room than a kitchen chair

            Price **£42 10 0**
Or delivery on first payment of **£3 14 5** and the remainder in 11 monthly instalments of **£3 14 5**

ELECTRIC 'RAYDO HAIR BRUSH

Needs no wire connection as it contains a dry battery which can be easily renewed. Invaluable for Hair or Scalp treatment **£3 3 0**

ARTIFICIAL SUNLIGHT

HOMESUN LAMP

The HOMESUN Lamp is designed for home use, and those subject to overstrain, nerve weakness, insomnia and such conditions are reinvigorated and restored by a course of artificial sunlight.

The HOMESUN is a smaller model of the famous Hanovia medical lamps, known in medical use for over 20 years. Supplied for any current and voltage (state full particulars of supply when ordering). Consumption ¼ unit.

Price, Alternating Current Model, **£15**

Price, Direct Current Model **£19**

(Ask for special booklet 'Sunlight all the year round ').

ALL PRICES ARE SUBJECT TO MARKET FLUCTUATIONS

HARRODS LTD   *Telephone SLOANE 1234*
Telegrams 'EVERYTHING HARRODS LONDON'   **LONDON S W 1**

ELECTRICAL DEPARTMENT
'EVER READY' Portable Electric Specialities Fitted with Dry Batteries

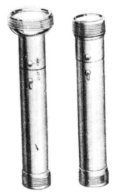

COMBINED HAND AND READING LAMP

With adjustable reflector

Polished Mahogany case. Nickel fittings
No. 2092. Large model. Fitted with 3 cell battery, giving 60-80 hours lighting service **27/6**
Refills (No. R 481) **7/6**
No. 2094. Small model. Fitted with 3 cell battery giving 12-15 hours lighting service **17/6**
Refills (No. 15) **1/6**

SPOTLIGHT TORCHES
Nickel-plated with 2½ in. reflector
No. 2004 With 2 unit cells, 6½ ins. long .. **9/6**
No. 2003 " 3 " " 8¼ " " .. **10/6**
With 1½ in. reflector
No. 2002 With 2 unit cells, 6½ ins. long .. **7/6**
No. 2001 " 3 " " 8¼ " " .. **8/6**

U 2 REFILL UNIT CELLS .. .. each **5d**
REFILL BATTERIES.. 2 cell, **10d**; 3 cell, **1/3**; 5 cell, **2/6**

STANDARD TORCHES
Corrugated fibre with 1½ in. Bull's eye lens
No. 1839 2 cell, small, 5½ ins. long **4/-**
No. 1829 2 cell, large, 6½ ins. long **5/-**
No. 1828 3 cell, large, 9 ins. long **6/-**
Refill Batteries: No. 1839, **8d**; No. 1829, **10d**; No. 1828, **1/3**

HALL TABLE LANTERNS
Nickel-plated
No. 1820 Large model. Fitted with 2½ in. Bull's eye lens **12/6**
Refill Batteries, 3 cell **2/-**
No. 1920. Small model. Fitted with 1½ in. Bull's eye lens **9/6**
Refill Batteries, 3 cell **1/-**

PORTABLE SEARCHLIGHTS
Nickel-plated with 3 in. reflector. Octagonal head
Fitted with spare bulb in lower end cap
No. 2202 With 2 unit cells, 8½ ins. long .. **11/-**
No. 2203 " 3 " " 10½ " " .. **12/6**
No. 2204 " 5 " " 15½ " " .. **15/-**

GENERAL UTILITY POCKET LAMPS
Leather covered in red, green or brown. Nickel-plated fittings, 1 in. Bull's eye
No. 1612 2 cell, 3¾ × 1⅞ × 1 in. **3/-**
No. 1613 3 " 3¾ × 2¼ × 1 in. **3/6**
Refill Batteries: No. 730, **6d**; No. 121, **1/-**

PORTABLE BELL SETS
Polished Mahogany Case, with 12 yards flexible wire
Nickel-plated domes and fittings
No. 1949 De Luxe model (as illustrated) .. **30/-**
No. 886 Popular upright model **15/-**
No. 155 Popular Bell set **10/6**
Refill Batteries (2 cell) **1/6**

ELECTRIC NIGHT LIGHT
Polished dark oak case—opal globe
No. 1979 (as illustrated) **7/6**
3 cell refill Batteries **1/6**

INSIST ON 'EVER READY' BRITAIN'S BEST BATTERIES FOR SATISFACTORY SERVICE

PEARL OSRAM LAMPS

The Clear Osram Gas-filled Lamp 40 watt

Standard Watts.	Standard Cap.	VOLTAGE RANGE AND PRICE PER LAMP.						
		25-30 v.	35-55 v.	60-80 v.	100 to 130 v.		200-260 v.	
		Gasfilled.	Gasfilled.	Gasfilled.	Vacuum.	Gasfilled.	Vacuum.	Gasfilled.
		s. d.	s. d.	s. d.	s. d.	s. d.	s. d.	s. d.
15		*2 0	*2 6	—	2 0	—	2 2	—
25		2 6	2 10	3 6	—	2 1	2 2	—
40	BC	2 10	2 10	3 6	—	2 1	—	2 3
60		3 4	3 4	4 3	—	2 3	—	2 3
75		—	—	—	—	3 6	—	3 6
100		—	5 9	7 3	—	4 3	—	4 3

* These sizes are supplied in Vacuum type only
These lamps can also be supplied in clear glass bulbs at the same price

The Pearl Osram Gas-filled Lamp 60 watt

OSRAM VACUUM LAMPS

Standard Watts	Standard Cap.	VOLTAGE RANGE AND PRICE PER LAMP.				
		25 & 30	50	60, 65, 70, 75, 80, 85.	100—130	200—260
		s. d.	s. d.	s. d.	s. d.	s. d.
15		2 0	2 6	2 10		
25	BC	2 0	2 6	2 10	2 0	2 2
40		—	—	—		
60		—	—	—		

Full Price List of Lamps on application All standard makes at same price

OSRAM CANDLE TYPE

Standard Watts	Voltage Range	PRICE PER LAMP	
		Plain	Crinkled
		s. d.	s. d.
	25 & 30	3 0	—
	50	3 6	—
20	60, 65, 70 & 80	4 0	—
	100 to 130	3 0	3 6
	200 to 260	3 8	4 2

ALL PRICES ARE SUBJECT TO MARKET FLUCTUATIONS
Telephone SLOANE 1234
Telegrams 'EVERYTHING HARRODS LONDON'

HARRODS LTD   **LONDON S W 1**

BUILDING AND DECORATING DEPARTMENT

SCHEMES PREPARED AND ESTIMATES SUBMITTED BY COMPETENT ARTISTS, SURVEYORS AND ENGINEERS

ALTERATIONS, DECORATIONS, SANITATION, HEATING AND ELECTRICAL INSTALLATIONS

ESTIMATES FREE

LET HARRODS MODERNIZE YOUR HOME

ALTERATIONS

Alterations and additions to Houses are skilfully executed by Harrods. The converting of two rooms into one. The installation of new bathrooms, garages, etc., and every kind of marble and general tiling work will be gladly estimated for and plans submitted on request

DECORATIONS

Period Interiors are faithfully reproduced and adapted to modern requirements—an art in which Harrods excel. Whatever your requirements, whether for one room or a whole house, Harrods will submit schemes and estimates

REPAIRS

Harrods have a special staff of skilled Carpenters, Plumbers, Fitters, Electricians, Bricklayers, Painters, etc., who carry out repairs of every kind

Special care is taken to give satisfaction in jobbing repairs of every description

ELECTRIC WIRING

The installation of power plants, the wiring or re-wiring of Houses the installation of bells and telephones are undertaken for the smallest or largest building. Harrods Building and Decorating Department will gladly advise and submit schemes and estimates

SANITATION

Harrods have a spacious showroom where the most up-to-date baths, lavatories, etc., may be inspected and selected. Full particulars and advice concerning all matters appertaining to sanitation will be furnished on request

DOMESTIC ENGINEERING

Water supplies, domestic hot water installations, central heating, sewage disposal plants and general plumbing are undertaken in any part of the country Free estimates and plans submitted

BUILDING & DECORATING DEPARTMENT

Re-creating the Beauty of Other Days

To bring back the beauty of a bygone period and to adapt its soft mellowing
influences to the modern home, is the purpose
of Harrods skilled Interior decorators

OAK PANELLED ROOMS AT MODERATE PRICES

Approximate prices for a room similar to the above illustration measuring 18 × 12 × 9 ft. high

Oak panelled walls with plate shelf, fixed and polished	..	..	**£100 0 0**
Beamed ceiling in oak	..	..	**£25 0 0**
Stone mantel and hearth with red brick fireplace opening	..	..	**£30 0 0**
Oak parquet floor as straight oak boards	..	..	**£30 0 0**

ALL PRICES ARE SUBJECT TO MARKET FLUCTUATIONS

HARRODS LTD

Telephone SLOANE 1234
Telegrams 'EVERYTHING HARRODS LONDON'

LONDON S W 1

BUILDING & DECORATING DEPARTMENT

A Fine Example of Modern Furniture and Period Reproduction

AN OAK LIBRARY OF JACOBEAN INFLUENCE

Finely figured oak panelling, with carved fruit wood ornamentations, makes a pleasing background for this restful library in which the dignified atmosphere of the Jacobean era has been reproduced

Leaded glazings in the bookcases and hand moulded plaster beams contribute to the atmosphere characteristic of the period. The stone Chimney Piece is noteworthy because of its generous opening, interestingly arranged in old brick and tiles. Carefully chosen Furnishings complete the inviting effect

The decorative scheme for this room was designed in Harrods Studio, and the work was executed by Harrods throughout

HARRODS LTD

Telephone SLOANE 1234
Telegrams 'EVERYTHING HARRODS LONDON'

LONDON S W 1

BUILDING & DECORATING DEPARTMENT

Harrods are Specialists in Period and Modern Decoration

A SEVENTEENTH CENTURY SALON

This magnificently appointed room—a reproduction of the work of Grinling Gibbons and his contemporaries—was built, decorated, and furnished by Harrods. The predominating colour tone from ceiling to floor is old ivory, which emphasises the rich beauty of the 'blue belge' marble bolection Chimney Piece and the Grinling Gibbons carving above. Note the elaborate ceiling of the period and the braces of Corinthian Pilasters placed symmetrically round the room

Antique Settees and Chairs in Needlework, Silver Fittings reproduced from Hampton Court Palace, beautiful furniture and an oriental carpet complete a distinctive Salon

BUILDING & DECORATING DEPARTMENT

Let Harrods Instal Your Electric Generating Plant

COMPLETE INSTALLATIONS FOR COUNTRY HOUSE POWER AND LIGHTING

The quality of the Electric Lighting and Heating contributes in no small degree to the success of the modern country or town House. Harrods long experience in carrying out electrical installations of every kind, and the exhaustive investigations which they have made into the various types of generating sets, enables them to submit schemes and estimates which will meet satisfactorily the requirements of every modern installation

You are invited to consult Harrods on every matter relating to the lighting or heating of your house

HARRODS LTD   *Telephone SLOANE 1234*
Telegrams 'EVERYTHING HARRODS LONDON'   **LONDON S W 1**

BUILDING & DECORATING DEPARTMENT

Harrods Modern Cooking and Heating Equipment

A Gas Cooker and an independent Boiler are by far the easiest and most economical means of cooking and of supplying hot-water in a house
Harrods offer expert advice as to removing out-of-date and extravagant Kitchen Ranges and the installation of modern equipment. Estimates Free

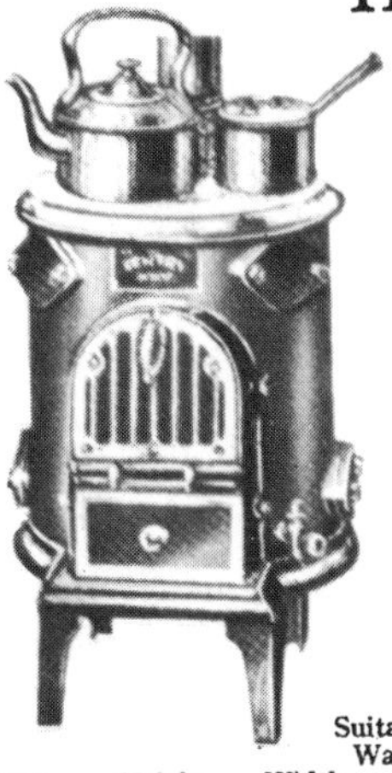

SENTRY BOILER
The No. 1 Sentry Boiler is designed with large and well placed mud covers readily facilitating thorough boiler cleaning. The size illustrated is suitable for heating a hot water storage tank or cylinder up to 50 gallons capacity

Size	Height	Width	Suitable Size Hot Water Storage Gals.	Prices Cast Iron
A	17½ ins.	15¾ ins.	25 or 30	£4 7 6
B	19½ ins.	15¾ ins.	30 or 40	£7 7 6
No. 1	22 ins.	18½ ins.	50 or 60	£12 10 0
No. 2	28 ins.	18½ ins.	70	£14 10 0
No. 3	34 ins.	18½ ins.	80	£17 0 0

SUNDRIES—Base and Legs for A and B (8 in.) 10/-
Legs for Nos. 1 and 2 (6 in.) .. 5/-
Stoking Tools A and B 2/9 ; other sizes 6/6

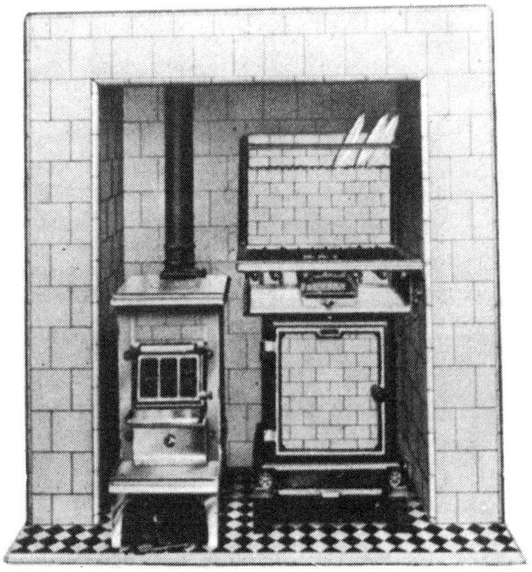

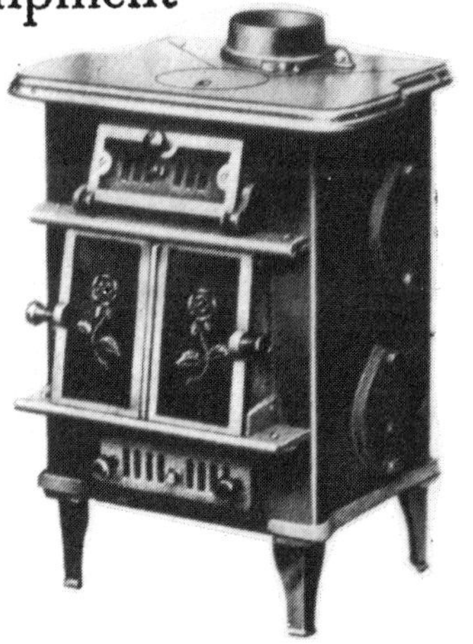

WHITE ROSE BOILER (*above*)
The No. 1 size illustrated, is a popular heater, chiefly on account of its convenient height. A special feature is the easy stoking through a feed door, obviating the removal of the top cover or use of filler.

SIZES AND PRICES

Description	No. 0 £ s. d.	No. 1 £ s. d.	No. 2 £ s. d.
Boiler with polished top and beadings	5 0 0	8 10 0	10 0 0
High Base, as illustrated, extra	11 0	11 0	11 0
Boiler treated by rustless process	1 12 6	2 0 0	2 7 6
Stoking Tools	4 0	4 0	4 0

Sizes of hotplate—

	Height ins.	Width ins.	Depth ins.
No. 0	22½	21	14
No. 1	26½	21¼	15
No. 2	32½	21¼	15

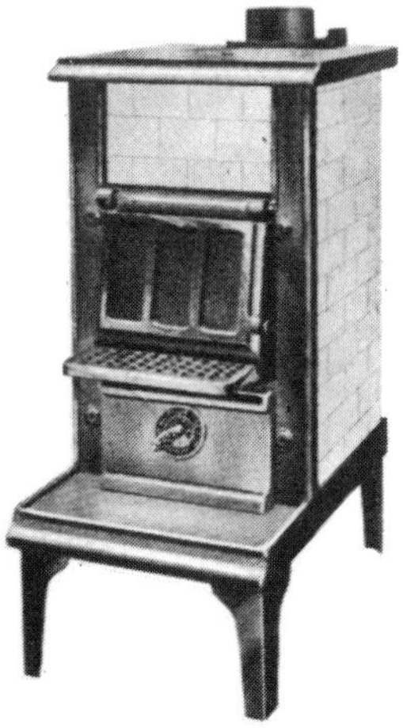

NAUTILUS BOILER
BI Pattern Nautilus Independent Boiler (*illustrated*). The bottom bars are rotated by a special device which crushes the clinkers into an enclosed ashpan. The porcelain enamelled steel casing, finished like white tiles, promotes cleanliness in appearance and use. An illustrated list, obtainable on application gives full details

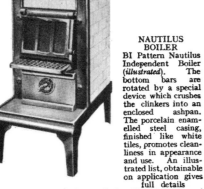

'A' PATTERN—Grey Body, Hot-plate ground Mouldings of Door, Top moulding of Ashpan, Trivet, and cornice of Hot-plate, ground and polished. White tile-pattern porcelain enamelled panel fitted above the door

'B' PATTERN—Same as 'A' pattern, but has in addition White tile pattern porcelain enamelled sides

	No. 1	No. 2	No. 3
'A' Pattern ..	£12 12 0	£15 15 0	£19 19 0
'B' Pattern ..	£13 7 0	£16 10 0	£21 0 0

IDEAL CLASSIC RADIATORS (*below*)
Ideal Classic Radiators made in sizes to suit all requirements. Particulars on application

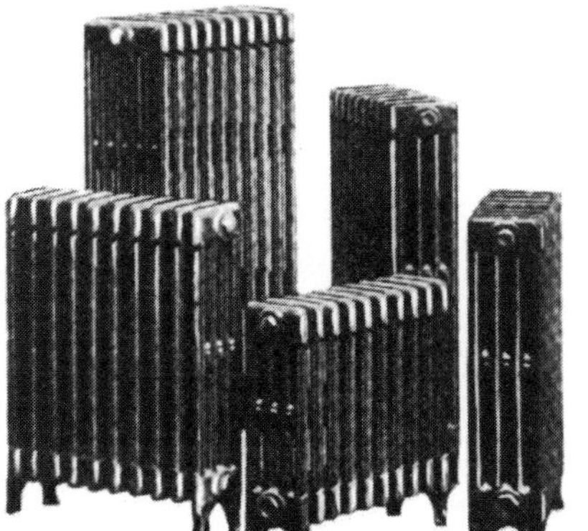

Harrods have many other types of radiators and boilers, and will gladly send full particulars on request

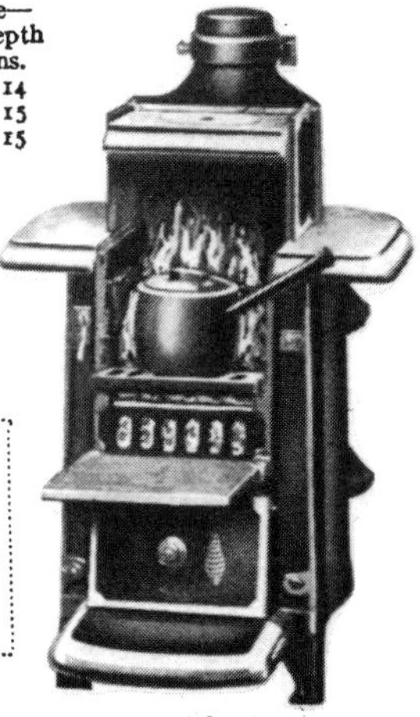

IDEAL BOILER (*above*)
The No. 0 illustrated here is a new and inexpensive type allowing a large open fire for heating and cooking It is particularly useful in a room which is used both for cooking and as a Maid's Sitting Room

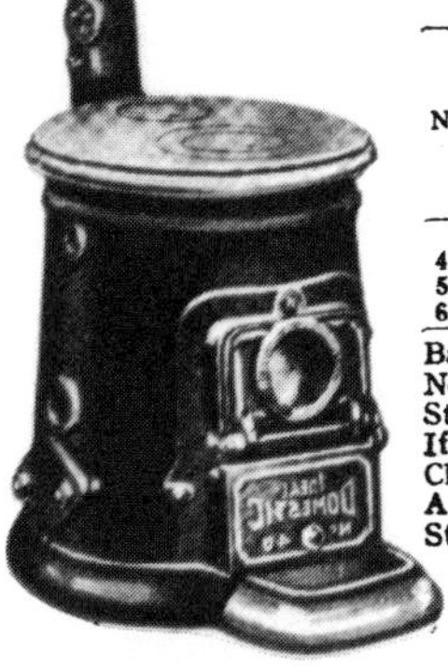

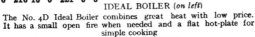

IDEAL BOILER (*on left*)
The No. 4D Ideal Boiler combines great heat with low price. It has a small open fire when needed and a flat hot-plate for simple cooking

RATINGS AND PRICES

No.	Hot Water Supply Only: British Thermal Units per hour.	Hot Water Supply Only: Gals. per hour 50-120°	Hot Water Supply Only: Gals. per hour 50-150°	Heating Only: British Thermal Units per hour.	Prices: With Polished Top £ s. d.	Prices: Extra if Firepot Rustless (Bower-barffed). £ s. d.
4D	38,500	55	38	15,200	5 3 9	2 6 6
5D	49,500	70	49	19,200	5 18 9	2 9 0
6D	66,000	94	66	26,800	7 8 9	3 5 9

Baseplate Nos. 4D and 5D .. 12/- .. No. 6D 13/9
No. 802 Ideal Damper Regulator £2 6 9
Stoking Tools, per set .. 2/9 Draw-off Cock 4/3
If Top dull nickel-plated with edges polished, extra .. 13/3
Cleaning Chisel 5/6
A set of Stoking Tools consists of Poker, Slice Bar, Shovel and Lifter.
Stoking Tools and Draw-off Cock are supplied unless otherwise ordered

GLOW-WORM BOILER
No. 02 Glow-Worm Junior Boiler (*on right*). Fitted with a 'shaking grate' which obviates all dust and is a great labour saving device

No.	Height ins.	Width at Base ins.	Suitable Size H.W. Cylinder or Tank. Gals.	Cast Iron £ s. d.
01 Junior	25	16	20 to 25	6 10 0
Minor	21½	18	25 to 30	8 0 0
02 Junior	26	15	30 to 35	9 9 0
1	*19¾	18	45 to 50	10 0 0
2	*24¾	18	60 to 70	11 10 0

Extras—
Cast Iron Tray, Nos. 1 and 2 12/-
*Set of 4 feet, Nos. 1 and 2 .. 5/-
Ashpan for Nos. 01, 1 and 2 .. 3/-
Stoking Tools 4/-

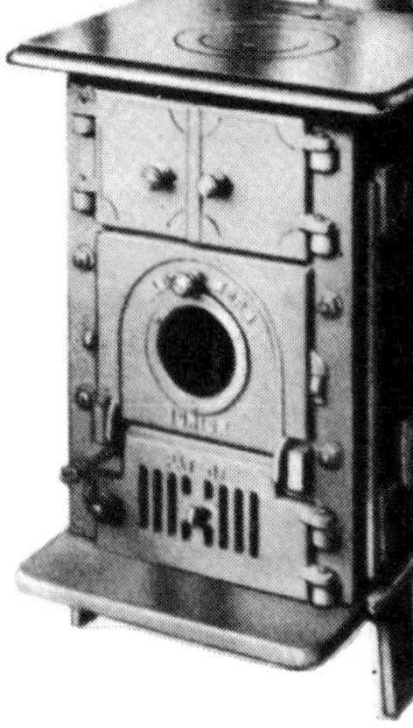

ALL PRICES ARE SUBJECT TO MARKET FLUCTUATIONS

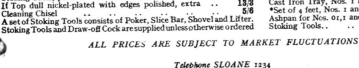

BUILDING & DECORATING DEPARTMENT
Attractively Made Baths and Thoroughly Reliable Geysers

THE 'KNIGHTSBRIDGE' BATH

A very favourably priced bath typical of Harrods remarkable values. Heavy cast iron British made. White porcelain enamelled inside and plain painted outside. Size overall 5 ft. 6 ins. × 2 ft. 5 ins. × 3 ins. roll

Price with brass fittings	**£4 15 0**
Price with nickel-plated fittings	**£4 19 6**

THE 'CASTLE' BATH

An inexpensive model of the popular square end bath. Side panels in white opal glass or imitation marble. Bath White porcelain enamelled inside. Sizes overall 5 ft. 6 ins. × 2 ft. 4 ins. × 1 ft. 10½ ins. high

Complete with nickel-plated fittings **£9 15 0**

Where desired the feet can be removed and the bath will be lowered by 6 ins.

Also shown is a new pattern pedestal lavatory basin, 27 ins. × 19 ins. Complete with nickel-plated fittings **£6 12 6**

THE 'BIJOU' BATH

Cast iron porcelain enamelled. A suitable size for a room where space is limited. Complete with nickel-plated fittings

Length	Width	Depth	Length	Width	Height	Roll
Inside sizes			Overall sizes			
3' 9"	1' 9¼"	1' 4"	4' 2"	2' 2¾"	1' 10"	2½"

£7 19 6

VICTOR

An inexpensive but thoroughly reliable geyser of the sealed type, whereby water does not come in contact with gas fumes. Interlocking taps allow gas to be turned on only after the water tap has been opened and the latter cannot be shut down without first turning out the gas. Heats 2½ gallons per minute

On wall bracket	£6 17 6
On floor stand ..	£7 13 6

Larger size to heat 4 gallons per minute

On wall bracket	£13 19 0
On floor stand	£14 17 0

Also supplied with automatic valve which cuts off gas if through any reason water ceases to flow. Prices on application

> *Write for complete list of Geysers*

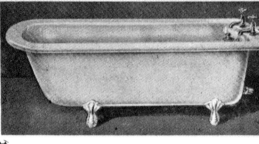

THE 'GLEN' BATH

White porcelain enamelled inside, plain painted outside, with flat rolls and extended rim at end for fittings. Complete with heavily plated valves and combined standing waste and overflow

Length	Width	Depth	Length	Width	Height	Roll
Inside sizes			Overall sizes			
5' 6"	2' 0"	1' 6"	6' 4½"	2' 8"	2' 0¼"	4"

£15 11 0

'LIGHTNING GEYSER'

Hot water instantly night or day whenever required. A hot bath can be obtained in five ten or fifteen minutes according to the size of the geyser

Heats per min.	Price
1½ galls. ..	£8 0 0
2 ,, ..	£12 0 0
3 ,, ..	£16 0 0
4 ,, ..	£20 0 0
8 ,, ..	£35 0 0
16 ,, ..	£90 0 0

'CALIFONT'

An instantaneous Water Heater capable of supplying hot water to one or more taps or throughout the entire house according to the size of heater installed

Heating per minute :—

1½ galls. ..	£14 0 0
2 ,, ..	£18 0 0
3 ,, ..	£22 0 0
4 ,, ..	£27 4 0
6 ,, ..	£40 16 0
8 ,, ..	£48 16 0
10 ,, ..	£64 8 0
16 ,, ..	£88 0 0

ALL PRICES ARE SUBJECT TO MARKET FLUCTUATIONS

HARROD LTD

Telephone SLOANE 1234
Telegrams 'EVERYTHING HARRODS LONDON'

LONDON S W 1

BUILDING & DECORATING DEPARTMENT

Attractive Wallpapers in a Wide Range of Prices for the Simplest or the Most Elaborate Setting

WRITE FOR SPECIAL PATTERN BOOKS, SENT POST FREE ON REQUEST

No. 1 BOOK

A general selection of wallpapers for repapering a house throughout.   Prices range from **6d—9/6** per piece There are also many delightful decorative backgrounds for Staircase, Drawing Room, Dining Room, etc.

No. 2 BOOK

Fine background effects—Plain, stipple, jaspe, canvas, leather and decorative embossed papers, etc. Prices range from **2/6** to **42/-** per piece. A large variety of coloured hand-printed borders always in stock

EXPERT ADVICE GIVEN ON ALL INTERIOR DECORATIVE WORK

Wallpapers and Decorative Panelling, etc.

HAND AND MACHINE MADE PAPERS

A wonderful range of every type of hand and machine made paper, including the newest decorative and plain effects with borders to match

CEILING PAPERS

Large variety of Printed Ceiling papers, also Anaglypta and Lignomour relief designs which effectually hide all cracks in plasterwork.   These can be repainted or distempered at any time

NURSERY DECORATIONS

Harrods have an interesting variety of Nursery Decorations including 10½ friezes and highly coloured panels illustrating popular fairy stories and scenes of interest to children

PARQUET FLOORING

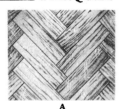

A

B

Harrods send expert workmen to fix flooring in any part of the country. Suggestions and estimates submitted on request

A—' Herringbone ' design can be supplied and laid in London districts for **15 -** per square yard, including a two line Walnut border. Country clients are invited to send a rough plan of a room or to ask for an estimator who will call by arrangement

B—Removable Parquet design which can be laid by local labour at a small cost. It is supplied in sheet size 3 ft. × 1 ft. at **9 9** per square yard A suitable border supplied at **6d** per foot run

FURTHER DESIGNS AND PRICES ON APPLICATION

Wallpapers and Decorative Panelling, etc.

A WASHABLE WALLPAPER

' Salubra,' a washable fadeless paper made with Artists Oil Colours, has a delightfully fresh and clean appearance and is an ideal choice for Nursery or Bedroom

OAK PANEL SCHEME

' Lincrusta ' is an exceptionally fine material for decorative work and is especially effective in giving a wonderful representation of solid oak

HAND BLOCK PAPERS

These can be printed in any desired colour at slightly extra cost

ALL PRICES ARE SUBJECT TO MARKET FLUCTUATIONS

HARRODS LTD

Telephone SLOANE 1234
Telegrams 'EVERYTHING HARRODS LONDON'

LONDON S W 1

INSURANCE DEPARTMENT
32 Hans Crescent
and
AT LLOYD'S

HARRODS INSURANCE DEPARTMENT occupies an outstanding position in the Insurance World, acting as Agents for all the principal Insurance Companies and being represented at Lloyd's by a thoroughly competent manager

Every class of Insurance is effected and information, expert advice and 'quotations' are freely tendered to Clients

Harrods have no preferential arrangement with any Insurance Companies or Underwriters, but advise their clients purely on the merits of the various companies, thus always obtaining the best possible terms consistent with security

FIRE, BURGLARY, HOUSEBREAKING AND LARCENY

For Private Residences and Business Premises

PUBLIC LIABILITY

Golfers, Sporting Guns, Wireless

PERSONAL ACCIDENT, DISEASE AND ALL SICKNESS

For both sexes, Annual or Permanent Contracts

ALL RISKS

Jewellery, Furs, Pictures and Valuables

LIFE ASSURANCES AND ANNUITIES

With or without Medical Examination—Children's Educational Endowments

MARINE AND BAGGAGE

Motor Craft, Travellers' Luggage

MOTOR CARS AND MOTOR CYCLES

Comprehensive Policies for all classes of risks

EMPLOYERS' LIABILITY

Domestic servants and all other employees

HOUSEHOLDERS' AND HOUSE OWNERS' COMPREHENSIVE POLICIES

Covering All Household Risks, Including Damage by burst Water Pipes, Storm, Tempest, Flood, Riots, Aircraft, Loss of Rent, Legal Liability to Third Parties

REDUCED RATES FOR LARGE VALUES

SPECIAL SCHEMES FOR SCHOOLS AND BOARDING HOUSES

LIVESTOCK, LIFTS, PEDAL CYCLES, STEAM AND OIL ENGINES, PLATE GLASS, LOSS OF PROFITS

BOILERS AND ELECTRICAL MACHINERY LEASEHOLD AND CAPITAL REDEMPTION

PARTICULARS OF ANY CLASS OF INSURANCE FURNISHED ON APPLICATION TO THE INSURANCE MANAGER

HARRODS ESTATE OFFICE

Auctioneers, Estate Agents, Valuers and Surveyors

Harrods Estate Office specialises in the sale of country estates, agricultural properties, town and country houses, factories, shops, trade premises, investments, Etc. Enquiries are invited

HARRODS ESTATE OFFICES
62 and 64 BROMPTON ROAD SW1
(Opposite Harrods Main Building)

Surrey Office :
WEST BYFLEET

Telegrams :
ESTATE c/o *HARRODS LONDON*

Telephone :
(Estate Office only) KENSINGTON *1490*
and SLOANE 1234

HARRODS AUCTION GALLERIES

For the Sale by Auction of

Antique Furniture, Works of Art, Bronzes, Silver Plate and Jewellery, Oil Paintings, Engravings, Prints, Water-Colours, Musical Instruments, Old Lace, Old Armour, Guns and Weapons, Books and Libraries, Furs, Etc.

ENQUIRIES ARE INVITED

VALUATIONS
of Works of Art, Antique and Decorative Furniture, etc., made by Experts for Insurance, Probate and other purposes

CONTENTS OF PRIVATE HOUSES
either in London or the Country sold by Auction on the premises

All Communications to

HARRODS LTD., 62-64, BROMPTON ROAD, S W 1

MOTOR HIRE DEPARTMENT
Confine your Car Cares to the Writing of a Monthly Cheque

For shopping expeditions, for business or for pleasure, 'phone Harrods Motor Hire Service (Sloane 1234) at any hour of the day or night. A luxuriously appointed car will be sent immediately to your door with a private liveried chauffeur whose carefulness and courtesy may be implicitly trusted

HARRODS HIRE TARIFF

DAILY HIRE RATES

				£	s	d				
2 hours up to	10 miles			1	1	0	Excess miles			1/6
3 ,, ,, ,,	15 ,,			1	10	0	,,	,,		1/6
5 ,, ,, ,,	30 ,,			2	12	6	,,	,,		1/3
10 ,, ,, ,,	60 ,,			4	10	0	,,	,,		1/0
12 ,, ,, ,,	100 ,,			6	5	0	,,	,,		10d
12 ,, ,, ,,	150 ,,			8	2	6	,,	,,		6d

EVENING HIRE RATES

Dinner, Theatre and Home (from 6 p.m. to midnight) allowing 25 miles **£1 5 0**

STATION RATES

To or from any London Terminus up to 10 miles and for one hour only between 8 a.m. and 8 p.m. .. **15/-**
Between 8 p.m. and 8 a.m. **£1 1 0**
Excess time on any of the above rates 10/- per hour

WEEK END RATES

Saturday 9 a.m. to Monday 6 p.m. up to a distance of 150 miles **£12 12 0**
Excess miles, each **1/-**
CARS ON HIRE BY WEEK of 7 days from **£21 0 0**
CARS ON HIRE BY MONTH of 4 weeks from **£63 0 0**

Yearly rates according to requirements

CARS FOR RACES

To hold six Passengers and Driver to and from Races in comfort. Harrods charge their Ordinary Daily Rates for all Race Meetings except Ascot and the Derby, when special prices are quoted on request

HARRODS PRIVATE CAR HIRE SERVICE

This 30 h.p. Armstrong-Siddeley Saloon-Landaulet at your Service day or night for 70 guineas a month

This handsome Car accommodates six passengers in perfect comfort. The two auxiliary seats, which face in any direction, fold up when not required

Electrically lighted throughout and provided with four doors

On a yearly contract reckoning on a mileage not exceeding 9,000 miles, the over-all inclusive charge for this Car is **70 guineas per month**

This 18 h.p. Armstrong-Siddeley Saloon-Landaulet exclusively at your Service for 60 guineas a month

Though of smaller power this Car yields nothing in finish and equipment to the higher-powered Car shown opposite

The Car is electrically lighted, velvet-smooth in running, and in every respect of superlative quality and appearance

On a yearly contract reckoning on a mileage not exceeding 9,000 miles, the charge for this Car inclusive of Harrods full Service is **60 guineas a month**

ALL PRICES ARE SUBJECT TO FLUCTUATIONS

HARRODS LTD

Telephone SLOANE 1234
Telegrams 'EVERYTHING HARRODS LONDON'

LONDON SW1

MOTOR HIRE DEPARTMENT
Harrods Finely Equipped Motor Ambulance

There is no vibration in this roomy, well-sprung ambulance, and, in addition to every possible comfort and convenience for the patient, ample accommodation is provided for the accompanying nurse and attendant. These Ambulances are sent out in charge of two Chauffeurs trained for this specialized work and may be commanded—except for infectious cases—any hour of the day or night

Minimum charge 2 hours or 10 miles	..	**42/-**	
Additional Time per hour	.. ..	**12/6**	

Additional Miles charged per mile **2/-**
Special rates quoted for long distances

LET HARRODS MAINTAIN YOUR OWN CAR

Harrods are prepared to take over and maintain customers' own Cars for a single inclusive sum

Under this arrangement Harrods supply a first-class chauffeur in private livery, a good garage and insurance against all third-party and other risks. In addition, the customer's Car is kept in excellent condition, cleaned and repaired without extra charge and is held ready for the owner's service at any hour of the day or night In the event of accident or breakdown another Car of similar style and power will be supplied free of cost

Harrods guarantee that Cars taken over under this scheme are never used except by owners' direct orders Harrods Garage Manager will gladly call and give fuller particulars of this scheme free of charge, on receipt of a card

HARRODS PRIVATE CARS FOR HIRE BY THE YEAR

Under their Yearly Contract System Harrods place a Car absolutely at your 'beck and call,' with a trained Chauffeur in private livery, ready to go anywhere, any distance, any hour of the day or night, the year round You can choose a magnificent Limousine or Landaulet with accommodation for five or seven passengers as required
You need not give one moment's thought to any detail of garaging, cleaning, petrol, oil, tyres or repairs You need not worry about the Chauffeur's wages or insurance, even against third party risks
You retain the same Car and the same Chauffeur all the year or you may change either or both. Should any mishap befall either the Chauffeur or the Car Harrods will effect immediate replacement
A representative will call to furnish an estimate on request

BUY YOUR NEW CAR AT HARRODS

Harrods Motor Car Sales Section will supply any make of Car for cash or on deferred terms. Your purchase will be followed by the finest possible ' After-Sales ' service
If Harrods have not got the Car of your choice in stock, a special Car is placed at your disposal to take you to the showrooms of the make you may select. The qualified representative who accompanies you will give

disinterested free advice, will arrange for registration, insurance, delivery and instruction in driving free of any extra expense

DEFERRED TERMS

Harrods easy payments are one-fifth down ; the balance, plus five per cent. per annum, in twelve or eighteen monthly instalments

ALL PRICES ARE SUBJECT TO FLUCTUATIONS

HARRODS LTD

Telephone SLOANE 1234
Telegrams ' EVERYTHING HARRODS LONDON '

LONDON S W 1

BOOK AND BOOKBINDING DEPARTMENT

Harrods have a large collection of Books in handsome Bindings, the latest novels by leading Authors and all well known Classics, Works of History, Travel, Biography, Theology, etc.

TO ORDER BOOKS by telephone, ask for the Book Department. Books are forwarded by return

NEW NOVELS AND BOOKS OF GENERAL INTEREST All new books of any importance are put into stock on publication. Books may be ordered in advance, to be forwarded to you immediately they are published

'OUT OF PRINT' BOOKS Harrods will advertise free of charge for any book required by a customer which is unobtainable from the Publisher. By this method very often 'out-of-print' and rare books can be obtained through the Trade

BOOKS published in **FOREIGN COUNTRIES** are supplied to order. If not obtainable in London Harrods will order them from abroad

MAGAZINES, NEWSPAPERS AND WEEKLY PUBLICATIONS are sent to subscription orders and are charged in advance

ANNUAL BOOKS OF REFERENCE

Badminton Diary	3/-
Bailey's Hunting Directory	10/6
Burke's Peerage	105/-
Crockford's Clerical Directory	42/-
Daily Mail Year Book	1/-
Debrett's Peerage, Baronetage and Knightage	75/-
Dod's Parliamentary Companion	7/6
Dod's Peerage	7/6
Directory of Directors	25/-
Golfer's Handbook	7/6
Kelly's Handbook to the Titled Classes ..	30/-
London Post Office Directory	55/-
Royal Blue Book	7/6
Royal Red Book	7/6
Stateman's Year Book	20/-
Stock Exchange Year Book	50/-
Whitaker's Almanack. Paper 3/-. Cloth ..	6/-
Whitaker's Peerage	25/-
Who's Who	45/-
Wisden's Cricketer's Almanac	5/-
Writers and Artists Year Book	3/6

BOOKBINDING, AND THE RESTORATION OF OLD BOOKS AND BINDINGS

Harrods undertake all branches of Bookbinding. Whether it is a priceless old Manuscript you wish to protect against depreciation, or a newer book the cover of which has been damaged, or if your Library Scheme requires all Books to be bound in a uniform fashion, let Harrods carry out the work for you. Estimates, with Samples of Leather and rough tracings of Patterns will gladly be sent on application

Harrods restore Old Books and Records in such a manner as to preserve their Antique appearance. All work of this character is executed by specialists

---

Customers desirous of having any valuable Fine Art Works, Editions de Luxe, etc., bound, can be supplied with designs suitable to the work, and samples of leather or other materials

The greatest care is taken with every detail, and only the best materials are used, to ensure a binding that will last

Harrods will not hold themselves responsible for books left to be bound if unclaimed after a lapse of twelve months. The edges of all books will be cut and trimmed, unless instructions are given to the contrary

---

LEATHER BOUND BOOKS

A large and handsome stock of Books in Leather Bindings, finished in the best style and workmanship, is on sale in this Department

---

A large and well chosen selection of

BIBLES, PRAYER BOOKS, CHURCH SERVICES, Etc.,

with or without Hymns always kept in stock

Lists of New Works and New Editions sent post free on Application

ALL PRICES ARE SUBJECT TO MARKET FLUCTUATIONS

Telephone SLOANE 1234
Telegrams 'EVERYTHING HARRODS LONDON'

HARRODS LTD   LONDON S W 1

BOOK DEPARTMENT
Price List

ART, BOOKS ON

The National Gallery. Edt. by T. Leman Hare, P. G. Konody, M. W. Brockwell, and F. W. Lippman. 100 plates, in colour. 2 Vols. **42/-**
The Louvre. By P. G. Konody and M. W. Brockwell. 50 superb plates in full colour **42/-**
The Uffiz. Gallery. 50 reproductions in colour of the most famous pictures. Text by P. G. Konody **42/-**
Six Centuries of Painting. By Randall Davies. 50 plates in colour **21/-**
Brown, J. H. Sketching without a master. Illustrated .. **6/-**
Steuart, J. Sketching in Water Colours. A Book for Amateurs, by An Amateur, fully illustrated **3/6**

THE 'MASTERPIECES IN COLOUR' SERIES

Reproducing the Treasures of Art in full colour. Attractive Cloth Binding with Art Colour Wrapper **2/6** each

Botticelli	Rembrandt
Burne-Jones	Reynolds
Constable	Romney
Corot	Rossetti
Franz Hals	Rubens
Gainsborough	Sargent
Holman Hunt	Titian
Leighton	Turner
Leonardo da Vinci	Van Dyck
Millais	Velasquez
Millet	Watts
Raphael	Whistler

Bully, M. H. Pictures and Painting **7/6**
Mather, F. J. Jnr. A History of Modern Painting. From Goya to Picasso **16/-**
Tonk, O. S. A History of Italian Painting **15/-**
Salway, J. The Art of Drawing in Lead Pencil **12/6**
Drawing for Art Students and Illustrators **12/-**

ATLASES

Bartholomew's Handy Reference Atlas of the World .. **12/6**
Touring Atlas of the British Isles **3/-**
Survey Atlas of Scotland **63/-**
Cassell's New Atlas with introduction. 144 Maps and Index **21/-**
Dunlop Touring Maps of the British Isles (32 Maps). In 1 Vol. **3/-**
Johnston's The World Wide Atlas **21/-**
Philips' Handy General Atlas and Gazetteer, with descriptive gazetteer of over 100,000 names **73/6**
New Systematic Atlas for General Readers **16/-**
Quarter bound leather **21/-**
Handy Volume Atlas of the World, with 72 Maps .. **4/-**
New Popular Atlas, with gazetteer index **6/-**
New School Atlas of Comparative Geography **4/-**
Record Atlas **10/6**
Pictorial Pocket Atlas of the World **2/-**
Handy Volume Atlas of London **6/-**
A.B.C. Pocket Atlas Guide to London **2/-**

GLOBES

Philips' 6-inch Terrestrial Globe on Polished Stand with solid brass half-meridian **8/-**
'British Empire' Globe, 8 inches diameter. In solid brass semi-meridian, on polished pedestal stand .. **12/6**
Nine-inch Globe. On stained wood pedestal, tilted axis **15/-**
With polished brass plain half-meridian .. **17/6**
With graduated half-meridian **18/6**
12-inch Globe. Mounted on polished wood pedestal stand, with engraved brass half-meridian **25/-**
14-inch Large Print Globe on metal stand, bronzed with inclined axis **45/-**
On polished wooden pedestal stand with brass half-meridian **47/6**
19-inch Clear Print Globe, mounted on Ebonised Pedestal Stand with brass graduated half-meridian **115/-**

COOKERY BOOKS

BEETON'S, MRS.
Household Management **12/6**
Family Cookery **8/6**
Everyday Cookery **6/-**
All-about Cookery **4/6**
Cookery Book **2/6**
Cake Making **2/6**
Puddings and Pies **2/6**
Cold Sweets **2/6**
Sauces and Soups **2/6**
Hors D'œuvres and Savouries **2/6**
'Bestway' Cookery Gift Book **4/6**
The 'Daily Mail' Cookery Book, edt. by Mrs. Peel .. **3/6**
Escoffier, A. A Guide to Modern Cookery **21/-**
Fairclough, M. A. The Ideal Cookery **35/-**
Kirk, Mrs. E. W. Tried Favourites Cookery Book. Paper **2/6**
Cloth **3/6**
Lindsay, J. and V. H. Mottram. Manual of Modern Cookery **4/6**
Little, May. A Year's Dinners. 365 Seasonable Dinners with Instructions for Cooking. A handy Guide Book for worried Housekeepers. Usually 6/- Harrods price **2/6**
Cookery up-to-date. Containing over 600 tested Recipes and other useful Cookery hints **1/-**
Leyel, Mrs. C. F. Puddings, Boiled, Baked, Fried, Steamed and Iced **1/6**
Cold Savoury Meals **1/6**
Meals on a Tray **1/6**
Drinks and Cordials **1/6**
Salads **1/6**
Jams **1/6**
Marshall, Mrs. A. B. Cookery Book **5/-**
Book of Ices **2/6**
Senn's Century Cookery Book **31/6**
The Menu Book **10/6**
Recherche Entrees **7/6**
Luncheon and Dinner Sweets **5/-**
A Book of Salads **2/6**
Eggs and Omelets **2/6**
Breakfast Dishes and Savouries **2/6**
Chafing Dish and Casserole Cookery **2/6**
Warne's New Model Cookery **7/6**

DICTIONARIES, ENGLISH

Harrods English Dictionary. Etymological and Pronouncing. Contains 75,000 words and meanings. Extra large print of Keywords. Strongly bound in leather-grained cloth **7/6**
Annandale's Large Type Concise Dictionary of the English Languages, etymological and pronouncing .. **7/6**
Cassells' New English Dictionary edited by E. A. Baker .. **7/6**
Chambers Etymological Dictionary **2/6**
Large Type Dictionary, pronouncing, explanatory and etymological. Illustrated **21/-**
Twentieth Century Dictionary **7/6**
Fowler, H. W. Dictionary of Modern English Usage .. **7/6**
India Paper edition **10/-**
Nuttall's Standard Dictionary, revised and extended by Rev. J. Wood **5/-**
Ogilvie's Student's Dictionary revised and edited by C. Annandale **15/-**
Oxford Dictionary, The Concise, adapted from the Oxford Dictionary **7/6**
Oxford Pocket Dictionary of Correct English **3/6**
Webster's New International Dictionary. Illustrated: buckram, **65/-**, or India Paper buckram, **115/6**, Full leather **147/-**
Webster's Little Gem Dictionary **1/6**

DICTIONARIES, FOREIGN

Bellow's French and English Dictionary for the Pocket with table and Maps. Roan, 12/6 India Paper Morocco **14/6**
German-English and English-German Dictionary .. **10/-**
Leather **13/-**
Cassell's New French-English and English-French Dictionary. Edited by E. A. Baker **7/6**

ALL PRICES ARE SUBJECT TO MARKET FLUCTUATIONS

BOOK DEPARTMENT

BOOK DEPARTMENT

Pocket Editions

'SAKI' (H. H. MUNRO)
Cloth 3/6 each

Reginald and Reginald in Russia	Beasts and Super-Beasts
The Chronicles of Clovis	The Toys of Peace
The Unbearable Bassington	The Square Egg
When William Came	

WALPOLE, HUGH
Novels. Cloth, 3/6   Leather, 5/-

The Cathedral	Fortitude
The Young Enchanted	Maradick at Forty
The Captives	The Duchess of Wrexe
The Green Mirror	The Wooden Horse
The Secret City	Mr. Perrin and Mr. Trail
The Dark Forest	

WEYMAN, S.
Thin Paper Edition. 22 Vols. With an Introduction in the First Vol. by Mr. Weyman. Cloth, 3/6   Leather, 5/-

The House of the Wolf	Sophia
The New Rector	Count Hannibal
The Story of Francis Cludde	In Kings' Byways
A Gentleman of France	The Long Night
The Man in Black	The Abbess of Vlaye
Under the Red Robe	Starvecrow Farm
My Lady Rotha	Chippinge
Memoirs of a Minister of France	Laid up in Lavender
The Red Cockade	The Wild Geese
Shrewsbury	The Great House
The Castle Inn	Ovington's Bank

STAMP ALBUMS

The 'IDEAL' ALBUM
No. 1011	All the World to 1914 complete. Bound in Cloth	17/6
No. 2101	All the World from 1915. New edition. Bound in Cloth	20/-

THE STRAND POSTAGE STAMP ALBUM
No. 2176	Attractive Pictorial binding. Guarded. Will hold 10,000 Stamps	5/-
No. 2177	Cloth binding, bevelled edges. Well Guarded. Will hold 10,000 Stamps	6/6
No. 2178	Cloth binding, gilt lettered, well Guarded. Will hold 11,500 Stamps	7/6
No. 2179	Artistic Cloth binding, gilt lettered, bevelled boards, well Guarded. Will hold nearly 13,000 Stamps	8/6
No. 2180	Leather back, gilt lettered, bevelled boards, well Guarded. Will hold nearly 13,000 Stamps	10/-

THE 'IMPROVED' STAMP ALBUM
No. 1001	Attractively bound in Art Cloth. Spaces for 5,000 Stamps	2/-
No. 2144	Bound in Cloth, fully Guarded throughout. Spaces for nearly 5,500 Stamps	3/-
No. 2191	Strongly bound, 4 maps in Colour. Fully Guarded throughout	4/-

THE GIBBONS CATALOGUE
Whole World Vol.	15/-
Part I. British Empire	6/6
Part II. Foreign Countries	10/-

Assorted packets of Postage Stamps
6d, 1/-, 2/-, 2/6, 3/6, 5/-, 7/6, 10/-, 15/- per pkt.

GUIDE BOOKS

BAEDEKER'S GUIDE BOOKS, WITH MAPS AND PLANS
Alps, The Eastern	15/-	Italy, Northern	12/-
Austria-Hungary	15/-	Italy, Southern, & Sicily	12/-
Belgium and Holland	10/-	London and its Environs	10/-
Berlin and its Environs	5/-	Mediterranean, The	16/-
Canada, The Dominion of	16/-	Norway, Sweden and Denmark	13/-
Egypt	20/-	Palestine and Syria	18/-
France, Northern	15/-	Paris and its Environs	10/-
France, Southern	15/-	Rhine, The	15/-
Great Britain	12/-	Spain and Portugal	16/-
Greece	12/-	Switzerland	16/-
Italy (Alps to Naples)	12/-	United States	20/-
Italy, Central, and Rome	12/-		

BLACKS FOREIGN GUIDE BOOKS
Belgium	7/6	Paris	2/6
Brittany	7/6	The Riviera	7/6
Holland	7/6	Rome and Environs	5/-
Normandy	7/6		

THE BLUE GUIDES
Edited by F. Muirhead, with Maps and Plans

Belgium and the Western Front	10/-	France, North-East	12/-
		„ North West	12/-
Brittany	7/6	„ Southern	15/-
England	16/-	The French Alps	10/-
Italy, Northern. From the Alps to Rome (Rome excepted)			15/-
Italy, Southern, including Rome, Sicily and Sardinia			15/-
London and its Environs			14/-
London, abridged			6/-
Normandy			7/6
Paris and its Environs			14/-
Switzerland, with Chamonix and Italian Lakes			15/-
Wales			9/-

HIGHWAY AND BYWAYS SERIES
(List on application)
Pocket Edition. Leather. 7/6 each.   Cloth 6/- each

THE LITTLE GUIDES
With Maps and Plans
(Complete List of Series on application)

WARD LOCK'S GUIDES
(List on application)

All the newest and best **Maps and Guides** for Tourists, issued by the well-known Publishers always kept in stock.   Lists upon application

BOOKS FOR TOURISTS

Bagot, R. The Lakes of Northern Italy	8/6
Belloc, H. The Pyrenees	8/6
Paris	8/6
Baring Gould, S. The Riviera	7/6
A Book of Cornwall	7/6
A Book of Dartmoor	7/6
A Book of Devon	7/6
Bradley, A. G. A Book of the Severn	15/-
Round about Wiltshire	8/6
The Avon and Shakespeare Country	8/6
The Romance of Northumberland	10/6
Brabant, F. G. Rambles in Sussex	7/6
Cox, J. C. Rambles in Surrey	7/6
Rambles in Kent	7/6
Douglas, H. A. Venice on Foot	12/6
Fletcher, J. S. A Book about Yorkshire	8/6
Hind, C. Lewis. Days in Cornwall	7/6
Hutton, E. Country Walks about Florence	7/6
Rome	7/6
Venice and Venetia	8/6
Naples and Southern Italy	8/6
The Cities of Lombardy	8/6
The Cities of Umbria	8/6
Siena and Southern Tuscany	8/6
The Cities of Spain	7/6
Lucas, E. V. A Wanderer in London	10/6
London Revisited	10/6
A Wanderer in Florence	10/6
A Wanderer in Venice	10/6
A Wanderer in Paris	10/6
A Wanderer in Holland	10/6
Roving East and Roving West	5/-
Lees, F. A Summer in Touraine	8/6
Morley, F. V. Travels in East Anglia	7/6
Norway, A. H. Naples, Past and Present	8/6
Newell, H. A., Lt.-Col. Footprints in Spain	10/6
Wade, G. W. Rambles in Somerset	10/6

ALL PRICES ARE SUBJECT TO MARKET FLUCTUATIONS

HARRODS LTD

Telephone SLOANE 1234
Telegrams 'EVERYTHING HARRODS LONDON'

LONDON S W 1

HARRODS CIRCULATING LIBRARY
AND SECONDHAND BOOK DEPARTMENT

INTERIOR SHEWING SECTION OF LIBRARY AND LOUNGE

The Library Service guarantees the immediate supply of all popular new literature, and offers other advantages at moderate rates of membership. A Prospectus and Sale Catalogue of books at greatly reduced prices will be posted to any address at home or abroad

RAILWAY AND STEAMSHIP OFFICES
NO BOOKING CHARGES

HARRODS issue Ordinary Tickets for all the Principal Lines from London and date them to suit the needs of passengers, thus avoiding the trouble and inconveniences of crowded Railway Stations

Steamship Tickets may be booked to all parts of the world

RESERVED SLEEPING COMPARTMENTS

These can be engaged upon all the different Railways, including all Continental Lines. Cabins can also be reserved on Steamers provided sufficient notice is given

CANCELLING OF SLEEPING ACCOMMODATION

Fifteen days' notice must be given, prior to departure, if passengers wish to cancel their sleeping accommodation, otherwise cancellation fees will be charged

INFORMATION AS TO TRAINS, ETC.

Although every care is used to ensure accuracy of information regarding the times of departure and arrival of trains, changing of carriages, routes and connections, Harrods do not hold themselves responsible for any mistakes that may arise

PASSPORTS AND INSURANCE

Harrods undertake the details regarding the securing of passports for their clients and will insure passengers baggage for a small premium for any period

CALL OR 'PHONE SLOANE 1234 FOR ALL INFORMATION

DRUG DEPARTMENT
Hot Water Bottles Guaranteed of British Manufacture

Best quality White Rubber English make

10 × 6 ins.	4/6	14 × 8 ins.	6/6
12 × 6 ,,	5/-	12 × 10 ,,	6/9
10 × 8 ,,	5/-	14 × 10 ,,	7/6
12 × 8 ,,	6/-	14 × 12 ,,	8/6

In Drab Rubber, British make guaranteed

10 × 8 ins.	...	3/11
12 × 8 ,,	...	4/3
12 × 10 ,,	...	4/11

Best quality Red Rubber

10 × 8 ins.	...	8/-
12 × 8 ,,	...	9/-
12 × 10 ,,	...	9/11

Seamless Moulded Bottle in soft Red, Golden or Jazz Rubber

11 × 8 ins ... 4/6

THE 'RONOLEKE' Hot Water Bottle, neck moulded into bottle. With stopper not requiring a washer
In Drab

10 × 8 ins.	6/6	12 × 8 ins.	6/9
12 × 10 ,,	7/6		

Red

10 × 8 ins.	7/6	12 × 8 ins.	8/6
12 × 10 ,,	9/9		

INDIA-RUBBER BUCKET

Collapsible ... 12/-

RAZOR WIPE
Solid Red Rubber 3/- each

INDIA-RUBBER COLLAPSIBLE TRAVELLING BATH
(Including Case)

No. 1	27 ins. across top	...	...	...	28/-
No. 2	30 ,,	,,	,,	...	30/-
No. 3	33 ,,	,,	,,	...	33/6
No. 4	36 ,,	,,	,,	...	37/6

Waterproof Case included with bath

RAZOR WIPE
Solid red rubber
Large size ... 3/- each

HOT WATER BOTTLE COVERS

Soft Velour in Blue, Pink Helio, Rose or Yellow

10 × 6 ins.	1/9	12 × 10 ins.	3/-
10 × 8 ,,	2/-	14 × 8 ,,	2/9
12 × 6 ,,	2/3	14 × 10 ,,	3/3
12 × 8 ,,	2/6		

Also with Bird Design in Silk

10 × 8 ins.	3/9	12 × 8 ins.	4/3
12 × 10 ,,	4/9		

In plain Ripple Wool, in Blue, Pink, Helio, Rose or Grey

10 × 6 ins.	9d	12 × 10 ins.	1/6
12 × 6 ,,	1/-	14 × 8 ,,	1/6
10 × 8 ,,	1/-	14 × 10 ,,	1/9
12 × 8 ,,	1/3		

RUBBER SOAP STAND
'The Pinnacle' Patent. Round or Oval ... 1/- each

INDIA-RUBBER MUFF WARMER
3/6
Also in soft Red or Blue Rubber ... 4/6

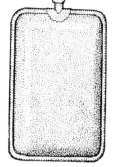

RUBBER 'FACE' BOTTLE
In soft Red, Blue and Jazz coloured Rubber
Size 6 × 4½ ins. ... 4/6

WATERPROOF CASE
This is included with the bath described above

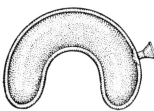

WATER NECK PILLOW
Stock sizes

16 × 23 ins.	...	...	13/6
16 × 25 ,,		...	15/-
18 × 25 ,,		...	17/-

RUBBER SOAP STAND
'The Pinnacle' Patent.
Oblong ... ...1/- each

WATER PILLOW
Stock sizes

18 × 15"	13/6	18 × 18"	15/6
18 × 20"	17/-	18 × 24"	21/-
18 × 26"	22/6	18 × 28"	24/-

INDIA-RUBBER BASIN
Collapsible, with iron ring at top 12/-

CIRCULAR WATER PILLOW
Maximum diameter

16 ins.	...	11/6	19 ins. ...	14/6
17 ,,	...	12/6	20 ,, ...	15/6
18 ,,	...	13/6		

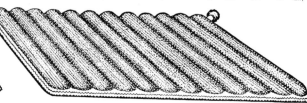

WATER SQUAB
For Hot or Cold Water
36 × 32 ins. £3 15 0

WATER BED
For Hot or Cold Water
72 × 36 ins. £8 8 0

ALL PRICES ARE SUBJECT TO MARKET FLUCTUATIONS

RUBBER AND WATERPROOF REQUISITES

A Page of Interesting Household and Toilet Goods

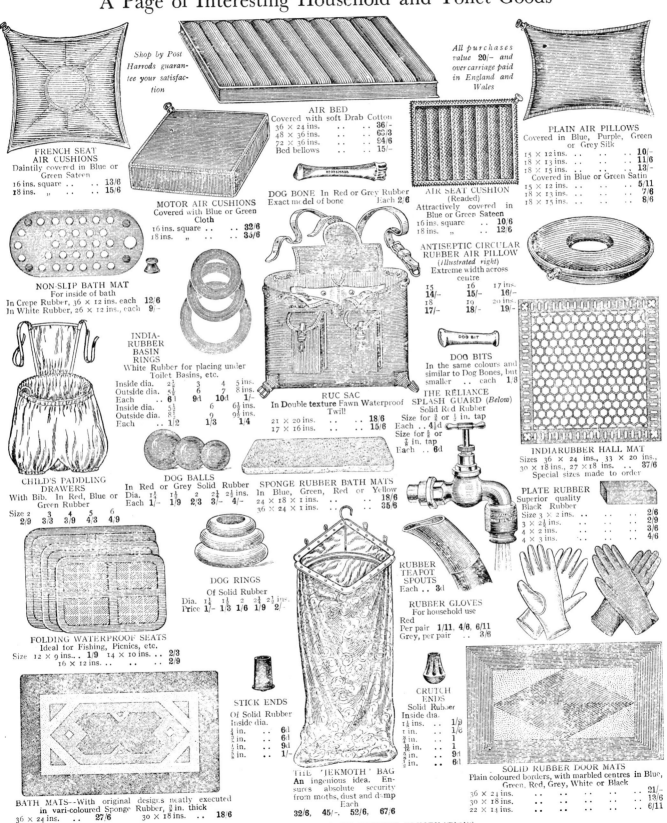

Shop by Post Harrods guarantee your satisfaction

All purchases value 20/- and over carriage paid in England and Wales

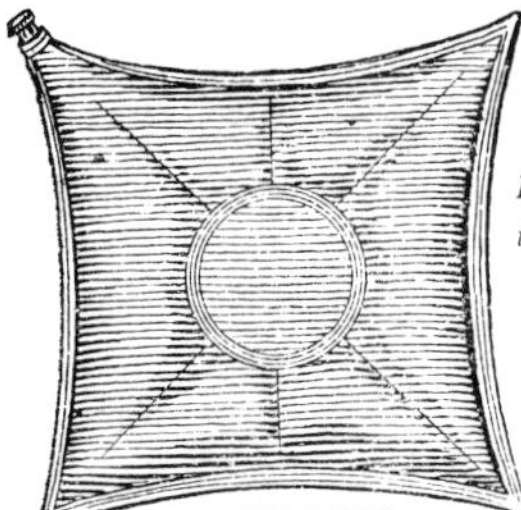

FRENCH SEAT AIR CUSHIONS
Daintily covered in Blue or Green Sateen

16 ins. square	13/6
18 ins. „	15/6

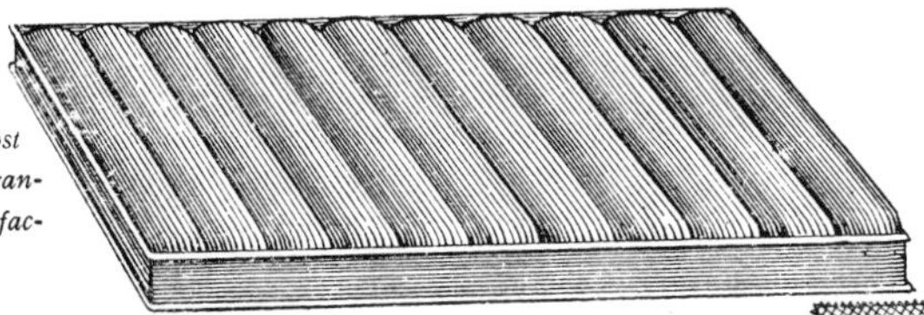

AIR BED
Covered with soft Drab Cotton

36 × 24 ins.	36/-
48 × 36 ins.	63/3
72 × 36 ins.	94/6
Bed bellows	15/-

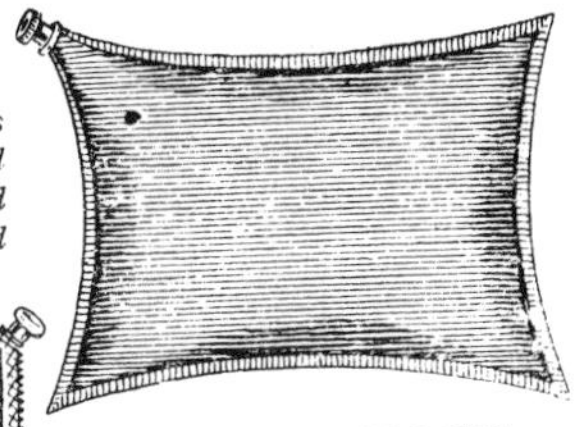

PLAIN AIR PILLOWS
Covered in Blue, Purple, Green or Grey Silk

15 × 12 ins.	10/-
18 × 13 ins.	11/6
18 × 15 ins.	13/-

Covered in Blue or Green Satin

15 × 12 ins.	5/11
18 × 13 ins.	7/6
18 × 15 ins.	8/6

MOTOR AIR CUSHIONS
Covered with Blue or Green Cloth

16 ins. square	32/6
18 ins. „	35/6

DOG BONE In Red or Grey Rubber
Exact model of bone Each 2/6

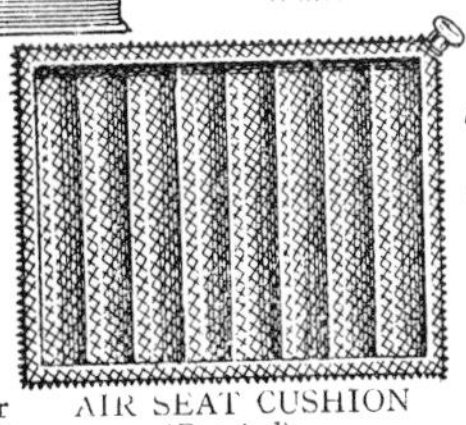

AIR SEAT CUSHION
(Beaded)
Attractively covered in Blue or Green Sateen

16 ins. square	10/6
18 ins. „	12/6

ANTISEPTIC CIRCULAR RUBBER AIR PILLOW
(*Illustrated right*)
Extreme width across centre

15	16	17 ins.
14/-	15/-	16/-
18	19	20 ins.
17/-	18/-	19/-

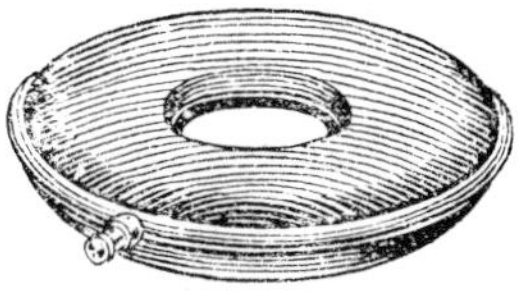

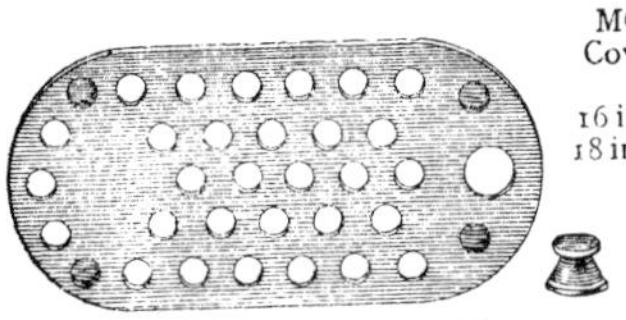

NON-SLIP BATH MAT
For inside of bath

In Crepe Rubber, 36 × 12 ins. each	12/6
In White Rubber, 26 × 12 ins., each	9/-

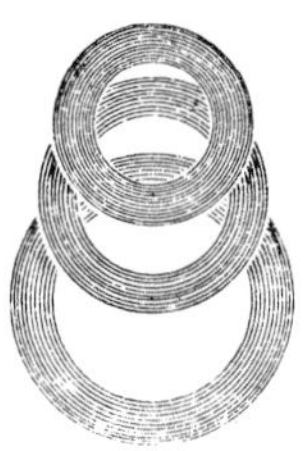

INDIA-RUBBER BASIN RINGS
White Rubber for placing under Toilet Basins, etc.

Inside dia.	$2\frac{1}{2}$	3	4	5 ins.
Outside dia.	$5\frac{1}{2}$	6	7	8 ins.
Each ..	6d	9d	10d	1/-
Inside dia.	$5\frac{1}{2}$		6	$6\frac{1}{2}$ ins.
Outside dia.	$8\frac{1}{2}$		9	$9\frac{1}{2}$ ins.
Each ..	1/2		1/3	1/4

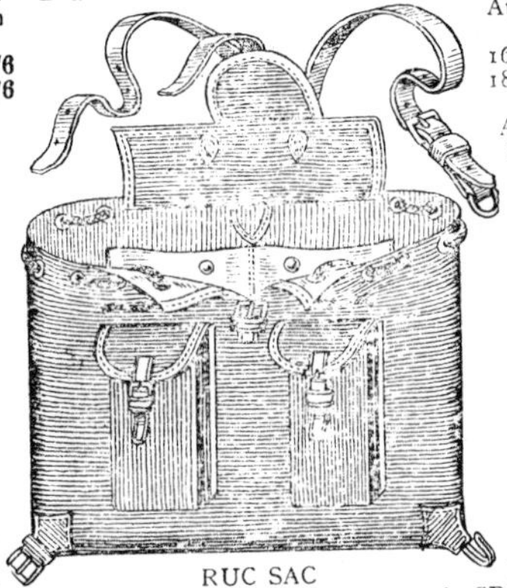

RUC SAC
In Double texture Fawn Waterproof Twill

21 × 20 ins.	18/6
17 × 16 ins.	15/6

DOG BITS
In the same colours and similar to Dog Bones, but smaller .. each 1/3

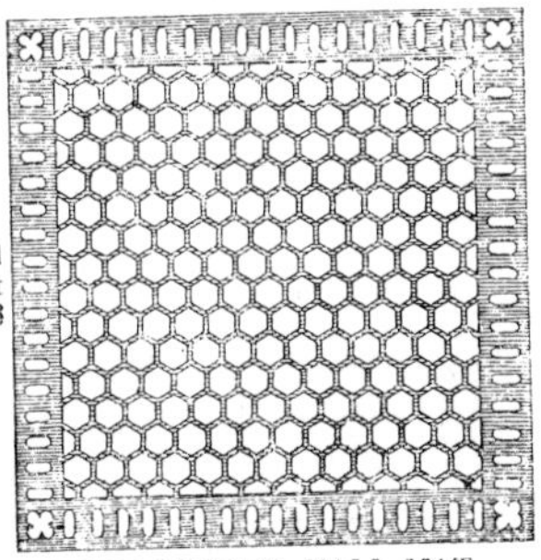

INDIARUBBER HALL MAT
Sizes 36 × 24 ins., 33 × 20 ins., 30 × 18 ins., 27 × 18 ins. .. 37/6
Special sizes made to order

CHILD'S PADDLING DRAWERS
With Bib. In Red, Blue or Green Rubber

Size 2	3	4	5	6
2/9	3/3	3/9	4/3	4/9

DOG BALLS
In Red or Grey Solid Rubber

Dia.	$1\frac{1}{4}$	$1\frac{1}{2}$	2	$2\frac{1}{4}$	$2\frac{1}{2}$ ins.
Each	1/-	1/9	2/3	3/-	4/-

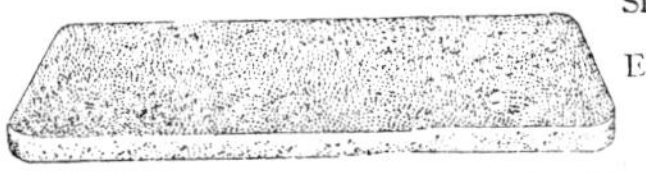

SPONGE RUBBER BATH MATS
In Blue, Green, Red or Yellow

24 × 18 × 1 ins.	18/6
36 × 24 × 1 ins.	35/6

THE RELIANCE SPLASH GUARD (*Below*)
Solid Red Rubber
Size for $\frac{3}{8}$ or $\frac{1}{2}$ in. tap
Each .. $4\frac{1}{2}$d
Size for $\frac{5}{8}$ or $\frac{7}{8}$ in. tap
Each .. 6d

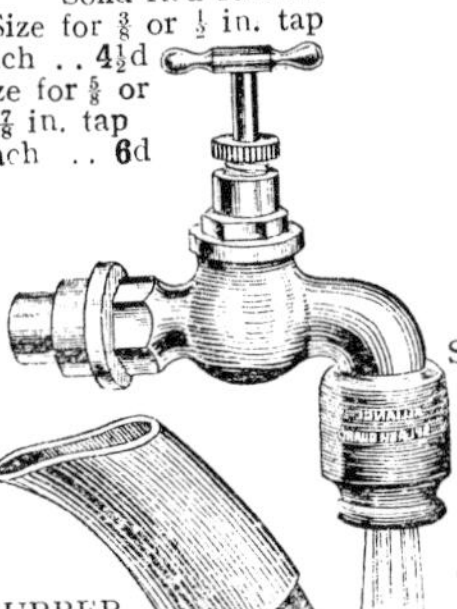

PLATE RUBBER
Superior quality Black Rubber

Size 3 × 2 ins.	2/6
3 × $2\frac{1}{2}$ ins.	2/9
4 × 2 ins.	3/6
4 × 3 ins.	4/6

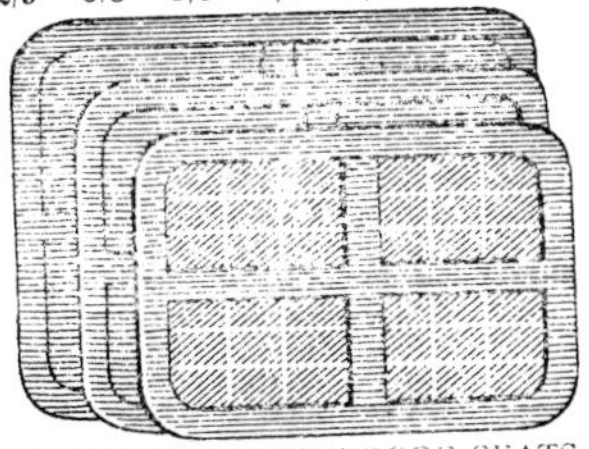

FOLDING WATERPROOF SEATS
Ideal for Fishing, Picnics, etc.
Size 12 × 9 ins.. . 1/9 14 × 10 ins. .. 2/3
16 × 12 ins. 2/9

DOG RINGS
Of Solid Rubber

Dia.	$1\frac{1}{4}$	$1\frac{1}{2}$	2	$2\frac{1}{4}$	$2\frac{1}{2}$ ins.
Price	1/-	1/3	1/6	1/9	2/-

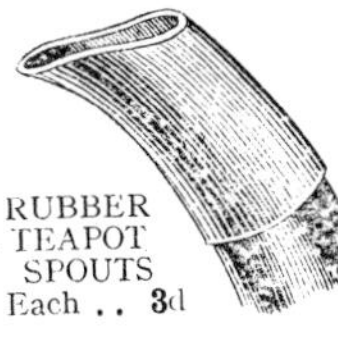

RUBBER TEAPOT SPOUTS
Each .. 3d

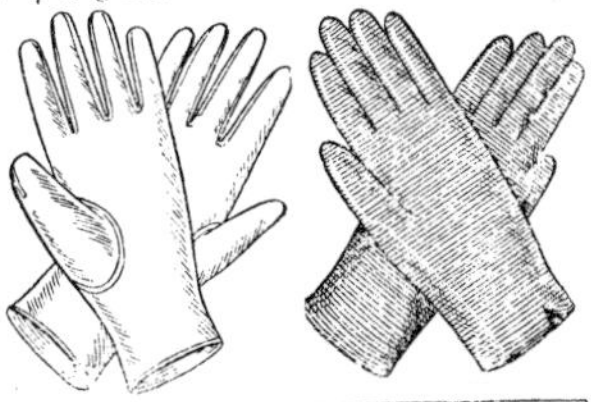

RUBBER GLOVES
For household use
Red
Per pair 1/11, 4/6, 6/11
Grey, per pair .. 3/6

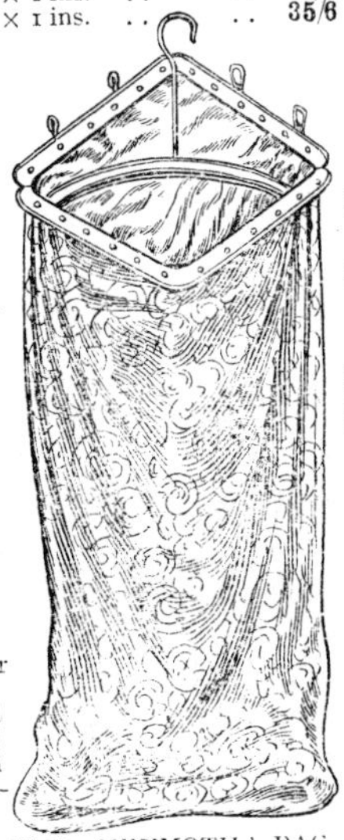

STICK ENDS
Of Solid Rubber
Inside dia.

$\frac{1}{4}$ in. ..	6d
$\frac{3}{8}$ in. ..	6d
$\frac{1}{2}$ in. ..	9d
$\frac{5}{8}$ in. ..	1/-

CRUTCH ENDS
Solid Rubber
Inside dia.

$1\frac{1}{8}$ ins. ..	1/9
1 in. ..	1/6
$\frac{7}{8}$ in. ..	1
$\frac{11}{16}$ in. ..	1
$\frac{5}{8}$ in. ..	9d
$\frac{1}{2}$ in. ..	6d

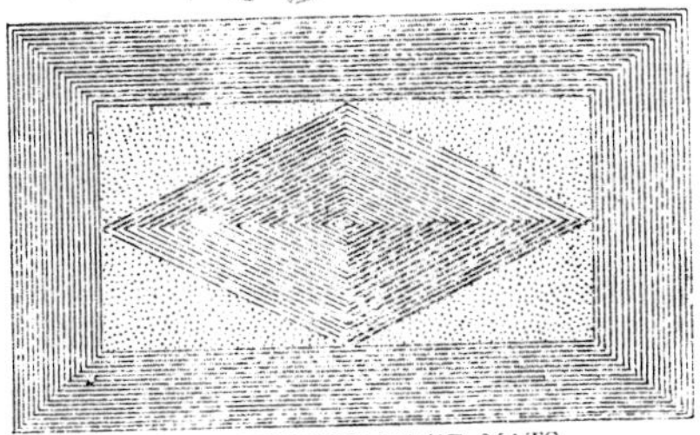

SOLID RUBBER DOOR MATS
Plain coloured borders, with marbled centres in Blue, Green, Red, Grey, White or Black

36 × 24 ins.	21/-
30 × 18 ins.	13/6
22 × 14 ins.	6/11

BATH MATS--With original designs neatly executed in vari-coloured Sponge Rubber, $\frac{3}{8}$ in. thick
36 × 24 ins. .. 27/6 30 × 18 ins. .. 18/6

THE 'JEKMOTH' BAG
An ingenious idea. Ensures absolute security from moths, dust and damp
Each
32/6, 45/-, 52/6, 67/6

ALL PRICES ARE SUBJECT TO MARKET FLUCTUATIONS

MOTOR WRAP DEPARTMENT
Motor Rugs Luxuriously Comfortable and Thoroughly Practical

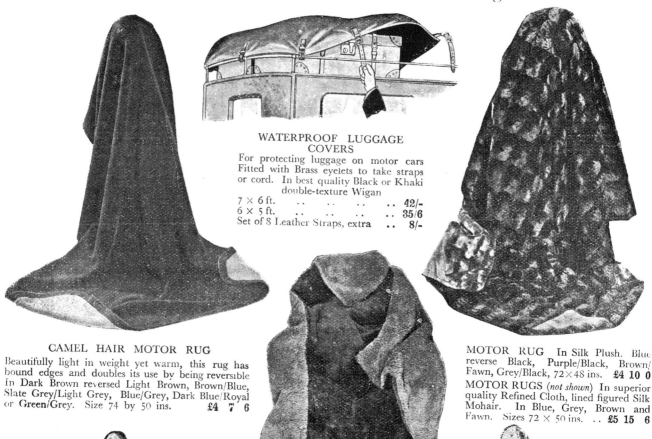

WATERPROOF LUGGAGE COVERS

For protecting luggage on motor cars Fitted with Brass eyelets to take straps or cord. In best quality Black or Khaki double-texture Wigan

7 × 6 ft.	42/-
6 × 5 ft.	35/6
Set of 8 Leather Straps, extra ..	8/-

CAMEL HAIR MOTOR RUG

Beautifully light in weight yet warm, this rug has bound edges and doubles its use by being reversible In **Dark Brown** reversed Light Brown, Brown/Blue, Slate Grey/Light Grey, Blue/Grey, Dark Blue/Royal or **Green/Grey**. Size 74 by 50 ins. **£4 7 6**

MOTOR RUG In Silk Plush. Blue reverse Black, Purple/Black, Brown/Fawn, Grey/Black, 72 × 48 ins. **£4 10 0**

MOTOR RUGS (*not shown*) In superior quality Refined Cloth, lined figured Silk Mohair. In Blue, Grey, Brown and Fawn. Sizes 72 × 50 ins. .. **£5 15 6**

THE 'MOTOLUXE'

Snug and warm, this Motor Rug in Real Alpaca Wool affords the warmth and protection of fur, without its oppressive weight and bulk. In Brown/Fawn, Blue/Grey, Fawn/Fawn stripe and Plain Grey. Size 72 × 50 ins. **£5 5 0**
Foot Muffs to match .. **£1 19 6**

MOTOR RUGS (*not shown*)
In Bedford Cord, in Grey or Fawn shades, unlined. Size 72 × 50 ins. .. **£2 17 6**
Lined Silk Mohair **£4 14 6**

WATERPROOF MOTOR APRONS

In superior quality Black Rubber, lined Dark Blue or Green

Size 72 × 48 ins.	**£2 12 6**
,, 60 × 48 ins.	**£2 2 0**

MOTOR RUGS (*not shown*)
In Plain Silk Mohair. In Blue reverse Grey. Size 72 × 50 ins. .. **£4 4 0**

MOTOR RUG

In Blue, Green or Drab Box Cloth, lined Silk Mohair. Size 72 × 48 ins. **£10 10 0**
In Rubber-proofed Melton Cloth, in Blue or Green. Lined Check Wool
72 × 48 ins. **£5 5 0** 60 × 48 ins. **£4 14 6**

ALL PRICES ARE SUBJECT TO MARKET FLUCTUATIONS

HARRODS LTD

Telephone SLOANE 1234
Telegrams 'EVERYTHING HARRODS LONDON'

LONDON S W 1

MEN'S WEAR SECTION
Serviceable Waterproof Mackintoshes, Cycling Capes and Motor Cycling Outfits, etc.

WATERPROOF SHOOTING CAPE
Double texture Fawn Indiana
36 ins. to 46 ins. long **45/-**

Orders by Post promptly and satisfactorily executed

MACKINTOSH COAT
Strong Black Rubber. Cut with double-breasted fronts, full skirt, and all-round belt Guaranteed waterproof
42/-

CHAUFFEUR'S MACKINTOSH COAT
Double texture Blue Rubbered Cashmere. Cut with double-breasted fronts, full skirt, and all-round belt
£5 5 0

CHAUFFEUR'S MACKINTOSH COAT
Single texture Blue Cashmere
£2 5 0

WATERPROOF CYCLING PONCHO
(*Illustrated on left*) Very light in weight Fawn shades. 36 ins, 39 ins. and 42 ins. long **15/-**

MOTOR CYCLING SUIT
(*Illustrated on right*) Strong Double texture Fawn Waterproof Twill Jacket cut with double-breasted fronts, and all-round belt. Seatless Trousers, with spat front to protect boots **52/6**
Jacket only **32/6**
Trousers only **23/6**

MACKINTOSH RIDING APRON
In Double texture Fawn Indiana Fitted with waist strap, and leg loops
18/6

WATERPROOF MOTOR CYCLING TROUSERS
Double texture Fawn Twill. Fitted with lightning fasteners at side Per pair **25/6**
In Legging style **21/-**

CHAUFFEUR'S MACKINTOSH COAT
Double-breasted fronts, cut with full skirt, and storm collar. In Double texture Black Rubbered Cashmere
65/-, 84/-, 94/6

When ordering, please state Height and Chest measurement

ALL PRICES ARE SUBJECT TO MARKET FLUCTUATIONS

HARRODS LTD

Telephone SLOANE 1234
Telegrams 'EVERYTHING HARRODS LONDON'

LONDON S W 1

MEN'S WEAR SECTION
Bespoke Tailoring

MEN who have their clothes made-to-order may place implicit confidence in Harrods Bespoke Tailoring Department, a Department which numbers amongst its patrons leading business and professional men, as well as distinguished members of the Military, Naval, Air and Diplomatic Services

Harrods Bespoke Tailoring is characterised by 'correctness' of detail and unfailing service, and there is a range of prices which affords ample scope for selection

Whilst the Authentic Styling of Modern Fashions is rigorously followed, individuality in choice of patterns and style is encouraged and supplemented by a thorough knowledge of the requirements of an exacting clientele

---

For Motorist or Golfer

CHROME LEATHER MOTOR COATS

Snug fitting yet providing ample room for freedom of movement, they afford complete protection in any weather
Full Chrome selected First Quality Skins. Light or Dark Tan and Black; lined Camel Fleece; Chamois Wind cuffs; Selvyt Pockets
£15 15 0
Similar Coat less ample in Skirt
£12 12 0
Light or Dark Tan Chrome Leather Coat; lined Teddy Bear Fleece; Wind Cuffs; Cloth Pockets
£9 9 0

LEATHER GOLF JACKETS

An ideal coat affording full protection in showery weather and tailored to ensure complete freedom of movement

Brown Mock Antelope Skins
£5 5 0

Dark Tan Mocha, very soft finish and slightly lighter than the Mock Antelope Skin
£4 15 0

Tan or Putty Coloured Persian Leather
£3 15 0

Showerproof Gaberdine
£2 2 0 and £2 15 0

WHEN ORDERING PLEASE SEND CHEST AND WAIST SIZE, ALSO HEIGHT

ALL PRICES ARE SUBJECT TO MARKET FLUCTUATIONS

HARRODS LTD
Telephone SLOANE 1234
Telegrams 'EVERYTHING HARRODS LONDON'
LONDON S W 1

MEN'S WEAR SECTION
Harrods Complete Range of Ready-for-Service Chauffeurs' Uniforms

The Importance of well Tailored Uniforms cannot be overestimated, for they are not only thoroughly comfortable and a source of pride to the wearer, but they reflect the good taste and discrimination of the owner

OVERCOATS
DOUBLE BREASTED MELTON
Made from a thoroughly reliable hard-wearing Melton Cloth Open or closed fronts. Warm Woollen lining and finished with wind cuffs and belt at back Blue, Grey, Black, Brown and Green. All sizes .. **£5 5 0**

DURATEX WHIPCORD
Double Breasted with 'two-way' collar. Can be worn open or closed. Lined medium weight Tweed. Belt at back and wind cuffs. Blue only .. **£6 6 0**

SPECIAL QUALITY
Double breasted, open or closed fronts. Made from All Wool yarn-dyed, Melton and specially tailored in Harrods own workshops. Lined through Dark Wool Fleece. Blue only .. **£7 7 0**

ALL WOOL GABARDINE
Blue Overcoats. Check lining interlined with Rubber. Raglan shoulders and all-round belt Medium weight and waterproof **£6 6 0**

JACKETS AND BREECHES
This smart looking Uniform is made from the world-renowned Duratex Whipcord in the open or closed front style. Colours : Blue, Black, Green, Brown and Grey All sizes **£5 15 6**

JACKETS AND TROUSERS
Made from the famous Duratex Whipcord. Open or closed fronts With double-breasted tunic and easy fitting trousers Colours : Blue, Light or Dark Grey, Green and Brown. All sizes **£5 15 6**

MELTON CLOTH
Jackets and Breeches and Jacket and Trousers in good quality, hard-wearing Melton Cloth. Open or closed fronts. Blue, Black, Green or Grey. All sizes **£5 5 0**

SUPER QUALITY WHIPCORD
Jackets and Trousers of the finest Blue Worsted Whipcord. Open fronts All sizes .. **£7 7 0**

PRIVATE LIVERIES, CHAUFFEURS UNIFORMS, ETC.

MADE TO ORDER

Harrods Tailoring Department has a special section devoted to the equipment of every description of Uniform, and estimates will gladly be given for State, Club, Hotel and Private Liveries

CHAUFFEURS' CLOTHING OUTFITS

CRASH LINEN DUST COATS
Double-breasted, closed fronts. Plain .. 25/-
With Blue Panel collar and cuffs .. 30/-

ALPACA DUST COATS
Blue and Grey. Either open or closed fronts Double Breasted. Belt at back 32/6
Heavier quality in Blue, Light or Medium Grey, Claret, Green and Black 47/6
Superior quality Coat made in Harrods own workshops. Sleeves lined Sateen. Belt all round. Open front 57/6

PANTRY JACKETS
Lilac and White Striped Jean .. 14/-

OVERALLS AND CLEANING COATS
BROWN OR BLUE HEAVYWEIGHT DUNGAREES
Bib, Trousers and Jacket. All sizes **£1 1 0**
Blue or Brown Boiler Suits ,, 18/6
Khaki Drill Cleaning Coats ,, 15/6

PATTERNS AND SELF-MEASUREMENT FORMS MAY BE HAD ON APPLICATION

ALL PRICES ARE SUBJECT TO MARKET FLUCTUATIONS

HARRODS LTD

Telephone SLOANE 1234
Telegrams 'EVERYTHING HARRODS LONDON'

LONDON S W 1

MEN'S WEAR SECTION

Formal Wear—Tailored to Meet the Requirements of an Exacting Clientele

The importance of perfectly tailored Evening Clothes need not be emphasised, but there is something more than correct tailoring in the perfect finish and distinctive touch which Harrods expert cutting ensures. Sizes for every type of figure — short, tall, slender or stout

DRESS WAISTCOAT

Single breasted 3 button style. Backless mod l. Note the V-shaped opening and wide open lapel
16/6 and 30/-

DRESS WAISTCOAT

Double breasted 2 button model in white Marcella. Conforms admirably to the lines of the new Dress Coat
30/- and 16/6

MEN'S EVENING DRESS WEAR

Harrods Ready to Wear Evening Clothes whilst offering all the style of the best West End tailoring, save time and lessen expense

FUR LINED OVERCOATS

A large selection of fur lined overcoats including Musquash, Nutria, Coney and other well-known furs. Single or double breasted models with plain or fur collars
Price from .. .. **18 gns.**

THE EVENING DRESS SUIT

This is an altogether smarter model than that of a year or two ago. The military silhouette, broader lapels, square shoulders, and short front are the outstanding characteristics. In Black Barathea
All sizes and fittings
Dress Coat and Trousers
11 and 14 gns.

DINNER JACKET SUIT

Note the broader lapels covered in cord silk, square shoulders, greater width across the chest, and the close-fitting over the hips.
In Black Barathea
All sizes and fittings
Dinner Jacket, Waistcoat, and Trousers
8½, 10 and 13 gns.

DAY OR EVENING COAT

A single breasted Chesterfield Overcoat, conservative in style and from light to medium in weight. Oxford Grey and Black lined throughout with rich quality satin
All sizes and fittings. Ready to wear .. **10 gns. and 9 gns.**

ALL PRICES ARE SUBJECT TO MARKET FLUCTUATIONS

Telephone SLOANE 1234
Telegrams 'EVERYTHING HARRODS LONDON'

HARRODS LTD

LONDON S W I

MEN'S WEAR SECTION

Distinguished Tailoring in Clothes Ready for Wearing

Harrods Ready-to-Wear Clothes have attained such a degree of perfection that many men always choose suits which can be worn right away. They know that whatever their type of figure there will be a size and fitting which will ensure a perfectly made suit at prices which are consistently moderate

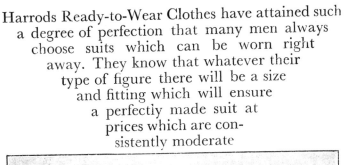

Ready-for-Service Suits that make choosing at Harrods a Simple Matter, and a Sure Success

SUITS FOR BUSINESS AND FORMAL WEAR

BLACK JACKET AND VESTS For wear with striped trousers. Vicunas and fine Twill Cheviots. All sizes
Single Breasted
4 Gns. **5** Gns. and **7** Gns.

STRIPED CASHMERE TROUSERS

Good Worsteds in neat stripe designs. All sizes and fittings
From .. **35/-** to **3** Gns.

LOUNGE SUITS
Tailored from the finest quality materials in both single and double-breasted styles. All prevailing weaves and shades of Grey, Brown, and Blue. Sizes and Fittings for every man **6** Gns. to **13** Gns.

FLANNEL SUITS
Lounge Suits, tailored in smooth all-wool 'West of England' flannel. Silver or medium Grey shades, also Blue, Brown and Grey with neat stripes. Ready-to-Wear
Single Breasted **5** Gns. and **7** Gns.
Double Breasted **£5 10 0** & **£7 12 6**

FOUR PIECE SUIT Tailored from fine Scotch and Harris Tweeds
Jacket, Vest, Trousers and Knickers .. .. .. **9½** Gns.
Jacket, Vest and Knickers .. .. **8** Gns.
Jacket and Knickers .. .. **7** Gns.

BLUE SERGE SUITS
An exceptionally fine hard-wearing Serge of dependable colour and quality
Single Breasted, **6**, **8** and **9½** Gns.
Double Breasted .. **5/-** extra

HARRIS TWEEDS
Sturdy excellence of material is combined with expert tailoring in these splendid wearing Harris tweeds. Tailored on comfortable easy fitting lines they are the most serviceable of all materials for sports and country wear
Single Breasted Lounge Suits **8** Gns.

BLACK MORNING COAT AND VEST

Authentically correct in every detail and perfectly finished
All sizes and fittings
8 Gns. and **9** Gns.

WOOL AND COTTON WAISTCOATS

Plain Biscuit colour, Grey, etc.
15/6 to **2** Gns.

ALL PRICES ARE SUBJECT TO MARKET FLUCTUATIONS

HARRODS LTD

Telephone SLOANE 1234
Telegrams 'EVERYTHING HARRODS LONDON'

LONDON S W 1

MEN'S WEAR SECTION

Sports Suits that Ensure Accurate Fitting and Yet Allow for Strenuous Action

GREY FLANNEL BLAZER SUITS

Jackets and Trousers only. Jackets unlined with exception of sleeves. Medium shade of Grey. Tailored in all sizes and fittings

Single Breasted **63/-**
Double Breasted **3/-** extra

BLUE FLANNEL BLAZERS AND TROUSERS

BLAZERS   Made in Pure Wool Flannel of a medium shade blue—reliable dye.   Lined sleeves.   All sizes and fittings

Single breasted	..	..	..	**42/-, 63/-**
Double breasted	..	..	..	**45/-, 66/-**

FLANNEL TROUSERS

All Wool Flannel.   Faultlessly tailored and designed to give complete freedom of movement.   White and three shades of Grey. Every inch waist measurement from 30 ins. to 46 ins. and leg lengths from 27 ins. to 36 ins. **45/-, 30/-, 21/-**
   White Gabardine **45/-, 37/6**

PLUS FOUR SUITS

All the newest colourings and patterns in sporting tweeds. Greys, Lovats, Fawns and Bracken Brown.   Ready-to-wear in all fittings from **4½** Gns.

TROPICAL SUITS

Harrods offer expert advice on the selection of suitable outfit for every climate.

JACKETS AND TROUSER SUITS in Poplin, Silk, Wool, Panella and Drill. In Fawn, Drab, Grey, Cream, Biscuit and White.

WHITE DRILL SUITS **30/-**
POPLIN SUITS from **2** Gns.
PANELLA SUITS from **70/-**
TUSSORE SILK .. **4** Gns.
ALPACA JACKETS
Black or Grey **21/-** and **35/-**
KHAKI DRILL SHORTS **10/6**

SKI-ING SUITS

BLOUSE MODEL.   Made of ALL Wool Gabardine in Navy, Black or Fawn.   This Style is exceptionally smart and allows ample freedom of movement.   The front, pockets and cuffs are protected against wind and snow, and the collar can be worn closed or open as shown.   Choice of either Buttons or Zip Fasteners for pockets and front

THE TROUSERS are made in the Plus Four style and fit snugly over the boots. Lining of Natural Wool or Silkene **8** Gns. and **7** Gns.

GABARDINE CAPS in Navy or Fawn **12/6**

Self Measurement Form on page 605

ALL PRICES ARE SUBJECT TO MARKET FLUCTUATIONS

Telephone SLOANE 1234
Telegrams 'EVERYTHING HARRODS LONDON'

HARRODS LTD

LONDON S W 1

MEN'S WEAR SECTION

The Exceptional Variety of Underwear in Every Weight and Texture, from the Softest of Silks to the Warmest of Woollens, has given Harrods a Reputation for the Finest Underwear Obtainable Anywhere

SUMMER WEIGHT

SILK AND MERINO

Anglo-Indian Gauze Lace. Vests	.. ..	18/6
" " " Shorts	.. ..	18/6
Sizes up to 38 ins. Larger sizes rising 1/- every 2 ins.		
White Lisle Thread Vests ..	.. ..	11/6
Pants	.. ..	13/6
Trunk Drawers	.. ..	12/6
All sizes up to 38 ins. Larger sizes 1/- every 2 ins.		

LOOSE CUT UNDERWEAR

All-Linen Shorts ..	.. ..	10/6
Calico Shorts ..	.. ..	4/6
Poplin Vests } White only	..	9/6
" Shorts } All sizes	..	9/6
" Combinations } 34 ins. to 44 ins.	..	14/6

Anglo-Indian Silk and Merino Underwear (Smedley's) in White

Vests, half or long sleeves ..	.. ..	18/6
Pants, 26 or 30 in. leg ..	.. ..	20/6
Knee Drawers ..	.. ..	20/6
Trunk Drawers	.. ..	19/6
Sizes up to 38 ins. Larger sizes rising 1/- every 2 ins. up to 44 ins.		

COMBINATIONS

Super 'TECTOR' Self-Grey Wool. Trunk legs.
Summer weight 26/6
Sizes 36 to 44 one price
Harrods 'TECTOR' Natural Wool. Guaranteed unshrinkable. Summer weight. All sizes 36 to 44 ins. 21/6
Self-Grey Wool, Long legs. Winter weight 31/6
'TECTOR' Natural Wool. Long legs. Winter weight. Guaranteed Unshrinkable. All sizes 36 to 44 ins. 25/6
All Vests or Combinations may be had with long or short sleeves

NATURAL WOOL UNDERWEAR

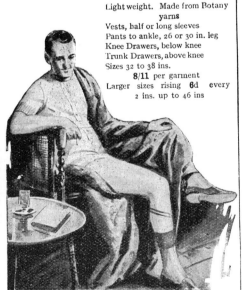

Light weight. Made from Botany yarns
Vests, half or long sleeves
Pants to ankle, 26 or 30 in. leg
Knee Drawers, below knee
Trunk Drawers, above knee
Sizes 32 to 38 ins.
8/11 per garment
Larger sizes rising 6d every 2 ins. up to 46 ins

SUMMER WEIGHT

Anglo-Indian Gauze. Vests	..	17/6
Silk and Egyptian Cotton. Pants ..	..	18/6
Shorts ..	..	17/6
Sizes up to 38 ins. Larger sizes rising 1/- every 2 ins. up to 46 ins.		

TROPICAL WEIGHT

Indian Gauze White Silk and Merino Underwear

Shirts, half sleeves	..	16/6
Trunk Drawers	..	16/6
Sizes up to 38 ins. Larger sizes rising 1/- every 2 ins. up to 46 ins.		

'Pesco' Silk and Wool. Light weight, in Blue or White

Shirts, half or long sleeves ..	..	19/6
Trousers	..	21/6
Trunk Drawers	..	20/6
Sizes up to 38 ins. Larger sizes rising 1/- every 2 ins. up to 46 ins.		

MEDIUM WEIGHT

Pure Natural Wool, specially blended yarn, fine gauge

Vests, half or long sleeves, 34 to 38 ins. ..	10/6
Pants to ankle, 26 or 30 in. leg. Sizes 32 to 38 ins.	10/6
Also Knee or Trunk Drawers ..	10/6
Larger sizes rising 1/- every 2 ins. up to 46 ins.	

Natural Wool Wolsey Underwear

Shirts	..	13/6
Trousers	..	14/6
Trunk Drawers ..	..	13/6
Sizes up to 38 ins. Larger sizes rising 1/- every 2 ins. up to 46 ins.		

'SUPER-TECTOR' Self-Grey Wool. Vests 17/6
" " " " Pants 17/6
" " " " Shorts 17/6
Sizes 32 to 46 ins.

WINTER WEIGHT

PURE WHITE Botany Wool. Scotch make. Vests half sleeves or long sleeves. Sizes 34 to 38 .. 18/6
Trousers 34 to 38 .. .. 19/6
Rising 1/- every 2 ins. up to 44 ins.

Pure Natural Cashmere, Winter Weight

Vests, half or long sleeves ..	.. ..	36/6
Trousers	.. ..	38/6
Sizes up to 38 ins. Larger sizes rising 1/- every 2 ins. up to 46 ins.		

Silk and Wool. 'TECTOR' Sky Blue, also in White Scotch manufacture

Vests, half or long sleeves, 34 to 46 ins. .. 26/6
Pants to ankle, 26 or 30 in. leg, 32 to 46 in. waist 26/6
All sizes 32 to 46 ins.

Also Trunks

SUMMER WEIGHT

SILK UNDERWEAR

Cream or Blue Vests. Medium weight ..	..	36/6
" " Pants. " "	..	39/6
" " Shorts. " "	..	37/6
Sizes up to 38 ins. Larger sizes extra, rising 1/6 every 2 ins.		

SILK 'TECTOR.' All sizes 34 to 44

Flesh colour Spun Silk Pants. Light weight ..	26/6
" " " " Vests. "	26/6
" " " " Shorts. " "	26/6
Flesh colour Spun Silk Vests. Winter weight ..	42/6
" " " " Pants " ..	45/6
Also Trunk Drawers	42/6

Larger sizes extra. Vests up to 38 ins. rising 2/6 every 2 ins. Pants up to 36 ins. rising 2/6 every 3 ins.

WAIST GRIPPING SHORTS with a New special band round the waist. Exceptionally comfortable. Can be adapted in any make to special order .. 16/6

ALL PRICES ARE SUBJECT TO MARKET FLUCTUATIONS

HARRODS LTD

Telephone SLOANE 1234
Telegrams 'EVERYTHING HARRODS LONDON'

LONDON SW 1

MEN'S WEAR SECTION
Harrods Splendid Variety of Shirts for Every Season and Occasion

Men who select their Shirt-Wear at Harrods may be confident that the fit style, finish, and comfort will fulfil their highest expectations. All sizes are in stock and men of practically every proportion can be fitted without delay

SHIRTS MADE-TO-ORDER

An exceptional variety of patterns in Zephyrs, Poplins, Taffetas, Flannels and Silks carefully tailored and finished in accordance with individual requirements

OXFORD SHIRTS

Double cuffs. Shirts in plain shades of Biscuit and Blue. Also neat striped effects of Black, Blue, Mauve and Brown on White grounds **15/6**

DRESS SHIRTS

Plain stiff Linen fronts and cuffs, 1 and 2 stud **10/6**
Plain stiff Linen fronts and cuffs, 1 and 2 stud, 3 lengths of sleeve **15/6**

PLAIN WHITE SHIRTS

Mercerised Cotton Twill, double cuffs **10/6**
Zephyr. White with White stripes Double cuffs **15/6**
Longcloth Uniform shirts, stiff Linen cuffs **12/6**
Longcloth Uniform shirts, fine quality, stiff Linen cuffs **18/6**

POPLIN SHIRTS

Superior quality Poplin, with two soft collars and Double cuffs .. **15/6 and 21/-**
White Poplin with pleated fronts and double cuffs **21/-**

CEYLON TWILL SHIRTS

Very light in weight. Neat stripes of Black, Blue, Mauve, Brown on White ground. Double cuffs **10/6**

TWILL SERGE SHIRTS

Fine quality, all Wool, hard wearing and very comfortable. Good range of choice designs and colours **21/-**

VIYELLA SHIRTS

Exclusive variety of designs. Coloured stripes on White ground, coloured ground effects, and plain shades. Double cuffs **20/-**

ZEPHYR

Excellent wearing quality shirts in all the newest designs and colourings. Exclusive to Harrods. Soft double cuffs and 2 collars with twin tabs and whalebone supports **10/6**

ZEPHYR SHIRTS

Stiff cuffs in neat coloured stripes of Black, Blue, Mauve and Brown on White ground **10/6**

DRESS SHIRTS

Sunk Marcella front, 'Cowheel' shape Linen cuff, 2 studs .. .. **15/6 and 21/-**
Plain stiff, 1 and 2 stud. All Linen .. **21/-**
Plain stiff, 2 stud only. Best Linen.. **25/6**
Stiff Pique fronts and Longcloth bodies **21/-**
Stiff Marcella fronts **15/6**
Soft pleated .. .. **10/6, 15/6 and 21/-**

UNION FLANNEL

Neat coloured stripes of Black, Blue, Mauve and Brown, on White grounds Single cuffs **12/6, 15/6**

CASHMERE SHIRTS

Best Cashmere made from the finest quality Wool. Smart striped effects in choice designs and colours **27/6**

UNION FLANNEL SPORTS SHIRTS

Made expressly for outdoor wear. Especially suitable for Golfing, Fishing, Shooting and for Sea Voyages. In all the fashionable colours. Collar attached
Single wrists **15/6**

ALL WOOL FLANNEL

Neat coloured stripes on White ground, Blue, Black, Mauve and Brown. Single wrists **10/6, 15/6, 21/-**

ALL PRICES ARE SUBJECT TO MARKET FLUCTUATIONS

HARRODS LTD

Telephone SLOANE 1234
Telegrams 'EVERYTHING HARRODS LONDON'

LONDON S W 1

MEN'S WEAR SECTION
Harrods Lead for Value in Men's Outfitting

TENNIS SHIRTS

Mercerised Cotton Twill	.. ..	10/6
Cream Poplin ..	.. ..	16/6
Fine White Repp	.. ..	10/6
Fine Union Twill	.. ..	13/6
All Wool Taffeta	.. 16/6,	25/6
All Wool Flannel	.. ..	16/6
Viyella ..	.. ..	19/6
Fugi Silk ..	.. ..	21/-
Heavy Silk ..	.. ..	35/-

TENNIS COMBINATIONS
Union Taffeta 15/6

SPUN SILK TAFFETA SHIRTS
Neat stripes in Black, Blue, Mauve and Brown, on White ground, also close striped effects. Two soft collars with twin tabs and whalebone supports. Double Cuffs
27/6, 37/6, 47/6

CREAM FUGI SILK SHIRTS
With two soft collars fitted with whalebone supports. Double Cuffs 27/6

WHITE JAP SILK SHIRTS
Double Cuffs
White Taffeta Silk with two soft collars	47/6
Plain front	55/-
Pleated front	63/-

WHITE TAFFETA
Plain White, with Double Cuffs
Superior Quality	25/6
Medium Weight..	21/-
Light Weight	16/6

ALL WOOL TAFFETA
Warmth without weight. Neat coloured stripes on White ground. Also close striped effects in Black, Blue, Mauve and Brown, with Double Cuffs 21/-

PROMINENT FEATURE
All Wool Taffeta, including two soft collars backed with longcloth to prevent shrinkage. Smart range of neat designs on white grounds 21/-

HEAVY CREPE DE CHINE SHIRTS
In close striped effects on White and coloured grounds. Two soft collars fitted with twin tabs and whalebone supports Double Cuffs .. .. 5/- and 63/-

POPLIN
Double Cuffs. Mercerised Poplin Shirts. Two soft collars with twin tabs and whalebone supports. Fancy stripes of Black, Blue, Mauve and Brown, on coloured grounds in medium and narrow widths .. 10/6
Also 12/6

POPLIN
Double Cuffs. Mercerised Poplin Shirts and two soft collars with twin tabs and whalebone supports. Plain shades of Biscuit, Blue, Grey and Helio also a wide assortment of exclusive striped effects in Black, Blue, Mauve and Brown, on White grounds in medium and narrow widths, etc. .. 15/6

POPLIN
Double Cuffs. Mercerised Poplin Shirts Two stiff double collars in plain shades. Buff and Blue only 15/6

SUPERFINE POPLIN
Double Cuffs. Mercerised Poplin Shirts made of the finest Egyptian yarns. Two soft collars with twin tabs and whalebone supports. Large assortment of close stripe designs, colourings of Black, Blue, Mauve, Brown and Red, etc. 21/-

TWILL CASHMERE
Finest quality. A variety of coloured stripes on white grounds, Blue, Black, Mauve, Brown, also close striped effects with same colourings. Double Cuffs 27/6

KHAKI BUSH SHIRTS
Khaki Poplin	15/6
Ceylon Twill Wool and Cotton mixture with two soft collars	16/6
Viyella. Collar attached ..	22/-
Fine all Wool, Two detachable collars	21/-

ALL PRICES ARE SUBJECT TO MARKET FLUCTUATIONS

HARRODS LTD

Telephone SLOANE 1234
Telegrams 'EVERYTHING HARRODS LONDON'

LONDON SW1

MEN'S WEAR SECTION
Collars to Suit Every Individual Preference

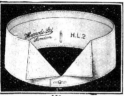

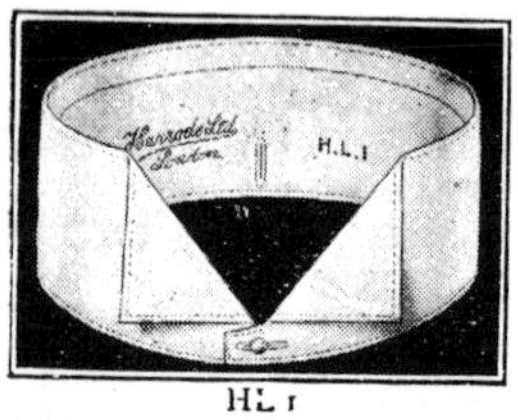

HL 1

HL 2

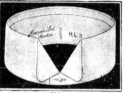

HL 3

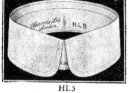

HL 4

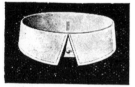

HL5

HL 6

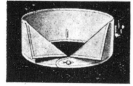

HL 7

HS 3

VAN HEUSEN

These Collars are exceptionally light and comfortable, yet always retain a smart appearance

Style 11 Semi Polo; white; quarter sizes

Style 11—6 Semi Polo; blue; half sizes

Style 11—7 Semi Polo; buff; half sizes

Price **18/-** per doz.

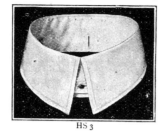

HS 1

SOFT COLLARS

HS 1   Linen-faced Polo
Price 1/3 each, 14/- per doz.
HS 2   Linen-faced Double
Price 1/3 each, 14/- per doz.
HS 3   Poplin, Semi Polo tabs and stiffeners
Price 1/6 each, 17/- per doz.
HS 4   All Wool Taffeta Polo
Price 1/9 each, 20/- per doz.
HS 5   All Wool Taffeta Double
Price 1/9 each, 20/- per doz.
HS 6   Jap Silk Polo
Price 2/6 each, 27/6 per doz.
HS 7   Jap Silk Double
Price 2/6 each, 27/6 per doz.
HS 8   Matt, Polo
Price 1/- each, 11/- per doz.

H 9

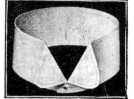

H 44, 55, 56

H 2

H 14A

LINEN COLLARS

In the newest and smartest designs
Sizes 14 to 18
Quarter sizes from 14 to 17

HL 1   2¼-in. Square Wing, wide
HL 2   2-in. Square Wing, medium
HL 3   2-in. Round Wing, medium
HL 4   1¾-in. Round Double
HL 5   2-in. Round Double
HL 6   1¾-in. Square Double
HL 7   Semi Polo, 2½-in. point
HL 9   2-in. deep, Wide wing style, Square Wing

Price 1/6 each, or 17/- per doz.

Customers' own shapes copied and patterns registered from 16/6 to 33/- per doz.

Any description or shape of collar made to special order at short notice

H 8

H 19

H 15, 16, 17.

H 4, 5, 6

FINE EGYPTIAN COTTON COLLARS
9/- DOZEN

H 1 2-in. Square Wing, wide drop	H 12 1½-in. Round Double
H 2 2-in. ,, ,, wide ,,	H 14A Semi Polo
H 3 2-in. ,, ,, medium ,,	H 15 1¾-in. Round Double
H 4 1¾-in. ,, ,, small ,,	H 16 2-in. ,, ,,
H 5 2-in. ,, ,, ,, ,,	H 17 2¼-in. ,, ,,
H 6 2¼-in. ,, ,, ,, ,,	H 18 1½-in. Square ,,
H 7 1¾-in. ,, ,, medium ,,	H 19 1¾-in. ,, ,,
H 13A 1¾-in., wide Square Wing	H 20 2-in. ,, ,,
H 8 1¾-in. Square Double	H 21 Polo
H 9 Semi Polo, 2-in. point	H 44 1¾-in. Round wing, small
H 10 ,, ,, 2¼-in. ,,	H 55 2-in. ,, ,, ,,
H 11A Flexible Semi Polo Made from specially woven cloth that will not stiffen in redressing, 11/- dozen	H 66 2¼-in. ,, ,, ,,

ALL PRICES ARE SUBJECT TO MARKET FLUCTUATIONS

HARRODS LTD

Telephone SLOANE 1234
Telegrams 'EVERYTHING HARRODS LONDON'

LONDON S W 1

MEN'S WEAR SECTION
Comfortable Smoking Jackets, Bath Robes and Travelling Rugs

DRESSING GOWNS
of every description in stock

CAMEL FLEECE
Natural Colour. Very soft and comfortable **42/-**

REAL CAMEL HAIR
Natural Colour. Warm and cosy
63/-, 84/-, 5 gns., 6 gns. and 9 gns.

SELF COLOUR WOOL GOWNS
Colours :—Grey, Mole, Brown, and Navy   **42/-**
  ,,   Fawn, Grey **63/-**
  ,,   Grey, Brown and Navy   ..   **75/-**
  ,,   Brown, Tan, Navy   ..   **126/-**

SELF COLOUR GOWNS
Check Collar and Cuffs. Fawn, Brown, Grey
and Navy..   ..   ..   **30/-, 65/- and 5 gns.**

SILK FOULARD GOWNS
Paisley designs
Very convenient for travelling
45/-, 63/-, 75/-, 90/-

UNLINED SILK BROCADE GOWNS
In characteristic designs in a wide range of
colourings..   ..   ..   **5 gns., 6 gns., 8 gns.**

UNLINED ARTIFICIAL SILK GOWNS
New design and colour schemes
45/-, 63/- 84/-

DRESSING GOWNS
The newest designs and colours
always in stock

BROCADE GOWNS LINED CASHMERE
Exceptionally warm and comfortable
5 gns.

BROCADE GOWNS LINED SILK
Superb designs and colourings
6 gns., 8 gns., 12 gns.

QUILTED BROCADE GOWNS
Luxuriously comfortable. Rich old Paisley
design with soft quilted lining
7 gns. and 14 gns.

QUILTED JAPANESE GOWNS
Plain Shades, **70/-**

FLANNEL AND CASHMERE GOWNS
Unlined. Wide assortment of attractive designs
in smart stripes and plain colours
50/-, 63/- and 90/-

BATH ROBES
Terry Towelling. Block stripes on White,
Mauve, Pink, Sky, Fawn and Grey   ..   **19/6**
Plain Coloured with contrasting collars and cuffs
21/-, 42/-

Jacquard designs. An exceptional variety in
characteristic colours   ..   **30/-, 37/6, 45/-**
Plain White **21/-, 35/6**

SMOKING JACKETS

Plain Cloth. Black, Navy and Brown, trimmed frogs
63/-
Plain Cloth with Quilted Collar and Cuffs, in Black
and Navy **126/-**
Self Colour Wool Smoking Jackets with 2 frog
fastenings. Navy, Tan. Purple and Brown   ..   **95/-**
Rich Brocade, lined Silk ..   ..   ..   **95/-, 7½ gns.**
Rich Brocade, Lined and Quilted
throughout ..   ..   ..   **5½ and 9½ gns.**
Velveteen. Brown, Black, Navy..   ..   **57/6**
Japanese Quilted Silk **42/-**

Illustrated is a Silk Brocade and a Woollen Dressing Gown

Illustrated is a Striped Terry Travelling Bath Robe

When ordering please state height and chest measurements

When ordering please state height and chest measurements

FRINGED RUGS
CHECK WOOLLEN Large variety of check designs
21/-, 30/-, 45/-, 63/-, 84/-, 5 gns., 6 gns.
TARTAN Plain backs   ..   **30/-, 45/-, 5 gns., 6 gns.**
FINE CASHMERE   ..   **63/-, 70/-, 84/-, 6 gns.**
LADY PLAID Plain and Tartan. Light weight **45/-**
PLUSH MOHAIR RUGS **4 gns., 6 gns., 9 gns., 14 gns.**
SILK PLUSH 'MOTEX' RUGS. Suitable for
either Car or Boudoir **95/-**

ALL PRICES ARE SUBJECT TO MARKET FLUCTUATIONS

HARRODS LTD

Telephone SLOANE 1234
Telegrams 'EVERYTHING HARRODS LONDON'

LONDON S W 1

MEN'S WEAR SECTION
All that is Expected of Good Footwear—Comfort, Style and Lasting Service

DRESS OXFORDS
Plain Dress Shoes without toe-caps
45/- and **63/-**
Hand-made quality **69/-** and **84/-**

Boots and Shoes made to order

BOX CLOTH SPATS
Light Fawn, Dark Fawn and Grey .. **8/6**
Super quality, half lined **11/9**
Canvas Spats, White, Biscuit and Drab .. **6/9**

OXFORD SHOES
Box Calf, Tan Willow or Patent
Leather. Medium Weight Soles **21/-**

Purchases **10/-** *and over Post Free in Great Britain*

DRESS SHOES
An inexpensive Dress Shoe with
light flexible sole .. **25/-** and **35/-**

HAND-MADE OXFORDS
Particularly smart hand-made shoes
that are much in demand for city
wear. Box Calf, Tan Willow Calf
or Patent Leather **69/-**

MEDIUM WEIGHT OXFORDS
These Oxfords may be had in either
Box Calf, Tan Willow or Patent
Leather **27/6**

COURT SHOES
Beautifully designed, light and flexible
Patent Leather Court Shoes
21/- and **30/-**

HAND-MADE OXFORDS
A neatly designed Oxford with a
slightly ornamented toe-cap. Tan
Russian Calf or Black Calf .. **69/-**

ALBERT SLIPPERS
Strongly made, leather soles
10/9, 18/9 and **25/-**
Soft leather soles. In Tan, Red and
Blue **6/11**

DOUBLE SOLED OXFORDS
These Shoes have stout double soles
and are Drill lined. Box Calf or
Tan Willow Calf **63/-**

HAND-MADE OXFORDS
Perfectly shaped Oxford Shoes, hand-
made throughout in Tan Russian
Calf or Black Calf. Medium weight
69/-

OXFORD SHOES
Medium weight substance soles
Leather lined. In Box Calf, Tan
Willow Calf or Patent Leather **35/-**

SEMI-BROGUES
Medium weight in Box Calf or Tan
Willow Calf **25/-**
Superfine quality **63/-**

SMART OXFORDS
Exceptionally smart and just the
right weight for city or business
wear. Tan Willow Calf, Box Calf
or Patent Leather **45/-**

PATENT LEATHER OXFORD SHOES
Medium weight **27/6**
Superior quality **35/-**

**All Boots and Shoes are
stocked in a variety of
fittings, and half sizes
from 6's—12's**

BOX CALF BOOTS
Drill lined **45/-**
Superfine quality. Drill lined
and medium weight .. **69/-**

MEN'S BOOTS
Box Calf or Tan Willow boots. Drill
lined. Medium weight soles
21/-, 27/6 and **35/-**

BOYS' BOOTS
Strong, comfortable, School Boots in
Black Box Calf. Sizes: Boys' 2 to
Men's 8. All sizes one price .. **17/9**
Also Shoes: same price

SELF MEASUREMENT FORM
Customers who wish to order by post may be assured of a perfect
fit by applying for the self measurement form which will be sent
on request

HARD WEARING BOOTS
Stout Box Calf Boots with a double
weight waterproof sole .. **45/-**

ALL PRICES ARE SUBJECT TO MARKET FLUCTUATIONS

HARRODS LTD

Telephone SLOANE 1234
Telegrams 'EVERYTHING HARRODS LONDON'

LONDON S W 1

MEN'S WEAR SECTION
Hats that Express Style and Individuality

Men who are particular about their attire will appreciate the importance
of choosing a hat which is in keeping with a well-groomed appearance
Whatever style is chosen from Harrods Hat Department,
and every type of hat is represented, there is always
the full assurance that in style, quality and price,
the utmost satisfaction will be afforded

'CAWNPORE TENT CLUB'
Pith body. Quilted Khaki Drill
detachable cover **25/-**

'RANELAGH' POLO CAP
Special consolidated body .. **42/-**

'WOLSELEY'
Cork body. Covered White or
Khaki Drill **27/6**

'THE MINTO'
Cork and Rubber body. Covered
White or Khaki Drill .. **30/-**
Pith body **25/-**

'LADIES' DOUBLE TERAI'
Fine Quality sun-resisting Fur
Felt, lined Red. Drab or Fawn **55/-**

'FULL CURL BOWLER'
Fine quality **25/-**

'THE DERBY'
Anglesey Curl .. **18/6, 21/-, 25/-**

'MEN'S DOUBLE TERAI'
Fine Quality sun-resisting Fur Felt
lined Red Satin. Drab or
Fawn **55/-**

SOFT FELT HAT
Curled brim. Light and Dark Greys,
Browns and Fawn **21/-. 25/-, 30/-**

TWEED SPORTS HAT
Made from fine quality Tweed.. **12/6**

'THE PORTLAND'
Tweed Caps. New designs and colourings
Silk lined **10/6, 12/6**

SOFT FELT SPORTS HAT
Adaptable brim, in Greys
Fawns and Browns **18/6, 21/-, 25/-**

'THE OPERA'
In fine quality Merino, lined
hard-wearing Satin, Best quality
collapsible springs **22/6**
In specially woven Corder Silk **32/6**

'THE SHINGLE'
Ladies' Riding Hats, curl narrowed
at back **30/-**

'CENTAUR 28'
Ladies' Riding Hat, drop brim **30/-**

'THE ANGLESEY'
Silk Hat. Fine quality **35/-, 45/-**
Hunting quality **42/-**

ALL PRICES ARE SUBJECT TO MARKET FLUCTUATIONS

HARRODS LTD

Telephone SLOANE 1234
Telegrams 'EVERYTHING HARRODS LONDON'

LONDON S W 1

HARRODS SELF-MEASUREMENT FORMS
Measurements required for Gentlemen's Clothing

When ordering OVERCOATS or JACKETS always include Chest and Waist Measurements over Waistcoat

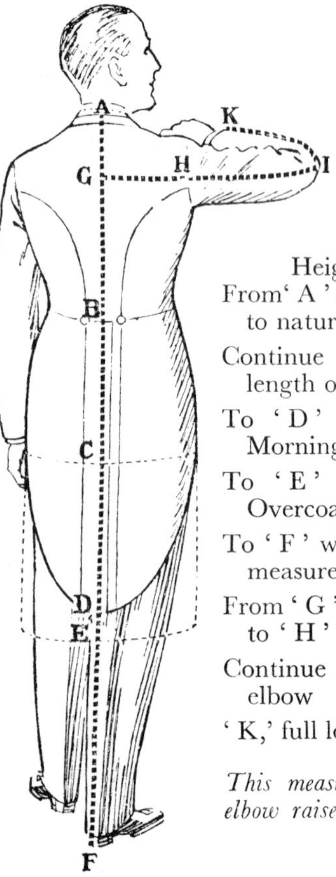

COAT

Inches

Height, Feet

From 'A' at Collar Seam to natural waist 'B' ....

Continue to 'C' for length of Jacket ....

To 'D' for length of Morning or Dress Coat ....

To 'E' for length of Overcoat ....

To 'F' which is ground measure ....

From 'G' centre of Back to 'H' at sleeve seam ....

Continue to 'I' for elbow ....

'K,' full length of sleeves ....

This measure should be taken with elbow raised and bent as illustration

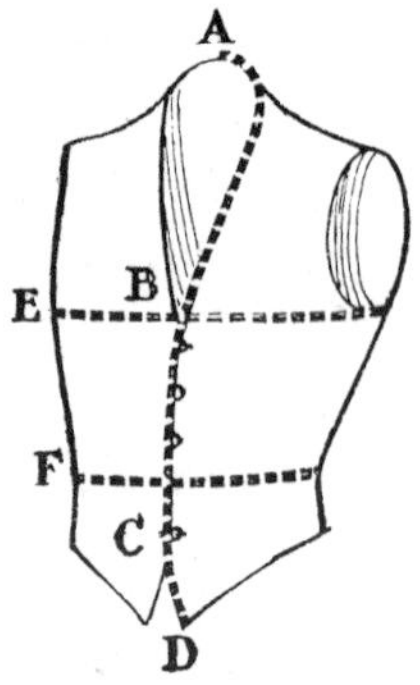

TROUSERS

Inches

'A' top of Waistband to 'B' ground at heel ....

'C' close up under fork to 'D' ground at heel ....

'E' Waist measure ....

'F' Seat measure ....

'G' width of Trousers at thigh ....

'H' at knee ....

'I' at bottom ....

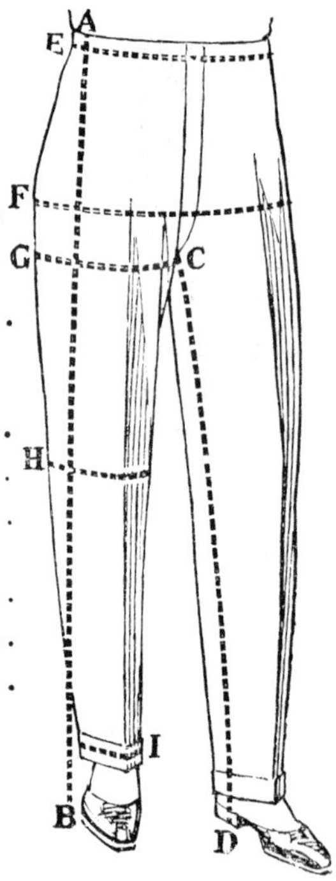

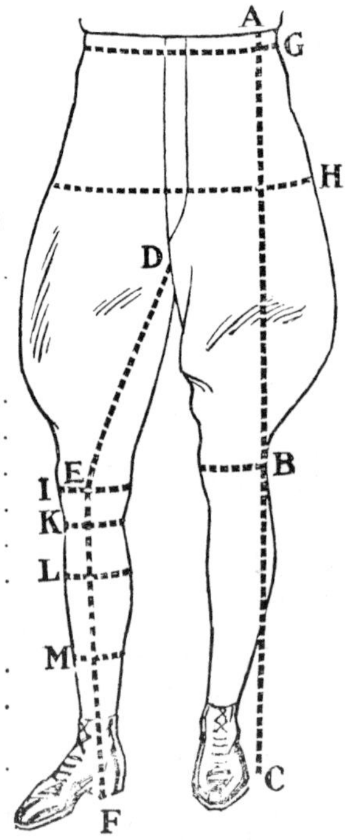

WAISTCOAT

Inches

'A' to 'B' length of opening at top button ....

To 'C' bottom button ....

Then to 'D' ....

'E' Chest measure ....

'F' Waist measure ....

RIDING BREECHES

Inches

'A' top of waistband to 'B' opposite knee cap ....

Then to 'C' ground measure at heel ....

'D' close up in fork to 'E' opposite knee bone ....

Then to 'F' at ground ....

'G' Waist measure ....

'H' Seat measure ....

'I' Measure over knee cap .... (with knee slightly bent) ....

'K' Close measure around small (below knee and above calf) ....

'L' Measure over calf ....

'M' Measure, half-way below calf and above ankle ....

Name ....

Address ....

....

Date ....

Height ....

HARRODS LTD

Telephone SLOANE 1234
Telegrams 'EVERYTHING HARRODS LONDON'

LONDON S W 1

BOYS' CLOTHING DEPARTMENT
Complete Outfits for Boys of All Ages

Boys as well as Parents know that whatever they need in clothing, be it School Suits, Sports Togs, Formal Wear, and all the necessary accessories for school or holiday wear they will be correct if they come from Harrods. Harrods understand school clothes—they know exactly what is decreed by the great public schools. Entrust then to Harrods the outfitting of your boys and you will then be certain that everything is right, everything as good as it can be

RUGBY SUITS. Regulation School Suits for boys of 7 to 14 years. Well cut from good trustworthy materials. All Suits are provided with generous turnings for lengthening. In Tweeds in Light and Dark Greys, Browns, Fawns and Lovats. All sizes.. **35/-**
Superior qualities
First size **67/6, 59/6, 55/6, 50/-, 45/-**
Rising **1/-** and **1/6** per size.
In all Wool Navy Serge.
First Size,
78/3, 66/9, 58/6, 50/9
Rising **2/6** and **1/6** per size.

RUGBY SUITS. Sturdy Suits designed for the bigger boy with the knickers fastening below the knee. Styled in substantial Tweeds in Grey, Brown, Fawn and Lovat. Sizes for boys 8 to 14 years. All sizes .. **37/6**
Superior qualities. First sizes .. **69/6, 59/6, 47/6**
Rising **1/-** and **1/6** per size.

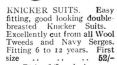

KNICKER SUITS. Easy fitting, good looking double-breasted Knicker Suits. Excellently cut from all Wool Tweeds and Navy Serges. Fitting 6 to 12 years. First size **52/-**
Rising **1/3** each size.
Other qualities **77/-** and **61/6**
Rising **2/3** and **1/6** each size.

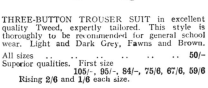

THREE-BUTTON TROUSER SUIT in excellent quality Tweed, expertly tailored. This style is thoroughly to be recommended for general school wear. Light and Dark Grey, Fawns and Brown.
All sizes **50/-**
Superior qualities. First size
105/-, 95/-, 84/-, 75/6, 67/6, 59/6
Rising **2/6** and **1/6** each size.

THE 'MARLBOROUGH' JACKET AND VEST is the regulation everyday Suit for many of the Public Schools. Tailored with skilful care from fine quality Black Vicuna Cloth and available in sizes to fit boys age 10 to 20 years. All sizes **37/6**
Superior qualities. First size **62/6, 59/6, 50/6, 45/6**
Rising **2/6** each size.

TROUSERS to wear with the 'Marlborough' Jacket and Vest, made from neat striped Worsted of reliable quality. All sizes **21/6**
Superior qualities. First size **42/6, 37/6, 34/6**
Rising **6d.** each size.

DOUBLE-BREASTED TROUSER SUIT. Tailored with the precision associated with the name of Harrods. Stocked in a large range of dependable Tweeds and Fancy Worsteds. Sizes for all average boys age 12 to 21 years. First size. **122/6, 105/6, 95/6, 89/6, 84/6**
Rising **3/6** and **2/6** each size.

ETON JACKET AND VEST perfectly tailored in trim regulation style from fine Black All Wool Vicuna Cloth. Sizes to fit boys from 7 to 15 years. All sizes **35/-**
Superior qualities. First size .. **72/6, 59/6, 48/6**
Rising **2/-** each size.

ETON TROUSERS. Made from medium and Dark Grey regulation hairline Trousering. First size for 7 years **22/-, 19/6, 15/6**
Rising **6d.** each size.

BOWLER HATS **16/6, 12/6, 10/6**
SILK HATS **29/6**

ALL PRICES ARE SUBJECT TO MARKET FLUCTUATIONS

HARRODS LTD

Telephone SLOANE 1234
Telegrams 'EVERYTHING HARRODS LONDON'

LONDON S W 1

BOYS' CLOTHING DEPARTMENT
Overcoats, Suits, and Gaiters for Little Boys

'CHESTER' Riding Coat of Fawn Covert for boys 4 to 14 years. First size 32/6
Rising 1/6 per size.

Other qualities 76/-, 60/-, 55/-, 43/6 Rising 1/6 and 3/- per size.

RIDING BREECHES, strong Fawn Cord 23/9. Rising 9d.

Bedford Cord 33/3. Rising 6d.

Best Whipcords strapped Buckskin, 62/6. Rising 2/6 per size.

Tan Gaiters 15/6

Boxcloth Gaiters 25/6

'THE NEW MAC' (guaranteed waterproof). Specially designed by Harrods with an eye to the health and comfort of the small boy is the 'New Mac' of Proofed Poplin. Either as a Dustcoat or Waterproof it is ideal. Double breasted, and lined Artificial Silk Check. In Red, Green, Dark Saxe and Fawn. To fit boys 2 to 7 years. Lengths 20 to 30 ins. Complete with Hat to match. All sizes 25/6

'ALGY' Attractive Coat for the little boy of 2 to 4 years. In materials of new designs, trimmed with collar of contrasting shades. First size 47/6
Rising 1/6 each size.
Also 57/6 Rising 2/- each size.
Hat to match 16/6

For special self-measurement Chart for all Boys' Suits and Overcoats, *see page 614.*

'DEREK' Beautifully cut and finished Tweed Coat with a Velvet or self collar. This style is made for little men of 2 to 4 years and is available in Brown, Grey Fawn or Blue. In various qualities. First size .. 46/6, 52/6, 65/- 75/-
Rising 1/6 and 2/6 per size.

Felt Hats to wear with this Coat 8/11 to 18/6

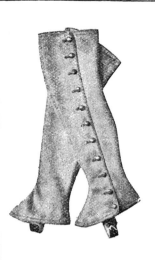

JACK. A warm Reefer Coat well cut from fine quality Navy Nap Cloth in the approved manner. For Jack Tars of 3 to 8 years. First size 30/6
Rising 1/- each size.

Other qualities 51/6 rising 2/-, and 43/6 rising 1/6 each size.

FINE NAVY SERGE COAT 24/6 and 36/6
Rising 6d. and 1/- each size.

OVERKNEE GAITERS in Beaver Cloth; cut high over the knee. Sizes 2 to 9 years. First size .. 9/6
Rising 6d. each year.

In superior quality. White, Beaver or Fawn shades. First size .. 14/6
Rising 1/- each size.

In Tan leather 13/6, rising 1/- each size. In Stockinette with fleecy backs: White or Covert shades. Sizes 2 to 6 years. All sizes 5/6.
In All Wool, all sizes 6/6. In Knitted Wool, Cream shade only .. 8/11

PANTA LEGGINETTES of warm, strong Stockinette. In Cream, Covert, Brown, Black or Fawn. Sizes for 2 to 10 years. First size .. 6/6
Rising 6d. each size.

In Corduroy: White, Mole, Grey, Drab or Brown. First size .. 9/-
Rising 6d. each size.

SAILOR SUIT. All Wool Navy Serge for sailors of 3 to 10 years. First size .. .. 42/- and 47/6
Rising 2/- each size

JUMPER AND KNICKERS. First size .. .. 35/- and 42/6
Rising 1/6 per size.

Jumpers in White Cotton Drill. First size 12/6
Trousers, First size 7/9
Knickers, First size 5/-
Rising 3d. per size.

Sailor Tams. Navy 7/6
White 3/11

ALL PRICES ARE SUBJECT TO MARKET FLUCTUATIONS

HARRODS LTD

Telephone SLOANE 1234
Telegrams 'EVERYTHING HARRODS LONDON'

LONDON S W 1

BOYS' CLOTHING DEPARTMENT
Warm Woollies and Cool Tub Suits for Smaller Boys

'DAVID' (*On left*)

Knit from fine quality Wool yarns in a pleasing stripe design, this snug Jersey is splendid for nursery wear. In Saxe/Tan Grey, Fawn/Saxe Tan, Sky/Fawn. For little lads of 3 to 8 years

First size of 22 ins. **13/6**

Rising **1/–** per size

'RONNIE' (*On right*)

Gay Silk stripes finish this cheery little Jersey Suit designed for little boys of 2½ to 5 years. Shades of Nile Green/White, Sky/White, Saxe/White, Biscuit and Sky

First size 20 in. chest **19/6**

Rising **1/6** every 2 inches

'HECTOR'

Jolly little Suit in fine Scotch yarns knit in attractive two-colour combinations, striped at collar and cuffs. Saxe Blue/Mole, Powder Blue/Sand, Scarlet/Covert, Tan/Covert. Sizes 22 to 26 in. chest. First size .. **23/6**

Rising **1/–** each size

Ties to match **1/6**

'ROY'

This Jersey Suit is made from the softest of Wool. The Sweater fastens at the shoulder with buttons (*as illustrated*). In Pale Blue, Saxe, Fawn, Brown, Helio and White

20 in. chest size **21/6**

Rising **1/6** every 2 inches

'HERBERT'

A square-necked Sweater is the feature of this trim Jersey Suit, carried out in fine Silk/Wool. Stripes band it effectively. For little boys of 3 to 6 years old. In Sky, Saxe, Fawn, Apple, Tan and White 22 inch chest size **23/6**

Rising **2/–** every 2 inches

'GRANTHAM'

Trim little Jacket Suit, which can be worn with shirt or blouse. In shades of Brown, Fawn and Grey. Sizes for boys 5 to 7 years

First size .. **45/–, 55/–, 65/–**

Rising **1/6** each size

'ROY' BLOUSE

A very smart Silk Blouse, stitched with a contrasting colour. Pastel shades of Biscuit, Powder Blue and Cedar in sizes for the little boy of 4 to 6 years

First size **48/6**

Rising **2/3** per size

'AUSTIN' (*On left*)

Smart Linen Suit opening over a White Vest In Apple Green, Fawn, Blue or Tan. Sizes 4 to 8 years. First size **30/6**

Rising **1/–** each year

In all Wool Gabardines and Serges, **41/–** and **44/6**

Rising **1/–** and **1/6** each year

THE 'BRISTOL' BLOUSE (*On right*)

Cotton Poplins in Tussore, Grey, Sky, Saxe and White. All sizes, 3 to 7 years **10/6**

Tussore Silk **10/6**

Crepe Flannel **12/11**

Silk/Wool in neat stripes of Saxe, Red and Helio **15/6**

Plain or striped Silk .. **21/–** and **25/6**

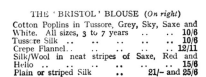

ALL PRICES ARE SUBJECT TO MARKET FLUCTUATIONS

Telephone SLOANE 1234

Telegrams 'EVERYTHING HARRODS LONDON'

HARRODS LTD   **LONDON S W 1**

BOYS' OUTFITTING DEPARTMENT

Nowhere will You Find a Greater Choice of Costumes than at Harrods

'COWBOY'

The fringed Trousers are made of strong Khaki Drill, while a Red Shirt and bandana kerchief add the necessary note of colour. Complete with Leather Belt and Holster, Pistol and Hat

Sizes 6 to 10 years 25/-
Sizes 11 to 15 years 27/6

'DICK TURPIN'

Red Coat with Lace ruffles. Black Breeches and a three-cornered Hat

Sizes 8 to 14 years 50/-
Men's sizes .. .. from 63/-
Black Patent Leather Gaiters .. Per pair 15 6

'Rajah'

'Cowboy'

'White Rabbit'

'WHITE RABBIT'

Soft White Fur-fabric Costume
Sizes 3 to 8 years
First sizes .. .. 42/- and 63/-
Rising 3/- each size.

'Dick Turpin'

'Coster'

'RAJAH'

Gold braid lends a truly Oriental richness to this striking Costume in vivid Sateen. Complete with Turban

Men's sizes .. 30/-
The same style is very effective in Brocaded Silk .. 60/-

'NAVAL OFFICER'

Very smartly tailored uniform which includes Navy Cloth Tunic, Trousers, Hat and Sword. Sizes 4 to 10 years
First size .. 70/-

Rising 1/6 each size

'PATCHWORK'

The Prince of Clowns—his colourful 'get up' establishes his claim to the title beyond dispute. In multi-toned Sateen, with White ruffle. Men's sizes .. 25/6

'Naval Officer'

'Patchwork'

'COSTER'

The Pearly King himself in Black and White Check Suit. Complete with Red striped vest, kerchief and cap. Men's sizes .. 35/-
Also in Black Velveteen 50/-
Boys' Costumes in Black Sateen 8 to 14 years 35/-

'PIRATE CHIEF'

Very colourful costume with typical Pirate's Headdress and Pistol. Complete with Tights.
Boys' sizes 65/-
Men's sizes 84/-

Fancy Dress Catalogue sent on request

'Pirate Chief'

ALL PRICES ARE SUBJECT TO MARKET FLUCTUATIONS

HARRODS LTD

Telephone SLOANE 1234
Telegrams 'EVERYTHING HARRODS LONDON'

LONDON S W 1

HARRODS SELF-MEASUREMENT FORMS
Measurements Required for Boys' Clothing

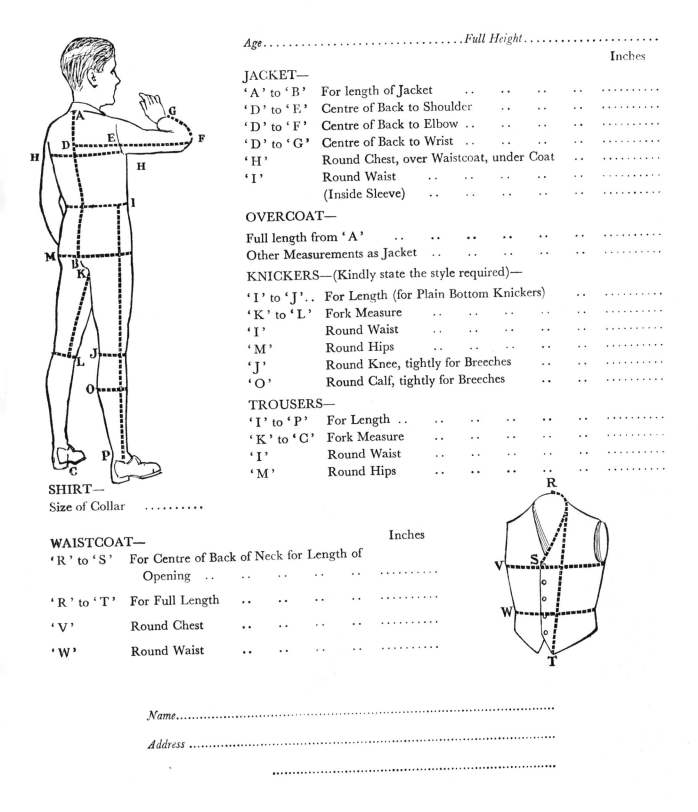

Age. . . . . *Full Height*. . . . .

Inches

JACKET—

'A' to 'B'	For length of Jacket	.. ..
'D' to 'E'	Centre of Back to Shoulder	.. ..
'D' to 'F'	Centre of Back to Elbow ..	.. ..
'D' to 'G'	Centre of Back to Wrist	.. ..
'H'	Round Chest, over Waistcoat, under Coat	.. ....
'I'	Round Waist	.. ..
	(Inside Sleeve)	.. ..

OVERCOAT—

Full length from 'A' .. ..

Other Measurements as Jacket .. ..

KNICKERS—(Kindly state the style required)—

'I' to 'J'..	For Length (for Plain Bottom Knickers)	.. ..
'K' to 'L'	Fork Measure	.. ..
'I'	Round Waist	.. ..
'M'	Round Hips	.. ..
'J'	Round Knee, tightly for Breeches	.. ..
'O'	Round Calf, tightly for Breeches	.. ..

TROUSERS—

'I' to 'P'	For Length ..	.. ..
'K' to 'C'	Fork Measure	.. ..
'I'	Round Waist	.. ..
'M'	Round Hips	.. ..

SHIRT—
Size of Collar   . . . .

WAISTCOAT—

Inches

'R' to 'S'	For Centre of Back of Neck for Length of Opening ..	.. ..
'R' to 'T'	For Full Length ..	.. ..
'V'	Round Chest ..	.. ..
'W'	Round Waist ..	.. ..

Name. . . . .

Address . . . .

. . . .

HARRODS LTD

Telephone SLOANE 1234
Telegrams 'EVERYTHING HARRODS LONDON'

LONDON S W 1

GIRLS' OUTFITTING DEPARTMENT

Every Need of the 'Youthful Miss' Satisfactorily Fulfilled at Harrods

SCHOOL BLOUSES
For girls 6 to 15 years. Made of best White Cotton Taffeta, with shaped collar. Sizes 3, 4, 5, 6, 7, 8 and 9. All sizes one price **8/9**

SERGE SKIRTS
To wear with these blouses, well tailored in Navy Blue Serge. Buttoned on White Cotton bodice and smartly box-pleated all around. Sizes 24 to 36 ins. All sizes one price .. **17/6**

SCHOOL FROCK
Copy of a model specially designed for School Wear and suitable for all ages. Made in fine Repp, smartly pleated. The trim little collar is finished with ribbon bow. Belted front with straight back. In Navy only. To order in other colours. Sizes 27 to 42 ins. All sizes one price .. **42/-**

Prettily Designed Frocks and Cloaks for Party Wear

DAINTY LITTLE PARTY FROCK
A—In Hatienne Taffeta, trimmed with Lace Collar and buttoned down the front. Colours, Blue, Green, Pink, Ivory. Sizes 24, 26, 28 and 30 ins. All sizes **63/-**

PIERRETTE
B—This fascinating costume is in Velvet and Organdie. Trimmed with a row of brass buttons on bodice, and gold horseshoes to match on cap and skirt. Can be obtained in Black and White, and Black and Red. Sizes 33, 36 and 39 ins. All sizes one price **94/6**

VELVETEEN CLOAK
C—Youthful in style is this Velveteen Cloak lined with dainty Artificial Silk to tone. Colours are Blue, Rose, Green or Old Gold. Sizes 26, 28, 30, 32, 34 ins. All sizes **52/6**

FOR CHILLY WEATHER
D—Attractive Coat for the little one. In double-breasted style with adaptable collar trimmed Velvet. Made in Velour trimmed Tweed, lined throughout with best quality Sateen. Back has centre box pleat and is finished with half belt and buckle to tone. Can be obtained in shades of Brown and Bois. Sizes 24, 26, 28 and 30 ins. All sizes one price **52/6**

READY FOR THE RAIN
E—An inexpensive Mackintosh combining good style with absolute reliability. Fashioned of All-Wool Cashmere, lined with Rubber, light in weight and perfectly finished in every detail. In shades of Saxe, Brown and Navy. Sizes 27, 30, 33, 36 and 39 ins. All sizes one price **23/6**
Hat to match **5/6**

ALL PRICES ARE SUBJECT TO MARKET FLUCTUATIONS

HARRODS LTD

Telephone SLOANE 1234
Telegrams 'EVERYTHING HARRODS LONDON'

LONDON S W 1

GIRLS' OUTFITTING DEPARTMENT
Riding Habits Tailored with Trim Correctness

JAUNTY RIDING COAT

Expertly cut and tailored from fine West of England covert in the correct Fawn shade. Also adaptable for walking. Sizes 26 to 40 ins. First size **63/-**. Rising **2/6** every 2 ins.

ASTRIDE HABIT

Ready-to-wear, in Fawn or Brown proofed covert. Note the smart swing lines: breeches are correctly strapped with self fabric. Sizes 24 to 45 ins. First size **£6 18 6.** Rising **8/6** each size

For the ' Morning Canter '
or a
Glorious Day in the Hunting Field
A WELL-CUT HABIT ADDS GREATLY TO HER COMFORT

SIDE SADDLE HABIT

Consisting of coat, skirt and breeches, tailored with exquisite precision of detail. Made to measure, in covert coating For all ages. From **15** gns. In whipcords from **15½** gns.

JODHPURS *(Illustrated left)*
Expertly tailored in hard wearing covert coating, trimmed with strappings of self material First size 24" **65/-**. Rising **3/-** each size. A lower priced quality for children 6 to 14 years. All sizes .. **39/6**
JOCKEY CAPS
Black or Brown Velvet, **16/6**
HUNTING CAPS
Black Velveteen. Stiff Crowns Cork-lined **35/6**

POINT TO POINT

(Illustrated on right)

A Useful Rainproof Coat **of** sporting cut, **styled** with storm collar and closed full vent at back

Recommended for enduring wear

Sizes 36, 38 and 40 ins.. . **49/6**

ALL PRICES ARE SUBJECT TO MARKET FLUCTUATIONS

HARRODS LTD

Telephone SLOANE 1234
Telegrams 'EVERYTHING HARRODS LONDON'

LONDON S W 1

CHILDREN'S OUTFITTING DEPARTMENT
Comfy, Warm, 'Wooly' Garments and other Necessities for Baby

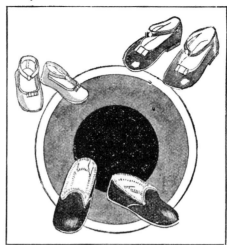

OB 22
BABY'S SOFT KID SHOES Colours—Red, Sky, Brown and Champagne. Sizes 2—5 .. **4/11**
Similar design to the above with hard sole and heel Sizes 3—6 .. .. **7/11**

CHILD'S DRESSING GOWN In Ripple Cloth. An excellent wearing material. Colours—Sky, Red and White. Size, 19 ins. .. .. **18/9** Rising 2/- each size

BEDROOM SLIPPERS
Sizes 3—6 .. **3/11**
Sizes 7—13 in Red and Sky only **4/11**

OB 17 BIBS, well made in quilted Cotton .. **1/9½d.**
WHITE TURKISH TOWELLING .. **9½d.**
Fancy Embroidered Lawn, to tie round under arms .. from **6/11**

Here's a group of useful little things that no nursery should be without
Powder Bowl **2/11—6/11**
Powder Puff .. **1/11—3/11**
Soap .. .. **1/—2/11**
Brush .. **1/11—3/11**
Comb .. .. **6d.**

(Not illustrated)
OB 19 LINEN FEEDERS with coloured Linen Appliqued Nursery Rhymes .. **3/9**

CHILD'S SLEEPING SUIT in Ceylon Flannel, delight and cosy. In plain colours Pink, Lemon and Mauve. All one Price **8/11** Also in good quality Cotton. fully soft of Sky, Sizes 2—7

OB 16 RUBBER PANTIES
Pale Pink, Baby Blue, Daffodil and White
Large size .. **1/11**
Extra large .. **2/6**

OB 19
LEGGINETTES Hand knitted throughout and of the finest quality Wool. Made with or without feet **9/11**
Rising **1/-** each size
Bonnet to match

OB 18
CLAXTON'S EARCAPS to train Baby's ears in the way they should go. All sizes .. **5/-**

OB 12 WOOL JACKETS Harrods have an exceptionally wide range of these Jackets in various lovely colourings. The one illustrated is **6/11** Various other qualities at different prices
Wool Bonnets from **4/11**

OB 20 SILK AND WOOL GLOVES Choice of two colours only— Camel & White Sizes 0—4 **2/11** per pair

OB 10 CHILDREN'S SOCKS Best quality White Lisle. Sizes 1—10 .. .. .. **2/11**
Rising 3d. per size
FANCY SOCKS with coloured stripe. Sizes 1—10 .. **1/6**
Rising 1d. per size
SPUN SILK SOCKS with openwork clocks. Sizes 2—10 .. **2/11**
Rising 3d. per size

ALL PRICES ARE SUBJECT TO MARKET FLUCTUATIONS

HARRODS LTD
Telephone SLOANE 1234
Telegrams 'EVERYTHING HARRODS LONDON'
LONDON SW1

HARRODS HAIRDRESSING SALONS

In Harrods beautifully appointed Salons there are 47 cubicles for the convenience of customers with not merely a few experts to advise but an EXPERT HAIRDRESSER in charge of each room

For the Permanent Wave Par Excellence

*H*AVE you seen the new 'ringletted' Permanent Wave that is so successful in Paris? It is inexpressibly *chic* and youthful— and Harrods will do it for you in the most becoming way. Or, if you prefer lustrous, loose, natural-looking waves, Harrods will give you those. So expert is this service that there is no danger of your hair losing anything of its sheen and colour, or of it becoming brittle in the process

A Permanent Wave at Harrods takes only about two hours of your time, and it will repay you with *months* of increased loveliness

Bobbed Hair - - 6 *Gns.*	*A highly qualified Specialist will advise on all hair troubles, free of charge*
Shingled Head - *from* 3 *Gns.*	
Full Head (long hair)- 5 *Gns.*	*Harrods Transformations and Shingled*
Half Head- - - 3 *Gns.*	*Wigs are made from finest natural*
Side Pieces- - *from* 1½ *Gns.*	*hair* - - - - *From 8 Gns.*

White hair treated without the slightest risk of its turning yellow

HIGH-FREQUENCY TREATMENT

The most gratifying results are being achieved daily by Harrods 'High Frequency' Hair Treatment

Where there is any tendency for the hair to fall, as it so often does after influenza, fever, or when the system is below par, this treatment swiftly revives vitality and growth, restores tone and brilliancy, and arrests a state of affairs which it is always unwise to neglect

FOR GREATER LOVELINESS

In practically every case Harrods are able to guarantee a wonderful improvement, whether by the restoration of the hair's natural beauty, or by tinting or waving, or by the artistic combination of additional tresses made up by Harrods own expert *posticheurs*

LADIES' HAIRDRESSING
PRICE LIST

	£	s.	d.
Haircutting	0	1	0
Singeing	0	1	0
Shampooing	0	2	0
Waving and Dressing .. .. from	0	2	0
Special Waving	0	3	6
Water Waving	0	3	6
Electric Treatment of the Hair (course of 5)	1	1	0
One Electric Treatment	0	5	0
Hairometer Treatment	0	10	6
Medicated Shampoo	0	3	6
Camomile Shampoo	0	5	0
Brightening Shampoo	0	5	0
Henna Shampoo	0	7	6
Oil Massage and Shampoo	0	7	6
Bleaching .. .. .. from	0	10	6
Hair Dyeing (inclusive of Dye) .. ,,	1	10	0
First Shingle	0	5	0
Shingle Trim	0	2	6
Shingle Wave	0	2	6
Henna application complete .. from	1	1	0
Henna slight application .. .. ,,	0	10	6
Lessons in Waving	0	10	6
Lessons in Hairdressing	0	10	6
Haircutting at Residence .. from	0	7	6
Manicure at Residence .. .. ,,	0	5	6
Historical character or poudre .. ,,	0	10	6
Electrolysis. Removal of superfluous hair per sitting, from	0	10	6
Manicure	0	2	0
Electric Face Massage	0	5	0
Electric Face Massage (course of 5) ..	1	1	0
Mud Massage 7/6,	10/6		
Chiropody each foot .. .. from	0	3	6
Foot Massage .. .. .. ,,	0	3	6
Pedicure des Ongles .. .. ,,	0	2	6
Permanent Waving, Side Pieces	1	11	6
,, ,, Half Head	3	3	0
,, ,, Whole Head	5	5	0
,, ,, Bobbed Head	5	5	0
Permanent Waving, Shingled Head £3 3 0 to £4	4	0	
Sunlight Treatment	0	10	6
Radiant Heat	0	10	6

CHILDREN'S HAIRDRESSING

Children look forward with delight to visiting Harrods Hair Dressing Salon. No tiresome waiting in chairs, but lots of amusing books to read, and jolly rocking horses to ride—more important still there is a highly skilled staff of Hairdressers in attendance and charges are extremely moderate

Shingle (first time)	..		5/-
Afterwards ..	..	..	2/6
Bob (first time)	..	..	3/-
Afterwards ..	..	..	1/6
Boy's Haircut	..	..	1/-
Boy's Shampoo	..	..	1/-
Girl's Shampoo	..	..	2/-
Hair cut and singe..		..	2/-

MEN'S HAIRDRESSING

A large and expert staff always in attendance. Excellent service and moderate charges

HARRODS LTD

Telephone SLOANE 1234
Telegrams 'EVERYTHING HARRODS LONDON'

LONDON SW1

LADIES' SHOE DEPARTMENT
Beautifully Fashioned Shoes to Grace the Season's Functions

This handsome shoe is made of the finest Silver or Gold Kid in the one bar style with metallic heel. 2, 3, and 4 fittings. Sizes 3—8 .. .. **49/6**

Fascinating model in Black Satin. The strap fastens at the side with a pretty paste buckle. Best London hand made Sizes and half sizes. All fittings **49/6**

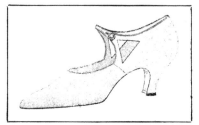

Exceedingly smart model in Silver Tissue with fashionable cut-out sides, and medium Louis heel. Particularly comfortable. All sizes and half sizes **29/6**

Exquisitely embroidered Black Satin Shoe. Best London hand made. Sizes and half sizes from 3—8. All fittings **59/6**

Silver Brocade with Silver Kid strappings, Spanish heel and medium toe. This design is exclusive to Harrods. Sizes and half sizes, 3—8 .. .. **49/6**

Well cut Court Shoe in Black Satin, with smart Louis heel. A striking example of Harrods value. Sizes and half sizes 3—8. All fittings. Also in White **21/-**

An ultra-smart model in rich Silver Brocade, with dainty Louis heel. Best London hand made. Also obtainable in Oxidized Silver. All sizes and half sizes All fittings **49/6**

Attractive model in Black Satin, with the approved flat heel. Fashionably cut-out sides. Sizes and half sizes. All fittings, sizes 3—8 .. .. .. **30/-** Also in Gold and Silver Kid **45/9**

Skilfully designed Court Shoe in Nude Satin, carefully cut round the sides, ensuring a perfect heel fitting. Trim Louis heel. Also in Dawn Satin and White Satin. Sizes, 3—8. All fittings **29/6**

Tan Willow Calf in one bar style with military heel. Designed on a perfect fitting last that ensures the 'last word' in foot comfort. Sizes and half sizes, from 3—8. Medium and wide fittings **29/6**

Beautifully designed Brocade Shoe with Louis heel and the short French toe. Also in Black Satin. Sizes 3—8. **49/6**

Perfectly cut One-Bar Shoe in Black Satin, with daintily stitched edges and strap. Finished with pretty paste button Sizes and half sizes, 3—8. All fittings **49/6**

ALL PRICES ARE SUBJECT TO MARKET FLUCTUATIONS

HARRODS LTD

Telephone SLOANE 1234
Telegrams 'EVERYTHING HARRODS LONDON'

LONDON S W 1

HOSIERY DEPARTMENT

Smart Hosiery in the Newest Textures and Favoured Shades

MERCERISED LISLE
LH 145
Good wearing Lisle stocking, fully fashioned Mercerised finish. Black, White, Mid-Grey, Beige, Wood, Beaver, Nude and Biscuit Sizes 8½–10½ .. .. per pair **2/11**

TENNIS SOX
LH 132
An excellent selection of White Tennis sox with fancy Rabbit Wool and plain coloured tops. All sizes
All White and plain coloured tops per pair **2/11**
Fancy Tartan tops, etc. per pair **4/11**

LISLE
LH 150
Mercerised Lisle stocking, medium weight with lace clock. Exceptionally serviceable. Fawn, Beaver, Nude. French Nude, Flesh, Wood, Grey, Silver. Sizes 8½–10½ Per pair **3/11**

BOTANY WOOL
Full fashioned Cashmere stocking in fine Botany Wool. Black, Grey, Silver, Beige, Fawn, Nude. Sizes 8½–10½
Per pair **3/11**
Heavier make, per pair .. **4/11**
Embroidered clocks, extra .. **1/-**

FOR COUNTRY WEAR
LH 131
Medium weight Lisle, highly mercerised, recommended for country wear Can be had with a lace or an embroidered clock. Beige, Fawn, Nude, Beaver, French Nude, Grey. Sizes 8½–10½, per pair .. **3/11**

CHIFFON LISLE
LH 140
Fine quality Chiffon Lisle stocking with lace clock. All shades of Flesh, Beige, Fawns, Beavers, Greys and Nude. Sizes 8½–10
Per pair **3/11**

'CELFECT' HOSE
LH 77
Excellent value stocking in strong 'Celfect' mixture. Grey, Silver, Fawn, Beige, Flesh, Mushroom and Dark Grey. Sizes 8½–10½
Plain .. .. .. per pair **3/11**
Embroidered clock .. per pair **4/11**

LISLE HOSE
LH 155
Excellent value in fine quality Lisle stockings, fully fashioned. A choice of either lace or embroidered clocks. Shades of Black, White, Nude, Grey, Beaver, Fawn, Beige. All sizes 8½–10 .. .. per pair **4/11**

FINE GAUGE CHIFFON LISLE
LH 160
Chiffon Lisle stockings, very sheer and fine, with dainty fancy lace clock. All the prevailing shades. Sizes 8½–10
Per pair **4/11**

SMART GOLF SOX
LH 129
Variety of short turnover top Golf sox to tone or contrast. Excellent quality Wool, in all shades of Heather, Beige and Fawn mixtures
From .. .. .. per pair **2/11**
Fancy and Jacquard top, per pair **4/11, 5/11**

SPORTS HOSIERY
LH 44
Good wearing stocking in Silk and Wool mixture suitable for sports and country wear Black, Black/White, Grey, Silver, Beige, Fawn, Nude, Mushroom and White Sizes 8½–10½
Plain .. .. .. per pair **5/11**
Embroidered clock .. per pair **6/11**

FINE GAUGE SILK
Splendid quality with beautifully worked lace clocks. The feet and top suspender hem are of Lisle for strength. In shades of Gunmetal, Beaver, Grey, Flesh, Nude, Beech and Gold. All sizes 8½–10½
Per pair **7/11**

'LEDA' SILK 1
Well-known 'Leda' Silk stockings made in England. The full fashioned Pure Silk leg is particularly long. Hem and feet are of Lisle for added strength. In Black White, Mist Grey, Zinc Grey, Cocoa, Beige, Light Beaver, Dark Beaver, Ash, Rosita Skin, Dark Skin, Nude and Gunmetal .. .. per pair **8/11**
With embroidered clock per pair **10/9**

'LEDA' 2
Fully fashioned British Silk stocking. Silk panel and suspender hem of Lisle for additional strength. Shades : Black, White, Mist Grey, Zinc Grey, Cocoa, Beige, Light Beaver, Dark Beaver, Ash, Rosita Skin, Dark Skin, Nude and Gunmetal. Sizes 8½–10. Per pair **6/11**
With embroidered clock per pair **8/11**

SILK HOSIERY
LH 56
Medium weight Silk stocking with long Silk panel and fashionable lace clock Fully fashioned, with Lisle feet and suspender hem for strength. In Rosewood, Diamante, Nude, Onion, Mushroom, Tinsel Silver and Tinsel Gold, Medium Grey, Black and White. Sizes 8½–10½
Per pair **8/11**

SILK AND WOOL
LH 170
Very fine gauge Silk and Wool stocking in pretty Marl mixture. Nude, Fawn, Beige, Grey and Biscuit shades. Sizes 8½–10
Plain .. .. .. per pair **9/11**
Fancy embroidered clock per pair **10/9**

'LYS HOSIERY'
LH 59
French Silk stocking of the well-known Lys make. Lisle lining to hem only and hand embroidered Fleur de Lys clock A splendid wearing stocking. Shades available Black, White, Smoke Grey, Silver Grey, Beaver, Nude, Flesh, Biscuit, Gunmetal and Rachelle Sizes 8½–10.
Per pair **14/6**

FRENCH SILK STOCKINGS
LH 126
French Silk stocking in excellent wearing quality. Silk throughout with the exception of Lisle lining to suspender hem. Dainty lace clock. Available in all the new Beaver, Fawn, Beige and Nude shades Sizes 8½–10½ .. .. per pair **14/6**

EXQUISITE SILK
LH 116
Fine Silk stocking, very elastic and wonderfully durable. Finished with a fancy lace clock. The suspender hem only is lined with very fine Lisle. Colours : Gunmetal, Beaver, Flesh, Gold, Tinsel Silver, Mid-Grey, Opera Pink, Nude and Black. Sizes 8½–10½ .. .. per pair **14/9**

ALL PRICES ARE SUBJECT TO MARKET FLUCTUATIONS

HARRODS LTD

Telephone SLOANE 1234
Telegrams 'EVERYTHING HARRODS LONDON'

LONDON S W 1

LINGERIE DEPARTMENT
Graceful Garments, Beautifully Made and Attractively Priced

US 82
SHADOWPROOF SLIP
Heavy quality shadowproof Crepe-de-Chine Slip, with 18 in. hem. Opera top style, finished with hemstitching. In Beige, Flesh, Peach, Mushroom, Lemon, Ivory and Black. Lengths 38, 40 and 42 .. .. **25/9**
O.S. Lengths 44—46 .. .. .. **29/6**

US 87
PRINCESS SLIP
In Crepe-de-Chine, trimmed with Cream Lace. Pink, Peach, Coral, Nil, Beige, Maize, Nattier, Ivory and Black. Lengths 38, 40 and 42 **21/9**
Directoire Knickers to match **16/9**
O.S. Slip. Lengths 44—46 .. .. **25/9**
Knickers to match **21/9**

US 84
WASHING SATIN SLIP
In good quality Washing Satin, finished at the top and bottom with Ruleau. Beige, Mushroom, Nil, Lemon, Nattier. Peach, Parchment, Ivory and Black. Lengths 38, 40 and 42 .. .. **29/6**
Round neck. Lengths 40, 42 and 44 **35/9**
Directoire Knickers to match .. **18/9**

US 83
PRINCESS SLIP
In Non-ladder Artificial Milanese Silk, with opera top and finished with elastic under the arm. In Beige, Mushroom, Pink, Coral, Nil, Beaver, Ivory and Black. Lengths 38, 40 and 42 **12/11**
O.S. Lengths 44—46 .. .. .. **15/11**
Round neck style. Lengths 38, 40 and 42 **14/11**
Round neck. O.S. Lengths 44—46 .. **18/11**
Directoire Knickers to match. O.S. **10/11**
S.W. **9/11**

US 86.
PRINCESS SLIP
In Celanese Satin, finished with elastic under the arm. Opera top style. In Pink, Peach, Nattier, Nil, Maize, Beige, Beaver, Navy, Grey, Ivory and Black. Lengths 38, 40 and 42 .. .. **12/11**
Directoire Knickers to match **10/9**

US 85
PRINCESS SLIP
Lovely Crepe-de-Chine Slip, finished with Georgette and beautifully embroidered. Opera top style, and new godet skirt. In Pink, Peach, Maize, Beige, Beaver, Nattier, Nil, Ivory and Black. Lengths 36, 38, 40 and 42 .. .. **39/6**
Directoire Knickers to match **29/6**

ALL PRICES ARE SUBJECT TO MARKET FLUCTUATIONS

HARRODS LTD

Telephone SLOANE 1234
Telegrams 'EVERYTHING HARRODS LONDON'

LONDON SW1

LINGERIE DEPARTMENT
Dainty Underwear of Silken Loveliness

LO 127

LO 123

LO 126

LO 129

LO 125

LO 124

LO 128
PRINTED GEORGETTE NIGHTGOWN

LO 128

LO 125. CAMI-BOCKER
In superior quality Crepe de Chine and Needlerun Lace, designed with the low cut back for evening wear. In Peach, Pink, Coral, Lemon, Beige, Nil, Ivory and Black **39/6**

Also in Silk Georgette, **39/6**

LO 126. CHEMISE
In Artificial Milanese daintily trimmed with Cream Lace and finished with elastic under the arm. Opera top. In Pink, Peach, Nil, Beige, Mushroom, Ivory, Maize and Black **10/9**

Directoire Knickers to match, **12/9**

LO 124. PYJAMAS
Heavy quality Crepe de Chine Pyjamas in the very newest design. Lovely hand-smocking on both Jumper and Trousers. Colours: Peach, Coral, Nattier, Lemon, Nil and Black .. .. .. **4½ Gns**

LO 127. TAILORMADE PYJAMAS
Very smartly designed in stripes or in plain colours.
Pure Silk Crepe de Chine

	S.W. & W.	O.S.
Pure Silk Crepe de Chine	**59/6**	**69/6**
Silk Taffeta ..S.W. & W.	**39/6**	**45/9**
Lista Silk ..S.W. & W.	**42/6**	**47/9**
Artificial Silk ..S.W. & W.	**21/9**	**25/9**
Wool and Cotton Mixtures S.W. & W.	**18/9**	**25/9**

LO 123. NIGHTGOWN
Beautiful quality Crepe de Chine with yoke of Needlerun Lace exquisitely designed. In shades of Pink, Coral, Peach, Nil, Lavender, Maize and Ivory **39/6**

Also in Silk Georgette, **39/6**

LO 129. KNICKERS AND CAMISOLE
Georgette Knickers daintily trimmed with Cream Lace. In Pink, Peach, Lemon, Nil, Heliotrope, Ivory and Black .. **35/9**

Camisole to match, **16/9**

LO 128 PRINTED GEORGETTE NIGHTGOWN
Daintily bound with contrasting shades and finished with ribbon girdle. In all the newest Lingerie shades .. **49/6**

ALL PRICES ARE SUBJECT TO MARKET FLUCTUATIONS
Telephone SLOANE 1234
Telegrams 'EVERYTHING HARRODS LONDON'

HARRODS LTD

LONDON S W 1

WOVEN UNDERWEAR
Underwear that Ensures Graceful Lines and Freedom of Movement

WU 15 & 16

WU 13 & 14

WU 9 & 10

WU 11 & 12

WU 15   LADIES' SPENCERS All well-fitting shapes.   In Wool

	Sizes	W.	O.S.
Low neck, no sleeves ..	..	6/11	7/11
High neck, short sleeves	..	7/11	8/11
V neck, short sleeves ..	..	8/11	9/11

Heavier quality Wool

Sizes	S.W.	W.	O.S.	X.O.S.
V neck, short sleeves	10/9	11/9	12/9	13/9
V neck, long sleeves	12/9	13/9	14/9	15/9

Made to open down front 1/- extra each size and shape

Also in fine Cashmere, Silk and Wool and Spun Silk, in a variety of styles

WU 16   Ribbed Wool EQUESTRIAN KNICKERS   Knee length, elastic at waist In Grey, Beige, Dark Brown, Light Brown, Cornflower, Sky, Covert, Nigger, Light and Dark Fawn, Purple, Mole, Navy, Black and White ..   .. Sizes : W. 6/11, O.S. 8/11

WU 13   Dainty Lisle VESTS Reliable and hard wearing. Opera top or low neck, no sleeves. Finished picot edge In Pink or White.   Sizes : W. and O.S. .. **5/11**

WU 14   Artificial Silk and Cotton KNICKERS Excellent wearing quality with double splicing and elastic at waist and knee. Lilac, Sky, Navy, Sahara, Pink, Silver, Fawn, Biskra, Sunrise, Apple, Pink, Black and White ..   Sizes : W. 7/11, O.S. 8/11

WU 9   Swiss Ribbed VESTS in Spun Silk. Dainty and close fitting. Sizes 34 and 36 ins. Opera top or low neck, no sleeves. Finished band or beaded top. Pink or White   **9/11**

Chemise length	..	..	.. **10/9**
Lighter weight ..	..	..	.. **8/11**
Chemise length	..	..	.. **9/11**

WU 10   Striped Silk and Wool KNICKERS Close fitting and snug. Light weight, with elastic at waist and finely ribbed at knee In Fawn, Silver, Tan, Pink, Sky, etc. with contrasting stripes **23/9**

WU 11   Ribbed Wool VESTS   Light, warm and beautifully soft. Finished band or beaded top. Opera top, low neck, no sleeves or low neck, short sleeves. In White only. Sizes 34 and 36 ins. **7/11**

Chemise length **8/11**

WU 12   Artificial Silk and Wool DIRECTOIRE KNICKERS   Elastic at waist and knee and double splicing at wearing parts In Fawn, Beige, Sahara, Dawn, Sky, Cloud, Pink, Navy, White and Black Sizes : S.W. and W. 11/9, O.S. 12/9

ALL PRICES ARE SUBJECT TO MARKET FLUCTUATIONS

HARRODS LTD

Telephone SLOANE 1234
Telegrams 'EVERYTHING HARRODS LONDON'

LONDON S W 1

WOVEN UNDERWEAR

Carefully Designed Garments for Every Type of Figure

WU 22 'TECTOR' WOOL VESTS

Replaced if they shrink. Summer weight. Opera top trimmed lace; low neck, ribbed arm; low neck, no sleeves

Sizes	Slr.	W.	O.S.	Ex.O.S.
	9/11	10/9	11/9	12/9
With V-neck, short sleeves				
	10/9	11/9	12/9	13/9

Winter Weight. Opera top, trimmed lace, low neck no sleeves; low neck, ribbed arms; low, high or V-neck short sleeves

Sizes	Slr.	W.	O.S.	Ex.O.S.
	10/9	11/9	12/9	13/9
With high neck, long sleeves				
	11/9	12/9	13/9	14/9

Chemise length 1/- extra

WU 23 ALL-WOOL KNICKERS

Well cut, with gusset. Elastic at knee and waist. In all shades. Also White and Black

Sizes	Slr.	W.	O.S.
	6/11	6/11	8/11
Superior quality ..	9/11	9/11	11/9
Heavier	11/9	11/9	12/9

WU 21 EQUESTRIAN KNICKERS

Soft Cashmere. To come below knee. Elastic at waist and ribbed knee. In all shades also White and Black

Sizes	Slr.	W.	O.S.
	16/9	17/9	18/9

WU 26 ANGLO GAUZE VESTS

For Summer wear. Excellent wearing quality. Plain opera top or trimmed silk lace. White only

Sizes	Slr.	W.	O.S.	Ex.O.S.
	15/9	16/9	17/9	18/9
Low neck, no sleeves; plain or lace trimmed ..	16/9	17/9	18/9	19/9

Chemise length, 2/- extra. Same shapes and sizes

WU 27 ANGLO GAUZE DRAWERS

To come below knee Carefully fashioned and finished with ribbing at knee and waist. White only Open shape

	Slr.	W.	O.S.	Ex.O.S.
	15/9	15/9	16/9	17/9

In heavy Silk and Wool, open shape White only

	Slr.	W.	O.S.	Ex.O.S.
	25/9	26/9	27/9	29/6

WU 24 'COUNTESS TOP' CHEMISE VEST

In light Silk and Wool, strengthened by fine cotton thread Lace top, insertion and ribbon straps

Sizes	Slr.	W.	O.S.	Ex.O.S.
White	18/9	18/9	19/9	20/9
Pink	19/9	20/9	21/9	22/9

Also in Spun Silk, same design, chemise length
White, size W. 17/9, O.S. 18/9. Pink, size W. 18/9, O.S. 19/9
Also in medium weight Silk and Wool, same design

Vest length.	Slr.	W.	O.S.	Ex.O.S.
White	21/9	22/9	23/9	—
Pink	22/9	23/9	24/9	—
Chemise length.	Slr.	W.	O.S.	Ex.O.S.
White	27/6	27/6	28/6	29/6
Pink	28/6	28/6	29/6	30/6

WU 25 NEW SHAPE UNDER PANTIES

Made to fit snugly above knee. Open or closed shape

Silk and Merino.	Slr.	W.	O.S.	Ex.O.S.
White only ..	12/9	13/9	14/9	15/9
Fine Wool, White only ..	12/9	13/9	14/9	15/9
Fine Anglo Gauze				
White ..	16/9	16/9	17/9	18/9
Pink ..	18/9	18/9	19/9	20/9

WU 20 SPUN SILK VEST

With lace top. Splendid wearing quality

Sizes	Slr.	W.	O.S.	Ex.O.S.
Opera top	19/6	19/6	22/6	23/6
Low neck, no sleeves	21/9	21/9	22/9	23/9

In Pink, 2/- extra
Chemise length, 5/- extra

WU 18 ALL-WOOL NIGHTDRESS

Made from selected yarns; very cosy and warm. All sizes. In square neck, V-neck or turn-over collar with long sleeves 29/6
Heavier quality, W. size .. 32/6, O.S. 35/9
Finest quality, W. size, 45/9   O.S. 49/6

WU 18

WU 24 & 25

WU 22 & 23

WU 26 & 27

WU 20 & 21

ALL PRICES ARE SUBJECT TO MARKET FLUCTUATIONS

Telephone SLOANE 1234
Telegrams 'EVERYTHING HARRODS LONDON'

HARRODS LTD   LONDON SW 1

CORSET DEPARTMENT
Supple Grace and Snug Fitting Comfort for the Well Dressed Women

Model 8042

Model 4074

Model 1563

Model 1308

Model 952

Model 930

Model 506

Model 0698

Model 8001

Model 2205

Model 1308
Cleverly designed Pink Rayon BRASSIERE. Very dainty and moulds the bust in perfectly natural outline Sizes 30 to 36 .. .. .. **9/6**

Model 952
Pink Broche and elastic side hooking GIRDLE. Deep fitting over hips, boned and lined over abdomen for support. Also boned at back Perfect fitting garment raised at front to control diaphragm. Three pairs suspenders **37/6**

Model 8042
French UPLIFT BANDEAU in string coloured Lace, lined with Net. Very narrow at the back. This garment is specially suitable for evening wear Sizes 28-36 ins. **16/9**

Model 930
Deep fitting Cream Lace BRASSIERE lined throughout with Net. Fastens with hooks at the back. Sizes 30-42 ins. **5/6**

Model 506
Wrap-around Pink Broche and Elastic CORSELET, suitable for sports wear. Two pairs of suspenders. Sizes 24-32 ins. .. **16/9**

Model 4074
A beautiful hand-made SATIN GARMENT with Elastic panels Step-in belt with novel zip fastening at the front and firmly boned over abdomen and back. Two pairs of suspenders. Sizes 26-34 ins. .. **67/6**

Model 0698
Attractive COMPLETE garment that gives graceful support together with utmost comfort. The hip portion is made of Broche and Elastic correctly boned; the top of Silky Rayon. Pink only. Sizes 26-36 ins. **25/9**

Model 1563
COMPLETE garment, made in a rich Pink Satin Broche, with elastic insets which cup the figure. The brassiere top is Satin Tricot. Three pairs suspenders. Garment invisibly boned. Sizes 28 to 36 .. **63/-**

Model 8001
Dainty Cream Lace French UPLIFT BANDEAU with elastic at the back. A perfect fitting garment. Sizes 28-36 ins. .. **5/6**

Model 2205
Step-in hand-made Cotton ELASTIC BELT beautifully fashioned and quite boneless, Depth at back 15½ ins. Two pairs of suspenders. Pink only. Sizes 23-32 ins. **32/6**

ALL PRICES ARE SUBJECT TO MARKET FLUCTUATIONS

HARRODS LTD

Telephone SLOANE 1234
Telegrams 'EVERYTHING HARRODS LONDON'

LONDON S W 1

LADIES' GLOVE DEPARTMENT
Fabric Gloves and Sports Gloves selected from Harrods Remarkable Variety

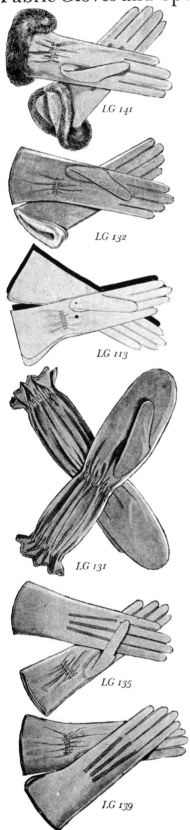

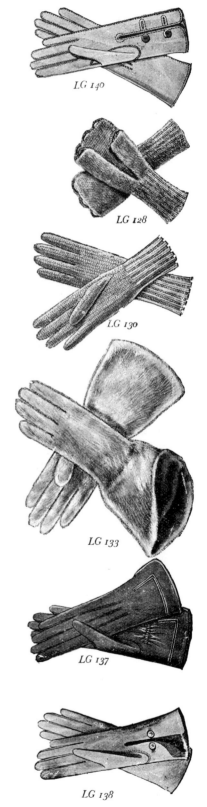

LG 140   REINDEER FABRIC GLOVES. Two button style, smartly finished with 'Magpie' sewing in shades of Sandalwood, Grey and Beige.   Sizes 6, 6½, 7, 7½ .. **4/11**

LG 141   FUR TRIMMED GLOVES. Delightfully soft fabric warmly lined with a fleecy lining.   Gauntlet style.   In shades of Beaver and Grey.   Sizes 6, 6½, 7, 7½ **3/11**

LG 128   WOOLLEN GOLF MITTENS. Made from soft Wool in shades of Brown and Fawn **4/6**
Also Angora Rabbit Wool in shades of Cherry, Blue, Orange and Beige .. **8/11**

LG 132   FABRIC LINED WOOL. A warm glove made of a smooth soft fabric lined with fleecy wool.   In shades of Beaver and Grey.   Sizes 6, 6½, 7, 7½ **2/6**

LG 113   FRENCH CUT WASHABLE SUEDE FABRIC GLOVES.   Fine texture and excellent fitting, they have every appearance of 'skin' gloves.   Open cuffs. In shades of Ficelle, Silver Grey, Rose, Beige and Sandalwood **3/11**

LG 130   KNITTED HUNTING GLOVES Specially designed for Hunting and general country wear.   In Drab, White or Chamois. Sizes 6, 6½, 7, 7½ **3/11**

LG 131   SKI-ING GLOVES. Gabardine lined with fleecy Wool.   Blue, Red, Navy, Black and Green **10/9**
Also in Waterproof Cloth with fleecy Wool lining.   In Drab and Grey **8/11**

LG 133   WOOLLEN   GAUNTLETS. Harrods have a large selection of Woollen gauntlets in both plain and fancy designs. Sizes 6, 6½, 7, 7½.   From **2/11** to **29/-** per pair

LG 135   FINE SUEDE WASHABLE FABRIC GLOVES. Ideal for shopping or morning wear.   Beige, Sandalwood, Silver Grey and Ficelle.   Sizes 6, 6½, 7, 7½ **1/9**

LG 137   FRENCH FABRIC GLOVES in pretty Gauntlet shape.   Rose, Beige, Drab, Ficelle and Silver Grey.   Sizes 6, 6½, 7, 7½ .. .. .. per pair **3/3**

LG 138   FRENCH FABRIC GLOVES. Smartly finished at the wrist with links and cuff.   In Rose, Beige, Fawn and Silver Grey.   Sizes 6, 6½, 7, 7½ .. **4/6**

LG 139   SILK LINED FABRIC GLOVES Pull-on style with elastic at wrists.   In Sandalwood, Silver Grey, Drab, Ficelle. Sizes 6, 6½, 7, 7½ **4/6**

LG 111   WASHABLE   REINDEER FABRIC GLOVES (not illustrated).   Hand Sewn.   Heavy suede finish—easy to wash and perfect fitting.   Elastic wrists.   In Sandalwood, Drab and Ficelle.   Sizes 6, 6½, 7, 7½ Per Pair **4/11**

LG 112   WASHABLE   REINDEER FABRIC   GLOVES (not illustrated). Gauntlet Shape.   Thoroughly practical gloves for morning wear—easy to wash and excellent fitting.   In new shades of Sandalwood, Silver Grey, Drab and Ficelle.   Sizes 6, 6½, 7, 7½ **2/11**

LG 141

LG 132

LG 113

LG 131

LG 135

LG 139

LG 140

LG 128

LG 130

LG 133

LG 137

LG 138

ALL PRICES ARE SUBJECT TO MARKET FLUCTUATIONS
Telephone SLOANE 1234
Telegrams 'EVERYTHING HARRODS LONDON'

HARRODS LTD   LONDON S W 1

FANCY JEWELLERY DEPARTMENT
Pearl Necklets and Fancy Jewellery from Harrods Exceptional Variety

'ROYAL RANEE' PEARLS

Ranee Pearls have ever been renowned for their exquisite colouring and wonderful texture, but even their beauty has been enhanced in the creation of the new 'Royal Ranee' Pearls. The misty loveliness revealed in these pearls is so natural in tone and radiance that even when placed alongside genuine pearls it is almost impossible to detect the difference

FJ 174
THREE ROW PEARL FESTOON
With fine paste clasp. Length 16 ins.
20 ins., 24 ins. .. .. **2 guineas**
FJ 175
'RANEE' PEARL BALL EARRINGS
Surmounted with fine paste. For pierced or unpierced ears .. .. Per pair **21/-**

FJ 170 'ROYAL RANEE' PEARLS
Carrying the soft lustre and deep gleaming radiance of the real treasures of the Orient. Complete with clasp
16 ins. .. .. .. **2 guineas**
19 ins. .. .. .. **3 ,,**
24 ins. .. .. .. **4 ,,**
FJ 171 'RANEE'
PEARL BOUTON EARRINGS
For pierced or unpierced ears
Per pair **21/-**

FJ 178
PRINCE OF WALES FEATHERS
Charming design in very fine paste
39/6

FJ 185
EARRINGS
Real stone and Marcasite. Carnelian, Chrysophase, Onyx and Amozite. For pierced or unpierced ears **39/6**

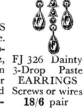

FJ 325
Smart Pearl and Paste Drop EARRINGS for Screws or wires
35/- pair

FJ 184 EARRINGS
In real stone. Crystal with Chrysophase, Rose Quartz, Amethyst, Carnelian or Topaz. For pierced or unpierced ears **21/-**

FJ 326 Dainty 3-Drop Paste **EARRINGS** Screws or wires **18/6** pair

FJ 183
DAINTY NOVELTY BROOCH
Fine paste on silver bar with pearl ends
10/6

FJ 179 DAINTY BOW BROOCH
In all White paste diamonds. Silver setting
21/-

FJ 176
THE GREYHOUND BROOCH
Fine paste. Silver setting **30/-**
Real Marcasite **35/-**

FJ 172
PEARL ROPE

Length 58 inches. Cream or Flesh Pink
Three different sizes—small, medium or large **21/-**

FJ 173
EARRINGS

Finest quality long paste Earrings for pierced or unpierced ears. Silver setting
Per pair **2 guineas**

FJ 177 ATTRACTIVE BOW BROOCH
In all White paste diamonds, or with Emerald, Sapphire or Onyx **55/-**

ALL PRICES ARE SUBJECT TO MARKET FLUCTUATIONS

HARRODS LTD

Telephone SLOANE 1234
Telegrams 'EVERYTHING HARRODS LONDON'

LONDON SW1

HANDKERCHIEF DEPARTMENT
Handkerchiefs of Exquisite Quality, in Every Conceivable Pattern and Design

Silks in dainty colours; Linen, hand-embroidered;
real Lace, Batiste or Crepe-de-Chine—you
will find good-wearing Handkerchiefs
of every description in Harrods
Handkerchief Department

SHEER LINEN
Self-coloured handkerchief with hand-embroidered initial and hemstitched hem
Size about 11⅛ inches
5/11 dozen

IRISH LINEN
Two-letter Monogram. Hand embroidered
8/9 per box of six

FRENCH BATISTE
Coloured rolled hem and border with hand-embroidered coloured initial on White ground
per dozen **11/6**

EMBROIDERED INITIAL HANDKERCHIEFS
Fine Lawn .. .. **4/11 per doz.**
Irish Linen Cambric .. **6/11, 10/9** ,,
Sheer Linen .. .. **11/6, 15/6, 25/9** ,,

IRISH LINEN
Fine quality Linen, with 3 row spoked border. Size about 10½ ins.
per doz. **8/6**

PLAIN IRISH LINEN
Size, approximately 11 ins.
5/11, 7/6, 10/6, 12/6 per doz.
Size, approximately 14 ins.
6/11, 9/11, 12/9, 15/9 per doz.

IRISH LINEN SPOKE STITCHED
11/6 per doz.

SELF COLOURED LINEN HANDKERCHIEFS
In gay or subdued colourings **4/6 and 10/6 per doz.**

FANCY COLOURED LINEN
1/-, 1/3, 1/6, 2/6 each

SELF COLOURED CREPE-DE-CHINE
Cord Borders, with a choice of 40 shades
12-inch .. **2/3 each**   **25/6 per dozen**

MONOGRAMS, CRESTS, INITIALS, ETC.
Embroidered at Moderate Charges
Specimens sent on application

FANCY COLOURED SILK HANDKERCHIEFS
1/6, 2/6, 2/11, 3/6 each

WHITE CHINA SILK
20 ins., **5/6**; 22 ins., **6/9**;
24 ins., **7/6**; 26 ins., **8/6**

SILKEEN HANDKERCHIEFS
Lovely soft texture

	Per doz.
9 × 9 ins. ..	**3/11**
12 × 12 ins. ..	**5/11**
13 × 13 ins. ..	**7/6**
20 × 20 ins.—½ and 1 inch hem .. Per doz.	**12/6**

SHEER IRISH LINEN
Spoked hem and centre, with reproduction Binche Lace border. Size including lace 10 ins.
Each **1/6**

'SILVER FLAX' PURE IRISH LINEN FOR LADIES
These beautiful Linen Handkerchiefs spun from the purest Irish Flax, hand woven, hand thread drawn, and hemstitched, are offered in two sizes

Size 12 ins., **16/6, 18/9, 22/6, 25/6 and 30/-** per doz.
Size 15 ins., **22/9, 25/6, 29/-,** and **32/6** per doz.

'SILVER FLAX' MEN'S HANDKERCHIEFS
Men will appreciate the splendid quality and snowy whiteness of this pure Irish Linen

Size, 20 ins. with 1-in. hem and 21 ins. with ½-in. hem
32/6, 41/6 and **63/-** per doz.

LADIES' HAND EMBROIDERED MONOGRAM HANDKERCHIEFS
Extra fine Irish Linen. Embroidered by hand with any two-letter combination. Finished with 7/16 in. hand thread drawn, hemstitched hems. Neatly boxed in half-dozens
Per box **8/9**

MEN'S MONOGRAM HANDKERCHIEFS
Size about 19 ins., ½ inch hemstitched hem.
Per box of six **14/3**

SHEER LINEN
Hemstitched. Hand embroidered initial
Size, 11 ins. with ¼-in. hem
per doz. **11/6**

SHEER LINEN HANDKERCHIEFS
Midget hems. Size 11 ins.
11/6, 13/6, 16/6, 21/-, 29/6 and **35/-** per doz.
Midget hems. Size 8½ ins.
8/11, 12/6, 15/6, 21/- per doz.
Cord borders. Size 11 ins.
7/6, 10/6, 14/6, 19/6, 24/6, 28/6, 33/6, 37/6 per doz.

REAL ARMENIAN LACE
1/6, 2/3, 2/11, 3/11, 4/6, 5/11, 7/6, 7/11 each

SELF COLOURED GEORGETTE
Picot-edged, 40 Shades
Each **1/6**

HARRODS 'LEDA' SILK HANDKERCHIEFS
Beautifully designed patterns in harmonizing and contrasting colour tones
Size, 12 ins. square .. .. **1/11 each**

MEN'S 'LEDA' SILK HANDKERCHIEFS
Similar to the above
18 ins. each **4/11**; 22 ins. each **7/11**

MEN'S HANDKERCHIEFS
CAMBRIC
With Hand-Embroidered Initial
Size 18 ins. with ⅞-in. Hem   Per dozen **7/11**

IRISH LINEN
Hand-Embroidered Initial Hemstitched
17/6 and 21/6 per dozen

IRISH LINEN, HEMSTITCHED		
19 ins.	**18/6, 24/6, 31/6** per doz.
21 ins.	**21/9, 28/6, 35/6** ,,

FANCY COLOURED LINEN
Newest designs and colourings
1/3, 1/11, 2/3, 2/9, 3/6 each

SHEER LINEN
Cord Borders
17/6, 21/6, 23/6, 25/6, 34/6, 45/- and **87/6 per doz.**

FANCY COLOURED SILK HANDKERCHIEFS
3/6, 4/6, 6/6, 6/11, 7/6, 9/6 each

MEN'S IRISH LINEN HANDKERCHIEFS
Hand embroidered Initial Size 18 ins. ⅜ inch hemstitched hem
per doz. **21/6**

ALL PRICES ARE SUBJECT TO MARKET FLUCTUATIONS

HARRODS LTD

Telephone SLOANE 1234
Telegrams 'EVERYTHING HARRODS LONDON'

LONDON S W 1

LADIES' OVERALL DEPARTMENT
Practical Overalls of Colourful Charm

For work about the house, for odd moments in the garden, for all
the thousand-and-one busy incidents of a woman's day, these
colourful Overalls are delightfully trim and practical

'JUNE'
A thoroughly practical Overall
in Check Overall Cloth in the new
style to slip over the head, and
fitted with elastic at the side and
waist. Easily adjustable, it serves
as a complete Overall Apron
Colours:—Navy, Red, Mauve
and Brown **4/6**
Dusting Caps to match **1/11**

'ELSIE'
A new style of sleeveless Overall
with 'crossover' bodice and two
button fastening. The slenderising
effect of this Overall makes it
especially suitable for Matron's
wear. In artistically subdued
colour tones and patterns
Sizes:—SW 42, W 44 .. **5/11**

'ADA'   **'IVY'**   **'JOYCE'**   **'AGNES'**

The Illustrations give some idea of the many smart Overall
models, but they cannot convey the full beauty of
the toning and contrasting colourings

'SAIDIE'

'ADA'
Tailored Coat Overall with detachable buttons; in
durable French Cretonne. Wide range of attractive designs in every conceivable colour. Sizes,
S.W. 42; W. 44; O.S. 46. 1st quality, **8/11**;
2nd quality, **12/9**. Superior Linen Cretonne **15/9**

'SAIDIE'
Smartly tailored Overall made in Mercerised Poplin
with reversible 'crossover' front and long roll
collar. Colours:—Green, Mauve, Rose, Brown,
Navy and Grey. S.W. and W. .. **14/9**

'IVY'
Artists' Smock Overall with 'Peter Pan' collar
and hand smocking. In pretty shades of Green,
Mauve, Orange, Cherry, Brown and Buff. Sizes
S.W. 40 and W. 42. Fadeless Casement Cloth **12/9**
Mercerised Poplin **21/-**

'JOYCE'
Casement Cloth 'Crossover' Overall. Hand-
smocked in contrasting colours. The collar and
front are piped of the same shade as the smocking
Colours:—Saxe, Cinnamon, Navy, Rose and
Mauve. L. 42 and 44 .. .. .. **12/9**
Mercerised Poplin **21/-**

'AGNES'
Attractive Overall in Printed Cotton. Oriental
designs and colourings with plain colour Casement
roll collar, and cuffs to tone. L. 42 and L. 44 **8/11**
French Cretonnes .. .. **12/9—15/9**

'COLLEEN'
Practical Coat Overall made in durable Linen
finished Overall Cloth. Detachable buttons and
smartly smocked on each side. Colours:—Saxe
Mauve, Rose, Brown, and Green
S.W. and W. .. **7/11** O.S. .. **8/11**
Lower priced quality
S.W. and W. .. **5/11** O.S. .. **6/11**

'COLLEEN'

ALL PRICES ARE SUBJECT TO MARKET FLUCTUATIONS

HARRODS LTD

Telephone SLOANE 1234
Telegrams 'EVERYTHING HARRODS LONDON'

LONDON S W 1

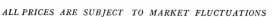

NURSES' UNIFORM DEPARTMENT

Harrods have Every Requirement for Nurses' Outfits

Harrods not only offer an extensive selection of Nurses' Wear, but they
see that every article, down to the smallest accessory,
is made from reliable materials

A

'STROUD'
A—A well tailored Uniform
Overall of good quality
White Drill. Coat sleeves
and detachable buttons.
Sizes S.W., W. and O.S.
15/9
Also Coat shaped. Overall
Cloth with Linen finish.
Sizes S.W. and W. **5/11**
Outsize, **6/11**

B

C

D

E

F

'GLOUCESTER'
F—Practical Uniform
Costume well cut and
tailored in Grey Flannel
or Tweed. Sizes S.W.
and W. **79/-**
O.S., **84/-**
Black Velour Hats with
band **15/9**

The fine quality of the materials and the faultless
styles of the uniforms are a complete
assurance of enduring wear

'HILLMOUNT'
B—Uniform Dress made in best quality Alpaca.
Inserted pleats at the front and back allow perfect
freedom of movement, yet the dress always has a
neat, trim appearance. Detachable Drill collar
and cuffs. Grey, Navy, Saxe, Brown or Black
Sizes S.W. and W. **30/-**

'EVA'
D—Detachable sleeves are a new feature of this
Fadeless Duro Cotton Uniform. Finished at tops
with elastic, which may be removed to allow extra
freedom of movement. Shades of Green, Mauve,
Rose, Blue-Grey, Black-Grey. Sizes W. 28 ins.
and 30 ins. **18/9**
Dora Cap with frills **2/3**

'ANTRIM'
C—Crossover style which may be worn as an overall or dress. Long roll collar and slots so that the
front panel can be reversed. Thoroughly tested
for washing. Sizes S.W. and W. .. **12/9**
O.S., **14/9**
Also made in Fadeless Duro Cotton .. **12/9**

'DOREEN'
E—Well tailored Coat Frock in good quality
Sicilian, designed for matron's wear. Shades of
Grey, Navy, Royal Cinnamon, Green, Saxe, Purple;
also in Black. Made and fitted in Harrods own
workrooms **£3 19 6**

SELF MEASUREMENT FORM ON PAGE 642

H

'BEATRICE'
H—Perfectly cut Uniform
Apron in Linen-finish
Apron Cloth. Invisible
pockets and gored skirt.
Lengths 30, 32, 34 **5/6**
Veils, 27 × 27 ins., **1/11**;
31 × 31 ins., **2/6**; 36 ×
36 ins., **2/11**

CORRECT STYLES FOR STATE REGISTERED NURSES

Harrods specialize in the Uniform for State Registered Nurses
Every prescribed type will be found here, correctly styled
according to regulation. Made to measure at following prices:—

Navy Gabardine Costume **4½ Gns.**	Navy Serge Overcoat, half lined **79/-**
	Navy Serge Storm Cap **10/6**
Navy Gabardine Overcoat, half lined .. **4½ Gns.**	Navy Gabardine Coat-frock and Cape .. .. **5 Gns.**
Navy Gabardine Storm Cap **10/6**	Navy Winter-weight Serge Coat-frock and Cape **75/-**

Patterns and further price list on application

'LYTLETON'
G—Showerproof Gabar-
dine Uniform Coat cor-
rectly styled with inverted pleat at the back. Half
lined. Lengths 42, 44, 46
4 Gns.
Similar style in Serge and
Tweed from **55/-**
Veils in Grey, Navy,
Brown and Black to
match the coats .. **12/9**

G

ALL PRICES ARE SUBJECT TO MARKET FLUCTUATIONS

HARRODS LTD

Telephone SLOANE 1234
Telegrams 'EVERYTHING HARRODS LONDON'

LONDON S W 1

MAIDS' UNIFORMS DEPARTMENT
A Smart and Serviceable Selection of Maids' Uniforms

Dainty yet thoroughly serviceable, Harrods outfits for
Maids are of a quality that is proved by an
attractive appearance and lasting wear

A—Dainty Afternoon Set (NU1)
consisting of spotted Muslin
Apron, Peter Pan Collar Set and
French Mob Cap trimmed with
fancy hemstitching. Apron, 5/11
Collar Set, 2/11   Cap, 2/6

F—Heavy quality Mercerised Rep
Dress (NU 6) Coat frock style. A well-
cut and perfectly finished uniform
Colours :—Navy, Grey, Saxe, Cinnamon and Black

Lengths 42, 44, 46 .. .. 18/9
Alpaca, 35/-

Attractive Uniforms of which every mistress will approve

The illustrations only show a few selections taken from
Harrods large assortment of Maids' Uniforms, a further
selection of which, together with patterns,
will be forwarded on request

B—Cotton Nurse Cloth Dress (NU2) with ' made in '
waist and Peter Pan collar. A thoroughly reliable
washing material.   Colours :—Blue/Grey, Black/
Grey, Mauve, Saxe, Blue/White stripe and
Mauve/White stripe. Sizes W. 28 and W. 30   8/11
Same shape in Alpaca 30/-
Other prices in Cotton Dresses 10/9, 14/9, 18/9
Dora Cap 1/6

Lengths 28 in., 30 in. 32 in., 34 in.

E—Uniform Apron (NU 5) Strong Washing Apron
Cloth with round or square bib 3/11

H—A new, smartly-cut model in Rep (NU 8)   The
bodice is made with round neck and is trimmed self
buttons.   The skirt has top pleats stitched down
half way.   In Navy, Black, Grey, Saxe, Cinnamon
Lengths 42, 44, 46 .. .. 39/6
Collar Sets in Embroidered Lawn .. The Set 2/11

C—House Maid's Apron (NU 3) in superfine quality
Cambric. Trimmed tucks and scalloped edge 6/11
New style embroidered Coronet Cap with Black
Velvet 2/3
Peter Pan Collar Set 2/11

D—Smart White Organdie Set (NU 4) Apron made
of striped Organdie Muslin trimmed with plain
Muslin and fancy hemstitching .. Apron 4/11
Coronet Cap with Black Velvet ribbon .. 2/11
Peter Pan Set 2/11

G—Parlourmaid's Uniform Dress (NU 7) In either
Sicilian or Gabardine in shades of Grey, Navy,
Green, Royal, Saxe, Purple and Black
Sicilian, 3/19/6   Gabardine, 5 gns
Fancy Ecru Spot Apron, 4/11. Collar Set, 2/11
Coronet Cap to match, 2/11
Tailored in Harrods own workrooms and designed
with loose panel back

ALL PRICES ARE SUBJECT TO MARKET FLUCTUATIONS

HARRODS LTD

Telephone SLOANE 1234
Telegrams 'EVERYTHING HARRODS LONDON'

LONDON S W 1

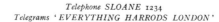

HARRODS SELF-MEASUREMENT FORMS

Measurements required for Nurses' wear

By adhering to these simple instructions, those unable to
make a personal visit to Harrods can safely
order garments to measure by post,
and receive every satisfaction

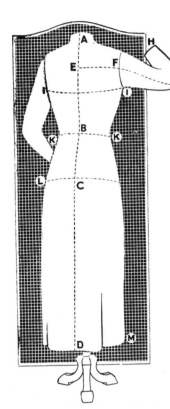

Excellent materials, faultless cut and
splendid workmanship guarantee lasting
and satisfactory service with every
garment offered in the Nurses' Section

IMPORTANT

With the exception of Lengths, all
measurements must be measurements of
the Figure and not of the garment
Harrods make the necessary allowances

Customers are requested to take these
measurements over the Dress

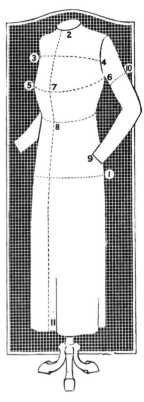

BACK MEASUREMENTS

		Inches
A to B	Neck to Waist	....
B to D	Waist to Bottom of Dress ..	....
E to F	From centre of Back to Arm Hole	....
	Arm Hole to Elbow	....
F to H	Arm Hole to Wrist	....
I to K	Under Arm to Waist	....

FRONT MEASUREMENTS

		Inches
	Size of Neck	....
3 to 4	Across Chest	....
5 to 6	Round Bust under Arms ..	....
8	Round Waist	....
I	Round Hips	....
2 to 8	Neck to Waist	....
8 to 11	Waist to Bottom of Dress ..	....
6 to 9	Inside Sleeve	....

HARRODS LTD

Telephone SLOANE 1234
Telegrams 'EVERYTHING HARRODS LONDON'

LONDON S W 1

RIBBON DEPARTMENT
Georgette Frillings and Collarings by the Yard

ARTIST'S BOW
Always in great demand, these bows are made from a fine quality Crepe-de-Chine in an almost unlimited choice of colour tones. Sand Tan, Brown, Nigger, Saxe, Powder, Royal, Navy, Scarlet, Cherry, Apple, Almond, Reseda, Vieux Rose, Wine, Stone, Rust, Grey, Hyacinth, Mauve, Bottle, Mulberry or Black .. **2/11**

CREPE-DE-CHINE TIES
Good quality Crepe-de-Chine in all the newest shades and colour tones. Lilac, Beige, Vieux Rose, Hydrangea, Saxe, Cyclamen, Tan, Rust, Grey, Fuchsia, Bois de Rose, Almond, Cherry, Brown, Wine, Cedar, Apricot, Rose, Sand, Lemon, Mushroom, Navy or Black **4/6**

FASHIONABLE FRONTING
When considering the choice of a 'Smart Fronting' for Modesty Vests, this beautiful quality Georgette with daintily trimmed tucks will find favour both for its charming simplicity and distinctiveness. Colour tones, Pink, Grey, Ivory, Sand and Black. Width 12 ins. .. Per yard **15/11**

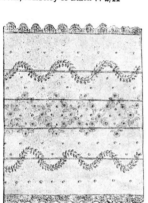

GEORGETTE PLASTRON FRONTING
Trimmed with Silk embroidered design and Lace edging. Ivory or Rose Sand Width 9 ins. .. .. Per yard **16/6**

'DUBOIL' CREPE WINDSOR TIE
A beautifully designed Crepe-de-Chine in a wide range of new and interesting coloured stripe effects. All the fashionable shades in harmonising and contrasting colour tones. Guaranteed to launder perfectly. Width 5½ ins. Length 54 ins. .. Each **3/11**

WIDE MOIRE RIBBON
This ribbon is specially suitable for Bags and Sashes and may be had in the following colours. Brown, Grey, Saxe, Navy, Pale Blue, Pink, Cyclamen, Fuchsia, Sand, Cream, White, Mauve and Black. Width 10½ ins. Per yard **6/11**

SMART WINDSOR TIES
Lovely Spun Crepe Silk Tie, cut on the bias. The colours which are guaranteed colour fast are Light and Dark Fawn, Cherry, Blue or Green, with diagonal bars to tone. Size 10 ins. wide by 1½ yards long. **7/11**

SILK EMBROIDERED GEORGETTE FRONTING
This beautifully embroidered Fronting is trimmed with picot edged Net frills In Beige only. Width 18 ins. Per yard **29/6**

COLLARING
Straight collaring to match Width 3½ ins. .. Per yard **6/6**

ORDER BY POST
Customers may order by Post, Telegraph or 'Phone with the same assurance of satisfaction as if they personally shopped at Harrods

POSTAGE
Postage paid on Drapery purchases of 10/- and over anywhere in Great Britain

COLLARING
Straight collaring to match. Width 4 ins. .. Per yard **7/11**

WASHING CREPE DE CHINE RIBBON
(On left)
With printed Rose Bud design on White, Blue, Pink, Coral, Salmon, Yellow or Mauve grounds

Width	½ in.	¾ in.	1⅛ in.
Per yard ..	5½d	8½d	1/-
Roll of 18 yds.	8/-	12/3	17/-

LINGERIE RIBBON
Satin Mouselini Lingerie Ribbon in 12 yard and 6 yard lengths. White, Pink, Blue, Mauve and Yellow.

	12 yard lengths			
Width	¼"	⅜"	½"	¾"
Price	1/10	2/8	3/8	4/9
	6 yard lengths			
Width	1"	1½"		
Price	3/9	5/3		

TAPESTRY RIBBON
Whether for Pochettes or Handbags the wonderful oriental colourings on Black, Navy or Beige grounds will give just that touch of colour which so enhances the ensemble. 7½ ins. wide Per yard **4/11**

LINGERIE RIBBON IN PRETTILY DESIGNED GIFT BOXES
These compact and neatly designed boxes contain 36 yards of lingerie ribbon in assorted colours, and each box contains six yards of the following colours :—White, Pink, Blue, Mauve, Champagne and Nil
Per box .. **6/11**

ALL PRICES ARE SUBJECT TO MARKET FLUCTUATIONS

LACE DEPARTMENT
Lovely Examples of Hand Made and Machine Made Laces

REAL TORCHONS

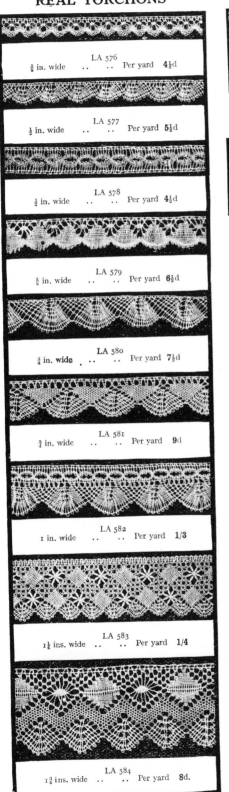

LA 576
⅜ in. wide .. .. Per yard **4½d**

LA 577
½ in. wide .. .. Per yard **5½d**

LA 578
½ in. wide .. .. Per yard **4½d**

LA 579
⅝ in. wide .. .. Per yard **6½d**

LA 580
¾ in. wide .. .. Per yard **7½d**

LA 581
¾ in. wide .. .. Per yard **9d**

LA 582
1 in. wide .. .. Per yard **1/3**

LA 583
1½ ins. wide .. Per yard **1/4**

LA 584
1¾ ins. wide .. .. Per yard **8d.**

LINGERIE LACES

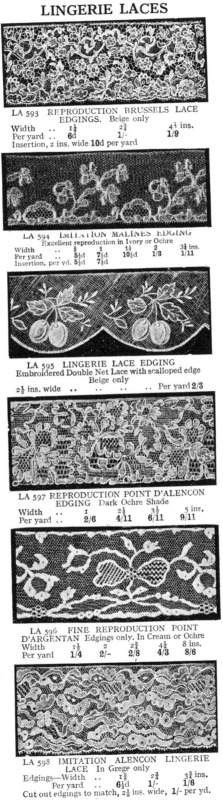

LA 593 REPRODUCTION BRUSSELS LACE EDGINGS. Beige only

Width ..	1¼	2¾	4¼ ins.
Per yard ..	6d	1/-	1/9

Insertion, 2 ins. wide **10d** per yard

LA 594 IMITATION MALINES EDGING
Excellent reproduction in Ivory or Ochre

Width ..	⅝	1	1½	2	3½ ins.
Per yard	5½d	7½d	10½d	1/3	1/11
Insertion, per yd.	5½d	7½d			

LA 595 LINGERIE LACE EDGING
Embroidered Double Net Lace with scalloped edge
Beige only
2½ ins. wide .. .. Per yard **2/3**

LA 597 REPRODUCTION POINT D'ALENCON EDGING Dark Ochre Shade

Width ..	1	2¼	3½	5 ins.
Per yard ..	2/6	4/11	6/11	9/11

LA 596 FINE REPRODUCTION POINT D'ARGENTAN Edgings only. In Cream or Ochre

Width	1½	2	2¾	4½	8 ins.
Per yard	1/4	2/-	2/8	4/3	8/6

LA 598 IMITATION ALENCON LINGERIE LACE In Grege only

Edgings ..	1⅜	2¼	3¾ ins.
Per yard ..	6½d	1/-	1/6

Cut out edgings to match, 2½ ins. wide, 1/- per yd.

REAL LACES

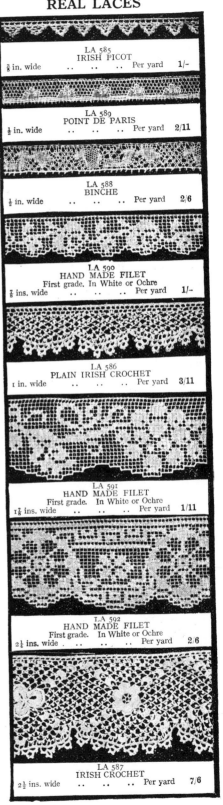

LA 585
IRISH PICOT
⅜ in. wide .. Per yard **1/-**

LA 589
POINT DE PARIS
½ in. wide .. .. Per yard **2/11**

LA 588
BINCHE
½ in. wide .. .. Per yard **2/6**

LA 590
HAND MADE FILET
First grade. In White or Ochre
⅞ ins. wide .. .. Per yard **1/-**

LA 586
PLAIN IRISH CROCHET
1 in. wide .. .. Per yard **3/11**

LA 591
HAND MADE FILET
First grade. In White or Ochre
1⅞ ins. wide .. .. Per yard **1/11**

LA 592
HAND MADE FILET
First grade. In White or Ochre
2¼ ins. wide . . . . Per yard **2/6**

LA 587
IRISH CROCHET
2½ ins. wide .. .. Per yard **7/6**

HARRODS LTD

Telephone SLOANE 1234
Telegrams 'EVERYTHING HARRODS LONDON'

LONDON S W 1

LACES AND EMBROIDERIES DEPARTMENT

EMBROIDERIES

PRETTY HEMMED EMBROIDERY
LA 617
3½ ins. wide .. .. per yard **10½d**

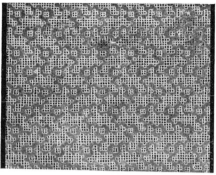

ALL OVER EMBROIDERIES
LA 613
Suitable for Brassiere. Strong Cambric
Width of work 20 ins. .. per yard **12/9**

DAINTY MUSLIN ALLOVER
LA 614
Width of work 20 ins. .. per yard **8/6**

FRILLED ORGANDIE FLOUNCING
LA 620
Suitable for Cot Trimming .. 22 ins. wide
In all colours and White .. per yard **4/11**

LINGERIE IDEAS

UNMADE CREPE DE CHINE PETTICOAT
LA 621
Unmade. Trimmed with imitation Needle-
run Lace. Pleats at side. In Champagne,
Pink or Ivory. Lengths, 29 ins., **19/6**;
31 ins., **21/9**; 34 ins., **25/9**
Unmade Nightdress to match .. **37/6**
Cami-Bocker **19/6**

CAMBRIC EMBROIDERY
LA 619
Camisole embroidery. 17½ ins. Suitable for
Camisole or Baby Petticoats .. per yard **3/6**

LINGERIE IDEAS
LA 618
For the Jumper Camisole. Crepe trimmed
imitation Mechlin Lace
18 ins. wide .. .. per yard **6/11**
26 ins. wide For Knickers per yard **8/11**
Colours—Peach, Rose or Champagne

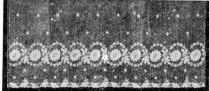

ORGANDIE FLOUNCING
LA 622
25 ins. wide .. .. per yard **4/11**

FOR THE LAYETTE

EMBROIDERED MUSLIN FLOUNCING
LA 625
With imitation Valenciennes lace edge
26 ins. wide .. .. per yard **5/6**

EMBROIDERED MUSLIN FLOUNCING
LA 623
26 ins. wide .. .. per yard **7/11**

EMBROIDERED MUSLIN ROBING
LA 624
A reproduction of Appenzell
26 ins. wide .. .. per yard **9/11**

ALL PRICES ARE SUBJECT TO MARKET FLUCTUATIONS

HARRODS LTD

Telephone SLOANE 1234
Telegrams 'EVERYTHING HARRODS LONDON'

LONDON S W 1

ART EMBROIDERY DEPARTMENT
Charmingly Artistic and Thoroughly Practical

1081 MATTRESS PINCUSHION
Good quality Satin. Royal, Scarlet, Yellow, Emerald, Tango, Rose. With cord to hang

3 × 3 × 1	2/-	4 × 4 × 1	2/11
3 × 5 × 1	2/6	3 × 7 × 1	3/3

A BIG VARIETY
OF TRACE
NEEDLEWORK
ALWAYS IN STOCK

1078 PADDED HANGER
Thinly padded and light in weight, it is specially suitable for travelling. Artificial Silk covering. Pinks, Blues, Mauves, Gold, etc. Width 16 ins. 1/-

1105 CASEMENT LAUNDRY BAG
Embroidered word 'Linen' in White. 28 ins. long, 19 ins. wide. Colours—Sky, Saxe, Rose, Pink, Mauve, Yellow, Orange, Fawn, Brown or Green 2/3

A LARGE VARIETY
OF TAPESTRY
NEEDLEWORK
ALWAYS IN STOCK

1077 PADDED HANGER
Padded in fancy patterned Voile. Rose, Mauve, Blue, Pink, etc., 1/-. Also covered in Satin, same colours Width 16 ins. 2/11

CASEMENT SHOE BAG
Embroidered 'Shoes' in White, Colours—Sky, Saxe, Rose, Pink, Mauve, Yellow, Orange, Brown or Green. 1/3
Without embroidery and in same colours. 1/-

1108 MILK JUG COVER
Double thickness fine White Net trimmed coloured beads
5 in. diameter 1/3
6 in. diameter 1/6
7 in. diameter 2/-

**1103
TAFFETA WORK BAG**
Shot Taffeta, lined with good quality Sateen and trimmed with coloured fruit spray effects in Mauve, Pink, Blues, etc. **14/6**

1104 DRESS WRAP
Good quality Sateen, complete with padded hanger to match. Length about 50 ins. Sky, Saxe, Grey, Fawn, Ivory, Black, Rose, Pink, Mauve or Brown .. **5/6**

**1106 CRETONNE
WORK BAG**
Exactly as sketched, in an exceptional variety of gaily coloured floral designs and patterns **2/6**

1110 SWEET LAVENDER
Lavender Sachets in Mauve Organdie, trimmed with deeper shade of ribbon. Three sizes. Also Pot Pourri in Orange, Lemon, Pink, Rose, Saxe or Green Organdie **1/9, 2/9, 3/9**
Small flat sachets, Lavender only **1/-**

1107 LINEN HANDKERCHIEF CASE
Hand embroidered as sketch. Many other beautifully designed patterns 7 ins. by 7 ins. **2/-**
(White only)

1109 CRETONNE BOXES
Attractive 'Bramble' design on Orange, Black or Fawn ground

Handkerchief box, 6½ × 6½ × 2 ..	2/-
Glove box, 12 × 4½ × 2 ..	2/3
Lace box, 12½ × 6½ × 2½ ..	3/11
,, ,, 13½ × 7½ × 3 ..	5/11
,, ,, 14½ × 9 × 4 ..	6/11
Blouse box, 16½ × 12½ × 4 ..	10/9

Drapery purchases value 10/- and over sent Post Free in Great Britain

1061 NIGHTDRESS SACHET
Made in Black Jap Silk, with embroidered rose spray, as sketch. 17 ins. × 14 ins. .. **18/9**

Customers may order by Post, Telegraph or 'Phone with complete assurance of satisfaction

1100 HOT WATER COSY
White frieze, embroidered in Rose, Saxe, Pink, Sky, Yellow, Red or Mauve, lined Sateen to match—detachable cover. 15 ins. across and 14 ins. deep, **11/9**
Coloured Terry cloth, Saxe, Sky, Rose, Yellow, Apricot, Mauve, Sateen pad to match 17 ins. across and 14 ins. deep, **18/9**

1102 TEA COSIES
Willow pattern Cretonne, Blue on White ground
Morning size .. 2/-   Medium size .. 5/11
Full size .. 6/11

1101 MORNING TEA COSY
White Muslin trimmed imitation Filet Lace squares and edge, on coloured Sateen pad. Ribbon to match Blue, Pink and Mauve. 10 ins. across, **5/11**

ALL PRICES ARE SUBJECT TO MARKET FLUCTUATIONS

Telephone SLOANE 1234
Telegrams 'EVERYTHING HARRODS LONDON'

HARRODS LTD

LONDON SW1

MANCHESTER DEPARTMENT

FLANNELS, GINGHAMS, MADAPOLLAM, MUSLIN, COLOURED LAWNS AND LINEN LAWNS, ETC.

FANCY COTTON GOODS

VOILES, PRINTED RADIANTS, PERLE DE CHINE, POPLINS AND THE LATEST PARISIAN EMBROIDERED NOVELTIES

MUSLINS

ROBE MUSLIN 45 ins. wide
Per yard 1/6, 1/11, 2/3, 2/6, 3/3, 3/6, 3/9

BUTTER MUSLIN 36 ins. wide
Per yard 6d, 8d, 10d

ORGANDIE MUSLIN 42 ins. wide (White)
Per yard .. 1/11, 2/6, 2/11, 3/6, 3/9, 4/6
Colours, 42 ins. wide
Per yard 1/11
50 Shades

SPOT MUSLIN 30 ins. wide
Per yard 1/11, 2/3, 2/6, 2/9, 2/11, 3/3, 3/6, 3/11

HARNESS MUSLIN 50 ins. wide .. per yd. 1/11
In Spots and Checks

HARD BOOK MUSLIN 38 ins. wide
Black and also White .. .. .. per yd. 10d

SPOT MUSLIN White, with coloured spots in Blue, Pink, Mauve and Lemon
30 ins. wide .. .. .. per yd. 2/11

SOFT BOOK MUSLIN 38 ins. wide
Per yard 1/3, 1/6, 1/9, 2/6

TARLATAN In all colours
36 ins. wide .. .. per yd. 9d

MADAPOLLAM

40 ins. wide
Per yard .. 1/-, 1/3, 1/6, 1/9, 1/11, 2/3

UNBLEACHED CALICO

30 ins. wide ..	..	..	per yard	9d
36 ins. „ ..	..	..	„	1/-
36 ins. „ ..	..	..	„	1/3
36 ins. „ ..	..	..	„	1/6
39 ins. „ ..	..	..	„	1/9
45 ins. „ ..	..	..	„	1/11
54 ins. „ ..	..	..	„	2/3

HORROCKSES NAINSOOK

40 ins. wide

PB 12 ..	..	..	per yard	1/9
PB 14 ..	..	..	„	2/3
PB 16 ..	..	..	„	2/6

SWANSDOWN CALICO

32 ins. wide ..	..	..	per yard	2/11
32 ins. „ ..	..	..	„	3/6
36 ins. „ ..	..	..	„	3/11
32 ins. „ ..	..	..	„	4/11

TARANTULLE

36 ins. wide

Standard ..	..	..	per yard	1/4½
Fine ..	..	..	„	1/9
Superfine ..	..	..	„	2/3

COLOURED LAWNS, ETC.

COLOURED LAWN 40 ins. wide
Per yard .. .. 1/- Per doz. yards .. 11/6
In all Pastel Shades

COLOURED LINGERIE LAWN 40 ins. wide
Per yard .. .. 1/6 Per doz. yards .. 17/6
Excellent quality. Pastel Shades

SUPERFINE LINGERIE LAWN 40 ins. wide
Per yard 1/11
Made from finest Egyptian Cotton. Guaranteed fast colour. In pastel shades and White

---

HARRODS GINGHAM

A fine, faultlessly finished cloth that lends itself admirably to many uses. Colourings and designs are clear and amazingly varied: stripes, checks, plaids and plain. Guaranteed fadeless and unshrinkable. Harrods will replace free any length should it fade through exposure to sunlight, sea air or repeated washings

140 Designs from which to choose

36 ins. wide .. .. per yard 1/6
Per doz. yards 17/6

MISCELLANEOUS

TOOTAL PIQUE In fine, medium and thick cords
42 ins. wide. .. .. .. per yard 3/11½

HARRODS PIQUE In three cords. 42 ins. wide
Per yard 3/6

TRICOT For Corset Making. 36 ins. wide
Per yard 14/11
In Pink, Mauve, Sky and White

COUTIL 50 ins. wide
Per yard 14/11

DRILL 38 ins. wide (White)
Per yard 2/3, 2/6, 2/11

DRILL Navy and Khaki, 30 ins. wide
Per yard 2/6

TURKEY TWILL 36 ins. wide
Per yard 1/6, 1/9, 1/11, 2/3

TOBRALCO Full range of stripes, spots and small floral patterns in White. Plain and fancy patterns in all colours
38 ins. wide .. .. .. per yard 1/11½

WRITE FOR PATTERNS

COLOURED LAWNS, ETC.

MERCERISED LAWN 44 ins. wide
Per yard 1/6
All Colours

COLOURED TARANTULLE 36 ins. wide
Per yard 1/11½

COLOURED SPOT MUSLIN 30 ins. wide
Per yard 2/11
In Mauve, Blue, Salmon, Navy, Black with White Spots.

FINE LAWN

45 ins. wide
Per yard 2/11, 3/3, 3/11, 4/6

MEDIUM LONGCLOTH

36 ins. wide

LS 10	..	..	..	per yard	1/4
LS 11	..	..	..	„	1/6
LS 12	..	..	..	„	1/8
LS 13	..	..	..	„	1/9
LS 14	..	..	..	„	1/11
LS 15	..	..	..	„	2/-
LS 16	..	..	..	„	2/3

FINE LONGCLOTH

36 ins. wide

H 11	..	..	..	per yard	1/6
H 12 ..	..	..	..	„	1/9
H 13 ..	..	..	..	„	1/11
H 14 ..	..	..	..	„	2/3
H 15 ..	..	..	..	„	2/6

APRON CLOTH

50 ins. wide ..	..	..	per yard	1/9
50 ins. „ ..	..	..	„	2/6

DORCAS CAMBRIC

40 ins. wide .. .. .. per yard 1/11½

DOWNPROOF SATEEN

White, 30 ins. wide .. .. per yard 2/11

LINEN CAMBRIC

39 ins. wide
Per yard 3/11, 4/3, 4/6, 5/6, 6/6, 6/11, 7/11

SHEER LINEN

39 ins. wide
Per yard 3/11, 4/11, 5/6, 5/11, 6/6, 7/11

COLOURED TARANTULLE

Colour Fast
In Pink, Sky, Helio, Orchid, Jade, Peach, Sunset
36 ins. wide .. .. per yard 1/11

COLOURED LINEN LAWN

8/40 ins. wide. In range of pastel shades, per yard 3/11

ALL PRICES ARE SUBJECT TO MARKET FLUCTUATIONS

HARRODS LTD

Telephone SLOANE 1234
Telegrams 'EVERYTHING HARRODS LONDON'

LONDON S W 1

MANCHESTER DEPARTMENT
Flannels, Linings, and Other Dress Materials of Faultless Quality at Specially Attractive Prices

FINE ALL WOOL CREAM FLANNELS

27 ins. wide	.. 3/3	40 ins. wide	..	6/6
29 ins. „	.. 4/3	45 ins. „	..	7/6
32 ins. „	.. 4/11	54 ins. „	..	7/11
36 ins. „	.. 5/11			

SUPER ALL WOOL CREAM FLANNELS

30 ins. wide	.. 4/6	36 ins. wide	..	6/6
30 ins. „	.. 4/11	36 ins. „	..	6/11
31 ins. „	.. 5/11			

NATURAL FLANNEL

28 ins. wide	.. 2/11	36 ins. wide	..	3/11
29 ins. „	.. 3/9			

MEDIUM ALL WOOL FLANNEL

26 ins. wide	.. 2/6	29 ins. wide	..	4/3
27 ins. „	.. 2/11	36 ins. „	..	3/11
27 ins. „	.. 3/3			

SCARLET FLANNEL

28 ins. wide ..	.. .. per yard	2/11

CREAM WINCEY

30 ins. wide ..	.. .. per yard	1/11
38 ins. „	.. per yard 2/11, 3/6, 3/11,	4/6

SILK AND WOOL PLAIN COLOURS

38 ins. wide ..	.. .. per yard	6/6
In Sky, Cream, Pink, Helio, Nil, Apricot		

CREPE FLANNEL

40 ins. wide ..	.. .. per yard	4/6
Cream and Colours		

WELSH FLANNEL

28 ins. wide ..	.. per yard	2/11
31 ins. „	.. .. „	3/6
34 ins. „	.. .. „	4/3

STRIPED WINCEY

30 ins. wide ..	.. per yard	2/3

STRIPED UNION SHIRTING FLANNEL

28 ins. wide ..	.. .. per yard	1/11

STRIPED ALL WOOL SHIRTING FLANNEL

30 ins. wide ..	.. .. per yard	3/9
Wonderful range of stripes and plain colours suitable for Shirts and Pyjamas		

FRENCH FLEECY DOMETTE

White and Black, 50 ins. wide	.. per yard	3/6

FLANNELETTE

35 ins. wide ..	.. per yard	1/-
36 ins. „	.. per yard 1/6, 1/9,	2/3

WINCEYETTE

36 ins. wide ..	.. per yard	1/-
36 ins. „	..	1/6
In Pink, Mauve, Lemon, Sky and Cream		

STRIPED WINCEYETTE

36 ins. wide ..	.. .. per yard	1/3
Suitable for Pyjamas, etc.		

CREAM DELAIN

38 ins. wide ..	.. .. per yard	5/11

MOLLETON FLANNEL

45 ins. wide ..	.. .. per yard	5/11

RIPPLE CLOTH

45 ins. wide ..	.. .. per yard	5/11

TWILL FLANNEL

40/42 ins. wide ..	.. .. per yard	5/11

VIYELLA CREAM

31 ins. wide,	Standard Weight	.. per yard		3/6
36 ins. „	„	„	„	4/3
44 ins. „	„	„	„	4/11
31 ins. „	Medium	„	„	3/11
36 ins. „	„	„	„	4/6
44 ins. „	„	„	„	5/6
31 ins. „	Heavy	„	„	4/9
36 ins. „	„	„	„	5/6
44 ins. „	„	„	„	6/9
31 ins. „	Tropical	„	„	3/6
36 ins. „	„	„	„	4/3
31 ins. „	Crepe Viyella	„	„	3/3
36 ins. „	„	„	„	3/9
31 ins. „	Clydella „		„	1/11½
36 ins. „	„		„	2/3½
31 ins. „	Aza ..	„	„	2/11½
36 ins. „	„	„	„	3/9
44 ins. „	„	„	„	4/6

STRIPED VIYELLA

31 ins. wide,	Standard Weight	.. per yard		3/11
31 ins. „	Medium	„	„	4/3
31 ins. „	Heavy	„	„	5/3

LUVISCA

38/40 ins. wide.

Plain Colours	.. .. .. per yard	3/6
Stripes	.. .. .. „	3/3

FADELESS CANTON CLOTH

Substantial and hard-wearing: excellent for Nurses' Uniforms, Overalls, Rompers, Curtains and Loose Covers. Fast-dyed in Light and Dark Saxe, Grey, Champagne, Fawn, Brown, Rose, Helio, Navy, Ivory and Cream. Also Black or White

48 ins. wide ..	.. .. per yard	1/11

SPUNJAMA

30 ins. wide ..	.. .. per yard	4/11

COTTON POPLIN

A strong hard-wearing fabric woven from highly mercerised Egyptian Cotton warp. Permanent Cords Grey, Green, Mauve, Saxe, Brown, Rust, Fawn, Navy, Black, White

39 ins. wide ..	.. .. per yard	3/6

WRITE FOR PATTERNS

PRINTED ART SILKS

36/40 ins. wide. All designs for Dresses and Lingerie
Per yard .. 3/6, 3/11, 4/6, 4/11, 5/6, 5/11

LININGS, ETC.

ART SILK TWILL LINING Shot effect

40 ins. wide ..	.. .. .. per yard	4/3

BROCADE LININGS various designs

40 ins. wide ..	.. per yard 3/11, 4/11,	5/6

TAILORS' PADDING In Black, White or Brown

24 ins. wide ..	.. .. .. per yard	1/6

BUCKRAM Brown only

38 ins. wide ..	.. .. .. per yard	2/-

HOLLAND

38 ins. wide ..	.. .. per yard	2/6
38 ins. „ ..	.. .. „	2/11
38 ins. „ ..	.. .. „	1/11

ITALIAN CLOTH White, Black, Grey and Brown only

50 ins. wide ..	.. .. .. per yard	2/11

DOMETTE INTERLINING

Black and White, 48 ins. wide	.. per yard	2/6

HOUSE FLANNEL

24 ins. wide ..	.. .. .. per yard	1/6

NUNS VEILING

36 ins. wide ..	.. .. .. per yard	3/6
Cream and Colours		

DRESS LINEN

DRESS LINEN All Colours

40 ins. wide ..	.. .. per yard	3/6

HARRIS LINEN All colours

36 ins. wide,	Light Weight .. per yard	3/11
36 ins. „	Heavy „ .. „	4/6

NURSE CLOTH

Suitable for Professional and Domestic wear. In stripes and plain colours. 39 ins. wide .. per yard 1/9
Fast Colours

DUROMAYD

Fast Colour. Floral designs. Patterns suitable for Children's Frocks

36 ins. wide ..	.. .. .. per yard	1/11½

SATEEN

40 ins. wide ..	.. .. per yard	2/3
In all Colours		

CREPE CORONA

Rich finish resembling Crepe de Chine. Exceptional washing and wearing qualities. Pink, Sky, Lemon, Champagne, Helio, Eau de Nil, Light Saxe, Rose, Navy, Black or White

40 ins. wide ..	.. .. .. per yard	4/11

PRINTED VOILES

38/40 ins. wide. For Lingerie and Dresses.
Per yard 2/6, 2/11, 3/6, 3/11, 4/6, 4/11, 5/11, 6/11

SHIRTING POPLIN

Excellent washing, durable and soft in texture. Suitable for shirts, blouses and children's garments. Neat stripes and coloured grounds

32 ins. wide ..	.. .. .. per yard	3/11

ALL PRICES ARE SUBJECT TO MARKET FLUCTUATIONS

DRESS MATERIALS DEPARTMENT

Harrods Dress Materials Section offer an infinite variety of the most fashionable materials from the foremost British and European Markets. Splendid wearing materials in a range of prices and patterns to meet every need and preference

Write for free patterns which will be sent immediately on application

ALPACA

A strong and durable British manufactured fabric, well dyed, and finished with an attractive sheen. For Uniforms, Dresses, etc. Ivory, Saxe, Sapphire, Light or Dark Navy, Wine, Purple, Moss, Bottle, Light, Mid or Dark Grey, Nut, Nigger and Black

50 ins. wide .. .. Per yard **4/11**
Super quality, 54 ins. wide .. .. „ **6/11**

SICILIAN

A well made fabric, specially suitable for Uniforms and Dresses Colours are :—Saxe, Sapphire, Wine, Brown, Green, Grey, Navy and Black

54 ins. wide .. .. Per yard **6/11**

BLACK FACE CLOTHS

Fine all wool cloths perfectly dyed and finished. Well shrunk and thoroughly recommended in every way for Dresses, Coats and suits

54 ins. wide .. .. Per yard **8/11, 12/9, 14/9, 16/9, 19/6**

TOILE CANVAS

Light weight, all wool fabric in a fine Canvas weave for Jumper Suits, Light Coats, etc. In delicate shades of Beige, Biscuit, Blue, Grey, Lemon, Rose and Green

54 ins. wide .. .. Per yard **12/9**

SERGES

Hardwearing, well dyed all wool Serges. Black or Navy
54 ins. wide
Per yard **4/11, 5/11, 8/11, 10/9, 12/9, 14/9, 16/9, 19/6**

GABARDINES

Pure wool in a fine clear rib. Suitable for Dresses, Costumes, Coats, etc. Black or Navy
54 ins. wide. Per yard **6/11, 8/11, 10/9, 12/9, 14/9, 16/9, 19/6**

BLACK AND NAVY FABRICS

A good selection of the newest fabrics in various weaves always in stock. Black, Navy or Ivory

PANAMETTE POUDRÉ

Strong and serviceable wool fabric with a neat self-coloured check design. Specially suitable for smart Costumes, Coats and Frocks. In Biscuit, Caramel, Beaver, Saxe Blue, Leaf Green, Reseda Green, and Light, Medium or Dark Grey

54 ins. wide .. .. Per yard **12/9**

SUPER STOCKINETTE

Made of pure soft wool, finely knit, British manufactured 50 different shades, including :—Fawn, Beige, Brown, Red, Blues, Greens, Mauve, Lemon, Rust, Wine, Ivory, Navy and Black

54 ins. wide .. .. .. Per yard **7/11**

KASHMIR

Delightfully soft wool fabric with a fine Hopsack weave, suitable for Suits, Coats and Frocks. Colours :—Beige, Beaver, Leaf Green, Powder Blue and Rose Beige

54 ins. wide .. .. Per yard **12/9**

WEST OF ENGLAND SUITINGS

A splendid range of the newest designs and colourings in fine wool suitings for Costumes. In Brown, Fawn and Black and White

54/56 ins. wide .. .. Per yard **12/9, 14/9, 16/9**

FRENCH SUITINGS

Excellent range of all wool suitings for serviceable Tailored Garments, in various designs and mixtures. Colours :—Blue, Green, Red, Brown, Fawn, also Black/White

54 ins. wide .. .. Per yard **12/9**

TRELYA

An entirely new soft wool crepe for Jumper Suits and Dresses. Very light in weight and exceptionally supple. Colours include Ivory, Biscuit, Beige, Fawn, Brown, Lemon, Powder, Leaf Green, Reseda, Red, Navy or Black

44 ins. wide .. .. Per yard **12/9**

FRISCA

The original fabric in a new weave which includes the following shades for smart Coats, Suits and Dresses :—Blue, Red, Beige, Brown, Green, Navy and Lemon. All colours are speckled with Black and White

51 ins. wide .. .. Per yard **16/9**

CREPE ARAIGNON

This light weight all wool crepe introduces a new weave for light Suits, Dresses and Jumpers and is very effective in smart shades of Green, Lemon, Brown, Blue, Fawn, Beige, Navy and Black

42/44 ins. wide .. .. Per yard **8/11**

WOOL JUMPER FABRICS

Harrods have a wonderful range of exclusive designs in light weight knitted and woven fabrics for Jumper Suits as well as a complete range of plain materials to tone or match. Colours :—Blue, Brown, Green, Lemon, Beige, Fawn, Black/White, Grey, Navy and Red. Various widths and sizes
Per yard **5/11, 8/11, 10/9, 12/9, 14/9, 19/9 and 25/9**

FRISCOTTA

A light weight woollen fabric with a faint speckled effect and the new openwork weave. For Coats and Suits. Colours :—Beige, Fawn, Brown, Blue, Green, Lemon, Navy and Black/White

54 ins. wide .. .. Per yard **9/11**

CANVAS FRIEZE

An all wool fabric with a small self coloured check design. Just the right weight for Coats, Suits and Children's Coats, Colours :—Powder, Saxe, Lido, Lemon, Leaf Green, Reseda. Beige, Fawn, Brown and Navy

54 ins. wide .. .. Per yard **8/11**

BASKET SUITINGS

Strong and serviceable all wool suitings in a neat basket design. Exceptionally smart for Costumes, Coats and Skirts. Two tone colourings in :—Nigger/Beige, Rust/Beige, Green/Beige, Nut/Beige

54 ins. wide .. .. Per yard **10/9**

SENIO CANVAS

Fine all wool Hopsack, in delightful melange effects. Colours are :—Rose and Grey, Blue and Grey, Fawn and Brown, Red and Black, Light Grey and Mid Grey, Natural, etc.

54 ins. wide .. .. Per yard **16/9**

FLANNEL SUITINGS

British made, all wool and well shrunk. For Tailored Suits, Skirts, etc. In light, medium or dark Grey

56 ins. wide .. .. Per yard **12/9, 14/9**

BON VELEEN (Regd.)

Silky-piled and supple with a soft bright sheen, this smart fabric makes up charmingly for Coats, Frocks, Evening Wraps and Children's Wear. Colours :—Fawn, Brown, Green, Red, Blue, Cherry, Wine, Purple, Bottle, Grey, Sapphire, Lemon, Ivory and Navy

36 ins. wide .. .. Per yard **5/11**

Also in Black

22 ins. wide .. Per yard **2/11**		36 ins. wide .. Per yard **5/11**	
27 ins. wide .. „ **4/11**		44 ins. wide .. „ **8/11**	

ALL PRICES ARE SUBJECT TO MARKET FLUCTUATIONS

HARRODS LTD

Telephone SLOANE 1234
Telegrams 'EVERYTHING HARRODS LONDON'

LONDON S W 1

SILK DEPARTMENT
Harrods Remarkable Values in Silken Fabrics

Nowhere will you find a more wonderful collection of the finest silks that the markets of the world afford, than at Harrods

Fashion's Favoured Fabric in a range of glorious colours from soft pastel shades to the deepest and richest colour tones awaits your selection. Silk for Evening Frocks, Fashionable Dresses and Wraps, for soft, dainty Underwear, and serviceable Linings—all may be chosen in a range of prices that are extremely moderate for fabrics of such perfection

---

CREPE-DE-CHINE

Harrods pride themselves on having established a record in Crepe-de-chine values during the last few years—and this, the latest of the series, sets a new standard of worth! It is a really reliable all silk crepe, unique in 'life' and lustre and possessed of splendid draping qualities. Excellent range of day and evening shades. Full 39 ins. wide

Per yard **6/11**

LINGERIE SATIN

For daintiest lingerie—A lovely all silk weave that will give long service and retain its lustre through repeated launderings. A wonderful range of over 20 beautiful shades. Width 39 ins.

Per yard **8/11**

SILK GEORGETTE

Surpassingly lovely in its soft lustre and crepe finish —a Georgette that will give excellent service. Enchanting choice of colours—no fewer than 114! 38 ins. wide

Per yard **9/11**

COLOURED JAPANESE SILK

A really reliable quality in this most useful and popular silk—for value and assortment of colours quite without rival! It has a firm soft finish and cannot be bettered for Linings, Lampshades, Children's Wear, Quilt Covers, etc. No less than 150 shades represented. Send to-day for Harrods complete Pattern Card. 36 ins. wide

Per yard **3/11**

TRIPLE NINON

Undoubtedly the most luxurious and caressing of lingerie fabrics, gossamer light, yet exceptionally good-wearing. In the latest of soft lingerie tones 38 ins. wide

Per yard **9/11**

'WHITE WARP' CHIFFON TAFFETA

This Taffeta is shot with white, softening the beautiful shades. In a reliable quality of the requisite stiffness and brightness for Dance Frocks and Evening Wear. 38 ins. wide

Per yard **8/11**

ALL SILK LINGERIE CREPE

Soft and full-bodied with a charming crepe-finish. Greatly in demand for Underwear. In a large range of dainty underwear shades. 38 ins. wide

Per yard **4/11**

CHIFFON VELVET

Delightfully supple in texture and with a deep silk pile, it is a velvet that will make up charmingly and wear well. In 40 of the smartest shades, including Ivory and Black. Width 36 in.

Per yard **9/11**

SATIN BEAUTE

A very fine weave crepe-back Satin, with a brilliant surface, delightfully soft for draping. In all the newest colourings. 38 ins. wide

Per yard **12/9** and **15/9**

A COMPLETE RANGE OF PATTERNS SENT ON REQUEST

ALL PRICES ARE SUBJECT TO MARKET FLUCTUATIONS

HARRODS LTD

Telephone SLOANE 1234
Telegrams 'EVERYTHING HARRODS LONDON'

LONDON S W 1

SILK DEPARTMENT
Silken Fabrics at Prices which Effect Real Economies

WOOL BACK SATIN
(Super quality)

This delightful British made Satin with its wool back preserves in every respect the delicate sheen, warm and glossy draping attractiveness that has always been its chief characteristic. Obtainable in various shades. 39 ins. wide .. .. Per yard **6/11**

PRINTED CREPE DE CHINE AND CREPE SATIN

Harrods have always a marvellous selection of beautiful printed Crepe de Chines and Satins from Lyons—world famous for lovely silks. The patterns which are charmingly decorative in design, range from demure floral designs to new and immensely smart geometric effects. Exquisite colour blending 38 ins. wide .. Per yard **9/11**, **12/9** and **15/9**

WASHING CREPE DE CHINE
(British made)

A rich heavy washing Crepe de Chine thoroughly recommended for hard wear and repeated washing. Specially suitable for Sports Dresses, River Frocks or heavier weight Lingerie. Choice of over 40 beautiful shades. 38 ins. wide .. .. Per yard **9/11**

STRIPE AND CHECK WASHING CREPE DE CHINE

In the most fashionable small checks and neat stripes woven on a heavy quality British Washing Crepe de Chine. The colours will not fade when washed. Unsurpassed for Spring and Summer Outdoor Frocks, Sports Dresses and Pyjamas. 38 ins. wide
Per yard **9/11—12/9**

PRINTED GEORGETTES AND MOUSSELINE

In patterns ranging from neat Pompadour designs on coloured grounds to lovely combinations of the latest colourings in large floral and conventional designs. Printed on gossamer light Mousseline or heavier Crepe Georgette, they're ideal for Evening Wear or Summer Dresses. 38 ins. wide
Per yard **10/9** and **13/9**

TINSEL BROCADES

Harrods possess a wonderful assortment of Tinsel Brocades. Rich medallion effects in beautifully blended colourings agleam with Tinsel, handsome floral designs on rich satin background and shimmering conventional fruits. Elegance itself for Bridge Coats and Evening Wraps. 36 ins. wide
Per yard **25/9** and **29/6**

THREE OUTSTANDING VALUES !
The kind of Value upon which Harrods Stake and Build their World-Wide Reputation

'GALITA' SILK LONGCLOTH

Unquestionably the finest lingerie value in London. A British made Spun Silk that possesses a rich sheen combined with marvellous wearing qualities. The serviceable weight recommends it for Washing Dresses and Children's Wear as well as for Lingerie of all descriptions. In a wide range of excellent washing colours. 38 ins. wide .. .. Per yard **4/11**

DYED SHANTUNG

Has the crispness, sheen and the slightly crinkled finish characteristic of the best Tussah silks, and is unrivalled for Soft Furnishings, Children's Wear, etc. Over 70 different shades. Harrods claim that no finer value can be obtained elsewhere at the price 33 ins. wide .. .. Per yard **3/9**

HARRODS FAMOUS CREPE DE CHINE

The wonderful popularity of this beautiful Crepe de Chine is the real proof of its quality. Wonderfully rich, heavy and lustrous with delightful draping qualities and an exquisite softness. Write for Harrods shade card containing over 150 glorious shades. 39 ins. wide .. .. Per yard **10/9**

A COMPLETE RANGE OF PATTERNS SENT ON REQUEST

ALL PRICES ARE SUBJECT TO MARKET FLUCTUATIONS

HARRODS LTD

Telephone SLOANE 1234
Telegrams 'EVERYTHING HARRODS LONDON'

LONDON SW1

HOUSEHOLD LINEN DEPARTMENT
Harrods Wonderful Display of Household and Family Linens

HARRODS have always been famous for the quality and the exceptional variety of their Linens, but never before have they offered such a splendidly assorted stock of reliable goods from the best Manufacturers

Damask Table Cloths and Serviettes, Linen and Cotton Sheets, Towels, Kitchen Cloths, Blankets, Down Quilts and Bedspreads, and every requisite for Household or Family use

ALL LINEN PLAIN HEMMED, MARKED IN INK, and Machine Stitched in Red Cotton, Free of Charge

DAMASK TABLE CLOTHS with SERVIETTES to MATCH

HL 1   DOUBLE DAMASK
Exclusive design of Louis XV period
Size 2 × 2 yds.   Each **26/9**   Size 2 × 2½ yds.   Each **32/6**
Size 2 × 3 yds.   Each **39/6**
SERVIETTES TO MATCH
22 × 22 ins.   Per dozen **31/9**   24 × 24 ins.   Per dozen **37/6**
26 × 26 ins.   Per dozen **43/6**

PURE LINEN DAMASK CLOTHS
Size 68 × 72 ins.
Each **10/9**
Size 68 × 90 ins.
Each **13/6**
Size 68 × 108 ins.
Each **15/9**

SERVIETTES TO MATCH
Size 20 × 20 ins.
Per dozen **10/9**
Size 24 × 24 ins.
Per dozen **15/9**

A finer quality, All Linen assorted designs
Size 36 × 36 ins.
Each **3/9**
Size 45 × 45 ins.
Each **5/11**
Size 54 × 54 ins.
Each **8/6**
Size 63 × 63 ins.
Each **11/6**
Size 68 × 72 ins.
Each **14/6**
Size 68 × 90 ins.
Each **17/6**
Size 68 × 108 ins.
Each **21/-**
SERVIETTES TO MATCH
Size 20 × 20 ins.
Per dozen **12/9**
24 × 24 ins.
Per dozen **18/6**

HL 2   PURE LINEN DAMASK
An interesting design with plain centre, introducing Adam's style
Size 2 × 2 yds.   Each **23/6**   Size 2 × 2½ yds.   Each **29/6**
Size 2 × 3 yds.   Each **35/6**   Size 2 × 3½ yds.   Each **41/6**
Size 2 × 4 yds.   Each **47/6**
SERVIETTES TO MATCH
Size 24 × 24 ins.   Per dozen **30/-**

HL 3   PURE LINEN DAMASK
Design of Maidenhair fern, border of ferns and foliage
Size 72 × 72 ins.   Each **16/9**   Size 72 × 90 ins.   Each **21/-**
Size 72 × 108 ins.   Each **25/-**
SERVIETTES TO MATCH
Size 20 × 20 ins.   Per dozen **15/6**   Size 22 × 22 ins.   Per dozen **18/9**
Size 24 × 24 ins.   Per dozen **21/6**

HL 4   PURE LINEN DAMASK
Exclusive design, with circular trail of Roses and Foliage
Size 70 × 70 ins.   Each **14/6**   Size 70 × 90 ins.   Each **18/6**
Size 70 × 108 ins.   Each **22/6**
SERVIETTES TO MATCH
Size 24 × 24 ins.   Per dozen **25/-**

ALL PRICES ARE SUBJECT TO MARKET FLUCTUATIONS

HARRODS LTD

Telephone SLOANE 1234
Telegrams 'EVERYTHING HARRODS LONDON'

LONDON S W 1

HOUSEHOLD LINEN DEPARTMENT
The Secret of Effective Bedrooms Lies in Well-Designed Bedspreads

HL 13
PRINTED BEDSPREADS
A bold tapestry design on a good quality Fawn Jaspe ground. In predominating colours of Rose, Blue, Mauve and Gold.

Single bed size
70 × 90 ins. .. **13/9**
Double bed size
90 × 100 ins... **18/9**

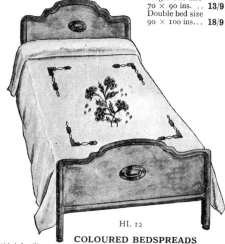

HL 12
COLOURED BEDSPREADS
Artificial silk, with embroidery and applique, as illustrated. In Rose, Saxe Blue, Old Gold, Helio and Fuchsia.

Single bed size
70 × 104 ins. .. **29/6**
Double bed size
100 × 104 ins. .. **37/6**

HL 17
ATTRACTIVE BEDSPREAD ON CREAM LINEN
With a wonderful reproduction of Cluny Lace.

Single bed size about 72 × 100 ins. **35/-**
Double bed size about 90 × 100 ins. **42/6**

A Choice Selection of Beautifully Designed Bedspreads

INEXPENSIVE BEDSPREADS
On Ecru Jaspe Cotton with dainty design in Blue, Pink or Helio

Single bed size about 70 × 90 ins.
each **5/11, 8/11, 10/9, 12/9** to **18/9**
Double bed size 90 × 100 ins.
12/9, 15/9, 18/9, 21/9 to **39/6**

ARTIFICIAL SILK SPREADS
In rich colours of Rose, Blue, Green, Mauve, Gold, Fuchsia, beautifully embroidered; also with applique to tone with the background.

Single bed size 72 × 100 ins.
29/6, 39/6, 49/6, 63/-, 67/6 to **159/6**
Double bed size 90 × 100 ins.
39/6, 49/6, 65/-, 75/-, 76/9 to **179/6**

IRISH EMBROIDERED LINEN BEDSPREADS
(White)

Single bed size 72 × 100 ins.
each **41/6, 47/6, 52/6** to **89/6**
Double bed size 90 × 100 ins.
each **49/6, 55/6, 69/6** to **105/-**

DAINTY DESIGN IN REPRODUCTION FILET LACE SPREADS
Ivory shade

Single bed size 75 × 100 ins.
each **15/9, 17/6** to **29/6**
Double bed size 96 × 112 ins.
each **24/9, 26/9** to **39/6**

ARTIFICIAL SILK LACE BEDSPREADS
Rose and Gold, Saxe and Gold, Helio and Gold, Tabac and Gold, Black and Gold, Honey and Gold, and Green and Gold

Single bed size 72 × 92 ins. each **52/6**
Double bed size 92 × 110 ins. ,, **75/-**

ALL WHITE SATIN MARCELLA COUNTERPANES
Single bed size
each **15/6, 19/6, 22/6, 25/6, 29/6**
Double bed size
each **19/9, 25/6, 29/6, 37/6, 42/6**

CREAM LINEN AND REAL LACE SPREADS
Cluny, Filet and other Real Laces
Single bed size
59/6, 79/6, 95/6, 115/6 to 20 Gns.
Double bed size
79/6, 95/6, 119/6, 132/6 to 33 Gns.

HL 14
COLOURED BEDSPREADS
Artificial silk, with Vase Design attractively embroidered and appliqued in Rose, Saxe Blue, Old Gold, Helio and Fuchsia

Single bed size
70 × 104 ins. .. **42/6**
Double bed size
100 × 104 ins. .. **49/6**

HL 16
COLOURED BEDSPREADS
Beautiful Artificial Silk Taffeta, with rich raised silk applique as illustrated. Hand made in pastel shades of Rose, Blue, Gold, Mauve and Green

Single bed size
70 × 108 ins...**130/-**
Double bed size
108 × 108 ins..**150/-**

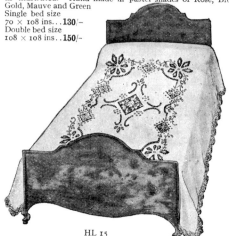

HL 15
LINEN AND LACE BEDSPREADS
On a good quality Linen, natural shade, with Filet Motifs, and handsomely embroidered with openwork. The edge is trimmed with a pretty Cluny Lace.

Single bed size 72 × 100 ins. **63/-**
Double bed size 90 × 100 ins. **75/-**

ALL PRICES ARE SUBJECT TO MARKET FLUCTUATIONS
Telephone SLOANE 1234
Telegrams 'EVERYTHING HARRODS LONDON

HARRODS LTD   **LONDON S W 1**

HOUSEHOLD LINEN DEPARTMENT
Guest Towels, Bath Towels, and Towelling of Every Description

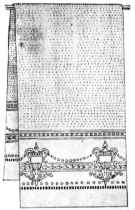

HL 18   PURE LINEN TOWELS
In Huckaback or Diaper, Hemstitched with Damask borders. (Exclusive design)
Size 24 × 40 ins. . . per doz. **36/-**

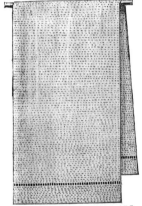

HL 20   HEMSTITCHED ALL LINEN HUCKABACK TOWELS
Size 20 × 40 ins.	. . per doz.	**25/6**
,, 24 × 40 ins.	. . ,,	**29/6**
,, 24 × 40 ins.	. . ,,	**39/6**
,, 27 × 40 ins.	. . ,,	**52/6**
,, 27 × 40 ins.	. . ,,	**75/9**

HL 22   VERY FINE PURE LINEN TOWELS
In Huckaback or Diaper, Hemstitched, with Damask borders. (Exclusive design)
Size 24 × 40 ins. . . per doz. **55/-**
HEMSTITCHED HUCK TOWELS
(not illustrated)
Pure Linen with coloured borders, Pink, Blue, Gold or Helio
Size 24 × 40 ins.	. . per doz.	**42/-**
,, 24 × 40 ins.	. . in diaper	**39/9**

BATH TOWELS, TOWELLING, ETC.

CHRISTY'S BEST QUALITY HEMMED
All White
Size 27 × 47 ins.	. . each	**4/4**
,, 33 × 49 ins.	. . ,,	**5/8**
,, 33 × 61 ins.	. . ,,	**7/3**
,, 41 × 63 ins.	. . ,,	**9/4**

CHRISTY'S BEST QUALITY
Hemstitched
Size 23 × 46 ins.	. . each	**4/4**
,, 28 × 50 ins.	. . ,,	**5/10**
,, 32 × 53 ins.	. . ,,	**7/9**
,, 41 × 57 ins.		**10/-**

COLOURED BATH TOWELS
(Christy's), Helio, Gold, Pink, Orange, Green, and Blue
Size 21½ × 44 ins.	. . each	**2/11**
,, 27 × 47 ins.	. . ,,	**3/11**
,, 32 × 53 ins.	. . ,,	**5/6**
,, 41 × 57 ins.	. . ,,	**7/11**

CHRISTY'S WHITE BATH TOWELS
With deep coloured Lined borders, in Blue, Yellow, Red and Helio
Size 30 × 50 ins.	. . each	**6/-**
,, 40 × 60 ins.		**10/9**

CHRISTY'S NATURAL COLOUR (WITH WHITE STRIPES) UNION TURKISH TOWELS
Size 23 × 45 ins.	. . each	**2/9**
,, 26 × 50 ins.	. . ,,	**3/4**
,, 30 × 54 ins.	. . ,,	**4/4**
,, 41 × 57 ins.	. . ,,	**6/9**

NATURAL WITH RED OR BLUE STRIPES, UNION TOWELS
Size 23 × 45 ins.	. . each	**2/9**
,, 28 × 52 ins.	. . ,,	**4/2**
,, 41 × 57 ins.	. . ,,	**6/11**

GUEST TOWELS
In fine Hemstitched Linen Huckaback or Diaper
Size 14 × 22 ins.		**17/6, 19/6, 23/9**
,, 15 × 24 ins.		**23/6, 29/6, 31/6**

Hemstitched and Embroidered with Pink, Blue, Gold or Helio borders
Size 16 × 24 ins.	. . each	**2/3, 3/-**

ALL LINEN HUCKABACK
By the Yard
18 ins. wide	. . per yard	**1/6, 2/-, 2/3**
24 ins. wide	,,	**2/3, 2/9, 2/11**
27 ins. wide		**3/-, 3/3, 3/9, 4/6**

ALL LINEN DIAPER TOWELLING
By the Yard   Birds Eye
18 ins. wide	. . per yard	**2/2, 2/6, 3/3**
24 ins. ,,	. . ,,	**2/9, 3/3, 4/-**
27 ins. ,,	. . ,,	**2/11, 3/6, 4/6**
36 ins. ,,	. . ,,	**3/6, 4/6, 5/6**

Russia
18 ins. wide	. . per yard	**1/9, 2/2, 2/6**
24 ins. ,,	. . ,,	**2/3, 2/9, 3/3**
27 ins. ,,	. . ,,	**2/6, 2/11, 3/6**
36 ins. ,,	. . ,,	**3/-, 3/6, 4/6**

CHRISTY'S BATH TOWELS
White, with Red or White Headings (Fringed). Suitable for maids
Size 24 × 48 ins.	. . each	**2/6**
,, 28 × 55 ins.		**3/4**

ALL WHITE, PLAIN HEMMED
Size 23 × 46 ins.	. . each	**2/6**
,, 27 × 52 ins.	. . ,,	**3/6**
,, 30 × 52 ins.	. . ,,	**4/6**
,, 32 × 56 ins.	. . ,,	**5/6**
,, 41 × 57 ins.	. . ,,	**7/4**

CHRISTY'S BROWN UNION FRICTION TOWELS
Hemmed
Size 22 × 47 ins.	. . each	**3/8**
,, 25 × 48 ins.	. . ,,	**4/2**
,, 26 × 52 ins.	. . ,,	**4/8**
,, 30 × 54 ins.	. . ,,	**5/9**
,, 32 × 63 ins.	. . ,,	**7/-**
,, 41 × 57 ins.	. . ,,	**8/3**

ALSO CREAM UNION TOWELS
Hemmed
Size 22 × 42 ins.	. . each	**5/3**
,, 26 × 48 ins.	. . ,,	**5/11**
,, 30 × 54 ins.		**9/2**

TURKISH LAVATORY TOWELS
(Typed down centre)
Size 13 × 22 ins.	. . per doz.	**10/6**
,, 18 × 33 ins.		**18/6**

RAZOR TOWELS
Typed Red, and taped
Size 12 × 12 ins. . . per doz. **5/11**

TURKISH TOWELLING BY THE YARD
All White
18 ins. wide	. . per yd.	**1/2½, 1/6**
24 ins. wide	,,	**1/5½, 1/10½**
27 ins. wide	,,	**1/7, 2/1½**
36 ins. wide		**2/9**

NATURAL STRIPED UNION ROLLERING
Red, Blue, Green or White Stripes
16 ins. wide . . per yard **1/5**
Better quality, 16 ins. wide, **1/9** per yard, in Red and Blue stripe only
Coloured Cotton Terry roller towelling in Helio, Gold, Pink, Orange, Green or Blue
16 ins. wide . . per yard **1/9**

CHRISTY'S BATH SHEETS
Good medium quality, all white, hemmed
Size 42 × 70 ins.	. . each	**8/9**
,, 48 × 78 ins.	. . ,,	**10/9**
,, 56 × 82 ins.	. . ,,	**13/6**
,, 66 × 84 ins.	. . ,,	**17/6**

Best quality, Hemstitched
Size 48 × 70 ins.	. . each	**16/6**
,, 60 × 76 ins.	. . ,,	**19/9**
,, 72 × 86 ins.		**27/6**

CHRISTY'S WHITE BATH SHEETS
Deep coloured Lined borders, Yellow, Blue, Red and Helio
Size 48 × 80 ins. . . each **16/9**

COLOURED BATH SHEETS
Helio, Pink, Gold, Green, Orange and Blue
Size 42 × 72 ins.	. . each	**10/9**
,, 52 × 80 ins.	. . ,,	**14/9**

HEAVY BROWN UNION BATH SHEETS
With Red borders, fringed
Size 48 × 80 ins.	. . each	**12/6**
,, 60 × 80 ins.		**15/6**

BATH MATS
All of good wearing qualities and Fast Colours. Tile pattern. In Red and White, Pink, Blue, Orange, Green, Black and Helio
Size 20 × 30 ins.	. . each	**4/11**
,, 27 × 37 ins.	. . ,,	**8/6**
,, 45 × 45 ins.		**16/11**

PLAIN COLOURS WITH BARRED BORDER
Pink, Blue, Helio, Gold, Orange and Green
Size 23 × 37 ins. . . each **5/11**

HL 19   ALL LINEN HUCKABACK TOWELS
With White, Red or Blue borders
Size 22 × 38 ins. . . per doz. **16/6**
Heavier and superior quality
Size 24 × 40 ins. . . per doz. **24/6**

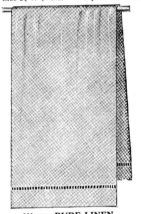

HL 21   PURE LINEN HEMSTITCHED DIAPER TOWELS
Size 18 × 34 ins.	. . per doz.	**37/6**
,, 22 × 40 ins.	. . ,,	**38/9**
,, 24 × 40 ins.	. . ,,	**49/6**
,, 27 × 40 ins.	. . ,,	**57/6**
,, 27 × 42 ins.	. . ,,	**73/6**

HL 23   PURE LINEN HEMSTITCHED HUCKABACK TOWELS
With Damask borders (exclusive design)
Size 24 × 40 ins. . . per doz. **37/6**
PLAIN HEMMED HUCKABACK TOWELS
Size 24 × 40 ins.	per doz.	**27/9, 37/9**
,, 27 × 40 ins.	per doz.	**42/6**

ALL PRICES ARE SUBJECT TO MARKET FLUCTUATIONS

Telephone SLOANE 1234
Telegrams 'EVERYTHING HARRODS LONDON'

HARRODS LTD   **LONDON S W 1**

HOUSEHOLD LINEN DEPARTMENT
Harrods World Renowned Hand and Power Loom Damask Table Cloths
with Serviettes
to Match

HL 5

HAND WOVEN DOUBLE DAMASK

Fleur de Lys centre with Greek Key Border, also striped

Size 2 × 2 yds. Each 37/9	Size 2¼ × 2¼ yds. Each 47/9
Size 2 × 2½ yds. Each 47/6	Size 2¼ × 2½ yds. Each 59/6
Size 2 × 3 yds. Each 56/6	Size 2½ × 3 yds. Each 71/6
Size 2 × 3½ yds. Each 66/6	Size 2½ × 3½ yds. Each 83/6
	Size 2½ × 4 yds. Each 94/6

SERVIETTES TO MATCH

Size 22½ × 22½ ins.	Per dozen	49/6
„ 24 × 24 ins.	„	56/6
„ 26 × 26 ins.	„	69/6

HL 6

A beautiful circular design of Roses and festooned border with Empire Wreath

Size 2 × 2 yds. Each 24/-
Size 2 × 2½ yds. Each 30/-
Size 2 × 3 yds. Each 36/-
Size 2 × 3½ yds. Each 42/-
Size 2 × 4 yds. Each 48/-

SERVIETTES TO MATCH

Size 24 × 24 ins.
Per dozen 33/-

HL 7

SUPER QUALITY ALL LINEN DAMASK HAND WOVEN

Stripe with Adams Border

Size 2 × 2 yds. Each 46/-	Size 2½ × 3 yds. Each 87/6
Size 2 × 2½ yds. Each 57/6	Size 2½ × 3½ yds. Each 103/-
Size 2 × 3 yds. Each 69/-	Size 2½ × 4 yds. Each 115/-
Size 2 × 3½ yds. Each 80/-	Size 2½ × 4½ yds. Each 130/-
Size 2½ × 2½ yds. Each 72/-	Size 2½ × 5 yds. Each 147/6
	Size 2½ × 6 yds. Each 178/-

SERVIETTES TO MATCH

Size 22½ × 22½ ins.	Per dozen	59/6
Size 24 × 24 ins.	„	67/6
Size 26 × 26 ins.	„	84/9

HL 8

COLOURED CLOTHS

Granite Cloth with Handsome colours, hemmed. In Blue, Gold, Green and Rose

Size 54 × 54 ins. Each 12/6
„ 70 × 70 ins. 18/9

SERVIETTES TO MATCH

Size 16 × 16 ins. Per dozen 12/6
„ 22 × 22 ins. „ 21/-

IN PURE LINEN

Damask Border, fast colours

Size 70 × 90 ins. Each 23/6
„ 70 × 108 ins. „ 29/6

KITCHEN TABLE CLOTHS

In Heavy Unbleached All Linen. Various good designs, plain hemmed

Size 54 × 54 ins. Each 5/6 and 7/9
Size 54 × 70 ins. Each 7/6
Size 60 × 60 ins. Each 7/6 and 10/9
Size 70 × 70 ins. Each 10/6 and 14/9
Size 70 × 90 ins. Each 12/9 and 17/9
Size 70 × 108 ins. Each 14/9 and 21/9

Also by the Yard
54 ins. wide Per yard 3/11 and 5/9
60 ins. wide Per yard 4/6 and 6/6
70 ins. wide Per yard 5/3 and 7/9

HAND WOVEN BLEACHED SLIP DAMASK

By the Yard
Spot (no Border)
27 ins. wide. Per yd. 5/6
36 ins. wide. Per yd. 8/9
Stripe and Empire Wreath centre, Floral Border Snowdrop Border with Spot centre
Passion Flower Border With Ivy centre
22½ ins. Per yard 6/9
27 ins. Per yard 7/11

HL 9 PURE LINEN

Beautiful French design with border

Size 45 × 45 ins. Each 9/6
„ 54 × 54 ins. „ 13/6
„ 63 × 63 ins. „ 18/-

SERVIETTES TO MATCH

Size 22 × 22 ins.
„ 24 × 24 ins.

DOUBLE DAMASK

Fruit and Festoon border

Size 72 × 72 ins. Each 23/9
„ 72 × 90 ins. „ 29/6
„ 72 × 108 ins. „ 35/6
Size 90 × 90 ins. Each 42/-

SERVIETTES TO MATCH

Per dozen 27/6
„ 31/9

HL 10 PURE LINEN

In longitudinal stripes

Size 72 × 72 ins. Each 19/6

DOUBLE DAMASK

with Adam Border

Size 72 × 90 ins. Each 24/6
Size 72 × 108 ins. Each 29/6

SERVIETTES TO MATCH

Size 20 × 20 ins. Per dozen 17/6 Size 22 × 22 ins. Per dozen 21/-
24 × 24 ins. Per dozen 24/6

HL 11 HEMSTITCHED

Empire Wreath design, with border

Size 36 × 36 ins.	Each 13/6
„ 45 × 45 ins.	„ 21/-
„ 54 × 54 ins.	„ 27/-
„ 68 × 68 ins.	„ 39/6
„ 68 × 90 ins.	„ 48/9
„ 68 × 108 ins.	„ 58/6
Size 15 × 15 ins.	
„ 24 × 24 ins.	

DAMASK CLOTH

striped and festoon

Size 68 × 126 ins.	Each 67/6
„ 68 × 144 ins.	„ 78/-
„ 86 × 86 ins.	„ 64/-
„ 86 × 108 ins.	„ 78/-
„ 86 × 126 ins.	„ 90/-
„ 86 × 144 ins.	„ 103/6

SERVIETTES TO MATCH

Per dozen 29/6
„ 72/-

ALL PRICES ARE SUBJECT TO MARKET FLUCTUATIONS

HARRODS LTD

Telephone SLOANE 1234
Telegrams 'EVERYTHING HARRODS LONDON'

LONDON S W 1

HOUSEHOLD LINEN DEPARTMENT
· Lovely Hand Embroidered Sheets with Pillow Cases to Match

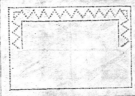

HL 40
LINEN & CLUNY LACE TOP SHEET

Size 70 ins. × 3½ yds.	each	55/-
,, 80 ins. × 3½ yds.	,,	63/-
,, 90 ins. × 3½ yds.	,,	72/6
,, 100 ins. × 3½ yds.	,,	79/6

Pillow Cases to match—

Size 20 × 30 ins.	each	29/6
,, 22 × 32 ins.	,,	32/6
,, 27 × 27 ins.	,,	33/6

HL 43
FINE LINEN
Interesting hand embroidery in Spot design

Size about 72″ × 3½ yds.	each	29/6
,, 90″ × 3½ yds.	,,	35/6

Pillow Cases to match—

Size 20 × 30 ins.	each	7/6
,, 22 × 32 ins.	,,	7/11

HL 32
MADEIRA HAND EMBROIDERED SHEETS
On Good Quality Linen—

Size 72 ins. × 3½ yds.	each	69/6
,, 80 ins. × 3½ yds.	,,	77/6
,, 90 ins. × 3½ yds.	,,	87/6
,, 100 ins. × 3½ yds.	,,	92/6

Pillow Cases to match—

Size 20 × 30 ins.	each	17/6
,, 22 × 32 ins.	,,	19/6
,, 27 × 27 ins.	,,	19/9

HL 33
HEMSTITCHED LINEN SHEETS
Plain Spokestitch—

Size about 72 ins. × 3 yds.	per pair	25/9
,, ,, 72 ins. × 3½ yds. per pair 37/6, 42/6, 53/6, 56/6, 69/6, 79/6, 89/6		
,, ,, 80 ins. × 3½ yds., per pair 42/6, 52/6, 65/-, 69/6, 79/6, 105/-		
,, ,, 90 ins. × 3½ yds., per pair 42/6, 47/6, 57/6, 69/6, 72/-, 87/6, 115/6		
,, ,, 100 ins. × 3½ yds., per pair 57/6, 75/-, 89/6, 92/6, 109/6, 145/-		
,, ,, 108 ins. × 3½ yds., per pair .. 69/6, 79/6, 97/6, 122/-, 152/6, 159/6		

HL 34
FANCY HEMSTITCHED LINEN SHEETS

Size about 72 ins. × 3½ yds.	per pair	59/6, 79/6
,, ,, 80 ins. × 3½ yds.	,,	69/6, 89/9
,, ,, 90 ins. × 3½ yds.	per pair	79/6, 97/6, 105/-
,, ,, 100 ins. × 3½ yds.	,,	97/6, 107/6, 135/-
,, ,, 108 ins. × 3½ yds.	,,	135/6, 152/6, 215/-

HL 36
SCALLOPED LINEN SHEETS
With Spoke-hemstitch—

Size about 70 ins. × 3½ yds.	per pair	57/6
,, ,, 80 ins. × 3½ yds.	,,	67/6
,, ,, 90 ins. × 3½ yds.	,,	79/6
,, ,, 100 ins. × 3½ yds.	,,	95/6

HL 37
LINEN PILLOW CASES
Plain Hemmed—

Size 20 × 30 ins.	each	2/6, 2/11, 3/11, 4/6, 4/11, 5/6
,, 22 × 32 ins.	each	3/11, 4/11, 5/11, 6/3
,, 27 × 27 ins.	each	5/3, 5/9, 6/3

Hemstitched—

Size 20 × 30 ins.	each	4/6, 5/6, 6/11, 7/9, 8/9, 9/9, 11/6, 13/9, 14/9
,, 22 × 32 ins.	each	5/11, 6/11, 7/11, 8/9, 9/9, 11/9, 13/6, 14/9, 15/9, 18/6
,, 27 × 27 ins.	each	6/11, 7/11, 8/9, 9/11, 10/9, 12/9, 14/9, 16/9, 19/9, 21/-
,, 25 × 31 ins.	each	8/6, 9/6, 10/9, 12/6, 14/9, 18/6

Fancy Hemstitching—

Size 20 × 30 ins.	each	9/9, 10/6, 11/9, 18/9
,, 22 × 32 ins.	,,	11/6, 12/9, 14/6, 21/-
,, 27 × 27 ins.	,,	11/6, 12/9, 14/6, 21/-
,, 25 × 31 ins.	each	12/9, 14/6, 21/-

HL 38
FINEST HAND EMBROIDERED
On Best Linen—

Size 72 ins. × 3½ yds.	each	69/6
,, 90 ins. × 3½ yds.	,,	95/-
,, 100 ins. × 3½ yds.	,,	119/6

Pillow Cases to match—

Size 20 × 30 ins.	each	28/6
,, 22 × 32 ins.	,,	31/6
,, 27 × 27 ins.	,,	32/6

HL 39
SCALLOPED LINEN PILLOW CASES
With Spokestitch—

Size 20 × 30 ins.	each	7/11
,, 22 × 32 ins.	,,	9/6
,, 27 × 27 ins.	,,	9/6

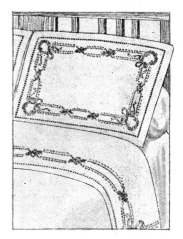

HL 35
MADEIRA HAND EMBROIDERED SHEETS
On Fine Linen—

Size 72 ins. × 3½ yds.	each	65/-
,, 80 ins. × 3½ yds.	,,	73/6
,, 90 ins. × 3½ yds.	,,	82/6
,, 100 ins. × 3½ yds.	,,	87/6

Pillow Cases to match—

Size 20 × 30 ins.	each	15/9
,, 22 × 32 ins.	,,	17/9
,, 27 × 27 ins.	,,	18/6

HL 41
Embroidered on good Linen. Design of Bow and Empire wreath

Size 70 ins. × 3½ yds.	each	42/6
,, 80 ins. × 3½ yds.	,,	49/6
,, 90 ins. × 3½ yds.	,,	58/6
,, 100 ins. × 3½ yds.	,,	67/6

Pillow cases to match—

Size 20 × 30 ins.	each	17/6
,, 22 × 32 ins.	,,	19/6
,, 27 × 27 irs.	,,	20/6

HL 42
HEMSTITCHED LINEN BOLSTER CASES
Plain Spokestitch—

Size 20 × 60 ins., single bed	each	11/6
,, 20 × 80 ins., double bed	,,	14/6

Fancystitch—

Size 20 × 60 ins., single bed	each	14/6
,, 20 × 80 ins., double bed	,,	17/6

ALL PRICES ARE SUBJECT TO MARKET FLUCTUATIONS

HARRODS LTD

Telephone SLOANE 1234
Telegrams 'EVERYTHING HARRODS LONDON'

LONDON SW 1

DYEING & CLEANING

Let Harrods Experts Renovate your Garments and Fabrics

New Freshness, new Colour, new Charm for all that's dull and dingy ! It's a sort of magic, really, that Harrods Dyeing and Dry-cleaning Service works—but magic with a thoroughly scientific foundation

Particular attention is devoted to the cleaning of all House Furnishings. Everything in the way of Personal Apparel, too, receives highly skilled care

Advice in any matter of Dyeing or Dry-cleaning will be supplied upon request ; also estimates of cost, where required

MEN'S WEAR

Of supreme importance in Men's Clothes is that perfection of detail which is preserved so faultlessly and economically by Harrods Dyeing and Dry-cleaning Service

	Cleaned from	Dyed from
Lounge Suits	6/6	12/6
Jackets, lounge	4/-	7/-
Trousers	1/9	4/-
Overcoats (light)	6/6	10/6
Raincoats reproofed	7/6	12/6
Sweaters and Cardigans	3/-	5/6

HATS	Cleaned from	Re-tinted from
Soft Felts, Re-blocked	3/-	—
Velours	4/6	—

GLOVES		
White or Coloured	4d	1/6

WOMEN'S WEAR

Everything, from the dyeing of a Fashionable Frock to the cleaning of a Pair of Gloves, may be entrusted to this Service with assurance of satisfaction

	Cleaned from	Dyed from
Dresses, Wool and Mixture ..	6/6	12/6
Skirts, Wool and Mixture ..	3/6	6/6
Coats, Cloth (light)	6/6	10/6
Gowns (Crepe de Chine)	8/6	12/6
Jumpers, Knitted Wool	3/-	4/6
Dressing Gowns, Wool	5/-	7/6

HATS—	Cleaned	Dyed
Felt	3/6	4/6
Velours	4/6	5/6
Straw	3/6	4/6

New Bands, 2/6 ; Head Linings, 1/- to 1/6

GLOVES, BELTS AND BAGS—		Cleaned from	Re-tinted and re-dressed
Short Gloves	pair	4d	1/-
Long Gloves	„	6d	1/6
Fur-lined Gloves	„	1/-	2/6
Suede Handbags	upwards	—	2/6
Belts, White and Coloured Leather ..		1/-	2/-

HARRODS 'LADDA-MEND' PROCESS

The 'Ladda-Mend' Process of Mending is quite different from darning. Ladders are mended 'invisibly' and Socks and Stockings are re-footed with such success that they cannot be distinguished from new. There are no uncomfortable darns to chafe the foot, and no weakened fibres to necessitate re-darning

REPAIRING LADDERS—	First 3 ins: or less	Additional ins.
Silk, ordinary	6d	1d per in.
Extra fine (40 gauge or over) ..	9d	1¼d „

RE-FOOTING—	White or Black	Coloured
Lisle .. .. .. per pair	2/-	2/6
Cashmere .. .. .. „	2/9	3/3

Other prices on application

RE-HEELING, RE-TOEING OR LENGTHENING—	White or Black	Coloured
Lisle .. .. .. per pair	1/6	2/-
Cashmere .. .. .. „	1/6	2/-
Silk .. .. .. „	2/6	3/-

Other prices on application

SPONGING AND PRESSING

A tonic for tired clothes

Here is a quick, efficient and inexpensive Clothes-Renovation Service. By a new method of pressing, dry steam is passed through the fibres of the material, purifying and freshening the garments. This treatment is not intended to supplant thorough cleaning by chemicals, but it does, in cases where Clothes are not too heavily soiled, help to restore their original smart appearance

A few example prices

For MEN		For WOMEN	
Suits	2/6	Costumes (plain) ..	3/-
Jackets	1/6	Jackets (plain) ..	2/-
Waistcoats	1/-	Outdoor Coats ..	2/6
Trousers	1/-	Skirts	1/6
Overcoats	2/6		

All garments are collected and delivered free within range of Harrods Motors

INVISIBLE MENDING

A Burn or Tear may make a Suit or a Costume absolutely unwearable, and darning always shows and spoils the appearance

Harrods method of Invisible Mending consists in reweaving the cloth in practically the same way as it was made, and no trace is left

The craftsmen are highly skilled, and work is executed in the shortest possible time

HOLES—	Tweeds and Velours	Finer Materials
¼ in. or less	2/-	3/-
Up to 2 ins.	9/6	10/6

TEARS—		
½ in. or less	1/9	3/-
Up to 5 ins. or less	10/6	15/6

Harrods Limited London S W 1

HABERDASHERY DEPARTMENT

If It's Anything in Smallwares—Harrods Have It

TOILET COMB STROPS
each .. 1/-

MENDING WOOL
Good quality strong
Mending Wool
Black, Tan, Clerical
Natural or White
Per ball .. 9½d

COAT HANGERS
Specially designed for travelling. Illustration shows
how easily and compactly it can be folded. Each 2/-

ELASTIC Six yards on card
Suitable for lingerie
6 cord. White only Per card 7½d
8 ,, ... ,, 9½d
10 ,, ... ,, 10½d
12 ,, ... ,, 1/0½
14 ,, ... ,, 1/4½
16 ,, ... ,, 1/6½

DRESSING GOWN GIRDLE
Good selection of colours
Wool .. .. each 1/11
Silk 9/11
Special colour combinations designed to order
in 7 days .. .. each 3/11

MENDING SILK
Fine or medium quality in boxes containing
12 reels of assorted coloured silks. Each reel
contains 10 yards of silk .. per box 10½d

SCISSORS
Strong and durable—Manicure, Dressmakers,
etc. Per pair 1/-

HAIRPINS
For bobbed or shingled hair, obtainable in
either bronze, black, silver or gold
Per Card of 4 pins Black or Bronze .. 2d
Gilt or Silver .. 3d

PEARL HEADED PINS
White, Pearl or coloured Heads
Per Card of 1 dozen pins .. 3d

TIE-ON DRESS SHIELDS
Brassierette Garment Shields in White or
Flesh coloured Nainsook. Small, medium or
large sizes 3/11

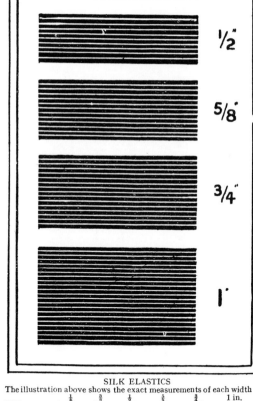

SILK ELASTICS
The illustration above shows the exact measurements of each width

	¼	⅜	½	⅝	¾	1 in.
White, per yd.	6d	7d	9d	1/-	1/2	1/6
Black ,,	6d	7d	9d	11d	1/-	1/4

GILT SAFETY PINS
Length .. ¾ in. .. Price 10½d per card 1 doz.
,, .. ⅞ in. .. ,, 1/0½ ,, ,, ,,
,, .. 1 in. .. ,, 1/0½ ,, ,, ,,
,, .. 1⅜ ins. .. ,, 8½d ,, ,, 6 pins

BRASSIERETTE
Jap Silk and Nainsook in 12 different colours, including White and
Flesh. Plain or Opera shape 4/11
Double Jap Silk, White or Flesh colour only 7/6

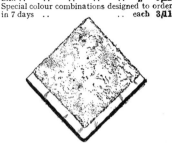

FACE CLOTHS
Beautiful soft quality Turkish Towelling
Each 6½d

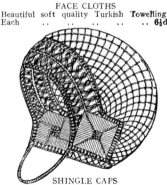

SHINGLE CAPS
Made of crocheted silk. A choice of many
delightful colours .. .. .. each 1/-

DRESS SHIELD
Double Nainsook Plain or Opera Style. White
or Flesh colour

			Black Panne Material	Double Jap Silk
Size 1	..	1/8	2/-	2/10
,, 2	..	1/10	2/3	3/4
,, 3	..	2/-	2/6	3/9
,, 4	..	2/3	2/9	4/3
,, 5	..	2/6	3/3	5/-
,, 6	..	2/11	—	5/11

ALL PRICES ARE SUBJECT TO MARKET FLUCTUATIONS

HARRODS LTD

Telephone SLOANE 1234
Telegrams 'EVERYTHING HARRODS LONDON'

LONDON SW 1

ARTIFICIAL FLOWERS DEPARTMENT
Expert-made Reproductions
Natural in Appearance

ORANGE TREES
12 ins. high. Tree only .. **4/11** Complete in gilt pot .. **7/11**
17 ins. high. Tree only .. **7/11** Complete in gilt pot .. **11/9**
32 ins. high. Tree only .. **21/9** Complete in gilt pot .. **27/6**

TULIPS
Two blooms with foliage, in natural colours **1/6**
DAFFODILS
3 blooms and foliage .. **1/3**

LILAC
Mauve or White **3/11**
MIMOSA
Most realistic. Per spray **1/11**

CAMELLIA AND RHODODENDRON TREES
In natural Pink or Red
24 ins. high .. **16/11** With gilt pot .. **21/9**
33 ins. high .. **21/9** With gilt pot .. **27/6**

DELPHINIUM
Dark Blue, Saxe, or Light Blue .. **1/11**
GUELDA ROSE
Natural White only **1/6**

CHRYSANTHEMUMS
Orange, Yellow, Fuchsia, Pink or Mauve. From **1/11**

CARNATIONS
In Orange, Yellow, Mauve, Rose Pink, Tache or Clove
Per doz. .. **7/6**
ANEMONES
In natural colours
Per doz. .. **7/-**
HYDRANGEA
Blue, Mauve or Pink
Per spray .. **1/-**
HOLLYHOCKS
Yellow, Cerise, Fuchsia, Pink, Mauve or Red
Per spray .. **2/3**

TIGER LILY
In Pink, Orange. One bloom and bud with foliage **1/3**
APPLE BLOSSOM
In Pink .. **1/11**
FOLIAGE
Beech, Mahonia, Oak, Creeper, Birch and Maple in Green or Autumn tints
From **1/11**
DAHLIAS
Single blooms. Fuchsia, Pink, Bronze or Gold
From **1/6**

RHODODENDRON
Mauve, Pink, Cerise **1/6**
CATKINS
Orange or Green **1/-**
HIPS AND HAWS
Per spray .. **1/11**
MONTBRETIA
Orange or Yellow
Per spray .. **1/-**

CAPE GOOSEBERRY
With Green or Orange foliage, or Cape Gooseberries only
Per spray .. **1/6**

POINSETTIA
In natural Red. One large or two small blooms **1/3**

ALL PRICES ARE SUBJECT TO MARKET FLUCTUATIONS

HARRODS LTD
Telephone SLOANE 1234
Telegrams 'EVERYTHING HARRODS LONDON'
LONDON S W 1

PERFUMERY & TOILET DEPARTMENT
Perfumes Express Personality—Choose them at Harrods

THE QUEST OF THE BEAUTIFUL

THE exquisite daintiness of Harrods Toiletries and the subtle charm of the Perfumes make an irresistible appeal to the women who realize that though beauty may be a gift of the Gods, it is also a cult which is within the means and power of everyone

PARFUM SILHOUETTE

PARFUM
In dainty glass bottles, elegantly cased .. 10/6, 17/6, 42/-

POWDER
Enhances the beauty of the complexion. In the following shades: Blanche, Naturelle, Rachel, Rachel-foncé, Rosée, Soir, Mauresque and Ocre .. .. Per case 2/6

BATH DUSTING POWDER
For use with a large puff, after the bath
In artistic boxes 3/6, 6/6, 12/6

BATH SALTS
Invigorate the system, and render the bath doubly refreshing
In bottles 8/6, 14/6, 21/-
In tins 6/6, 10/6, 18/6, 35/-

BATH SALTS
In capsule form. One capsule sufficient for a bath
Six in box 2/-

COMPRESSED BATH SALTS TABLETS
For week-end use
Per box of twelve tablets 2/9

EAU DE TOILETTE
In bottles with sprinkler attachment .. 10/6, 19/6, 37/6

TOILET SOAP
A pure super-creamed soap of finest quality
Three tablets in box 2/9

PARFUM A BRULER
8/6, 18/6

PARFUM RUSSE

PARFUM
An odour of enduring charm
In crystal glass bottles, artistically cased 5/6, 10/6, 19/6, 35/-

POWDER
A harmless complexion powder, well perfumed
In eight shades : Blanche, Naturelle, Rachel, Rachel-foncé, Rosée, Soir, Mauresque and Ocre .. .. Per case 2/6

SACHETS
In silk
Each 9d and 1/6. Doz. 8/6 and 17/-
For Wardrobe. In paper .. .. Each 1/3 Doz. 14/-

EAU DE COLOGNE
A refreshing perfumed Cologne
Per bottle 8/-, 15/6, 20/-, 37/6, 72/6

EAU DE COLOGNE BATH SALTS
Soften and perfume the bath water
In bottles 8/6, 14/6, 21/-
In tins 6/6, 10/6, 18/6, 35/-

BATH SALTS
In capsule form. One capsule sufficient for a bath
Six in box 2/-

EAU DE COLOGNE COMPRESSED BATH SALTS TABLETS
For week-end use or for travellers. 12 tablets in box .. 2/9

EAU DE COLOGNE BATH DUSTING POWDER
For use after the bath. In artistic boxes .. 3/6, 6/6, 12/6

EAU DE COLOGNE TOILET SOAP
A pure super-creamed soap of finest quality. Three toilet tablets in box. Per box 2/9

EAU DE COLOGNE BATH SOAP
Fine quality soap, well perfumed
Six tablets in box 5/6

EAU DE COLOGNE VISITORS' SOAP
Six tablets in box 2/3

PARFUM A BRULER
8/6, 18/6

ALL PRICES ARE SUBJECT TO MARKET FLUCTUATIONS

Telephone SLOANE 1234
Telegrams 'EVERYTHING HARRODS LONDON'

HARRODS LTD   LONDON S W 1

PERFUMERY AND TOILET DEPARTMENT
Harrods Sprays are Unequalled in Variety and Beauty of Design

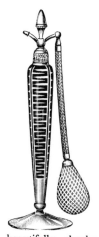

From Galle of Paris—
Patterned in floral design in rich Red tones
Height 8½ ins. .. **35/-**

A beautifully slender shaped Spray in Gold and Black
10 ins. high .. **45/-**

Madonna Spray made in lovely colours—rich Orange and Gold or Madonna Blue and Gold
Height 5½ ins. .. **12/6**

Tall, elegant Spray of Black and Gold, with floral design in Orange and Green
10 ins. high .. **77/6**

Cut Glass in an exquisite Mauve shade
Height 9½ ins. .. **21/-**

Iridescent and Crystal Spray, gracefully designed and patterned in Gold. Height 9 ins.
54/-

Beautifully cut Crystal Spray, with brass top in new design
5 ins. high .. **8/6**

Small Spray in Blue, Green, Purple or Red crystal
3½ ins. high .. **9/6**

Cut Crystal Spray. May be chosen in pale Pink, Rust or Maroon. 5½ ins. high ..**12/6**

Galle Spray showing an attractive floral design in beautifully blended colours
9½ ins. high .. **42/-**

Deep Blue baccarat Cut Glass Spray, with Gold finished top and silk covered bulb
Height 6 ins. .. **27/6**

Tall, graceful, Spray in rich Blue, Gold and Black. Jewelled silk-covered bulb
9 ins. high .. **54/-**

Uniquely-designed Spray in pale Sea-green and Black
Height 6½ ins. .. **17/6**

Artistic Spray in Black Glass attractively silhouetted in Gold. Golden base and top, finely engraved
Height 10 ins. .. **45/-**

The 'Bunch of Violets' Spray, in tones of Violet and Green. Solid brass top and silk covered bulb
Height 5½ ins. .. **11/6**

ALL PRICES ARE SUBJECT TO MARKET FLUCTUATIONS

HARRODS LTD
Telephone SLOANE 1234
Telegrams 'EVERYTHING HARRODS LONDON'
LONDON S W 1

PERFUMERY AND TOILET DEPARTMENT

Toilet Preparations that are Known the World Over

THE HÉLÈNE BEAUTY PREPARATIONS

THE HÉLÈNE PREPARATIONS FOR THE CLEANSING, NOURISHING AND BEAUTIFYING OF THE SKIN ARE A 'BEAUTY INSURANCE' FOR THE MODERN WOMAN. EACH PREPARATION IS MADE OF THE PUREST INGREDIENTS AND DELICATELY PERFUMED

HÉLÈNE PORE CREAM

An astringent cream which closes enlarged pores and prevents blackheads. Apply at night where pores are noticeable. .. Per pot **3/6**

HÉLÈNE ASTRINGENT LOTION

Has a most beneficial effect on the skin; it braces up the muscles and at the same time keeps the pores small and fine. To be used after Cleansing Cream **2/6, 4/6, 10/6**

HÉLÈNE TISSUES

Absorbent silky tissues to be used for removing cleansing cream. More hygienic than a face towel. A packet of 50 for **1/-**. Per ream **7/6** 200 for **3/6**

HÉLÈNE BENZOIN AND CUCUMBER LOTION

A cooling and refreshing lotion which tones and preserves the skin. Ideal for use after exposure to wind or sun. In three sizes .. **2/-, 3/-, 5/6**

HÉLÈNE CLEANSING CREAM

A refreshing cream to cleanse the skin from all impurities and nourish the tissues. To be used at night and first thing in the morning **3/6, 6/6, 9/6, 17/6**

HÉLÈNE LIP STICK

A new indelible lip stick in a double-fitting gilt case. In three shades: Light, Medium and Dark .. **3/6**

HÉLÈNE ROUGE SUPRA

A new cream rouge, easy and delightful to use, lending a soft, flattering tint to the skin. In light or dark shades .. Per pot **4/6**

HÉLÈNE POUDRE SUPRA

Delicately perfumed and exceptionally fine, giving a soft bloom to the skin. In Rachel, Rachel-foncé, Naturelle, Rosée, Blanche, Ochre, Ochre-Rose and Péche. .. Per box **5/6**

HÉLÈNE LOTION SUPRA

For making the skin soft and velvety. To be applied before powder **2/6, 4/6**

HÉLÈNE SKIN FOOD

Is particularly suitable for massage. Builds and nourishes the tissues underneath the skin, generally improves and strengthens it, also greatly aids in the prevention of lines and wrinkles. In four sizes **3/6, 6/6, 12/6, 22/6**

HÉLÈNE COMPLEXION LOTION

A liquid powder, delicately perfumed, of unusual fineness Almost invisible and does not rub off. Excellent for use before a dance Obtainable in all shades

In three sizes **3/6, 6/6, 12/6**

HÉLÈNE DAY CREAM

A vanishing cream of rare purity, delightfully fragrant. It gives a soft radiance to the skin and makes a good powder foundation In two sizes **2/6, 4/6**

HÉLÈNE BLEACH CREAM

This preparation will be found excellent for whitening the skin and acts beneficially on all discolorations **2/6, 4/6**

ALL PRICES ARE SUBJECT TO MARKET FLUCTUATIONS

HARRODS LTD

Telephone SLOANE 1234
Telegrams 'EVERYTHING HARRODS LONDON'

LONDON SW1

PERFUMERY AND TOILET DEPARTMENT
Perfumes, Toilet Powders, Bath Toiletries and Face Creams

BATH POWDER

Softens and perfumes hard water and renders the bath delightfully refreshing. In Cologne, Lavender, Rose, Verbena, Violet, Ideale. In barrels .. 1/9, 3/3, 6/-

GLYCERINE AND MILK OF CUCUMBER

A liquid cream of the greatest benefit. Will smooth away discomfort and leaves the skin refreshed and soft as velvet 1/-, 1/6, 2/6

EAU DE COLOGNE NO. 1

The finest Eau de Cologne, double distilled in Great Britain from selected French Essences

	2 oz.	4 oz.	8 oz.	Pint	Qt.
In plain glass bottles					
	3/9	7/-	13/6	32/6	62/6
In stoppered square bottles					10 oz.
					18/6
In wickered bottles	Reputed	½ Pint	Pint	Qt.	
		13/6	23/6	46/6	

Foaming Cologne, for perfuming and softening hard water 8/6
Mentholated Cologne 2 oz. bot. 4 oz. bot. 8 oz. bot.
4/- 7/6 14/6

LANOLINE AND CUCUMBER

An ideal preparation for keeping the skin soft and smooth
2/-, 3/-, 5/6

TOILET OATMEAL

Violet scented. A splendid water-softener, and an ideal preparation for the toilet 1/3, 2/-, 3/6, 6/-

FLOWER ESSENCES

Concentrated (without Alcohol)
These essences provide the natural flower odour more faithfully than the more diffused alcoholic extracts. Carnation, Heliotrope, Jasmin, Geranium, Lilac, Lily of the Valley, Sweet Pea. In bottles fitted with glass rod attachment to stopper. Each bottle elegantly cased 3/6, 6/9

BATH SALTS

Perfumed Verbena, Cologne, Violet and Lavender. In glass stoppered bottles .. .. 4/6, 8/6 and 11/6
In gilt tins : 3/6 approx. 3 lbs., 5/6 approx. 5 lbs., 9/6 approx. 9 lbs., 22/6 approx. 24 lbs.

SILK CORSAGE SACHETS
(Not illustrated)

Various perfumes. 9d & 1/6 each
8/6 and 17/- per dozen
Wardrobe Sachets. Paper 1/3 each
14/- per dozen
Lavender Bags, or Lavender and Verbena Bags, 10½d each
10/- per dozen
Sachet Powder in Bottles. In any of the above perfumes
1 oz., 1/9 ; 2 oz., 3/- ; 4 oz., 5/6

COMPLEXION POWDERS

Perfectly harmless, soft, and smoothly adherent. Carnation, Cyclamen, Jasmin, Lilac and Violette, per box .. 2/6
These complexion powders are issued in the following eight shades : Blanche, Naturelle, Rachel, Rachel-foncé, Rosée, Ocre, Ocre-Rosée, Pêche

FROZEN EAU DE COLOGNE NO. 1

The genuine fragrance in stick form, in frosted glass bottles with nickel screw caps 3/-
Also Frozen Lavender Water .. 3/-

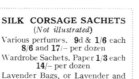

VIOLETTE DE PARME

A harmless complexion powder, delightfully soft and smoothly adherent Gives a delicious fragrance of violets. Per box 1/6, 2/9
In various shades :
Blanche, Rachel, Rose and Naturelle

COLD CREAM (Otto of Rose)

A cleansing cream and skin tonic combined, much better than soap and water for cleansing the face and preserving its softness and texture
Per jar 1/6, 2/6, 4/6, 8/6
Tubes 1/-

DUSTING POWDER

Fragrant and refreshing, for use with a large puff, after the bath. In Lily of the Valley, Rose, Geranium, Lilac, Lavender, Verbena and Violet
In barrels 3/-, 5/6

'NONODOR'

For preventing excessive perspiration and destroying all odour
Liquid, per bottle 1/6, 2/9, 5/-
Cream, per pot 1/6
Powder, per tin 1/9

PATE AMYGDALINE

An excellent preparation containing oil and almonds Heals chapping and roughness Keeps the hands and skin smooth, soft and white
2/3, 3/6, 6/6

TOILET VINEGAR

An aromatic vinegar for softening water and whitening the skin. An excellent deodorant
Per bottle, in two sizes
2/9, 5/-

COMPRESSED BATH SALTS *(In Tablets)*

A convenient size for travellers Softens hard water, perfumes the bath, and renders it doubly refreshing. In the following perfumes : Cologne, Lavender, Verbena, Violette
12 tablets in box 2/6

OLD ENGLISH LAVENDER WATER

Distilled from the finest Mitcham Flowers. Each bottle daintily cased

2 oz.	4 oz.	6 oz.	8 oz.	Pint	Quart
4/6	8/6	12/6	16/6	32/6	62/6

In square-stoppered bottles
10 oz. 18/6 20 oz. 32/6 32 oz. 50/-

THEATRICAL COLD CREAM

Ideal for use after grease paint, rouge, etc. 1 lb. tins 5/6

TOILET WATER

Available in the following perfumes : Verbena, Turkish Lavender, Violette and Muguet
9/6, 18/-, 35/6
Reuben's, Lilac, Chypre
10/6, 19/6, 37/6

ALL PRICES ARE SUBJECT TO MARKET FLUCTUATIONS

PERFUMERY AND TOILET DEPARTMENT
An Attractive Selection of Toilet Requisites

BATH BRUSHES

With strap, without handle. Best quality Bristles (Hard). 4¾ × 2¾ ins. **11/6 & 9/-**
With strap, without handle. Pure Bristles (Medium). 5½ × 3 ins. .. **6/6 & 8/6**

With strap and detachable handle. Pure Bristles (Medium). 5¼ × 2¾ ins. .. **8/6**
With strap and detachable handle. Pure Bristles (Medium). 5¾ × 3½ ins. **11/9 & 12/6**
With fixed, straight handle. Best quality Fibre **4/6**

With fixed (bent) handle. Best quality Bristles (Hard). 4¾ × 2¾ ins. .. **13/6**

With fixed handle (slightly curved). Best quality Bristles (Hard). Bristles on both sides (Convex and Concave). Size of head 4½ × 3½ ins. (square shaped) .. **17/6**
With long handle **17/6**

BATH STRAPS

Loofah and Turco. 23 ins. long .. **2/-**
Double Loofah. 23 ins. long .. **2/6**
Fibre. To be used wet .. **3/6**

Lawrence's Horse Hair, for dry use only **6/-**
Loofahs .. .. 9d and **1/-**

Miniature Bath Brush with fixed handle. Best quality Bristles (Medium) .. **8/6**

BATH WHISK

Best quality fibre, mounted in hand-turned boxwood handle **7/6**
'Ruba' Bath Brush **10/6**

NAIL BRUSHES

Satinwood Nail Brushes. Best unbleached Siberian Bristles

Roach Back

4 row, 3	inches long	..	..	**2/9**
4 ,, 4	,,	,,		**3/-**
5 ,, 4¼	,,	,,	..	**4/6**
6 ,, 4¼	,,	,,	..	**5/3**
7 ,, 4½	,,	,,		**6/-**
8 ,, 4¾	,,	,,	..	**8/-**
9 ,, 5	,,	,,	..	**9/-**
10 ,, 5¼	,,	,,	..	**11/6**
11 ,, 5½	,,	,,	.. 15/6 &	**16/6**

Concave Back

4 row, 4	inches long		..	**5/-**
5 ,, 4¼	,,	,,	..	**5/6**
6 ,, 4½	,,	,,	..	**6/6**
7 ,, 4¾	,,	,,	..	**7/6**
8 ,, 4¾	,,	,,	..	**8/9**
9 ,, 5	,,	,,	..	**9/9**
10 ,, 5¼	,,	,,	..	**11/6**
11 ,, 5¾	,,	,,	..	**12/6**
12 ,, 6	,,	,,	..	**15/6**

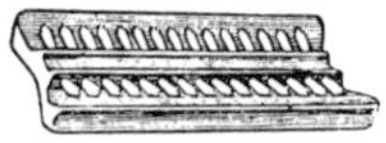

'Duplex,' two single rows of bristles .. **1/3**

Hardwood (unpolished), with one row of bristles on the back. 6 row, 4 inches long **4/6**

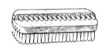

Unpolished wooden back with concave short bristles. 6 row, 3¾ inches long .. **2/6**
Polished wooden back. Best quality grey bristles. 6 row, 4½ inches long .. **2/3**

Polished wooden back. Best quality grey bristles (2½ inches square), 13 row **3/6**
Erinoid Nail Brushes Very best quality bleached bristles. Blue, Red, Green, Tortoiseshell and other colours

4 row, 4	inches long	..	..	**7/9**
5 ,, 4¼	,,	,,	..	**9/-**
6 ,, 4½	,,	,,	..	**10/9**
7 ,, 4¾	,,	,,	..	**12/6**

Erinoid Nail Brushes with one row of bristles on back and short bristles on front 6 row, 2¾ inches long **5/9**

MANICURE NECESSITIES

Orange Sticks .. .. Per box **1/3**
Orange Sticks with rubber hoof end
Each 9d and **1/3**
Emery Boards, short .. Per box **7½d**
Emery Boards, medium.. ,, **1/-**
Emery Boards, long .. ,, **1/6**
Cuticle Cream .. .. 1/- and **1/9**

FACE SQUARES

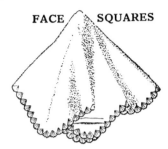

Double Sided Turco. Fringed edge. 13 × 12 ins. **5d**
Double Sided Turco. Coloured scalloped edge. 12 ins. square **9d**
Single Sided Turco. Coloured scalloped edge. 12 × 11 ins. .. 7½d, 10½d & **1/6**

FACE GLOVES

White Turco, bound edge, best quality
Small size .. .. .. pair **9d**
Ordinary size .. .. ,, **1/3**
White Turco, scalloped edge, best quality
Ordinary size .. .. pair **1/3**
Coloured Turco (White/Pink and White/Blue), bound edge, best quality, pair **1/6**
Turco and Loofah. Small .. each **1/-**
Ordinary .. .. each 1/3, 1/6 & **1/9**
Double Loofah. Small .. each **1/3**
Ordinary .. each 1/6 & **1/9**
Turco and Rubber. Small .. each **1/9**
Loofah and Rubber. .. ,, **9d**
Lawrence Flesh Gloves, for dry use only. Per pair .. .. **6/-** 
Hyde's Complexion, Small .. each **1/6**
Ordinary ,, **2/9**
With thumb piece each **3/6**

COMPLEXION BRUSHES

Rubber
'Ruba' **5/-**

HOLDALLS

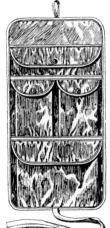

Plain or Shot Silk Full length pocket at back .. **22/6**
India Cloth. Full length pocket at back. Small **6/6**
Large .. **12/6**
Plain Rubber. Full length pocket at back. Small **3/11**
Medium .. **4/11**
Large .. **6/11**
Check. Full length pocket at back
Small .. **3/9**
Medium .. **5/-**
Large .. **6/6**
Oiled skin. Full length pocket at back .. **6/6**

ALL PRICES ARE SUBJECT TO MARKET FLUCTUATIONS

HARRODS LTD

Telephone SLOANE 1234
Telegrams 'EVERYTHING HARRODS LONDON'

LONDON S W 1

PERFUMERY AND TOILET DEPARTMENT

Toilet Puffs, Sponges, Shaving Brushes, and Glass Toilet Goods

TOILET REQUISITES—*continued*

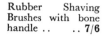

Bone Turn-back Handle (for Travelling) (*as illustrated*) filled with best Badger
13/6, 15/6, 17/6, 19/6, 25/-

Rubber Shaving Brushes with bone handle **7/6**

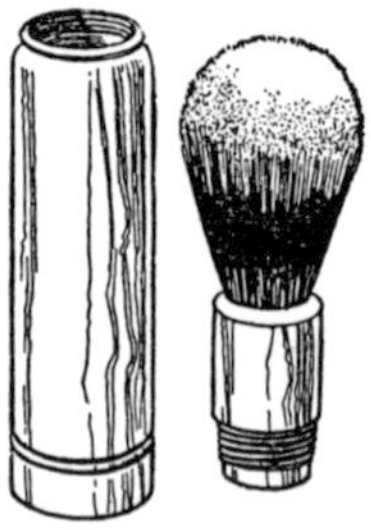

SOAP CASES

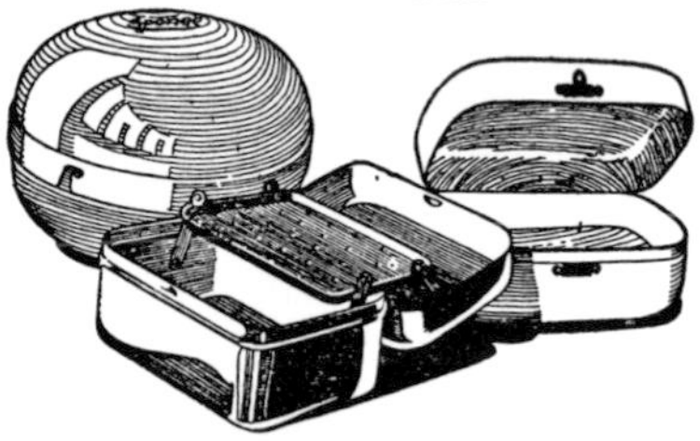

Aluminium **1/6**
Xylonite. Pink, Blue or White .. **2/-**
With hinged lid. White only .. **2/6**

SPONGE BAGS

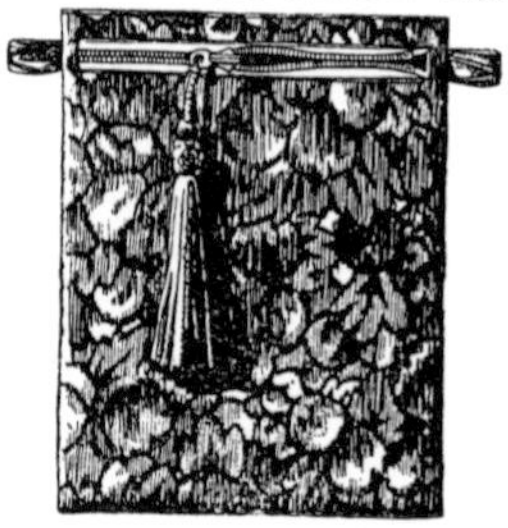

Check. Best Rubber proofed **1/1, 1/4, 1/6, 1/9, 2/-**

'Elite.' Plain Rubber in various colours **2/-, 2/3, 2/6, 2/9, 3/-**

India Cloth. Best rubber proofed. Khaki **2/-, 2/6, 2/9, 3/6**

Silk, best quality. Various colours. Shot or plain .. **3/6, 4/6, 5/6, 6/6, 7/6, 8/6**

Taffeta Silk. Various colours **3/11, 4/11, 5/6**

Oiled Skin. Yellow only . **1/-, 1/3, 1/6, 2/-, 2/3, 2/6**

SPONGE NETS

Each **1/8, 2/-, 2/3, 2/6**

SPONGE SQUARES
With Pocket

Check **2/6, 3/11, 4/11**
India Cloth **3/6, 4/6, 5/6**
Silk. Various colours .. **8/6, 13/6, 17/6**

SPONGES

Turkey Sponges, perfectly formed
3/6, 4/9, 6/6, 7/9, 8/6, 10/6, 15/-, 17/6, 21/-, 25/-, 30/-, 35/-

Honeycomb Sponges
2/6, 3/6, 5/6, 6/6, 7/6, 10/6, 12/6. 14/6, 17/6, 21/-, 25/-, 30/-, 35/-, 45/-, 50/-, 55/-

Flat Sponges, commonly known as Elephants' Ears. These sponges take the place of washing gloves .. **1/6, 2/6, 3/9, 4/6**

SPONGES

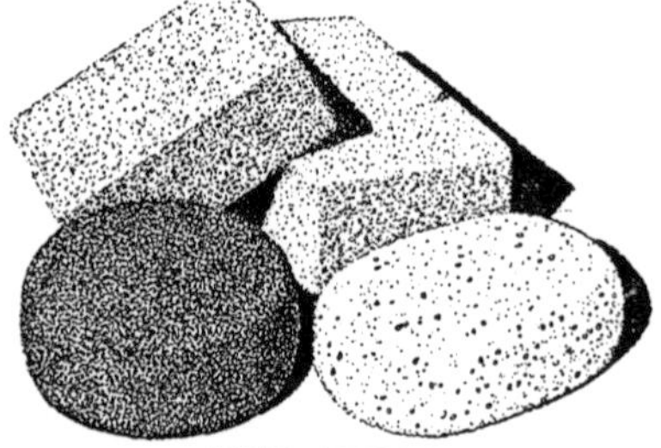

RED (OVAL)

2½ × 4 ins. **7½d, 10½d**
4½ × 6 ins. **1/3**
5 × 7 ins. **1/9**

COLOURED (OBLONG)

With butterfly in corner. Pink, Green and Mauve

4½ × 3 × 1½ ins. **1/6**
5 × 3¼ × 1¾ ins. **2/-**
5½ × 3½ × 2 ins. **2/6**

COLOURED (ROUND)

Hand-cut. Green, Pink, Mauve and Light and Dark Blue

3½ ins diameter **2/-**
4¼ ins. ,, ... **2/6**
5 ins. ,, ... **3/6, 4/6**

SORBO

1 in. **1/-**, 2 ins. **1/9**, 3 ins. **2/6**, 4 ins. **3/9**, 5 ins. **6/-**

RUBBER SPONGES
Red (Oblong)

3¾ × 2⅜ × 1½ ins. **9d**
4¼ × 2¼ × 1⅜ ins. **10½d**
4½ × 3 × 2 ins. **1/3**
5 × 3½ × 2 ins. **1/6**
5½ × 3¾ × 2⅛ ins. **2/-**
5½ × 4¼ × 2¼ ins. **3/3**

TOILET PUFFS

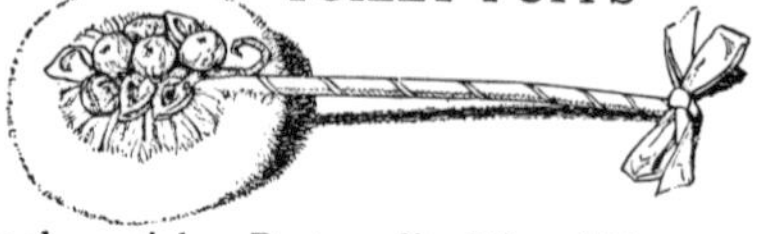

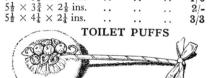

Back or stick. Best quality Tinted Down on handles of various designs

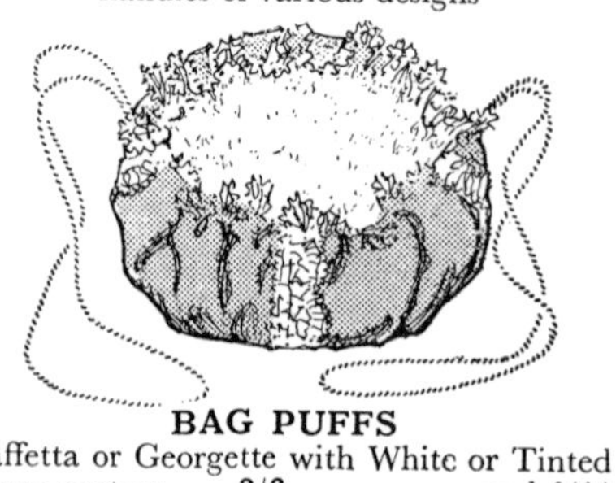

BAG PUFFS

Taffetta or Georgette with White or Tinted Down centres .. **3/6** and **4/11**

FLAT DOWN PUFF

2 ins. **3d**, 3 ins. **7½d**, 3¼ ins. **1/-** 3½ ins. **1/3**, 4 ins. **1/9**, 4½ ins. **2/3**, 5 ins. **4/-**

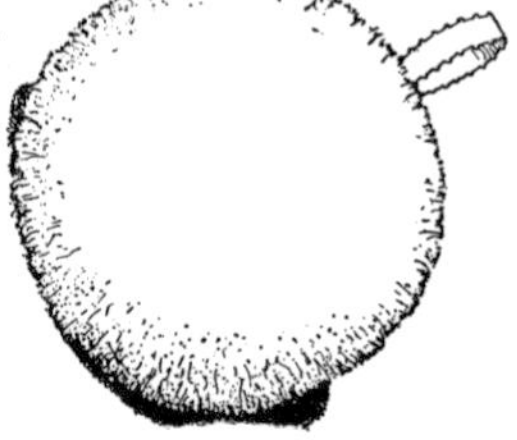

HANDKERCHIEF PUFF

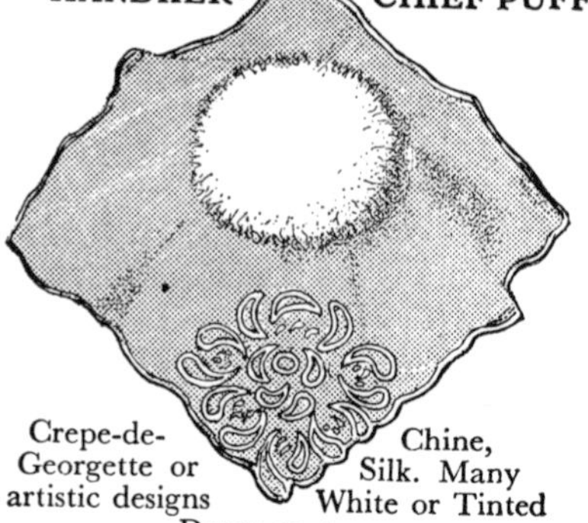

Crepe-de-Georgette or Chine, Silk. Many artistic designs White or Tinted Down centres

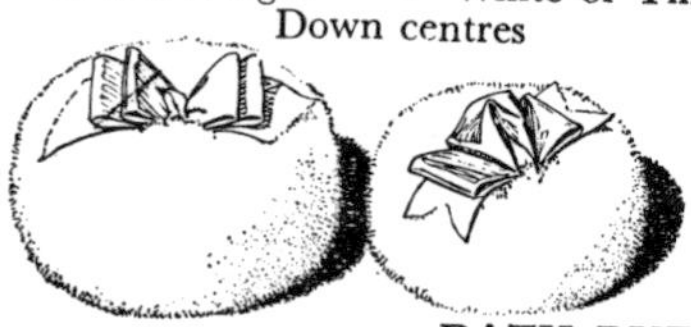

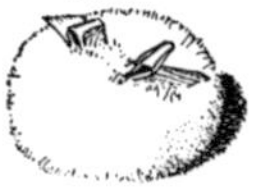

BATH PUFFS

Best quality Tinted Down with satin ribbon bow
3 ins. **2/-**, 3½ ins. **2/3**, 4 ins. **2/11**, 4½ ins. **3/11**, 5 ins. **5/9**, 5½ ins. **6/9**, 6 ins. **8/9**, 6½ ins. **10/6**, 7 ins. **11/6**

Best quality White Down with satin ribbon bow
3 ins. **1/9**, 3½ ins. **2/-**, 4 ins. **2/3**, 4½ ins. **2/9**, 5 ins. **3/11**, 5½ ins. **5/6**, 6 ins. **7/6**, 6½ ins. **9/6**, 7 ins. **10/6**

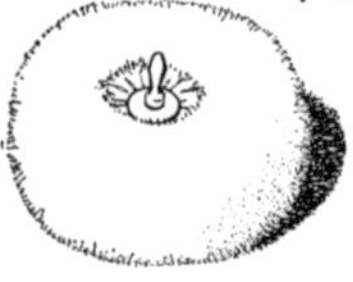

SNOWBALL PUFFS

2 ins. **6½d**, 3 ins. **1/-**, 3½ ins. **1/6**, 4 ins. **1/11**, 4½ ins. **2/6**

BEAVER PUFFS

Finished with silk back and bow to match puff
2 ins. dia. **2/9**
3½ ins. ,, **5/6**
4½ ins. ,, **7/6**

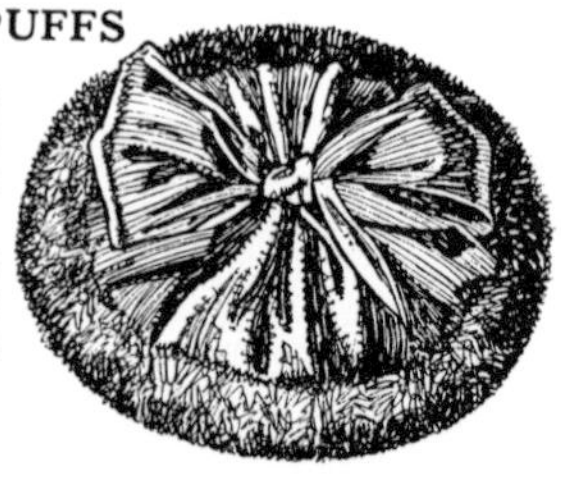

ALABASTER GLASS AND ENGLISH CRYSTAL TOILET GOODS

ALABASTER GLASS

Apricot, Blue (Dark and Turquoise), Green (Jade), Mauve, Nacre de Pearl, Orange, Pink (Rose) and Tortoiseshell

Bowls. 4 ins. **17/6**, 5 ins. **22/6**, 6 ins. **27/6**, 7 ins. **37/6**, 8 ins. **45/-**

Bottles **21/-**
Cream Jars **7/9**
Pomade Jars **17/6**
Bath Salts Jars. 9½ ins. high .. **57/6**
Bath Salts Scoops **5/6**

FINEST ENGLISH CRYSTAL Richly Cut

Bowls. 5 ins. **22/6**, 6 ins. **27/6**, **7** ins. **35/-**
Bath Salts Jar to match, height 8 ins. **45/-**

PAPIER MACHE BOWLS. Blue (Light and Dark), Cream, Eau de Nil, Mauve, Pink and Red
5 ins. **3/6**, 6½ ins. **5/11**, 8 ins. **6/11**

ALL PRICES ARE SUBJECT TO MARKET FLUCTUATIONS

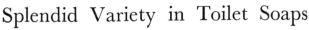

PERFUMERY AND TOILET DEPARTMENT

Splendid Variety in Toilet Soaps

CASTILE TOILET SOAP

Made in Italy from the finest Tuscan Olive Oil

12 tablets in box	.. .. ..	**5/6**
Six boxes for	.. .. ..	**32/6**

BELGRAVIA TOILET SOAP

Delicately perfumed in Curd, Lavender, Old Brown Windsor, Glycerine and Cucumber, Cold Cream, Eau de Cologne or Oatmeal ; also assorted

Per box of 12 tablets	.. ..	**3/–**
Six boxes for	.. ..	**17/6**

CLOVE CARNATION TOILET SOAP

Triple milled and heavily perfumed A Soap that will appeal to dainty tastes. In boxes of 12 tablets

Per box	.. ..	**3/9**
Six boxes for	.. ..	**22/–**

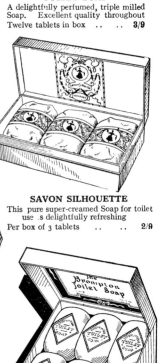

ROSE GERANIUM TOILET SOAP

A delightfully perfumed, triple milled Soap. Excellent quality throughout

Twelve tablets in box	.. ..	**3/9**

ALBANY CREAM TOILET SOAP

A high-class toilet soap, perfumed with lavender. Each tablet wrapped in transparent paper. 12 tablets in box

Per box	.. ..	**4/6**
Six boxes for	.. ..	**26/6**

GOLD MEDAL OATMEAL TOILET SOAP

Excellent quality. Ideal for delicate skins. In boxes of 3 tablets

Box..	.. ..	**1/6**
Per doz. boxes	.. ..	**17/–**

VERBENA TOILET SOAP

Delightfully perfumed

Per box of 12 tablets	..	**3/9**
Six boxes for	..	**22/–**

CHYPRE TOILET SOAP

Finest quality, delicately perfumed with the odour of Amber perfumed Moss

Per box of 3 tablets	.. ..	**2/9**

CURD SOAP

For toilet purposes. In bars of three tablets, weight about 1 lb.

Per bar	.. ..	**8d**
12 bars for	.. ..	**7/6**

SAVON SILHOUETTE

This pure super-creamed Soap for toilet use is delightfully refreshing

Per box of 3 tablets	.. ..	**2/9**

LADY TATTERSALL TOILET SOAP

A pure super-creamed Soap, suitable for the most sensitive skins. Exquisitely perfumed. Boxes of 3 tablets .. **2/9**

BUTTERMILK TOILET SOAP

Pure white triple milled, exceptionally well perfumed

In boxes of 12 tablets (3 ozs. each) ..	**3/6**
Six boxes for ..	.. ..	**20/6**

MUGUET TOILET SOAP

A fragrant, triple milled Soap Suitable for all skins, no matter how delicate

3 tablets in box	.. ..	**2/9**

OLD BROWN WINDSOR TOILET SOAP

Well perfumed, triple milled. In boxes of 3 tablets. Per box.. .. .. **1/6**

Six boxes for	.. ..	**8/6**

BROMPTON TOILET SOAP

English manufacture. Made from a pure base and cannot be equalled in price or quality. In boxes of 12 tablets

Per box	.. .. ..	**2/6**
Per dozen boxes	.. ..	**29/–**

ALL PRICES ARE SUBJECT TO MARKET FLUCTUATIONS

HARRODS LTD

Telephone SLOANE 1234
Telegrams 'EVERYTHING HARRODS LONDON'

LONDON SW 1

PERFUMERY AND TOILET DEPARTMENT

Harrods Visitors' Soaps—A Compliment to Your Guests

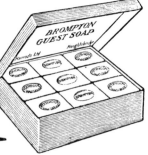

SANDALWOOD VISITORS' SOAP

Finest quality milled and well-scented with this favourite odour. Six tablets in box
Per box .. 2/9   Six boxes for .. 16/-

BROMPTON GUEST SOAP

Pure white, fine quality, milled, cold-cream toilet Soap.   36 tablets in box
Per box .. 3/9   Four boxes for 14/6

RANWORTH VISITORS' SOAP

Triple milled, well perfumed.   Twelve tablets in box.   Perfumed with Verbena, Carnation, Jasmin or assorted
Per box .. 2/6   Six boxes for .. 11/6

DAINTY GUEST SOAP

A beautifully perfumed, triple milled Soap.   Three dozen tablets in box
Per box .. 2/6   Six boxes for 14/6

VIOLETTE DE PARME VISITORS' SOAP

High-grade, super-creamed soap for sensitive skins.   In boxes of 6 tablets
Per box .. 2/3   Six boxes for .. 13/-

REGALIA VISITORS' SOAP

In handy-sized tablets, daintily scented.   In boxes of 6 tablets
Per box .. 1/9   Six boxes for 10/-

MITCHAM LAVENDER VISITORS' SOAP

A super-fatted, well-perfumed Soap Six tablets in box
Per box .. 2/3   Six boxes for 13/-

RUSSIAN COLOGNE VISITORS' SOAP

Delicately perfumed
Per box of 6 tablets   .. 2/3
Six boxes for 13/-

VIOLETTE DE PARME TOILET SOAP

Suitable for the most sensitive skins, fragrantly perfumed
Per box of 3 tablets   ..   2/6
Six boxes for 14/6

OTTO OF ROSE TOILET SOAP

An exquisitely perfumed, triple milled, superior quality Soap
Per box of 3 tablets   ..   2/6
Six boxes for   ..   14/6

MITCHAM LAVENDER TOILET SOAP

Exquisitely perfumed, triple milled Soap Artistically packed in boxes of 3 tablets
Per box .. 2/6   Six boxes for .. 14/6

VIOLET OATMEAL TOILET SOAP

A soap for hard water.   Delightfully soothing to the skin
Per box of 3 tablets 1/6
Six boxes for 9/-

SHAVING SOAPS

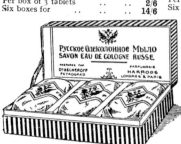

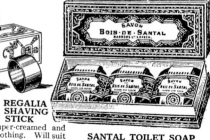

RUSSIAN EAU DE COLOGNE TOILET SOAP

A toilet Soap highly recommended and appreciated.   Most suitable for the complexion and skin.   Refreshingly perfumed with a very fine brand of Eau de Cologne
Per box of 3 tablets   ..   2/9
Six boxes for 16/-

HARRODS SHAVING SOAP

In wooden bowls.   A perfumed superfine soap, producing a copious lather ... 1/6

REGALIA SHAVING CREAM

For sensitive skins .. Per pot 2/-

REGALIA SHAVING STICK

Super-creamed and soothing.   Will suit the most sensitive skins.   In nickel cases   .. 1/3

SANTAL TOILET SOAP

Delicately perfumed with this favourite odour
Per box of 3 tablets   ..   2/6
Six boxes for 14/6

ALL PRICES ARE SUBJECT TO MARKET FLUCTUATIONS

HARRODS LTD

Telephone SLOANE 1234
Telegrams 'EVERYTHING HARRODS LONDON'

LONDON SW1

TOILET BRUSH DEPARTMENT

Ebony, White Xylonite and Imitation Tortoiseshell Brushes and Mirrors

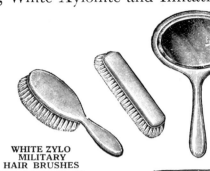

ENGLISH CUT GLASS
Bottle with Ivory Cap
35/6, 45/-

ENAMEL SHINGLE SET
Various Coloured Pieces
Complete in Fitted case
£2 7 6

**WHITE ZYLO
MILITARY
HAIR BRUSHES**
Filled with a good Quality
Bristle
12/-, 16/6, 25/- each
TOILET PIECES
TRAYS 5/-, 9/6 each
MIRRORS
11/6, 17/6, 21/- each

WHITE XYLONITE TOILET SETS.
CLOTH BRUSHES .. 6/-, 10/6, 12/6 each.
HAT BRUSHES .. .. 7/6, 9/6 ,,
LADIES' HAIR BRUSHES
12/-, 18/6, 20/-, 21/-, 22/-, 27/-, 30/- ,,

**HAND
MIRRORS**
17/6, 21/- each
**PRINCESS
SHAPE** 11/9
16/- each
**POWDER
BOXES** 2/6
SHOE LIFTS
2/3
HAIR TIDY
3/9
**DRESSING
COMBS**
2/-, 2/3

**IMITATION
TORTOISESHELL
JEWEL CASES**
7/11, 9/-

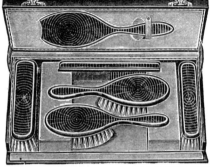

ENAMEL MEDIUM-SIZED SIX PIECE SET
Various Colours
£4 10 0

ENAMEL FOUR PIECE SET
Various Coloured Pieces
Complete in case £3 15 0

**IMITATION
TORTOISESHELL
HAIR BRUSHES**
12/-, 16/6, 20/-, 21/-

**LADY'S
EBONY BRUSH**
Filled with Pure Bristles **12/-**

(Not illustrated).
**IMITATION
TORTOISE-
SHELL—**
Brush Trays 28/-
Powder Bowls 7/6
Hand Mirrors
(Round) 8/9, 10/-
Hand Mirrors
(Princess Shape)
16/-, 18/6

**IMITATION
TORTOISESHELL
SHOE LIFT** .. 3/-

**IMITATION
TORTOISESHELL
MILITARY HAIR
BRUSHES** 13/6, 16/6, 25/6

**LADY'S
EBONY BRUSH**
Pure Bristles. Medium Cut.
15/6, 16/6, 17/6, 21/-,
25/-, 33/6

**IVORY MILITARY
COMBS**
4/9, 6/9, 7/9, 10/6

**IVORY DRESSING
COMBS**
6/9, 9/-, 12/-, 18/6, 21/-

**IMITATION
TORTOISESHELL
CLOTH BRUSHES**
9/-, 11/6

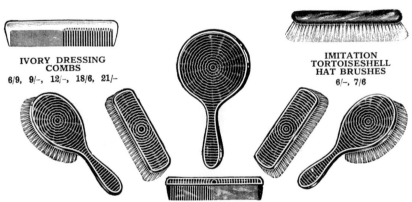

**IMITATION
TORTOISESHELL
HAT BRUSHES**
6/-, 7/6

TRAVELLING MIRRORS
(Folding) covered Pigskin.
Morocco ; Crocodile Leather
to Stand, Hang, or Hold with
moveable metal strut back,
in Leather case.
21/-, 26/-, 31/6, 42/-

**TRAVELLING FOLDING
MIRRORS**
Covered in Fancy Leather.
17/6, 18/6, 20/-, 26/-

ENAMEL TOILET SETS IN A VARIETY OF COLOURS, WITH GILT EDGES
Exceptionally good quality bristles.
SIX PIECES.—Two Hair Brushes, Cloth Brush, Hat Brush, Mirror and Comb £6 6 0
Complete in case £6 18 6

ALL PRICES ARE SUBJECT TO MARKET FLUCTUATIONS

HARRODS LTD

Telephone SLOANE 1234
Telegrams 'EVERYTHING HARRODS LONDON'

LONDON S W 1

DRUG DEPARTMENT
Harrods Dispensing Department

PRESCRIPTIONS are dispensed under the supervision of a qualified chemist, assisted by a fully qualified staff. The utmost care and accuracy are exercised in carrying out physicians' orders, and all medicines are carefully checked before being sent to the customers. Prescriptions to the value of 10s. and over are sent carriage paid to any address in Great Britain

PRICE LIST

DENTAL PREPARATIONS

AROMATIC TOOTH TABLET

In celluloid case. Fragrant and antiseptic .. 1/3

CACHOUS (Harrods)

Finest quality, delightfully perfumed in either Floral or Violet
Per box   8d

CAMPHORATED CHALK

In cartons .. .. .. 10½d and 1/6

CARBOLIC MOUTH WASH

Antiseptic, deodorant, detergent; meets all requirements of dental and oral hygiene
Per bottle .. 3/6, 6/6, 15/-

CARBOLIC DENTIFRICE

Per box .. 6d, 1/3, 1/9, 3/6

DENTAL PLATE CLEANER
Prepared from a unique formula. Specially devised for artificial teeth. Per tube .. 1/6

CHLORATE OF POTASH TOOTH PASTE

Science's discovery against 'Acid-mouth,' the forerunner of decayed teeth. Per tube 10d

DENTONA

(*On left*) (Salol Mouth Wash)
Per bottle 2/6, 4/6, 9/-

DENTAL PREPARATIONS

ORIGINOL

(Glycer. Thymo Alkaline Co.)

An Alkaline antiseptic and non-irritating solution for medical and dental purposes. (Highly recommended)
Per bottle
1/3, 2/3, 4/6, 8/6

PYORRHŒA PASTE

Neutralises the poison which causes the gums to become soft, inflamed and painful. Apply the paste with the tip of finger, massage lightly and afterwards clean the teeth in the usual way
Per tube .. 1/6

STANLEY'S TOOTHACHE CURE
For instantaneous cure of toothache .. Per bottle 1/3

TOOTH PICKS
The famous Le Negri Brand. Each in a sealed envelope, sterilised. In boxes
25, 7d; 50 1/1; 100 2/-; 500 7/6

KEMPSTER TOOTH POWDER

Pleasant to the taste and guaranteed harmless. Beneficial to tooth structure
In sprinkler tins .. 1/6

VIOLET MOUTH WASH

An antiseptic solution which arrests decay of the teeth, and imparts firmness to the gums. The active properties of this preparation ensure a thoroughly hygienic condition of the mouth
4/6 and 8/6

EAU DENTIFRICE

(Dr. Becherre)
Per bottle
4/9, 7/-, 13/6

MYRRH AND BORAX

Prepared with Eau de Cologne. The ideal astringent mouth wash. Per bottle
1/6, 2/9, 4/9, 8/6

DENTAL PREPARATIONS

WINTHERIA

An antiseptic deodorant and prophylactic solution containing Wintergreen, Thyme, Eucalyptus, Menthol, Boric and Benzoic acids
Per bottle 1/6, 2/6, 4/6

WINTHERIA TOOTH PASTE

In tubes. Antiseptic and tooth preserving. Cleans and polishes dental enamel

Per tube 1/-

DISINFECTANTS

BROMPTON DISINFECTING FLUID

Per bottle.. .. 1/6, 1/10
Per gallon.. .. 5/-
The true germicide as suggested by Pasteur. In a concentrated form. Tins not returnable

CARBOLIC DISINFECTING POWDER

In large sprinkler tins   1/6
28 lbs. 6/-; ½ cwt. 10/-

FUMIGATING PASTILLES
(Aromatic)
With stand .. Per box 1/6

FUMIGATION AND DISINFECTION
of rooms and premises carried out by skilled Sanitary Specialists. Phone or write the DRUG DEPT.

EXTERMINATION OF PESTS
such as beetles, mice, etc. undertaken by skilled operatives

LYSOL

The universal Antiseptic. In bottles
4 oz. 10½d; 8 oz. 1/6; 16 oz. 2/6; 32 oz. 4/3

ALL PRICES ARE SUBJECT TO MARKET FLUCTUATIONS

HARRODS LTD

Telephone SLOANE 1234
Telegrams 'EVERYTHING·HARRODS·LONDON'

LONDON S W 1

DRUG DEPARTMENT

DISINFECTANTS

OZONATEUR
An automatic disinfector. Indispensable in sick rooms, lavatories, etc. Ozonises the air continuously Height 10 ins., width 4 ins. **8/6**

OZONATINE
Ozonising Fluid for use with above
In cans **8/6**

PERFECT PINE FLUID
An excellent disinfectant and deodorant
Per bottle **1/9**

PERFECT PINE POWDER
In sprinkler tins **1/-**

PIVENA DISINFECTANT
A new disinfectant made from the essences of pine and verbena. A wonderful repellent for flies, ants etc. Per bottle **1/10½**

'RANWORTH' OZONISING OUTFIT
An ideal method of purifying and deodorising Sick Rooms, Lavatories, Hotels, Public Places, Bathrooms, etc. The Outfit consists of a Terra Cotta Porous Pot; a polished Aluminium Stand, or an Enamelled Wall Bracket with polished Aluminium fittings.

The 'Ranworth' Ozonising Fluid specially prepared for use in the Ranworth Porous Pot, gradually percolates through, diffusing into the air a disinfecting vapour having powerful purifying and deodorising properties.

The 'Ranworth' Wall Bracket and Porous Pot. Complete **19/-**
The 'Ranworth' Stand and Porous Pot. Complete **16/-**
The 'Ranworth' Ozonising Fluid; Lavender, Pine or Verbena. Per tin **5/6, 10/6, 39/6**

HAIR PREPARATIONS

'BAYROL'
Royal Bay Rhum and Cantharides, for the hair. The regular use of 'Bayrol' preserves the hair and makes it look its best. In sprinkler bottles **1/9, 3/3**

BAY RUM
White or Brown genuine American, distilled from the leaves. Excellent as a dressing for the hair and for promoting its growth.
Per bottle **3/6, 6/6, 12/6**

BIRCH BALSAM
The wonderful antiseptic and detergent hair wash; prevents scurf
Per bottle **2/6, 4/6, 7/6**

BRILLIANTINE (Solid)
In flat tins. Does not go rancid .. **1/3**

CANTHARIDINE HAIR TONIC
This tonic prevents the hair falling off, makes it grow long and thickens it when thin or impoverished .. Per bottle **3/6, 6/6, 10/6**

CAMOMILE SHAMPOO POWDERS
For making delightfully perfumed egg julep for washing the hair
Packet of 5 .. **1/6** Each **4d**

EAU DE QUININE
An excellent tonic for the hair, agreeably perfumed
Per bottle **4/6, 8/6**

HAIR RESTORER
This preparation is justly celebrated for restoring grey hair to its original colour. It is not a dye, and therefore does not stain the scalp or hands during use
Per bottle **3/9**

HAIR PREPARATIONS

EGG JULEP
For washing the head and cleansing the hair
Per bottle **1/6, 2/6**

ERASMUS WILSON'S HAIR WASH
An original formula for this preparation is in Harrods possession
With oil
Per bot. **3/6, 7/-**
Without oil
Per bot. **3/6, 7/-**

HARRODS HAIR CREAM
The ideal hair fixative. Free from oil and grease
Per bottle .. **1/8**

'JABORANDI' HAIR WASH
'Jaborandi' stops the hair falling and renders the scalp healthy .. .. .. Per bottle **3/-**

HENNA GLOSSA SHAMPOO
(Obtainable only from Harrods). An exquisite preparation; contains sufficient Henna to give the hair a bright glint without in any way altering its colour.
Per pkt. of 5 .. **1/6**
Each .. **4d**

FLOWERS AND HONEY
Essence of Pampas Flowers and Honey in concentrated form. A pomade and hair wash combined. Gives the hair a soft lustrous appearance. In sprinkler bottles
4/6, 8/6, 15/6

JASMIN OIL (Mineral)
For the hair. A pure, specially selected oil of high quality .. .. .. Per bottle **1/6, 2/6, 4/6**

LIME JUICE AND GLYCERINE
Allays irritation, softens the hair
Per bottle **1/-, 1/9, 3/-**

DR. LOCOCK'S PARAFFIN
Per bottle **1/3, 2/3**

LOTION VEGETAL
Violet .. .. .. Per bottle **7/6**

OLIVE OIL SHAMPOO
An ideal preparation for women's and children's hair It does not alter the colour of the hair nor leave it brittle .. Per bottle **2/6**

MADAME ORLOFF'S PETROLEUM HAIR TONIC
For promoting a luxurious and lasting growth of the hair
Per bottle **1/9, 3/-, 5/6**

POMADES FOR THE HAIR
	Per pot	
Cantharidine ..	10d	1/6
Castor Oil ..	10d	1/6
Pomade Crystalline	10d	1/6
Marrow ..	10d	1/6

'ROSARIDINE'
Rosemary and Cantharidine Hair Wash. For renewing and strengthening the hair
Per bottle **2/6, 4/6**

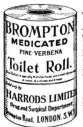

HAIR PREPARATIONS

SAPO (Liquid Soap)
A pure and highly concentrated liquid soap. For manicure and other toilet purposes .. **2/-, 3/6**

SAPONACEOUS SHAMPOO POWDERS
Makes a sweetly perfumed egg wash for the hair
Per box of 8 powders **1/-**

VIGNON BRILLIANTINE
Prepared with the finest quality oil and spirit. Perfumed with White Rose, Lily of the Valley, Jasmin, or Violet

Per bot. **1/6, 2/6, 4/6**

VIOLET OIL
(Mineral) for the hair. A pure, specially selected oil of high quality
Per bot. **1/6, 2/6, 4/6**

WINTHERIA SHAMPOO POWDERS
The ideal hair cleanser. Makes the hair soft and silky
Per packet of 7 .. .. **1/3**

HOUSEHOLD REQUISITES

ANTI-FLY SPRAY SOLUTION (Concentrated)
Exterminates flies, mosquitoes, moths, ants and all winged pests .. .. .. Per bottle **2/6**

ANTI-MOTH
Formerly known as Moth Killer. A very successful moth preventative **2/9, 4/9**

BEETLE POWDER
For destroying cockroaches, black beetles, crickets, etc.
In perforated tins **2/-, 3/9**

BROMPTON PINE-VERBENA TOILET PAPER
A pure Toilet Paper of good quality at a remarkably low price In packets. Size 7½ × 5½ ins.
Dozen .. **8/6** Each .. **9d**
In rolls .. .. each **6d**
Dozen for **5/6**

CLOTH BALL
Dry Cleaner. In White, Black, Nigger Brown, light or dark Grey, Navy Blue, Fawn or Champagne
Each **1/3**

'DEWDROP' PORTABLE HOME WATER-SOFTENER
This apparatus is extremely simple and hygienic, has no moving parts, nothing to adjust or break, and operates without rubber tubes or syphon systems. Made of white porcelain enamelled ware. Size approximately 20 ins. high, 8 ins. diameter. Approximately one gallon of water can be drawn off in 30 seconds when required **£3**

ALL PRICES ARE SUBJECT TO MARKET FLUCTUATIONS

HARRODS LTD

Telephone SLOANE 1234
Telegrams 'EVERYTHING HARRODS LONDON'

LONDON SW 1

DRUG DEPARTMENT

HOUSEHOLD REQUISITES

DORRAH' CREPE TOILET PAPER
Pure, soft and strong. The softest sanitary paper made
In rolls .. Each 5d   Per dozen .. 4/6

DRINKING STRAWS
Boxes of 100 straws .. 10½d

FUMIGATING PASTILLES (Aromatic)
Complete with stand .. .. .. Per box 1/3

GORDON CARBOLIC
An excellent quality paper, 600 sheets. In
packets .. Each 10d
Dozen for .. 9/6
Three dozen .. 25/-
In rolls .. Each 8d
Dozen for .. 7/6
Three dozen .. 21/-

HOUSEHOLD AMMONIA (Cloudy)
For all cleaning purposes. Softens hard water, removes grease and dirt, excellent for cleaning fabrics, etc.
6 bottles 12/-
Per quart bottle .. 2/3
Per gallon .. 6/6
Jars 3/- extra

PERFUMED TOILET AMMONIA
In the following odours : Eau de Cologne, Verbena, Lavender, Rose or Violet
Per dozen 31/6
Per bottle 2/9

INSECT POWDER
In sprinkler tins .. .. .. 8½d and 1/3
In paper .. .. Per lb. 3/6

'KLEANITOFF'
The new, safe and non-inflammable cleaner. Removes dirt, grease, tar, paint, etc. from all articles of clothing
Per bottle 1/3

LAVATORY SEAT COVERS
24 in. .. .. Per pkt. 1/-

MOTH-BANISH
Repels moths, flies, wasps, etc. Leaves no objectionable odour 1/6

ORIENTAL INSECT POWDER
In perforated tins.. 6d and 1/-
1 lb. in paper 3/6

PERMUTIT' WATER SOFTENER
For giving a constant supply of soft water for drinking washing, etc.
Bijou,   20 × 10¾ × 4½ ins. £5 0 0
Standard, 28½ × 13 × 4½ ins. £7 10 0
'Complete Household' .. .. From £29 10 0
Full particulars from Drug section

'QUILLAIA'
Kid Glove Cleaner .. .. .. Per Tin 1/-

HOUSEHOLD REQUISITES

SELTZOGENES
Best quality Screw Pattern— wire covered
3 pints £2 2 0
5 ,, ...   2 5 6
8 ,, ...   3 5 0
Accessories for use with above Funnels and Plug, per set 1/6

SELTZOGENE CHARGES
Per box of 12
2 pints 2/9   3 pints 3/-
5 ,,   3/- 8 ,,   4/-
Packed in tins for export, 6d extra on above prices

THE SODA STREAM
An apparatus for making aerated water. Complete outfit comprises :—Machine, compressed gas and bottles £12 12 0
Further particulars from Drug section

SPARKLET SYPHONS
Complete electro-plated Syphons, 'B' pattern, fitted valve pin
Each 7/6
Also double size 'C' Syphons, as illustrated on right for using 'C' bulbs .. .. Each 8/9
'C' Syphon silver-plated
Each 15/-

SYPHON PARTS
Wearing Parts (Spares) for Sparklet Syphons, easily renewable and ensuring apparatus being kept in constant use. Bulb-neck washer, pin and 1 tube washer .. .. Each 4d
Glass Tubes, 'B' size, with washer .. .. Each 9d
Glass Tubes, 'C' size, with washer .. .. Each 1/-
Sparklet Bulbs, 'C' size for 'C' Syphons. Per box of 6 1/9
Per box of 12 .. .. 3/6
'B' size Bulbs for 'B' Syphons
Per box 2/4

SPARKLOIDS (Mineral Water Tablets)
Containing in their correct proportions the essential ingredients of the following waters :—Soda, Potass, Seltzer, Vichy and Carlsbad, Lithia .. Per bot. 1/6

YEUKLENE
A preparation for removing stains and grease spots from chair covers, clothing, carpets, and for renovating silks. Cannot be sent by rail or post .. Per bot. 1/3

MEDICINAL PREPARATIONS

ANALGESIC BALSAM
Highly esteemed for its analgesic properties in sciatica, lumbago, rheumatism and neuralgia .. Per tube 2/6

ANTISEPTIC THROAT PASTILLES
Per tin 1/3

MEDICINAL PREPARATIONS

APATONE
A British Aperient and Tonic Water specially bottled for Harrods. A wine-glassful of Apatone in the early morning keeps one in good health
Per bottle 1/3

APERIENT PILLS
Per box 4d, 7d 100 for 2/-

ASTHMA POWDER (Gordon's)
Per tin 2/6

BISMUTHATED MAGNESIA POWDER
Per bottle 1/-

BISMUTHATED MAGNESIA TABLETS
Per bottle 1/-

BLOOD CHERRIES
For the nerves and blood. A tonic for men, women and children. Containing red bone marrow
LECITHIN AND HÆMOGLOBIN
Per bottle 1/6

BLOOD PURIFYING MIXTURE
3/-, 5/-

BROMPTON LOZENGES
Per box 9d

BRONCHIAL MIXTURE
Per bottle 2/-

BRONCHIAL PASTILLES
Per box 1/3, 2/6

CALIFORNIAN FRUIT SALINE
Effervescent, health giving, pleasant, cooling, refreshing and invigorating Per bottle 1/6, 2/11

CARLSBAD SALTS
10d, 1/6

CARLSBAD SALTS (Effervescing)
2/9

CHILBLAIN CAPSULES
Per box 1/6

CHILBLAIN LINIMENT
Per bottle 1/3, 2/3

CINNAFORM TABLETS
(Cinnamon and Formalin)
Per bottle 1/-

COLD MIXTURE
Per bottle 1/-

HARRODS COCA WINE
Prepared from Erythroxylon Coca Gives refreshing sleep. Specially recommended for actors, singers, public speakers, etc.
Per bottle .. 5/-   6 bottles .. 29/-

COLOL
Purified Liquid Petroleum Medicinal Paraffin in Jelly form (Raspberry Flavour)
4/-

CORYZA CREAM
A nasal ointment for cold in the head, catarrh, hay fever, etc. In a tube with a nasal nozzle .. 1/6

ALL PRICES ARE SUBJECT TO MARKET FLUCTUATIONS

HARRODS LTD

Telephone SLOANE 1234
Telegrams 'EVERYTHING HARRODS LONDON'

LONDON SW 1

DRUG DEPARTMENT

MEDICINAL PREPARATIONS

CORN CURE
(Harrods)
This preparation is almost infallible
Per bot. **1/3**

'CREOPIN'
A safe and speedy remedy for throat and nasal affections by simple inhalation from a handkerchief or pocket inhaler
Per bottle .. **1/3, 3/-**

'CREOPIN' EMBROCATION
Per bottle **1/3**

'CREOPIN' INHALER
Each **1/-**

'CREOPIN' TABLETS
Invaluable for prevention and cure of sore throat
Per bottle **1/3**

DIARRHŒA MIXTURE **1/9**
DIGESTIVE MIXTURE .. .. **1/9 and 3/-**
DIGESTIVE LOZENGES .. Per box **1/6**

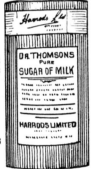

DR. THOMSON'S BATH SALTS
For fat reducing
Per packet **1/3**
Per dozen packets .. **12/6**

DR. THOMSON'S SUGAR OF MILK
Best quality
Per tin .. **2/6, 4/6, 8/6**

EPTIANBAD Anti-obesity Tablets .. Per box **2/3**

EYE LOTION Antiseptic. Soothing and healing .. .. .. Per bottle **1/6**

FOOT CREAM Alleviates the discomfort of hot and tired feet. Invaluable to those who suffer during warm weather
Per bottle **1/-, 2/6**

FOOT POWDER
In sprinkler tins .. **5½d, 10½d**

DR. FORBES BRONCHIAL PASTILLES
This famous formula has earned the complete approval of all who have tried the pastilles
In boxes
Per box **1/3, 2/6**

FORMALINS
Per bottle **1/3**

GORDON'S TONIC PILLS .. .. Per box **1/3**
HÆMOGLOBIN CAPSULES **1/7**
HÆMORRHOIDAL SUPPOSITORIES
Invaluable in treatment of piles .. .. Per box **2/6**

HAY FEVER
Spray solution .. .. .. Per bottle **1/6**

MEDICINAL PREPARATIONS

GASTRIC ANTI-ACID LOZENGES
Per box .. **9d**

GORDON'S ASTHMA POWDER
Per tin .. **2/6**

HEPATIC MIXTURE (Liver) .. Per bottle **1/6**
HERMANNSBAD SALTS .. Each **2/-**
INFLUENZA MIXTURE .. Per bottle **1/6**
LIVER PILLS
Per box .. **4d and 7d** Per 100 **2/-**
LIVER PILLS (Little) .. Per tube **9d**

LEMON SQUASH TABLETS
For making home made lemonade
Per tin **1/6**

ORANGOL
Medicinal Paraffin mixed with the juice of choice oranges Specially suitable for children as it tastes like orange jelly
Per pot **4/-**

PODOPHYLLIN PILLS
A safe and easy laxative Per box **5d, 9d, 2/6**

MARIENBAD TABLETS
(Harrods)
Per box **2/6**

MIDGE LOTION
For allaying the inflammation caused by stings of gnats, mosquitoes, etc.
Per bottle .. **10½d, 1/6**

PARLEMOL
A medical preparation containing 90 per cent. of liquid Medicinal Paraffin in lemon jelly form
Per pot **4/-**

'RAPID' QUININE TABLETS
To cure colds and influenza quickly
Per box .. **1/6**

QUININE AND IRON TONIC
A specially improved preparation. Medically recommended
Per bot. **1/3, 2/3**

RED BRONCHIAL ELIXIR
Eases irritating coughs immediately
Per bottle **1/-, 1/9, 3/-, 4/6**

MEDICINAL PREPARATIONS

'RODORA' (Harrods)
A perfumed insect specific. Non-poisonous, prevents the bites of mosquitoes, gnats, midges, etc.
Per bottle **1/6, 2/6**

ORANGE AND QUININE WINE
An excellent appetising bitter, recommended as the best vehicle for taking cod liver oil
Per bottle .. **3/-** Per dozen **35/-**

ST. PATRICK'S ELIXIR
A well-known Irish remedy for neuralgia, tic-douloureux and similar complaints
Per bottle **1/9**

DR. THOMSON'S SPECIALITIES
Salts, Fat-reducing
Bath .. Per pkt **1/3**
Dozen pkts. .. **12/6**
Sugar Milk .. Per tin **2/6, 4/6, 8/6**

THROAT GARGLE
Antiseptic and astringent. Should be used regularly
Per bottle **1/6**

SYRUP OF FIGS
Pure, reliable, Per bottle **1/-, 2/-**

WINTER PASTILLES
For sore throats and chest colds
Per tin **1/3**

YEAST-LIFE TABLETS
A tonic and lightning restorative
Per tin **1/3, 2/9**

VINBOVINE
A combination of old crusted port, finest malt extract and meat juices. A fine restorative after influenza, and nerve tonic
Per bot. .. **5/-** 6 bots. for **29/-**

SURGICAL APPLIANCES

ACCOUCHEMENT SETS, SOUTHALL'S
	No. 1	No. 2	No. 3	No. 4
Each	**15/-**	**35/-**	**75/-**	**120/-**

ACCOUCHEMENT SHEETS, SOUTHALL'S
	22×18	28×25	33×33	36×36 ins.
Each	**1/3**	**2/3**	**3/-**	**4/-**

ACID TUBES Bent or Straight **6d**

AIR CUSHIONS, CIRCULAR
Best red rubber
Diameters, 14 ins., 15 ins., 16 ins., 17 ins., 18 ins., 19 ins., 20 ins.
Prices **13/6, 14/6, 15/6, 16/6, 17/6, 18/6**

ALL PRICES ARE SUBJECT TO MARKET FLUCTUATIONS

HARRODS LTD

Telephone SLOANE 1234
Telegrams 'EVERYTHING HARRODS LONDON'

LONDON SW1

DRUG DEPARTMENT

SURGICAL APPLIANCES

APRONS, MACKINTOSH ..	..	..	**4/3**
,, ,, With Bib	..	..	**4/9**

ANTI-RHEUMATIC RINGS

Rolled Gold .. .. .. From **7/6** each

ARM SLINGS

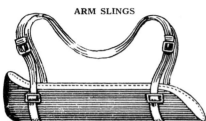

Patent Leather, with Elbow Piece	..	Each	**17/6**
,, ,, without Elbow	..	,,	**10/6**
Triangular Arm Slings, Black Sateen	..	,,	**3/6**
Simplex ,, ,, ,, Webbing		,,	**2/-**

ARTIFICIAL SUNLIGHT LAMPS
From **£5 10 0**

BALANCES (Baby), with Net **7/6**

BANDAGES

Cotton, Bleached, 1 in. by 6 yds.	Each **2d**	Doz.	**1/9**
,, ,, 1½ in. by 6 yds.	,, **2½d**	,,	**2/3**
,, ,, 2 in. by 6 yds.	,, **3d**	,,	**2/9**
,, ,, 2½ in. by 6 yds.	,, **4d**	,,	**3/9**
,, ,, 3 in. by 6 yds.	,, **5d**	,,	**4/9**
,, ,, 3½ in. by 6 yds.	,, **6d**	,,	**5/6**
,, ,, 4 in. by 6 yds.	,, **7d**	,,	**6/6**
,, ,, 6 in. by 6 yds.	,, **9d**	,,	**8/6**

Crepe—2 in.	2½ in.	3 in.	3½ in.	4 in.	6 in.	8 in.
1/6	**2/-**	**2/3**	**2/6**	**2/9**	**4/6**	**5/6**

Domette, 3 in. by 6 yds. ..	..	..	..	**1/6**
,, 6 in. by 6 yds. ..	..	..	..	**2/6**
Elastic Web, 2 in., Blue line, yd.	..	..	**1/6**
,, ,, 2½ in. ,, ,,	..	..	**1/9**
,, ,, 3 in. ,, ,,	..	..	**2/-**
,, Best White, 2 in. ,,	..	..	**1/4**
,, ,, 2½ in. ,,	..	..	**1/6**
,, ,, 3 in. ,,	..	..	**2/-**

Flannel, each 6 yards long—

Width	3 in.	4 in.
	1/9	**2/6**

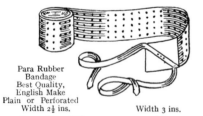

Para Rubber
Bandage
Best Quality,
English Make
Plain or Perforated
Width 2½ ins.   Width 3 ins.

Length	Plain	Perforated	Length	Plain	Perforated
5 ft.	**3/6**	**4/3**	5 ft.	**4/3**	**5/-**
7½ ,,	**4/6**	**5/6**	7½ ,,	**5/6**	**6/3**
10½ ,,	**6/3**	**7/-**	10½ ,,	**6/9**	**7/6**
15 ,,	**8/-**	**8/9**	15 ,,	**10/-**	**10/9**
21 ,,	**10/6**	**11/3**	21 ,,	**11/6**	**12/3**

Stockinette, **1/-** per yard
Triangular, **1/-** Unbleached, **1/6**

BASINS, SURGICAL
Enamelled Iron (circular)

Diameter	4 in.	6 in.	8 in.	10 in.	12 in.
	9d	**1/3**	**1/6**	**2/3**	**3/3**

SURGICAL APPLIANCES

BANDAGE WINDERS

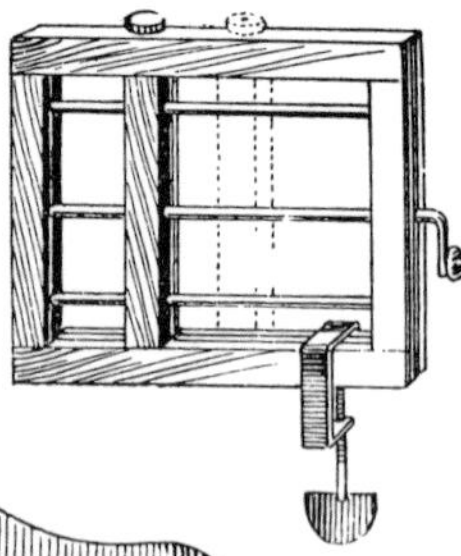

Bandage Winder, strongly made; will wind bandages of any width up to 6 ins. Complete with Clamp for attaching to table .. **4/-**

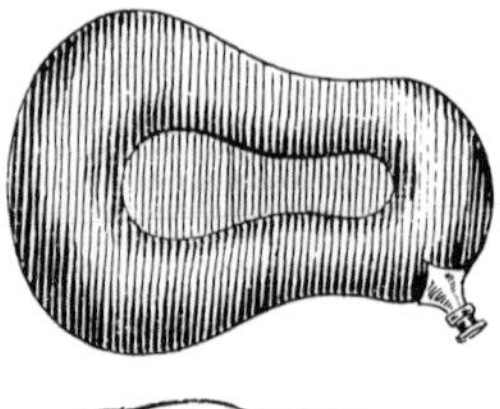

BED BATHS
India-Rubber
Small, Each **17/6**
Large ,, **21/-**

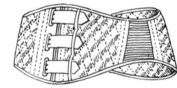

BED BATHS, Enamelled and Padded	Each **17/6**
BED CRADLE, Metal	.. **8/6, 10/6**
,, PANS, Circular, Porcelain	.. .. **12/6**
,, ,, Slipper ,,	.. **7/6, 12/6**
,, ,, ,, Enamelled Iron	**9/6, 12/6**
,, ,, Perfection ..	.. **7/6, 9/-**

SUPPORTING BELTS FOR LADIES
15/-, 17/6, 21/-, 25/-, 37/6

BELTS, ABDOMINAL (MEN'S)

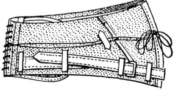

Lumbago Belt, Lined and Interlined with Flannel
Each **12/6**

BELTS, ABDOMINAL (LADIES')

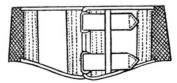

Cotton Belts, for supporting and preserving the shape
To lace at back, with side straps .. Each **25/-**
In Best Silk .. .. .. ,, **37/6**

'The Imperial,' Belt, 6 in. Dove Web, Elastic Sides
Each **7/6**

SURGICAL APPLIANCES

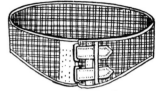

'The Zepyrine' Belt In Cellular Cloth Each **7/6**

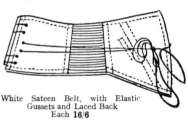

White Sateen Belt, with Elastic
Gussets and Laced Back
Each **16/6**

BELTS (UMBILICAL HERNIA)

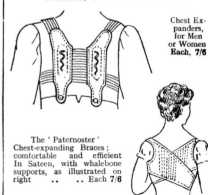

India-Rubber Belts for
Children **3/6**
*Give full measurements
when ordering*

BINDERS Southall's ..	..	..	..	**3/6**
BLACKHEAD REMOVERS	..	..	**6d, 9d**
BOTTLE CAPS Best Rubber	..	..	**4½d**

BOTTLES (in Boxwood Cases)

Ozs.	½	1	2	4	6	8	10
	2/3	**2/9**	**3/3**	**5/-**	**6/6**	**8/6**	**10/6**

(In Nickel Cases)

Ozs.	½	1	2	4	6	8
	2/-	**2/-**	**2/6**	**3/6**	**5/-**	**5/6**

BOUGIES

Gum Elastic, Olivary		
Sizes 1 to 12	Each	**1/6**
Gum Elastic, Cylindrical		
Sizes 1 to 12	Each	**1/-**

BRACES, CHEST EXPANDING

Chest Expanders, for Men or Women
Each, **7/6**

The 'Paternoster' Chest-expanding Braces; comfortable and efficient In Sateen, with whalebone supports, as illustrated on right .. .. Each **7/6**

BREAST GLASSES
For self-use
Each **1/6**

ALL PRICES ARE SUBJECT TO MARKET FLUCTUATIONS

HARRODS LTD

Telephone SLOANE 1234
Telegrams 'EVERYTHING HARRODS LONDON'

LONDON S W 1

DRUG DEPARTMENT

SURGICAL APPLIANCES

Breast Relievers .. .. Each **2/6, 3/6**
,, Shields (Southall's) .. ,, **4/-**

BRUSHES, CAMEL HAIR

Please quote size number when ordering

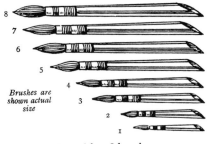

Brushes are shown actual size

From **1d** to **8d** each

Throat. Straight or bent shape **6d, 8d**

BUNION PLASTERS

Blue Jay .. .. .. Packet **2/-**
Allcock's .. .. .. ,, **1/3**

BUNION SHIELDS

Felt, thin .. .. .. Box **5½d**
,, thick .. .. .. ,, **6½d**
Maw's Felt, thin .. .. ,, **6½d**
,, ,, thick .. .. ,, **7½d**
Rubad (self-adhesive) .. ,, **10½d**

CATHETERS

When ordering, please state index number of pattern required

Red Rubber Catheters, straight or funnel end (Sizes 1-12) .. .. Each **1/6**
Brown Elastic Gum Catheters, with Wires complete. Best quality (Sizes 1-12) .. **1/6**

Female Catheters

Glass, Straight **6d**
Glass, Curved (Queen Charlotte's Hospital pattern) **6d**
Glass, in Nickel-plated case .. **1/-**

CHEST PROTECTORS

Single, Grey Flannel .. .. Each **2/6**
Double, ,, ,, ... ,, **4/6**

CATHETER BOXES .. Each **4/9**

Catheter Cases, for carrying Catheters in the pocket. Centre Box for Carbolised Lubricant Each **2/6**
Catheter Cleaners, for fixing to Tap .. .. .. ,, **3/6**
Catheter Stretchers .. .. ,, **6/6**
Caustic Pencils .. .. ,, **9d**
Charts for Temperature.. .. Doz. **9d**
Chart Boards .. .. .. Each **2/6**

SURGICAL APPLIANCES
CLINICAL THERMOMETERS

Owing to their fragile nature we cannot send these Thermometers by Post or Carrier except at Purchaser's own risk

2-minute, plain, 2/-	Lens Front	..	2/6
1 ,, ,, 2/6	,, ,,	..	3/-
½ ,, ,, 3/-	,, ,,	..	3/6
	"With Kew Certificate, 4/6"		
Centigrade, ½ minute, Lens Front		..	3/6
Repello, ½ minute Lens		..	8/-
Veterinary, plain, 2 minute		..	4/6
Clinical Thermometer Resetter		..	1/3
,, ,, Acello Resetter		..	2/6

CORN PLASTERS

Allcock's **9d, 1/3**
Blue Jay .. .. .. Per pkt. **2/-**
Felt, thin .. .. .. Per box **6½d**
,, thick .. .. .. ,, **7½d**
Maws' thin .. .. .. ,, **6½d**
,, thick .. .. .. ,, **7½d**
Olympic Corn Dots .. .. ,, **7d, 1/3**
Perfection .. .. .. ,, **7d, 1/3**
Rubad (self-adhesive) .. .. ,, **10½d**

CORN SILK .. .. Per packet **7½d**

COTTON WOOLS

Superfine .. Per lb. **3/9**, ½ lb. **1/11**, ¼ lb. **1/-**, 2 oz. **7d**
Hospital .. .. .. Per lb. **2/-**
Johnson & Johnson's .. ¼ lb. **1/3**, ½ lb. **2/4**, 1 lb. **4/6**
Unbleached .. .. .. Per lb. **1/3**

CUPPING GLASSES Fine quality (Set of three) **4/6**

DENTABATHS **4/6**

DENTA REFILLS **2/6**

DENTAL MIRRORS **2/6**

DENTAL SILK

Waxed or unwaxed, per reel of 12 yds. **1/-**, 150 yds. **8/6**
Lister's (tube) .. 12 yds. **1/1½**, 24 yds. **1/10½**

DENTAL SUCTION CUPS .. 12 for **1/6**

,, **SYRINGES** .. **4/6, 7/6, 8/6**
,, ,, With sterilizer **10/6, 12/6**

DENTAL WAX .. .. Per stick **4½d**

DOUCHES (Combination)

Rubber Douche and Hot Water Bottle Combined In Pouches
Pints 2 3 4
12/6, 13/6, 14/6
Enamelled Steel (white)

All Douches are fitted with 6 ft. India-Rubber Tubing and Vulcanite Mounts, including Vagina Tube, Rectum Tube and Tap

2 pint .. **5/-**
3 pint .. **5/6**
4 pint .. **6/-**

SURGICAL APPLIANCES

FOUNTAIN ENGLISH-MADE RUBBER DOUCHE

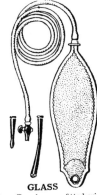

In Pouches, 2, 3, 4 Pint
Complete **9/6, 10/6, 11/6**

GLASS

All these Douches are fitted with 6 ft. India-Rubber Tubing and Vulcanite Mounts, including Vagina Tube, Rectum Tube and Tap
Glass, with Enamelled Tin Holder—
2 pint, each **4/6** 3 pint, each **5/6**
4 pint ,, **6/6** 6 pint ,, **8/6**

PORCELAIN

Finest Quality, complete
3 pint, **7/6** 4 pint, **8/6**

No. D R 89 S.

Set of 3, Vagina Tube, Rectum Tube, and Tap .. **1/3**
Glass Vaginal Tubes, curved or straight .. each **9d**
Gum Elastic Vaginal Tubes **6d**
India-Rubber Tubes, Rectal, each **10½d, 1/3**, ,, **2/3, 3/3**
India-Rubber Tubing 2 yard **1/9**
Tube Clip .. .. .. each **9d**
DRAINAGE TUBING .. .. Per yard **10d**
DREDGERS, GLASS .. .. Per yard **10d**
,, **WOOD** **4½d, 1/-, 3/-**
DROPPERS, EYE .. .. In box **6d**
,, **MEDICINE** .. .. In box **6d**

EAR CAPS

The 'Claxton' Patent Improved. When ordering send measurements from round the forehead to back of head, and from lobe of one ear, over the head, to lobe of other ear .. .. Each **5/-**

EAR DEFENDERS — (Mallock Armstrong's Patent).—Made in five sizes: oo extra small, o small, 1 medium, 2 large, 3 extra large, Per pair, in metal case with cleaner **4/-**
EAR MOPS .. .. .. Each **1/6**
,, **PLUGS** .. .. Per packet **1/-**
,, **SPECULUMS (TOYNBEA)** Set of 3 **7/6**
,, **SPONGES** .. .. Each **6d**
,, **SYRINGES, GLASS**
(Curved or straight) ½ oz. **10½d**
1 oz. **1/3**
,, Red Rubber
Long Nozzle .. Each **1/9**

EAR APPLIANCES FOR THE DEAF
CONVERSATION TUBE

A well-tried and successful appliance. Cotton Covered, with vulcanite ends. Simple in construction, clean **10/6, 18/6, 21/-**
Ear Phone, Brompton, **63/-**
Ear Phone Globe **70/-**

ALL PRICES ARE SUBJECT TO MARKET FLUCTUATIONS

HARRODS LTD

Telephone SLOANE 1234
Telegrams 'EVERYTHING HARRODS LONDON'

LONDON S W 1

DRUG DEPARTMENT

SURGICAL APPLIANCES

ELECTROPHONES

Otophone, Marconi £25
Ossiphone, „ extra £2 2 0

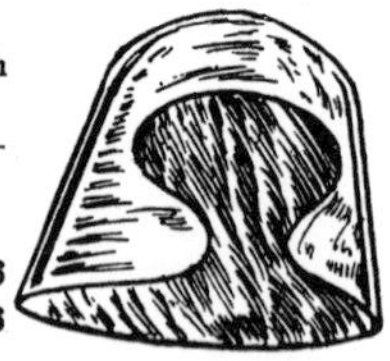

Ear Shells. When in use both hands are left quite free
Each 25/-

'Dorrah' Ear Shells
Pair 10/6
Each 5/6

EAR TRUMPETS

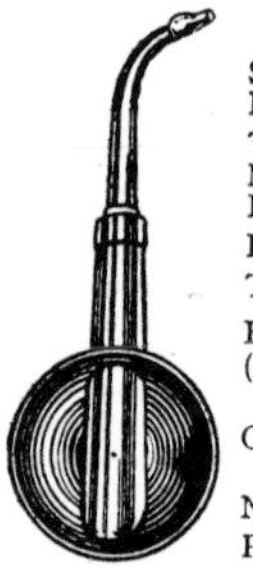

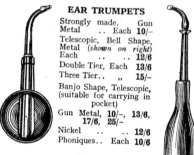

Strongly made. Gun Metal .. Each 10/-
Telescopic, Bell Shape, Metal (*shown on right*) Each 12/6
Double Tier, Each 13/6
Three Tier.. „ 15/-
Banjo Shape, Telescopic, (suitable for carrying in pocket)
Gun Metal, 10/-, 13/6, 17/6, 25/-
Nickel 12/6
Phoniques.. Each 10/6

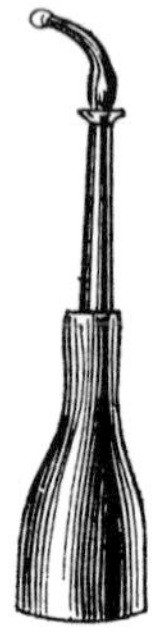

ENEMAS

The 'Syphon' Enema. Best Quality, Seamless Black. Warranted not to split. In oval hinged box Each 5/9
The 'Dorrah' Enema, made specially for Harrods Ltd. .. .. Each 8/6
Ingram's Sterilendum Best Quality Rubber. Fitted best Glass Valves .. .. .. Each 5/6
Suction End Enema.. .. .. .. Each 5/6
Seamless Black Rubber Hospital Enema, in cardboard box .. .. Each 4/6

EVERHOT

Bottle 12/6
„ Refill 1/-

EYE BATHS

Glass 6d, 1/3
Aluminium 9d
Porcelain 6d
Rubber 1/6

EYE DROPPERS

In box (Glass) 6d
Ointment Rods .. .. $4\frac{1}{2}$d

EYE SHADES

For wear when reading .. .. Each 1/6
Celluloid, single 6d
Silk, Black „ 1/-
„ „ double 1/6
Straw, „ single 1/6

EYE SPONGES 6d

FEEDERS

The 'Allenbury's' Feeder, complete in cardboard box .. .. Each 1/6
Bottles (spare) .. .. .. „ $10\frac{1}{2}$
Valves („) .. .. .. „ $3\frac{1}{2}$d
Teats („) .. .. .. „ $4\frac{1}{2}$d
Glaxo Feeding Bottle .. .. „ 1/6
„ Teats .. .. .. „ $4\frac{1}{2}$d
„ Valves .. .. .. „ $3\frac{1}{2}$d

FEEDING CUPS

White China .. .. Each 2/6
Decorated Earthenware .. .. „ 2/9
The Ideal Feeding Cup (Glass) .. „ 1/3
„ „ „ „ (Earthenware) .. „ 1/6
„ „ „ „ (China) .. „ 2/6

FINGER STALLS

Chamois 9d
Leather 1/-
Rubber 4d
Silk 9d
Suede 1/-

SURGICAL APPLIANCES

FORCEPS

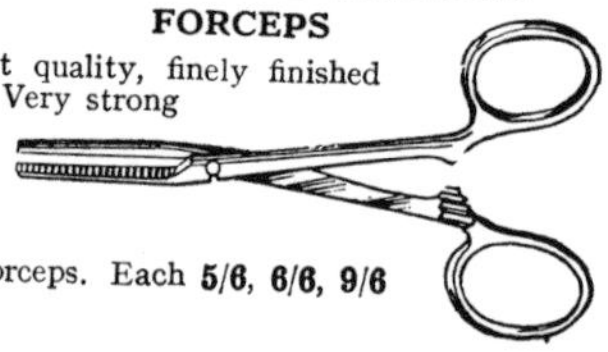

All of best quality, finely finished
Very strong

Dressing Forceps. Each 5/6, 6/6, 9/6

For General Surgical use
Each 1/9

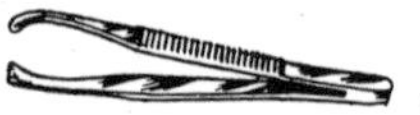

For Removing Hairs, etc. Each .. 10½d, 1/3
For Removing Splinters Each .. $10\frac{1}{2}$d, 1/3
Forceps, Artery, curved or straight ..Each 4/6, 5/6

FIRST AID CASES

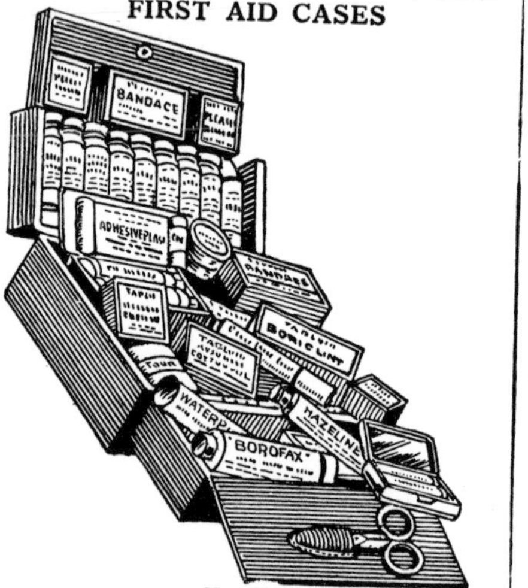

No. 702
'TABLOID' BRAND FIRST AID CASE

$7\frac{1}{4} \times 5\frac{1}{4} \times 3$ inches. Contains 'Tabloid' Bandages and Dressings, 'Vaporole' Aromatic Ammonia for use as Smelling Salts, 'Borofax,' 'Hazeline' Cream, Sal Volatile, Carron Oil (solidified), Tourniquet, Jaconet, Castor Oil, Plaster, Protective Skin, Scissors, Pins, etc. and eight tubes of 'Tabloid' and 'Soloid' Brand products. In Rex Red, Royal Blue or Imperial Green Enamelled Leather £5

No. 709 'TABLOID' FIRST AID
(*The Boy Scout's*)

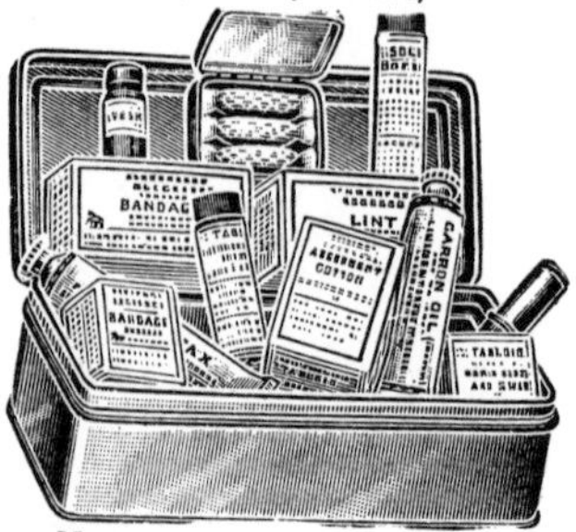

Measurements: $6\frac{5}{8} \times 3\frac{1}{8} \times 2$ in.

CONTENTS

'Tabloid' Brand Compressed Dressings—
1 Bandage 1 in. × 3 yds.
1 „ 1 in. × 6 yds.
1 „ Triangular
2 packets Absorbent Cotton ¼ oz.
1 packet Lint, 1 oz.
1 packet Cotton, Boric, 1 oz.

Ointments—
'Borofax'
Carron Oil (*solidified*)

Instruments, Etc.—
Camel-hair Brush
Safety Pins
Sundries—
Jaconet
Plaster, Adhesive
Protective Skin
'Vaporole' Brand Products—
Aromatic Ammonia (*for use as Smelling Salts*)
Iodine Tincture (*for use as an Antiseptic*)

In Rex Red or Royal Blue Enamelled Metal .. 11/-

SURGICAL APPLIANCES

No. 706
'TABLOID' BRAND FIRST AID CASE
('The Aviator's' Regd.)

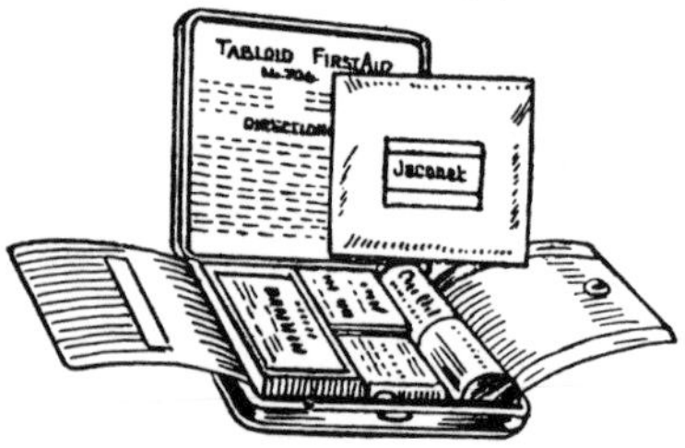

Aluminium Case: $3\frac{1}{2}$ by 3 by $\frac{3}{4}$ inches

Contains a 'Tabloid' Bandage, 'Tabloid' Boracic Gauze, Carron Oil (solidified), 'Vaporole' Aromatic Ammonia for use as Smelling Salts, Adhesive Plaster, Court Plaster, Jaconet, Pins, etc. This equipment is carried by many well-known aviators 20/-

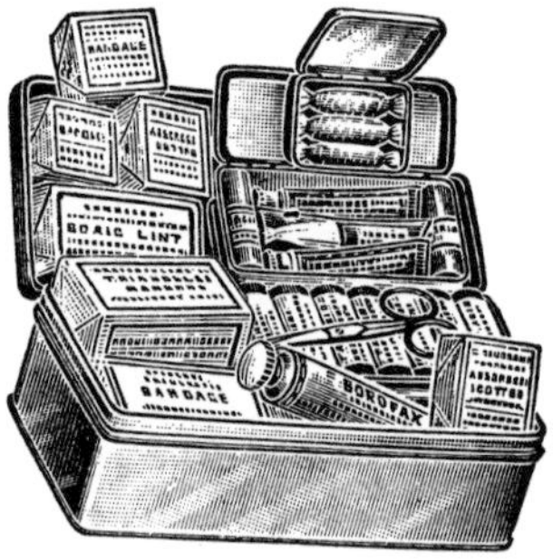

No. 707 'TABLOID' BRAND FIRST AID

$6\frac{5}{8} \times 3\frac{1}{8} \times 2$ inches. Contains: 'Tabloid' Bandages and Dressings, 'Vaporole' Iodine Tincture, 'Vaporole' Aromatic Ammonia for use as Smelling Salts, 'Borofax' Brand Boric Acid Ointment, Carron Oil (solidified) and Jaconet, Castor Oil, Plaster, Protective Skin, Scissors, Pins, etc., and seven tubes of 'Tabloid' and 'Soloid' Brand products. In Rex Red, Royal Blue or Imperial Green Enamelled Metal, or in Aluminised Metal 16/6

No. 708
'TABLOID' BRAND FIRST AID CASE
('The Nurse's' Regd.)

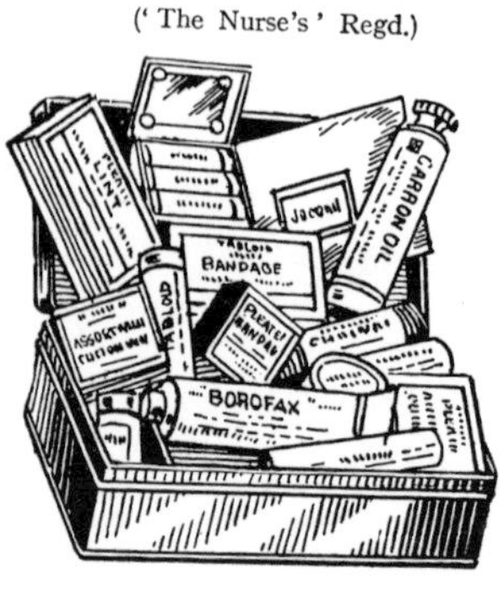

Measurements: $6\frac{5}{8} \times 3\frac{1}{8} \times 2$ inches

Contains: 'Tabloid' Bandages and Dressings, 'Vaporole' Aromatic Ammonia for use as Smelling Salts, 'Borofax,' Carron Oil (solidified), Jaconet, Plaster, Protective Skin, Pins, etc., and two tubes of 'Tabloid' and 'Soloid' Brand Products. In Aluminised Metal 11/-

Webbing Holder for attaching this equipment to the waist-belt or cycle handle-bar 1/-

ALL PRICES ARE SUBJECT TO MARKET FLUCTUATIONS

DRUG DEPARTMENT

SURGICAL APPLIANCES

Hosiery, Elastic—continued

THIGH STOCKING — Take Circumference at
IHGFABCDE. Length from ground to F, and F to
H or I according to the length required
The following are available from stock

			Per pair	
Anklets, Cotton	..	..	Per pair	9/6
,, Cotton and Silk	..	..	,,	12/6
,, Silk	..	..	,,	13/6
Dress Silk	..	..	,,	32/6
Knee Caps, Cotton	..	..	,,	10/6
,, Cotton and Silk	..	..	,,	13/6
,, Silk	..	..	,,	15/6
Dress Silk	..	..	,,	37/6
Leggings, Cotton	..	..	,,	11/6
,, Cotton and Silk	..	..	,,	13/6
,, Silk	..	..	,,	16/6
Dress Silk	..	..	,,	39/6
Stockings, Cotton	..	..	,,	15/6
,, Cotton and Silk	..	..	,,	19/6
,, Silk	..	..	,,	22/6
Dress Silk	..	..	,,	57/6

Additional charge for making to order, from 2/6 per
pair
Knee Stockings, Wristlets, Thigh Stockings, or Knee
Leggings only made to order. Special quotations
given on receipt of dimensions

HOT BOTTLES

Everhot	..	..	..	12/6
,, Refills	..	..	..	1/-

ICE BAGS

Best Check

8 in. ..	Each	2/6
9 in. ..	,,	2/9
10 in. ..	,,	3/3

INHALERS

In Earthenware—

½ pint 3/-	1 pint 4/6
1 quart	..	7/6
Burney Yeo	..	1/3
Pockett	..	1/3

INJECTION BOTTLES

Best Quality Rubber and
Bone Nozzle

1 oz.	2 oz.	3 oz
2/6	2/9	3/-
4 oz.	6 oz.	8 oz
3/3	3/6	3/9

INSULATORS

Vulcanite Stem	..	..	..	4/6

JACONET

Pink, 42 ins. wide	..	Per yard	3/6
White, 42 ins. wide	..	,,	3/6

KIDNEY DISHES

Enamelled Iron	1/-, 1/6, 2/6
Glass	2/6
Porcelain	2/6, 3/6, 4/-

SURGICAL APPLIANCES

KNAPKINETTES
.. .. 3/6, 4/6, 5/6

LACTOMETERS

For testing Milk	..	..	..	Each 3/6

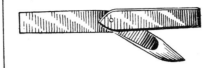

Lancets, Abscess	..	..	Each 1/8

Bistouries, Aseptic, Curved or Straight	..	..	5/6

LANCETS

Lancets, for Bleeding
Each 1/9

Lancets, Gum
Each, 5/9

LAMB'S WOOL

Genuine	..	Per oz. 1/-	Per lb. 10/6

LIGATURES
.. .. 3/-, 3/6

LINTS

Plain Absorbent	¼ lb 1/2,	½ lb 2/-,	1 lb. 3/9
Boracic	¼ lb. 10d,	½ lb. 1/6,	1 lb. 2/9

LITMUS BOOKS

Blue or Red	..	..	..	Each 3d

MAXIM'S, Sir Hiram, Pipe of Peace and Inhaler

complete	..	..	..	15/6
,, Pipe of Peace	..	..	..	8/6
,, Menthol Inhaler	..	..	..	7/6
,, Pocket Inhaler	..	..	..	5/-

MASSAGE ROLLERS

Kim Flexible Rollers	..	12/6
Pearl	..	7/6, 15/-
The Plunkt	..	7/6, 19/6, 25/-
The Swedish Rub-away	15/-, 15/6, 21/-, 30/-

MEASURES

Graduated Medicine
Tumbler, 4 Table-
spoons, Super
quality .. Each 7½d
Do. in Case Each 1/6
do. and Minim
Measure .. Each 2/-

Minim, Glass
Each 6d
(As shown on right)

Medicine Glass—
Graduated .. Each 1/9
Measures, Glass—
Conical. Ozs. 1 2 4 6
9d 1/3 3/6 9/-
Cylindrical
Ozs. 4 10 20 40
1/6 2/9 5/9 10/-
Measure Jug (Enamelled Iron)
Each 10 oz., 2/3 ; 20 oz., 3/- ;
40 oz. 4/6
Measure Jugs (Earthenware)
Each 10 oz., 2/- ; 20 oz., 2/9 ;
40 oz., 3/9

Measure (Allenbury Food)	..	..	Each 1/6
,, (,, Dry Food)	..	..	,, 1/6

SURGICAL APPLIANCES

MEDICINE Droppers	..	..	6d
,, Tubes, Glass, bent or straight	..	4½d
MOPS Absorbent Cotton	..	.. 1 doz.	1/6

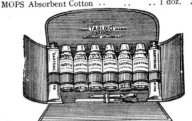

No. 114. 'TABLOID' BRAND MEDICINE POCKET CASE
The 'Alpine'

9¾ × 4¼ × 1¼ ins. For Alpine travellers, mountaineers
and tourists, this little case is exceptionally useful
It is fitted with four ½ oz. phials of 'Tabloid' products,
also Chlorodyne, Boric Acid Lotion, 'Dartring'
Lanoline, etc.—the equipment recommended by the
Alpine Club Committee. Weight, 9½ ozs. In Morocco
Leather .. .. Each 40/-

No. 115. 'TABLOID' BRAND MEDICINE POCKET CASE
Measurements 9¼ × 4¼ × 1½ ins. In Morocco Leather,
Contains ten ½ oz. phials of 'Tabloid' Brand products,
Ammonium Bromide, Chloral Hydrate, Dover Powder
Iron and Arsenic Compound, Laxative Vegetable,
Potassium Chlorate, Quinine Bisulphate, Rhubarb and
Soda, gusset pocket for dressings or papers, etc. 50/-

No. 112. 'TABLOID' BRAND MEDICINE POCKET CASE

Measurements 4 ×
3 × 1 ins. Specially
adapted for cyclists,
tourists, etc. Will be
found to meet all ord-
inary requirements.
Made of nickel-plated
metal. Fitted with
five glass-stoppered
bottles of 'Tabloid'
Brand products,
Bismuth and Soda,
Lead and Opium,
Potassium Chlorate,
Tonic Compound and
Laxative Vegetable
15/6

No. 1 TRAVELLER'S MEDICINE CASE

Containing two glass-
stoppered bottles,
two screw-cap bottles,
one glass Pot Scissors
and Bone Spoon. In
Leather .. 21/-

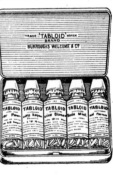

ALL PRICES ARE SUBJECT TO MARKET FLUCTUATIONS

HARRODS LTD

Telephone SLOANE 1234
Telegrams 'EVERYTHING HARRODS LONDON'

LONDON S W 1

DRUG DEPARTMENT

SURGICAL APPLIANCES

No. 3 TRAVELLER'S MEDICINE CASE
Containing 2 by 1 oz. wide-mouthed glass-stoppered bottles, 5 by 1 oz. glass-stoppered bottles, 2 by ½ oz. ditto, Medicine Measure, Scissors, Bone Spoon and Camel Hair Pencil. In Leather **49/6**

No. 2 TRAVELLER'S MEDICINE CASE
Containing four glass-stoppered bottles (2 by ½ oz. and 2 by 1 oz.), Scissors, Camel Hair Pencil and Bone Spoon. In Leather **21/-**

NASAL DOUCHES

Kress & Owen	..	**1/-**
Harrods	..	**9d**

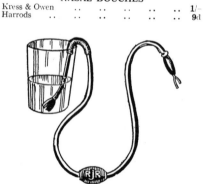

Nasal Douche, in box complete .. .. Each **4/3**

NASAL SYRINGES

Glass, with Vulcanite Fittings	..	**4/6**
Rubber	..	**1/9, 2/3**

NEEDLES, SURGICAL .. Per packet **1/6**

Surgical and Silk (in tube).. ..	**2/6**
Hypodermic	**9d, 1/-, 1/3**
Hypodermic, Flat	**7/6**

SURGICAL APPLIANCES

NIPPLE SHIELDS

India-rubber..	.. Each	**6d**
Glass	.. ..	**1/6**
Metal..	Per pair	**1/-**

NOZZLES

Rectal, Glass	**4½d**
Rectal, Vulcanite	**11½d**
Vaginal, Vulcanite	**6d**
Vaginal, Glass	**6d**
Vaginal, Rubber	**6d**

OBESITY REDUCERS

Jordan Roller	**35/- 42/-**
Vaco Cup	**20/-**

ŒSOPHAGUS TUBES.. .. From **3/6** to **6/6**

OILED SILK

Green. Size, yard				
	⅛/9d	¼/2/3	½/4/-	1/7/6

OINTMENT INTRODUCERS

Boxwood **1/9**

OUTAPLASMA **3/-**

PEDICURE **1/3**

PESSARIES

Pro-Race, Check, Solid rim	**3/-**
,, ,, Air rim	**5/-**
In three sizes, Small, Medium, Large	

PLASTERS

Belladonna, Breast	**10½d**
Back	**10½d, 1/4**
Court (black, white, pink or tri-colour)	**10½d, 1/3**
Gold Beater' Skin	**6d**
Taylor's Adhesive—5 yard spools—	

	½ in.	1 in.	1½ in.	2 in
	1/3	1/9	2/3	2/6
10 yard spools	2/-	2/9	3/3	—
Menthol (Burroughs, Wellcome & Co.)				2/-

POULTICE BAGS .. .. .. Each **6d**

POWDER BLOWERS

De Vilbiss Powder Blower, No. 36

For powder applications. The adjustable tip on this Powder Blower is a De Vilbiss feature. The powder is diffused perfectly and evenly and a counter current of air prevents bunching **6/6**

PROBES

Silver	**1/3, 3/-**
Director	**1/9**

PULSE GLASSES **1/3, 2/6**

RECTAL FEEDERS **3/6**
,, Tube (Vulcanite) **6d**

REJUVENATOR, OVERBECK'S

Portable Model	**£6 0 0**
Standard	**£6 6 0**
High Power	**£7 10 0**
Batteries for above **17/6 ; 30/- ; 45/-**	

SURGICAL APPLIANCES

RESPIRATORS

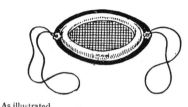

As illustrated **3/-**

SAFETY PINS

Maw's assorted	Per box	**9d**
'Ongard'	,,	**7d**
'M.D.'	,,	**1/-**

SANITARY BELTS

Sanita Belt	**1/6**
Phellose	**1/6, 2/6**

SANITARY TOWELS

	Size 0	1	2	3	4
'Dorrah'	—	1/-	1/3	1/9	2/-
'Hosezene'	—	1/3	1/8	2/3	2/6
'Mene' ..	1/-	1/2	1/7	2/-	2/3
'Santose' (Cellulose)	Ord. size 1/9		Extra large 2/4		

'Southall's	0	1	2	3	4	5	x	xx
	1/-	1/2	1/7	2/-	2/3	3/-	3/3	3/6

Southall's Compressed **1/6 2/- 2/6 3/-**

SANITARY SPONGES .. .. Each **1/-**

SANITARY SPONGES

SCALPELS

Plain handles, Aseptic .. .. .. six sizes **4/6**

SCISSORS, SURGICAL

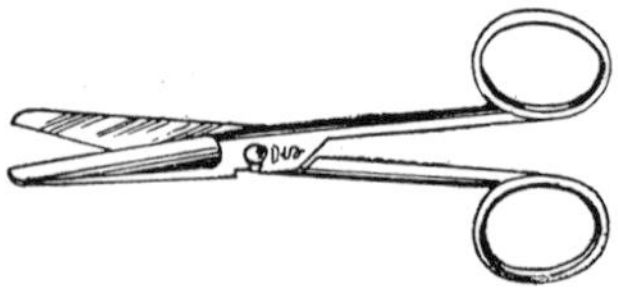

Blunt, straight Size 5 in. Screw **2/3** Detachable **6/6**

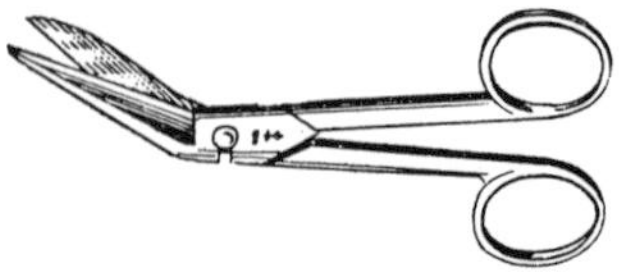

Bent, blunt or one or both points Screw Joints Size 4½ ins. **3/6**

Curved, blunt one or both points Screw joints Size 4½ ins. **3/6**

Scissors (Baby) **1/6, 2/-** Silkworm Cut **1/9**

SOOTHERS

A—India-Rubber Ring and Pad, and Non-collapsible Teat .. .. .. Each **10½d**
B—India-Rubber, one hard and one soft Teat .. .. Each **10½d**
C—Bone Ring and Shield, Non-collapsible Teat .. .. .. Each **6d**
C—India-Rubber Ring and Teat, with Bone Shield .. .. .. Each **7½d**
C—All Rubber .. .. Each **7¾d**

ALL PRICES ARE SUBJECT TO MARKET FLUCTUATIONS

HARRODS LTD

Telephone SLOANE 1234
Telegrams 'EVERYTHING HARRODS LONDON'

LONDON S W 1

DRUG DEPARTMENT

SURGICAL APPLIANCES
STETHOSCOPES

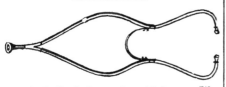

Superior Quality Stethoscope, Ivory fitted .. 7/6

STIRRING RODS

Glass or Vulcanite, Flat End	..	Each	6d

STYPTIC PENCILS 6d
SWAB HOLDERS 3/6
SWAB STICKS 1/6

SYRINGES

Ear, All Glass	8d, 9d, 1/3, 2/6
Ear, Rubber	1/6, 1/9

Glycerine, Vulcanite and Glass—

Size	2 dram.	½ oz.	1 oz.
	1/3	1/6	1/9

The 'Record' Hypodermic and Serum Syringes, every part sterilizable, including Metal Case .. from 3/6

Hypodermic, All Glass 3/6, 4/6
Injection (see Injection Bottles)
Nasal (see Nasal Syringes)

Urethral, Glass	9d, 1/3
,, Glass and Vulcanite ..	1/6, 2/-, 2/6
,, Rubber	1/6, 2/-, 2/6
Veterinary	17/6

SUSPENSORY BANDAGES

F.S. ..	.. Cotton ..	..	2/6
F.S. ..	.. Silk ..	..	3/6
No. 62 ..	.. Silk ..	..	4/6
Sports ..	.. Cotton ..	..	2/6
O.P.C. ..	.. Silk ..	..	4/6

WHIRLING SPRAYS

Marvel ..	.. .. ..	Each	15/-
Ingrams ..	.. .. ..	,,	13/6
Good Quality ..	.. ..	,,	5/-

WRIST STRAPS

Suede	..	1/3, 1/9
Leather	..	1/6
Elastic	..	2/6

SURGICAL APPLIANCES
THERMOMETERS

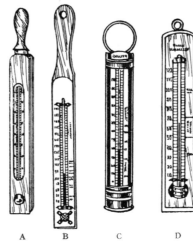

A   B   C   D

A	For Bath	..	1/6
B	,,	..	3/3
C	,,	..	2/3
D	For Room ..	1/3, 3/6, 4/6
Food ..	..	..	2/3

Thermometers, Clinical, see page 700

TONGUE DEPRESSORS

Glass ..	.. .. ..	1/9
Nickel	.. .. ..	3/6

TONGUE SCRAPERS 1/6

TOW .. .. Per lb. 1/6

TRUSSES

Trusses of any kind made to order

NOTE.—It is most important when ordering to state whether for the right or left sides and whether a Single or Double Truss is required. Measurement required is the circumference taken one inch below top of hips

Washable Truss, made of Vulcanite Rubber

Single..	.. .. ..	Each	18/6
Double	.. .. ..	,,	25/6

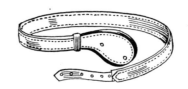

Ordinary Truss Single	.. ..	Each	9/6
,, ,, Double	.. ..	,,	10/6

SURGICAL APPLIANCES

Salmon and Ody's Pattern, with Movable Pads
Single 12/6
Double 16/6

URINALS

Boat Shape
China .. 3/6

Boat Shape
Rubber .. 8/6

Perfection
(Female) .. 6/-

Male or Female
Enamelled Iron
6/9
Male or Female
Earthenware 3/6

Urinal, Male, for Travelling purposes. etc. For Night and Day Use
All Rubber .. .. Each 21/-
Rubber and Canvas .. ,, 21/-

Female, for Night and Day Use Straps to be Self-adjusted
All Rubber .. .. Each 21/-
Rubber and Canvas .. ,, 21/-

URINOMETERS 3/-
Spare Glass 1/3

VACCINATION PADS Each 7½d
Shields, Small.. .. .. 10½d
,, Large 1/6

VIOLET RAY

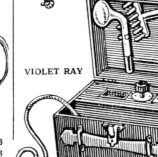

Type A	Size 9½ × 6 × 6 ins.
In black leatheroid case	£4 0 0
Voltage, 32, 50, 110 and 120
Type B	Size 9½ × 6 × 6 ins.
Universal voltage mahogany case ..	£5 5 0

ALL PRICES ARE SUBJECT TO MARKET FLUCTUATIONS

HARRODS LTD

Telephone SLOANE 1234
Telegrams 'EVERYTHING HARRODS LONDON'

LONDON S W 1

DRUG DEPARTMENT

Harrods Price List of Drugs and Chemicals

Agar Agar .. .. 4 oz., **3/–** ; ½ lb., **5/6** ; 1 lb. **10/6**
Almond Oil .. .. Per bottle **1/6**, **2/6**, **4/9**, **9/3**
Alum, Powdered .. 4 oz., **2½d** ; 8 oz., **4d** ; 1 lb. **7d**
Ammonia, Aromatic Spirits of Per bot. **1/3**, **2/2**, **4/–**
,, Carbonate .. .. .. Per lb. **1/6**
,, Chloride (Sal Ammoniac) .. Per lb. **1/2**
,, Liquid .. .. Per bot. **5½d**, **10½d**
,, Strongest, 0·880 .. Per bot. **1/3**, **1/9**
Ammoniated Tincture of Quinine Per bot. **1/3**, **2/–**, **3/6**
,, ,, ,, ,, Capsules Per box **1/6**

ANALYSES (Urine, etc.)

Urine, complete analysis **£1 1 0**
,, qualitative, for sugar and albumen **£0 10 6**
,, bacteriological investigation .. **£0 10 6**

Analyses of every description undertaken. Charges for analyses other than those mentioned above, given on application

Water, Ordinary Analysis and Report as to suitability for dietetic purposes .. **£1 11 6**
The above with Analysis of Mineral Matter **£3 3 0**
Ordinary Analysis, with Microscopical Examination **£2 2 0**
Ordinary Analysis with Bacteriological Examination **£5 0 0**
Bacteriological Examination of Drinking Water for Evidence of Sewage Pollution **£3 5 0**

Stoppered bottles, specially cleaned, together with instructions for use sent on application to the Dept.

Aspirin Tablets Bot. 25, **6d** ; 100, **1/6** ; 250, **3/–**
Basilicon Ointment .. .. Pot **8d**
Bay Rum, White and Brown Per bot. **3/6**, **6/6**, **12/6**
Beeswax, pure, Yellow ¼ lb., **10d** ; ½ lb., **1/7** ; 1 lb. **3/–**
,, White .. .. .. oz. **4d**. ; 1 lb. **4/–**
Beetles—Harrods undertake by annual contracts to keep premises clear of these pests. Prices quoted on application
Beetle Powder .. .. .. Per tin **2/–**, **3/9**
Benzine .. .. .. Per tin **1/–**, **1/9**, **3/–**
Benzoin Gum .. .. Per oz. **6d**
,, Tincture .. .. Per bot. **1/–**, **1/9**, **3/3**
Bicarbonate of Soda Pkt., 4 oz., **2d** ; 1 lb., **4½d**
Bismuthated Magnesia, Powder .. Per box **1/–**
,, ,, Tablets .. ,, **1/–**
Bismuth Lozenges .. .. .. Per box **9d**
Bitter Apple, Whole or Powder .. .. Per lb. **5/–**
Blaud's Pills .. .. Per bot. **10d**, **1/6**
,, Capsules .. .. .. ,, **1/–**
Boracic Ointment .. Per pot **8d**, **1/–**, **1/6**, **2/9**, **5/–**
,, Powder .. Per ¼lb. **5d**, ½lb. **9d**, lb. **1/4**
,, Lotion .. .. Per bot. **6d**, **1/–**
Borax, Lump / ,, Powdered } 4 oz., **3d** ; 8 oz., **5d** ; 1 lb., **9d**
Boric, Zinc and Starch 1 oz., **3d** ; 4 ozs., **8d** ; 8 ozs., **1/2** ; 1 lb., **2/2**
Calcined Magnesia .. .. .. Per bot. **1/–**
Camomile Flowers .. 1 oz., **3d** ; 4 ozs., **9d** ; 8 ozs., **1/3** ; 1 lb. **2/–**
Camphor .. .. 1 oz., **6d** ; 2 ozs., **11d** ; 4 ozs., **1/6** ; 8 ozs., **2/9** ; 1 lb. **4/6**
,, Compound Liniment .. Per bot. **3/–**
,, Pills .. .. .. Per bot. **1/–**, **1/9**
,, Spirit of .. .. .. ,, **1/9**, **3/–**
Camphorated Chalk .. .. Per bot. **10½d**, **1/6**
Camphorated Oil .. .. .. Per bot. **1/6**, **2/6**
Cantharidine Hair Tonic .. Per bot. **3/6**, **6/6**, **10/6**
Carbolic Powder Disinfectant .. .. Tin **1/6**
,, Acid .. .. Per bot. **9½d**, **1/5**, **2/6**
,, Ointment .. .. .. Per pot **8d**, **1/–**
,, Lotion .. .. .. Per qrt. bot. **1/6**
Carbonate of Ammonia .. .. .. Per lb. **1/6**
,, ,, Magnesia (Heavy) .. .. ,, **2/6**
,, ,, ,, (Light) .. .. 4 ozs. **8d**

Cardamom Seeds .. .. Per oz. **1/–**
Carlsbad Salts .. .. Per bot. **10½d**, **1/6**
,, ,, Effervescent .. Per bot. **2/9**
Carmine .. .. Per pkt. **1/–**
Carron Oil .. .. Per bot. **8d**, **1/–**
Cascara Capsules .. .. .. Per box of 24 **1/–**
,, Sagrada, Liquid Per bot. **1/–**, **1/9**, **3/–**, **5/6**
Castor Oil .. .. .. Per bot. **9d**, **1/3**, **2/–**
,, ,, Vet. .. .. .. Per lb. **1/–**
,, ,, Capsules .. .. Per box **1/2**
Caustic Soda .. .. .. Per lb. tin **10½d**
,, Potash .. .. .. ,, **2/–**
Chalk and Orris .. .. Box **6½d** ; bot. **1/6**
Charcoal Powder .. .. .. Per lb. **1/–**
Chemical Food (Parrish's) .. Per bot. **1/–**, **2/9**, **6/–**
Chlorate of Potash Lozenges .. Per box **9d**
Chlorinated Lime .. .. Bot. **1/–** ; 7 lb. tin **6/9**
Cinnaform Tablets .. .. .. Per bot. **1/–**
Cinnamon and Quinine .. .. Per bot. **1/9**, **3/–**
,, ,, Capsules .. .. Box **1/9**
Citrate of Iron and Quinine .. .. Per oz. **2/–**
,, Magnesia, Eff. .. Per bot. **1/4**, **2/6**, **4/6**
Citric Acid .. 4 oz., **1/3** ; 8 ozs., **2/3** ; 1 lb. **4/–**
Citriodora Oil .. .. .. Per bot. **1/–**
Citronella Oil .. .. .. Per bot. **9d**, **1/6**
Cocoa Butter .. .. Per lb. **4/6**
Cocoa Nut Oil .. Per pot **6d**, **10½d**, **1/6**, **2/6**
Cod Liver Oil Capsules Box of 24, **1/4** ; box of 6 doz. **3/6**
Cod Liver Oil Cream Emulsion, with Hypophosphites (Harrods) Specially prepared, and quite palatable Per bot. **1/9**, **3/–**
Cod Liver Oil, 'Cream Brand.' Extra pure, from selected fish only. This oil is specially imported by Harrods. Bots. 8 oz. **1/6**, 16 oz., **2/9** ; 32 oz., **5/–** ; ½-gal., **12/6** ; 1 gal., **22/6**
Colocynth, or Bitter Apple, Whole **5/–**
,, ,, ,, Powder **5/–**
Compound Glycerine Thymol Per bot. **1/3**, **2/3**, **3/3** **6/–**, **11/6**
Confection of Senna **1/–**, **2/–**, **3/6**
,, ,, Sulphur .. .. .. Per lb. **5/6**
Cream of Tartar **5d**, **9½d**, **1/6**

Diarrhœa Mixture (Harrods) .. Per bot. **1/9**
Digestive Mixture .. .. Per bot. **1/9**, **3/–**, **5/9**
Dill Seed Water .. .. .. Per bot. **7d**, **1/–**

Easton's Syrup .. .. .. Per bot. **2/–**
Elder Flower Water Bots. 8 oz., **1/–** ; 16 oz., **1/9** ; 1 qt. **4/–**
Emulsion of Cod Liver Oil with Hypophosphites Per bot. **1/9**, **3/–**
Epsom Salts .. 4 oz., **2½d** ; 8 oz., **3½d** ; 1 lb. **6d**
,, ,, Vetinary .. .. .. Per lb. **4½d**
Essence Camphor (Rubini) .. Per bot. **1/6**, **2/9**
,, Ginger, Jamaica Per bot. **1/–**, **1/8**, **2/10**
,, Peppermint .. .. Per bot. **2/–**
,, ,, Extra strong ,, **2/9**
Eucalyptus Oil **8d**, **1/9**
,, Pastilles .. .. oz. **4d** ; lb., **4/6**

Flowers of Sulphur .. .. Per lb. **9d**
Formalin Tablets .. .. .. Per bot. **1/3**
French Chalk .. 4 oz., **2d** ; 8 oz., **3½d** ; 1 lb. **6d**
Friar's Balsam .. .. Per bot. **1/–**, **1/9**, **3/–**
Fuller's Earth Powder .. .. .. Per lb. **5d**

Gall and Opium Ointment .. .. Per pot **8d**, **1/–**
Glauber Salts 4 oz. **2d** ; 8 oz., **3d** ; 1 lb., **5d**
Glycerine and Borax .. .. Per bot. **1/–**, **1/9**
,, and Black Currant Pastilles Per box **1/–**
,, Jujubes .. .. .. ,, **1/–**
,, Medicinal .. Bot. **9½d**, **1/6**, **2/11**, ; qt. **6/6**
,, Pastilles .. .. .. Per box **1/–**
,, and Rose Water .. .. Bot. **1/–**, **1/9**

Glycerine Suppositories, box, Adults, **1/2** ; Childs, **10½d** ; Infants **7½d**
,, and Tannin .. .. Per bot. **1/3**, **2/–**
,, of Thymol Compound Per bot. **1/3**, **2/3**, **3/3**, **6/–**, **11/6**
Goulard Extract .. .. .. 1 oz. bot. **6d**
,, Water .. Per bot. **6d**, **9d** ; pt. **1/3**
Gregory Powder .. .. .. Per bot. **1/–**
Gum Arabic or Acacia (Powder or Lump). Best quality .. .. .. 4 oz., **1/6** ; 1 lb. **4/6**
Gum Benzoin .. .. Per oz. **6d**
,, Tragacanth, Powdered—
Best quality .. .. .. Per oz. **1/6**
Second quality .. .. oz. **9d** ; 4 oz. **2/6**

Hæmoglobin Capsules .. .. Per box **1/7**
Henna, powdered .. .. 4 oz. **1/–**, 1 lb. **3/9**
Hydrochloric Acid, Commercial (Spirits of Salts) Per bot. **1/3**, **2/–** ; qt. **3/–** ; gal. **6/6** Jar **3/–** extra
Hydrogen Peroxide, 20 vols. Per bot. **10½d**, **1/1**, **1/8**
,, ,, 10 vols. Per bot. **1/3**, **2/–**, **3/9**
Hypophosphites Compound Syrup Per bot. **1/6**, **2/6**

Insect Powder .. .. Sprinkler tin **8½d**. **1/3** Per lb. in paper **3/6**
Iodine Liniment .. .. .. Per bot. **1/6**, **2/9**
,, Solid **2/–**
,, Sticks **1/6**
,, Tincture of .. Per stop. bot. **1/–**, **1/9**, **3/–**
,, ,, Colourless ,, **1/–**, **1/9**, **3/–**
Ipecacuanha Wine .. .. .. Per bot. **1/4**, **2/6**
Irish Moss .. .. Per lb **1/6**
Iron and Quinine Citrate .. .. .. Per oz. **1/9**

Lavender Oil .. Per bot. 1 oz. **3/–** ; 2 oz. **5/6**
Lime Water .. .. Qt. **1/2** ; gal. **5/6** Returnable jar, **3/–**
Liniments Camphor Compound Per bot. **3/–**
,, Iodine .. .. Per bot. **1/6**, **2/9**
,, Soap .. Per bot. **1/3**, **2/3**, **4/3**
Linseed, Crushed .. .. Per lb. **6d**
,, Whole .. .. ,, **6d**
,, Oil Per bot. **1/2** ; pt. **2/–** ; qt. **3/–** ; gal. **10/–**
Liquid Paraffin (Medicinal). Bot. **1/6**, **2/6**, **4/6** ; ½-gal. **8/9** ; 1 gal. **17/–**
,, Paraffin Capsules. Box of 24, **1/6** ; 6 doz. **3/6** ; gross **5/6**
,, Ammonia .. .. Per bot. **5½d**, **10d**
,, Soap (Sapo) .. .. .. Per bot. **2/–**, **3/6**
Liquorice Powder Compound .. Per bot. **1/8**
Liquorice, Finest Solazzi .. .. 4 oz. stick **1/6**

LOZENGES & PASTILLES

	per oz.	per lb.
Antacid	0/4,	4/6
Benzoic Acid	0/6,	6/6
Bismuth	0/5,	5/–
,, & Soda	0/4,	4/6
Black Currant	0/6	5/6
Brompton Hospital	0/3,	3/6
Bronchial	0/5,	5/–
Bronchial Pastilles	0/5	5/–
Camphor	0/5,	6/–
Carbolic Acid	0/4,	4/6
Cayenne	0/4,	4/6
Charcoal	0/5,	5/–
Chlorate of Potash	0/4,	4/–
Chlorodyne	0/4,	4/–
Delectable	0/4,	4/6
Digestive Tablets	0/5,	5/6
Eucalyptus Lozenges	0/4,	4/6
,, Pastilles	0/4,	4/6

ALL PRICES ARE SUBJECT TO MARKET FLUCTUATIONS

HARRODS HIRE AND CATERING DEPARTMENT

Contracts Undertaken in Any Part of the United Kingdom

CATERERS

AND

COMPLETE BALL FURNISHERS

HARRODS Hire and Catering Department is fully prepared to undertake the complete arrangements for any furnishing and catering contracts in any part of the Country, and if desired, will gladly send either the Catering Manager or a competent Official appointed by him to estimate and give full particulars. Arrangements are made for Dance and Hunt Ball Suppers, Coming of Age Festivities, Theatre Suppers, Private and Public Luncheons, Dinners, Weddings, Afternoon and Evening Receptions, Garden and Children's Parties, Race Meetings, Cricket Weeks, Regattas, etc.

GENERAL HIRE

Glass, China, Silverware, Seating, Napery, etc., are supplied on hire for any period

Estimates sent by return of post for the equipment of Town and Country Houses

Temporary Ball Rooms, Marquees, Pavilions, etc., erected and furnished

BAZAARS—Halls decorated and Stalls erected and supplied at the shortest notice

CONCERTS—Stages, Scenery, Platforms supplied and erected. Arrangements made for lighting effects

CATERING SECTIONS

Estimates sent, include the hire of necessary Tables, Chairs, Napery, China, Glass, Plate, Cutlery, Flowers for the Table and the services of Competent Waiters under personal supervision

MENUS—On receipt of details, Menus will be submitted for any Social functions

Chefs, Butlers, Parlour Maids, Waitresses, etc., sent on shortest notice for temporary engagements in either Town or Country

No contract too small, none too large and all contracts undertaken are carried out by a well-trained and thoroughly reliable staff

SPECIAL QUOTATIONS FORWARDED ON APPLICATION

HARRODS
ENTERTAINMENT BUREAU

Artistes, Concerts, Cinematograph and Firework Displays
and Indoor and Outdoor Entertainments provided
for every Occasion

DANCE, ORCHESTRAL AND MILITARY BANDS

Harrods are agents for well-known London Orchestras and all Continental and American Bands visiting London

HARRODS ENTERTAINMENT BUREAU

Harrods make all arrangements for Concerts, Garden Parties, At Homes, Banquets, Fetes, etc., and enlist the services of the finest Orchestral, Dance, or Military Bands in the Country

Not only are the services of the most accomplished London Artistes obtained, but through the co-operation of other agencies those artists who are now world-famous may also be engaged

Quotations given for any form of Entertainment

PIANISTS FOR DANCES AT SHORT NOTICE

Musicians for private dances obtained at shortest notice

CHILDREN'S ENTERTAINMENTS

Harrods specialize in providing entertainment and amusement for Children. Conjurors, Marionettes, Performing Animals, Child Dancers, Pip, Squeak and Wilfred, Felix the Cat and a host of others, are all included in a series of attractive and amusing interludes for Children's parties

SCHOOLS AND COLLEGES

Cinematograph entertainments of an instructive and educational character are arranged for all schools and colleges, and when requested competent Lecturers will lecture during the presentation of the films

CINEMATOGRAPH

Always a popular feature with Children, this form of entertainment has the advantage of being adaptable to almost any sized room

Harrods have the most up-to-date apparatus which projects pictures that are perfectly clear and steady All subjects that are of special interest to children are included amongst the films and in many cases they are beautifully coloured. Animal and Zoo studies, Fairy Stories, Humorous Pictures, etc., may be selected from an extensive list (sent on request)

FIREWORK DISPLAYS

Firework Displays with trained expert in attendance Terms quoted on application

HORTICULTURAL DEPARTMENT
Harrods Have Everything You Need for the Garden

BULB AND SEED SECTION

HARRODS offer a splendid variety of Bulbs, Lilies, and Flowering Roots which can always be obtained when in season. All stocks are obtained from the foremost cultivators who are specialists in their own particular varieties, thus a uniform standard of excellence is assured

Export orders are dealt with by men who thoroughly understand the kind of plants most suitable for the country in which they are required. List of Vegetable and Flower Seeds published in January. Bulb Lists in August

GARDEN SUNDRIES

Harrods range of reliable Weed killers, Insecticides and Fertilisers is particularly comprehensive. Full list will be sent on request

TYING, SHADING AND PROTECTING MATERIALS

MATS for frames, and for protecting fruit trees from frosts.   Prices on application
BAMBOO CANES .. .. per 100 ; 4 ft. **5/6**, 5 ft. **10/6**, 6 ft. **12/6**, 12 ft. **14/6**

MEDICATED SHREDS
per 100 ; 2-in. **9d**, 2½-in. **10½d**, 3-in. **1/3**, 3½-in. **1/6**, 4-in. **2/–**, 5-in. **2/9**, 6-in. **3/6**

DAHLIA STAKES   Extra Hard Wood, painted Green, tarred ends
per doz. ; 4 ft. **3/6**, 5 ft. **4/6**, 6 ft. **5/6**

FLOWER STICKS Plain
per 100 ; 1 ft. **8d**, 1½ ft. **1/–**, 2 ft. **1/6**, 2½ ft. **2/–**, 3 ft. **3/–**, 4 ft. **5/6**

FLOWER STICKS Green
per 100 ; 1 ft. **1/3**, 1½ ft. **1/6**, 2 ft. **2/9**, 2½ ft. **4/–**, 3 ft. **5/6**, 3½ ft. **7/6**, 4 ft. **10/–**

GARDEN GLOVES   Ladies' Tan Leather .. .. .. Per pair **2/6**
    ,,   ,,   Men's ,,   ,, ... ,, **2/6**

INDELIBLE GARDEN PENCILS .. .. each **4**d, per doz. **3/6**

LABELS FOR POTS Painted .. .. per 100 ; 4-in. **10**d,
5-in. **1/–**, 6-in. **1/2**, 7-in. **1/5**, 8-in. **1/9**, 9-in. **2/2**, 10-in. **2/9**, 12-in. **3/–**

ZINC LABELS .. .. prices on application

SUPER GARDEN INK for marking on metal, wood, paper, etc.
per bot. **1/–**

WATERPROOF PLANT LABELS .. per 100 **1/6**, 500 **6/6**, 1,000 **12/–**

RAFFIA (Horticultural tape) on reels .. .. each **1/6**

  ,,   best picked .. .. .. per lb. **1/6**, 7 lbs. **8/9**

  ,,   dyed. Blue, Green, Red, etc. .. .. .. per lb. **2/6**

SUMMER CLOUD for shading, Green or White per tin **1/6**, per doz. **16/–**

TARRED TWINE thick, medium and thin .. .. per ball **9**d, **1/5**

WEED KILLERS (non-poisonous)

HARRODS POWDER Can be used with safety even when there are domestic animals about

Small Tin to make 12½ gallons, Sufficient for 40-50 sq. yds, ... **1/9**
Medium Tin ,, 25 ,, ,, ,, 75-100 sq. yds, ... **3/–**
Large Tin ,, 100 ,, ,, ,, 300-400 sq. yds. **10/6**

McDOUGALLS liquid .. per qt. **2/6**, ½-gall. **4/–**,
1-gall. **6/6**, 2-galls. **12/–**, 5 galls. **25/–**

CORRY'S WEED DEATH (Powder)
To make 12½ galls. **2/–**, 25 galls. **3/6**, 50 galls. **6/6**

SAND AND FIBRE

BEST COARSE POTTING SAND .. per cwt. **3/–**
COCOANUT FIBRE .. .. per bushel **2/6**
LAWN SAND for eliminating moss and daisies in lawns .. .. .. per 7 lbs. **3/–**, 14 lbs. **5/–**
28 lbs. **7/6**, 56 lbs. **13/–**, 1 cwt. **24/6**

ADCO   To make manure from garden rubbish
ACCELERATOR .. per 28 lbs. **4/6**, 56 lbs. **8/–**,
112 lbs. **15/–**

STANDARD .. 28 lbs. **6/3**, 56 lbs. **11/6**, 112 lbs. **22/–**

Every garden should use this. Ask for particulars

CAGE BIRD, POULTRY AND GAME FOOD

Harrods supply all foods for Cage Birds both Foreign and English also Poultry foods. Let us know your requirements and we shall be pleased to quote prices.

INSECTICIDES (non-poisonous)

ABOL .. per 1 pt. **2/1**, 1 qt. **3/2**, ½ gall. **5/–**,
1 gall. **9/–**, 3 galls. **22/10**, 5 galls. **36/6**

GISHURST COMPOUND .. per box **1/6**, **4/3**

SOLOMIA .. .. per ½ pt. **1/2**, pt. **2/–**, qt. **3/2**
½ gall. **5/–**, 1 gall. **9/–**

XL-ALL .. .. per ½ pt. **1/9**, pt. **3/–**, qt. **5/3**,
½ gall. **9/6**, 1 gall. **16/3**

XL-ALL EXTRACT OF QUASSIA
per tin **1/–**, **1/9**, ½ gall. **4/6**, 1 gall. **7/6**

ABOLENE TAR OIL WINTER WASH
per 1 gall. **6/–**, 3 galls. **16/6**, 5 gall. drum **25/-**

XL-ALL WINTER WASH per 1 lb. tin **1/6**, 7 lbs. **7/3**

XL-ALL WHITE FLY VAPOUR
1/3, **2/–**, **3/6**, **6/–**, **10/6**, **19/–**. Size **1/3** for 2,000 cubic feet

OSTICO TREE BANDING COMPOUND
tins each **1/6** and **6/6**

KATAKILLA POWDER .. .. each **2/–**, **6/–**

VAPORITE   For destroying pests in soil

tins	7 lbs.	14 lbs.	28 lbs.	56 lbs.	112 lbs.
	1/3	**3/9**	**5/6**	**8/–**	**11/3**	**17/6**

WORM KILLER

7 lbs.	14 lbs.	28 lbs.	56 lbs.	112 lbs.
2/6	**4/–**	**6/6**	**11/–**	**19/6**

ARTIFICIAL FERTILISERS

FERTOLA for general use

7 lbs.	14 lbs.	28 lbs.	56 lbs.	112 lbs.
3/–	**5/6**	**10/–**	**18/–**	**30/–**

CLAY'S FERTILISER .. .. in tins **10**d, **1/6**

7 lbs.	14 lbs.	28 lbs.	56 lbs.	112 lbs.
3/6	**6/–**	**10/–**	**18/–**	**32/–**

CANARY GUANO

Tins	7 lbs.	14 lbs.	28 lbs.	56 lbs.	112 lbs.
2/–	**3/–**	**5/6**	**10/–**	**17/–**	**32/–**

HOP MANURE .. .. per bag **3/–**, **7/–**, 5 bags **33/9**

VINE MANURE (THOMSON'S) .. in tins **1/3**

7 lbs.	14 lbs.	28 lbs.	56 lbs.	112 lbs.
3/–	**5/–**	**9/–**	**16/–**	**30/–**

LAWN MANURE

14 lbs.	28 lbs.	56 lbs.	112 lbs.
3/6	**6/–**	**10/6**	**18/6**

AGRICULTURAL SALT .. .. per cwt. **8/–**, 56 lbs. **4/6**, 28 lbs. **2/6**

	14 lbs.	28 lbs.	56 lbs.	112 lbs.
BASIC SLAG	**1/6**	**2/9**	**5/–**	**7/6**
BONE MEAL	**2/6**	**4/6**	**8/–**	**15/–**
KAINIT	**1/6**	**2/9**	**5/–**	**7/6**
NITRATE OF SODA	**3/6**	**6/6**	**11/6**	**21/–**
SUPERPHOSPHATE OF LIME	**1/6**	**2/6**	**4/–**	**7/6**
SULPHATE OF AMMONIA ..	**3/6**	**6/6**	**11/6**	**21/–**

COAL DEPARTMENT

As the price of coal and coke constantly fluctuates Harrods are unable to quote here. They will, however, on receipt of your enquiry, gladly quote for delivery in London or by the truck load to your nearest station.

ALL PRICES ARE SUBJECT TO MARKET FLUCTUATIONS

HARRODS LTD

Telephone SLOANE 1234
Telegrams 'EVERYTHING HARRODS LONDON'

LONDON S W 1

DOG ACCESSORIES DEPARTMENT

Everything for Your Dog's Comfort at Harrods

ROUND BASKET

No.		Walnut		Buff
No. 1.	11 ins.	4/-		4/3
No. 2.	12 ins.	4/3		4/6
No. 3.	13 ins.	6/-		5/6
No. 4.	14 ins.	7/-		6/6
No. 5.	15 ins.	9/-		8/6
No. 6.	16 ins.	10/6		10/-
No. 7.	17 ins.	12/-		11/-
No. 8.	18 ins.	13/6		13/-

EARTHENWARE DRINKING VESSEL

Size 1 .. **5/-**   Size 2 .. **6/9**

EARTHENWARE SPANIEL BOWL
Specially designed for long-eared dogs
5/-

DOG KENNEL
Strongly made and well-finished throughout

For Terriers. Length 2 ft. 6 in. Width 1 ft. 4 in. Height 2 ft. 5 in. **£3 5 0**
For Bulldogs and Airedales. Length 3 ft. 0 in. Width 1 ft. 9 in. Height 2 ft. 10 in. **£3 10 0**
For Collies. Length 3 ft. 6 ins. Width 2 ft. 3 in. Height 3 ft. 8 in. **£4 4 0**

THE 'REGENT'
On Legs, with Cushion
13×7 ins. **13/3** ; 15× 8 ins. **15/6** ; 17×9 ins. **17/9** ; 19× 9½ ins. **20/9** ; 21 × 10 ins. **23/9** ; 23 × 10½ ins. **27/-**
Staining, any colour, extra **2/3**

THE 'SUTHERLAND'
Lined with Poplin, and with Cushion

16 ins.	18 ins.	20 ins.
22/6	24/9	29/3
22 ins.	24 ins.	
33/9	38/3	

In Colour, extra .. **2/3**

THE 'BROMPTON
In Buff Wicker, upholstered

Size 1	..	..	21/-
Size 2	..	..	24/-
Size 3	..	..	27/-

If in Colour, Price extra

THE 'CRESCENT'
Round Basket on stand. In Buff, upholstered in Serge. Measurements are diameter at top

No. 1. 16½ ins.	13/6	No. 4. 20½ ins.	19/-
No. 2. 17½ ins.	15/-	No. 5. 21 ins.	21/-
No. 3. 19 ins.	17/6	No. 6. 22 ins.	25/-

SHOW HAMPER
In Buff Wicker with Talc front which enables the dog to be seen without unfastening the hamper
Unlined **56/-**

> For Dog Collars and Leads, etc., see pages 214 and 215
>
> ———
>
> When ordering, please state size and breed of your dog

BEEHIVE KENNEL
Buff varnished. Galvanized Wire Doors

Outside measurements		Outside measurements	
12×11×12 ins.	18/-	20×14×16 ins.	23/-
14×11½×13 ,,	19/3	22×15×17 ,,	24/9
16×12×14 ,,	20/3	24×16×18 ,,	29/3
18×13×15 ,,	21/9	26×17×19 ,,	32/9

THE 'BARREL' SLEEPING BASKET
Buff 21/6, Walnut 22/6, Cushion extra

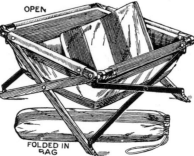

THE 'TRINGHAM' FOLDING BASKET
Very convenient for travelling. In two sizes
1st size, various colours **29/6**
2nd size, Black and Orange .. .. **30/6** and Plain Brown

THE 'TIDBURN' TRAVELLING BOXES
These boxes are exceptionally well made and may be had in all sizes according to the special breed of dog for which they are to be used
Prices range from 24/- to 105/-
Please state Breed of Dog when ordering

ALL PRICES ARE SUBJECT TO MARKET FLUCTUATIONS

HARRODS LTD

Telephone SLOANE 1234
Telegrams 'EVERYTHING HARRODS LONDON'

LONDON S W 1

HARRODS—FOR THE DOG LOVER

A Well cared for Animal is a Pleasure to All

To keep dogs healthy great care must be given in the selection of a wholesome and well-balanced food ration. Given this and regular exercise the health of your dog is assured.

MARRABLES

Lactic Puppy Milk Food. Tins 1/3, 2/-, 3/10

SHERLEY

Lactol Puppy Food. Tins 1/8, 6/-, 25/- each

HARRODIAN FOODS

	112 lbs.	56 lbs.	28 lbs.	7 lbs.
Dog Cakes ..	34/0	17/6	9/6	2/4
Puppy Cakes ..	36/6	18/9	9/6	2/6
Hound Meal ..	36/0	18/9	9/6	2/5

	112 lbs.	56 lbs.	28 lbs.	7 lbs.
Terrier Meal ..	36/0	18/9	9/6	2/5
Ship Biscuits, broken ..	33/0	17/0	8/9	2/3

SPRATTS PATENT

				112 lbs.	56 lbs.	28 lbs.	7 lbs.
Dog Cakes ..	..	..	..	36/0	18/9	9/6	2/5
Terrier Cakes ..	..	..	..	38/6	19/6	10/0	2/7
Ovals ..	..	..	..	44/0	22/6	11/6	2/11
Puppy Cakes ..	..	..	..	40/6	20/6	10/6	2/8
C.L.O. Dog Cakes	..	..	..	37/0	18/9	9/9	2/6
C.L.O. Puppy Cakes	..	..	..	40/6	20/6	10/6	2/8
Rodnim ..	..	..	..	40/0	20/6	10/6	2/8
Pet Rodnim ..	..	..	..	40/6	20/9	10/9	2/9
Weetmeat, No. 1 & 2	..	..	..	40/0	20/6	10/6	2/8
Fibo ..	..	..	..	40/6	20/9	10/9	2/9
Bulldog and Terrier Meal	..	..	..	40/0	20/6	10/6	2/8
Greyhound Biscuits	..	..	..	36/6	18/9	9/6	2/5
Plain Round Biscuits	..	..	..	33/0	16/9	8/9	2/3
Alsax (Alsatians)	..	..	..	40/0	—	—	2/8
Pepsinated Puppy Meal	..	..	..			per pkt.	1/0
Charcoal Biscuits	..	..	..				2/0
Pet Dog Biscuits	..	..	..			per box	1/0

CLARK'S

				112 lbs.	56 lbs.	28 lbs.	7 lbs.
Melox ..	..	..	..	40/0	20/6	10/6	2/9
Melox Marvels ..	..	..	..	43/0	22/0	11/3	2/11
Melox Puppy De Luxe	..	..	..			boxes	1/0
Buffalo Bars Biscuits ..	..	..	..			"	1/0

SPILLER'S

			112 lbs.	56 lbs.	28 lbs.	7 lbs.
Osoko	..	..	41/0	21/0	11/0	3/0
Victoria Dog Cakes ..	..	..	35/0	18/0	9/4	2/5
Victoria Puppy Cakes	..	..	40/0	20/6	10/6	2/8
Saval, No. 1 and No. 2	..	..	48/0	24/6	12/6	3/3
Victoria Pet Dog	..	..	41/0	21/0	10/6	2/8
Plasmon Pet Dog Cakes	..	..	—	—	—	4/2
Victoria Extract.Malt	..	..	43/0	22/0	11/6	3/0
Victoria Hound Meal	..	..	36/0	18/6	9/9	2/7
Victoria Sippets	..	..	41/0	21/0	11/0	3/0
Victoria Fish Cakes	..	..	35/0	18/0	9/4	2/5
Victoria Terrier Meal	..	..	37/0	19/0	10/0	2/8
Assorted Sippets	..	..			per carton	1/0

ELASTENE WOOD WOOL BEDDING FOR DOGS

			100 lbs.	50 lbs.	12 lbs.	pkt.
For Pet Dogs, No. 4 K.	..	..	31/0	16/9	6/0	3/9
For Terriers, No. 5 K.	..	..	25/0	13/9	5/0	3/0
For Large Dogs, No. 5 BK.	..	..	22/6	12/6	4/9	2/9

MOLASSINES

				112 lbs.	56 lbs.	28 lbs.	7 lbs.
Dog Cakes ..	..	..	..	36/6	18/9	9/6	2/5
Puppy Cakes ..	..	..	..	40/6	20/6	10/6	2/8
Terrier Food ..	..	..	..	40/0	20/6	10/6	2/8
Vimlets ..	..	..	..	36/6	18/9	9/6	2/5
Carton Dog and Puppy	..	..	..			each	1/0

WALKER HARRISON

				112 lbs.	56 lbs.	28 lbs.	7 lbs.
Viscan ..	..	..	..	40/0	20/6	10/6	2/9

LOWE & SONS

			112 lbs.	56 lbs.	28 lbs.	7 lbs.
Carta Carna ..	..	..	36/6	19/6	10/6	2/9

FREEMAN'S

Digestive Rusks .. .. .. boxes 5/0 & 1/9

SHERLEY

Lactol Puppy Biscuits .. .. per box 1/8

ENTWISTLE'S

Morsels.. .. .. carton 1/0

NEW MEAT RATIONS IN TINS

Ken-L-Rations	1 lb. tin 8d, 48 tins 30/0
Pup-E-Rations	1 lb. tin 8d, 48 tins 30/0

A FEW WELL KNOWN REMEDIES AND MEDICINES, Etc.

	Per pkt.
Kur Mange, Skin Cure	2/6
Sopex Shampoo ..	1/6
Pulvex Dry Cleaner ..	9d.
Ruby Balm Ointment ..	1/0
Ruby Remedy Worm Cure ..	3/6
Sherley Wet Shampoo ..	2/0
,, Dry Shampoo ..	1/6
,, Skin Cure ..	1/6
,, Tonic and Condition Powder	1/3
,, Aperient Powder ..	1/3
,, Castor Oil Capsules ..	1/3
,, Gastrine Tablets ..	1/3
,, Canker Lotion ..	1/6
Hyreco Dog Soap ..	per tin 9d. & 1/6
Hyreco Dry Clean ..	per tin 1/0
Lyptrol, Eucalyptus Shampoo ..	1/0
Castrique Worm Powder ..	1/6 & 3/0
Benbow Blood Mixture ..	bottles 2/6
Benbow Blood Mixture ..	capsules 3/0
Bob Martin Condition Powder ..	6d. & 1/0
Karswood Condition Powder ..	1/0
Lintox Distemper Cure	2/6 & 5/0
Vandy Dry Cleaner	1/6 & 2/6

ZOOLOGICAL DEPARTMENT

'INSPECTION AND ENQUIRIES INVITED'

Pedigree Dogs and Cats—Cage Birds or Poultry—whatever your needs Harrods can supply them. Expert advice given on all matters connected with the purchase and welfare of your pet.

DOGS TRIMMED, WASHED OR SHAMPOOED BY APPOINTMENT

Harrods have a wonderful collection of Cage Birds including many rare varieties seldom seen in this country

ALL PRICES ARE SUBJECT TO MARKET FLUCTUATIONS

HARRODS LTD

Telephone SLOANE 1234
Telegrams 'EVERYTHING HARRODS LONDON'

LONDON S W 1

FUNERAL DEPARTMENT
Funerals Conducted in Town, Country or Abroad

SALOON MOTOR HEARSE

Graves Purchased and all Arrangements Made at Cemeteries

Harrods undertake all funeral arrangements reverently and at moderate charges. Competent assistants are sent at any time to take instructions and give all the information required by the various authorities at home and abroad

ESTIMATES AND FULL PARTICULARS SUBMITTED ON REQUEST

ESTIMATES FOR FUNERALS

Clients are respectfully urged to state their requirements clearly when giving orders for funeral arrangements particularly as to distance and number of cars required. Harrods will gladly advise or take full charge of all arrangements in accordance with their clients' wishes

EMBALMING

Embalming or Temporary Preservation undertaken by thoroughly skilled men. Full particulars on application to the manager of Harrods Funeral Department

CREMATION

The utmost care is required in preparing the forms and obtaining the necessary certificates for Cremations For this special work Harrods have an experienced manager, thus saving clients needless trouble and inconvenience. In all cases where cremation is desired the earliest possible notice should be given. Urns for Cremated Ashes in Marble, Alabaster and Bronze

MOTOR HEARSES

Suitably equipped Motor Hearses and Private Cars are always available for the conveyance of remains to any part of the Town or Country

TELEPHONE : SLOANE 1234 DAY OR NIGHT

HARRODS LTD

LONDON S W 1

GROCERY DEPARTMENT

HARRODS FOOD SERVICE HAS NO EQUAL IN BRITAIN

Whether you live in London, the suburbs, or in any part of the country there is no requirement in Groceries that cannot be secured at Harrods. In Harrods wonderful Grocery Section are found the finest products of every country in the world, an astonishing variety of which this list is merely representative

GROCERIES DELIVERED TO YOUR DOOR

Free delivery to your door of all goods within the radius of Harrods Motor Delivery (see pages 9, 10, 11) and free carriage on all purchases value 20/- and over to any part of England and Wales, and value 60/- to Scotland

---

ALMONDS

Bitter	per lb. **2/4**. Nibs, per lb. **3/-**
Ground, sweet, Harrods ..	.. ½ lb. tin, **1/5**, 1 lb. **2/9**
,, ,, Marshall's ..	.. .. .. 1 lb. tin **3/-**
,, ,, Loose.. ..	.. .. .. per lb. **2/7**
Jordan	finest, per lb. **3/4**, fine **2/9**
Salted	pr. bot. **2/6, 2/2** ; Devilled per bot. **2/6**
Valencia	fine per lb. **2/6** ; finest, per lb. **2/9**

ALUMINIUM CLEANERS

Aurora	.. per drum **1/-**
Crease's..	per drum **4d**, **8½d**
Noma	,, **8d, 1/-**
Rid	per pkt. **6d**

ANCHOVIES

Boneless, in Oil

HARRODS..	per bot. **1/8, 2/3, 3/2**
Burgess'	.. .. per bot. **1/8**

In Brine

Burgess'	.. ½ bot. **2/4**, bot. **4/5**
C. & B.'s	,, **2/3**, ,, **4/4**
Keddies'	,, **2/-**, ,, **3/10**
Lazenby's	,, **2/3**, ,, **4/4**
Cresca,' in Oil	.. per tin **7½d**
,, in Butter	.. ,, **1/3**
,, with Lemon ..	.. ,, **1/3**
In Regalia, Amieux Freres ..	per tin, **7½d, 1/-**
With Ravigote ,, ,, ..	.. per tin **1/-**

Sauce, see page 744
Paste, see page 743

APPLES

Peeled and Cored

Canadian	.. nom. gallon tin **2/10**
English	.. ,, **2/9**
English	nom. 2½ tin **1/-**

Evaporated

S. African Pippins	per lb. **1/3**, 3 lbs. **3/8**
Rings..	per lb. **1/3**, 3 lbs. **3/8**
Whole Cored	per lb. **1/2**, 3 lbs. **3/5**
Apple Sauce..	.. per tin **1/1**
Apple Juice (Pomol)	per bot. **2/3, 4/3**

APRICOTS (Evaporated)

Australian	per lb. **1/6**, 3 lbs. **4/5**
South African	.. ,, **1/2**, ,, **3/5**
,, ,, ...	.. ,, **1/5½**, ,, **4/3**
Californian (Fancy Quality).. ..	.. ,, **1/8**, ,, **4/11**
In Syrup, see page 733	
Pulp, see page 734	

AROMATIC SEASONING

Maggis'..	.. per bot. **1/1, 1/9, 9/6**
Senns'	.. .. per bot. **11d**

ARROWROOT

Bermuda, genuine	.. 1 lb. tin **8/-**
Plasmon .. .. .. a. ..	.. ½ lb. pkt. **9½d**
St. Vincent	Loose, per lb. **1/-**, 1 lb. tin **1/3**
West Indian .. .. .. ,,	per lb. **1/3**, 1 lb. tin **1/6**
Speed's..	per 1 lb. tin **1/9**

ALL PRICES ARE SUBJECT TO MARKET FLUCTUATIONS

GROCERY DEPARTMENT

BALL ROOM POWDER

Ronuk	per tin 1/–
Slipperine	per tin 1/6, 2/6
Stevenson's	per tin 1/–

BAKED BEANS WITH TOMATO

Clark's	No. 2 tin 5½d, doz. 5/3
Heinz	per tin 6d, 8½d, 1/3
,, Vegetarian ..	per tin 6d, 8½d

BAKING POWDER

HARRODS ..	tin 7d, 1/1, 3/–
Alfred Bird & Son's ..	tin 7d, 1/2
Borwick's.. ..	per tin 7½d, 1/3, 3/2, 6/4
Marshall's, in drums ..	1 lb. 1/6, 10-oz. 1/–
Raisley Flour ..	per tin 10d
Royal .. per ½ lb. tin 1/7, 1 lb. tin 3/–
Yeatman's ..	per tin 7½d, 1/3, 3/2, 6/4

BANANAS (Dried)

.. ..	per lb. 1/–

BARLEY

Pearl ..	per lb. 2¾d, 7 lbs. 1/6½
Robinson's Patent ..	per tin 7½d, 1/3

BATH BRICKS

Bath Bricks	each 3d
Powder	per drum 2½d

BATH CUBES (Reckitts):

Lavender, Verbena or Ess. of Flowers ..	per pkt. of 6 cubes 1/–

BEANS

	Per lb.	7 lbs.
Butter, Hand-picked	4d	2/3
Flageolets	9d	5/1
Haricot, Genuine, Small ..	4d	2/3
,, ,, Medium	4d	2/3

BEE CANDY

.. ..	per 2 lb. block 2/–

BEEF FLUID

	2-oz.	4-oz.	8-oz.	16-oz.
Bovril	1/2	2/1½	3/9	6/2
,, Seasoned.. ..	1/3	2/2½	4/1	7/2
,, Campaign ..			per tin 2/6	
'Beefex'	1/1	1/11	3/6	5/6
Oxo	1/1	1/11	3/6	5/6
'Photo' Liebig	11d	1/7	2/9	5/–

BEEF EXTRACT, ETC.

	2-oz.	4-oz.	8-oz.	16-oz.
HARRODS	1/1	1/11½	3/9	7/–
Baron Liebig	1/2½	2/3	4/3	7/9
Jardox	—	1/11½	3/6	5/9
Lemco	1/5½	2/8	4/11	8/10
Tooth's Liebig			box of 12 small jars 4/–	

BEEF TEA CUBES, ETC.

'Allies'	12 cubes 10½d, 6 cubes 5½d
Armour's Cubes	per tin 6d, 3/–
Bovril Lozenges.. ..	per box 9d
,, Tablets	3 tab. 9d, 6 tabs. 1/5
Ivelcon	bot. 1/9, cubes 6 for 5½d, 12 for 10½d
Oxo Cubes	6 cubes 6d, 50 cubes 4/–

BISCUITS

*Kinds marked * can now be supplied in ½ lb. packets.*

	About 7lb. Tin per lb.	½ Square Tin each	No. 2 Tin each	Special Tin each	No. 1 Tin each
*Abernethy, Thin, H. & P. ..	1/5	—	2/6	—	1/7
,, ,, McV. & P. ..	—	—	4/–	—	—
Academy Creams, McV. & P.	1/7	8/6	4/1	—	2/2
Acorn, H. & P.	—	—	—	1/10	—
Afternoon Tea, McF., L. & Co.	2/7	8/11	—	2/10, 4/7	—
			¼-flt. McV.,P. 5/3		
,, ,, H. & P. ..	2/7	10/8	—	2/10	—
Akoll, H. & P...	—	—	—	—	3/9
Albert, H. & P.	—	—	3/2	—	—
*Arrowroot, Thin, H. & P. ..	1/5	6/4	3/2	—	1/9
Assorted, Hughes ..	—	—	—	2/–	—
*Assorted Creams, H. & P. ..	1/7	7/6	4/2	—	—
Assorted Gingerbreads, H. & P.	—	—	4/1	—	—
Baltic Crackers, Hughes	1/–	—	—	—	—
Bath Olivers, Fortt's Original ..	—	—	—	1/10, 2/9	—
,, ,, ,, ,, small	—	—	—	2/3, 4/2	—
,, ,, ,, Chocolate	—	—	—	3/6	—
,, ,, H. & P. ..	—	—	—	2/2	—

BISCUITS—*continued*

	About 7lb. Tin per lb.	½ Square Tin each	No. 2 Tin each	Special Tin each	No. 1 Tin each
Bath Olivers, Wafers, Amery	—	—	—	1/6	—
*Boudoir, McV. & P.	2/7	5/2	—	—	—
,, H. & P. ..	—	—	2/11	1/11	—
*Bourbon, P.F. & Co... ..	1/7	—	5/6	—	—
Braemar, Gray Dunn's	—	—	3/3	—	—
Brandy Snap, Fox's ..	—	—	—	2/4	—
*Breakfast, H. & P.	2/–	3/8	—	—	—
,, Small, McV. & P.	—	3/5	—	—	—
Butterette, McV. & P.	—	3/6	—	—	—
*Butter Puffs, Crawford's ..	1/4	3/4	—	—	—
* ,, Fingers, ..	1/7	7/9	3/9	—	2/3
Butter, Rich., Milnes..	—	—	—	2/–	—
,, Hard, Simmers	—	—	—	per pkt. 7½d	
*Cabin, H. & P.	11d	—	—	—	—
,, Crawford's ..	11d	—	—	—	—
,, Brown's Super.. ..	—	2/9	—	—	—
Cafe Noir, Carr's	—	—	4/–	—	—
*Captains, Thin, H. & P. ..	1/4	2/9	—	Round tin 1/11	—
* ,, Oval, Thin, H. & P.	1/2	4/9	2/7	—	1/7
,, Lemann's, Thick ..	—	—	—	2/6, 7/–	—
,, ,, Thin	—	—	—	3/–	—
,, Simpson's ..	—	4/–	—	7/6	—
Casino, H. & P. ..	—	—	—	1/11	—
Cheese, H. & P.	1/3	—	2/3	—	1/5
* ,, Assorted ..	1/4	3/9	—	2/11	1/5
,, Fingers, Windrock, per tin 1/6 ; Cheese Sticks, Helders, tin 2/6; Cheese Sticks. H. & P's, tin 1/9; Cheese Straws, Harpers, tin 1/9					
Chocker Jack .. per box 1/–					
Chocolate Brunette ..	—	—	4/10	—	2/6
,, Fingers, Rowntree's	—	—	2/6	—	—
,, Vienna, McF., L. & Co.	—	—	2/10	—	—
,, Mixed, Bournville	—	—	—	—	2/6
,, ,, H. & P.	2/4	11/8	—	2/7	—
,, Assorted, McF., L. & Co.	—	—	Box 1/6	2/7	—
,, ,, McV. & P.	—	—	—	2/7	—
,, ,, P. F. & Co.	—	—	—	1/8, 3/–	—
,, ,, Jacobs	—	—	—	2/7	—
,, ,, G. Dunn's	—	—	—	1/6, 2/7	—
,, Table	—	—	6/1	—	3/1
,, Tennis, McF., L. & Co.	—	—	2/–	—	—
,, Vita Wheat, P.F. & Co.	—	—	—	per pkt. 1/–	
,, Wafer, Cadbury's ..	—	—	—	2/6	—
City Assorted, Crawford's	—	6/5	—	2/8	—
Club Crackers, H. & P. ..	1/6	2/6	—	2/4	—
* ,, Cheese, Carr's ..	2/1	5/5	3/–	1/6	1/7
Cold Water Crackers, McV. & P.	—	3/10	—	—	—
Cornish Wafers, H. & P. ..	—	—	2/4	—	—
Coronation, H. & P. ..	—	—	—	3/6	—
*Cracknels, Toy, H. & P. ..	3/–	—	3/4	—	—
,, Fancy, H. & P. ..	3/–	—	3/7	—	—
,, Puff, H. & P. ..	3/4	—	2/3	—	—
,, Jacob's ..	—	—	—	2/7	—
Cream Brazils, P. F. & Co. ..	1/6	—	4/–	—	2/1
,, Cheese, Assorted, H. & P.	1/4	3/8	—	2/–	—
,, Crackers ..	1/3	3/6	—	2/6	—
Choice Assorted, Jacob's	—	—	—	2/9	—
Crepes Dentelles (Pancakes) ..	—	—	—	2/6	—
*Custard Cream, P.F. & Co. ..	1/6	—	4/10	—	—
*Cuddy	1/–	4/8	—	—	—
'Daren'	—	—	—	pkt. 8d	
Dessert, H. & P.	3/–	—	6/10	—	3/8
*Digestive, McV. & P.	1/6	6/–	—	3/–, 5/1	—
,, H. & P. ..	—	—	3/4	2/9	2/–
,, Gray Dunn's ..	—	—	—	5/2	—
,, Rusks, Robb's Sweetened or unsweetened	—	—	—	3/9	—
Dinner, H. & P.	2/2	4/6	—	3/5	—
,, Toast, McF., L. & Co.	2/–	—	—	3/7	—
Emblem Assorted, Carr's	—	6/6	—	2/1	—
Empire Assorted, H. & P. ..	1/6	6/3	—	2/6	—
Ensign Assorted, McF., L. & Co.	—	—	3/2	2/–	—

ALL PRICES ARE SUBJECT TO MARKET FLUCTUATIONS

HARRODS LTD

Telephone SLOANE 1234
Telegrams 'EVERYTHING HARRODS LONDON'

LONDON S W 1

GROCERY DEPARTMENT

BISCUITS

	About 7 lb. Tin per lb.	½ Square Tin each	No. 2 Tin each	Special Tin each	No. 1 Tin each
Ufillet, Crawfords	—	—	2/9	—	—
Universal Assorted, McV. & P.	—	6/5	—	2/8	—
Vitalveg	—	—	—	3/9	—
Wafers—Sugar, *Vanilla, Raspberry, Strawberry, Coffee, Chocolate, Lemon, H. & P.	*3/3	—	—	1/7	—
,, Assorted, H. & P... ..	2/9	9/6	—	2/1	—
,, Ice, H. & P.	3/2	4/8	—	1/3	—
,, Opera, H. & P. ..	—	—	—	2/11	—
,, Rugby, H. & P. ..	—	—	—	2/8	—
,, Princes, P.F. & Co. ..	—	—	—	1/2	—
,, Carmencita, H. & P. ..	—	—	—	1/6	—
,, Cheese or Celery, Fette's..	—	—	—	1/3	—
,, Water, McV. & P. ..	1/2	3/11	—	2/4	—
,, Oyster 1/5, Venice 1/2, Oatmeal 4/-, Tunbridge Wells 2/6,					
,, Altesse 2/-, Ginger (American) 2/6, Educator 2/6, Nabisco 1/-,					
,, Uneeda 7d					
*Water Biscuits, Jacobs.. ..	1/2	3/2	—	2/3	—
,, ,, Large, McF. Lang	1/2	—	—	—	1/11 Drum
,, ,, H.B. Oval, H.&P.	1/2	3/6	—	—	—
* ,, ,, Fine, Gray Dunn's	1/2	—	—	2/3	—
* ,, ,, Table, Carr's ..	1/4	3/-	—	1/7	—
,, ,, McV. & P. ..	—	—	—	2/10	1/11 Drum
*Wave Crest, Jacob's ..	1/5	3/10	2/5	—	—
Wheatmeal, H. & P. ..	1/6	7/9	4/2	—	2/4
Wheat, Chapman's Entire	—	—	—	2/-	—
Wine, Wood's	—	—	—	2/6	—
,, Mixed, P.F. & Co. ..	1/8	7/4	3/9	—	—
,, ,, H. & P. ..	—	—	—	2/1	—
York, Lemann's	—	—	—	5/-	—
Zu Zu Snaps .. Packet 7d	—	—	—	—	—

ALLOWANCE ON TINS WHEN EMPTY { Per Large Square 1/-. No. 2 tin 3d No. 1 tin 1d Per ½ square 8d Special tin 2d Cabinet tin 1d }

BLANC MANGE POWDER

Bird & Son (Various)	per box 6½d, 1/- ; tin	1/3½
Borwick's ,, ...	per tin	1/2
Carltona ,, ...	per pkt.	4½d
Cerebos ,, ...	,,	4d
Chivers ,, ...	,,	2½d
Cook's ,, ...	,,	5½d
Creamola ,, ...	,,	4d
'Flakna' ,, ...	,,	1½d
Foster Clark's ,, ...	,,	4½d
Green's (Chocolate)	,,	4½d
,, (Assorted)	,,	3d
Plasmon	,,	6½d

BLOATER PASTE, see page 743

BLUE

HARRODS Squares	per lb.	1/2
Nixey's 'Soho'	8 squares	7½d
,, Cervus..	6 bags	5½d
Reckett's Squares .. per lb. 1/3 ; bags 6 for	5½d
Colman's ,, ...	per lb.	1/2

BOMBAY DUCK .. .. per tin 2/3

BONE DUST .. .. .. per tin 1/3

BORAX

Lump or Powdered	per lb.	7d
Household Treasure	per pkt.	6d

BOWEN'S FOOD POWDER .. .. per tin 2/9

BRAND'S SPECIALITIES

Beef Tea, Invalid	per bot. 1/4
,, ,, Home made	per tin 1/-
,, ,, Jelly	per tin 1/6, 2/9
,, ,, Tabules	per doz. 2/6
Chicken Jelly	per bot. 2/1, per tin 1/9, 3/3
Concentrated Beef Tea	per tin 1/3, 2/6, 5/-
Essence of Beef ..	per tin 2/6, 4/8 ; bot. 2/9, 5/-
Essence of Chicken ..	per tin 2/9, 5/2
,, ,,	per bot. 3/- 5/6
Essence of Mutton ..	per tin 2/6, 4/8 ; bot. 2/9
Essence of Veal	per tin 2/6
Extract of Meat	2 ozs. 1/6
Invalid Turtle Soup	per tin 2/-, 3/6
,, Chicken Broth ..	per bot. 1/4 ; ½ tin 1/-
,, Calves Foot Jelly (Wine)	bot. 2/8, ½ bot. 1/6
Meat Juice	per bot. 3/9
Mutton Broth	1/4
Savoury Meat Lozenges ..	per box 1/3, 1/9, 3/6
Turtle Jelly	per bot. 2/9
,, Soup (real)	per bot. 2/3 ; tin 4/-

BOOT CREAM AND PASTE

HARRODS Black, Brown or White Cream, per bot. 7½d, 11½d, 1/7 ; per doz. 7/3, 11/3, 18/-

Paste .. .. .. per tin 5½d, 10d ; doz. 5/3, 9/9

E. Brown & Son's

De Guiche	per bot. 9d, 1/9
Meltonian Cream, Black, White	'Dumpy' Jar 9d, 1/-
,, ,, ,,	tubes 1/- ; bots. 1/-, 1/9
Lutetian Brown	per bot. 1/-, 1/9
Meltonian Paste	per tin 6d
Parian White	per bot. 1/-
White Cleaner	per tin 6d
,, ,, ...	De Luxe tin 1/-

Caswell & Co.'s

Cream	bots. 7½d, 1/-, 1/9
Dubbin, Black or Brown ..	per tin 8½d, 1/-
Kid Reviver	per bot. 10½d
Paste	per tin 6½d, 10½d
White Ho	per bot. 1/-

Everett's

Electric Black	per carton 1/2
Jetta or Nutta	per tin 6d, 8d
New Century	per bot. 10½d
White Cleaner	per tin 6d
,, Paste	,, 9d
Russian Cream	per bot. 1/2

Various

Brown's Satin Polish	per bot. 1/-
Carr's Boot Creams	per bot. 8d
,, Paste	per tin 3d, 6d
,, Snowflake	per bot. 8d
Cherry Blossom	per tin 2½d, 4½d
'Cobra' Black or Brown ..	,, 3d, 6d, 1/-
Crease's Scientific White Cleaner ..	per bot. 1/-
Day & Martin's Creams ..	per bot. 8d
,, ,, 'Just Out' ..	per tin 4d
,, ,, Wax Polish ..	,, 4½d
,, ,, White Dressing ..	,, 6d
Gishurstine	per tin 10½d
'Goldband' Cleaner ..	per tube 8d
,, Cleaning Set ..	each 1/-
Nugget Boot Polish ..	per tin 3d, 6d
,, White Cleaner ..	per bot. 9d
,, Outfits (Metal) ..	each 2/-
Ronuk Boot Polish, Black and Brown ..	per tin 6d
'Regent'	tubes 7d
,, ...	bots. 9d
S.A.P. Black and Brown	per tin 6d, 1/-

ALL PRICES ARE SUBJECT TO MARKET FLUCTUATIONS

GROCERY DEPARTMENT

COFFEE (PURE)

When ordering, please state whether Whole or Ground is required

HARRODS PURE COFFEES Nos.		Roast per lb.	Raw per lb.
3.	Blend. Full Flavoured	1/10	1/8
4.	Central American and Mocha	2/4	2/2
5.	Colombian. Choice	2/8	2/6
6.	Finest Kenya	2/8	2/6
7.	Choice Mysore	2/8	2/6
8.	Finest Costa Rica	2/8	2/6
9.	Black Coffee..	2/8	2/6
10.	Vera Paz	2/10	2/8
11.	Mocha	3/–	2/10
12.	Peaberry	3/2	3/–
13.	Old Government Java	3/2	3/–
14.	Jamaica. Finest Blue Mountain	3/4	3/2

'Ameer' Blend   per ½ lb. tin, 1/5½, 1 lb. tin 2/10, 5 lb. tin 13/10
'Cafe'   ,,   ,,   1/5½,   ,,   2/10,   ,,   13/10
'Origny'   ,,   ,,   1/6½,   ,,   3/–,   ,,   14/8

VARIOUS
'Bendor'   .. .. per 1 lb. tin 2/9
'Ibex'   .. .. per ½ lb. pkt. 1/1½
H.A.G., free from Caffeine   .. .. per tin 1/8, 3/2
Beechnut (American)   .. .. .. per tin 3/2

COFFEE ESSENCES & EXTRACTS
HARRODS Essence of Coffee and Chicory   .. per bot. 1/6, 4/9
Bantam   .. .. per tin 1/6, 7/–
Cafolin   .. .. per bot. 4/8
Branson's (Pure)   .. .. per bot. 10d, 1/7, 2/5
Cafe au Lait   .. .. .. per ½ tin 8½d, tin 1/3
Camp Coffee   .. .. .. per bot. 10½d, 1/7, 3/9
Chiver's   .. .. per bot. 10½d, 1/7
Clark's Optimus   .. .. per bot. 9½d
,,   Super   .. .. ,, 1/11
Drysdale's Rum Coffee   .. .. per bot. 1/8, 1/–
,,   Coffee and Chicory   .. .. per bot. 1/8
Kolacafe 10½d
Wallace P.R.   .. .. per lb. 2/9
Symington's (Pure)   .. per bot. 9½d, 1/7, 2/11
,,   Dandelion   .. .. per bot. 1/5
,,   Coffee and Chicory   .. ,, 1/7

COFFEE, FRENCH
HARRODS Finest   per ½ lb. tin 1/1½, 1 lb. tin 2/2, 3 lb. tin 6/3
,,   Breakfast Blend   ,,   1/0½,   ,,   2/–,   ,,   5/9
,,   Extra Fine   .. per 1 lb. tin 1/10, 3 lb. tin 5/3
,, ... per 1 lb. tin 1/8, 3 lb. tin 4/9
,,   Special School Blend   .. per lb. 1/6, 7 lb. 10/3
'Frenchman'   .. .. .. per 1 lb. tin 2/1
'Garcon'   .. .. ,, 2/8
Red, White and Blue   .. .. per lb. 2/2

CORN FLOUR
HARRODS finest quality   per 1 lb. pkt. 6d, 3½ lb. linen bag 1/1
Berger's   .. .. per 1 lb. pkt. 9d
Brown and Polson's   .. per lb. 9d, 4 lb. tin 3/–, ½ lb. pkt. 4½d
Colman's Rice   .. .. .. per lb. pkt. 9½d
Johnston's   .. .. ,, 9d
Marshall's Kasama 6½d
Plasmon   .. .. .. per ½ lb. pkt. 1/–
Windrock (with Arrowroot)   .. .. per 1 lb. pkt. 9d

CRAB
Natural   .. .. per ½ tin 1/4
Dressed   .. .. per ¼ tin 1.d
Natural   .. .. ,, 10½d

CRAYFISH   .. .. per tin 1/–

CREAM
Nestle's   .. .. per ½ tin 10d, tin 1/3
Dano   .. .. ,, 8½d, ,, 1/2

'CRESCA' PRODUCTS
Asparagus   .. .. per bot. 3/9
Creme de Marrons   .. .. per tin 1/–, 1/8½d
,,   ,,   with Brandy and Vanilla   per jar 5/–

'CRESCA' PRODUCTS—continued
Corn on Cob (Baby)   .. .. per bot. 1/10½
Mousee de Anchois   .. .. .. per jar 1/9
Olives, Stuffed with Almonds   .. .. per bot. 2/–
Truffle Sauce   .. .. ,, 1/6

CREME DE RIZ
Marshall's   .. .. per tin 1/6

CREX   .. .. per 7 lb. 11d, 14 lb. 1/9, 30 lb. 9/9

'CRISCO' Frying Fat   .. .. per tin 1/8

CROCUS POWDER   .. per ¼ lb. pkts. 2d, per lb. 6d

CURRANTS
Australian   .. .. .. per lb. 9d, 3 lbs. 2/2
,, ... per pkt. 10½d
Choice Vostizza   .. .. per lb. 9d, 3 lbs. 2/2
Fine Quality   .. .. .. 8d, ,, 1/11

CURRY PASTE
Daw Sens Packed by HARRODS   .. per bot. 1/–, 1/9, 3/3
Capt. White's   .. .. .. jars 1/6, 2/6
Cook's   .. .. large jars 2/5, small jars 1/6
Halford's   .. .. per jar 1/11
Nizam 2/6
Vencatachellum's ..   .. .. per bot. 3/4

CURRY POWDER
Daw Sens 'Calcutta.'   Packed by HARRODS
per 1 lb. tin 2/3, 1 lb. glass 2/6
Ahmutys & Co.'s   .. .. per 1 lb. tin 3/4, bot. 1/3, 2/5
Atkinson's   .. .. .. per bot. 2/6, 3/3
Barber's   .. per 1 lb. tin 2/4, bot. 2/6, Empress bot. 1/–
Capt. White's   .. .. .. per bot. 1/–
Cooke & Co.'s 1/2
Crosse & Blackwell's   .. per 4 oz. bot. 10½d, 8 oz. bot. 1/5½
Halford's   .. .. .. per tin 1/–, 1/9½
Heinz   .. .. per tin 10½d
Loose..   .. .. per bot. 2/–
Lazenby's   .. .. per 4 oz. bot. 10½d
'Nizam'   .. .. .. per tin 1/6, 2/6
Madras   .. .. per tin 2/3, per bot. 11d
Marshall's   .. .. .. per bot. 1/6, 9d
Sharwood's   .. .. .. per 1 lb. tin 1/–
Stembridge's   .. per 1 lb. tin 3/9, ½ lb. bot. 2/2
Tiger, 'Calcutta'   .. .. .. per ½ lb. tin 1/3
Vencatachellum's Genuine..   .. .. per tin 1/11, 3/4
,,   Loganath's   .. .. .. ,, 1/6, 2/9

CURRIED PREPARATIONS
Halford's Crab   .. .. .. per ½ tin 2/6
,,   Fowl   .. .. per ½ tin 2/8, per tin 4/11
,,   Lobster   .. .. ,, 2/8½ ,, —
,,   Mutton   .. .. ,, 2/6 ,, —
,,   Prawns   .. .. ,, 2/6 ,, 4/7
,,   Rabbit   .. .. ,, 2/6 ,, 4/7
,,   Sauce   .. .. ,, 1/5 ,, 2/5

CUSTARD POWDER
HARRODS..   .. per tin 10½d, 7 lb. tin 4/–
Bird's   per box 6½d, 1/–, per tin 1/3½, 4/9
Brown & Polson's   .. .. .. per tin 1/2
Carltona   .. .. .. per tin 1/–, pkts. 6½d
Colman's   .. .. per tin 1/2
Cerebos   .. .. ,, 1/–
Chiver's   .. .. ,, 10½d
Creamola   .. .. per pkt. 6d, per tin 1/3
Foster Clark's   .. .. per tin 10½d
'Flakna'   .. .. per pkt. 5½d
Fulcream (Sweetened)   .. .. .. per pkt. 10½d
,,   (Unsweetened)   .. .. ,, 8d
Green's   .. .. ,, 6d
Borwick's   .. .. ,, 5d
Monk & Glass   .. .. per pkt. 10½d, per tin 1/3
'Oma'   .. .. per tin 1/–
'Peterkin'   .. .. .. per pkt. 9d, per tin 1/3
Plasmon   .. .. per pkt. 7½d

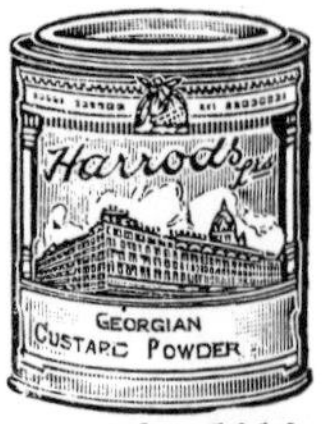

ALL PRICES ARE SUBJECT TO MARKET FLUCTUATIONS

HARRODS LTD

Telephone SLOANE 1234
Telegrams 'EVERYTHING HARRODS LONDON'

LONDON SW 1

GROCERY DEPARTMENT

FLOUR

(Subject to alteration without notice)

	7 lbs.	14 lbs.	½ sack 140 lbs.
HARRODS Finest Household	**1/5½**	**2/10**	**27/6**
Hungarian	**1/10**	**3/7½**	**34/–**
Pastry Whites	**1/6**	**2/11**	**28/6**
Wheatmeal	**1/5½**	**2/10**	**27/6**

(½ sacks **1/6** extra, returnable)

	7 lbs.	14 lbs.	½ sack 140 lbs.
Australian	**1/5½**	**2/10**	**27/6**
Canadian	**1/5½**	**2/10**	**27/6**

(Sacks free)

Buckwheat, Heckers	per pkt. **1/7**
Graham	per 3½ lb. bag **1/8**
Household Millenium	7 lbs. **1/6**, ½ sack, including sack **30/6**
,, Colman's	per 5 lb. bag **1/6**
,, 'Red Shield'	,, 3½ lb. ,, **1/1½**
Prewett's Household	,, 7 lb. ,, **1/8**
,, Whites	,, 7 lb. ,, **1/8**
,, Wheatmeal	,, 7 lb. ,, **1/8**
Rye, American	,, 3 lb. ,, **1/9**
Wholemeal, 'Artox'	,, 7 lb. ,, **1/11**
,, 'Allison's'	,, 3 lb. ,, **1/0½**
,, ,,	,, 7 lb. ,, **1/11½**
,, Hovis	,, 7 lb. ,, **1/11½**
,, Hindhaughs	,, 3 lb. ,, **1/–**
,, Peterkins' 3's	per pkt. **1/1**
,, Daren	per 7 lb. bag **2/2**
,, 'Red Shield'	,, 3½ lb. ,, **1/1½**

FLOUR (Self Raising)

HARRODS . . . . 7 lbs. **1/8**, 14 lbs. **3/3**, ½ sack, 140 lbs. **31/9**

(½ sacks free, not returnable)

'Colman's'	per 5 lb. bag **1/8**
'Eureka'	,, 3 lb. ,, **11d**
'McDougal's' 3 lb. bag **9½d**, 6 lb. bag **1/6½**,	,, 12 lb. ,, **3/–**
'Lito'	,, 3 lb. ,, **1/–**
Peterkin, 3's, Self Raising	per pkt. **10½d**
Queen Fisher	per 3 lb. bag **1/–**, 6 lb. bag **1/11**
'Seraflo'	per 3 lb. bag **11½d**

FURNITURE POLISH

HARRODS 'Harpola'	per tin **10d**, **1/7**, **3/2**
Adams'	per bot. **10d**, **1/6**
Blessita	per tin **6d**
Carr's	per bot. **9d**
Chiver's	,, **9d**
Cobra	per tin **5d**, **10d**
Day & Martin	per bot. **8d**
Durax	,, **1/3**
Everett's	,, **10½d**
Furmoto	per bot. **1/6**, and tins **2/–**, **5/–**
Hannah's Magic	per bot. **1/6**
Hargreaves'	,, **10d**
Jackson's	per bot. **9½d**, **1/6**, **2/6**
'Karpol'	per tin **1/–**
'Komo'	per jar **10d**
Milton Glaze	per bot. **2/–**
'Min'	per jar **1/6**
'N.N.'	per bot. **10d**
Oakey's	per jar **10d**
Premier	per bot. **1/3**
Romar	per tin **1/–**, **2/–**, **4/–**
Ronuk	per jar **1/–**, **1/9**
S.A.P.	per tin **6d**, **11½d**, **1/6**
Shinelite	per bot. **1/3**
Slick	per tin **10d**
Stephenson's	per bot. **4½d**, **9d**, **1/6**
Stone's	per bot. **1/4**
Terezol	per bot. **11d**, **1/6**
Tuxedo	per tin **6d**
Venus	per bot. **1/–**, **2/–**

DESSERT FRUITS IN TINS AND BOTTLES

HARRODS 'Marguerite' Brand, Extra Choice Quality, Perfect Fruits—

Apricots	No. 2½ tin **1/9**, No. 3 tin **2/3**
Fruit Salad	No. 2½ tin **2/1**
Hawaiian Pineapple Slices	No. 2 tin **1/2**, No. 2½ tin **1/5**
Pears	No. 2½ tin **1/10**, No. 3 tin **2/4**
Peaches	No. 2½ tin **1/9**, No. 3 tin **2/3**

(12 tins of any of the above **1/–** per doz. less)

Other Brands—

Apricots	Nos. 2½'s Choice **1/5**, 2½'s Fine **1/2½**, 1¼'s Fine **8d** picnic tin **6d**
Blackberries	per No. 2 tin **1/4**
Blackcurrants (Australian)	No. 2½ tin **1/10½**
Cherries, 'Cirio'	per ½ tin **10d**, per tin **1/6**, picnic tin **6½d**
,, Royal Anne	per tin **1/10½**
Fruit Salad	No. 2½ tin **1/11**, 1½ tin **1/1**
Grape Fruit	picnic tin **7½d**, per tin **1/3**
Gooseberries (Australian)	No. 2½ tin **1/2**
Guavas	,, **2/3**
Lichees (Indian)	per tin **2/6**
Loganberries	picnic tin **7½d**, No. 2 tin **1/3**
'Mammee'	No. 2 tin **1/8**
Mangoes (Ripe)	No. 2½ tin **2/8**
Oranges, Tangerine	per tin **8½d**
Pears, 2's (Canadian) **11½d**, 2½'s Choice **1/6½**, 2½'s Fine **1/4½**	1¼'s **9½d**, picnic tin **6½d**
Peaches 2½'s Choice **1/3**, 2½'s Fine **1/1½**, 1¼'s **7½d**, picnic tin **6d**	
Pie Peaches	tin about 7 lbs. **3/3**
Pineapple Slices per tin **7½d**, 2½ Choice, **1/2½**, 2½ Extras **1/4½**	Choice, per No. 2 tin **11½d**, Extras, per No. 2 tin **1/1**
,, Chunks	large tin **1/6½**, small tin **7½d**
,, Gold Reef Slices	No. 2½ tins **1/3**
,, ,, Chunks	,, **1/3**
,, Crushed Hawaiian	per tin **1/–**
,, ,, South African	No. 1 tin **9d**
Peeled Grapes	per tin **9½d**
Plums, Egg	No. 2½ tin **1/4½**
,, Greengage	No. 2½ tin **1/4½**, No. 2 tin **9½d**
,, Dripack	No. 2½ tin **1/6**
Raspberries	No. 2 tin **1/6**
,, (Australian)	per No. 1 tin **1/–**
Strawberries	No. 2 tin **1/9**

(12 tins of any of the above **6d** per doz. less)

'Old Homestead' (in Heavy Syrup)

Apricots	per bot. **6/3**, **3/9**, **2/3**
Cherries	per bot. **2/9**
Fruit Salad	,, **2/3**
Figs	,, **3/9**
Loganberries	,, **3/3**
Peaches	per bot. **6/3**, **3/9**, **2/3**
Pears	,, **6/3**, **3/9**, **2/3**
Pineapple Slices	per bot. **2/3**

ALL PRICES ARE SUBJECT TO MARKET FLUCTUATIONS

GROCERY DEPARTMENT

GELATINE

HARRODS Finest Quality French White Sheet, 1 lb. **4/6**, ½ lb. **2/6**	
,, Fine Sheet	,, **4/3** ,, **2/4**
Crosse & Blackwell's Leaf ..	per 1 lb. pkt. **3/4**
Cox's (Sparkling)	per pkt. **6d**, **1/-**
,, Powdered	per drum **1/3**, **2/4**, **4/3**
Gelinglass	per ¼ lb. pkt. **1/-**
Knox's	per pkt. **1/3**
Marshall's Leaf .. per 1 lb. **7/6**, ½ lb. **3/10**, ¼ lb. **2/-**	
,, Flake	per 1 lb. pkt. **6/3**
Nelson's A1 Sheet	per lb. **4/6**
,, Amber	,, **5/-**
,, Opaque	per pkt. **6d**, **11d**
,, Powdered	per 4-oz. tin **1/2**
,, Waterleaf	per pkt. **6d**
Swinborne's	per pkt. **6d**, **11½d**

GINGER BEER

Adam's Concentrated	per bot. **2/4**

GINGER (Preserved in Syrup)

Finest Cargo	No. 1 jar **1/5**, No. 3 jar **2/9**, No. 6 jar **5/3**
Finest Dry Preserved	per lb. **1/4**
Finest Stem	No. 1 jar **1/10**, No. 3 jar **3/4**, No. 6 jar **6/6**
	per glass **2/3**, **4/4**
Heinz	per bot. **1/4½**, **2/3**
Young Stem ..	No. 3 Blue and White Hawthorne jar **5/8**
,, ,, 'Mandarin'..	2½'s **5/6**, 5's **10/6**

GLASS CLOTH AND PAPER

Oakey's, Red Cloth, O, F, 1	per quire **3/6**
London, ,, ,, O, F, 1	,, **3/-**
Oakey's, White ,, O, 1, 1½, 2, 3 ..	,, **3/6**
,, ,, Paper O, 1, 1½, 2, 3 ..	,, **2/6**

GLAZE

C. & B.'s or Lazenby's	per bot. **1/-**

GLUCOSE

Water White	per 7 lb. tin **3/3**

GRAPE JUICE

Marsh's	per bot. **1/9**
Welch's	,, **1/10**
Grappe de France ..	per bot. **2/4**, **4/6**
Mostelle (Golden) ..	per bot. **3/9**
,, (Red)	,, **3/6**

GRAVY POWDER

'Betzol'	per tin **7½d**

GROATS

Robinson's Prepared	per tin **7½d**, **1/3**

GROULT'S PREPARATIONS

Alphabetiques	Per ½ lb. pkt. **7d**
Chestnut Flour	,, ,, **9d**
Cream of Rice	,, ,, **7d**
Cream of Barley	,, ,, **6½d**
Macaroni, Moyens	,, ,, **7½d**
Nouilles aux Oeufs ..	,, ,, **7½d**
Nouilles Blanches ..	,, ,, **7d**
Perles du Nizam	,, ,, **10d**
Petites Pates	,, ,, **6d**
Potato Flour	,, ,, **6½d**
Sago	,, ,, **9d**
Semoule de Riz ..	,, ,, **7½d**
Spaghetti	,, ,, **6½d**
Tapioca	,, ,, **7d**
Vermicelli	,, ,, **7d**
Wheat Semoule	,, ,, **6½d**

GUAVA JELLY'S. AMERICAN

.. ..	per box **1/8½**, **3/2**
Daw Sen's Indian	per bot. **2/6**, **5/-**
'Pucca' Indian	,, **1/9**
West Indian..	,, **2/-**
Speed's Indian	per 1 lb. tin **1/9**

GUAVA CHEESE

Daw Sen's (Indian)	per bot. **2/6**
West Indian.. ..	,, **2/-**

HEARTHSTONE

Rough	per doz. **10d**
Squares	,, **1/3**
Powder	per drum **3d**

HERBS, DRIED

Keddies'—Basil, Marjoram, Thyme, Mixed, Parsley ..	per bot. **10½d**
Bayleaves, Chevril, Mint, Sage, Tarragon, Winter Savoury	,, **1/1**
C. & B.'s or Lazenby's—	
Mixed, Parsley, Thyme ..	,, **10½d**
Mint, Sage, Tarragon ..	,, **1/1**
Herbaceous Mixture ..	,, **9½d**
Turtle Herbs ..	per pkt. **1/2**

HERRINGS

Bruce (Scotch) (in Tomato) ..	per tin **8½d**
Fillets in Olive Oil (Harrods) ..	per bot. **1/9**, **3/-**
Fresh Scotch ..	per tin **8d**
Marshall's Fillets (in Tomato) ..	,, **4d**
Roes (Soft)	per glass **1/-**, **1/11**, tins **10½d**
,, ,, C. & B...	,, **1/-**
Tyne Brand (in Tomato) ..	per tin **10½d**

HOMINY

.. ..	per lb. **3d**, 7 lb. **1/8**
American ..	5 lb. linen bag **1/4**
,, ..	pkts. **1/-**

HONEYCOMB MOULDS

Original	per pkt. **6½d**
Various—Chocolate Fruit Salad, Imperial, Lemon, Orange, Royal, Raspberry, Strawberry ..	,, **7½d**

HONEY

HARRODS Finest Amber No. 1 jar **1/5½**, No. 2 **2/9**	
,, Hybla-Fancy (Tango Colour) Jar	**3/6**
Australian, Fancy jar, about 1 lb ..	**1/3**
Per glass jar ..	**1/6**, **1/3**, **8½d**
7 lb. tins ..	**8/-**
Aberdeenshire ..	per jar **2/6**
Be-Ze-Be ..	per jar **9d** and **1/4**
,, Ginger ..	per glass **1/7**
Canadian White ..	1 lb. tin, each **1/2**
2 lb. 3 oz. tin, each **2/4½**, 4½ lb. tin, each **4/4**	
Fine Quality No. 1 crocks **10½d**, No. 2, **1/7½**	
	No. 4 **2/9**
Finest English ..	per glass **2/3**
Heather, Scotch ..	,, **4/3**
,, New Forest ..	,, **3/-**
Hymetian	,, **3/-**
Imperial Bee (N. Zealand) per jar **10½d**, **1/4½**, **2/9** 7 lb. tins each **8/3**	
Jamaica ..	per bot. **1/6**
Munton's Malted ..	per jar **1/4½**
Narbonne (Noel's) ..	per glass jar **2/3**
,, C. & B.'s ..	per crook **2/6**
New Zealand ..	per glass **1/4**
Orange Blossom ..	per jar **1/10**
Quebec	per glass **2/-**
Scotch (Baxter's) ..	,, **3/9**
Sections (Glazed) ..	,, **3/-**
,, (Californian) ..	,, **1/10**
White Clover ..	,, **1/8**

ALL PRICES ARE SUBJECT TO MARKET FLUCTUATIONS

HARRODS LTD

Telephone SLOANE 1234
Telegrams 'EVERYTHING HARRODS LONDON'

LONDON S W 1

JAMS AND JELLIES

	No. 1 Jar	No. 2 Jar
C. & B.'s		
Apricot Jam	10d	1/7
Blackcurrant Jam	1/0½	2/-
Cherry Jam	1/4½	2/8
Damson Jam	11½d	1/10
Gooseberry Jam	9d	1/5
Greengage Jam	10d	1/7
Plum Jam	8d	1/3
Raspberry Jam	1/-	1/11
,, and Currant Jam	11d	1/9
Strawberry Jam	1/-	1/11
Blackberry Jelly	10½d	1/8
Blackcurrant Jelly	¼'s 5½d, ½'s 9d, 1's 1/2½	
Red Currant Jelly	¼'s 5d, ½'s 7½d, 1's 1/1	

HARTLEY'S		
Apricot Jam	9½d	1/6
Blackberry Jelly	10½d	1/8
Blackcurrant Jam	1/-	1/10½
Damson Jam (Stoneless)	10d	1/6½
Gooseberry Jam, Red	8½d	1/4
Greengage Jam (Stoneless)	10d	1/7
Blackcurrant Jelly	¼'s 4½d, ½'s 7½d, 1/2	—
Red Currant Jelly	¼'s 4d, ½'s 7d, 1/-	—
Plum Jam (Red)	9d	1/4½
Raspberry Jam	11d	1/8½
Raspberry and Currant Jam	10½d	1/7½
Strawberry Jam	11½d	1/10

KEILLER'S SUGARLESS	No. 1 jar
Apricot Jam	2/3
Blackcurrant Jam	2/8
Damson Jam	2/2
Greengage Jam	2/2
Gooseberry Jam	1/10½
Plum Jam	1/10½
Raspberry Jam	2/6

LENSBOURG (Swiss)	1 lb. Jar
Cherry, Black or Red	1/6½

'OLD HOMESTEAD'	No. 1 Jars
Apricot Jam	1/4
Blackcurrant Jam	1/10
Damson Jam	1/6
Greengage Jam	1/3
Raspberry Jam	1/7½
Strawberry Jam	1/7½
Loganberry Jam	1/3
Plum Jam	1/4
,, ,, Victoria	1/5
Quince Jam	1/9
Cherry Jam	2/4

	Large	Medium	Small
Apple Jelly	1/8	1/-	8d
Blackberry Jelly	1/8		
Blackcurrant Jelly	3/3	1/9	1/-
Crab Apple Jelly	1/8	1/-	8d
Cranberry Jelly	2/1	—	—
Damson Jelly	1/6	—	—
Quince Jelly	1/8	1/-	—
Red Currant	3/-	1/7½	1/-

ROBERTSON'S	No. 1 Jar	No. 2 Jar
Apricot Jam	9d	1/5
Bramble Jelly	10½d	1/8
Blackcurrant Jam	11½d	1/9½
Raspberry Jam	11d	1/8½
Strawberry Jam	11½d	1/10

SCOTT'S JAMS	No. 1 Jar	No. 2 Jar	No. 3 Jar	No. 7 Jar
Apricot Jam	9d	1/4	1/11	4/8
Blackcurrant Jam	11d	1/8½	2/5	6/-

JAMS AND JELLIES—continued

SCOTTS—continued	No. 1	No. 2	No. 3	No. 7
Bramble Jelly	9½d	1/6	—	—
Damson Jam (Stoneless)	10d	1/7	2/3	
Gooseberry Jam	8½d	1/4	1/11	4/8
Greengage Jam (Stoneless)	8½d	1/4	1/10	
Raspberry Jam	11d	1/8½	2/5	6/-
Raspberry and Currant Jam	10d	1/7½	2/4½	5/9
Red Plum Jam	8½d	1/3½	1/10	4/6
Strawberry Jam	11d	1/8½	2/5	6/-
Red Currant Jelly	small 4d, medium 7d, large 1/-			
Blackcurrant Jelly	,, 4d, ,, 7d, ,, 1/-			

SOUTH AFRICAN	2 lb. tin
Apricot Jam	1/8
,, and Pine Jam	1/8
Cape Gooseberry Jam	per glass 1/3, 2/3 1/10½
Fig Jam, Ripe	1/8
,, ,, Green	1/8
Peach Jam	1/8
,, and Pine Jam	1/8
Plum Jam	1/8
Pineapple Jam	1/8
Quince Jam	1/8

ST. MARTINS	No. 1 Jar	No. 2 Jar
Apple Jelly	9d	—
Apricot Jam	9d	1/4
Blackcurrant Jam	11d	1/8½
Damson Jam	10½d	1/7½
Plum Jam (Red)	8½d	1/3½
Red Currant Jelly	1/2	—
Raspberry Jam	11d	1/8½
Strawberry Jam	11d	1/8½

TIPTREE CONSERVES, ETC.	No. 1 Jar
Apricot Preserve	1/3
Blackberry Conserve	1/4
Blackcurrant Conserve	1/6
Damson	1/6
Cherry Conserve, Blackheart	2/6
,, ,, Whiteheart	2/6
,, ,, Morello	2/6
Fig Preserve	1/6
Greengage Conserve	1/6
Gooseberry Conserve (Red)	1/2
,, ,, (Green)	1/3
Loganberry Conserve	1/10
Orange Conserve	1/4
Mirable Conserve	1/6
Mulberry Conserve	2/11
Plum Conserve, Purple	1/5
,, ,, Philippine	1/6
,, ,, Egg	1/4
Raspberry Conserve, Tiny Tip	1/7
,, and Currant Conserve	1/6
Red Currant Conserve	1/5
Jelly, Apple Golden	1/2
,, Quince	1/10
,, Blackcurrant	1/9
,, Red Currant	1/8
,, Blackberry	1/5
,, Loganberry	2/-
,, Raspberry	1/11
,, Orange	1/2
Quince Conserve	1/9
Pineapple Preserve	1/10
Peach Preserve	1/9
Strawberry Conserve, Scarlet	1/9
,, ,, Favourite	1/7
Seedless Blackberry	1/6
,, Blackcurrant	1/8
,, Raspberry	1/11
,, Strawberry	2/2

ALL PRICES ARE SUBJECT TO MARKET FLUCTUATIONS

HARRODS LTD

Telephone SLOANE 1234
Telegrams 'EVERYTHING HARRODS LONDON'

LONDON S W 1

GROCERY DEPARTMENT

LIME JUICE

Rose's .. .. per bot. **2/-**
'Crestona' Concentrated .. .. ,, **8½d**
Montserrat .. .. per bot. **1/8**, **3/-**
'Kia-Ora' .. .. per bot. **2/-**

LIME JUICE CORDIAL

Feltoe's .. .. per bot. **1/9**
Idris .. .. ,, **1/11**
'Kia-Ora' .. .. per bot. **1/1**, **2/-**
Montserrat .. .. per bot. **2/-**
Rose's .. .. ,, **2/2**
Rowntree's .. .. ,, **2/-**
Schweppes' .. .. ,, **2/-**
Southwell's .. .. ,, **1/6**
Stower's .. .. ,, **2/-**

LOBSTER

'Creel Brand' .. .. .. med. tin **2/2**, lge. tin **4/3**
Other Brands .. sml. tin **1/3**, med. tin **2/-**, lge. tin **3/11**
C. & B.'s or Lazenby's .. .. med. tin **2/5**
Glass .. .. each **3/-**

MARMALADE

	No. 1 Jar	No. 2 Jar	No. 3 Jar	No. 7 Jar
HARRODS ..	7d	1/1½	1/7	3/9
,, per doz.	6/9	13/-	18/-	—
,, Jelly ..	7½d	1/2	—	—
,, Coarse Cut	9d	1/5	2/-	5/-
Atkinson's ..	1/2	—	—	—
Baxter's	1/-	1/11	—	—
Cairn's Home Made	8½d	1/3½	—	—
,, Coarse Cut	1/-	1/11	—	—
,, Ginger ..	1/1	—	—	—
,, Gold Fish ..	8½d	1/3½	(Globe 9d)	
,, Scotch ..	8½d	1/3½	—	—
,, Tangerine ..	11½d	—	—	—
Cooper's 'Oxford'	1/2	2/2	3/-	6/6
,, Dark Blue	1/0½	2/-	—	—
Cooper's Vintage	1/1	2/6	—	—
Childrens' Choice (Pannier) ..	1/-	1/10	—	—
Chiver's 'Old English'	8d	1/3	1/9½	4/1
,, Grape	11d	1/9	—	—
,, Jelly	7½d	1/2	—	—
'Claremont,' Scotch (screw top jars)	1/2	2/-	—	—
Fleming's Grape Fruit	1/4½	—	—	—
,, Orange	1/-	—	—	—
Ginger	11½d	1/9½	—	—
Golden Shred	7½d	1/2	—	4/3
Grape Fruit	..	per jar 1/-,	1/4,	2/9
Hartley's	8d	1/3	1/9½	4/-
,, Jelly	8d	1/3	—	—
Keiller's (White Pots)	9½d	1/5½	2/1½	4/6
,, (Glass Pots)	8½d	1/4	1/11	—
,, Little Chip	8½d	1/4	—	—
,, Sugarless..	2/-	—	—	—
Ladies' Choice (Pannier).. ..	1/-	1/10	—	—
Old Homestead Dower House ..	..	per No. 1 Jar		1/4
,, ,, Grape Fruit ..	..	..	,,	2/-
,, ,, Orange	No. 1 Jar 1/2,	No. 2 Jar		2/4
,, ,, ,, Bitter ..	..	..	No. 1 Jar	1/4
,, ,, Tangerine ..	..	..	,,	1/4
,, ,, Thatched House..	..	..	,,	1/1
Scott's	7d	1/1½	1/7	3/9
,, Jelly	7½d	1/2	—	—
Silver Shred	7½d	1/2	—	—
Squires' Choice (Pannier) ..	1/-	1/10	—	—
St. Martin's	7½d	1/2½	—	4/-
,, Bitter..	1/-	1/11	—	—
Tickler's	7d	1/1½	1/7	3/9
Tiptree	1/3	—	—	—
,, Crystal	1/2	—	—	—
,, Everyday	9d	—	—	—
,, Fine Cut	1/-	—	—	—
,, Grape Fruit	1/8	—	—	—

MARMALADE—*continued*

	No. 1 Jar
Tiptree Invalid	1/3
,, Juicy	1/4
,, Lemon	1/3
,, Sliced Orange	1/4
,, Old Times	1/1
,, Breakfast..	1/1
,, Tonic	1/3
,, Doctor's	1/2
,, Tangerina..	1/4

MACARONI

Finest (Long Pipe) .. 1 lb. **4½d**, 7 lbs. **2/6**, pkts. each **6d**
Creamettes.. .. .. per pkt. **4½d**
Alphabets .. .. per lb. pkt. **7d**
Stars .. .. per lb. pkt. **7d**
Shelloni (Canadian) .. .. per pkt. **5d**
Heinz, with Cheese in Cream Sauce .. .. per tin **8½d**, **1/-**
De Barberi's .. .. per 4 lb. box **3/-**
Energen .. .. per pkt. **1/6**
Italian .. .. per 4 lb. box **2/3**
Quaker, Milkaroni.. .. .. per pkt. **9½d**

MACASSAR (Red Fish) .. .. .. per bot. **2/4**

MALLOW FLOAT .. .. .. per tin (4¼ lb.) **9/6**

MASONS DUST .. .. per bag **6d**, **1/-**, per bushel **4/-**

MAPLE BUTTER .. .. per jar **1/8**, per tin **2/6**

Sugar .. .. per pkt. **10½d**, **1/9**
Syrup .. ..per bot. **1/6** and **2/6**; per tin **4/3**, **5/9** and **8/6**
Log Cabin Syrup .. .. per tin **1/10½**, **3/11**

MAPLEINE .. .. per 1 oz. bot. **1/3**

MARBLE CLEANERS

Marbalette.. .. .. per bot. **1/-**
Marbleine .. .. per tin **7½d**
Marblerito .. .. per bot. **1/-**
Marble Powder .. .. per tin **10d**

MARMITE per 2 oz. jar **10d**, 4 oz. jar **1/6**, 8 oz. jar **2/6**, 16 oz. jar **4/6**

MATCHES

'Army & Navy' .. .. per doz. **10½d**
Bryant & May's .. .. .. per doz. **10d**, **11d**, **1/5**
'Bluecross' .. .. per doz. **10½d**
'Dunyerbit' .. .. ,, **10½d**
'Planters' .. .. ,, **10d**
'Remember' .. .. ,, **11d**
Moreland's 'John Bull' .. .. ,, **11d**
Safeties, Foreign .. .. ,, **9d**

(*Delivered in radius of our own vans only*)

MAYONNAISE

HARRODS .. .. per bot. **2/6**
Brand's .. .. ,, **10½d**
Crosse & Blackwell's .. .. .. per bot. **10½d**, **1/7**
Escoffier's .. .. per bot. **11d**
Heinz .. .. ,, **1/-**
Keddie's .. .. per bot. **10½d**, **1/8**
Lazenby's .. .. ,, **10d**, **1/5½**
'Old Homestead'.. .. .. per bot. **2/6**

MEATS

Bacon (Sliced) .. .. per glass **3/2**, **2/1**
Beef (Sliced) .. .. ,, **1/8**, **2/8**
Chicken (Devilled) .. .. per tin **2/-**
Ham (Devilled) .. .. per tin **1/6**, **2/6**
Tongue (Devilled) .. .. ,, **1/4**, **2/2**

ALL PRICES ARE SUBJECT TO MARKET FLUCTUATIONS

GROCERY DEPARTMENT

OIL FOR FRYING, Etc.

Jacob's .. .. ½ gall. **3/8**, per gall. **7/3**
gall. can extra **4/–**, ½-gall. can extra **2/6**
'Saladin' .. .. per tin **1/4** and **2/4**
Pure Vegetable (HARRODS) per ½-gall. can, not returnable **4/3**
nom. qt. can **2/3**
'Wesson' .. .. per tin **3/9**

OIL MINERAL FOR LAMPS

'Royal Standard,' 'Crown Diamond'
5 gall. drum **4/5**, cask about 40 gall. **43/–**
'White May,' 'White Rose'
5 gall. drum **4/10**, cask about 40 gall. **46/6**

Drums allowed for as marked. An allowance 8/– will be made on empty Casks if returned in sound condition (carriage paid) to the Oil Warehouse. Address Card for same will be forwarded by post

Carriage on 5 gall. drums in London area **1/2**. Outside London area carriage forward

OILS

Colza .. .. per bot. **2/3**, *per gall. **7/6**
Huttonizing Fluid .. .. per tin **2/–**
Linseed Oil .. .. per qt. bot. **2/–**
Neatsfoot .. .. ,, **2/9**
Sperm Oil .. .. ,, **1/8**

* Cans 1/6 extra, allowed when returned

OLIVE OIL

HARRODS Finest Quality Huile d'Olive
per bot. **3/4**, ½-bot. **1/9½**, ¼-bot. **1/2**, gallon **16/–**,
½-gall. **8/3**, gall. jars **3/–**, ½-gall. **2/–** extra, returnable
Brand's .. .. ½-bott. **2/1**
Barton & Guestier's .. per bot. **4/6** and **2/6**
Heinz .. .. qrt. tin, **4/9**
Italian Sasso
½-bot. **2/10**, qt. tin **3/10**, gall. tin **14/6**
Lucca, C. & B.'s or Lazenby's ½-bot. **1/9½**, bot. **3/4**
Marshall's .. .. per bot. **2/–**
Provence, C. & B.'s or Lazenby's
½-bot. **1/9½**, bot. **3/4**
Riviera .. .. bot. **1/10**, **3/4**
Sante .. .. per bot. **5/9**, ½-bot. **2/11**
Sandolivia .. .. per bot. **5/3**

OLIVES

HARRODS, Stuffed .. .. 6 oz. bot. **1/7**
,, Assorted .. 9 oz. bot. **2/2**
,, Olive Farcies .. per bot. **1/3**, **1/8**
,, French .. .. ,, **1/4**, **2/–**
,, Spanish .. .. ,, **1/1**, **1/8½**
Californian Ripe .. .. .. per bot. **1/11**
Colossal, Plain .. .. ..nom. pt. bot. **3/9**
,, Stuffed .. .. ,, **4/–**
De Luxe (C. & B.'s) .. .. per bot. **1/4**
French Amieux Freres .. .. ,, **1/6**
Indian, in Vinegar .. .. ,, **2/3**
Jacob's .. .. per large bot. **2/–**
King Olives .. .. ,, ,, **2/4**
Mammoth, Plain.. .. .. per 12 oz. bot. **2/6**
,, Stuffed .. .. ,, ,, **2/10**
Pitted .. .. per bot. **2/9**
Spanish, C. & B.'s or Lazenby's .. ½-pt. bot. **1/1**
,, Queen, Heinz .. .. .. per bot. **1/4½**
Stuffed .. ..per bot. **1/–**, **2/5**
,, Lazenby's .. .. per bot. **1/6**
,, Heinz .. .. per ½-bot. **1/3**, bot. **1/8**
,, Libby's .. .. .. per bot. **1/3½**
Queen, ,, ... ,, **1/2½**

ONIONS

Powdered .. .. per tin **1/–**

ORANGE JUICE

P. J. L. Sweetened .. .. .. per bot. **3/–**
,, Unsweetened .. .. .. ,, **3/–**

ORANGE SQUASH Etc.

Be-Ze-Be .. .. per bot. **2/–**
Caley's .. .. ,, **1/6**
Cochrane's .. .. ,, **3/–**
Fleming's .. .. ,, **1/11**
Idris .. .. ,, **2/3**
Kia-Ora .. ..per bot. **1/1**, **2/–**
,, Unsweetened .. .. per bot. **2/–**
,, Crush .. .. per decanter **2/–**
'Mission Orange Juice'
16 oz. bot. **2/3**, 32 oz. bot. **4/–**, 128 oz. bot. **13/6**
Orange Cup (C. & B.'s).. .. per bot. **1/10½**
Orange Pierjac .. .. ,, **2/–**
'Oros' S. African .. .. .. ,, **2/–**
'Purity' .. .. ,, **3/6**
Schweppes' .. .. ,, **2/–**
Stower's .. .. ,, **2/–**

OVENO .. .. per tin **1/–**

OYSTERS .. .. per tin **1/1**

PANCAKE MIXTURE

Aunt Jemima's .. .. per pkt. **10d**
Green's .. .. ,, **5d**

PANIR FLOUR .. .. .. per pkt. **11d**

PARAZONE Bleach.. .. .. per bot. **1/6**

PARISIAN ESSENCES (For Gravies)

HARRODS .. ..per bot. **2/2**, **1/2**
Lazenby's.. .. .. ,, **1/4**, **2/3**

PASSION FRUIT

Australian.. .. .. per bot. **1/6**, **2/9**, **5/–**

PATÉ DE FOIES GRAS—

Terrines, Finest French

No. 5 High	**37/6**	No 10 Flat	**9/–**
No. 6 ,, ...	**30/–**	No 12 ,, ...	**6/6**
No. 7 ,, ...	**21/6**	No 13 ,, ...	**5/6**
No. 8 ,, ...	**16/–**	No 14 ,, ...	**4/6**
No. 9 ,, ...	**12/6**	No 15 ,, ...	**3/6**
Miniature	**2/–**	No 16 ,, ...	**2/–**

Amieux Freres Foie d'oie Entier au Natural .. .. tins **16/–**
Ballotin de Faisan .. .. per tin **10/–**
Bloc de Foie Gras Entier Doyen's .. No 1 tin **14/–**
Doyens Paté de Foies Gras .. No 14 tins, per tin **4/–**
Paté de Foies Gras (Amieux Freres) .. ,, **2/4**
Puree de Foies Gras (Amieux Freres) .. tins **11½d**, **1/7½**
Puree de Foies Gras (Doyen) .. per tin **11½d**, **1/7½**

PAW PAW PRESERVE

W. Indian .. .. per jar **2/8**

PEACHES

Evaporated .. .. per lb. **1/4**
In Syrup, tins and bottles, *see page 733, 734*

PEANUT PASTE .. .. .. glass **8½d**, **1/1**, **1/10**

PEANUTS (Salted)

American .. .. per bot. **2/6**

PEARS

PEARS, Evaporated .. .. .. per lb. **1/4**
In Syrup, tins and bottles, *see page 733, 734*

ALL PRICES ARE SUBJECT TO MARKET FLUCTUATIONS

GROCERY DEPARTMENT

SOAP EXTRACT, POLISHING POWDERS, Etc.—

Wylie's Disinfectant No. 4	7 lb. bag 2/9
,, ,, No. 1	,, 3/-
Hudson's No. 1 quality per lb. 6½d, doz. ¼ lb. pkts. 1/7½, 14 lb. box 7/6	
,, No. 2 quality	per doz. ¼ lb. pkts. 1/6
Kleendish	per pkt. 4½d
'Vim'	per drum 2d, 6d, 10d
'Kleenoff'	per tin 10d
Sapolio	each 5½d
Lively Polly	per lb. 6½d, 14 lb. box 7/6
'Longa Life'	per pkt. 3½d
'Kleno'	per bot. 1/3, 2/-
'Ofome'	tubes 1/3, 2/-
Old Dutch Cleanser	per tin 7½d
'Omo' (Hudson's)	per carton 3d, 6d
'Persil'	6d
'Panshine'	per pkt. 5½d
'Quick'	per drum 4½d
Quic Hand Clean	8d
'Restu'	per pkt. 3½d
'Roo' Powder	per 7 lb. bag 1/9
,, Plates	each 6d
'Duzzall'	per bot. 7½d
'Kit'	per tin 6d
'Rustimova'	,, 1/6
'Sambo' Cleaner	per tin 6d, 1/-
'Sapon'	per drum 8d
'Sparkla'	per tab. 2½d, drum 5d
'Tetralene'	per tube 9d, per tin 1/6
'Westrapol'	tubes, each 1/-
'Wisk'	per drum 6d
'Jaxo'	,, 7d
'Blessita'	per tin 6d
'Handslick'	per drum 1/-
Smith's Disinfectant Soap Powder	per pkt. 1½d
'Dispa'	per tin 6d
'Golden Rod'	per pkt. 6d
'Glitto'	per pkt. 2½d, 6d
'Rinso'	,, 10d, 3½d
'Dosol'	per pkt. 6d
'Wizard'	per drum 6d
'Kurlo'	per pkt. 3d
'Compo'	,, 6d
'Handclene'	,, 8d
'Wolsil'	,, 3d
'Bumpo'	,, 3½d
'Whiteshine'	per tin 7½d, 1/-
'Gospo' Powder	per tin 7½d, 28 lb. box 10/-
,, Block	each 3½d
'Scourine'	per drum 6d
'Flikitoff'	,, 6d
'Soako'	per pkt. 3½d
'Magpie'	per drum 7d
'Grip'	,, 6d
'Tozol'	per tin 1/-
'Sanoper'	per drum 7d
'101' Scourer	,, 6d
'Vitrella'	per tin 1/-
'Gumption'	,, 1/3
'Iclean'	,, 6d
'Pavitts'	per drum 4½d
'Moval'	per tube 6d, 1/-
'Gazelle'	per pkt. 3½d
'Klenolene'	per bot. 1/-
'Tuxedo'	per pkt. 6d
'Socleno'	,, 7½d
'Lightning' Cleanser	per drum 6d
'Eezal'	per pkt. 4d
'Solveno'	per tin 7½d
'Kingsol'	,, 6d
'Acto'	,, 6d
'Huttonizing Fluid'	,, 2/-
'Esco'	,, 9d
'Austin' Wash Easy	per pkt. 1½d

SOAP EXTRACT, POLISHING POWDERS, Etc.—
continued

Gossage's Dry Soap	per lb. 6½d, per doz. ¼ lb. pkts. 1/6½
Armour's Cleanser	per drum 5½d
'Paintclene'	per tin 6d
'Lystra'	per drum 6d
'Spic and Span'	,, 5½d

SOAP FOR CARPETS, ETC.

Chivers'	per tab. 9d
Carr's	per tin 4½d, 1/3
Carpetine	,, 11½d, 1/6
Proctor's	per tab. 9d
Stephenson	,, 6d

SOAP FLAKES

HARRODS Washing Wafers small pkt. 2½d, med. pkt. 4½d, large pkt. 7½d	
Loose	per 1 lb. 8½d, 7 lbs. 4/10
Flakettes, Bibby's	per pkt. 6d
'Ivory'	,, 6½d
Lux	per pkt. 9d, 6d, 3d
'Feather'	per pkt. 4d
'Flako'	,, 4½d
Goodwin's	per drum 1/-
Wilkie & Soames'	per 1 lb. pkt. 8½d
Silver Leaves	per pkt. 5d
Jolli Chips	,, 2½d
Fairy Flakes	per pkt. 6d

SODA (Washing)

per 7 lb. 6½d, 14 lb. 1/0½, 28 lb. 2/-, ½ cwt. 3/10½, 1 cwt. 7/8

SODA, BI-CARBONATE

per 1 lb. 3d, 7 lbs. 1/6

Calasko, Bleaching ... per pkt. 2d

SPAGHETTI

Finest Italian	per lb. 5d, 7 lb. 2/9
Heinz, in Tomato	per tin 6½d, 9½d, 1/3
Italian Dinner, containing pkt. Spaghetti, bot. Tomato Sauce, bot. Grated Cheese, sufficient for 4 persons	2/6
Premier, in Tomato	per bot. 1/4½
'Merrisalco,' in Tomato	per glass 9½d
Van Camp's ,,	per tin 10½d

SPONGE MIXTURE

Green's (Chocolate or Raspberry)	per pkt. 6d
,, (Various)	,, 5½d
'Tricol'	,, 5½d
'Peterkin'	,, 5½d
Symington's	,, 5d
Foster Clark's	,, 4½d
Crestona	,, 5½d
Spongeoma	,, 5d
'Spongie'	,, 5½d
'Viota'	,, 6½d
,, Honeycomb	,, 3½d

SUGAR

(See Weekly List for Current Prices)

	1 lb.	7 lb.
Afternoon Tea Cubes	3¾d	2/1½
Cane, Mauritius	3¼d	1/10
Castor	3¾d	2/1½
,, Cane	4¼d	2 5
,, Glebe	4 lb. bag	—
,, (Banquet)	*14 lb. tin 8/6	
Coffee Crystals	4d	2 3
,, ,, 'Dapple'	1 lb. pkt. 1/-	—

* 1/- allowed on tins if returned in good condition

ALL PRICES ARE SUBJECT TO MARKET FLUCTUATIONS

GROCERY DEPARTMENT

SUGAR

		1 lb.	7 lb.
Cubelets (Fairries)		4¼d	2/5
Dark Brown		3¼d	1/10
Demerara		3½d	1/11½
Domino Cubes	per 2 lb. pkt. 1/3	—	—
'Glebe' Gran.		—	—
Granulated		3d	1/8½
" Cane		3¼d	1/10
" Domino	per 2 lb. pkt. 1/-	—	—
Icing		4d	2/3
" Bridal	*12 lb. tin 8/-	—	—
" Bride Cake	7 lb. tin 5/-	—	—
" Marshall's	2 lb. tin 2/4	—	8/2
Lump		3½d	1/11½
" Cane		3¾d	2/1
Preserving		3¼d	1/10
Cane		3½d	1/11½
Soft Cooking		3¼d	1/10
Spinning, Marshall's	2 lb. pkt. 3/6	—	—
Sugar Candy, Light or Dark	per lb.	6½d	3/8
" " Crushed	per 1 lb. pkt. 1/3	—	—
" " " Loose		7½d	—
Yellow Crystals		3¼d	1/10

* 1/- allowed on tins if returned in good condition

SPICES

- Pimento, Ground .. per lb. 1/4
- Ground .. " 1/3
- Carraway Seeds .. " 6d
- " " ground .. " 10d
- Cinnamon, Finest .. " 4/-
- " Ground .. per ¼ lb. tin 1/2
- Cloves, Finest Penang .. per lb. 4/6
- " Ground .. per ¼ lb. tin 1/1, 1 lb. 3/8
- Coriander Seeds .. per lb. 11d
- " Ground .. " 1/-
- Ginger, Finest Picked .. " 2/6
- " Ground .. " 2/6
- Mace, Whole .. " 7/9
- " Ground .. per ¼ lb. tin 1/11
- Mixed Spice .. per 1 lb. tin 2/-, ¼ lb. tin 8d, 2 oz. tin 5d
- Nutmegs .. per lb. 3/9
- " Ground .. per ¼ lb. tin 1/1
- Pickling .. per lb. 1/2
- Turmeric .. " 2/2

SOOT DESTROYER

- 'Imp' .. per pkt. 4½d

SOUPS IN TINS AND BOTTLES

	HARRODS tins	HARRODS bots.	C. & B.'s tins.	C. & B.'s bots.	Lazenby's tins	Lazenby's bots.
Consomme, Hare, Kidney, Ox Tail (thick or clear), Mock Turtle (thick or clear), Mulligatawny or Chicken Broth	1/3	1/9	1/3	1/9	1/3	1/9
Gravy, Tomato or Julienne	1/1	1/7	1/1	1/7	1/1	1/7

- Marshall's Sildeen Consomme .. per bot. 2/3
- Amieux Freres—Ox Tail, Petit Marmite, Bouillion Gras, Potage Julienne .. per tin 10½d, 1/8
- Armour's Tomato .. per tin 6d, per doz 5/9
- Campbell's—Asparagus, Beef, Celery, Consomme, Bouillion, Julienne, Chicken, Ox Tail, Mulligatawny, Tomato, Pea, Vegetable, Mock Turtle per tin 7½d, per doz. 7/3
- Clark's—Celery, Consomme, Julienne, Mulligatawny, Mock Turtle, Ox Tail, Pea, Green Pea, Tomato, Vegetable, Scotch Broth per tin 7½d, per doz. 7/3
- Clark's Chicken .. per tin 1/-
- Real Turtle (Crosse & Blackwell's) per ½ pt. bot. 1/8, pt. bot. 3/2, ½ pt. tin 1/6, pt. tin 2/9, qt. 4/11

SOUPS IN TINS AND BOTTLES—*continued*

- Edwards' Desiccated—Brown, White, Tomato per doz. pkts. 2/-, ¼ lb. tin 8½d, ½ lb. tin 1/4, 1 lb. tin 2/6
- Edwards' Gravina .. per tin 1/-
- Escoffier's Creme Tomato .. per pt. tin 1/1
- Heinz's Green Pea, Celery .. per med. tin 1/-
- " Tomato .. per tin 6d, 9d, 1/2½
- " Cream of Bean .. per tin 10d
- Real Turtle Soup, Lusty's Clear per qt. tin 14/-, pt. tin 7/4, ½ pt. tin 4/-, bot. 4/-, 7/4; 2 portion tin 2/3, 1 portion tin 1/4
- 'Sailor' (Various) .. per tin 7½d, 11½d
- " Real Turtle .. ½ pt tin 1/6
- Symington's Clear .. per bot. 9d
- Van Camp's (Various) .. per tin 8½d, per doz. 8/3

SOUP SQUARES AND TABLETS

- 'Dirk Brand'—Julienne, Kidney, Scotch Broth, Lentil, Mulligatawny, Pea, Tomato, Mock Turtle, Hare, Green Pea, Mutton Broth, Ox Tail per pkt. 2d, per doz. 1/10
- HARRODS Turtle Soup Tablets .. per box of 4 tabs. 1/-
- Ivelcon, St. Ivel, Consomme 6 tabs. in tin 5½d, 12 tabs. 10½d
- Standard Food Co., Consomme .. tin containing 12 tubes 1/8
- Maggis' Consomme .. 6 cubes 6d, 12 cubes 11½d
- Symington's—Scotch Broth, Kidney, Mulligatawny, Pea, Lentil, Tomato, Ox Tail, Mock Turtle, Hare, Celery, Onion, White Vegetable pkt. to make 1 qt. 6d, per doz. 5/11
- Lusty's Turtle Tablets .. per box of 4 tabs. 1/-
- Brand's Squares—Gravy, Tomato, Mock Turtle, Mulligatawny, Julienne, Ox Tail 6 in box 2/6
- Maggis'—Green Pea, Pea, Pea and Bacon, Julienne, Lentil, Mock Turtle, Mulligatawny, Mushroom, Scotch Broth, Spring Vegetable, Tomato, Ox Tail, White Haricot per pkt. 2d, per doz. 1/11
- Foster Clark's—Scotch Broth, Kidney, Mulligatawny, Pea, Lentil, Tomato, Ox Tail, Mock Turtle, Hare, Green Pea .. per pkt. 2½d, per doz. 2/5

STARCH

- Colman's White (Loose) per lb. 7½d, ½ lb. box 4½d, 1 lb. box 8½d, 4 lb. box 2/9
- " Blue .. 1 lb. box 8½d
- " Cream .. " 8½d
- Glenfield's .. per lb. 8d
- Dutch (Loose) .. " 4½d
- O. Jones' Blue .. 1 lb. box 8½d
- " Cream .. per lb. 8½d
- Reckitt's Blue .. 1 lb. box 8½d
- " Ecru .. " 8½d
- " White .. " 8½d
- Robin .. per box 5d, 10d

STARCH GLAZE

- Borax .. per pkt. 3d

STARCH GLOSS

- Redford's .. per box 1/3

STEEL POWDER .. per box 7½d

SUCCOTASH .. per tin 1/3

SUGAR CORN .. per tin 10½d, per bot. 2/1

- Corn on Cob, Maine .. No. 4 tin 2/9
- " " Canadian .. No. 3 tin 2/4
- " " .. " 1/9

SULTANAS .. per lb. 11d, 1/-, 1/4

- Australian .. per lb. 11d, 1/-
- " .. per 1 lb. carton 1/1

ALL PRICES ARE SUBJECT TO MARKET FLUCTUATIONS

GROCERY DEPARTMENT

TEAS

Teas generally used for mixing

Nos.	1 lb. tin		5 lb. tin	10 lb. tin	20 lb. tin
20	5/-	Oolong. (Formosa) ..	24/8	48/4	94/8
21	5/-	Scented Orange Pekoe	24/8	48/5	94/8

Carriage paid on Tea orders value **10/-** or over anywhere in Britain
We shall be pleased to supply Free Samples of all Teas upon application with the exception of Nos. 18, 20, 21, 22, 27, 28 and 30

TRUFFLES (Extra Choice)

Black Glass Bots. ..	⅛-bot. **1/7½**, ¼-bot. **3/2**, ½-bot. **5/9**, bot. **10/6**
Peelings, tin **4/3**	Pieces, per tin **5/9**
Tins, 1 in tin	**1/6½**
Tins	Each **2/6, 4/6, 8/6, 15/9**
White Glass Bots. ..	⅛-bot. **1/9**, ¼-bot. **3/4**, ½-bot. **6/-**, bot. **11/-**

TURPENTINE

.. .. quart **2/2**, gall. **7/9**

*Quart Jars **9d** extra but returnable. Cans **1/6** extra*

TURTLE PREPARATIONS

See also Soups, page 748

Crosse & Blackwell's (Herbs) ..	per pkt. **1/1**
Sun-dried	½-lb. box **9/-**, 1 lb. box **17/6**
Turtle Green (Fat) ..	per bot. **5/4**
,, Jelly (Lusty's) ..	**2/3**
,, Extract (Lusty's) ..	per bot. **1/-, 2/-, 6/-**

VANILLA

.. per oz. **2/6**, pod **6d**, 1 in glass tube **9d**, 2 in glass tube **1/4**

VEGETABLES (Free from Colouring)

Asparagus, Large Green ..	per tin **1/5½**
,, Medium Tips ..	,, **1/6**
,, French ..	bots. **4/3**
,, ,, Amieux Freres ..	per tin **1/10½, 3/3**
Artichokes Fonds ..	per bot. **4/-**, per tin **1/10½**
Beans, Lima ..	per tin **1/2**
Beetroot ..	per tin **1/7½**
Carrots (French shaped) ..	per tin **8½d**, per bot. **1/10½**
Celery (French) ..	per tin **1/9, 10½d**
Champignons ..	tins **7½d, 1/2, 2/-**
,,	bots. **1/2, 1/7½, 2/6**
Flageolets ..	per tin **1/6**
Haricot Verts ..	per bot. **2/-**, per tin **10½d, 1/3**
Jardinere ..	per bot. **2/-**
Macedoine de Legumes ..	per tin **1/6**
,, Amieux Freres ..	per bot. **1/10**
Okra (Cut) ..	per tin **1/3**
,, in Tomato ..	,, **1/4**
,, Whole ..	,, **1/6½**
Petits Pois, Amieux Freres ..	per bot. **1/10½**, per tin **1/-, 1/10½**
Peas in Butter, Amieux Freres ..	per tin **1/9**
,, Early June ..	per tin **10½d**
Petit Pois, Tres Fin ..	per tin **1/-, 1/10½**
,, ,, Fins ..	per tin **10½d, 1/8½**
,, ,, Moyens ..	per tin **9½d, 1/6**
Sweet Potatoes ..	per tin **1/3**
Spinach ..	per tin **8½d, 1/3**

VENETIAN RED

1 lb. packets **6d**

VERMICELLI

Finest Loose ..	per lb. **7d**
De Barberi's ..	4 lb. box **3/-**
Italian ..	,, **2/3**

VINEGAR

HARRODS, Pure Malt

*Best ½ gal. **1/4**, gal. **2/6**, pt. bot. **9d**, qt. bot. **1/2**
,, Second Quality ..	per gal. **2/1**
,, Distilled ..	pt. bot. **10½d**, qt. bot. **1/4**
French Wine, HARRODS ..	per qt. bot. **1/8**
Desseaux, French ..	per bot. **1/7**
Essence (Burgoyne Burbidge's) ..	,, **1/10**
Bordins (French) ..	**1/4½**
Champions ..	per qt. bot. **1/3**
Mailles (French) ..	per bot. **1/1½, 1/10**
French Wine (Escoffier's) ..	per bot. **1/4**
Grimble's Malt ..	pt. bot. **9½d**, qt. bot. **1/3½**
,, 'Orleans' ..	per bot. **1/6**
Mailles' ..	,, **1/1½**
Raspberry, Blackcurrant ..	½-bot. **1/1½**, bot. **1/11**
,, (Roses) ..	per bot. **2/9**
Sarson's ..	pt. bot. **9½d**, qt. bot. **1/3½**
Tarragon, White, Marshall's ..	per bot. **1/6**
Keddies, Tarragon, Eschalot, Garlic, Chilli, Elder
	¼-bot. **7½d**, ½-bot. **1/-**, bot. **1/10½**

C. & B.'s or Lazenby's—

Pure Malt ..	pt. bot. **9½d**, qt. bot. **1/2**
Chilli ..	per bot. **8½d, 1/2½, 2/3**
Garlic ..	,, **8½d, 1/2½, 2/3**
Distilled ..	per pt. bot. **10½d**, qt. **1/4**
Elder ..	,, ,, **8½d, 1/2½, 2/3**
Eschalot ..	,, ,, **8½d, 1/2½, 2/3**
Tarragon ..	,, ,, **7½d, 1/0½, 1/11**
Raspberry ..	per bot. **1/3, 2/2**
Black Currant ..	,, **1/3, 2/2**

Half Gallon Jars **1/7½, Gallon Jars **2/3** extra, returnable*

*Allowance on Empty Bots. qrt. size **1/6** doz., pt. size **1/-** doz.*

WAX

White Round Cakes ..	per lb. **3/3**
S.A.P., Prepared ..	per tin **—**
Beeswax (Genuine) ..	per lb. **3/-**
Laundry ..	per pkt. **8d**
Vegetable ..	per lb. **2/-**

WEBB'S EXTRACT

For Claret Cup .. .. per bot. **4/-, 7/6**

WHITING

.. .. 7 lbs. **7½d**, 28 lbs. **2/1**, cwt. **7/9**

Prepared .. .. per pkt. **3d, 6d**

WHITEBAIT

C. & B.'s ..	per tin **1/3**
New Zealand ..	per tin **2/8**

WINDOW CLEANERS

Flo-Ry-Tin ..	per tin **1/-**
Windolene ..	,, **1/-**
Bimbo ..	,, **5½d**

YEAST CAKES

Makay's Powder .. per pkt. **6d**

.. per bot. **1/4**

YERBA MATE

'Ilex' Brand

½-lb. **1/9**, 1 lb. **3/-**, 2 lb. **5/4**, 3 lb. **7/9**, 4 lb. **10/3**, 7 lb. **17/6**

'Matte' .. ½-lb. **1/9**, 1 lb. **3/-**

ALL PRICES ARE SUBJECT TO MARKET FLUCTUATIONS

PROVISION DEPARTMENT
Harrods Food Service Means
Satisfaction Always

Wherever you live, Harrods wonderful Provision Department is at your service. The finest and freshest foods are carefully packed and promptly dispatched under conditions which more than satisfy the most exacting demand for cleanliness and hygiene. Harrods deliver all purchases to your door if you reside within the radius of Harrods Motor Service. Purchases of 20/- and over sent Carriage Paid in England and Wales, and 60/- and over in Scotland

FANCY CHEESE
For Prices see Weekly Food List

Stilton, Rich and Blue, Whole, about 14 lbs. per lb.
,, Half or Quarter Cheese ,,
Stilton in Jars .. .. per jar
Farmer's Cheddar Loaf (8 to 12 lbs.) per lb.
Finest English Farmer's Cheddar .. .. ,,
English Cheshire Farmhouse Cheese .. .. ,,
Cheshire Loaf, 5 to 6 lbs... ,,
Finest Canadian Cheddar ,,
Fine New Zealand Cheddar ,,
Finest Italian Parmesan, Old .. .. .. ,,
Parmesan, in bottles ..
Finest French Roquefort .. ,,
Real Italian Milan Gorgonzola .. .. .. ,,
McLaren's Imperial Cheese per jar
Emmenthaler Gruyere, finest Swiss .. .. per lb.
Wenslet .. .. .. each
Swiss Knight Gruyere, portions, 6 in box ..
Swiss Knight Gruyere, whole in boxes
Midget Cream Dutch, about 1 lb.
Cream Edam, about 4 lbs. per lb.
Double Gloucester .. ,,
Pommel .. .. box of 6
Suisse .. .. .. ,,
Port Salut .. .. per lb.
Kraft .. per box ..
,, in portions, 6 in box per box
Kraft .. .. .. per lb.
Camembert (French) Dutacq's.. .. .. each
Horner's Cream Cheese .. ,,
Moonraker.. .. .. ,,
St. Ivel Lactic .. .. ,,
Little Wilts .. .. ,,
Diploma Crustless Cheddar and Cheshire, 6 portions in box .. .. .. ,,
Charterhouse Cheddar and Cheshire, 8 portions in box
Chilvern Cottage Cheddar, 4 portions .. .. ,,
Horner's Cheddar and Cheshire, 6 portions in box

TINNED GOODS
FINEST OX TONGUES
Per tin 6/3, 7/1

PAYSANDU TONGUES
Size	C	E	F	H	
	5/6	6/6	7/3	9/9	Per tin

SHEEP'S TONGUES
Per tin 1/8

ENGLISH BRAWN
Per tin 1/-, 1/9

PRESSED BEEF
Per tin 2/6

LIBBY'S CORNED BEEF
12 oz. Nett .. .. per tin 10½d
1¾ lbs. ,, ... ,, 1/8
6 lbs. ,, ... ,, 4/6

BACON AND HAMS
ONLY THE BEST BRANDS STOCKED
We Purchase and Ship Direct from the Curing Houses, ensuring Perfection in Freshness and Flavour. All Bacon and Hams Smoked in Modern Hygienic Stoves
For Quality and Flavour English and Irish Bacon is superior to the Foreign Article and is less wasteful in cooking

	Harrods Canadian	Harrods Danish	Harrods Irish & Denny	Cole & Lewis & Harris Wiltshire
Sides (about 60 lbs.) per lb.				
Half Sides Fore End (about 32 lbs.) ,,				
Half Sides Gammon End (about 28 lbs.) ,,				
Fore Hocks (8 to 10 lbs.) ,,				
Collar (2 to 6 lbs.), Boneless ,,				
Back, Prime (any weight cut) .. ,,		*For Prices see Weekly Food List*		
Streaky, Prime .. ,,				
Streaky, Thin (2 lbs.) .. ,,				
Flank (2½ lbs.) .. ,,				
Gammon (Whole 15 lbs.) ,,				
Half Gammon, Knuckle End (7 to 8 lbs.) ,,				
Gammon, Corner and Middle(4 to 8 lbs.) ,,				
Fore End (about 16 lbs.) ,,				Bradenham
Finest Wiltshire Bath Chaps (3 to 4 lbs.) lb. Chaps, lb.				

LARGE STOCKS OF FINEST MATURED HAMS

Finest York Hams ..	..	10 to 14 lbs.	per lb.	
,, ,, ,, ..	..	15 to 16 lbs.	,,	
,, ,, ,, ..	..	17 to 19 lbs.	,,	
,, ,, ,, Medium				
Stout Selection ..	..	20 to 26 lbs.	,,	
Finest Smoked York Hams..		14 to 16 lbs.	,,	
Bigger's finest Irish Hams ..		12 to 14 lbs.	,,	
Seager's Real Suffolk Hams (Sweet Cured) ..	..	12 to 14 lbs.	,,	
Bradenham Hams ..	..	14 to 16 lbs.	,,	
Virginia Hams ..	..	12 to 14 lbs.	,,	
Smoked Breakfast Hams ..		10 to 14 lbs.	,,	
Finest Smoked Ox Tongues		5 to 6 lbs.	,,	

For Prices see Weekly Food List

OX TONGUES
	Size	A	B	C	Extra large
HARRODS	..	5/6	6/9	11/3	13/3
Harvey's	..	5/6	6/9	11/3	13/3
Poulton & Noel's		5/6	6/9	per glass	

CALVES TONGUES
2/8, 3/9 per glass

CHICKEN BREASTS
Brand's (in bottle) 4/6
Shippam's 5/6

PATÉ DE FOIE GRAS
Per jar 2/-, 3/-
Purette de Foie Gras, per glass .. 1/-

TABLE BUTTERS
For Prices see Weekly Food List

Real Cornish Farm House per lb.
Finest Danish (Direct Shipment) .. .. ,,
Finest Unsalted (Exquisite Brand) .. .. ,,
Harrodian Brand Creamery ,,
Fine Unsalted Creamery.. ,,
Best Cooking .. .. ,,
Victorian Brand Creamery ,,
Fancy N. Zealand Creamery ,,

MARGARINE
For Prices see Weekly Food List

HARRODS 'SPECIAL' TABLE MARGARINE in 1 lb. Rolls .. per lb.
Quality Perfect
Special Unsalted in Rolls per lb.
Finest Quality Salted ,, ,,
Fine Salted .. .. ,,
'Pheasant Brand' ½ lb. pkts.
Blue Band.. .. ,,

EGGS
All per doz.

Finest English New Laid
Best Imported New Laid *For Prices*
Best Cooking .. .. *see Weekly*
Eggs for Preserving during *Food List* April .. .. ..

COOK'S FARM EGGS
Dried, dram equal to 12 New Laid Eggs .. .. ; 24

BEEF SUET
For Prices see Weekly Food List

Hugon's Shredded or Block, 1 lb. packets.. .. ..
Cook's Shredded, 1 lb. packets
Nutter per lb. ; 3 lb. tin ..
Cashew and Hazel Nut Butter, in cartons .. ..
Yorkshire Pride, 1 lb. packets

FINEST QUALITY LARD
For Prices see Weekly Food List

Finest Wiltshire .. 1 lb. pkts.
Denny's Finest Irish, ½ lb., 1 lb. and 2 lb. pkts. .. per lb.
Denny's Bladder, 4-8 lbs. ,,
Swift's Silverleaf .. 1 lb. pkts.
Finest in 28 lb. pails .. per lb.
Altitude, for Puff Paste ½ lb. packet
CREAM (Direct from the Dairies) per jar , pint , qrt.
COW AND GATE MILK in Tins Full Cream ; Half Cream

ENGLISH BRAWN
Finest .. per glass 1/1, 1/9, 4/6
Boar's Head ,, 1/2, 1/10, 4/9
PRESSED BEEF, in glass .. 2/10
PRAWNS in Aspic .. 2/-

GALANTINE
Chicken & Ham, Turkey & Tongue, Ham & Tongue .. .. Glass 2/-, 3/6, 6/6

POTTED MEAT
Poulton & Noel's .. .. per jar 7½d
Shippam's .. .. ,, 9½d
HERRING ROES, New Seasons' Per glass 11½d

HARRODS SANDWICH PASTE
DELICIOUS AND APPETIZING
15 VARIETIES IN FISH & PASTE
Freshly made per large glass 7½d Per doz. 7/3

FOR CURRENT PRICES SEE WEEKLY FOOD LIST

HARRODS LTD

Telephone SLOANE 1234
Telegrams 'EVERYTHING HARRODS LONDON'

LONDON S W 1

COOKED MEATS DEPARTMENT
Harrods Freshly Cooked Foods are Despatched Daily. All Cooking is Done by Expert Chefs

Owing to Daily Market Fluctuations these prices are only intended as a guide

DRESSED BOAR'S HEAD
From 42/- to 63/-

FINEST PRESSED BEEF
Per lb. 3/-

SPICED DERBY ROUND OF BEEF
Per lb. 3/6

Hampers for races, boating, picnics, etc., prepared with the best selected viands

FINEST QUALITY ENGLISH OX TONGUES
Glazed and decorated for the table
Each 12/6 and 15/6

SOUPS
(Harrods own make)
Oxtail, Julienne, Consomme, Brunoise, Mulligatawny, Lobster Bisque
Per bottle 1/9
Real Turtle .. .. Per bottle 7/6, 4/-

FISH
Fish Cakes ..	..	Each 5d
Fried Fillets Fish	..	,, 1/-
Filleted Sole. Siberienne		
		Each portion 2/6
Lobster Cardinal ..		Each half 3/6
Coquille of Turbot Mornay ..		1/-

FRESH RUSSIAN CAVIARE
Served in stone jars
6/-, 8/6, 10/-, 15/-, 20/-

Salmon Mayonnaise .. ⎫
Coquille of Salmon .. ⎪
Salmon Troute in Aspic .. ⎪
Darne of Salmon Belle Vue .. ⎬ *When in season*
Lobster Mayonnaise .. ⎪
Salmon Cutlets .. ⎪
Lobster Cutlets .. ⎭
Prices obtained in department

PATÉ DE FOIE GRAS HUMMEL
3/6, 4/6, 7/6, 12/6, 16/6, 21/-

TERRINES PATÉ DE FOIE GRAS
Each 3/6, 4/6, 7/6, 9/6, 12/6, 16/6, 21/-

RAISED GAME PIES
(When in season)
Each 3/6, 5/6, 7/6, 10/6, 21/-

PATÉ DE FOIE GRAS EN CROUTE
(When in season)

ENTRÉES
Vol au vent Financière, Regence, Princesse, Toulouse ..	Per person 2/6
Braised Oxtail ..	Per lb. 2/6
Veal Cutlets Milanaise ..	Each 2/-
Lamb Cutlets Favourite ..	
Fricassees of Chicken ..	Per person 3/-
Curry of Lamb Madras ..	Per lb. 2/6
Curry of Chicken..	,, 2/6
Jugged Hare (when in season) ..	,, 2/6
Saddle of Hare (when in season)..	Each 2/-
Partridge in Casserole (when in season)	
Grouse in Casserole (when in season)	

ENTRÉES
Pheasant in Casserole (when in season)		
Boiled Fowls, Bechamel Sauce ..From 10/6		
Mousse of Ham ..	Each	6d, 1/-, 5/6
Mousse of Chicken	,,	6d, 1/-, 7/6
Mousse of Foie Gras	,,	6d, 1/-, 6/6
Lobster in Aspic ..	,,	6d, 1/-, 6/6
Prawns in Aspic ..	,,	6d, 1/-, 5/6
Tongue in Aspic ..	,,	6d, 1/-, 5/6
Eggs in Aspic ..	,,	6d, 1/-, 5/-
Sole in Aspic ..	,,	6d, 1/1, 6/6
Chicken Cutlets in Aspic ..		Each 6d
Lamb Cutlets in Aspic ..	..	,, 9d

ENTRÉES
Galantine of Veal..	..	Per lb. 4/6
,, Game (when in season)..		,, 4/6
Boars Head Truffled	..	,, 4/6
Stuffed Boned Turkey	..	,, 4/6

COLD MEATS
English Roast Beef	..	Per lb. 4/-
Silverside Beef	..	,, 3/6
Finest Corned Beef, glazed		Each 1/2, 10d
Collared Head ..	..	Per lb. 3/-
Harrods Own Made Brawn	..	,, 2/-
Ox Tongue, Sliced	..	,, 4/6
Ox Tongue, glazed whole	..	,, 3/9

THESE GOODS ARE PERISHABLE AND ARE SENT TO THE COUNTRY ENTIRELY AT CUSTOMERS' OWN RISK

DRESSED BREAKFAST HAMS
Weight 8 to 12 lbs...Per lb. 2/6

DRESSED YORK HAMS
Average weight 12 to 16 lbs.
Per lb. 3/6

HALF HAMS CUT IF DESIRED

GALANTINE OF CHICKEN
Per lb. 4/6

BONED STUFFED TURKEY
(When in season)
Per lb. 4/6

HAMS
Cooked Boneless Gammon, Danish or Irish Per lb. 2/10

PIES, ETC.
Melton Mowbray Pies
1/6, 3/-, 4/8
Harrods own made veal and ham and egg pies
1/6, 1/10, 2/4, 3/4
Steak and Kidney Pies in dish
5/6, 7/6
Chicken and Ham Patties
Per dozen 8/-
Lobster Patties Per dozen 8/-

POULTRY
Roast Chicken
Each 5/6 to 15/6
Chicken, boned and stuffed
Each 10/6, 12/6, 14/6
Boned Stuffed Pigeon Each 3/6
Boned Stuffed Quails
Whole 3/6, Half 1/9

Oyster Patties (when in season)
Per dozen 8/-

INVALID SPECIALITIES
Made with the finest obtainable viands
Chicken Broth, Beef Tea, Calves Foot Jelly 1/6 per bottle

SALADS
Russian ..	..	Per lb. 2/3
Potato ..	..	,, 2/-

SWEETS
(Made at shortest notice)
Charlotte Russe ..	Each 9d, 4/6
Cream Creole..	Each 6d, 3/6, 4/6
Fruit and Wine Jellies	Each 6d, 3/6, 4/6

Fruit Flans—Peach, Pineapple, Gooseberry, Cherry, Apricot, from each 1/6, 2/-
Pure Cream Ices—Vanilla, Chocolate, Strawberry and Coffee .. Per qt. 6/6
Special prices for large quantities

BAKERY DEPARTMENT
Delicious Cakes Made Fresh Daily in Harrods OWN Bakeries
Order by 'Phone or Post if a Visit is Inconvenient

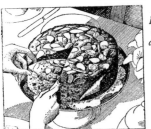

Harrods pay carriage on all purchases value 20/- and over to any Station in Britain

DUNDEE CAKES (*illustrated above*)
Sultanas and Peel only

1 lb. 2 ozs. ..	2/-	3 lbs. ..	.. 5/-
1½ lbs. ..	2/6	4½ lbs. ..	.. 7/6
2 lbs. ..	3/6	6½ lbs. ..	.. 10/6

Packed in Tins for export

About 2 lbs. ..	5/-	About 4½ lbs.	10/6
" 3 lbs. ..	7/6		

OLD ENGLISH PLUM CAKES

About 1½ lbs.	2/6	About 4½ lbs.	7/6
" 2 lbs. ..	3/6	" 8 lbs. ..	12/6
" 3 lbs. ..	5/-		

Packed in Tins for export

2 lbs. ..	5/-	4½ lbs. ..	10/6
3 lbs. ..	7/6		

MARQUERITE CAKES
With chopped raisons, preserved ginger and almonds. Weight about 2 lbs. .. Each 2/6

RICH CHERRY CAKES
Fruited with Alpine Cherries and peel Weight about 2 lbs. .. .. Each 3/6

GINGER CREAM CAKES
A very light cake containing chopped Ginger and Almonds. About 1½ lbs. .. Each 1/8

WHEATMEAL HONEY CAKES
A real old fashioned Honey Cake made with pure Wheatmeal and Honey. Weight about 2 lbs. .. .. .. Each 2/-

SEED LOAF CAKE
Weight about 2 lbs. .. .. Each 2/-

LUNCHEON LOAF CAKE
Filled with Empire Sultanas, Currants, etc. Weight about 2 lbs. .. .. Each 2/-

COLLEGE CAKES
Popular Cakes for the 'Tuck' Box. Fruited with Empire Sultanas, Currants, Cherries and peel, and topped with split Almonds Weight about 3 lbs. .. .. Each 3/6

GINGERBREAD LOAF
A delicious Ginger Cake to which chopped preserved Ginger has been added Each 1/3

MILAN
Plain buttery mixture .. .. Each 2/-

PRINCESS CAKES
Plain cake delightfully flavoured with marzipan .. .. Each 2/-

BROMPTON CAKES
A choice of three Cakes—Madeira, Seed or Fruit. Weight 1 lb. Each 1/- or 3 for 2/10

CUT CAKE
Per lb. A choice assortment of cakes including Sultana, Genoa, Madeira, Seed, Scotch Dundee at 1/8 per lb. and Cherry 1/10 per lb. Old English Plum 2/- per lb. In blocks each weighing approximately 6 lbs.

ICED GINGER CAKES
A very light ginger mixture with chopped Glace Ginger, layered with Ginger Cream and Iced with Fondant to which Ginger Cream has been added .. Each 2/6

GINGER NUTS
Made in Harrods own Bakeries from an original recipe .. .. .. Per lb. 1/3

WINE BISCUITS
Harrods own make. A fine assortment of Biscuits including Rich Traveller, Lemon, Rice, Cherry, Alexandra, Shrewsbury, Queen Drops, Seed Currant, and Cokernut, etc. Packed in neat Lace Box. Per lb. 2/-

HARRODS SHORTBREADS
Made of the finest materials procurable Per dozen 2/-, or each 2/-, 5/-, 7/6

HONEY CAKES (CONTINENTAL)
Made from pure honey and kept air tight Will keep moist for several days Each 2/-, 3/6
In small quarters .. .. Per doz. 2/-, 3/-

ALMOND GOODS
Only pure Almonds, Castor Sugar and Egg Whites are used

MACAROONS	Per doz.	2/6
CHOCOLATE MACAROONS	"	2/6
SMALL MACAROONS	Per lb.	2/6
RATIFIAS	"	3/6
MACAROON TARTS	Per doz.	2/6

RYE BISCUITS
A special dietetic Biscuit manufactured in our own Bakeries from pure Rye meal Very nutritious and appetising. Packed in neat lace box .. .. .. Per lb. 1/-

HARRODS CONTINENTAL FANCY CAKES
Dainty little cakes delicately flavoured and prettily designed for afternoon Tea Parties Packed in White boxes containing one dozen cakes .. .. Per doz. 2/6

DUTCH CHEESE TARTS	Each 1/6
FRANZIPANE TARTS	Each 1/-

FRENCH WAFER BISCUITS
Filled with delicious Fruit centres Per lb. 3/-

HARRODS PETIT FOURS
All kinds of almond sweetmeats, Glace and Chocolate dainties are included in this tempting variety. Packed in neat lace box Per lb. 3/6

WEDDING CAKES
Each Wedding Cake is made in Harrods own Bakeries by experts. Almond and sugar icings are not applied until cakes are fully matured, thereby maintaining perfect condition throughout

Wedding Cake .. .. Per lb. 2/9

Quotations for special designs or sizes will be gladly submitted on request

---

Top Ornaments Extra

Please ask for Catalogue

Free delivery to your door if you reside within the radius of Harrods Motor Delivery

SWISS ROLL
(*Illustrated above*) Fresh eggs, finest castor sugar, pure flour are the good things in Harrods Swiss Roll. Plain with various jam fillings or Chocolate flavour and filled with smoothest Viennese Cream .. Each 1/-

HARRODS GATEAU AND LAYER CAKES
Flavours and layers—Orange, Chocolate, Pineapple, Strawberry, Coffee, Walnut, Maraschino. All at 2/6 each

Gateau Havana	..	..	.. Each	2/6
" Apricot	..	..	.. "	2/-
" Duchesse	..	..	.. "	2/-
" Japanese	..	..	.. "	2/-
" Horse Shoe	..	..	.. "	2/6
" Walnut	..	..	.. "	2/-
" Chalet	..	..	.. "	5/-
" Football	..	..	.. "	4/6
" Marlboro'	..	..	.. "	2/6
" Meringue	..	..	.. "	2/-
" Cauliflower	..	..	.. "	3/6
" Mushroom	..	..	.. "	3/6
" Assorted colours and flavours	"	1/3
" Parisienne	..	..	.. "	1/9
" Russian	..	..	Each	1/-, 1/6

MARZIPAN FRUITS
Made from pure almonds, castor sugar and egg whites. Packed in white boxes containing one dozen fruits .. .. Per box 3/6

GRESSINI STICKS
A novel form of Dinner Roll kept air tight —will retain their crispness for many days Prettily tied with red ribbon. In bundles of 1 dozen .. .. .. Per bundle 9d

SPONGE CAKES, ETC.

Sponge Cakes ..	..	.. Per doz. 1/6
" Racks ..	..	.. Each 1/-, 1/6
" Rings ..	..	Each 10d, 1/3, 1/6
" Leamington	..	.. Each 1/-
" Moulds	..	From 2/6 each
Almond Sponge Cake	..	Each 1/-
Milk Chocolate Almond Sponge	"	1/-
Jam Sandwiches	..	Each 8d
Small Swiss Rolls	..	.. Per doz. 2/3

ALMOND SPONGE CAKE
A light Sponge Cake to which is added pure Butter and Ground Almonds .. Each 1/-
Flavoured with Chocolate couverture same price

BIRTHDAY CAKES
Rich dark fruit cake, almond iced and decorated. From 4 lbs. upwards Per lb. 2/6

CHILDREN'S BIRTHDAY CAKES
A rich layered Genoese with or without almond paste. Iced with fondant and decorated. From 3 lb. upwards Per lb. 2/6

CHALET CAKES
A rich madeira Cake layered with Viennese Cream and charmingly designed to represent a miniature Chalet .. .. Each 5/-
Larger sizes made to order

CONFECTIONERY DEPARTMENT
Superfine Quality Chocolates Attractively Boxed

SUPERFINE CHOCOLATE ASSORTMENT

Fresh made daily from the purest ingredients obtainable. Packed in a White Box, daintily ribboned and covered with transparent wrapper

No. 83 1 lb. box, **4/-** ; No. 82 2 lb. box, **8/-** ; No. 81 4 lb. box, **16/-**

SWEETMEAT CABINET

Prettily designed Cabinets containing eight drawers, each drawer containing a different sweetmeat, including Fondant Fourres, Caramels, Toffees, Imperial Gums, Sugared Almonds, Chocolates, etc., etc.
Per Cabinet, **10/-**

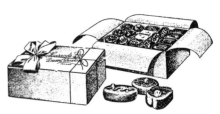

ROYAL DESSERT CHOCOLATES

The Chocolates in the Golden Box. These Delicious Chocolates comprise a variety of dainty centres with smooth couverture

No. 76 1 lb. box, **4/-** ; No. 75 2 lb. box, **8/-** ; No. 74 3 lb. box, **11/6**

No. 16 'HARRODIAN' CHOCOLATE ASSORTMENT

This well known variety is undoubtedly a remarkable value in moderately-priced chocolates
Many new and tempting varieties
4-lb. box, **10/-**

'PARISIEN' CHOCOLATE ASSORTMENT

An exceptional assortment of delicious chocolates packed in hygienic cartons, also in 4-lb. boxes
No. 71 1 lb. cartons, **3/-** 4 lb. box, **12/-**

PRINCESS CHOCOLATE ASSORTMENT

A delightful variety of chocolates in a beautifully designed Box with an Imperial Blue Centre tied with ribbon to match
No. 87 1 lb. box, **5/-** No. 86 2 lb. box, **10/-** No. 85 4 lb. box, **20/-**

FANCY DRUMS

Harrods have an exceptional variety of artistically designed drums which were executed by Paris Artists and are exclusive to Harrods. A most attractive gift. From **6/6** to **45/-** each

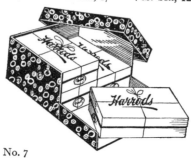

No. 7 HARRODS CLUB BOX

A Club Case containing four separate 1 lb. boxes 'Harrodian' Assorted Chocolates
4-lb. box, **10/-**

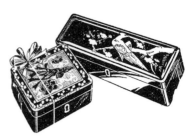

LACQUER BOXES

These boxes are beautifully designed in many different models, two of which are illustrated. Each box is filled with Harrods Superfine Chocolates
6/6 to **42/-** each

ALL ORDERS FOR CHOCOLATES AND CONFECTIONERY TO THE VALUE OF **10/-** *POST PAID IN GREAT BRITAIN*

ALL PRICES ARE SUBJECT TO MARKET FLUCTUATIONS

HARRODS LTD

Telephone SLOANE 1234
Telegrams 'EVERYTHING HARRODS LONDON'

LONDON S W 1

CONFECTIONERY DEPARTMENT
Choice Quality Chocolates and Assorted Sweets

PRINCESS CHOCOLATES
5/- per lb

All the Fruit Creams in this are made with real Fruit

Liqueur Creams	Mocha Caramel
Strawberry Panachee	Greengage Panachee
Montelimart, extra fin	Advocaat Cream
Praline Biscuit	Ginger Dessert
Apricot Cream	Parisian Nougatine
Chocolate Brazil	Raspberry Supreme
La Paris	Orange and Citron Dessert
Dessert Almond	
Praline Wafer	Butter Roll
Pate de Amandes	Marzipan Brazil
Chocolat Carola	Strawberry Cream
Chocolat Delyse	Chocolate Ginger Cube
Almond Whirl	
Raspberry Cream	Blackcurrant Cream
Chocolate Marsh-mallow	Walnut Whirl
	Philadelphian
Banana Cream	Chocolate Truffle

SILK BOXES
In exquisite designs and colourings, these boxes are perfect in every detail, and are of the finest French Manufacture. Filled with Harrods Princess Assorted Chocolates they will prove a most attractive gift
From 21/- to 105/- each

HARRODS SPECIAL TRUFFLES
Chocolate Truffles	.. .. Per lb.	**6/-**
Coffee Truffles ..	.. .. .. ,,	**6/-**

SLAB CHOCOLATE
Foiled and Wrapped, ½-lb. Slabs

Nut Milk at **1/-** each	Vanilla at **1/-** each
Orange Milk at **1/-** ,,	Vanilla Nut at **1/-** ,,
Coffee Milk at **1/-** ,,	Vanilla Fruit
Milk Fruit &	&Nut at **1/-** ,,
Nut at **1/-** ,,	Sante at .. **1/-** ,,
Milk Fruit at **1/-** ,,	Mocha at .. **1/2** ,,
Milk at .. **1/-** ,,	Brazil Nut Milk
	at **1/3** ,,

Milk Vanilla (Foiled and Wrapped)
6d Packets

HARRODS
BITTER SWEET CHOCOLATE
4/- per lb

HARRODS COOKING CHOCOLATE
Vanilla flavoured, sweetened or unsweetened in 1 lb. blocks, 2/- per lb

LANGUES DE CHAT

In two sizes
1/6 and **3/-** per box

A delightful assortment of confectionery, well flavoured and perfectly shaped. Comprising Fondants, Marzipan, Mosaic, Strawberries, etc. .. .. 4lb. box **10/-**

BOILED SWEETS
Harrods have always been noted for their Boiled Sugars and the ever-increasing demand for these wholesome sweets is a sufficient testimony to their value and quality

Tangerine Balls	Barley Sugar Balls
Brandy Balls	Carnival Balls
Clove Balls	Bulls Eye Balls
Aniseed Balls	Mixed Fruit Drops
Lemon Butterscotch Drops	Creme de Menthe Drops
Pear Drops	Pineapple Drops
Acid Drops	Barley Sugar Nibs
Barley Sugar Orange	Butterscotch Cubes
Lime Nibs	Barley Sugar Lemon
Jazz Rock	

Per lb., **1/8** ;   Small Bottle, **1/-** ;
Large Bottle, **1/10**

TURKISH DELIGHT
This delightful sweetmeat is manufactured exactly as made in Constantinople, and is guaranteed to be free from gum, glucose or gelatine
Per lb., **1/8**
Small Drums, **1/6** ; Large Drums **2/9**

2lb. boxes 'Mecca Brand'
Plain at **4/6** each
With Almonds at **5/-** ,,
With Pistachio at **5/6** ,,

All Orders for Chocolates and Confectionery to the value of 10/- post paid in Great Britain

HOME MADE TOFFEES
Delicious Toffees made in our own Model Factory. Pure, rich and full flavoured
Ten distinct flavours :—

Cream	Malted Milk
Chocolate	Treacle
Coffee	Almond
Walnut	Brazil
Mint	Assorted Nut

All one price, **2/-** per lb

SUPERFINE CHOCOLATES
4/- per lb

Cokernut Dessert	Orange Cream
Pistachio Cream	Raspberry Cream
Chocolate Pineapple	Cherry Cream
Milk Macaroon	Lemon Cream
Moulded Croquants	Milk Caraque
Vanilla Cream	Plain Caraque
Orange Royale	Chocolate Macaroon
Creme de Menthe Delight	Chocolate Nougatine
	Pineapple Cream
Seville Dessert	Chocolate Peppermint
Chocolate Marzipan	
Italian Cream	Hazel Whirl
Walnut Cream	Mocha Walnut
Chocolate Truffle	Noyeaux Royale
Croquante	Rose Cream
Chocolate Caramel	De la Creme Praline
Pistachio Marzipan	Ginger Truffle
Coffee Cream, etc.	Coffee Truffle

CHOCOLATE FIGURES
Well moulded figures made with Harrods finest chocolates
All at 6d each
Special Models :—

Cat Ribboned	.. .. Each	**9d**
Doll	.. .. .. ,,	**3/6**
Bride and Bridegroom	Per pr.	**2/6**
Footballs, 15 ins. in circumference	.. .. Each	**2/6**

HARRODS FRUIT FUDGES
A beautifully flavoured sweetmeat made with Real Fruit and containing no artificial flavouring

Blackcurrant	Raspberry
Strawberry	Pineapple
Orange	Lemon

All varieties, **3/-** per lb

DELICIOUS CREAMY CARAMELS
The real Creamy kind
½-lb. box, **1/3**   1-lb. box, **2/6**

EDINBURGH ROCK
Real Edinburgh Rock, a full flavoured and wholesome sweetmeat
2/- per tin

CRYSTALLIZED FLOWERS
Rose Leaves, Violets, Mimosa, Lavender, Lilac, Mint leaves, Carnations. Per lb **6/-**

CHOCOLATE PASTILLES
Made with Harrods finest Bitter Sweet Chocolates and neatly packed in attractive boxes
Three sizes,
1/-, 1/6, 3/- per box

ALL PRICES ARE SUBJECT TO MARKET FLUCTUATIONS

CONFECTIONERY DEPARTMENT
Dessert Sweets—Chocolates and Fancy Fruits

ASSORTED SWEETMEATS

Marzipan Bar	..	.. Each	1/-
Mocha Bread	..	.. Per lb	5/-
Mocha Beans	..	.. ,,	5/-
Peppermint Lumps	..	.. Per tin	2/-
Orchard Fruits	..	.. ,,	3/-
Peanut Brittle	..	.. ,,	2/3
Pistachio Fourres	..	.. Per lb	3/6
Violet Fourres	..	.. ,,	3/6
Rose Fourres	..	.. ,,	3/6
Marzipan Walnuts	..	.. ,,	3/-
Chocolate Fudge	..	.. ,,	2/6
Coffee Fudge	..	.. ,,	2/6
Almond Aboukir	..	.. ,,	3/-
Maple Candy	..	.. ,,	2/8
Mocha Walnuts	..	.. ,,	3/6
Opera Caramels	..	.. ,,	2/8
Peppermint Wafers	..	.. ,,	2/4
Per box, 8½d and 1/4			
Plain Nougat	..	.. Per bar	6d
Chocolate Nougat	..	.. ,,	6d
Cokernut Ice	..	.. ,,	9d
Cokernut Candy	..	.. ,,	9d
French Almond Rock	..	Per lb	2/8
French Almond Brittle	..	,,	2/8
After Dinner Mints	..	.. ,,	2/-
Ginger Crunch	..	.. ,,	2/-
Fruit Lumps	..	.. ,,	2/-
Peppermint Lumps	..	.. ,,	2/-
Chocolate Walnut Dragees	..	,,	5/-
Chocolate Almond Dragees	..	,,	5/-
Chocolate Brazil Dragees	..	,,	5/-
Brazilian Fourres	..	.. ,,	3/6
Glace Marshmallows	..	.. ,,	4/6

DESSERT NUTS

Fancy Baskets filled with Nuts for Dessert, and daintily ribboned
From **7/6** to **30/-**

ASSORTED NUTS

Salted Almonds	..	Per lb	5/-
Salted Walnuts	..	,,	4/6
Salted Peanuts	..	,,	2/4
Salted Pistachio	..	,,	10/6
Jordan Almonds	..	,,	3/9
Walnut Halves	..	,,	3/6
Pistachio	..	,,	8/3
Devilled Almonds	..	,,	5/-
Marrons Glaces	..	,,	5/-

FRUIT BASKETS

Fancy Fruit Baskets Packed with Choicest Fruits and tastefully ribboned
From **7/6** to **130/-** each

JOSEPH NEGRES CRYSTALLIZED & GLACE FRUITS
Specially packed for Harrods

Nom. 8 lb size	..	each	29/-
,, 4 lb ,,	..	,,	16/6
,, 2 lb ,,	..	,,	8/6
,, 1 lb ,,	..	,,	4/6

CRYSTALLIZED & GLACE FRUITS

Finest Fruits, grown in the South of France, specially packed for and imported by Harrods

Approx. 8 lb. boxes	..	Each	26/6
,, 4 lb. ,,	..	,,	13/6
,, 2 lb. ,,	..	,,	6/9
Assorted, loose	..	Per lb	3/9
Glace Apricots	..	,,	5/-
Crystallized Apricots	..	,,	5/-
Glace Golden Cherries	..	,,	2/3
Glace Green Cherries	..	,,	2/6
Peeled Figs, pink & white	,,		4/-
Small Black Figs	..	,,	4/-
Large ,, ,,	..	,,	4/-
Small Green ,,	..	,,	4/-
Large ,, ,,	..	,,	4/-
Japanese Medlars	..	,,	4/-
Whole Peaches	..	,,	4/6
Half Peaches	..	,,	4/6
Glace Greengages	..	,,	4/-
Crystallized Greengages	,,		4/6
Crystallized Strawberries	,,		4/6
Mandarines	..	,,	4/-
Glace Whole Pineapple	..	,,	4/-
Glace Pineapple Slices	..	,,	4/6
Glace Whole Melon	..	,,	4/6
Glace Melon Slices	..	,,	4/6
Glace Jaffa Oranges	..	,,	4/6
Glace Almonds	..	,,	4/-
Crystallized Walnuts	..	,,	5/-
Crystallized Angelica, finest round	..	,,	3/6
Crystallized Cherries	..	,,	3/-
Glace Cherries	..	,,	2/3
Lunettes	..	.. ,,	3/6
Brochettes	..	.. ,,	3/6
Knotts	..	.. ,,	3/6

ASSORTED SWEETMEATS—contd.

Glace Walnuts	..	.. Per lb	6/-
Peppermint Fondants	..	,,	2/4
Assorted Refreshers	..	,,	1/8
Harrods School Mixtures, comprising :—Jellies, Fondants & Cokernut dainties	,,		1/10
Glace Brazils	..	.. ,,	6/-
Harrods Assorted Twists	.. Per bott.		1/6

FRENCH CONFECTIONERY

Amandes Extra Rouge	.. Per lb		4/6
Amandes Excelsior	..	,,	4/6
Noisettes de Barbizon	..	,,	4/6
Chocolate Mouseline Lentils	..	,,	4/6
Dragees Tosca	..	,,	4/6
Praline Princesses	..	,,	4/6
Menthe Lentils, extra	..	,,	4/6
Dragee Poupon Sirop	..	,,	4/6
Arago Amande Grille	..	,,	4/6
Nougatines, extra	..	,,	4/6
Lysettes	..	,,	4/6
Arago Avelines	..	,,	4/6
Trocadero Dragees	..	,,	4/6
Arago Dragee Almonds	..	,,	4/6
Mint Lentils, extra	..	,,	4/6
Dragee Poupons	..	,,	4/6
Silver Boules, No. 0	..	,,	6/-
,, ,, ,, 1	..	,,	6/-
,, ,, ,, 2	..	,,	6/-
,, ,, ,, 3	..	,,	6/-
Gold Boules, No. 1	..	,,	25/-
,, ,, ,, 2	..	,,	25/-

FONDANT FOURRES

A beautiful sample of the Confectioners' art. Perfectly shaped in soft delicate colourings and well flavoured Fancy Baskets, daintily ribboned from **7/6** to **42/-** each

FRUIT CONFECTIONS

Choice quality fruits packed in drums Chinese Figs, Maltese Oranges, Palermo Lemons, Raspberries, Strawberries, **2/-** per drum

PRESERVED GINGER

Finest quality Crystallized and Glace

Young stem	..	.. Per lb	4/6
Finest Cube	..	.. ,,	3/11
Pieces	..	.. ,,	2/6
Chips	..	.. ,,	2/4

ALL PRICES ARE SUBJECT TO MARKET FLUCTUATIONS

HARRODS FOOD MARKET

The Largest and Most Completely Equipped Organization of its Kind in the World

PART OF INTERIOR OF HARRODS MEAT AND POULTRY HALL

HARRODS MEAT, FISH, POULTRY AND GAME

Always Fresh, Appetising and Delicious

HARRODS offer, beyond question, the largest choice of high-grade Meat, Fish, Poultry and Game to be found under one roof anywhere in the Kingdom. In the matter of Meat, they offer the pick of Smithfield Market and the Scotch Farms ; in the matter of Fish, the pick of Billingsgate. It is not possible to buy better quality Meat, Fish, Poultry or Game than is obtainable at Harrods, who have the honour of supplying many of the most distinguished residences in the land. For the benefit of Customers who are unable to do their shopping in person, a highly efficient staff of specially trained Telephone Operators is maintained who are acquainted with the ruling prices of all Foodstuffs and are solely engaged upon booking orders for the Food section

Harrods Motor Deliveries deliver daily in a wide London Area

See pages 9, 10, and 11 for list of districts covered

HARRODS LTD
*Telephone SLOANE 1234
Telegrams 'EVERYTHING HARRODS LONDON'*
LONDON S W 1

FRUIT AND VEGETABLE DEPARTMENT
A Weekly Price List of Fruit and Vegetables Will Be Posted to Customers Free on Request

The finest Fruit and Vegetables obtainable—the very pick of Covent Garden—are always to be found in Harrods Fruit and Vegetable Department, and, for the quality supplied, Harrods believe their prices to be the lowest in London. Free Deliveries daily throughout the wide radius of Harrods Motor Deliveries (*see* pages 9, 10, 11)

FLORAL SECTION
A beautiful selection of fresh cut Flowers and Plants is available daily. Floral Decorations for Balls, Receptions, Weddings, Concerts, etc., undertaken, and assistants sent to any London address to give advice. Wedding, Court and Ball Bouquets are specially designed to order

Mourning Orders are carefully and artistically executed by a special staff of Floral Artists

HARRODS LTD   *Telephone SLOANE* 1234
Telegrams 'EVERYTHING HARRODS LONDON'   LONDON S W 1

WINE DEPARTMENT
Harrods Wines and Spirits are Carefully Selected from the Finest Markets of the World

TERMS AND CARRIAGE ARRANGEMENTS

GOODS TAKEN :—Under the Licensing Act, 1921. Wines and Spirits can only be taken away between 11.0 a.m. and 3 p.m., or after 5 p.m.

CASES :—For Town and Suburban Deliveries. Bin Cases are used. The deposit for these is **3/6** each (Returnable)

JARS.—Jars are charged at **2/-** per gallon capacity (Refunded on Return)

EMPTIES :—All empty wine and spirit bottles (except Champagne, Liqueurs, and odd shapes) allowed for as follows :—
      BOTTLES, Per dozen **1/-**   HALF-BOTTLES, Per dozen **6d**
    NOTE.—Flagons, Aerated Water Bottles and Syphons, Beer Bottles, etc., see under quotations

PARCEL POST :—All Wines and Spirits sent by Parcels Post are at owner's risk

COUNTRY ORDERS :—Purchases of Wines and Spirits, value **£1** or over are sent Carriage Paid to any Goods Station in England and Wales. Purchases of **£3** value or over are sent Carriage Paid to any Goods Station in Scotland, or to any Port in the Channel Islands having direct steamer communication with London

SHERRIES

All guaranteed Full Strength

	Per doz.	Per gall.
YELLOW SEAL, full flavoured. Wine of good quality	40/-	—
Green Seal. Very good Pale Golden	46/-	20/-
Medium dry, No. 3 (Half botts. 29/- doz.)	52/-	23/-
Montilla, No. 5, very pale, delicate, light dryness	60/-	—
Old Bond Invalid. Soft and Mellow (Half botts. 33/- doz.)	60/-	—
Solera, No. 8, soft, nutty	64/-	29/-
AMOROSO, ' Red Seal,' good flavour and colour	66/-	30/-
Misa's ' Old Raya.' Excellent bouquet, medium body, full nutty flavour	66/-	—
Vino de Pasto, No. 7, a dry Dinner Wine, well matured	66/-	30/-
Bin 87 Reserve Old Brown Sherry. Shipped by Williams & Humbert (Half botts. 36/- doz.)	66/-	—
OLOROSO. Gonzalez Byass. Shipper's Label	72/-	—
' HARRODORA,' a choice Oloroso, medium, dry, with pleasant character and fair body	72/-	33/-
Solera, No. 10. Very fine old Selected	78/-	—
Garvey's Palma, full dry (Half botts. 42/- doz.)	78/-	36/-
' HARRODORA PALO CORTADO,' a fine robust vintage style Sherry, very attractive in character. A wine suitable for all occasions	80/-	—
Garvey's Vintage, Old Golden, full flavoured	82/-	—
Manzanilla, fine old dry	84/-	—
AMONTILLADO, No. 11, ideal dinner wine	84/-	—
Finest Old East India, No. 12	84/-	—
Williams & Humberts Walnut Brown	84/-	—
Garvey's ' Old Time ' Brown, very rare. A true type of Mid-Victorian Sherry, dry in character, with great body. A wine that matures well in bottle	90/-	—

Sherries—*continued*

	Per doz.	Per gall.
' EMBAJADOR.' An extra choice old Solera, has a wonderful aroma and full flavour Rich colour	90/-	—
' EXQUISITO.' A rare old East India Sherry Exquisitely delicate flavour with full character. Fully 50 years old in cask	102/-	—
' BRISTOL MILK.' Harvey's Extra superior Golden Sherry	120/-	—
' BRISTOL CREAM.' Harvey's Choicest old full Pale	144/-	—

PORTS
(MATURED IN WOOD)

The following excellent Values are specially recommended, being free from sediment and ready for immediate consumption

ALL GUARANTEED FULL STRENGTH

	Per doz.	Per gall.
No. 1 Sound Douro Wine	42/-	19/6
No. 3 Light Tawny	45/-	21/-
Red Seal, Fruity, Ruby, Exceptional Value	48/-	22/-
Green Seal, Medium Tawny	54/-	24/-
RUBY TAWNY (Blue Seal)	60/-	27/-
Bandiera White Port	60/-	—
Bandiera Ruby Port	60/-	—
Taylor's L.R. Light Ruby Port. Sound Wine, excellent value	60/-	—
Cockburn's. Fine Old Ruby Port. Pleasing Wine of soft matured character, with good flavour	66/-	—
Taylor's V.C. Vintage Character Port. A full bodied, fruity and luscious Wine	66/-	—
Martinez Old Tawny. A shipment of light Wine, reliable quality and recommended	66/-	—
OLD INVALID, Matured in Wood. Shipped direct and bottled in our Cellars. Highly recommended	66/-	30/-
Dow's Old Tawny, Branded Corks	66/-	—

ALL PRICES ARE SUBJECT TO MARKET FLUCTUATIONS

WINE DEPARTMENT

Champagne

	Vintage	Per dozen botts.	½-botts.
Goulet, George, extra quality, extra dry	1919		
,, ,, ,, ,,	1920		
,, ,, ,, ,,	1921		
Heidsieck, Charles, extra quality, extra dry	—		
,, ,, ,, ,, ,,	1921		
,, ,, Dry Monopole ..	1919		
,, ,, ,,	1921		
Henry Goulet, Cuvée de Reserve	1917		
Irroy, Ernest & Co., Carte d'Or, extra quality	1920		
Krug & Co., Private Cuvée	—		
,, ,, ,,	1919		
Laroche, Eugene, Grand Imperial	1920		
Lanson, Père et Fils, extra quality, extra dry	1920		
Lemoine, J., Cuvée Royale	1919		
E. Mercier, Private Cuvée	1919		
Moet & Chandon, Dry Imperial	1919		
,, ,, ,,	1915		
Montebello, Duc de, Maximum Sec	1915		
Mumm, G. H., Cordon Rouge	1920		
Paul Ruinart, extra quality, extra dry	1919		
Perrier, Jouet, Reserve Cuvée, extra dry	—		
,, ,, ,,	1919		
Piper Heidsieck, Très Sec	1919		
Pol Roger, extra dry	1915		
,, ,, ,,	1919		
Pommery & Greno, Nature	1917		
,, ,, ,,	1919		
,, ,, ,,	1921		
Roederer, Louis, extra dry	1914		
,, ,, ,,	1920		
St. Marceaux, very dry	1919		
,, ,, ,,	1920		
Victor Clicquot, extra dry	1915		
Ruinart Pere et Fils	1919		
Wachter & Co., Royal Charter	1914		
,, ,, ,,	1919		

Prices on application

CHAMPAGNE IN MAGNUMS

	Vintage
Moet & Chandon, Brut	1911
Duval, Charles, Extra Quality, Extra Dry	1915
Pommery & Greno, Nature	1915
Moet & Chandon, Dry Imperial	1914
Pol Roger, Extra Dry	1919
,, ,, ,,	1915
Paul Ruinart	1919

Prices on application

CHAMPAGNE IN QUARTER BOTTLES

	Per doz.
Laroche, Eugene, Grand Imperial, Vintage 1923	33/-
Paul Ruinart, extra dry	42/-
Moet & Chandon, White Dry Sparkling	36/-
Ayala, extra quality, extra dry	40/-
Charles Heidsieck, extra quality	40/-
Perrier Jouet, extra quality	40/-
Lanson, Pere et Fils	42/-

SPARKLING MUSCATEL HARRODORA

This wine has a much appreciated delicate flavour
Specially shipped by Harrods

Per dozen bottles .. 84/- Per dozen ½-bottles .. 47/-
,, ¼ ,, .. 28/-

SPARKLING SAUMURS

AND LIGHT FRENCH WINES

	Per dozen botts.	½-botts.
Good Quality	72/-	41/-
Sparkling Wine of Cognac	78/-	43/-
*Chaussepied's Monitor Brut	84/-	47/-

* Unsurpassed for its dietetic value, old prepared and entirely free from acidity

Sparkling Saumurs—*continued*

	Per dozen botts.	½-botts.
Bouvet-Ladubay Cuvée Excellence Brût	96/-	53/-
Sparkling Vouvray	96/-	53/-
Veuve Amiot, Cremant du Roi, dry and extra dry	102/-	55/-
Ackerman-Laurance Dry Royal or Brût-Royal (¼-botts., 30/- doz.)	108/-	57/-

SPARKLING ANJOU AND TOURAINE WINE

From the Garden of France

	botts.	½-botts.
Sparkling Grand Vin d'Anjou (Hock type)	100/-	55/-
Sparkling Grande Touraine (Moselle type)	100/-	55/-

SPARKLING BURGUNDY

	botts.	½-botts.
Sparkling Volnay Geisweiler	84/-	47/-
Sparkling Volnay	108/-	59/-
Sparkling Beaune	120/-	65/-

SPARKLING WHITE MEDOC AND BORDEAUX

	botts.	½-botts.
Sparkling Ducru (Nathaniel Johnston's)	84/-	46/-
Clos des Cordeliers (Collier Noir), Dry	90/-	49/-

SACRAMENTAL WINE

	botts.	½-botts.
Vino Sacro, Regd. in 1875. Altar Wine in perfection	50/-	29/-
Sacratinta (the perfect Sacramental Wine)	50/-	29/-

HOCKS AND MOSELLES
HOCKS, STILL

	Vintage	Per dozen botts.	½-botts.
Niersteiner	—	36/-	21/-
Bodenheim, H. Sichel Sohne	1917	40/-	23/-
Laubenheimer, Julius Kayser & Co.	1918	42/-	24/-
Liebfraumilch	1917	44/-	25/-
Niersteiner, J. Kayser & Co.	1921	48/-	27/-
Hockheim, Deinhard & Co.	1920	50/-	28/-
Nierstein Superior, H. Sichel Sohne	1921	52/-	29/-
Hockheim, Deinhard & Co.	1919	54/-	30/-
Rudesheimer, J. Kayser & Co.	1921	60/-	33/-
Nierstein, H. Sichel Sohne	1915	66/-	36/-
Rudesheim, H. Sichel Sohne	1921	66/-	36/-
Liebfraumilch, H. Sichel Sohne	1921	69/-	38/-
,, Superior, Deinhard & Co.	1921	72/-	39/-
Rauenthaler Berg, A. Koch Sohne	1917	78/-	—
Rauenthal Berg, Deinhard & Co.	1921	80/-	43/-
,, Cabinet, A. Koch Sohne	1917	84/-	—
Johannisberg, H. Sichel Sohne	1921	135/-	71/-

SPARKLING HOCKS

		botts.	½-botts.
Deinhard Cabinet, Extra Dry	—	116/-	62/-

MOSELLES, STILL

	Vintage	botts.	½-botts.
Zeltinger	—	36/-	21/-
Brauneberger	1921	40/-	23/-
Bernkasteler Riesling, Kayser & Co.	1917	42/-	24/-
Zeltinger, Julius Kayser & Co.	1921	45/-	25/-
,, Kayser & Co.	1917	48/-	27/-
Berncastel, Deinhard & Co.	1920	48/-	27/-
Zeltinger Superior, Deinhard & Co.	1921	52/-	29/-
Winnengen, Deinhard & Co.	1922	54/-	30/-
Berncastel, Deinhard & Co.	1919	54/-	30/-
Brauneberg, H. Sichel Sohne	1921	60/-	33/-
Piesporter	1918	60/-	33/-
Brauneberg, H. Sichel Sohne	1917	64/-	35/-

ALL PRICES ARE SUBJECT TO MARKET FLUCTUATIONS

WINE DEPARTMENT

Hocks & Moselles—Moselles Still

	Vintage	Per dozen botts.	½-botts.
Berncasteler Estate Wine, Deinhard & Co.	—	66/-	36/-
Berncasteler Schlossberg, J. Kayser & Co.	1921	72/-	40/-
Scharzberg, H. Sichel Sohne	1921	75/-	41/-
Berncasteler Rosenberg, J. Kayser & Co.	1921	78/-	42/-
Berncasteler, Extra quality, H. Sichel Sohne	1921	98/-	52/-

SPARKLING MOSELLES

	Per dozen botts.	½-botts.
Bernard Massard	96/-	53/-
Kayser & Co.	96/-	53/-
Muscatelle, Deinhard & Co.	100/-	56/-
Nonpareil, H. Sichel Sohne	108/-	59/-
Bernkasteler, Carl Graeger	100/-	55/-

SPARKLING MUSCATEL
(Produce of France)

Good Quality Special	78/-	44/-
'Harrodora,' Sparkling Muscatel (½-botts., 28/- doz.)	84/-	47/-
Big Tree, Extra Quality, Rich (½-botts. 36/- doz.)	108/-	60/-
Rayons d'Or, Delicate Muscat	108/-	59/-
Golden Guinea, Dry (½-botts., 38/- doz.) ..	126/-	69/-

COCKTAILS

	per bott.
Caperitif	4/-
Hercules	6/6

GORDON'S

	per bott.
Martini	10/6
Dry Martini	10/6
Fifty-fifty	10/6
Perfect	10/6
Piccadilly	10/6
Manhattan	10/6

HOLLOWAY'S

	per bott.
Bronx	10/6

BIG TREE BRAND

	per bott.
Martini Cocktail	9/6
Manhattan Cocktail	9/6

VIVA BRAND

	per bott.
Manhattan	7/-
Martinez	7/-

SOUTH AFRICAN
SOUTH AFRICAN (RED)

	Per dozen botts.	½-botts.

BURGOYNE'S
Veldt Burgundy, a delightfully soft light Burgundy from the Union of South Africa ..	36/-	19/-
Schoongezicht Hermitage, a wine held in high repute in South Africa. From the noted estate of the Hon. John X. Merriman, P.C.	54/-	28/-

WESTMACOTT & CO.
Hermitage, a pure natural dinner wine of Burgundy type	32/-	19/-
Carbernet Sauvignon, the finest South African Burgundies	39/-	—

SOUTH AFRICAN (WHITE)
BURGOYNE'S
Paarl Amber, Hock, a charming South African dinner wine of pleasing character	36/-	19/-
Tafelberg Hock, a peerless hock from the Union of South Africa	60/-	31/-

WESTMACOTT & CO.
Sauvignon Blanc, a light modern dry dinner wine	32/-	19/-
Very Old Drakenstein, a light wine of Hock character	32/-	19/-
Worcester Hock, a wine peculiar to South Africa of a rich Sauterne type	40/-	23/-

South African—*continued*
SOUTH AFRICAN (DESSERT)
WESTMACOTT & CO.

	Per dozen botts.	½-botts.
Constantia Frontignac, rich dessert wine made from the Frontignac grape	54/-	29/-
Red Muscadel, rich dessert wine with a muscat flavour	56/-	31/-

AUSTRALIAN (Red)
HARRODS AUSTRALIAN BURGUNDY

	Per flagon	Per ½ flagon	Per doz. botts.	Per doz. ½-botts.
Specially Selected, Shipped and Bottled by Harrods Limited. A fine Palatable Wine for Beverage use. Highly recommended for Invalids. To be obtained only from Harrods ..	—	—	36/-	21/-

HARRODS AUSTRALIAN RICH OLD RUBY WINE—PORT TYPE

Guaranteed full strength	—	—	34/-	—

FELL'S 'KOALA' BRAND

'Victorian' Burgundy. A fine genous, full-bodied wine	4/-	2/-	36/-	20/-
'Hermitage Grape' Burgundy. A specially selected full-type Burgundy	—	—	48/-	26/-
Emu Burgundy, full and generous ..	4/6	2/3	36/-	19/-
Keystone Burgundy	4/6	2/3	40/-	—

BURGOYNE'S
Harvest Burgundy, the standard of excellence amongst red flagon-wines	4/6	2/3	40/-	21/-
Ophir Burgundy, a wonderful Australian production from the model Burgoyne vineyard of Mount Ophir, Victoria, Australia ..	5/-	2/6	44/-	23/-
Tintara, ferruginous, the famous Australian natural tonic wine ..	6/-	3/-	48/-	25/-

3d extra is charged on all Flagons and will be allowed on return of Flagons, complete with stoppers

AUSTRALIAN (White)
HARRODS AUSTRALIAN WHITE WINE PORT TYPE

Guaranteed full strength	—	—	34/-	—

BURGOYNE'S
Harvest Burgundy, the standard of excellence amongst white flagon-wines	4/6	2/3	40/-	21/-
Chasselas, a light Australian type ...	—	—	36/-	19/-
Highercombe Amber, a beautiful Australian white wine of full hock type	—	—	48/-	25/-

FELL'S 'KOALA' BRAND

'Chablis' type, an elegant dry wine	4/-	2/-	36/-	20/-
Victorian 'Hock' type, a very fine wine with high-class character	—	—	48/-	26/-
EMU CHABLIS, soft and palatable	4/6	2/3	36/-	19/-

3d extra is charged on all flagons, refunded on return of flagons complete with stopper

ALL PRICES ARE SUBJECT TO MARKET FLUCTUATIONS

WINE DEPARTMENT

Whisky, Scotch

	Per bott.	Per doz.	Per gall.
Antiquary, J. W. Hardie's..			
Black and White, J. Buchanan's ..			
Blue Cap, John Begg			
Claymore, Greenlees Bros.			
Cluny, J. E. Macpherson's			
Cream of the Barley, Alexander Stewart..			
Highland Queen, Macdonald & Muir's, 10 years old			
John Haig			
Johnnie Walker Red Label			
Long John, Special Reserve			
Millburn, Finest Old Liqueur ..			
Old Glenlivet Blend, Lumsdens	12/6	150/-	—
Old Orkney			
Old Style 'Special'			
O.V.H., Greer's			
Perfection, McCallums			
Real Mountain Dew, W. & S. Strong ..			
Sandy Macdonald, 10 years old			
Strathdon, Williams' Liqueur			
Teacher's Highland Cream			
Uam Var			
V.O.B., Chas. Mackinlay's			
Vat. 69, Sanderson's			
White Horse Cellar, Mackie & Co.'s ..			
White Label, J. Dewar's			

PURE SCOTCH WHISKY
HARRODS V.O.H.

A soft mellow Whisky, 8 years old. Special Blend, highly recommended

Per dozen bottles **150/-**

CERTIFICATE OF ANALYSIS

I have examined a Sample of your V.O.H. SPECIAL BLEND, and find it to be a thoroughly sound Spirit, free from all impurities, and possessing those characteristics which are only found in fully matured Whiskies
It is soft, mellow, and fragrant. I have therefore no hesitation in recommending it as a GOOD and GENUINE Stimulant

(Signed) R. H. HARLAND, F.I.C., F.C.S.
Public Analyst

WHISKY, IRISH

	Per bott.	Per doz.
Harrods Irish Whisky	12/-	144/-
Dunville's V.R.		
Old Bushmills		
Paddy, Cork Distillery, 10 years old, guaranteed		
John Power & Son's Special 'Three Swallow'	12/6	150/-
John Jameson's ***		
Geo. Roe & Co.'s G.R. guaranteed 7 years old..		
Dunville's Special Liqueur	13/6	162/-

CANADIAN WHISKY

	Per bott.	Per doz.
Hiram Walker & Sons, Ltd. 'Canadian Club'	12/6	150/-

RUM

	Per bott.	Per doz.	Per gall.
Fine Old Jamaica	12/-	144/-	69/-
Dry Cane, very old..	12/-	144/-	—
Liquid Sunshine	12/-	144/-	—
Ron Bacardi (*see* Liqueurs)			

HOLLANDS

	Per bott.	Per doz.
De Kuyper, in Glass	13/6	162/-
Bols (Stone)	13/6	162/-
P. Loopuyt (Glass)	13/-	156/-
Wolfe's Schnapps	14/-	168/-

GIN

	Per bott.	Per doz.	Per gall.
Unsweetened Gin (Harrods)	11/-	132/-	63/-
Unsweetened (Nicholson's) or Old Tom			
Satinette Especial Old Gin			
Booth's Dry Gin	12/-	144/-	—
Gordon's Dry Gin or Old Tom			
Vickers' Sweetened Gin or Dry			
Boord's, Dry or Old Tom..			
Holloway's (London Dry) or Old Tom..	11/6	138/-	—
Coate's Plymouth			

TWO SPECIAL OFFERS

HARRODS AUSTRALIAN BURGUNDY

Supplied and bottled by Harrods. A fine palatable Wine, most suitable for beverage use Highly recommended for Invalids. This Burgundy can only be obtained from Harrods

Per dozen bottles	36/-
Per dozen half-bottles	21/-

PORT IN JARS

Wicker covered jars each containing one Imperial gallon pure Douro Ruby Port Jars free. Carriage paid in England and Wales .. .. Each **22/-**

BRITISH WINES

	Per bott.	Per doz.
Green Ginger, Orange, Raisin, etc. (Stower's)..	2/7	31/-
Rich Raisin, Cowslip, Elder (Stone's) ..	2/10	34/-
Green Ginger, Orange, Dry Raisin (Stone's)	2/10	34/-
Green Ginger (Crabbie's)	3/6	42/-
Ginger Liqueur (Stone's)	4/-	48/-

SUNDRIES

		Per bott.
Amer Picon		15/-
Byrrh	Per litre	6/-
Dubonnet		6/-
Dubonnet Quinquina	Per litre	7/-
Fernet Branca		20/-
Kina Lillet	Per litre	7/-
Junora (Wine of Health)	(½-botts. 3/3)	5/6
Vinho Vigor (Tonic Port)..		5/6

BRITISH CORDIALS, Etc.

Aniseed	8/-
Cinnamon	8/-
Cloves..	8/-
Ginger Gin	11/-
Cherry Brandy	12/6
Ginger Brandy	11/-
,, ,, Liqueur	12/6

ALL PRICES ARE SUBJECT TO MARKET FLUCTUATIONS

HARRODS LTD

Telephone SLOANE 1234
Telegrams 'EVERYTHING HARRODS LONDON'

LONDON S W 1

CIGAR AND TOBACCO DEPARTMENT

BRIAR PIPES IN CASES

THE ILLUSTRATIONS SHOW THE VARIOUS STYLES IN WHICH THE PIPES ARE MADE WHEN ORDERING PLEASE STATE THE STYLE NUMBER AS SHOWN

Unmounted pipes are not available in styles 203 or 205

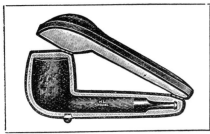

STYLE 201

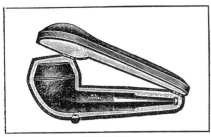

STYLE 202

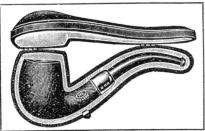

STYLE 203

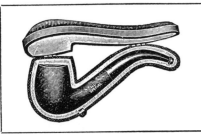

STYLE 204

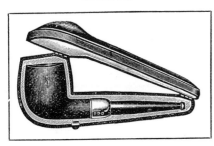

BLOCK GOUDRON PIPES

Case containing 1 of these processed Meerschaum Pipes. The pipes are of a dark polished finish and are not so fragile as White Meerschaum. Vulcanite mouthpiece. In style illustrated only. Three sizes .. .. .. 35/-, 40/- and 45/-

H.L. SPECIAL

Case containing 1 dark Walnut coloured, good quality, Briar. No mount. Vulcanite mouthpiece .. 10/6

H.L. DE LUXE

Case containing 1 light coloured Briar of fine grade Silver mount. Vulcanite mouthpiece 12/6

HANS

Case containing 1 dark-coloured Briar of fine quality No mount. Vulcanite mouthpiece.. .. .. 14/6

BRUYERE ANTIQUE

Case containing 1 dark-finished Old Briar. With aluminium tube. No mount. Vulcanite mouthpiece 18/6

BRUYERE ANTIQUE

Case containing 1 dark-finished Old Briar. With aluminium tube. Narrow Gold mount. Vulcanite mouthpiece 22/6

BRUYERE ANTIQUE

Case containing 1 rich dark-finished Old Briar with aluminium tube. Broad gold mount. Vulcanite mouthpiece 27/6

B.B.B. ULTONIA

Case containing 1 Briar of this well-known brand Dark colour. No mount. Vulcanite mouthpiece 13/6

B.B.B. BEST MAKE

Case containing 1 Briar of light-coloured finish Excellent quality. Silver mounted. Vulcanite mouthpiece 19/6

B.B.B. ULTIMA THULE

Case containing 1 dark-finished Briar with quill inner tube that can be replaced when foul. No mount. Vulcanite mouthpiece 21/-

Extra Quills per pkt. 6d

G.B.D. NEW ERA

Case containing 1 dark-coloured Briar from this well-known maker. No mount. Vulcanite mouthpiece,. 19/6

DUNHILL

Case containing 1 Standard Bruyere, dark-finished, polished Briar, or 1 rough-surfaced Shell Briar, from which all soft parts have been eliminated. Vulcanite mouthpiece. Either type .. .. Per case 32/-

'ROCK' BRIARS
(*Illustrated on left*)

These handsome pieces of Briar Root, polished and surfaced, are excellent for very cool smoking. Roughly 6 ins. in diameter with flexible tube 60 ins. long
Plain .. 30/-
With Meerschaum lined cup .. 37/6

BLOCK BRIAR PIPES
(*Illustrated on right!*)

A cool pipe that can be conveniently placed at a distance when reading, motoring, etc. Flexible tube 36 ins. long

Plain surface .. 10/6
Rock surface .. 12/6

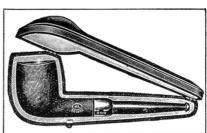

STYLE 205

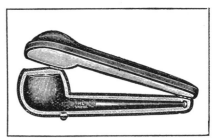

STYLE 206

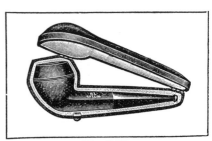

STYLE 207

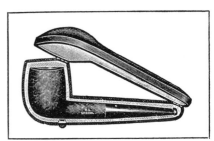

STYLE 208

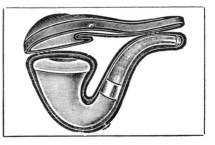

FINE CALABASH PIPES

Cut from selected Gourds and Meerschaum lined, these are very cool smoking. Vulcanite mouthpieces. Small sizes. Not in case 7/6

In case, as illustrated and with removable Meerschaum cup, Ambroid mouthpiece. Large size 37/6

ALL PRICES ARE SUBJECT TO MARKET FLUCTUATIONS

HARRODS LTD

Telephone SLOANE 1234
Telegrams 'EVERYTHING HARRODS LONDON'

LONDON SW1

CIGAR AND TOBACCO DEPARTMENT

COMPANION CASES
OF BRIARS

THE ILLUSTRATIONS SHOW THE VARIOUS STYLES
OBTAINABLE. WHEN ORDERING PLEASE STATE THE
STYLE NUMBER

Unmounted Briars are not available in Styles 102, 109, 112

H.L. SPECIAL

Case containing two dark Walnut coloured, good
quality Briars. No mounts

Per case	..	..	..	..	20/-
Case of four Pipes	..	..	..	..	37/6

H.L. DE LUXE

Case containing two light coloured Briars of fine
grade. Silver mounts

Per case	..	..	..	..	23/6
Case of four Pipes	..	..	..	..	45/-

HANS

Case containing two dark coloured Briars of fine
quality. No mounts

Per case	..	..	..	..	27/6
Case of four Pipes	..	..	..	..	50/-

BRUYERE ANTIQUE

Case containing two dark finished old Briars, with
aluminium tubes. No mounts

Per case	..	..	..	..	35/6
Case of four Pipes	..	..	..	..	67/6

BRUYERE ANTIQUE

Case containing two dark finished Old Briars,
with aluminium tubes. Narrow gold mounts

Per case	..	..	..	43/6

BRUYERE ANTIQUE

Case containing two dark finished Old Briars
with aluminium tubes. Broad gold mounts

Per case	..	..	..	53/6

B.B.B. ULTONIA

Case containing two Briars of this well-known brand
Dark colour. No mounts

Per case	..	..	..	23/6

B.B.B. BEST MAKE

Case containing two Briars of light coloured finish
Excellent quality. Silver mounted

Per case	..	..	..	37/6

B.B.B. ULTIMA THULE

Case containing two dark finished Briars with quill
inner tube that can be replaced when foul. No mounts

Per case	..	..	38/6
Extra Quills	..	.. per packet	6d

G.B.D. NEW ERA

Case containing two dark coloured Briars from
this well-known maker. No mounts

Per case	..	..	..	..	35/-
Case of three Pipes	..	..	..	..	52/6

DUNHILL

Case containing two standard Bruyere, dark finished,
polished Briars or two rough-surfaced shell Briars, from
which all soft parts have been eliminated. Either type

Per case	..	..	..	..	64/-

Cases can also be supplied containing one standard and
one shell Briar at same price

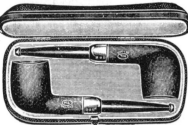

STYLE 101

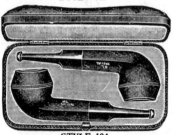

STYLE 102

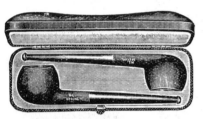

STYLE 103

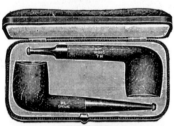

STYLE 104

STYLE 105

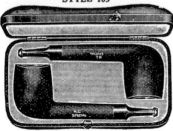

STYLE 106

STYLE 107

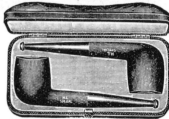

STYLE 108

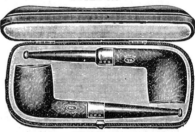

STYLE 109

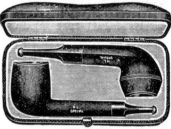

STYLE 110

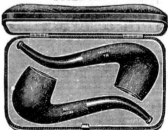

STYLE 111

STYLE 112

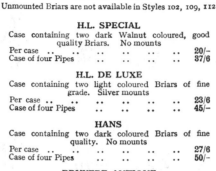

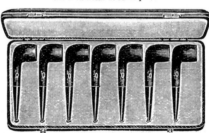

STYLE 113

Cases of three, four or seven Pipes

Containing three Dunhill Pipes	..	£4 16 0
" four G.B.D. New Era Pipes		3 10 0
" seven Bruyere Antique Pipes		6 0 0
" seven Dunhill Pipes	..	11 11 0

ALL PRICES ARE SUBJECT TO MARKET FLUCTUATIONS

HARRODS LTD

Telephone SLOANE 1234
Telegrams 'EVERYTHING HARRODS LONDON'

LONDON SW1

CIGAR AND TOBACCO DEPARTMENT
Tobacco Jars with Air-Tight Lids

Well made from fine mahogany, lead lined. ½ lb. size. Height 6 ins. .. **37/6**

Made from selected mahogany Will give lasting wear. Lined with lead. Capacity over 4 ozs. Height 6 ins. **37/6**

Earthenware body with expanding air-tight lid. Blue colouring. ½ lb. size. Height 4 ins. **10/6**

Turned from solid mahogany with weighted lid which is practically air-tight. Lined lead. Capacity over 4 ozs. Height 5½ ins. .. **37/6**

Mahogany box with weighted lid, lead lined. 6 oz. size Size 6 × 6 × 4⅜ ins. .. **37/6**

Doulton Toby ware jar with loose lid and damper for moistening tobacco. ¼ lb. size Height 4½ ins. .. **5/6**

Earthenware body with expanding air-tight lid. Blue colouring. ½ lb. size. Height 3½ ins. .. **10/6**

Earthenware body with expanding air-tight lid. Brown/Blue colouring. ½ lb. size Height 3½ ins. .. **10/6**

Earthenware body with expanding air-tight lid. Blue colouring. ½ lb. size. Height 4 ins. **10/6**

Doulton Toby ware jar with loose lid and damper for moistening contents. ½ lb. size. Height 4⅞ ins. .. **6/-**

Earthenware body with screw-in air-tight lid. Bronze-green coloured band. ½ lb. size Height 4¼ ins. **9/6**

Doulton ware with nickel clamp air-tight fitting to lid Brown and cream colourings ¼ lb. size. Height 4½ ins. **15/-**

Doulton ware with nickel clamp air-tight fitting to lid Brown coaching scene. ¼ lb. size. Height 4½ ins. .. **15/-**

Doulton ware with nickel clamp air-tight fitting to lid Coloured hunting scene ¼ lb. size. Height 4½ ins. **15/-**

Earthenware body with screw-in air-tight lid. Blue colouring ½ lb. size. Height 4 ins. **9/6**

Doulton ware with nickel clamp fitting to lid. Air-tight. Blue colouring. ½ lb. size. Height 6 ins. .. **18/-** ¼ lb. size. Height 3¾ ins. **15/-**

Doulton Toby ware with nickel clamp air-tight fitting to lid. ¼ lb. size. Height 3¾ ins. .. **10/6** ½ lb. size. Height 6 ins. **12/6**

Doulton ware with nickel clamp air-tight fitting to lid ½ lb. size. Height 6 ins. **16/6** ¼ lb. size. Height 3¾ ins. **14/3**

Doulton ware with nickel clamp air-tight fitting to lid Blue colouring. ¼ lb. size Height 3¾ ins. .. **20/3** ½ lb. size. Height 6 ins. **22/6**

Doulton ware with nickel clamp fitting to lid. Air-tight Brown colouring. ½ lb. size Height 6 ins. .. **14/3** ¼ lb. size. Height 3¾ ins. **12/6**

Earthenware body with air-tight fitting to lid. Brown with coloured band. 6 oz. size Height 4½ ins. .. **9/6**

Blue-brown Majolica ware with air-tight fitting to lid ½ lb. size. Height 5 ins. **7/6**

Blue-brown Majolica ware with air-tight fitting to lid 4 oz. size. Height 4½ ins. **6/6**

Blue-brown Majolica ware with air-tight fitting to lid ½ lb. size. Height 4 ins. **7/6**

Earthenware body with air-tight fitting to lid. Brown with blue top. 6 oz. size Height 4½ ins. .. **9/6**

ALL PRICES ARE SUBJECT TO MARKET FLUCTUATIONS

HARRODS LTD

Telephone SLOANE 1234
Telegrams 'EVERYTHING HARRODS LONDON'

LONDON S W 1

CIGAR AND TOBACCO DEPARTMENT
Smokers' Cabinets, Pipe Racks and Smokers' Stands

SMOKER'S CABINET
No. 1859   Size   15 × 9½ × 12¾ ins. high
Nickel fittings and two ash trays
Polished or Fumed Oak **112/6**
Inlaid Mahogany **138/6**

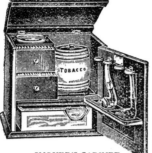

SMOKER'S CABINET
No. 1877   Size 11 × 8½ × 10½ ins. high
Nickel Fittings and 1 Ash Tray
Polished Oak **72/6**
Mahogany **77/6**

SMOKER'S CABINET
No. 1857   Size 11 × 8½ × 7¾ ins. high
Nickel fittings and one ash tray
Polished Oak **42/6**

SMOKER'S CABINET
No. 1858   Size 13½ × 8 × 10¾ ins.
Nickel fittings and one ash tray
Polished Oak **70/-**

SMOKER'S CABINET
No. 1878   Size 14 × 9 × 11¾ ins. high
Nickel fittings and two ash trays. Front
revolves to close
Polished Oak **120/-**

SMOKER'S CABINET
No. 1879   Size 12½ × 8 × 9½ ins. high
Nickel fittings. Without shield on top
Polished Oak **60/-**
Shield **3/6** extra

SMOKER'S CABINET
No. 1880   Size 15 × 7 × 16½ ins.
high.   Two nickel ash trays
Finished Dark Oak in Jacobean
Style..   ..   ..   **90/-**

SMOKER'S CABINET
No. 1860   Size   14 × 10 × 13 ins. high
Nickel fittings and four ash trays. Front
revolves to close. Polished Oak .. **£10 10 0**
Mahogany **£11 11 0** Inlaid Mahogany **£12 12 0**

SMOKER'S STAND
No. 1991   Size when closed
16½ × 10½ × 40½ ins. high
Nickel fittings and two ash
trays
Dark Oak in Jacobean Style
with twisted legs   **£9 9 0**

SMOKER'S STANDS
In rich Oak or Mahogany, china ash tray. The Oak Stands have twisted upright in Jacobean style
No. 1983
Oak.   23 ins. high (without table) .. **18/6**
No. 1981
Oak. 28 ins. high (with 10-in. round table as shewn) **21/-**
No. 1983
Mahogany, 23 ins. high (without table) .. **21/-**
No. 1982
Mahogany, 28 ins. high (with 10-in. round table as shewn) .. **25/-**

SMOKER'S TABLE
No. 1992   Size when closed
16½ × 18 × 28½ ins. high
Nickel fittings and four ash trays
Cigarette trays sink as top is closed
Fumed Oak **£15 15 0**
Polished Mahogany   ..   **£17 17 0**
Also in Jacobean style, Dark Oak
with twisted legs   ..   **£16 16 0**

SMOKER'S STANDS
'Smokador' bronze finished
Pedestal with match holder
on handle and two rests on
rim. Cannot be knocked over
or spill ashes.   Spent ends
pass down centre into base
Height overall 28 ins.   **47/6**

SMOKER'S STAND
No. 1993. Size when closed
15½ × 11 × 41½ ins. high
Front revolves to close
Nickel fittings and four ash
Trays
Polished Mahogany **£18 18 0**
Inlaid Mahogany **£20 0 0**

PIPE RACKS
Inlaid Mahogany. To hold six
pipes. Brass fittings .. **28/6**
Also in Fumed or Natural Oak
26/6

PIPE RACKS
Mahogany, with inlaid frame
To hold 6   ..   ..   **27/6**
,,   ,,   12   ..   ..   **31/6**

OAK PIPE RACKS
Jacobean Style. To hold seven pipes
Dark or Polished Oak finish **22/6**

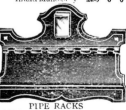

PIPE RACKS
Inlaid Mahogany. To hold seven pipes
With match holder **24/6**
Without match holder   ..   **22/6**
Also in Oak without holder   ..   **17/6**

ALL PRICES ARE SUBJECT TO MARKET FLUCTUATIONS

HARRODS LTD

Telephone SLOANE 1234
Telegrams 'EVERYTHING HARRODS LONDON'

LONDON S W 1